CANOEING THE CHURCHILL

A Practical Guide to the
Historic Voyageur Highway

CANOEING THE CHURCHILL

A Practical Guide to the

Historic Voyageur Highway

Greg Marchildon and Sid Robinson

Discover Saskatchewan Series Editor

Ralph Nilson

Canadian Plains Research Center
University of Regina
Regina, Saskatchewan
2002

Canadian Plains Research Center
University of Regina
Regina, Saskatchewan S4S 0A2
Canada
Tel: (306) 585-4758
Fax: (306) 585-4699
e-mail: canadian.plains@uregina.ca
http://www.cprc.uregina.ca

National Library of Canada Cataloguing in Publication Data

Marchildon, Gregory P., 1956–
Canoeing the Churchill

(Discover Saskatchewan series, ISSN 1484-1800 ; 3
Includes bibliographical references and index.
ISBN 0-88977-148-0

1. Canoes and canoeing--Churchill River (Sask. and Man.)--Guidebooks. 2. Churchill River (Sask. and Man.)--Guidebooks. 3. Churchill River (Sask. and Man.)--History. I. Robinson, Sid, 1954– II. University of Regina. Canadian Plains Research Center. III. Title. IV. Series.
GV776.15.S2M37 2002   797.1'22'0971241   C2001-911718-3

Cover photo by Greg Marchildon. This photo showing Nistowiak Falls was taken August 2, 1986.
Cover design by Donna Achtzehner, Canadian Plains Research Center.
All photos taken by the authors unless otherwise acknowledged.

Printed and bound in Canada by Houghton Boston, Saskatoon, Saskatchewan
Printed on acid-free paper

To Julian Marchildon, Haley Robinson, and Ragnar Robinson,

a new generation of voyageurs

TABLE OF CONTENTS

ROUTE MAPS

HISTORICAL MAPS

FOREWORD

We are very fortunate to have *Canoeing the Churchill: A Practical Guide to the Historic Voyageur Highway* as the third title in the "Discover Saskatchewan" series. The two authors, Greg Marchildon and Sid Robinson, have, through their extensive research and experiences on the river, provided a significant contribution to the literature for canoeists and outdoor recreation enthusiasts. Of equal importance, their book contributes to the historical and ethnographic understanding of lives lived along this northern Saskatchewan waterway.

On a personal level, each year I look forward to spending the long daylight hours of the northern Saskatchewan summer on wilderness waterways. The beauty of this lonely land draws me back year after year. I hope that through this book people from Saskatchewan and beyond will take the opportunity to understand more about this magnificent river and the people who, over the centuries, have relied on it for trade, transportation, and food.

While the Churchill is a relatively isolated river in an isolated land, it still needs to be understood in an historical as well as a current context. The authors of *Canoeing the Churchill* provide these contexts, and it is to be hoped that readers will be convinced to treat the river with respect, in order to ensure not only that the Churchill River continues to serve its fundamental and critical role in the northern ecosystems of Saskatchewan, but also that future generations can continue to enjoy and appreciate its beauty.

Publication of *Canoeing the Churchill* was assisted by a generous grant from the Saskatchewan Heritage Foundation. Special thanks go to the staff of the Canadian Plains Research Center, in particular Donna Achtzehner for her invaluable work in bringing this project to fruition.

Ralph Nilson
Series Editor
December, 2001
Regina, Saskatchewan

PREFACE

In the summer of 1985, we rented cabins on opposite sides of Lac la Ronge's Nut Point peninsula. By overland trail, we were only two kilometres apart, so we sometimes met on weekends to drink tea and discuss topics of interest. One August evening, the talk turned to canoeing and the possibility of a fall canoe trip. After sorting out the mechanics of the J stroke (our paddling skills were limited) and who had what gear, we determined we were in fact ready for a modest excursion. We then went on to discuss possible trip routes. A section of the Churchill River, just an hour's drive north of La Ronge, was our unanimous choice.

We were captured by the Churchill's rich history as part of the old trans-Canada voyageur highway. We looked forward to camping on the same rocks and portaging the same trails as the early traders and their voyageurs. At the same time, it occurred to us that we might benefit from a guide or handbook describing our intended route's history. As far as we knew, though, no such guide existed. We were familiar with the canoe trip booklets—originally written by canoeist Peter Gregg—that the provincial government offered free of charge to canoeists. However, while these booklets were (and still are) excellent navigational aids, their slim format left little room for history.

Sitting at the kitchen table under a kerosene lamp, we continued our trip planning into the night. But even as we concentrated on maps, food, and gear, we kept coming back to how handy a history guide would be. And gradually, as the lamp wick burned shorter, the idea for this book was born. We decided—without yet knowing a low brace from a knee brace—that we ourselves could canoe the length of Saskatchewan's voyageur highway and write up a paddler's guide to its history. The idea seemed so sensible, we wanted to get on the water right away. However, as it was clearly too late in the year to begin an extended canoe trip, we reluctantly agreed to postpone our adventure until the following spring. Although disappointing, the delay would give us a chance to read more about the fur trade, learn the rudiments of photography, and find the equipment needed for a summer-long trip.

In late May, 1986, we finally set out on our enlarged expedition. We hauled an aluminum Grumman Eagle to the Clearwater River and, from there, headed south and east on a seventy-day voyage to Cumberland House. We could not have wished for a better summer. We paddled and portaged, fished and swam, and talked to people we met along our way. We were always dead tired by nightfall, but each day taught us something new.

While our 1986 canoe trip was long, the actual writing of this book has been a far longer journey. The original plan was to have our research written up into a usable guide soon after our canoe trip. We started our writing fast enough, but within weeks, we seemed to have more questions than answers about our route. The next summer, despite our best efforts, we were still a long way from completion. By 1990, we had made enough progress to interest a publisher in our work. But three years later, we had not yet turned in a completed manuscript, and the publisher had moved on to other endeavours. As more years passed, we also moved on to other things and farther away from a wrap-up. While we continued to revisit our route and gather information about it, we were never able to put our collected information and photos into usable form.

In 1997, our project was resurrected from the dead by the Canadian Plains Research Center. That year, we were asked by Dr. Ralph Nilson, the Dean of Physical Activity Studies at the University of Regina, to finish the book up so that it could be included in his new "Discover Saskatchewan" series. Dr. Nilson's hope was that the book would appear by no later than 1998. Again, we were to fail to meet expectations. We did devote any spare time we had to finishing up our work. However, it seemed our time too often went into more research rather than writing final drafts. We thus caused more delays and, in doing so, surely tested the patience of our publisher and editor.

Now finally, with the help of CPRC and encouragement from family and friends, we have managed to put our collected material together. The finished product—with its maps, photos, and text—is thicker than we originally intended. Nonetheless, while it may be heavy to portage, we hope it finds its way into many canoe packs.

Greg Marchildon, Sid Robinson
January 2002

PREFACE TO THE THIRD PRINTING

In this third printing, *Canoeing the Churchill* remains essentially the same as it was when first published. There have been only two changes and one addition of note.

The first change, made in the second printing, concerns the way measurements are set out in the text. To assist visiting American paddlers and others who may not be familiar with the metric system, metric measurements are now followed by their American equivalents in parentheses.

The second change, also made in the second printing, is with respect to the spelling of Cree terms and place names in our guide. In the first printing, Cree words were spelt using "Colin's Modified Roman Orthography," developed by the Lac la Ronge Indian Band. The Band has since adopted the use of "Standard Roman Orthography" (SRO). As SRO is now standard throughout most of Saskatchewan, our original spellings have been converted to their SRO equivalents. We extend our thanks to Arok Wolvengrey – assisted by Solomon Ratt, Jean Okimâsis, and Bill Barry – for making the conversions. Readers can refer to Appendix C (page 408) for a pronunciation guide to both Cree and Dene words.

In this third printing, eight photos from the 2005 Saskatchewan Centennial Canoe Quest have been added to the colour photo insert. In the Quest, 30 teams raced "North" canoe replicas down the guide route from Lac la Loche to Sturgeon Landing, traveling 966 kilometres (600 miles) in 15 days. (A 16th day to Cumberland House was cancelled when flood waters forced that village to evacuate.) The race was an epic adventure and is now part of the route's history.

Greg Marchildon, Sid Robinson
May 2006

ACKNOWLEDGEMENTS

Writing this guide would have been impossible without the help of the dozens of people who have, over the past sixteen years, given us practical support and provided us with information. To the extent possible, we here wish to acknowledge and thank those persons. We will undoubtedly miss naming some who have helped us along the way, and we apologize for this oversight. The help of all contributors, named or unnamed, has been appreciated.

Thanks first to Gene Josephson and Wendy Stueck who accompanied us down the Clearwater River from Warner Rapids to Methy Portage at the start of our 1986 trip. In those first days, Gene—an old canoe hand by our standards—gave us much needed advice on when to run rapids and when to walk around them. Both Gene and Wendy did more than their share of camp chores while we examined and photographed rapids and portages.

Thanks, too, to Patsi Walton, now of Montreal, who was with us for the last third of our 1986 trip—the distance from Otter Rapids to Cumberland House. Patsi shared her knowledge of northern Saskatchewan's plants and showed us the ones we could safely add to our menu. Patsi also used her guitar, voice, and good humour to enliven our journey.

In the years since 1986, several canoeists have supported us on forays to revisit the route. Without exception, they have been endlessly patient during detours made to check and recheck information. They have also freely done more than their share of portaging and camp chores to allow us to pursue small explorations. These canoeists include Laurel Archer, Ryan Burdon, Joanne Epp, Noreen Gobeille, Judy Halyk, Bill Hilderman, Bill Jeffery, Hilary Johnstone, Vanessa Johnstone, Dorothy Josephson, Gene Josephson (again), Brad Koop, Leslie Mennie, Alain Michelet, and several Robinsons, namely, Faye, Gaye, Haley, Ragnar, Randy, Shelley, and Sherry.

In 1986 and in subsequent years, we also received a great deal of help from people on dry land. Sometimes, this help was of a practical nature as in the case of vehicle shuttles or proofreading written text. Most often, it was in the form of information—a commodity most vital to us. The help we received had a tangible value, but it also encouraged us to move forward with our project.

We are particularly indebted to the assistance we have received from Dale Russell of Saskatoon. In sharing his knowledge of Cree and Dene history, Dale reminded us that the human history of the Churchill and Sturgeon-weir goes back thousands of years and that the period from European contact to the present is only a small part of it. While the route's early history remains largely unknown to us, Dale has at least given us a sense of how rich it must be. Tim Jones, too, with his understanding of aboriginal pictographs, has helped us appreciate the great span of pre-contact history.

In researching the fur trade, we have had research assistance from the National Archives of Canada, the Saskatchewan Archives Board, the Hudson's Bay Company Archives (HBCA) and the Pahkisimon Nuye-ah Library in La Ronge. We owe a significant debt to the HBCA in Winnipeg. Much of our research at the HBCA was done by mail, and archives staff often went an extra mile to answer our written queries. HBCA staff who assisted us include David Arthurs,

Judith Beattie and Scott Reid. Special thanks go to Anne Morton, present Head of Research and Reference at HBCA, who faithfully answered long lists of questions.

Provincial civil servants often assisted us with answers to questions. These include Andrew Gracie and Pam Schwann of Energy and Mines, Dalvin Euteneier of Sask Water, Daryl Kraft of Information Services (SaskGeomatics Division), Peter Niven of SaskPower, John Boyd of Sask Housing, and Dennis Belliveau of Saskatchewan Highways and Transportation (who went to considerable length to give us the history of northern Saskatchewan's first provincial roads). Several Saskatchewan Environment staff, some of whom are listed below, also assisted us both while on duty and while on their free time.

We also benefited from the help of the Historic Trails Canoe Club of Regina, originally established in 1956 to explore the Churchill River. The members of this club have always had a keen interest in the history of the Churchill and have played a significant role in reviewing and updating the provincial canoe trip booklets for the river. We would like to thank members Jean Miketinac, Dave Christopherson, and Peter Whitehead for their comments on portions of our manuscript. Special thanks go to Marcel de Laforest (like Peter Whitehead, a charter member of the club) who read most of the manuscript and was most patient and helpful in the last stages of revision.

Others who gave us practical support or general information include Dave Armstrong, Cindy Barker, Lee Barker, Bill Barry, Marvin Bather, Father Beaudet, Thomas Billette, Mervin Bilquist, Verna Bilquist, the late Simeon Bloomfield, the late Louis Bouvier, Vi Bouvier, Bill Chanin, Scott Charles, Bev Cheechoo, Jeff Chiarenzelli, Doug Chisholm, Roly Chretien, Marie Jeanne ("MJ") Chuey, Ron Clancy, the late Jonas Clarke, Robert H. Cockburn, Karen Cojocar, Ron Cojocar, Ken Cornett, Mike Current, Lois Dalby, the late Fred Darbyshire, Nora Darbyshire, Jeff Davies, Howard DeLong, Irene Desjarlais, Ovide Desjarlais, Ric Driediger, Leighton Dunn, the late Father Durand, Beatrice Fecke, Charlie Fosseneuve, Dorothea Funk, Lyle Galloway, Louis George, Rick Glass, Joe Goodeyon, Bev Goulet, Gill Gracie, Walter Hainault, John Hansen, Carmen Harry, Norm Henderson (who went far beyond the call of duty in commenting on the first three chapters of the manuscript at one particularly difficult stage), Jack Hillson, Lynda Holland, Dr. Meinrad Hoffman, Norm Hoknes, Casey Howey, Gwyneth Hoyle, Anita Jackson, Bruce Joa, Leo Jacobsen, Sherry Jacobsen, J. Keith Johnstone, Harold Kirtzinger, Eugene Klein, Margaret Klein, Fritz Laliberte, George Laliberte, Mary Laliberte, Joyce Laprise, Mike Lariviere, Charles Lauterer, Jean (Jerry) Lavoie, Bill Layman, Harvey Legary, Carl Lentowicz, Grant Lohrenz, Audrey Mark, Dale McAuley, Father Jean Mégret, David Meyer, Dave McIllmoyl, Yvonne McIntyre, Isaac McKenzie, Father Bertrand Mathieu, Roy Morin, Vital Morin, the late Gisli Norman, Lilje Norman, Clarisse Petit, John Piper, Elaine Poulin, Roger Poulin, Allan Quandt, Alvin Reimer, Nancy Reimer, Alex Robertson, Scott Robertson, the late Fred Robinson, Ivor Robinson, Roland Robinson, Don Ryback, Virginia Scanlon, Wayne Schick, Ray Sernes, Angus Sewap, John Sheard, Jon Sigtema, Don Skopyk, Kelly Stevenson, Larry Stevenson, Dean Tait, Fred Thompson, Gary Thompson, Ron Thompson, George Thurlow, Eddie Tihonen, Jacqueline Toupin, Tim Trottier, Gord Wallace, Ron Ward, Don Watson, Randy Wells, and Charlie Willetts.

Photographs make up an important part of our work. If not otherwise indicated, the photos shown are our own—most being taken as either black-and-white prints or colour slides on our

1986 trip. However, in addition to our own photos and those obtained from archival sources, others have made significant photo contributions. Pilot Doug Chisholm of La Ronge took all of our aerial photos (excepting the archival shot of Buffalo Narrows on page 133). Dave Armstrong of Regina took many of the photographs shown in Chapter 8. Marg Beament of La Ronge provided us with the photo of her parents, John and Mary Ann McKay at Black Bear Island Lake. Lois Dalby and Lynda Holland, both of La Ronge, provided us with the photo of Solomon Merasty and P.G. Downes shown on page 331. Graham Guest, also of La Ronge, gave us his photos of Angelique and Bill Merasty shown on pages 359 and 360. (Graham has further given us a good deal of practical support.) John and Mary Morin of Prince Albert provided us with photos of the Sturgeon Landing residential school shown on page 383. Finally, Hilary Johnstone of La Ronge has contributed several photos and has also done the sketches of the food box on page 13, the voyageur on page 39, and the pack and paddle on page 404.

Many Dene have their home territories on western sections of the route. We have set out some local Dene history and have tried to give Dene names for places along the route. This would not have been possible without the help of Dene who live, or have lived, between the Clearwater River and Knee Lake. For information and names regarding the Clearwater River and La Loche regions, we relied heavily on advice from Greg Hatch (assisted by Celina Janvier and the late Pierre Lemaigre), Alphonse Janvier, Steven Lemaigre and Annette Montgrand. For names and information about the Peter Pond Lake area, we relied upon help from Hazel MacDonald and Monique Sylvestre. Paul Sylvestre provided us with names and information for the Churchill Lake area. Joe Black and Philip Wolverine proved to be invaluable resources with respect to English River Dene Nation territory. Mayor Margaret Aubichon provided us with information about her home community of Patuanak. Finally, Ben Garr, a Dene linguist originally from Patuanak, spent several hours reviewing our Dene names and helping us transcribe them into our rudimentary English phonetics.

Many, many people helped us with information about Cree territory and the Cree language. Without exception, they were ever patient as we asked to have stories and Cree words repeated time and again. Those informants that come especially to mind include Mike Durocher of Île-à-la-Crosse, the late Albert Hansen of Pinehouse, Martin Smith of Pinehouse, Bill Nelson of Trout Lake, the late John McKay of Black Bear Island Lake, Johnny S. McKenzie of Grandmother's Bay, Blake Charles of Stanley Mission, Big Jim McKenzie of Stanley Mission/Nistowiak Falls, John Charles of Stanley Mission/Keg Lake, Daniel Linklater of Pelican Narrows, the late Frank Linklater of Pelican Narrows, Martin Michel of Pelican Narrows, and the late Bill Merasty of Denare Beach. A very special thanks goes to John and Mary Morin, now of Prince Albert, who gave us information about Cree life on the Sturgeon-weir River and at Cumberland House. John was born on the West Weir and was intimately familiar with the Sturgeon-weir. Mary was born and raised at Cumberland House. We went back to John and Mary for information so often, John was once heard to ask, "How many books are those guys writing?" Our other Cree informants include Victoria Ballantyne, Allan Charles, Pat Chartier, Jim Churchill, Sarah Cook, Susan Cook, Louis Custer, Dick Hansen, John Halcrow, Maggie Halcrow, Adam Highway, Eli Highway, the late Louis Jobb, Vie Laffrenere, the late Arthur McCallum, Judy McCallum, Richard McKay, Becky McKenzie, Sam McKenzie, Ron Merasty, the late Solomon Merasty, Gerald M. Morin, James (Magic) Ratt, the late Joseph Ratt, Maggie Ross, the late Elizabeth Sewap, the late James Sewap, Ray Smith and Doreen Vancoughnett.

Nicole O'Byrne first made us aware of the possibility of publishing our book in the Canadian Plains Research Center's "Discover Saskatchewan" series. We want to thank the series editor, Dr. Ralph Nilson, Dean of Physical Activity Studies at the University of Regina, for immediately understanding what we were trying to accomplish and committing his support. We also wish to thank CPRC publisher Brian Mlazgar for his willingness to take on the risk of printing our work. And our warmest thanks go to our editor at CPRC, Donna Achtzehner, who put in countless hours of skilled labour to transform our original manuscript drafts into book form. She was always cheerful in the face of our delays and demands, and we ever appreciated her patience and understanding. We also owe special thanks to CPRC map-maker Diane Perrick for her many hours of painstaking work on the route maps.

Lastly, we wish to acknowledge the contribution of our respective families. From the very beginning, we have had ongoing encouragement from our parents—Anna, Joe, Violet, and Ivor. We have also had loyal backing from our immediate family members—Giovanna, Julian, Hilary, Haley, and Ragnar. Over the past years, they have encouraged our "canoe book" project even when it has taken time away from them. We are most grateful for that support.

Greg Marchildon, Sid Robinson

INTRODUCTION

There is magic in the feel of a paddle and the movement of a canoe, a magic compounded of distance, adventure, solitude and peace. The way of the canoe is the way of wilderness and of a freedom almost forgotten, the open door to waterways of ages past and a way of life with profound and abiding satisfactions.

Sigurd Olson, *The Lonely Land*[1]

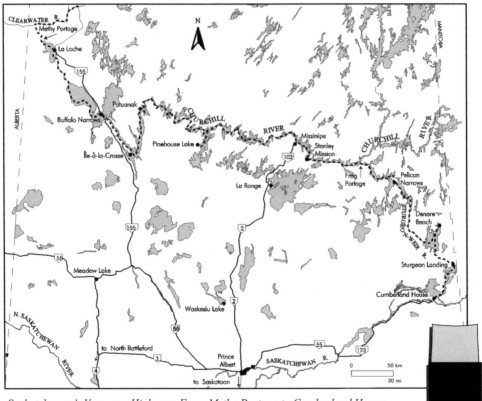

Saskatchewan's Voyageur Highway: From Methy Portage to Cumberland House

1

This book is a paddler's guide to a historic canoe route—a 1,000-kilometre (625-mile) chain of lakes and rivers stretching across northern Saskatchewan from Methy Portage in the west to Cumberland House in the east. The route was once part of the great voyageur highway which, at the height of the fur trade in North America, reached from the Atlantic all the way to the Pacific. As such, it was the very track followed by fur traders and explorers like Alexander Mackenzie, David Thompson, and George Simpson when they first came into Canada's North-West. We intend this guide to help you trace the path of these famous travellers and—just as they did—learn about the route as you proceed.

Our guide is meant for a varied audience. First, we hope it assists the ordinary canoeist who perhaps gets out in a canoe only once a summer. We also hope it is of some value to more experienced trippers, especially group leaders and school chaperons who need to know as much as they can about their route. Finally, we hope it offers something to students of aboriginal and fur trade history who, whether they paddle or not, have an interest in the voyageur highway.

We should be clear as to what this book is not. It is not a guide on how to camp or canoe. On these subjects, there are already many excellent books (some of which we have listed in Appendix A). Nor is this book meant to be a travel narrative. Back in 1986, while doing our initial research for this guide, we did paddle the length of the route in a seventy-day trip. We will sometimes refer to that trip (and to later trips), especially to mention people we have met, but our intended focus is the route itself and not our own paddling experiences.

The Guide Route

The route begins at the western edge of Saskatchewan on the continental divide separating the Arctic and Hudson Bay drainage basins. It then moves eastward towards Manitoba, following the natural downstream flow of its lakes and rivers. The early fur traders necessarily first paddled the route in an opposite, upstream direction to enter the North-West. However, since most present-day canoeists prefer to travel with the current, the route is best described in a west to east, downstream direction.

At its upstream end, the route begins with an 80-kilometre (50-mile) section of the Clearwater River that provides access to the north end of historic Methy Portage. It then follows the voyageur trail south over the portage (which crosses the Arctic-Hudson Bay divide) to Lac la Loche, one of the headwaters of the Churchill River. From Lac la Loche, it goes down the La Loche River, through Peter Pond Lake, and into Churchill Lake. Now recognized as the Churchill River, it continues on to Lac Île-à-la-Crosse and then follows a chain of east-flowing lakes and rapids to Frog Portage. Here, it leaves the Churchill basin via Frog Portage and heads southeast along waterways making up the Sturgeon-weir River. Finally, it ends where the Sturgeon-weir joins the Saskatchewan River at Cumberland House.

Two main features give the route a wild and rugged wilderness character. First, the route lies entirely within Canada's boreal forest—the "north woods." Secondly, much of it—that between the communities of Patuanak and Denare Beach—lies within the Canadian Shield. Here, where the glaciers of the last ice age scoured away much of the soil, there are bare outcrops of ancient, Precambrian rock. These outcrops produce picturesque shorelines as well as many good campsites.

Alexander Henry was one of the first white traders to reach the upper Churchill River. His description of the region, based on what he first saw in 1776, captures the physical essence of the route even if he exaggerates the ruggedness of the local geography:

> As we advanced, we found the river frequently widening into lakes, thirty miles long, and so broad, as well as so crowded with islands, that we were unable to distinguish the main land on either side. Above them, we found a strait, in which the channel was shallow, rocky and broken, with the attendant features of rapids and carrying-places. The country was mountainous, and thinly wooded; and the banks of the river were continued rocks. Higher up, lofty mountains discovered themselves, destitute even of moss; and it was only at intervals, that we saw afar off a few stunted pine-trees.[2]

If you were to paddle the entire route, including the initial Clearwater River portion, your trip would actually be 1,100 kilometres (684 miles) long. Since this may be more paddling than you want, we have divided the route into sections and have given each section its own chapter. With the exception of the initial Clearwater section, each section begins at a northern community accessible by road and ends at a similar community downstream. You can therefore use one or more chapters to fashion a trip that best fits your own circumstances.

The route offers some of the best wilderness paddling to be found anywhere in North America. Its relative isolation translates into a pristine canoeing and camping experience, far removed from the concrete and confusion of urban life. It is a place where natural vegetation still grows and where wildlife still finds the habitat it needs to survive. With the exception of areas immediately downstream of communities, you can still drink straight from the side of your canoe without fear of human pollution.

Unlike so many places in the world, the route is still open to use by all responsible travellers. You are free to paddle your canoe and pitch your tent where you wish without permit, licence, or fee. Such freedom is a rare thing these days, and it goes a long way toward making the route a special place.

Climate and Weather

The route lies entirely within the subarctic climatic region. This means that the route's waterways are typically sealed shut by ice in winter for as long as they are open in summer. Typically, spring breakup is not over until early May or later. The first fall frosts usually begin in early September. Actual freeze-up of small lakes and quiet bays begins in October and is well advanced everywhere except on large lakes by early November. In short, the regular canoeing season runs from about June 1 to October 1.

Paddling the route, you may encounter some days that are wet, cold, and miserable. But as a rule, you can expect good weather and at least a few days that are gloriously warm and sunny. Though the route is less arid than southern Saskatchewan, its rainfall is actually quite light with an average summer having a total of about 30 centimetres (12 inches).[3] At one point during our 1986 trip, it rained for four days straight, but this is uncommon. Usually, a day or two of cloud and rain will be followed by clear, sunny skies.

The temperature and precipitation statistics in Table 1.1 approximate summer weather conditions on the route.

Table 1.1   Three-year Average Temperature and Precipitation at Missinipe (1994-96)

Month	Average High	Average Low	Average Temperature	Precipitation
May	14.5°C (58.1°F)	0.1°C (32.2°F)	7.3°C (45.1°F)	44 mm (1.7 in)
June	23.2°C (73.8°F)	8.1°C (46.6°F)	15.6°C (60.1°F)	63 mm (2.5 in)
July	23.3°C (73.9°F)	10.4°C (50.7°F)	16.8°C (62.2°F)	72 mm (2.8 in)
August	21.1°C (70.0°F)	8.8°C (47.8°F)	14.7°C (58.5°F)	91 mm (3.6 in)
September	16.6°C (61.9°F)	4.7°C (40.5°F)	10.7°C (51.3°F)	48 mm (1.9 in)
October*	6.9°C (44.4°F)	-1.8°C (28.8°F)	2.5°C (36.5°F)	40 mm (1.6 in)

Data collected by Ric Driediger of Horizons Unlimited in Missinipe for Environment Canada.
*Note: October data is for the years 1993, 1994, and 1995. October data does not include snowfall.

Wind is always of special interest to canoeists since any wind strong enough to create white-caps is apt to keep a canoe on shore. In northern Saskatchewan, the prevailing summer wind is from the west with average wind velocity being between 12 and 14 kilometres per hour (7 and 9 miles per hour)—notably less than in southern parts of the province. In the fall, the wind comes more out of the north and increases in velocity.[4]

Although wind conditions can vary dramatically from day to day, the wind often follows a 24-hour cycle driven by the sun's energy. On clear days, the wind is typically very light at sunrise. The sun then begins to heat up the forest which in turn causes the air above it to warm and rise. As more and more air rises and cooler air comes in to take its place, the wind builds. This wind generally blows strong through the afternoon. Then, as the sun sets, the wind ordinarily diminishes to an evening calm. When the cycle is in effect, you can sometimes escape being windbound by embarking in the evening or early morning. At times, of course, the wind may blow strong both day and night and force you to stay put for a day or so. Here, the value of patience cannot be overstated. The wind *will* eventually drop and let you proceed safely.

The route is all but free from hurricanes and tornadoes. (A freak tornado did touch down on the Churchill in early July 2000.) Occasionally, though, during either day or night, severe thunderstorms and strong winds can hit like a freight train. These are rare, but you will want to keep them in mind. During the day, a weather watch will let you know if it is time to leave the water to seek refuge on land. In the evenings, pitching your tent in a place that is sheltered yet away from ready-to-crash trees will allow you to sleep safely.

Daylight

Because the route lies between 54° and 57° north latitude, it has long summer days. It is not quite the land of the midnight sun, but it should provide as much daylight as you need through most of the paddling season. At the summer solstice in late June, the Buffalo Narrows area has a sunrise time of 4:26 a.m. and a sunset time of 10:04 p.m.[5] Allowing for pre-dawn light and twilight, you can expect to have usable daylight by 4:00 a.m. and as late as 11:00 p.m. Into the fall, the days shorten rapidly, but even into October, you will have twelve hours of usable light.

Vegetation

The route lies entirely within Canada's boreal forest belt. Its main trees are aspen poplar (*Populus tremuloides*), black spruce (*Picea mariana*), and jack pine (*Pinus banksiana*). The aspens—favourite food of the beaver—proliferate along the route, most noticeably in the west before the route enters the Shield. Black spruce dominate low-lying areas, where they form a dense "rabbit bush," but they also grow extensively on the Shield's rock outcrops. Jack pines form thick stands on sandy soil and also survive well on Shield rock. Less common species include balsam poplar, white spruce, balsam fir, white birch, and tamarack. In the Cumberland House area, you will also find cottonwood, Manitoba maple, American elm, and green ash. Sometimes, an area will have only one tree species, but often several species grow together to form a mixed wood. For example, a hillside might have 60 percent aspen and balsam poplar, 30 percent black and white spruce, and 10 percent randomly spaced birch and jack pine.

The route's forest ordinarily has an understorey of shrubs. Near the water and in wet spots, you will find river alder, dwarf birch, red-osier dogwood (oddly, related to the little bunchberry), willows (whose species are hard to sort out), and sweet gale. Away from the water, at least in aspens and mixed woods, the green alder creates tangled thickets and encroaches on many portage trails. The alder offers no fruit, but several other shrubs sharing its territory have edible berries—saskatoons, gooseberries, raspberries, pincherries, and low bush-cranberries. In very dry situations, where little else will grow, creeping juniper (its small blue berries are actually cones) sometimes finds enough moisture to form thick green mats.

Below the shrubs, the forest floor is green with enough small plants to keep any amateur botanist busy. In low areas, shrub-like Labrador tea (whose leaves make a mild tea) are every-where. Blueberry (producing fine fruit) can be found on several different terrains. Other species easy to identify include fireweed (common in burnt areas), twinflower, bearberry, bog and dry ground cranberry, bunchberry, cloudberry, dewberry, strawberry, coltsfoot, and sarsaparilla. Immediately at ground level, there are also mosses and lichens (the pale green reindeer moss found on dry ground is really a lichen).

Not all the route's vegetation is on dry land. Many plants grow in or right next to the water. With the aid of a plant guide, you can learn to identify much of what you see from your canoe.

Plants common to the route's shallow water and shore margins include cattail, horsetail, great bulrush, giant bur-reed, water smartweed, yellow pond lily, sedges, and wild mint.

Horsetails in water. Photo taken June 28, 1986, downstream from the old Knee Lake settlement site.

Animals

The mammals you are most likely to see while canoeing and camping along the route are beaver, muskrat, otter, woodchuck, snowshoe hare, and red squirrel. (You can also count on being startled by beaver tails slapping the water on quiet nights.) Other fur bearers—lynx, coyote, fox, mink, ermine, fisher, marten, and wolverine—are secretive and rarely seen. The larger mammals—moose, woodland caribou, white-tailed deer, and black bear—also tend to stay hidden from view, but you may chance upon them around river bends and on portages. As for the legendary timber wolf, while you are not apt to see one, you might hear its stirring howl at nightfall.

PAUL GERAGHTY / SASKATCHEWAN ENVIRONMENT

Otters (above) and woodland caribou (below).

Over the centuries, these animals have all been hunted and trapped by people living on the route. However, with their habitat largely intact, most populations are at safe levels. Only two mammals living along the route—the wolverine and the woodland caribou—are considered vulnerable. These species require large tracts of wilderness to survive and are intolerant of habitat change caused by human intervention. In 1998, both species were listed as being at risk by the Committee on the Status of Endangered Wildlife in Canada.[6]

The route is rather short on amphibians and reptiles. The only amphibians resident on the route are the boreal chorus frog, the northern leopard frog, the wood frog, and the Canadian toad. The sole reptile is the red-sided garter snake which, happily, is harmless to humans.[7]

Birds

The route's birds are much more visible than its animals. Even if you are not a birdwatcher, you will easily identify several species. Most notable of these are the bald eagle, common loon, white pelican, raven, and grey jay (this dapper-looking bird is also known as the "Canada jay," "whiskey jack," and "camp robber").

The bald eagle is of special interest to many canoeists. The route—particularly its Shield section—has some of the best bald eagle breeding habitat in North America. A 1996 study showed

PAUL GERAGHTY / SASKATCHEWAN ENVIRONMENT

Bald eagle with eaglets on nest (above) and loons (below).

that between Otter Rapids and Trade Lake the route had a total of fifty-six nests with twenty-nine of these active (a breeding pair may change nests from year to year).[8] Bald eagles, both male and female, develop their white head and tail plumage by four or five years of age and apparently begin breeding about two years later.[9] On the route, when you see a white-headed eagle, you can keep an eye out for a nest—typically a huge platform of sticks built well above the ground in a large aspen. If the nest is active, you may see young eaglets (usually two) poking their heads up over the edge of the nest as they wait for their parents to bring more fish dinner.

Most canoeists will instantly recognize the common loon by its wild, haunting call. Loon pairs use the entire guide route as a summer home and breeding ground, hatching two chicks on a low mound of mud and plant material built alongshore. Fish-eating birds, loons are superb underwater swimmers. When one vanishes near your canoe, it is a challenge guessing how far away it will resurface.

Other individual bird species to watch for include the double-crested cormorant (often called the "crow duck"), belted kingfisher, common nighthawk, sandhill crane, and golden eagle (confusingly similar to an immature bald eagle). You are also likely to see various species of gulls, terns, ducks, geese, grebes, blackbirds, hawks, owls, woodpeckers, chickadees, grouse, and assorted shore birds. You will definitely hear many of the small songbirds who nest in the route's marshes and shore thickets, but hidden as they are, you will not easily catch more than a fleeting glimpse of them.

Fish and Fishing

Northern pike (*Esox luscius*), commonly known as "jack" or "jackfish," and walleye (*Stizostedion vitreum*), often referred to as "pickerel," are the main game fish you will encounter. Both are excellent eating fish. It is generally quite easy to catch walleye and a related species called sauger by casting a jig into the foot of rapids along the route. Pike can be caught almost anywhere, especially along the edges of shallow, reedy areas. They are voracious feeders and will strike just about any type of lure.

Other fish include the pretty Arctic grayling (found only on the Clear-water River section of the route) which can be caught on a wet or dry fly. The rather ugly burbot (also known as maria or ling cod) also counts as a game fish, but it is not often caught by summer anglers. Yellow perch are numerous, but they are very small along

PAUL GERAGHTY / SASKATCHEWAN ENVIRONMENT

Northern pike.

the route and seldom fished for. Although lake trout are found in the deeper lakes adjacent to the guide route, they usually only occur on the route as accidental migrants. As for whitefish, while they are a mainstay of the route's commercial fishery, they only rarely take an angler's hook. Goldeye are said to occur in the Pelican Narrows area and at Cumberland Lake. Lake sturgeon, once common from the Sturgeon-weir River to Cumberland Lake, are now very rare, and sport fishing for this prehistoric-looking monster is currently banned.

If you plan to fish along the route, you must purchase a provincial fishing licence, available at local Saskatchewan Environment offices (see Appendix B) and at many gas stations and retail stores in northern Saskatchewan. When you purchase your licence, you can ask for a copy of Saskatchewan's anglers' guide which sets out the daily limits and regulations for the current fishing season.

TRIP PLANNING

This guide is not a "how to plan your trip" book. We assume that you or your partner(s) already have experience in planning a canoe expedition. If you do not, we recommend that you read one or more of the good canoe tripping books on the market. In what follows below, we restrict our planning advice to a few topics pertinent to the route.

Skill Levels

Whatever your canoeing experience, it is fair to ask, "What skills do I need for this route?" The answer to this question depends on what section or sections of the route you wish to paddle. As a general comment, we can say that the route is well-suited to the ordinary canoeist. It is definitely challenging, but it does not have to be a white-knuckle adventure.

Since not all sections of the route are the same, this guide suggests the skill level required for each particular section—whether modest, advanced, or expert. These levels take into account factors such as the nature of any rapids and portages, available wind protection, and the section's remoteness. While the levels have no official status, we give them the following common sense definitions:

Modest: Good basic skills beyond the novice level, i.e., an ability to paddle flatwater in a straight line in fair weather and run Class 1 rapids.

Advanced: An ability to paddle flatwater in some wind, run Class 2 rapids, and negotiate moderate rapids by wading, lining, or tracking.

Expert: An ability to paddle flatwater in winds producing whitecaps, run Class 3 rapids, and negotiate difficult rapids by wading, lining, tracking, or poling.

The suggested skill level for a particular trip should be taken only as an approximate measure of what a trip may demand. Factors such as water levels, the time of year, and weather conditions can have a dramatic effect on a trip's level of difficulty. It should also be noted that a particular trip is often more difficult in an upstream direction. While upstream travel avoids the risks associated with running rapids, going up strong currents often calls for special skills and extra endurance. The skill levels required for the route sections are summarized in Table 1.2.

Table 1.2   Trip Planning Information

Chapter	Route Section	Skills Required for Downstream Travel	Skills Required for Upstream Travel	Distance km (mi)	Days Paddling	Portages
3	Clearwater River to La Loche	Advanced	Expert*	119 (74)	5-7	7-8
4	La Loche to Buffalo Narrows	Advanced	Advanced	127 (79)	5-8	0
5	Buffalo Narrows to Île-à-la-Crosse	Modest	Modest	64 (40)	2	0
6	Île-à-la-Crosse to Patuanak	Modest	Modest	63 (39)	2-3	1
7	Patuanak to Pinehouse	Advanced	Expert*	175 (109)	6-9	3-8
8	Pinehouse to Otter Rapids	Modest	Advanced	170 (106)	6-8	9-15
9	Otter Rapids to Stanley Mission	Modest	Modest	34 (21)	2	2
10	Stanley Mission to Pelican Narrows	Advanced	Advanced	125 (78)	5-6	9-11
11	Pelican Narrows to Denare Beach	Advanced	Advanced	127 (79)	5-7	5-8
12	Denare Beach to Sturgeon Landing	Advanced	Expert*	65 (40)	3-4	0-1
13	Sturgeon Landing to Cumberland House	Modest	Modest	52 (32)	2-3	0
Total				1,100 (684)	43-59	36-54

*Not recommended for ordinary canoeists.

Choosing your Party

We suggest that in choosing your party for a trip on the route you pay some heed to the above-recommended skill levels. Although this guide was prepared with the ordinary canoeist in mind, the term "ordinary" should not be equated with "inexperienced." We recommend against a group of novice canoeists attempting the route on their own. Novices can paddle and enjoy the route, but they should do so with a veteran partner who can compensate for their own inexperience. Even the most naturally able beginner can benefit from the company of an experienced mentor.

In planning a group trip, you should also take into consideration factors beyond the paddling and camping skills of your group. Are you extroverts or introverts? Are you all in good physical condition? How do you each handle psychological adversity or physical hardship? Being alone with people for days or weeks on end in the wilderness can be a trying experience (more trying than the wilderness itself), and you should do what you can to bring together people who can get along under difficult circumstances. You should also know in advance what each person's objectives for the trip are. Is it to paddle through every available hour of daylight? To run as many dangerous whitewater rapids as possible? To go fishing? To enjoy the quiet splendour of nature? To escape from family or work? To catch up on sleep? To talk and carouse with old friends? The answer to such questions will help determine the compatibility of your group.

What is the right size of group? You should try to keep to eight or fewer paddlers. Big groups make it hard to find campsites of sufficient size. They are also harder to organize in camp and on the water. And, the more people, the less likely that you will get to enjoy the solitude of your surroundings or to see wildlife. Of course, if you are leading a school or youth group, your party may be quite large indeed. If so, you will need to plan around your numbers, paying special attention to campsite selection.

To completely avoid group dynamics, you might decide to go solo. Keep in mind, however, that going it alone on the sparsely populated route means there may not be anyone around to help you in the event of difficulty or injury. That said, there is no law prohibiting solo paddling. Moreover, being alone in the wilderness can be a profound experience. How, then, can you reduce the risks of a solo trip on the voyageur highway? First, make sure that you have advanced canoe tripping skills. Second, make sure that you are not only in good physical condition but also psychologically prepared for being alone. Third, avoid long lake traverses and run only Class 1 and Class 2 rapids. Fourth, be extra careful around camp. Finally, have a friend back home who knows your trip route, schedule, and emergency rescue plan.

If you cannot find a suitable party to paddle with and you are not quite ready to go solo, you may wish to look to a professional canoeing outfitter for help. An outfitter can arrange for some preliminary training, the right equipment, and an experienced guide. You may wish to request a trip of your own design or else join an expedition already planned by the outfitter. Either way, an outfitted trip is an excellent option in many situations. Contact names for canoe outfitters serving the route can be found in Appendix B.

Trip Length

We have divided the route into sections or "trips" of varying lengths. Table 1.2 above sets out the required skill level, distance, estimated paddling time, and the number of portages for each. The estimated times in the table assume an average travelling speed of 25 kilometres (16 miles) per day, but they also allow for the risk of being windbound on big lakes and/or the extra time needed for bad rapids and tough portages. You can use Table 1.2, and the more detailed information contained in the route chapters, to tailor a trip that matches your particular situation.

When to Go

As already mentioned, the route's paddling season runs from about June 1 to October 1. You may plan your trip for any time within this window. However, if your trip includes the Clearwater River, the La Loche River, or the southern part of the Sturgeon-weir River, you should be aware that low water levels may cause problems as summer advances. These rivers have their peak flows in May or June and then sometimes see flow rates drop significantly enough to create serious rock gardens. Accordingly, trips on these rivers are best made in early summer.

What to Bring

Working from a list will speed up the packing process and may even save a sleeping bag from getting left behind in the hall closet. You may already have your own checklist matched to your personal preferences. In case you do not, we offer our own list on page 12 as a reference for a two-person team. The list is long, and you can perhaps safely pare it down. But keep in mind that if a handy item is small, you may want to bring it even if it is not really essential. And although you may never use your First Aid kit or spare eyeglasses, common sense dictates that you bring them anyway.

The canoe is perhaps the most important checklist item of all since, without a canoe, there is no canoe trip. Happily, there are many canoes on the market suitable for travel on the route. A canoe need not be fancy (we did our 1986 trip using the humble Grumman Eagle), but it should be large enough to provide ample freeboard when loaded and sturdy enough to bump over the occasional ledge without damage. Ideally, it should also be light enough for you and/or your partner (if you have one) to handle easily on dry land. If you wrench your back hoisting a heavy ark onto your shoulders, your trip could become more of a challenge than you really want.

Your tent will also be a main part of your outfit. We recommend you bring a good quality, two-layered tent—one with a breathable inner wall that is absolutely bug proof and an outer fly that will shed rain. Since many route campsites are on bare Shield rock, it is also a good idea to have a tent with a free-standing design, one that does not need a lot of pegs in the ground to support it. It is also very convenient to have a tent with zippered doors in both the front and the back (a back door might be good should a bear come calling at the front). Our only other tent advice is that you bring one rated for more people than you plan to put in it. We have found a four-person tent is about right for two people when laundry and wet maps are hung from the ceiling to dry.

Food

Like your canoe and tent, the food you will bring on your trip deserves special mention. While the average person needs between 2,000 and 2,500 calories a day for everyday living, this can easily jump to 5,000 calories a day if you are paddling for hours on end and muscling packs across portages. If you naturally have a high metabolism, then your caloric needs will be even higher. Plan to eat at least double what you would ordinarily. We know this equation from hard experience. When we began our 1986 trip, one of us had not an ounce of extra fat, while the other was a typical sedentary urbanite with several pounds of extra lard. Despite eating enormous volumes of food, we both lost weight daily to the point that, by the end of our trip, Mr. Fit-and-Trim looked anorexic, while Fat Boy had the build of a slim movie star. The moral of the story? Bring lots of extra food.

As for what food you bring, this is an intensely personal decision. Some canoe trippers believe in the moveable feast approach—they dine rather than eat. Everything, including expensive wine and even hors d'oeuvres, is brought along. Others—and we throw ourselves into this camp—see food as canoe fuel and prepare accordingly. But no matter what your menu, exercise

canoe
carrying yoke
bow and stern lines
large car sponge
bailer or water pump*
travel mugs (tied to
    thwarts)
4 paddles (only 1
    required by law)*
life jackets*
rain suits
◆ ◆ ◆ ◆
tent and fly
silicone
extra rope
light cord
◆ ◆ ◆ ◆
2 tarps
sleeping pads
sleeping bags
◆ ◆ ◆ ◆
food box
canoe packs
day packs
◆ ◆ ◆ ◆
maps
map case
route guide
◆ ◆ ◆ ◆
compass
◆ ◆ ◆ ◆
garbage bags
plastic bags and ties
◆ ◆ ◆ ◆
whistle (or other sound
    signalling device)*
flashlight
flares
buoyant heaving line
    (minimum 15 m or
    50 ft)*
binoculars
watch

sewing kit
sewing elastic
duct tape
tent seam sealer
small stuff sacks
◆ ◆ ◆ ◆
fishing rods and case
fishing tackle
fish hook remover
filleting knife
sharpening stone
fishing licences
◆ ◆ ◆ ◆
snare wire
axe
folding saw
jack knives
◆ ◆ ◆ ◆
campfire grill and
    canvas cover
campfire mitts
fire starter
matches (water-
    proofed)
◆ ◆ ◆ ◆
First Aid kit
scissors
tweezers
sun screen
lip balm
hand cream
medicinal brandy
◆ ◆ ◆ ◆
insect repellant
bug nets
◆ ◆ ◆ ◆
extra eye glasses   (as
    required)
contact lens kit   (as
    required)
sun glasses
glasses straps
laundry soap

hand soap
shampoo
hair brush
comb
mirror
nail clippers
tooth brushes
tooth paste
dental floss
razors
towels
wash cloth
toilet paper
◆ ◆ ◆ ◆
regular underwear
long underwear
shirts
sweaters
shorts
long pants (2 pairs)
footwear (2 pairs)
extra shoelaces
hats
toques
gloves
light parkas
waterproof
    clothing bags
◆ ◆ ◆ ◆
frying pan and lid
2 pots and lids
3 plates/bowls
3 cups
3 spoons
3 forks
3 knives
spatula
ladle
wooden spoon
cutlery container (e.g.,
    Rubbermaid or
    Tupperware)

water bottle or
    thermos
large bowl or basin
dish soap
dish cloth
scouring pads
tea towels
◆ ◆ ◆ ◆
flour
lard
baking powder
salt
pepper
margarine
pasta
rice
lentils
dried meat
cheese
ketchup
soup mixes
spices
cereal
raisins/currants
other dried fruit
powdered milk
sugar
tea
coffee
juice crystals
jam
peanut butter
chocolate/sweets
vitamin pills
◆ ◆ ◆ ◆
camera, film, and
    waterproof case
cards/board games
reading material
notebook
pens

*denotes equipment required by federal law

and fresh air will guarantee you will always be hungry enough to enjoy mealtime. As the old joke goes: What is the difference between a bad meal and a good meal? . . . Three days.

How you organize and carry your food and kitchen wares calls for some thought. A strong backpack is okay for bags of flour and macaroni, but not so good for things that squash or break. Many people prefer to use rigid plastic barrels with airtight lids that clamp or screw on. The barrels keep food dry and also keep food smells away from bears. We still use the old-style plywood grub boxes with hinged lids. They can be heavy (the box on our 1986 trip weighed 100 pounds loaded), and they may not seal in odours. On the other hand, a box opens wide for meal preparation, and later, with the lid closed, it makes a good table or chair.

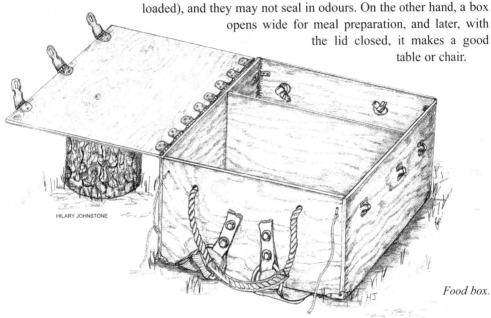

HILARY JOHNSTONE

Food box.

Entry and Exit Points

Once you have your party organized, your trip selected, and things packed up, you need to arrange getting to and from the route. Since the guide's trip chapters all begin at a point (usually a community) accessible by road, your arrangements will likely involve a vehicle "shuttle." The first part of the shuttle involves getting from your home base to the route. Road distances in both kilometres and miles to the route's main start/end points from four Saskatchewan centres are summarized in Table 1.3.

For most canoeists, the second part of the shuttle involves travel between the start and end points to ensure transportation home for crew and gear at the end of a trip. This travel can have different permutations. One option is to proceed first to your end point, pick up a driver from that community, proceed to your start point, and then have the driver return your vehicle to your end point.

One way to avoid the second part of the shuttle is to do a return trip by travelling out for a certain distance and then returning to the start point. A straight out and back trip on the route is worthwhile since you will always notice things on the comeback leg that you missed going out. You can also look at ways to loop off the route to see new country as you return to your start point.

Table 1.3 Distances by Road to Access Points from Selected Centres in km (mi)

Entry and Exit Points	Saskatoon	Regina	Prince Albert	La Ronge
Warner Rapids, Clearwater River	666 (413)	925 (575)	575 (357)	501 (311)
La Loche	601 (373)	860 (534)	510 (317)	436 (271)
Buffalo Narrows	496 (308)	755 (469)	407 (253)	333 (207)
Île-à-la-Crosse	473 (294)	732 (455)	384 (239)	310 (193)
Patuanak	496 (308)	755 (469)	407 (253)	311 (193)
Pinehouse	486 (302)	709 (441)	345 (214)	211 (131)
Otter Rapids	464 (288)	687 (427)	325 (202)	85 (53)
Stanley Mission	460 (286)	683 (424)	320 (199)	80 (50)
Pelican Narrows	529 (329)	686 (426)	388 (241)	301 (187)
Denare Beach	566 (352)	723 (449)	425 (264)	336 (209)
Sturgeon Landing	584 (363)	636 (395)	441 (274)	452 (281)
Cumberland House	437 (272)	525 (326)	304 (189)	488 (303)

Vehicles left behind while you are on your trip are best placed in the safekeeping of someone in the local community to avoid theft and vandalism. In some cases, the local village office, First Nation administration office, or Royal Canadian Mounted Police (RCMP) detachment may be able to direct you to reliable community members willing to help.

Because the route's main start points are all at or near northern communities, they offer a chance to pick up last-minute supplies, make telephone calls, and mail letters. The larger communities have some characteristics in common. Each will have one or more stores, a gas station, a post office, an RCMP detachment office, a main church (either Catholic or Anglican) and, except in Métis communities such as Buffalo Narrows and Île-à-la-Crosse, a First Nation administration office around which so much of the community's life revolves. As you might expect, smaller communities, such as Sturgeon Landing, have fewer facilities.

PADDLING THE ROUTE

Maps, Compass, and GPS

Unless you are fortunate enough to have been born and raised on the route, you will need one or more topographic maps for the trip you have chosen. This guide is meant to complement "topo" maps and not to take their place. Without proper maps, you run the risk of becoming hopelessly lost or going over a falls you did not want to see up close.

The federal government has mapped all of Canada using the National Topographic System which divides the country's landmass into large blocks numbered from 1 at St. John's, Newfoundland, in the southeast to 117 at the Beaufort Sea in the northwest (with some numbers skipped near the U.S. border and three odd numbers added in the high Arctic). Each large block is subdivided into sixteen lettered blocks (from A to P) which are in turn further subdivided into sixteen numbered blocks. Maps for the lettered blocks have a scale of 1:250,000, while maps for their subdivisions have a scale of 1:50,000.

The route is covered by eight polychrome (colour) maps of the 1:250,000 series and by about forty-five mainly monochrome (black and white) maps of the larger scale 1:50,000 series. These maps contain details of lakes, rivers, topographic relief, forest cover, human settlement, roads, and other man-made features. As a general rule, the larger scale the map, the better it will fill your navigational needs. You can get by with the smaller scale (1:250,000), but the more detailed (1:50,000) maps are better suited for route finding. In any case, while we will often refer to the 1:50,000 maps, we will assume that you may have only the 1:250,000 series.

You can order either 1:50,000 or 1:250,000 scale maps through Natural Resources Canada (NRCan) which has an on-line service listing regional distributors, map dealers, and on-line map stores. In Saskatchewan, you can get the maps through Environment offices throughout the province. Address and contact numbers for obtaining maps are provided in Appendix B.

A quick note regarding the map grid references used in this guide. Known as Universal Transverse Mercator (UTM) references, these six-digit numbers use the grid lines marked out on both 1:50,000 and 1:250,000 maps to describe the location of a particular point. A UTM number's first three digits—or easting—describe a point's position in an east-west direction, while its second three digits—or northing—identify the point's north-south location. Details of how to use UTM numbers can be found in the margin of every topo map (a good reason not to cut the margins off your maps). In the route chapters which follow, locations are frequently pinpointed by a bracketed reference to a map sheet and the six-digit UTM number.

Maps and water do not mix. Nonetheless, you will need to use your map regularly while paddling, even in rainy weather. The most effective way to protect your maps is to use a waterproof map case which you may purchase from an outdoor equipment store or from a map dealer. You could also laminate your maps in plastic, but this makes them difficult to fold or write on. Another option might be to paint your maps with a clear construction sealant to make them water repellant.

For both canoeing and hiking off portage trails, you should have a good compass. Inexpensive and easy to use, a basic orienteering compass can be a real help (and sometimes survival tool) in navigating island-studded lakes and unmarked or indistinct walking trails.

GPS—short for Global Positioning System—has brought a revolutionary change to navigation around the world. GPS receivers pick up signals with time and positioning information from twenty-four satellites orbiting Earth. With this information, GPS can tell you your location on the ground at any time within a margin of error of 100 metres (110 yards) or less. It can also give you the bearings for and distance to your intended destination and update this information for you as you paddle or walk. Despite its expense, some canoeists now have a GPS receiver as a part of their tripping outfit.

Rapids and Water Levels

This guide provides you with detailed information on the major rapids along the route and advice aimed at helping you determine when to run a rapid and when to portage. You should not, however, accept our advice on a significant rapid without first doing your own scouting and making your own decision as to how it should be handled. This is because water levels on the route can vary considerably, turning what is a rushing torrent one year into a trickle the next and vice versa. Our advice is based mainly upon the water levels we encountered in 1986 which happened to be a year with fairly average flow conditions. But average is not always normal, and there is a good chance you will find water levels quite different than what we describe.

Water levels along the route depend upon a number of factors, including the past winter's snowfall and the speed of spring runoff. Sask Water Corporation studies these factors, monitors present flow conditions, and forecasts future flows. It can provide you with streamflow summaries for the Clearwater, Churchill, and Sturgeon-weir rivers and comparison figures from other years (see Appendix B). By comparing the average water levels mentioned in this guide with the actual levels you will be confronting on your trip, you will be better able to gauge the relevance of our advice.

In discussing the rapids of the route, we use the standard rating system in the Saskatchewan canoe trip booklets available from Saskatchewan Environment. The rating system is as follows:

Class 1: Small and regular waves; easily navigated passages. Usually navigable by novice paddlers.

Class 2: Regular, medium-sized waves; low ledges; sweepers; log jams may be present; passages clear though narrow and requiring competent maneuvering. Inspection usually required. At least one member of team should be intermediate paddler.

Class 3: Waves numerous, high, and irregular; exposed rocks; strong eddies. Inspection strongly recommended. Upper limit for open canoe. Usually navigable by intermediate to expert paddlers.

Class 4: Waves high, powerful, and irregular; dangerous exposed rocks; boiling eddies; passages difficult to reconnoiter. Inspection mandatory. Powerful and precise maneuvering required. Rapids of this class, and over, should only be attempted by expert paddlers in covered canoes.

Class 5: River channel extremely obstructed; ledges; violent and fast current; abrupt corners. Reconnoitering mandatory but difficult.

Class 6: Difficulties of Class 5 carried to extremes of navigability. Definite risk of life involved.

Since we have written this guide for the ordinary canoeist, we assume that all rapids are run without spray skirts. Accordingly, we recommend against running any rapid greater than Class 3, and we suggest that Class 3 rapids, if run at all, might really best be run empty or lightly loaded.

If your trip is upstream, rapids will present you with special challenges. A rapid that might be an easy downstream run may require an upstream portage. However, wading or tracking your canoe can sometimes allow you to avoid carrying, and hence, where this is practical, we offer our suggestions. We do not do so for the preliminary Clearwater River section and Chapter 12's "South Weir" section since their long stretches of strong current discourage any upstream travel.

Portages

On the route, portages provide a way around almost every rapid of any size as well as paths across two important heights of land. Their lengths vary considerably—from just a few metres (or yards) past the shortest rapids to the 19-kilometre (12-mile) carry at Methy Portage. A significant part of the guide route, they are rich in history since most have changed very little through centuries of use. Tramping over a portage, you will tread in the very footsteps of pre-contact indigenous peoples, fur trade voyageurs, and famous explorers.

This guide provides the most common name for each portage, an estimate of its length in metres (with length in yards in parentheses) based on our own pacing (checked against any measure given in the Saskatchewan canoe trip booklets), and an explanation of how to locate both the upstream and downstream ends of a portage. It also gives a brief description of the portage's overall condition and, where applicable, its camping possibilities.

The more bags, bundles, and loose articles you bring along, the more trips you will have to make across each portage. By keeping your food and gear to a minimum and by consolidating it into a few packs, you can minimize the number of carries across each portage. Given the number and length of portages on the whitewater sections of the route, we recommend a maximum of two carries per person on each portage. Watch out for small, loose articles. Without special care, you can easily leave such gear behind on portages.

Camping

While the route has increasing canoe traffic (especially between Great Devil Rapids and Nistowiak Falls), it is still one of the least congested and least controlled canoe routes in the world. Currently, there are no specific canoe camping regulations on any part of the route. Camping permits are not required, and you are free to choose your campsite from a wide range of natural sites. Open campfires are allowed except when forest fires pose a hazard.

This guide will help you find many of the route's natural campsites. It will also give you an idea of what a particular site is like and how many tents it can handle. This information should help you plan your evening stops, especially if you are in charge of a big group and need to find larger campsites. The campsites are, of course, only available on a "first come" basis. It is therefore useful to consider what alternate sites might be available if a preferred site is already occupied.

Bears

What about the bears, you ask. While planning our 1986 trip, we found ourselves constantly returning to the subject of black bears (the route has no grizzly bears). In the end, we became so paranoid that we decided to bring an ancient single-shot shotgun with us for self-defence. Every night, we loaded up our gun and kept it between our sleeping bags. Every night, we waited for a bear to come. But we never had so much as a single visit in seventy nights.

The truth is that black bears are generally shy and avoid humans. Occasionally, their quest for food will bring them into a camp, but some basic precautions will reduce the risk of this happening. Clean your fish far from your campsite and discard fish remains into deep water some distance from shore. Do not bury fish offal or other food waste near your camp. Make sure that your kitchen area is cleaned up at night with food and pack-out refuse sealed in odour-proof containers. If your camp shows signs of regular bear visits, you may choose to suspend your food containers above ground. Our own practice has been to store our food in a spot which a bear could not easily approach without first going past our tent—our theory being that the bear might be warded off by our presence even if we are fast asleep.

If a bear does come into your camp, we suggest you make as much noise and racket as possible to scare it off. You then might as well pack up and move on to a more tranquil spot. If you decided to stay, the bear could come back and even if it chose not to, it is highly unlikely you would get any sleep while you awaited its next move.

Insects

Our own view is that you are much more likely to be bothered by insects than by bears. The route is a bug-free zone for half the year, but during the paddling season, it has a host of insects that love to bite—ranging in size from big horseflies and deerflies down to little blackflies and tiny no-see-ums. Happily, with the exception of the occasional far-ranging horsefly, these bugs will not bother you while you are on the water paddling.

You should bring along bug dope (Muskol or other DEET-containing mixtures are best) for use at the end of the day since the mosquitoes love to come out for a bite or two just as the sun is setting. As for black flies, a good hat can provide at least some protection. If you are particularly sensitive to insect bites, you may want to consider a "bug hat" with fine mesh screening to protect your face and neck. A specially designed "bug shirt" will offer you even more protection.

Safety

As the saying goes, "safety is no accident." Rather, safety is the ongoing, conscious management of risks to prevent these risks from spiralling into dangers, accidents, emergencies, or even tragedies. Such management is crucial on canoe trips where remoteness can magnify what might be a matter of little consequence back home into a real emergency. Ordinary common sense is a good risk management tool for canoeists. But a safety checklist can help too, and we recommend you make such a list. You can look to canoeing instruction books for guidance and also consider the following items on our own list:

- **Leave your trip plan with a trustworthy friend.** Include a practical action plan for your friend to follow if you do not arrive at your destination on schedule. The RCMP should be alerted in an apparent emergency. They in turn will contact a Search and Rescue unit of experienced northerners for assistance.

- **Keep dry and warm or, at least, maintain an ability to get dry and warm.** Have proper rain gear, avoid capsizing your canoe, keep your sleeping bag and spare clothes in waterproof bags or containers, and carry waterproofed matches or a lighter on your person at all times.

- **Wear your life jacket.** Even an Olympic swimmer can drown if knocked unconscious in a water mishap.

- **Respect the wind on lakes.** Never travel in wind conditions creating whitecaps. Never make any traverse which could leave you at the wind's mercy. Learn to enjoy a windbound camp.

- **Scout all significant rapids before deciding whether to shoot.** Remember that a downstream vantage point will show you obstacles not visible from above the rapids.

- **Get off the water when lightning threatens.**

- **Keep track of your canoe.** Never leave your canoe unattended without both bow and stern lines securely tied to rocks or trees. This advice applies even when your canoe is on dry land since the wind can blow a canoe overland an incredible distance.

- **Avoid camping under dead or dying trees that could fall or lose branches in a storm.**

- **Bring an up-to-date First Aid kit and be familiar with basic First Aid procedures.**

If we were to focus on only one safety issue, it would be the importance of keeping dry and warm on your trip. There are times when a cold wind, a driving rain, wet clothes, a cold water dunking, or even simple cool temperatures combined with fatigue, hunger, and/or dehydration can result in your body losing heat faster than it can produce it. The result is hypothermia—a serious condition which, in the extreme, can lead to death.

With mild hypothermia, body temperature falls to between 32° and 35° Celsius (between 89° and 95° Fahrenheit), and shivering and some loss of coordination results. If body temperature drops further, to below 32° Celsius, severe hypothermia sets in. Shivering then stops, pulse and respiration become slow, speech becomes slurred, and coordination becomes very poor. Loss of consciousness occurs if body temperature drops to around 30° Celsius (86° Fahrenheit).

If you experience mild hypothermia, take prompt action to prevent your condition from worsening. Get out of the wind and rain, get into dry clothes, make a fire, drink something hot, and start eating high-calorie foods. If you end up with severe hypothermia, perhaps as a result of an upset in cold water, the stakes are very high. Your companion(s) should quickly but gently wrap you in dry sleeping bags (any aggressive movement could cause heart failure), and then lie next to you to provide the extra heat that your body needs but can no longer generate on its own.

Pondering a risk as grave as hypothermia, you may wonder, "Should I bring emergency communications equipment?" The route does not yet have cell phone service (that day will no doubt soon arrive), but there are bush telephones, radios, and emergency locator transmitters (ELTs) which will allow you to send messages in the case of an emergency. If you canoe to escape the telephone and related technology, the thought of bringing a telephone or radio on a canoe trip may make you cringe. But such devices do offer a kind of safety to the remote traveller.

Environmental Ethics

The wilderness of the great North-West has shrunk rapidly during this century. We must do what we can to preserve what is left for future generations. The canoe itself presents few problems—skimming lightly atop the water while propelled by old-fashioned muscle-power, it is the supreme eco-vehicle. But we as canoeists do affect the environment. How can we minimize this impact? We offer some basic guidelines which you can supplement with your own:

- Plan a trip that pares down vehicle shuttle travel.
- Camp at existing campsites that fit your group size.
- Use existing campfire pits and a minimum of firewood. (The folding metal Environmental Firebox sold by Horizons Unlimited of Missinipe is a great wood saver.)
- Make sure your campfire is dead out when you leave it.
- Respect any government ban on open fires during hot, dry weather.
- If you smoke, butt your cigarettes away from all organic matter.
- Do not cut or wound live trees for bough beds or any other purpose.
- Use a proper latrine at a single site away from your camp and the water.
- Use biodegradable soap for yourself and your dishes.
- Leave no garbage. "Pack it in. Pack it out."
- Do not touch rock paintings or disturb sites having cultural or archaeological significance.

Our objective to make the route and its history more accessible to canoeists may itself seem less than environmentally friendly. Why not simply discourage canoeists from travelling the route? Our view is that anyone who sees and appreciates the route at paddling speed will likely become a friend of the route, and an ally of efforts to preserve it as southern-style development encroaches upon it.

HISTORY OF THE ROUTE

Indigenous Waterway

We hope this guide conveys some sense of the route's long aboriginal history. Indigenous people have occupied the route for thousands of years—possibly since soon after the last glacial retreat about 10,000 years ago—and do so to this day. By contrast, Europeans and Euro-Canadians are recent arrivals, having been on the route for less than 250 years.

Regrettably, much of the early history is lost in the mists of time. People on the route in the pre-European contact era had no writing system (that we know of). Instead, they relied on oral tradition to hand down knowledge and stories from one generation to another. This tradition no doubt served people well for centuries. However, after European contact, major events and influences—such as epidemics, missionary work, and residential schools—seriously interrupted the normal verbal transfer of ancestral knowledge.

We must be careful not to overstate the loss of traditional history and knowledge. From talking to people on the route, we know that a great deal of this information still exists and continues to be passed on by word of mouth. Since we cannot speak either Cree or Dene, we have likely heard only a tiny fraction of what could be told. Notwithstanding, we use what local people have shared with us as we try to illustrate the connection between indigenous peoples and the route, both in the past and today.

As you might expect, in the period since European contact, there has been a great deal of study and writing regarding the original peoples of the route. Early fur traders, explorers, and adventurers often recorded information (sometimes misleading) about the native people they met. Archaeologists, historians, and anthropologists have added to this information. We use these written works in our efforts to explain the route's aboriginal history.

Aboriginal Rock Paintings

Although early residents of the route have left us no written record of their lives, artists among them did develop a tradition of using red ochre (iron oxide) to paint figures on bare rock faces next to the water. Some of these paintings have survived for generations despite damage from sun, water, funguses, and the very occasional human vandalism. They can be found on that part of the guide route between Pinehouse Lake in the west and Amisk Lake in the east. Who made the paintings is not definitely known, but it is believed the artists were ancestors of the route's present-day Cree.[10]

In the route chapters, we give the precise locations of all the paintings known to us and briefly describe the figures depicted at each location. Some readers, fearing vandalism or inadvertent damage to the rock paintings, might well question whether the locations of the paintings should be made public. This is a thorny issue, and one we have looked at from several angles. In the end, we have concluded that the paintings will be best protected if people have an opportunity to learn about them and appreciate them from close up.

Map 1.1   Rock painting sites

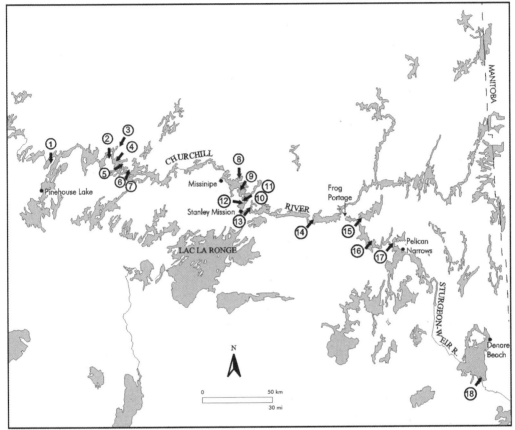

Number	Site	Map	Location	Number	Site	Map	Location
1	McDonald Bay	73-O	067751	10	Mountain Lake Peninsula #1	73P	303475
2	Kinosaskaw Lake	73P	414751	11	Mountain Lake Peninsula #2	73P	303475
3	Foster River Mouth	73P	478807	12	Four Portages	73P	266444
4	Silent Rapids	73P	469741	13	Stanley Rapids	73P	324424
5	Wamninuta Island	73P	522684	14	Inman Channel	73P	577403
6	High Rock Narrows #1	73P	559656	15	Manawan Lake	63M	039366
7	High Rock Narrows #2	73P	565655	16	Wood Lake	63M	109223
8	Rattler Creek	73P	287656	17	Medicine Rapids	63M	241202
9	Cow Narrows	73P	297545	18	Amisk Lake	63L	187389

Cree and Dene Place Names

Cree and Dene place names provide another way to highlight the long history that indigenous peoples have had with the route. Most of the official names for the route's geographical features come to us from the early fur trade or else from Saskatchewan men and women who lost their lives serving in Canada's military during World War II.[11] However, almost all lakes, rapids, and large islands also have one or more aboriginal names. Sometimes, these names simply reflect an obvious geographical feature of the place in question, but in other cases, they commemorate, or at least hint at, the occurrence of some long ago event. Relying mainly on conversations with people who have lived on the route, we have tried (using the orthographies discussed in Appendix C) to record as many of these names as possible.

Voyageur Highway

The route is indeed the old voyageur highway. From the 1770s onward, it was part of the trunk line that fur traders from both Montreal and Hudson Bay followed in order to tap the fur riches of the Canadian North-West. Every summer for a full century, iron-tough voyageurs manning birchbark canoes or York boats used the route to move trade goods inland and then bring out the preceding season's fur catch. Eventually, this traffic declined, and the route lost its role as part of Canada's first transcontinental highway. By then, however, it had already made a major impact on Canada's future.

The fur trade era was a colourful chapter in Canadian history, and there are a number of written accounts describing the Saskatchewan section of the voyageur highway. It is fascinating to read from a journal entry written perhaps two centuries ago by a fur trader or explorer who travelled the very route you are now on. In the next chapter, we introduce several of these adventurers. The route chapters include quotations from their journals and narratives, and these will help to give you a sense of what their lives might have been like. Reading these quotes as you travel should bring you about as close as you can get to a living history experience.

Voyageur Certificates

At the end of your trip, having become a modern-day voyageur, you may want something to mark your achievement. Saskatchewan Environment, in cooperation with La Ronge's Community Development Corporation, offers an excellent souvenir in the form of a "Saskatchewan Voyageur Certificate." The certificate, on parchment-like paper, sets out the canoeist's name, number of companions, the route travelled, its distance, and its portages. To be eligible for a certificate, you must pre-register your trip at participating Environment offices or the Tourist Information Centre at La Ronge. Certificates are given out when you and any companions return.

THE HISTORY OF
SASKATCHEWAN'S VOYAGEUR HIGHWAY

The place of the beaver in Canadian life has been fittingly noted in the coat of arms. We have given to the maple a prominence which was due the birch. We have not yet realized that the Indian and his culture were fundamental to the growth of Canadian institutions. We are only beginning to realize the central position of the Canadian Shield.

Harold A. Innis, *The Fur Trade in Canada* (1930)[1]

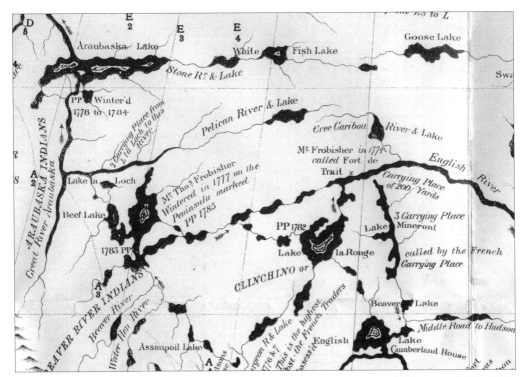

Detail of "Peter Pond's Map 1785"—as it appears in Peter Pond: Fur Trader and Adventurer *by Harold A. Innis (Irwin & Gordon, 1930).*

T
he purpose of this chapter is to tell, as concisely as possible, the history of the guide route. In the first section, we introduce you to the route's indigenous peoples—the earliest human inhabitants, the Cree who have lived in the region for centuries, the Dene who came in the late 1700s, and the Métis who were born of the fur trade. In the second section, we present a brief history of the fur trade, a history that turned an indigenous travel route into a major highway used by European fur traders and explorers. We devote the third section to the voyageur, the workhorse of the fur trade. In the last section, we introduce the fur traders and explorers whose journals and narratives give fascinating snapshots of the route as it was when Europeans first travelled through the North-West.

THE ROUTE'S INDIGENOUS PEOPLES

Earliest Inhabitants

While we cannot precisely date the first human habitation along the route, we do know that it could not have been earlier than 10,000 years ago. It was only then that North America's last major glaciation, named the Wisconsin, finally retreated north of the route after covering all of Saskatchewan (except the Cypress Hills) for perhaps 100,000 years.[2] By the time the route was ice-free, indigenous hunters, known to archaeologists as "Paleo-Indians," were already established in southern and central Saskatchewan.[3] These hunters may also have been close on the heels of the retreating ice since projectile points typical of late Paleo-Indian times—about 7,500 to 8,000 years ago—have been found at Buffalo Narrows.[4]

Unlike southern Saskatchewan, the north has seen only limited archaeological work. As a consequence, we know very little about the route's first Paleo-Indians and their early successors. We can assume, however, that once the post-glacial boreal forest was established, they soon began using the lakes and rivers for travel—by canoe during open water seasons and by tracking over the ice during the winter. Living beside the waterways, they could exploit fish, beaver, muskrat, and waterfowl for food. But they also would have occasionally travelled inland to hunt moose, woodland caribou, and wood bison. Harvesting tools included fish weirs, spears, atlatls (spear throwers, which came into use in North America as early as 7,500 years ago) and bows and arrows (first introduced about 1,500 years ago). Food preparation centred on the campfire and eventually involved (possibly as early as 2,000 years ago) the use of ceramic pottery.[5]

The Cree

Although we do not know exactly who the route's first peoples were, most archaeologists and historians now agree that the Cree have been living on the route for several centuries, certainly well before European contact. This is contrary to an earlier theory that the Cree had migrated into the region from the east during the fur trade, forcing out the local inhabitants.[6]

The Cree make up a major branch of the broad-based Algonquian language family, dialects of which are spoken all the way from the Maritimes to the Rocky Mountains. While the Cree have always called themselves *nîhithawak*, meaning "those who speak the same language,"[7] the word "Cree" comes from a shortened version of the name *Kiristino*. This latter name was first applied by Europeans to an obscure group of Indians who roamed the country south of James Bay in the early 1600s but was then somehow extended by both the French and English to refer to all Cree groups.[8]

By the time of European contact, the Cree had developed a hunting and gathering culture particularly adapted to the route's rigorous environment. They lived in small family units typically consisting of two to five families. The family shelter was a hide-covered tent or teepee (*mîkiwâhp* in Cree), but smaller lean-tos were also often used, especially when travelling. In summer, family-sized birchbark canoes were used for travel, while in winter, snowshoes, toboggans, and dog power allowed mobility on the frozen waterways.[9] The Cree were adept at finding sustenance in a country that lacked the south's vast buffalo herds and the far north's caribou migrations. Likely anything with caloric value was eaten, but some food sources were more important than others. Judging from early fur trade accounts, the moose was the most important large animal hunted. Beaver and waterfowl were important summer staples, while snowshoe hares and grouse were important in winter. During spawning runs, fish caught at stone weirs built in fast current were also a dietary mainstay.

At the time of European contact, Cree on the route spoke a *th* dialect, so called because it has a "th" consonant not found in other Cree dialects. This is sometimes known as "Rocky" Cree because it is now spoken mainly in the Shield regions of northern Saskatchewan and Manitoba. However, when explorers like Alexander Mackenzie first arrived, it existed all the way from Methy Portage (*mithay* is the word for "burbot" in *th* dialect) to Cumberland House, where a group known as the Basquia *(opâskwêyâw)* Cree spoke *th*.[10]

The guide route's early *th*-dialect Cree were more than simple hunters and gatherers. They are thought to be responsible for all or most of the pictographs found on bedrock outcrops along the route. The route's paintings are located at the far western fringe of a swath of similarly styled paintings found across the Canadian Shield from the St. Lawrence River and the Great Lakes to the upper Churchill River. They were made using a highly durable pigment (*wathaman* in Cree) consisting of processed iron oxide mixed with a binder (possibly isinglass, a strong glue made from fish bladders). Modern dating techniques have not yet been effectively applied to these paintings, but it is believed that most are from the pre-contact era since few show any sign of European influence. The Cree name for them—*masinâpiskahikîwin*—translates roughly as "writing on rocks," and the Cree today see them as a type of writing which most people can no longer interpret.[11] According to Tim Jones, the archaeologist who first surveyed the Churchill River paintings in 1965, the pictographs likely reflect the ancestral beliefs of Cree hunters and fishers who "emphasized vision-seeking" in their spiritual life. Whatever their meaning, they are fascinating reminders of another time.[12]

After fur traders and explorers first saw the route, other Cree peoples arrived. In the west, people speaking a Plains Cree *y* dialect—which substitutes a "y" consonant for any "th" sound—eventually made their way to the Lac Île-à-la-Crosse area, possibly coming from the south via the Beaver River. In the area of Cumberland House, Cree from the east moved in when the local Basquia Cree population was decimated by a major smallpox epidemic in 1781. These eastern immigrants were Swampy Cree who introduced their own *n* dialect which (as one might guess) substitutes an "n" consonant wherever a *th* speaker would use a "th" sound.[13]

The fur trade and more recent events have brought many changes to the route's Cree people. Nonetheless, Cree still live on the route and, in fact, make up most of its population. In the west, *y*-dialect speakers, mainly of Métis descent, live in the communities of Buffalo Narrows, Île-à-la-Crosse, and Pinehouse. East from Pinehouse, *th*-dialect speakers (members of the Lac la Ronge Indian Band and the Peter Ballantyne Cree Nation) occupy the route all the way to Sturgeon Landing. (Both these *y*-dialect and *th*-dialect groups are now often known as "Woods" or "Woodland" Cree.) And, at the southeast end of the route, *n*-dialect Swampy Cree, including both Métis and members of the Cumberland House Cree Nation, live in and around Cumberland House.

The Dene

The Dene, who live in northwest sections of the route, are not related to the Cree. Rather, they are part of a large and diverse family of indigenous peoples known as the Athapaskans who, it is now thought, can be traced back to a homeland situated in the vicinity of southern Alaska, southwestern Yukon, and northern British Columbia. The first Athapaskans long ago dispersed to occupy most of the sub-Arctic North-West as well as some oddly remote locations such as southern Alberta (the Sarcee) and the American southwest (the Apaches and the Navajos).[14]

The Hudson's Bay Company often referred to the Dene as "Northern" Indians to distinguish them from the Cree or "Southern" Indians. At the same time, traders and others also called them "Chipewyans," from the Cree term *wîcîpwayâniwak*, meaning "(those who have) pointed skins or hides"—possibly an allusion to the way in which the Dene cut their hunting shirts.[15] The Chipewyan name eventually saw wholesale usage by non-Dene, even though the Dene have always called themselves *Dene* meaning, simply, "the people." It is only very recently that outsiders have at last adopted the use of the Dene's own name.

The Dene are relative newcomers to the route. At most (and this is not certain), their pre-contact territories would have included only the northwestern fringe of our route—the Clearwater River and the headwaters of the Churchill River. The heart of their territory would have been further north where they could hunt the migrating herds of barren land caribou.[16]

Like the Cree, the Dene developed a culture and technologies suited to hunting and gathering in a harsh environment. The getting of food, clothing, and shelter had to be given high priority. Alexander Mackenzie has left a good account of the Dene emphasis on proper clothing:

> There are no people more attentive to the comforts of their dress, or less anxious respecting its exterior appearance. In the winter it is composed of the skins of deer, and their fawns, and dressed as fine as any chamois leather, in the hair.... This dress is worn single or double, but always in winter, with the hair within and without. Thus arrayed, a Chepewyan will lay himself down on the ice in the middle of a lake, and repose in comfort, though he will sometimes find a difficulty in the morning to disencumber himself from the snow drifted on him during the night.[17]

The Dene were drawn south in the late 1700s by the fur trade. Their movement southward was likely expedited by the 1781 smallpox epidemic that killed large numbers of Cree all along the guide route, leaving country vacant for immigrants. By the 1800s, many Dene were associated with Île-à-la-Crosse and visited it routinely to trade. In 1838, for example, a Hudson's Bay Company census found 489 Dene connected to the Île-à-la-Crosse post. They occupied regions in several directions from Île-à-la-Crosse, including an area as far downstream on the Churchill as Pinehouse Lake.[18]

Judging by the historical record, the mixing of Dene and Cree on the route produced at least some friction during the fur trade era. According to Alexander Mackenzie, "They [Dene] were for sometime treated by the Knisteneaux [Cree] as enemies; who now allow them to hunt to the North of the [guide route], from Fort du Traite upwards, but when they occasionally meet them, they insist on contributions, and frequently punish resistance with their arms."[19] Clearly, though, both groups eventually did learn to share the route.

In the early 1900s, the Dene reduced their range somewhat. They frequented Île-à-la-Crosse less after fur trade outposts and missionaries reached further north. The Dene also drew back upstream from Pinehouse Lake to Dreger Lake after epidemics hit the Pinehouse Lake area.[20] Nonetheless, their modern-day descendants still maintain a strong presence along the northwest sections of the route. Those descendants include the members of the Clearwater River Dene Nation of Lac la Loche, the Buffalo River Dene Nation of Peter Pond Lake, the Birch Narrows Dene Nation of Turnor Lake, the English River Dene Nation centred at Patuanak, as well as many Métis.

The Métis

The Métis are an important part of the route's indigenous population, and many have family trees with one or more roots in the fur trade. From the start, the fur trade in northern Saskatchewan made the birth of a Métis people inevitable. The very first white traders—men such as Louis Primeau—were essentially *coureurs de bois* ("wood runners") who went into the country to live with the Indians. It was thus natural for them to enter into relationships with aboriginal women and raise families. When the trade became more established, things were not so different. Voyageurs might have little time for family life during the summer, but those wintering inland had ample opportunity to meet and marry local girls and women. This often happened when men went to live *en derouine*—wintering with the Indians to drum up trade and to relieve their employers the expense of their own rations.

When fur traders did take an aboriginal wife, it was usually solemnized *à la façon du pays*—according to local custom. In addition to providing men with companionship, such marriages provided the fur trade with a female workforce capable of handling numerous important tasks. These unions as well helped to build trading relationships with local First Nations since a trader could reasonably expect his in-laws to bring their furs to him or his employer. They also produced children who would be the forebears of the modern Métis.[21]

Contemporary Métis with a fur trade heritage may be of Cree or Dene descent or even both. Similarly, their non-native origins go back to one or both of two groups. The first group is that of the French Canadian voyageurs hired by Montreal-based fur trade firms up until 1821 when the North West Company merged with the Hudson's Bay Company.[22] The second is that of the men brought from Europe by the Hudson's Bay Company to work inland. These recruits were most often hardy souls from the Orkney Islands off the north coast of Scotland (in 1800, 390 of the HBC's 498 employees were Orkneymen), but they sometimes came from other parts of Scotland, England, Ireland, and even Norway.[23]

Of course, Métis on the route also have origins unrelated to the early fur trade. In the early 1900s, many white trappers moved into northern Saskatchewan. Soon after, commercial fishing and mink ranching attracted other men (often Scandinavians) northward. In more recent times, there have been influxes of non-native pilots, miners, teachers, police officers, civil servants, and all manner of people just wanting to escape the south. Some such immigrants have come and gone quickly, but others have stayed long enough to marry into communities and add to the Métis mix.

There is no section of the route that does not have a Métis presence, but in some communities it is particularly strong. La Loche, Buffalo Narrows, and Pinehouse are notable among these, while the old fur trade centres of Île-à-la-Crosse and Cumberland House stand out as true bastions of Métis culture.

THE FUR TRADE

The Beaver

The beaver—the big-toothed, tree-felling, dam-building rodent who is depicted on every Canadian five-cent coin—should be given credit for starting the fur trade. To survive in his wet and often cold world, the beaver has a thick under-fur made up of fibres that are spiked or barbed at the root. Early on, well before Columbus reached the Americas, Europeans learned that this spiked fur was superb for pressing into a durable, water-resistant felt suitable for hats. Indeed, in the early days of hatting, felt from beaver fur was the only felt suitable for making large and durable hat brims.

Beaver pelts from Canada's North-West were of a particularly superior quality because the North-West's cold climate produced a thicker fur. Of these, the most valuable of all were the *castor gras* (greasy beaver) or "coat beaver" pelts, which had a greasy texture after being worn as winter coats by Indians living in the boreal forest. *Castor gras* pelts had two real advantages over regular *castor sec* (dry beaver) or "parchment" pelts. One was that the wearing process naturally removed the beaver's long guard hairs which could not be used in the felting process. The other was that the wearing process somehow caused keratin protein on the under-fur fibres to break down. Since the keratin interfered with the felting process, its breakdown markedly improved the under-fur's already good felting quality.

When Europeans first arrived in North America, the supply of beaver from the forests of Russia and Scandinavia was already becoming depleted. Therefore, indigenous North Americans found, to their surprise, that Europeans were anxious to give them new and useful items, from knives and kettles to blankets and muskets, in exchange for worn-out robes of beaver fur. This was the beginning of the fur trade. As the trade developed, indigenous people extended their limited supply of coat beaver by hunting and selling parchment beaver. Soon, the beaver became so central to the fur trade that its pelt actually became a currency unit, the "Made Beaver" (or MB) against which all other fur trade goods were valued. In this way, a hatchet might be valued at 1 MB and a gun at 12 MB.

The beaver hat would lose its prominence over time. Between 1720 and 1740, English hatters perfected a technology called "mercury carroting" which could remove keratin from poor quality furs such as hare and rabbit, making them suitable for felting for the first time. A secret at first, mercury carroting spread over time, and cheap substitute furs cut seriously into the beaver hat market. Later, in the 1840s, gentlemen began preferring silk hats over felted beaver hats, and a further decline occurred.

Beaver felt hats were made fashionable in Europe during the Thirty Years War (1618–48) by victorious Swedish cavaliers who sported wide-brimmed beaver slouch hats adorned with draping plumes. Hats were eventually of many types, such as these from the late eighteenth and early nineteenth centuries.

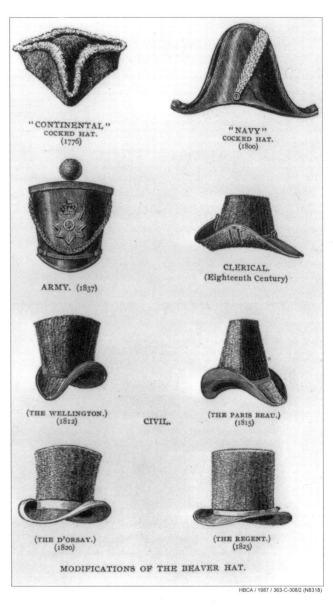

"CONTINENTAL." COCKED HAT. (1776)

"NAVY" COCKED HAT. (1800)

ARMY. (1837)

CLERICAL. (Eighteenth Century)

(THE WELLINGTON.) (1812)

CIVIL.

(THE PARIS BEAU.) (1815)

(THE D'ORSAY.) (1820)

(THE REGENT.) (1825)

MODIFICATIONS OF THE BEAVER HAT.

The end of the beaver hat era was significant, but it did not end the fur trade or the beaver's role in it. The loss of the hat market was offset by an increasing demand from furriers for beaver and other pelts to be used as fancy furs. The beaver thus continued to have a commercial value. Beyond that, it also remained—like the voyageur and the birchbark canoe—symbolic of the trade and a way of life.[24]

The Hudson's Bay Company

Canada's fur trade began at least as early as 1534, when explorer Jacques Cartier met indigenous people and traded with them for their furs in the vicinity of Chaleur Bay in the Gulf of St. Lawrence. It then became more regular after the founding of New France in the 1600s. However, in those early years, Canada's far North-West was still beyond the reach of even the French colony's wide-ranging *coureurs de bois*.

In 1668, the fur trade took a significant step towards the North-West when the French fur traders Radisson and Groseilliers, who had become frustrated with the regulations they found governing the fur trade in New France, masterminded an English trading venture into Hudson Bay. The venture was successful in sending the 36-foot ketch *Nonsuch*, commanded by Boston sea captain Zachariah Gillam (or Guillam) and guided by Groseilliers on board, into Hudson Bay and then James Bay, where it wintered at the mouth of the Rupert River. When, in 1669, the

Nonsuch returned to England with furs to trade, its backers were impressed. A group of them, led by the Bohemian-born Prince Rupert, moved to obtain long-term rights to Hudson Bay. And, on May 2, 1670, King Charles II granted Prince Rupert and his nineteen fellow "Adventurers" a Royal Charter giving them exclusive trading rights to Hudson Bay and its drainage basin, land to be known as "Rupert's Land" for the next two centuries.

Upon obtaining its Charter, the new Hudson's Bay Company (HBC) moved quickly to exploit trade possibilities. Within a decade, the company had posts (or "factories") at the mouths of the Albany, Moose, and Rupert rivers running into James Bay. Then, in the 1680s, it also built posts on the west side of Hudson Bay—at the mouth of the Nelson in 1682, the Hayes in 1684, the Severn in 1685, and the Churchill in 1688 (this first Churchill post was short-lived and was not re-established until 1717). Of these, York Factory at the mouth of the Hayes was of special significance. It had good water connections to the North-West and would eventually become the nerve centre of the company's Rupert's Land operations.

In its early years, despite its fine Charter, the HBC had to deal with much harassment from the French—who would either sail into Hudson Bay or come overland from the St. Lawrence. Indeed, by 1697, when the French soldier Pierre le Moyne d'Iberville captured York Factory, the

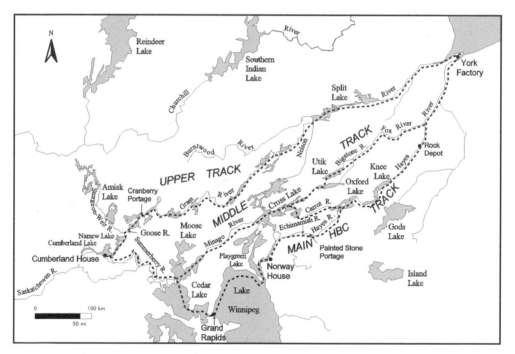

Map above, adapted from Eric W. Morse, Fur Trade Canoe Routes of Canada/Then and Now, *indicates three fur trade canoe routes from Cumberland House to York Factory. The "Upper" and "Middle" tracks were popular with Indian middlemen, while the "Main" track was the HBC's principal route after 1774.*

Map on facing page, drawn by Cree "Cha chay pay way ti" for the HBC's Peter Fidler in 1806, gives an aboriginal view of the canoe routes between Cumberland House and Split Lake on the way to York Factory using the Upper Track. The "Burntwood River" route (on left) lies even further north than Morse's "Upper Track." The "Grass River" route (at centre) and "Pine River" route (on right) correspond to Morse's "Upper" and "Middle" tracks respectively.

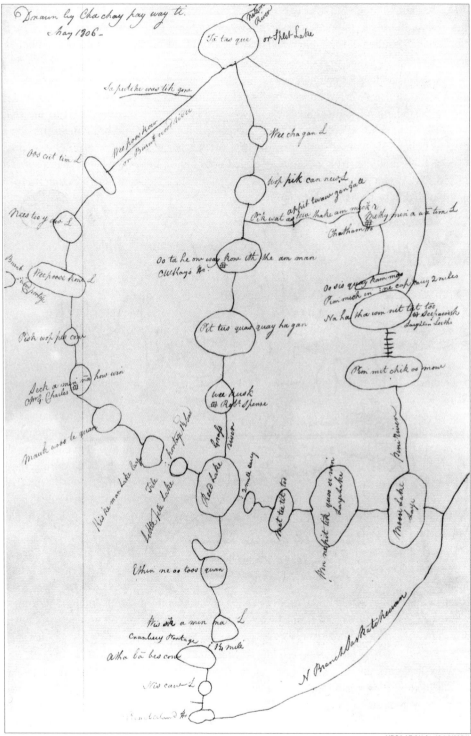

HBC was left with only its Albany post operating. This situation continued through to 1713 when the Treaty of Utrecht (signed in Holland by England and France to end the War of the Spanish Succession) resulted in the French withdrawing from Hudson Bay and the HBC gaining back its lost post sites.

Notwithstanding French incursions, the HBC was in time able to develop its trade. In doing so, it made almost no effort during the first eighty-four years of its history to go out and meet its Indian customers on their home turf. (Henry Kelsey's extraordinary travels to the prairies in 1690-92 are notable exceptions.) Rather, it expected that they would bring their furs down to the Bay to trade. This worked well enough for a time, especially since some Indians—principally Cree and Assiniboine (Nakota Sioux)—traded not only on their own behalf but also as middle-men for far distant groups. Trading parties in small birchbark canoes kept bringing fur to the Bay, and the HBC saw no need to venture inland.

The Montrealers and the North West Company

After the Treaty of Utrecht, the HBC had some competition from the Montreal-based traders of New France in the region south of James Bay, and this caused it to build Henley House upstream on the Albany River in 1743. At the time, the HBC still enjoyed a monopoly in the North-West, since traders from New France had not yet ventured so far. However, by the 1750s, French traders had advanced up the Saskatchewan River into present-day Saskatchewan. Their progress was stalled only when New France came under British siege during the Seven Years War and French fur merchants had to turn away from their normal vocation.

Once Britain was successful in taking over New France (Montreal fell to the British in September 1760), Montrealers resumed their interest in the fur trade almost immediately. While many French traders chose to return home to France rather than live under British rule, new traders—English, Scottish, Swiss, and American among them—came forward and set up small partnerships to exploit the old trade routes alongside the few remaining French merchants. These partnerships sensibly relied on the expertise of voyageurs who had already ventured to the *pays d'en haut* (literally the "upcountry," or the wilderness of the North-West) during the French regime. Hence, by the latter 1760s, Montreal interests were back on the Saskatchewan River, and by 1773, they had—with a contingent of eighteen men headed by Joseph Frobisher—moved north onto our guide route for the first time and were poised to begin a rapid leap-frog advance towards the rich Athabasca country.

At first, the Montreal partnerships were loose affairs tailored to the moment. For example, the Frobisher party of 1773 was apparently backed not only by the Frobisher brothers (Benjamin, Joseph, and Thomas) but also by James McGill (the university founder), Isaac Todd, and Barthélemi Blondeau. Such pooling of resources went a long way to insuring the success of risky ventures into the North-West. It was therefore natural that the original loose partnerships eventu-ally grew in size and structure.

The end result of the Montreal traders partnering was the well known North West Company (NWC). It is difficult to put a precise date to the NWC's birth, but the nucleus of the company was formed by 1775 when Benjamin Frobisher, James McGill, and Maurice Blondeau (cousin to Barthélemi) took out a single trading licence for twelve canoes and seventy-eight men going to the North-West. This joint venture model evolved to where, in 1779, nine Montreal trading partnerships (Benjamin Frobisher and James McGill being again involved) created a sixteen-share coalition called the "North West Company" to, as its name suggests, pursue the North-West trade. This "company" lasted one year and was then succeeded by a similar alliance. The latter then fell apart after two years because of internal dissension and because the terrible smallpox epidemic that swept the fur country in 1781–82 all but wiped out the year's trade. Finally, in the winter of 1783–84, Montrealers—likely under the guidance of the astute Scotsman Simon McTavish—put together a new North West Company which would survive to grow and prosper.

One strong firm that initially stayed out of the NWC was that of Gregory, McLeod and Company which gave Canadian explorer Alexander Mackenzie his start in the fur trade. Gregory-McLeod gave stiff competition to some NWC posts up until 1787. In that year, in an incident at Lake Athabasca, John Ross, a Gregory-McLeod trader, was shot and killed by an employee of the rival NWC post being run by the talented but temperamental Peter Pond. Wanting to avoid any more such unprofitable violence, the rival companies responded by merging. The enlarged NWC, reviewing Pond's checkered past and his possible role in Ross's death, chose to ease him out of the picture. While Pond's trading skills were legendary, the NWC could now rely on Gregory-McLeod men such as Mackenzie to take his place.

Another Montreal company outside the original NWC was that of Forsyth, Richardson & Co. The Forsyth concern had originally concentrated its efforts in what is now American territory, but after the American Revolution it turned its attentions northward. As Forsyth drew in partners and grew in size, the NWC gave it enough notice to derisively call it the "Little Company" and its men the "Potties" ("small pots"). In 1800, to gain more strength, the Forsyth concern joined with another small concern known as Parker-Gerrard-Ogilvy, and with Alexander Mackenzie who had himself been pushed out of the NWC the year before. This new combination was called the New North West Company but became better known as the XY Company because of the "XY" mark it used on its packs. The XY Company, at one-third the NWC's strength, competed fiercely with the NWC. This rivalry lasted until November 5, 1804, when the two companies merged to give a new NWC the form it would take during the years it went head to head with the HBC.[25]

For the Montrealers, the vast distance between Montreal and the North-West—5,000 kilometres (3,000 miles) to the Athabaska country—was a monumental challenge. Simply put, there were not enough ice-free days to let voyageurs travel to and from the North-West in one summer. As early as the French regime, the Montrealers had dealt with this problem by setting up forward depots at Grand Portage on the northwest shore of Lake Superior. Grand Portage was a natural waypoint on the voyageur highway since it was here the voyageurs had to leave the big water of Lake Superior to advance into the North-West via smaller waterways, the first being the Pigeon River. The portage itself was a 14-kilometre (9-mile) trail which took voyageurs past ugly rapids on the lower Pigeon River to a point where the river became navigable.

Under the NWC, Grand Portage was both the company's forward depot and its great inland headquarters. Every summer, NWC voyageurs from Montreal (*mangeurs de lard* or "pork eaters") brought trade goods to Grand Portage and carried them over the portage to a cache point known as Fort Charlotte. Their counterparts from the North-West (*hommes du nord* or "North men") then normally arrived at Grand Portage with the season's fur in early July. Their arrival prompted celebrations with drinking, singing, dancing, and occasional fighting. But it also meant more portaging and the work of putting together the trading outfits that would go back into the

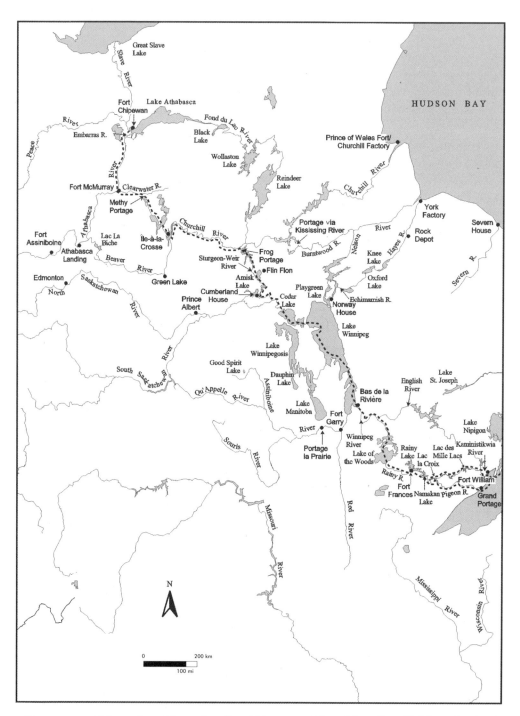

The voyageur highway from Montreal to Fort Chipewyan. Adapted from Eric W. Morse, Fur Trade Canoe Routes of Canada/Then and Now.

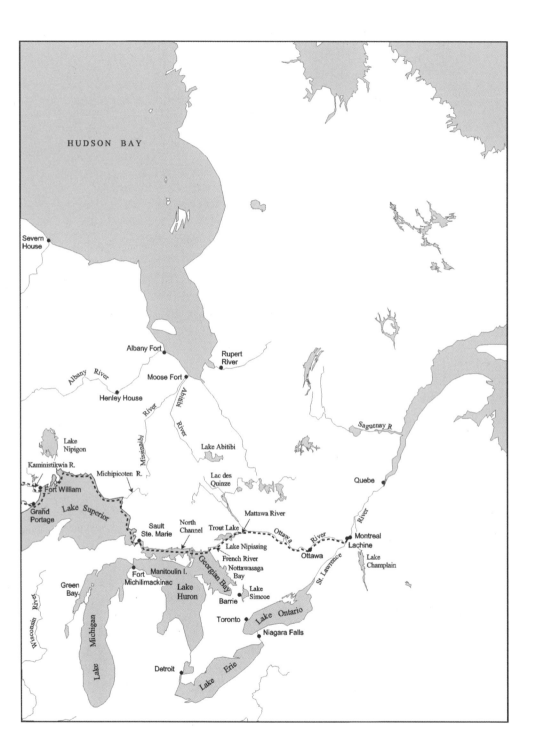

North-West for the ensuing year. While the voyageurs laboured, the NWC's Montreal agents and its "wintering" partners met to review the year past and plan for the next. Then, once work and business were complete, the North men headed back for their winter posts. Though they had been saved the distance to Montreal, they still had to race against freeze-up.

As a forward depot, Grand Portage was key to the NWC's operations. However, though it was far inland from Montreal, canoe brigades from the Athabasca still found it too far to make a round trip to Grand Portage in one season. The NWC dealt with this problem by setting up an extra, more westerly advance depot at Rainy Lake (near present-day Fort Frances, Ontario) for the posts in the Athabasca and beyond. A special contingent of pork eaters was given extra pay to move trade goods in from Grand Portage to Rainy Lake. This saved the Athabasca brigades— who no longer had to come all the way to Grand Portage—a crucial two weeks of travel and let them get home on open water.

In the aftermath of the American Revolution, Grand Portage (in present-day northern Minnesota) ended up on the American side of the American-British border. To avoid American customs regulations, the NWC decided to move its inland base onto British soil. It eventually found a new site, roughly 75 kilometres (50 miles) northeast of Grand Portage, where the Kaministikwia River flows into Lake Superior. The canoe track inland up the Kaministikwia was longer than the Grand Portage track, but it did provide an all-British route to Rainy Lake. Hence, in 1803, the NWC moved to the Kaministikwia where it built (at present-day Thunder Bay) an elaborate post complex centred around a spacious Great Hall. From 1807 onward, the new head-quarters was named Fort William in honour of William McGillivray who had, upon the death of his uncle Simon McTavish in 1804, become the NWC's chief executive officer.

Rivalry between the HBC and the NWC

The HBC saw competition coming into the North-West even before the fall of New France. Its initial response was not (if one exempts Henley House on the Albany River) to build inland trading posts. Rather, it chose to send men inland to persuade Indian traders to continue bringing their furs down to the Bay-side posts. In 1754, Anthony Henday left York Factory on the first such trip and, travelling by canoe and by foot with a Cree guide named Little Deer, made it to the vicinity of present-day Red Deer, Alberta, and then to the Edmonton area where he overwintered. Henday was to make two more trips inland in later years, and all together, between 1754 and 1774, the HBC would send at least fifty-six parties inland—mainly to the Saskatchewan River basin where Montrealers were trading—to bring customers back to the Bay. Unfortunately, this program, however ambitious, was simply no match for the Montrealers' program of bringing their wares straight to the customer.[26]

Finally, in 1773, by which time business was clearly ailing at the Bay, the HBC decided to move its operations inland. A year later, its servant Samuel Hearne succeeded in establishing Cumberland House, which he named after the HBC's original governor, Prince Rupert, Duke of Cumberland (by then long dead). In the years to follow, the HBC would set up more inland posts as it tried to play catch-up with the Montrealers who, having built their first post on the guide route a year before Hearne, moved ever deeper into the North-West without any regard for the HBC's Charter monopoly. In time, it became common to see both a Hudson's Bay Company post and a North West Company post side by side—not for protection against the Indians, but to compete for their furs.

Competition between the HBC and the NWC was strong but not particularly rancorous in its early stages. Occasionally, rival traders would assist each other with provisions or other aid should the need arise. For example, when the HBC sent a surveying party headed by Philip Turnor off to the Athabasca in 1791, Patrick Small of the NWC's Île-à-la-Crosse post first guided the Turnor people as far as Île-à-la-Crosse and then provided them with winter quarters there. However, in due course, even at Île-à-la-Crosse, strife began to break out as too much competition cut profits and frayed tempers. Assaults, hostage-taking, threats to Indian customers, and the burning and destruction of property became commonplace. The NWC was responsible for most of the high-handed behaviour, and the HBC was often left scrambling for an adequate response.

As the situation deteriorated, the HBC moved to adopt more aggressive business policies. The company then searched for someone who could ensure that those policies were carried out. The man it found was Scottish-born George Simpson who, because of his short stature and imperious nature, would become known as "the little Emperor." On February 26, 1820 in London, Simpson was accredited as acting Governor-in-Chief of Rupert's Land. Soon after, he sailed for North America to assume command of his new empire.[27]

Simpson arrived on the job with the view that unless the HBC could compete with the NWC in the rich English (Churchill) River and Athabasca districts, the company would fail. Thus, as he headed for the North-West by canoe in the summer of 1820, he had a keen eye for the current state of outfits heading to those districts:

[Tuesday, August 22 on the Saskatchewan River] Embarked at half past three AM; passed fourteen N.W. Canoes; I could not help remarking with much concern the striking contrast between our Brigade and that of our Opponents; all their Canoes are new and well built of good materials, ably manned, a water proof arm chest and cassette for fineries in each, and the baggage covered with new oil cloths, in short well equipped in every respect: on the other hand our Canoes are old, crazy, and patched up, built originally of bad materials without symmetry and neither adopted for stowage nor expedition; manned chiefly by old infirm creatures or Porkeaters unfit for the arduous duty they have to perform, the Arms wrapped up in Leather, so that the first shower of rain must damage them, and not more than half a dozen tottered Oil cloths in the whole Brigade: there is much room for improvement in this branch of the business.[28]

Appearances were deceiving, however. The Montrealers were in fact being crippled by the cost of their overextended transportation system. Montreal to the Athabasca was roughly 5,000 kilometres (3,000 miles), a staggering distance by canoe. Furs were also being depleted in many parts, and the HBC's new eagerness to compete promised to give it a larger share of what furs were left. It was only a matter of time before the HBC's geographic advantage and its changing business practices would give it a decisive advantage. Hence, by the time Simpson had settled in at Lake Athabasca where he was to winter in 1820–21, the NWC was already negotiating a merger with the HBC's London Committee. By 1821, cold calculations of future profits had won out over old competitive instincts—the result was a merger of the two companies.[29] The combined company kept the name of the Hudson's Bay Company in order to preserve any advantages that might still flow from the original monopoly charter over the waters that drained into Hudson Bay.

The Fur Trade after 1821

Simpson learned of the HBC–NWC merger from a North West Company canoe that he met on Lake Winnipeg while outbound for Norway House on June 18, 1821. He first thought that the news was a hoax, but upon confirming it, he was extremely pleased.[30] He could now turn his energies to streamlining the new company into a profitable fur-gathering machine. The fierce competition of the preceding years had favoured the aboriginal traders, so Simpson moved to raise the price of HBC goods relative to that of furs. He also brought economy—a word soon to be synonymous with his name—to all aspects of the HBC's operations. He replaced canoes wherever possible with larger York boats which delivered more freight per man and were more suited to the prosaic sailing skills of the company's many Orkneymen. And he closed many fur trade posts, preserving only those that would add to profits. The result was that on Saskatchewan's old voyageur highway, only the posts at Île-à-la-Crosse and Cumberland House were kept in continuous operation.

The merger and Simpson's changes gave the HBC a good balance sheet over the next several decades. True, the beaver hat industry fell into decline during Simpson's tenure. But in an age before synthetics, fur still remained in demand for both fashion and practical dress. Until Simpson's death in 1860 and for many years thereafter, "fur was king"[31] in the North-West, and the HBC was in charge of the realm.

Though it enjoyed an enduring success, the HBC never quite managed to gain a complete monopoly in the fur trade. The company often faced competition from individual traders who moved in whenever it made commercial sense. Other companies also challenged the HBC from time to time. Most notable of these was Revillon Frères. First established in Paris in 1723, it still operates today in fields as diverse as banking and perfumes ("Revlon"). Revillon entered the North American fur trade in 1899 with a post at Edmonton and went on to operate forty-seven Canadian posts. It was a sophisticated operation and gave the HBC a run for its money wherever it had a post. However, setbacks such as the loss in battle of Revillon sons during World War I and ongoing cutthroat competition from the HBC eventually weakened Revillon's fur trade operations. By 1926, the HBC owned 51 percent of Revillon's Canadian fur trade holdings, and by 1935, had total control of them.[32]

In 1987, the fur trade world was shocked by the announcement that the Hudson's Bay Company, after 317 years in the fur trade, was selling off its fur operations—the Northern Stores Division and related fur sale houses. Perhaps no one should have been overly surprised. The decision to abandon the fur trade was, one can reasonably guess, made by people who had never looked forward to freeze-up, graded a pelt, or heard a word of Cree. In the modern HBC, a company focused on department store retailing, the fur trade had become a quaint anachronism.[33]

The death of the HBC has not meant the end of the fur trade. Though the anti-fur lobby has hurt the industry, trappers along our route still go out in late October for early winter trapping and again in March to take beaver and muskrats. A new company, ironically named The North West Company, now operates what was the HBC's Northern Stores Division under the trade name "Northern." While Northern stores concentrate on regular retailing, they still buy fur as it comes in. A few independent fur buyers also buy fur in the old way. At Robertson Trading in La Ronge, just south of the Churchill, a Cree trapper can still deal in his own language with Alex Robertson or his son Scott and, if he chooses, trade his fur catch for groceries and other supplies.

The Voyageur and His Craft

The Voyageurs

The voyageurs, who could still find breath to sing at the end of a sixteen-hour day of paddling and portaging, provided the manpower necessary to drive the fur trade in the eighteenth and nineteenth centuries. If they were veterans of the voyage inland, they also acted as guides, ensuring that brigades did not end up swept over dangerous falls or hopelessly lost amid uncharted islands. Finally, if they had overwintered with Indian groups inland, they often filled key roles as interpreters of indigenous languages and dialects.

The most famous voyageurs were the French Canadians, most often referred to by their employers as "Canadians," "*Canadiens*" or "*engagés*." Recruited from the farms and villages near Montreal, these "natural water Dogs"[34] were typically young men keen to leave home in search of adventure and equal to the physical demands of voyaging. Though they had to be strong, as American traveller Thomas McKenney wrote in 1826, they were ideally small of stature:

Voyageur with sash, paddle, and tumpline.

> . . . I can liken them to nothing but their own ponies. They are short, thick set, and active, and never tire. A Canadian, if born to be a labourer, deems himself to be very unfortunate if he should chance to grow over five feet five, or six inches; – and if he shall reach five feet ten or eleven, it forever excludes him from the privilege of becoming a voyageur. There is no room for the legs of such people, in these canoes. But if he shall stop growing at about five feet four inches, and be gifted with a good voice, and lungs that never tire, he is considered as having been born under a most favourable star.[35]

Fur trade employers supplied almost everything the voyageurs needed while voyaging, but the *Canadien* voyageur traditionally supplied his own sash and paddle—possessions which were sometimes proudly handed down from father to son in the farms and villages of Quebec and the Métis settlements of the North-West. The brightly-coloured woven sash, or *ceinture fléchée*, was not only a decorative part of the voyageur's costume but also served to give abdominal and back

GLOSSARY OF VOYAGEUR TERMS

Agrès – basic equipment and accessories of a voyageur canoe

Avant – bowman in a canoe

Bourgeois – fur trade company officer

Bouts – literally "ends," referring to the bowman and steersman of a canoe; the bouts of a canot du nord were responsible for carrying it on portages

Canadien – a French Canadian

Canot du Maître – large "Montreal" canoe used on the voyageur highway from Montreal to Lake Superior; usually 10 to 11 metres (32 to 36 feet) long with a crew of 8 to 10 paddlers

Canot du nord – smaller voyageur canoe used north and west of Lake Superior; usually about 8 metres (25 feet) long with a crew of four to six paddlers

Castor gras – literally "greasy beaver," beaver pelts that had seen previous use sewn into winter coats; the wearing process removed a pelt's guard hairs and improved its underfur's felting characteristics

Castor sec – literally "dry beaver," a beaver pelt previously unworn

Ceinture flèchée – brightly coloured woven sash worn around a voyageur's waist

Chanson – song

Collier – tumpline or carrying strap consisting of a headband connected to long tie strips; the collier placed the weight of a voyageur's portage *pièces* on his forehead

Cordelle – a towing line used for lining or tracking a canoe

Coureurs de bois – literally "wood runners," referring to young men who left the colony of New France to live and trade among aboriginal peoples

Décharge – unloading a canoe completely in order to take it up or down rapids empty; alternately, rapids where only the cargo was carried

Demi-chargé – literally "half-loaded"; a canoe *demi-chargé* could sometimes go up or down a rapid too swift or shallow for a fully loaded canoe

support in the same way that wide belts assist weightlifters today.[36] The paddle was hand-carved from hard maple or other suitable wood. By today's standards, the blade on a standard voyageur paddle was uncommonly narrow, sometimes as little as 8 centimetres (3 inches) in width, though the paddle of a steersman would be much wider. Paddles were often painted with decorations, usually on the blade but sometimes also on the shaft and grip. These decorations could be a solid colour—brownish red, black, white, and green being the most used—or geometric designs of lines, bars, or dots.[37]

Though traders and explorers often complained about the *Canadiens'* "live for today" attitude, most recognized their voyaging prowess. The NWC trader Daniel Harmon wrote that "by flattering their vanities (of which they have not a little) they may be made to go through fire and water."[38] Similarly, the HBC's Colin Robertson described them as "the best voyagers in the World." He added:

> [T]hey are spirited, enterprising, and extremely fond of the Country…[H]owever dismal the prospect . . . [t]hey follow their Master….[They will] sing while surrounded with misery; the toil of the day is entirely forgot in the encampment; they think themselves the happiest people in existence; and I do believe they are not far mistaken.[39]

As Robertson notes, the voyageurs loved to sing, not only at their campsites at the end of the day, but also on the trip, to the rhythm of their paddles. Many of their *chansons* have survived to this day, and since the vast majority of *Canadien* voyageurs were illiterate and did not write of their own experiences through journals and narratives, these serve as an important record of voyageur life from the perspective of the voyageurs themselves. One such song is sung by two voyageurs, one playing the role of a young *engagé* and the other a veteran. The young man and his companions are embarking for the *pays d'en haut*, and the older, experienced man is dispensing advice as they leave. The eager young man sings: "We are voyageurs starting on our way. Don't you see the townsfolk watching from the walls?" The older and wiser man responds: "Put some patience in your wallet, for you will get dry from constantly paddling and portaging, and rest will seldom come." The young man remains joyful, so the older man again warns him that he is about "to go upstream and through lakes, always harnessed" to his paddle and his pack. Undaunted, the young man sings: "We are voyageurs and good fellows. We seldom eat but we often drink." To this, the older man replies, "If the mosquitoes sting your head and deafen your ears with their buzzing, endure them patiently, for they will show you how the devil will torment you in order to get your poor soul." Then, having finally chastened the youngster, the veteran voyageur adds a last, somewhat softer, piece of advice: "When you are in the worst rapids, let Mary be your guide. Make your vow to Her, and you will see the waves recede. And pray from the bottom of your heart that they may ever recede."[40] The optimism and the strength of body and spirit evident in this song is echoed in this reminiscence of one voyageur:

> I have now been forty-two years in this country. For twenty-four I was a light canoe-man; I required but little sleep, but sometimes got less than required. No portage was too long for me; all portages were alike. My canoe never touched the ground till I saw the end of it. Fifty songs a day were nothing to me. I could carry, walk, and sing with any man I ever saw.... No water, no weather ever stopped the paddle or the song.[41]

Despite their talents, *Canadien* voyageurs had little chance of rising to positions of power in fur trade society. Anglo-Saxon prejudices and their own lack of education conspired against them. At best, they could only hope to rise within their own ranks. A young man first hiring on as a voyageur would start as a *milieu*, or middle-man. In time, he could aspire to become an *avant* (bowman) or *gouvernail* (steersman). These two

En derouine (or *en dérouine*) – drumming up trade with aboriginal families by travelling and living in their home territories; sending men *en derouine* increased trade and also allowed posts to reduce the cost of feeding its employees over winter

Engagé – man under contract with a fur trading company or partnership to serve as a voyageur

Gouvernail – steersman in a canoe, commanding the same wage as an *avant*

Guide – literally "guide," the man in head charge of a canoe brigade

Hommes du nord – literally "North men," those voyageurs who travelled northwest of Lake Superior

Mangeurs de lard – literally "pork eaters," also known as *Allants et Venants* or "Goers and Comers," those voyageurs who shuttled trade goods and furs between Montreal and Grand Portage or Fort William

Mariage à la façon du pays – literally "country marriage," meaning a voyageur's common law relationship with an aboriginal wife

Milieu – middle paddler in a canoe, earning half the wage of an *avant* or *gouvernail*

Pays d'en haut – literally "high country" or "upcountry," meaning the wilderness northwest of Lake Superior

Perches – poles for poling a canoe

Pièce – a single portage pack ordinarily weighing about 40 kilograms (90 pounds)

Pipe – the voyageur's hourly smoke break; also a distance measure equalling the distance a canoe would travel in an hour, i.e., about 8 kilometres (5 miles)

Portage – to carry a canoe and all of its contents past rapids; alternately, a carrying trail

Poses – resting or "putting down" points on a long portage, allowing the work of carrying to be done in stages

Taureau – rawhide bag (usually buffalo hide with the hair out) containing about 40 kilograms (90 pounds) of pemmican

Vieille – literally, the "Old Woman," the voyageur's name for the wind

positions, at the front and back of the canoe, were equal in pay (double the wage of a *milieu*) and close in status. (Arguably, the *avant* position was slightly above that of *gouvernail* since it was common for a canoe to be referred to under the *avant*'s name.) Then, if an *avant* or *gouvernail* made enough trips inland, he might be promoted to guide of a brigade of several canoes. Or, he might gain the special position of interpreter. Beyond guide or interpreter, however, he would have few prospects.

While not so well known as the *Canadiens*, other nationalities also contributed to the voyageur labour force. For instance, Iroquois canoemen, also from the Montreal area, took up the voyaging tradition in much the same way as their *Canadien* neighbours. Colin Robertson, who described the *Canadiens* as the best in the world, held the Iroquois in similar esteem: "I have frequently heard the *Canadien* and Iroquois voyagers disputed as regards their merits, perhaps the former may be more hardy or undergo more fatigue, but in either a rapid or traverse, give me the latter, from their calmness and presence of mind which never forsakes them in the greatest danger."[42] Indian canoemen from many nations were also hired as needed to fill crew rosters and act as guides through their home territories.

Prior to the 1770s, the HBC had relied heavily on Indian canoemen hired on a per trip basis to escort its men inland. From the 1770s onward, especially from the time it established Cumberland House in 1774, the company had need of a regular voyageur service and thus looked to its own Orkney employees for help. Its Orkneymen had limited experience with canoes, but they quickly became proficient paddlers. In 1779, Philip Turnor, after canoeing to York Factory in the company of Orkneymen, wrote to his HBC superiors: "I should be guilty of injustice was I not to inform your Honors that I think your Servants that came from Cumberland House at this time are in my opinion a set of the best Men I ever saw togather as they are in general obliging, hardy, good Canoe Men."[43] Not surprisingly, with their boating background, Orkneymen continued as valuable voyageurs when York boats were introduced onto fur trade routes.

In time, as the fur trade gave rise to a Métis nation, Métis voyageurs became more and more common. In the York boat era, Métis voyageurs or "tripmen," based mainly at Red River, eventually supplied most of the muscle needed to transport HBC freight along the route. The "Portage la Loche" brigades led by Métis guides such as Alexis L'Esperance, Baptiste Bruce, and Jack Fidler made long voyages every summer to move goods and furs between York Factory and Methy Portage.

The Voyageur's Canoe

The early fur trade could not have developed were it not for the humble birchbark canoe of the Indian. Made entirely from local materials, the birchbark was light enough to portage past the rapids and falls that interrupted North America's water highways. Admittedly, fur traders enlarged the original Indian craft to outsize proportions, but even then, it remained light enough to be carried on men's shoulders.

Birchbark canoe construction was traditionally done on a "bed" of level ground surrounded by stakes aligned in the shape of the canoe's gunwales. Sheets of moistened birchbark were laid down on the bed and then stitched with spruce roots (*watapiy* in Cree) to a gunwale frame held up by the surrounding stakes. In later steps, the birchbark seams were sealed with spruce gum mixed with fat, while wooden sheathing and ribs were fitted to give the canoe an inside frame. The work was often a family affair, and aboriginal women played a major role in building early

NA / C-002772

Voyageurs repairing canoe at evening camp, ca. 1870. Oil painting by Frances Anne Hopkins (1838-1919).

Models of fur trade canoes, from top to bottom: Ottawa River Algonkin canoe; Hudson's Bay company express canoe; Têtes de Boule "Iroquois" canoe; Lake Timagami canoe; early fur trade canoe; Hudson's Bay Company canoe built in Quebec.

NA / C-021522

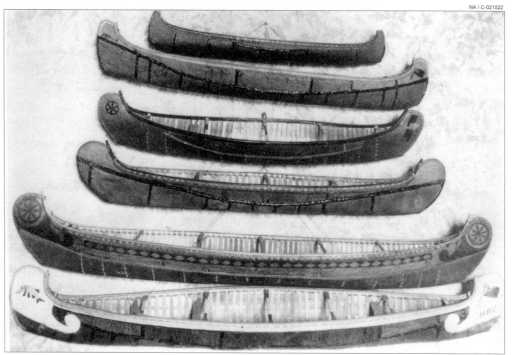

fur trade canoes. In time, as demand for canoes grew, fur companies had their own canoe building yards with skilled builders on staff. In 1821, the NWC's canoe yard at Fort William built sixty-seven "North" canoes.[44]

Two main types of fur trade canoe eventually developed. The first type was that used to go from Montreal to Grand Portage or Fort William via the Ottawa River and the Great Lakes. Known as *canots du Maître* or "Montreal canoes," these birchbark monsters were 10 to 11 metres (32 to 36 feet) long and weighed about 270 kilograms (600 pounds) empty. Usually powered by eight to ten voyageurs, they could carry sixty-five 40-kilogram (90-pound) packs (called *pièces*) of trade goods plus another ten packs of food stuffs. When the weight of the men and their personal belongings were added in, the canoe's total load might approach 4,000 kilograms (9,000 pounds).[45]

The *canot du nord*, or "North canoe," was the name given by the voyageurs to the second main type of canoe. It was the canoe used west and north of the Great Lakes where smaller waterways and numerous portages made the Montreal canoe impractical. The North canoe was about 8 metres (25 feet) long and weighed about 135 kilograms (300 pounds) empty. With a capacity roughly half that of a Montreal canoe, it carried an average of twenty-three packs of trade goods or furs plus another dozen packs devoted to food stuffs, baggage, and the like. The normal crew size was four to six men.[46]

Birchbark canoes of either design were incredibly strong yet very fragile. A heavy cargo evenly distributed on poles laid over a canoe's bottom would do no harm, but the least caress of a sharp rock in rapids could rend the all-important birchbark shell. Hence, every fur trade canoe carried a repair kit consisting of a roll of birchbark (*watapiy*) for sewing, and a spruce gum mixture and melting pot for sealing operations. In the course of a voyage, it was all too common for voyageurs to take their craft ashore and gum its hull. Indeed, on long voyages, frequent gummings often gave a noticeable increase to a canoe's portage weight.

Besides a repair kit, fur trade canoes carried other basic equipment or *agrès*. This equipment commonly included a sail and mast, oil cloths to protect packs from rain (and for use as a tent stretched out from an overturned canoe), a sponge for bailing, towing line, metal ferrules (end pieces used to save pole ends from wear), floor poles, axe, and cooking pot. Equipment sometimes included paddling seats, but voyageurs would at other times simply use their cargo for seating.

York Boats

After the merger of 1821, the HBC, under the economizing George Simpson, made a concerted effort to replace birchbark canoes with "York" boats—wooden rowboats about 12 metres (40 feet) long with pointed bow and stern. Although heavier and clumsier than canoes, York boats had several advantages over their birchbark cousins. They were stronger and could be counted on to last at least two full years, while canoes had life expectancies of little more than one season.[47] They could carry more sail and handle rougher water on the larger lakes. They also allowed the HBC to replace its expensive *Canadien* canoemen with its lower-waged Orkneymen who, fortuitously, had experience with both rowing and sailing. Most importantly, the boats could handle substantially more freight with only slightly larger crews—fifty to sixty 40-kilogram (90-pound) *pièces* with a crew of only six or seven men.[48] Overall, they were approximately 33 percent more efficient than canoes.[49]

Replica of a York boat afloat on the Bigstone River at Cumberland House in August 1993. After being built at Prince Albert, the replica was rowed to Cumberland to help the community host the Northern Saskatchewan Summer Games & Cultural Festival.

York boats quickly took over most of the HBC's transport requirements. Canoe freighting survived only on secondary trade routes too small or rugged to admit boats. On the main trade arteries, including the guide route, canoes were abandoned except for "express" canoes used to deliver mail and ferry important passengers. However, while York boats ended the canoe's golden age, they did not end voyaging traditions. True, they did call for some new ways. Men had to adapt to the feel of pulling the massive, Viking-style oars. They also had to learn how best to drag the boats over portages on log rollers. But most of the traditions, established by generations of paddlers, were passed on intact to the men who would row the big boats.

The Voyageur's Hard Day's Night

The voyageur workday started well before first light, often as early as 2:00 or 3:00 a.m., with the brigade guide rousing everyone—either with a contracted *"St'r lever! St'r lever!"* (*"C'est l'heure à se lever!"* or "time to get up") or with a less polite cry. Embarking without eating, the voyageurs then paddled (or rowed in the York boat era) for several hours before stopping at 6:00 or 8:00 a.m. for a hot breakfast. This was followed by more paddling until midday, when a brief stop might be made for a cold meal. Paddling then continued until about 8:00 p.m. when a final stop was made for a cooked supper and evening camp.

On the water, voyageurs swung their paddles at a rate of forty to sixty strokes a minute to produce a base speed of 7 or 8 kilometres (4 or 5 miles) an hour. If they raced to relieve boredom, speeds were even faster. Distances travelled depended on wind, current, and the number of portages, but accounts suggest that 50 to 60 kilometres (30 to 40 miles) per day was common on routes with an average number of portages. Express canoes with select crews would go even faster. For example, when George Simpson travelled from York Factory to the Pacific in 1828, his "light" canoes, manned by nine men each, travelled *upstream* on our route from Cumberland House to Methy Portage—1,000 kilometres (625 miles)—in twelve days, even though Simpson stopped along the way to conduct business. Other instances have been recorded of canoes exceeding 150 kilometres (100 miles) in a single day![50]

The voyageurs preferred the rhythm of paddling over the back-breaking work of portaging, and they went to considerable lengths to avoid unnecessary carrying. They preferred to run a rapid fully loaded, and Class 2 or even Class 3 rapids were run as a matter of course. If a rapid was to be run, the *avant* would ready himself by switching to a larger paddle and then, from his superior vantage point, direct the *gouvernail* as to the best line to follow. Most times, a canoe would reach the bottom of a rapid unscathed. But not every run was successful, and many voyageurs, as the crosses overlooking some rapids attested, were drowned in mishaps.

If a brigade guide decided that a rapid was too shallow to be negotiated fully loaded, there were still two paddling options to consider. The first option, which could apply to either downstream or upstream travel, was to lighten a canoe by half to increase its buoyancy and deal with the rapid in two trips or *demi-chargés*. The second option, for a yet more difficult rapid, required a canoe to be completely emptied before being paddled up or down—a so-called *décharge*.

If paddling was out of the question, the voyageurs had three other alternatives that still allowed them to avoid a full portage. The first was wading or "handing" the canoe—carefully walking it through shallow rapids while holding on to its gunwales. The second was "lining" (or "tracking" if travel was upstream) which involved pulling the canoe along the river bank with a

"Voyageurs and Raftsmen on the Ottawa about 1818," 1930-31, oil on canvas, by Charles William Jefferys (1869-1951). Reproduced with permission of the C.W. Jefferys Estate, Toronto.

cordelle (towing line) while a steersman and perhaps another man remained in the canoe to help guide it. The third was poling against the river bottom with *perches* (poles) if the bottom was shallow enough and the current not too swift. Three-metre-long (10-foot) poles suitable for poling were sometimes carried as equipment, but more often they were cut from the river bank as needed and tipped with metal ferrules to save them from wear. Fur trade accounts indicate that the wading, lining, and poling alternatives were often used in combination with a *demi-chargé* or *décharge*.

When a portage was absolutely necessary, the crew of a North canoe brought it alongshore and stood it off in good depth to prevent rocks from damaging its fragile birchbark skin. The *avant* then jumped into the water, steadying the canoe for the *gouvernail*, who jumped into the water next. With these two holding the canoe, the two or more *milieux* clambered out. Once the crew had thus disembarked, the passengers, if any, were carried to shore on the middlemen's shoulders, piggyback style. The voyageurs then unloaded their non-human freight, and the middlemen began the task of carrying loads to the other end of the portage, using a *collier* to aid them with the standard two 40-kilogram (90-pound) *pièces* per trip. The *avant* and *gouvernail* (together known as *bouts* or "ends") had the responsibility of carrying the canoe over the portage, in upright fashion, before taking up the general carrying. (In contrast, large Montreal canoes were carried upside down by four to six men.) A North canoe and its cargo ordinarily required each voyageur to make five trips across a portage—three with loads and two back unloaded—so that he actually walked 5 kilometres for every kilometre of portage. Assuming an average speed of 5 kilometres per hour, a 1-kilometre (2/3 mile) portage would take about an hour to complete.

If the length of a portage was greater than 800 metres (½ mile), the voyageur dropped his *pièces* at spaced intervals called *poses*, going back to bring up all of his loads before continuing on. The *poses*—which could be anywhere from 400 to 800 metres (¼ to ½ mile) long—served to even out the loaded and unloaded walks and to protect against theft. While they could be randomly chosen, it was common for the same *poses* to be used year after year. These would often have some favourable natural feature such as a water source or a view of the surrounding landscape. Most certainly, the constant caching of *pièces* would keep them free of undergrowth. If a portage had well-established poses, voyageurs might think of its length in *poses* rather than in terms of actual distance. At the same time, they might also know those *poses* by names handed down from one generation of voyageur to the next.

The voyageurs did not write down their own views of portaging, but other travellers have done so in admirable fashion. Describing his own canoe voyage north from Pelican Narrows in 1940, American adventurer P.G. Downes captured the essence of portaging:

> Portaging and the North are inextricably identified. When an obstruction is met in canoe travel, a falls or a land barrier to be crossed, the canoe beached, everything taken out and the canoe, turned over, is transported across first....The loads come next. The tump-line is fastened around as large an accumulation of boxes and bags as the person can manage. He then kneels, back to this, and slips the leather strap over his forehead until it pulls directly down on the front part of his head. At this juncture it is advisable to take the heaviest unpacked object near at hand, a fifty-pound bag of flour is admirable, and wedge it in against the back of the neck. The victim then struggles to his feet and staggers forward, gradually accelerating his pace until he achieves a shuffling scramble always on the verge of plunging to his knees. The hands, grasping loose miscellaneous objects which do not easily pack, such as guns, axes, and tea pails, are useless to comb off the hordes of

black flies and mosquitoes which seem by long patience and intelligence to have congregated from all parts of the North at these portages to attack their unarmed and defenseless victims.[51]

Their ruthless regimen of paddling and portaging in eighteen-hour stretches pushed the voyageurs to the limits of human endurance. They therefore looked for help wherever they could find it. Sometimes, that help came from the North-West's unpredictable wind which they knew as *La Vielle,* or "the Old Woman." A good tail wind allowed the voyageurs to hoist the sail which was standard equipment on every North canoe. They could then lean back and take a well-earned rest. If the wind blew too strongly for sailing or in the wrong direction, they might still hope to relax in a windbound camp. On portages, too, the wind was a friend who could cool a brow or fan away mosquitoes.

Food in the form of pemmican gave the voyageurs—some of whom made "Gods of their bellies"[52]—both energy and satisfaction. In the early days of the fur trade, voyageurs had to find their own food by stopping en route to hunt or fish or to trade for provisions from sympathetic Indians. This took precious time and limited the distance which could be travelled in a season. Traders therefore began to purchase high-energy Indian pemmican (*pimîhkân,* derived from the Cree word *pimiy,* meaning "grease"). Prepared mainly by aboriginal women in the Great Plains, it was a mixture of dried buffalo meat and fat. Berries were sometimes added to improve flavour, and in the north, moose, caribou, or even fish might be substituted for buffalo. The mixture was crammed into buffalo-skin bags called *taureaux* which were topped off with melted fat and sewn shut to produce compact, 40-kilogram (90-pound) parcels. Pemmican was extremely nutritious per unit of weight—a voyageur needed only 1 to 2 kilograms (2 to 4 pounds) per day—and would last for months and even a year or more without spoiling. Cooked into a stew called "rubbaboo" or chewed in its raw state, it was the voyageurs' staple diet from the 1780s until the decimation of the buffalo herds in the 1870s.

Apart from eating, the voyageurs had other pleasures that helped to brighten their days. The *Canadiens* had their *chansons* as constant companions and would sometimes sing throughout most of a working day. Another diversion was fur trade rum. While it was mainly used for trading purposes, it also served to motivate voyageurs. A rum ration was often given out at the end of a hard day. On George Simpson's gruelling 1828 trip to the Pacific, he allowed his men "drams four times a day."[53] But more important than either song or drink was tobacco. Paddling was interrupted every hour for a short break to allow voyageurs to light up their pipes for a welcome smoke. These breaks, called *pipes*, were so essential that distances came to be measured by *pipes* (for example, *deux pipes* meant about 15 kilometres or 9 miles of flatwater paddling).

At the very end of his day, the voyageur had one final pleasure, that being the luxury of sleep. He often had only bare ground and a few spruce boughs under his blanket and an upturned canoe above him. And mosquitoes surely plagued him. But when he lay down his head, hardly knowing which end of the day he was at, fatigue guaranteed him a few hours of sweet rest.

THE FUR TRADERS AND EXPLORERS: THEIR JOURNALS AND NARRATIVES

Some of the fur traders and explorers who travelled on Saskatchewan's voyageur highway left behind written accounts of their experiences. These generally took the form of either journals or narratives. Both reveal a great deal about the route and their authors' adventures on it. In the route chapters, we quote extensively from these journals and narratives to give you a close-up look at the route as it was in the early fur trade. In this chapter, we provide thumbnail sketches of the fur traders and explorers we quote from and some background on their writings. In special cases, such as that of Louis Primeau, we introduce characters who played crucial roles in the fur trade yet left behind little or no written record of their exploits.

Louis Primeau and the Frobisher Brothers

Who was the first white man to see the guide route? It is impossible to say for sure, but the distinction could belong to a little known yet clearly extraordinary woodsman named Louis Primeau, known to the Cree as "Nick'a'thu'tin" (*nikî-thôtin[isin]*) or "windbound."[54] Born in Quebec, Primeau entered the fur trade in the mid-1700s and served at New France's inland posts. His service was halted in about 1759 when the British Conquest of New France caused French inland traders to abandon their operations and go back to Quebec. Primeau himself, like some other French servants, chose to stay in the *pays d'en haut* and adopt an aboriginal way of life. He lived in this manner until 1765 when he came to York Factory to take up employment with the HBC. That year, the HBC sent him inland to trade with the Assiniboine, or Nakota Sioux. The next year, 1766, he was sent to "the famous…Beaver River." To get there, he probably first travelled inland from York Factory to the southeast end of our route, using the Indians' "Middle Track" canoe route or their alternate "Upper Track." He would then have gone upstream on the route all the way to the mouth of the Beaver River near present-day Île-à-la-Crosse.[55]

Primeau continued in the employ of the HBC until 1772, staying inland each winter and accompanying canoe brigades of Indian customers back to York Factory each spring. Finally, in the summer of 1772, Primeau deserted to the cause of Montreal traders who were becoming very active on the Saskatchewan River. During the following year, possibly on a trip east to Quebec, Primeau made contact with the fur trading Frobisher brothers of Montreal and joined them in a plan to launch the first significant fur trade campaign on our route.

Louis Primeau was a most energetic man. Between 1773 and 1776, with direction and support from the Frobishers, he played a lead role in establishing the first five trading posts seen on the route—upstream from Cumberland House in 1773, at Frog Portage in 1774, on Amisk Lake in 1775, on Dipper Lake in 1775, and at Île-à-la-Crosse in 1776. During these years, he was, as Samuel Hearne put it, "not master of the Gang," but a most skilful "chief Pilot and Trader."[56]

Primeau's masters, the Frobisher brothers—Joseph (1740–1810), Benjamin (1742–1787), and Thomas (1744–1788)—were from Yorkshire, England. They came to Montreal in the mid to late 1760s and, like others, found opportunities in the fur trade after the fall of New France caused some French traders to leave. The Frobishers worked well as a team, with Benjamin looking after business in Montreal while Joseph and Thomas went into the wilderness. They also had a talent for working with other people. They recognized Louis Primeau as a diamond in the rough and established a relationship with him which would, through the 1770s, allow them to open up the region to trade. They also partnered with several other Montreal traders to overcome the challenges of trading in the distant North-West. Indeed, they were largely responsible for tying together the original North West Company. And, when Benjamin and Thomas died in the late 1780s, Joseph joined with NWC director Simon McTavish to form McTavish, Frobisher & Co., a firm which would essentially manage the NWC over the next several years.[57]

Alexander Henry's Narrative

One Montreal trader who had a successful connection with the Frobishers was Alexander Henry (1739–1824), often called "the Elder" to distinguish him from his nephew of the same name. Originally a merchant working out of Albany, New York, Henry first came north to Canada to supply goods to the British army during its invasion of New France. After the war, he turned to the fur trade for his livelihood and, after a decade in the Great Lakes region, eventually made his way into the North-West. In June 1775, Henry headed inland with a large contingent of trading canoes and by fall had arrived on Lake Winnipeg where he fell in with other traders, including Joseph and Thomas Frobisher. At Cumberland House, the traders split off from each other to go to their intended wintering grounds. Most traders left for the prairies or parkland, but Henry and the Frobishers chose a different route. As Henry put it, "…we resolved on joining our stock [in a combined total of ten canoes], and wintering together. We steered for the river Churchill, or Missinipi, to the east of Beaver Lake, or Lake aux Castors."[58]

Henry wintered with the Frobishers on Amisk Lake in 1775–76, but he used a good part of the winter to take a journey on foot to visit the Great Plains and the Assiniboine (Nakota Sioux). In the spring of 1776, he and the Frobishers went to Frog Portage on the Churchill, where they traded their goods to Dene who had come down from the Athabasca country.

When Henry returned to Montreal with his handsome profits in 1776, he was quite taken with the North-West's trade potential. He sailed to England the same fall and presented a proposal to the HBC to have the company hire him to recruit French-Canadian voyageurs on their behalf. Unsuccessful in convincing the HBC to adopt his proposal, he returned to Montreal (after a side trip to meet the young Queen Marie-Antoinette of France) where he turned his energy and active imagination to other enterprises. In the next three decades, he married a widow and had five children, made and lost fortunes as a fur merchant and land speculator, and also found time to play an active role in community affairs.[59]

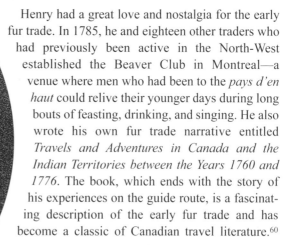

Henry had a great love and nostalgia for the early fur trade. In 1785, he and eighteen other traders who had previously been active in the North-West established the Beaver Club in Montreal—a venue where men who had been to the *pays d'en haut* could relive their younger days during long bouts of feasting, drinking, and singing. He also wrote his own fur trade narrative entitled *Travels and Adventures in Canada and the Indian Territories between the Years 1760 and 1776*. The book, which ends with the story of his experiences on the guide route, is a fascinating description of the early fur trade and has become a classic of Canadian travel literature.[60]

Alexander Henry, from Travels & Adventures in Canada and the Indian Territories between the Years 1760 and 1776.

Published in 1809, *Travels and Adventures*, with its tales of exploration and hardship, allowed Henry not only to recapture his youth but also to put fur traders of a new generation in their proper place. As he groused to an old friend the same year his book came out, "...All the new North westards are a parcel of Boys and upstarts, who were not born in our time, and suposes they know much more of the Indian trade than any before them."[61]

Samuel Hearne's Journal

Samuel Hearne (1745–1792) was born in London, England. He was hired by the HBC in 1766 to work as a mate on a trading ship attached to Prince of Wales Fort at the mouth of the Churchill River. By then, he was already an experienced sea dog since he had joined the Royal Navy at the age of twelve and had seen action in the Seven Years War. As it turned out, however, the HBC did not draw on his sailing abilities for long. Rather, because he was young and fit and had some knowledge of navigation, the company saw him as well suited for inland explorations.

In 1769 and early 1770, Hearne, sent out from Prince of Wales Fort by Chief Factor Moses Norton, made two initial attempts to reach the legendary Coppermine River. Then, making a third try in December 1770, Hearne embarked from Prince of Wales Fort on an amazing inland journey across the Barrens in the company of the Dene leader Mattonabbee and other Dene, including Mattonabbee's six wives. Over the course of the next year and a half, a time of much privation, Hearne and his companions succeeded in reaching the Coppermine River, the Arctic Ocean, and Great Slave Lake. They returned to their start point on June 30, 1792.

Because of his successful trip into the Barrens, the HBC selected Hearne to set up its first inland post west of Hudson Bay. In 1774, Hearne and his helpers travelled inland from York Factory courtesy of Cree canoemen and eventually reached the southeast end of our route. Hearne then proceeded to build a post he called Cumberland House, which today survives as Saskatchewan's oldest continuous community.

Hearne's journal account of both his voyage from York Factory to Cumberland House and the post's first season was published by the Champlain Society (a body specializing in publication of Canadian history) in 1934 as a section in the *Journals of Samuel Hearne and Philip Turnor*. Introduced, edited, and copiously footnoted by J.B. Tyrrell, Hearne's journal provides some very interesting observations on the HBC's own endeavour and on the competing Montrealers' early presence on our route.

NA / C-020053

Samuel Hearne, founder of Cumberland House.

After establishing the HBC's post at Cumberland in 1774–75, Hearne was recalled to Hudson Bay to take over command of Prince of Wales Fort. Although its thick stone walls suggested great goings on, Prince of Wales Fort was in fact a quiet posting, and Hearne spent some of his time writing a narrative of his earlier journeys to the Barrens. In 1782, his quietude was interrupted by a French naval attack on his fort. Hearne had no choice but to surrender, and Prince of Wales Fort was destroyed. However, the invading French commander Lapérouse did allow Hearne and his men to sail back to England on their own, and the next year, Hearne returned to rebuild a wooden post 8 kilometres (5 miles) upstream from the ruined stone fort. Hearne then commanded the new post, known as Fort Churchill, until 1787, when he retired in poor health to England where he died a few years later at the age of forty-seven. The narrative of his journeys to the Barrens, a fine example of eighteenth-century exploration literature, was published three years after his death.[62]

Matthew Cocking's Cumberland House Journal

Hearne's immediate successor at Cumberland House was a Yorkshireman named Matthew Cocking (1743–1799). Blessed with a better-than-average working man's education, Cocking was hired by the HBC in 1765 to work at York Factory as a "writer" looking after correspondence, keeping accounts, and transcribing post journals. In 1772, he was sent inland to improve upon the "incoherent and unintelligible" reports that HBC servants in the interior were sending back regarding the trade and the Montrealers' disruption of it. After leaving from York Factory, Cocking travelled into present-day western Saskatchewan, seeing the country with an observant eye as well as learning how to hunt buffalo and steer "Indian" canoes. Upon his return, he gave a clear account of his travels and stressed the need for the HBC to establish inland posts.

When the HBC directed Samuel Hearne to go inland to establish a post, it assigned Cocking to assist him. As it turned out, however, Cocking was of no assistance to Hearne in 1774. The HBC men were entirely dependant on Cree canoes for their transportation inland, and Cocking found himself travelling separate from Hearne. At one point, his original guides refused to proceed farther up the Saskatchewan River. Cocking and his European companions therefore had to hire different Cree canoes to continue. But they still had no control over their itinerary, and ended up finally at Good Spirit Lake (near present-day Canora, Saskatchewan) where they spent the winter. Cocking's party returned to York Factory on June 27, 1775, not having seen Samuel Hearne at all in the preceding year.

Cocking finally did make it to Cumberland House in October 1775, when he took over command of the post from Samuel Hearne. Despite suffering from a bad rupture, Cocking remained in charge at Cumberland through the next two trading seasons (1775–76 and 1776–77). His experiences at Cumberland were eventually published by the Hudson's Bay Record Society almost two centuries later as part of a two-volume series known as the *Cumberland House Journals*.[63]

In 1777, at last admitting that Cocking's rupture made inland service difficult for him, the HBC's London Committee permitted him to take charge of Fort Severn on Hudson Bay. Then, in his final years with the HBC, he had the command of York Factory itself. In 1782, he finally retired to York, England, leaving behind his aboriginal wife and their three daughters. Sadly, this was quite typical of the way that families of such "country marriages" were treated. Cocking did, however, send his family a remittance each year, and his last will remembered them. In it, he instructed that his daughters were each to receive £6 per year, the eldest to receive the full amount with the younger to share their portions with their mother. Part of the bequest was to be "laid out in Ginger Bread, Nuts &tc. as they have no other means of obtaining these little luxuries, with which the paternal fondness of a Father formally [sic] provided them."[64]

Peter Pond and His Map

Of all the fur traders and explorers to travel the route, none was more surrounded by controversy than the remarkable Peter Pond (1740–1807). Born in Milford, Connecticut, Pond left home at a young age to pursue an army career and was with General Amherst when the British general captured Montreal in the Conquest of New France. After the Conquest, Pond took up seafaring and sailed to the West Indies. However, upon returning to find his mother dead and his father off trading, he stayed home at Milford for three years to care for his younger siblings.

In about 1765, Pond entered the fur trade and traded for several years in the region of Detroit and the upper Mississippi. His hair-trigger temper showed itself during this time when he shot and killed a trader in a duel. Pond brought the incident to the attention of authorities but was not prosecuted. He then returned to the fur trade, maintaining an active interest in the Indian peoples he met. Finally, in 1775, he left the upper Mississippi to move beyond Grand Portage and into the North-West.

During Pond's initial 1775 venture into the North-West, he was one of the traders who fell in with the Frobisher brothers on Lake Winnipeg. However, he did not then choose to move north to the route. Rather, he branched off south to spend the winter trading at Dauphin Lake, just west of Lake Winnipegosis. In the following two years, 1776–77 and 1777–78, he returned to the North-West to winter, in the company of other Montreal-based traders, at the junction of the Sturgeon and North Saskatchewan rivers, just west of present-day Prince Albert.

In 1778, Pond embarked on a journey that would ensure him a place in fur trade history. That spring, instead of heading out from the Saskatchewan to Grand Portage with furs from the previous winter's trade, he took charge of a pool of trade goods that he and other Montreal traders, who were backed mainly by the Frobisher brothers and Simon McTavish, had left over from the previous winter's trade. On May 26, he turned north off the Saskatchewan at Cumberland House with five canoes loaded with goods and proceeded upstream to Frog Portage, Île-à-la-Crosse, and beyond. In due course, he came to Methy Portage and became the first white man to cross over it. He then continued northward on the Athabasca River to within 70 kilometres (45 miles) of Lake Athabasca, whereupon he stopped to winter and trade. Through the winter, Pond and his men secured 140 packs of fur from the Cree and Dene they met—a highly successful trade.

Unfortunately, Pond's Athabasca success was followed by trouble. He spent the winter of 1781–82 on Lac la Ronge, at the mouth of the Nemeiben River, trading alongside another Montreal-based trader, a Swiss named Jean-Étienne Wadin. Friction developed between Pond and Wadin during the winter, and in March 1782, a quarrel broke out between the two. Wadin was shot in the thigh, either by Pond or his clerk, and he bled to death. Five years later, Pond was implicated in yet another death when he was trading for the NWC on Lake Athabasca in competition with John Ross of the Gregory-McLeod concern. A dispute broke out between the rival factions, and Ross was shot and killed by one of Pond's voyageurs named Péché. This last killing prompted a merger between the NWC and Gregory-McLeod. Pond spent the winter of 1787–88 on Lake Athabasca working with Alexander Mackenzie, who had previously been in charge of the Gregory-McLeod post at Île-à-la-Crosse. Evidently, however, there were too many black clouds over Pond's head, and it turned out to be his last winter in the North-West.

Peter Pond was clearly a successful fur trader and explorer, but he ought also to be remembered as a map-maker. In the winter of 1784–85, which he spent in Montreal, he drew a map of the North-West based on his own travels and information collected from aboriginal people. The map was a great achievement and, in an early version presented to the United States Congress, gave a good general outline of the unexplored Mackenzie River. In later versions, Pond's map would suggest that a large river leading west from Great Slave Lake likely ran into the Pacific at Cook Inlet, Alaska. While this error would discredit Pond's mapping skills, it also inspired Alexander Mackenzie in his explorations of the river named after him.

Today, the lake west of Buffalo Narrows bears Pond's name. The largest lake on our route, its size reflects the considerable contributions of the irascible Peter Pond to Canada's North-West.[65]

Alexander Mackenzie's Epic Narrative

Born on a farm a short distance from Stornoway on the Isle of Lewis, Scotland, Alexander Mackenzie (1764–1820) was one of many highland Scots who joined the fur trade in the eighteenth century. When a severe depression hit his native island in the 1770s, young Alexander emigrated to the colony of New York with his family. Shortly after the family's arrival there, the American Revolution broke out. Since his family were Loyalists, Alexander was sent to boarding school in Montreal to ensure his safety. At about fifteen, he left school to learn the fur trade in the firm of Finlay and Gregory. In 1784, after five years in his firm's Montreal office, by which time it had become Gregory, McLeod and Company, Mackenzie was finally entrusted to go inland to Detroit with "a small adventure of goods." With success in this venture came a partnership share in the business.

In June 1785, Alexander Mackenzie met with his partners at Grand Portage and agreed to go to the English (Churchill) River and establish a headquarters at Île-à-la-Crosse. Once at Île-à-la-Crosse, he found himself competing with the NWC post under the command of Patrick Small. Small had already sent a young and ambitious clerk named William McGillivray down the Churchill River to set up an outpost at Lac des Serpents

HBCA 1987/363-M-4/7 (NA 123)

Sir Alexander Mackenzie, after the portrait by Lawrence.

(Pinehouse Lake). Mackenzie tried to check Small's move by sending his cousin Roderick McKenzie to set up a rival post at the same location. Isolation and compatible personalities were to make McGillivray and Roderick McKenzie fast friends, and they were pleasantly surprised when their firms merged in 1787.

As already noted, the NWC and Gregory-McLeod merger resulted in Alexander Mackenzie joining Peter Pond in the Athabasca for the 1787–88 season. The NWC probably wanted him to learn the local trade from Pond in advance of Pond leaving the region for good. However, Mackenzie could not help but listen to Pond's energetic views on how a great undiscovered waterway might allow inland navigation all the way to the Pacific. By the next spring, Mackenzie had become enthralled with the idea of becoming the first person to cross North America to the Pacific Ocean. To turn idea into action, he spent the next year organizing an expedition to accomplish his goal, and on June 3, 1789, he set forth from the NWC's new Fort Chipewyan on Lake Athabasca. After going up the Slave River to Great Slave Lake, he followed the river that Pond assumed flowed west to the Pacific. But the river, later named after Mackenzie, eventually turned north and in due course led him to the Arctic Ocean instead of the Pacific. By September 12, Mackenzie was back in Fort Chipewyan, having completed a round trip of over 4,800 kilometres (3,000 miles) in just 102 days.

Disappointed but undaunted, Mackenzie threw himself into preparing for a second attempt to reach the Pacific. An encounter with HBC surveyor Philip Turnor at Cumberland House in June 1790 made Mackenzie realize that he lacked proper navigational training and equipment. He took steps to correct this by spending the winter of 1791–92 in London to study and purchase some basic instruments—a compass, sextant, chronometer, and large telescope. Upon his return to the North-West, the HBC's Philip Turnor had already ascertained the proper longitude for Fort Chipewyan, and this information, coupled with Captain James Cook's longitudes for the Pacific coast, showed Mackenzie that Peter Pond had placed Lake Athabasca far too close to the Pacific. Mackenzie therefore realized that, to save summer travel time, he should start his next expedition from a jump-off point west of Fort Chipewyan. In the autumn of 1792, in preparation for a spring journey, he went up the Peace River from Fort Chipewyan and set up an advance base at the junction of the Peace and Smoky rivers (now Peace River Landing, Alberta).

On May 9, 1793, Mackenzie and his crew of nine—six voyageurs, one fur trader, and two Indian hunters and interpreters—started their momentous voyage. First ascending the Peace and Parsnip rivers, they eventually crossed over the continental divide and proceeded down the McGregor and Fraser rivers. Local Indians then convinced them that the Fraser was not their best option, so they backtracked up the Fraser to its junction with the West Road River. Here, they cached some of their supplies and began a trek overland to the west. In time, they reached the Bella Coola River which they followed to reach the Pacific coast. Here, using vermillion mixed with grease, Mackenzie painted on a rock: "Alexander Mackenzie, from Canada, by land, the twenty-second of July, one thousand seven hundred and ninety-three." Although of no immediate benefit to the NWC, his expedition had accomplished what none other had done before.

Mackenzie was keenly interested in writing an account of his inland travels. After his return from the Pacific, however, he spent much of the ensuing winter in a state of unexplainable melancholy, and his writing did not progress as he had hoped. Fortunately, inspiration eventually returned to him, and over the next several years, with help from an experienced travel editor and possibly his cousin Roderick, he completed an epic volume entitled *Voyages from Montreal to the Frozen and Pacific Oceans*.[66] Published in 1801, *Voyages from Montreal* was an instant success. It captured thousands of readers in Europe and North America with its simple and direct accounts of Mackenzie's voyages, the land and peoples of the North-West, and the fur trade. On February 10, 1802, only two months after publication, Mackenzie was knighted.

In 1799, Mackenzie had left the NWC after much friction between himself and the NWC's Simon McTavish. He played a key role in the XY Company which competed against the NWC. However, when that company merged with the NWC in 1804, Mackenzie was left out of the re-organized NWC. He then turned to local Quebec politics for a time but soon wearied of that pursuit. He eventually grew tired of life in Canada and moved back to Scotland where he married and had three children. His final years were relatively quiet, a striking contrast to his adventurous years in the North-West.[67]

Philip Turnor's HBC Journal

Philip Turnor (1751–1799/1800) came from Middlesex, England. He was brought up in farming but somehow acquired a knowledge of surveying and mathematics. In 1778, when he was twenty-seven, the HBC hired him to work as an inland surveyor and sent him to York Factory where he was first engaged in making a plan of that post. He then proceeded inland from York Factory to Cumberland House, escorted by Indians. He used their "Upper Track" via the Nelson and Grass rivers and surveyed that route as he went. He arrived October 11, 1778, at Cumberland and wintered there until March when he went upriver on the Saskatchewan's ice to survey the way to the HBC's Upper Hudson house. He then returned to Cumberland by canoe in spring and on June 9, 1779, left to return to York Factory by the Indians' "Middle Track." Thereafter, with his inaugural expedition behind him, he spent the next several years surveying for the HBC in the country around Hudson Bay.

In the fall of 1789, Turnor arrived in Cumberland House with orders to lead a major HBC survey expedition to Lake Athabasca, plotting the route there and ascertaining the exact location of the lake itself. Turnor's party was to comprise ten people—himself; Peter Fidler, a young man newly trained in the rudiments of surveying; Malcolm Ross, an experienced fur trader; Ross's country wife and two children; and four Orkneymen. Since the HBC had no posts on the route, Turnor and his people were to rely on their own resources and the goodwill of the rival NWC to provision them. The NWC would in fact aid Turnor's party, the *quid pro quo* being that the Turnor group would not engage in any fur trade business.

On September 13, 1790, Turnor and his party started out from Cumberland House. Their journey to the Athabasca—the "Athapiscow Country" as Turnor called it—and the return back to York Factory would take close to two years. The first fall, they made it as far as Île-à-la-Crosse where they wintered at the NWC post commanded by Patrick Small. They could not go any farther since freeze-up was near at hand and three of Turnor's men were crippled with injuries from their tough upstream journey. To Turnor's relief, Small generously provided his party with two houses in the NWC compound. In the spring of 1791, Turnor and his group continued their journey to the Athabasca. Reaching Lake Athabasca, they spent the summer exploring around the lake, and then spent the winter based at the NWC's Fort Chipewyan on the west end of the lake. They then made their journey homeward in the summer of 1792, reaching York Factory on July 17.

Turnor believed that the HBC should return to the Athabasca forthwith, and he volunteered himself and his men for the task. However, his attempt to convince his superiors of the necessity of this venture was unsuccessful. Disappointed, Turnor was to leave the North-West for good. In October 1792, he returned to England where he took up teaching navigation in London. He died just eight years later.

Philip Turnor's Athabasca journey provided a wealth of geographical information which was used to improve the HBC's maps of the North-West. But his journal from the trip—rivaled only by that of his companion Peter Fidler—also gives modern canoeists an excellent description of Saskatchewan's voyageur highway during the early fur trade. As will be seen, we refer to it many times in this guide. The journal was published in full as part of a volume edited by explorer J.B. Tyrrell and published by the Champlain Society as the *Journals of Samuel Hearne and Philip Turnor*.[68]

Peter Fidler's Journal and Maps

Born at Bolsover, Derbyshire, England, Peter Fidler (1769–1822) had an education that was better than average for his time. Although he was hired by the HBC as a labourer in 1788, the company soon realized that he had some ability with a pen and promoted him to the position of writer. It then sent him inland, first to Manchester House on the North Saskatchewan River and then to South Branch House on the South Saskatchewan.

In the spring of 1790, Fidler was sent to Cumberland House to receive a crash course from Philip Turnor in surveying and astronomy. Turnor had originally planned to take a young David Thompson as his assistant with him on his forthcoming expedition to the Athabasca. But Thompson had broken his leg in a sled accident in December 1788, and that fracture did not heal as expected. Hence, Turnor decided that Fidler would go in Thompson's stead and trained Fidler for that purpose.

Once on the Athabasca voyage, Fidler demonstrated his hardiness; the experienced Malcolm Ross described him as "a very fit man for surveying in this quarter, as he can put up with any sort of living, that is in eating and drinking." At the same time, Fidler exhibited an uncommon talent for journal writing and map-making, even when reduced to using scraps of birchbark for paper. When

LORNE BOUCHARD / HBCA / P-435 (N3563)

Philip Turnor (centre) and Peter Fidler (left) survey Lake Athabasca.

J.B. Tyrrell edited Turnor's Athabasca journal for publication, he used extracts from Fidler's journal to clarify or expand upon Turnor's daily entries. He also inserted some of Fidler's fascinating sketches of lakes along the voyageur highway to illustrate the Turnor party's progress. Taking our cue from Tyrrell, we also borrow from Fidler's journal and reproduce some of his maps in this guide.

After establishing his own reputation as a surveyor during the 1790–92 Athabasca expedition, Fidler spent almost thirty years surveying the North-West, from the Red River region of present-day Manitoba to the foothills of Alberta. At the same time, he was active as a Hudson's Bay Company trader. Unfortunately, throughout the period, his work was constantly made difficult by rival traders from the XY Company and the NWC. He faced vigorous opposition from these traders at Lake Athabasca between 1802 and 1806, at Île-à-la-Crosse in 1810 and 1811, and then at Red River between 1812 and 1817. Nonetheless, he persevered in the face of adversity and contributed a great deal to both the survey of the North-West and the fur trade.

Things should have improved for Fidler after the merger of the HBC and NWC in 1821. Instead, he was pensioned off, a surplus employee in a company now chiefly concerned with finding economies. He died at Dauphin Lake House (in present-day Manitoba) soon after, survived by his wife who had been with him on many of his travels and also by eleven of his fourteen children.[69]

David Thompson's Narrative

David Thompson (1770–1857) was born in London of Welsh parents. Thompson's father died when he was two, causing financial hardship for the family left behind. Thus, when Thompson was seven, his mother placed him in Grey Coat School, a London charity school near Westminster Abbey. Thompson stayed at the school until he was fourteen, by which time he had learned the basics of mathematics and navigation. The school then arranged for him to begin a seven-year apprenticeship with the HBC, and his life as fur trader and explorer began.

Thompson spent 1784–85, his first year in North America, under Samuel Hearne at Fort Churchill, where he quite likely obtained a working knowledge of the Dene language. He was then transferred to posts on the South and North Saskatchewan rivers where he learned to speak Cree. Soon after, in 1787–88, he wintered with Peigans in the Rocky Mountain foothills and learned their language too. In December 1788, he broke his leg at Manchester House on the North Saskatchewan, and in the spring of 1789, he was transferred to Cumberland House to continue a slow convalescence. He spent the winter of 1789–90 studying navigation under Philip Turnor in hopes that he would be able to go with Turnor on his 1790 Athabasca expedition. However, to Thompson's dismay, his leg did not get better in time for the trip, and Peter Fidler was chosen to take his place as Turnor's junior surveyor.

Fortunately, despite the disappointment of not going to the Athabasca, Thompson maintained his interest in surveying. He obtained a set of surveying instruments from the HBC's London Committee and put these to good use on a regular basis, becoming the HBC's official surveyor by 1794. As chief surveyor, Thompson was particularly intrigued by the possibility of charting a westerly route into the Athabasca that would avoid the back-breaking misery of Methy Portage. In 1796, he and two Dene guides—the energetic Kozdaw and the more placid Paddy—were finally successful in travelling via Reindeer Lake and Wollaston Lake to the east end of Lake Athabasca. The journey, which almost cost Thompson and his friends their lives, showed that the

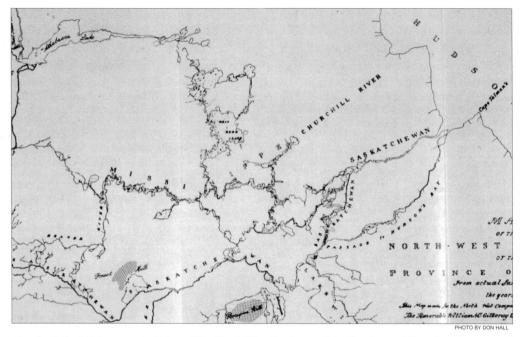

Detail of David Thompson's "Map of the North-West Territory of the Province of Canada." Reproduced from David Thompson's Narrative 1784–1812, *published by the Champlain Society, 1962.*

route was too difficult to be feasible for trade, but the story of the trip stands out as an epic saga in canoe travel literature.

In 1797, feeling unduly restricted in his surveying work by York Factory's Chief Factor Joseph Colen, Thompson deserted the HBC to join the NWC. With this move, his career as a surveyor and map-maker really took off. He began with a solid year of surveying in a huge tract of land lying west and south of Lake Superior. In 1798, he travelled upstream on the upper Churchill for the first time and, the following summer, travelled down the entire length of our route on his way to Grand Portage. In subsequent years, he did extensive explorations in the Rocky Mountains. By 1814, his grasp of the North-West's geography allowed him to complete a great map of the country between Lake Superior and the Pacific, and for years, this map hung in the Great Hall of the NWC's Fort William. It essentially confirmed Thompson's place as the greatest land geographer Canada has ever produced.

Thompson had a special connection to our route. It was at Île-à-la-Crosse in 1799 that Thompson met and married Charlotte Small, the 13-year-old Métis daughter of the NWC's Patrick Small. The marriage would produce thirteen children and, unlike many similar unions, would last Thompson's lifetime.

Thompson left the NWC in 1815 to purchase a farm in Upper Canada. He then spent several years surveying for a commission locating the Canada-U.S. border. When this work ended in 1820, he turned his hand to several occupations. But good fortune abandoned him, and in the last years of his life, financial setbacks left him and Charlotte penniless.

Despite his last years of poverty, Thompson was able to work on a narrative of his life's explorations. This work was interrupted when he went blind in 1851 and was not yet finished when he died in obscurity in 1857. It was many years later that surveyor and historian J.B. Tyrrell picked up the manuscript and had it published by the Champlain Society as *David Thompson's Narrative*.[70]

George Simpson's Athabasca Journal

George Simpson (1786/7–1860) was born in the Scottish Highlands and raised there by an aunt. He received a basic education from a parish school and then, perhaps about 1800, he moved to London to work in an uncle's sugar brokerage firm. The move brought Simpson into contact with the fur trade since, in 1812, one Andrew Wedderburn joined the sugar brokerage. Wedderburn had bought stock in the HBC in 1808 and thereafter came to play a main role in the company's management. Simpson must have impressed Wedderburn with his tough-minded approach to business. In 1820, when it emerged that the HBC needed a new Governor of Rupert's Land to face the NWC's competition, Wedderburn decided that Simpson was the man for the job, and saw to his hire, even though the latter knew virtually nothing about the fur trade.

In February 1820, Simpson sailed for North America, eager to learn the intricacies of the fur business and the geography of his new domain. He landed in New York in April, spent some time in Montreal and Fort William, and then moved inland to the North-West. Not wasting any time, he left Rock Depot (an HBC post just inland from York Factory) on July 30, 1820, to travel inland all the way to Lake Athabasca where he would winter. On this trip, which included the entire length of our route, Simpson kept a journal that documented his first impressions of the rivalry between the HBC and the NWC, his views on how the trade could be improved, and his sometimes caustic appraisals of the people he met. Eventually published by the Hudson's Bay Record Society as *Journal of Occurrences in the Athabasca Department by George Simpson, 1820 and 1821*, the daily record of his first North-West voyage makes for fascinating reading.

Simpson would preside over the HBC for the next forty years. In the first years after he started with the company, he competently managed the rationalization and re-organizing of operations that followed its merger with the NWC in 1821. Once he had the HBC's monopoly running smoothly, he did not slacken in his single-minded pursuit of profit. He continued to champion hard work and economy and drove the HBC's return on

George Simpson, 1857

investment to the 10–25 percent range. His status grew with company profits. In 1841, he was knighted to become "Sir George Simpson." At the same time, his almost complete control over HBC affairs led many to know him as the "little Emperor." Certainly, by the time he died in 1860, his reputation as one of the great business leaders of the century was firmly established.

Unfortunately, for all his talent, Simpson was not a nice man. He was a racist, even in the context of his own time. He described his own children born of country wives as "bits of brown" and, in later years, bragged that they had no claim on his estate. Nor did he have any qualms when, in 1829, he abandoned his country wife of the day, Margaret Taylor, and married his cousin Frances Simpson in England. After he brought Frances to Canada, he banned the non-white wives of his colleagues from his home. When he died, he left a fortune to his white heirs and nothing to his fur trade children.[71]

The Journals and Narratives of the Franklin Expeditions

The upper Churchill route to the Athabasca was not only a fur trade highway but also a gateway for scientific explorations of the far north. The most famous northern explorer to use the route was Captain John Franklin (1786–1847) who, on behalf of the British Royal Navy, made a total of four expeditions into the Arctic. The main goal of these expeditions was to fill in the blank spaces on maps of North America's Arctic region and, at the same time, find a navigable "Northwest Passage" between the Atlantic and Pacific oceans. The Royal Navy also hoped Franklin could advance scientific knowledge of geomagnetism and thus make it easier to use magnetic compasses for navigation in polar regions. Since the magnetic north pole's location was still unknown, navigators did not clearly understand why compass needles swung as they did in northern latitudes.

Franklin was born in England as the son of a textile merchant. His middle-class family was able to send him to good schools, but at the age of fourteen, he chose to volunteer for the British navy. In April 1801, only six months after signing up, he was with commander Horatio Nelson's fleet at the Battle of Copenhagen. He then moved on to serve on ships venturing as far as Australia, China, and South America. In the course of this service, he was shipwrecked in the South Pacific in 1803, was involved in the Battle of Trafalgar (during the Napoleonic Wars) off the Spanish coast in 1805, and was wounded at New Orleans (in the lead-up to the Battle of New Orleans) in 1814.

Franklin's meritorious naval record as a young man prompted the Royal Navy to give

Sir John Franklin

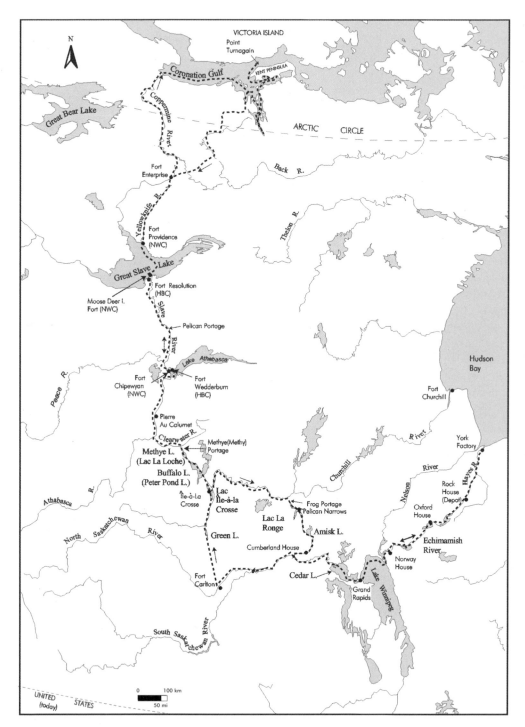

The route of Franklin's first inland expedition from the shores of Hudson Bay to the Arctic Circle. Map adapted from Franklin's First Arctic Land Expedition 1819–1822, *published by the Champlain Society.*

him a main role in its quest for a Northwest Passage. For his first expedition to the Arctic, Franklin was placed in command of one of two British ships that sailed from Norway's Spitsbergen Islands in 1818. This expedition ended without success after six months when both its ships were stopped by pack-ice. However, in a second expedition (1819–1821) and a third (1825–1827), Franklin was able to reach the Arctic coast via inland travel which, for both expeditions, took him on our route.

On his 1819 expedition, Franklin had a core team of fellow naval men including surgeon and naturalist John Richardson (1787–1865); midshipman and artist George Back (1796–1878); and midshipman, surveyor, and artist Robert Hood (1797–1821). The team initially sailed from England to York Factory on an HBC ship, arriving on August 30, and then travelled to Cumberland House by boat, reaching there on October 23, 1819. Franklin stayed at Cumberland until January 1820, at which time he and Back left by dog team for Lake Athabasca by way of the Saskatchewan River, Île-à-la-Crosse, and Methy Portage. Richardson and Hood overwintered at Cumberland and then followed Franklin in the spring, going by canoe along our route.

In some respects, Franklin was not ready for an overland Arctic expedition. The HBC's George Simpson predicted Franklin would have poor success and caustically noted, Franklin "must have three meals p diem, Tea is indispensable, and with the utmost exertion he cannot walk above Eight miles in one day...." These comments were unfair to Franklin, who was truly a sturdy individual, but they did point to his lack of experience with inland travel in the north's harsh environment.[72]

Eventually, on July 18, 1821, Franklin and his navy men—accompanied by NWC trader Willard Wentzel, fifteen voyageurs, eight Copper (Yellowknife) Indian guides, and four interpreters—reached the Arctic Ocean via the Coppermine River. Wentzel, four voyageurs, and the Copper Indians then returned south, while Franklin and the remaining nineteen men took two canoes to explore the Arctic coast eastward from the mouth of the Coppermine. They continued their explorations until August 18 when—after charting 1,000 kilometres (625 miles) of coastline never before seen by white men—the end of summer and dwindling supplies caused them to turn and start back south.

On the return trip, Franklin's lack of northern travel experience and his refusal to take advice from knowledgeable fur traders, voyageurs, and aboriginal guides finally caught up to the expedition. The journey southward on an inland route up the Hood River became an ordeal as autumn advanced and game grew scarce. With its food stocks depleted, the expedition resorted to a starvation diet which too often consisted only of nauseous *tripe de roche* (rock lichens). Nine voyageurs died from cold and hunger. On October 20, 1821, Robert Hood, already greatly weakened by the lichen diet, was shot through the head by Iroquois voyageur Michel Teroahauté. The killing was apparently precipitated by an argument occurring between the two starving men while they were left alone in a forlorn camp. Teroahauté was in turn shot to death by John Richardson who feared the man might kill again. Thus, by the time Franklin's party was rescued by Copper Indians and escorted to safety, it had lost a total of eleven men.

In 1823, shortly after he returned to England, Captain John Franklin wrote and published his account of the 1819–1822 expedition as *Narrative of a Journey to the Shores of the Polar Sea*. In writing the book, he borrowed extensively from the journals of John Richardson and Robert Hood and, to a lesser degree, from that of George Back. The book's sales were buoyed by horrific rumours of cannibalism occurring on the expedition. Its first edition had to be reprinted four times within eighteen months, while published translations fed a curious public outside the English-speaking world. Today, Franklin's *Narrative* remains a good read. Though it focuses on Franklin's Arctic adventures, its first chapters—describing Cumberland House and the Cree of that region; the 1820 winter dog sled journey by Franklin and Back between Île-à-la-Crosse and Methy Portage; and the 1820 summer canoe trip by Richardson and Hood between Cumberland House and Methy Portage—provide a great deal of information about our route.[73]

Readers wanting to know more about Franklin's 1819 expedition will appreciate the work of C. Stuart Houston, formerly a doctor and scholar at the University of Saskatchewan. Houston's *To the Arctic by Canoe* (1974) presents Robert Hood's diary of the expedition's activities to September 15, 1820 (which Hood had put into narrative form during the winter of 1820–21 at Fort Enterprise north of Great Slave Lake), paintings Hood did for the expedition, and valuable commentary on Hood's death and other topics.[74] In *Arctic Ordeal* (1984), Houston publishes—again with excellent appendices and comments—the journal of the erudite John Richardson for the period August 21, 1820 to December 19, 1821.[75] Finally, in *Arctic Artist* (1994), Houston completes a trilogy by setting out George Back's expedition journals and paintings.[76]

Though Franklin, Richardson, and Back barely survived the 1819 expedition, their ordeal did not deter them from exploration. They learned enough from their mistakes to execute a much better planned expedition to the Arctic in 1825–27, again travelling inland via our route to reach their destination. In 1826, working from the mouth of the Mackenzie River, Franklin and Back explored the Arctic coastline westward for 600 kilometres (375 miles). At the same time, a second party headed by Richardson traced the coastline east as far as the Coppermine River. Upon returning to England, Franklin published an account of his highly successful expedition in *Narrative of a Second Expedition to the Shores of the Polar Sea*. This second narrative (which gives our Saskatchewan route only brief mention to avoid repeating information in the first work) was well received and led to Franklin being knighted in 1829.[77]

Franklin is today most famous for his fourth Arctic expedition which, unfortunately, ended in tragedy for all involved. Planning to navigate the Northwest Passage by sea, Franklin left England in May 1845 with two ships and 134 men, never to be heard from again. Later investigations revealed that Franklin's ships became permanently locked in Arctic ice off Prince William Island in September 1846 and that Franklin died there June 11, 1847. Some of his men survived into 1848, but they too eventually perished, likely from the combined effects of cold, scurvy, starvation, and perhaps lead poisoning from canned provisions.

Some good did come from Franklin's disappearance. His status as a hero in England and the efforts of his widow resulted in numerous expeditions being sent to the Arctic to look for him. These expeditions made many contributions to mapping and to general science. One noteworthy venture was that of John Richardson who, with the tough and talented Orkneyman John Rae as his second-in-command, went in search of Franklin in 1848, using our route to reach the Arctic. (Interestingly, despite what Richardson might have thought of Michel Teroahauté, the voyageurs he hired to travel from Montreal to Methy Portage were mainly Iroquois.) Richardson did not find Franklin, but his two-volume narrative of the search, *Arctic Searching Expedition,* first published in 1851, made a major contribution to geography and science. Chapter 3 of the work gives a good description of Richardson's travel upstream between Cumberland House and Methy Portage in 1848.[78]

J.B. Tyrrell: Geologist, Surveyor, and Historian

Joseph Burr (J.B.) Tyrrell (1858–1957) was born and raised at Weston, Upper Canada (now part of Toronto), the son of a Loyalist mother and an Irish stonemason father. He attended Upper Canada College and then went to the University of Toronto where he obtained an Arts degree. To please his family, he then began articling with a Toronto law firm in order to become a lawyer. In 1881, however, he grew bored with his legal studies and hired on with the Geological Survey of Canada. Though he was quite deaf and nearly blind without glasses, Tyrrell was a robust and hardy individual well-suited to the outdoor life the Survey had to offer.

Tyrrell had no formal training in geology, but he quickly established himself as a good field geologist. He had his first taste of field work in 1883 as an assistant to geologist George Mercer Dawson in present-day southern Alberta and British Columbia. The following year, he was put in charge of exploring a vast region making up what is now central Alberta. Tyrrell began his work by travelling along the Red Deer River by canoe in hopes that the river's banks might reveal what lay below ground level. His strategy was a good one. On June 9, 1884, in the vicinity of Drumheller, he discovered what would prove to be Canada's largest field of dinosaur fossils. Then after travelling downstream for only three days more, he discovered a great deposit of workable coal which would one day make Drumheller boom. Today, Tyrrell's original find of dinosaur bones is recognized in the name given to Drumheller's Tyrrell Museum of Palaeontology, opened in 1985, which houses the world's largest collection of intact dinosaur skeletons.[79]

Tyrrell went on to explore huge tracts of North-West wilderness for the Geological Survey. He took his own findings and consolidated them with the information gathered by early fur traders and explorers to fill in many of the blank spots still showing up on maps at the end of the nineteenth century. Of special interest is his work of 1892, when he was assigned to the region between the Churchill River and Lake Athabasca and consequently travelled a portion of our route. Reaching Île-à-la-Crosse from Prince Albert, Tyrrell first hired three canoemen from Île-à-la-Crosse and then, on June 29, 1892, paddled down the Churchill to the mouth of the Mudjatik River. He then ascended the Mudjatik to reach Cree Lake and then Lake Athabasca. He later returned to Île-à-la-Crosse via the Geikie, Foster, and Churchill rivers, arriving there on September 14, 1892.[80]

After his 1892 journey, Tyrrell stayed on with the Geological Survey until 1898. His work during these years included expeditions to the Barren Lands in 1893 and 1894. It also saw him research and present a major paper on glacial theory in 1897. The paper—advancing the theory that

J.B. Tyrrell, 1886

the north had been glaciated on more than one occasion—was controversial at first but eventually won him accolades from the scientific community. Upon leaving the Survey, Tyrrell went on to pursue mining-related careers in both the Klondike and northern Ontario.

Throughout his life, Tyrrell had a keen interest in the history of fur trade exploration. He devoted considerable energy to editing and helping to publish the journals and narratives of early fur traders and explorers. Indeed, it was Tyrrell who raised David Thompson from obscurity and gave him the fame he so deserved. Tyrrell began his campaign in the 1880s, editing *A Brief Narrative of the Journeys of David Thompson in North-Western America* in 1888 and then seeing published the more complete *David Thompson's Narrative* in 1916.

In pursuing his passion for history, Tyrrell worked closely with the Champlain Society, an organization founded in 1905 (and still in operation) to publish manuscripts and other works of Canadian historical significance. It was the Champlain Society that first published *David Thompson's Narrative*, which Tyrrell had edited and provided with an exhaustive introduction. Years later, in 1934, the Society also published the *Journals of Samuel Hearne and Philip Turnor*, again under Tyrrell's editorship and with an introduction by him. Tyrrell was a driving force behind the Champlain Society for many years, and served as its president from 1927 to 1932. During his involvement with the Society, he championed the publication of fur trade journals and narratives. It is in good part thanks to his efforts that the Champlain Society has made so many of these fascinating works available to the modern voyageur.[81]

-3-

CLEARWATER RIVER TO LA LOCHE

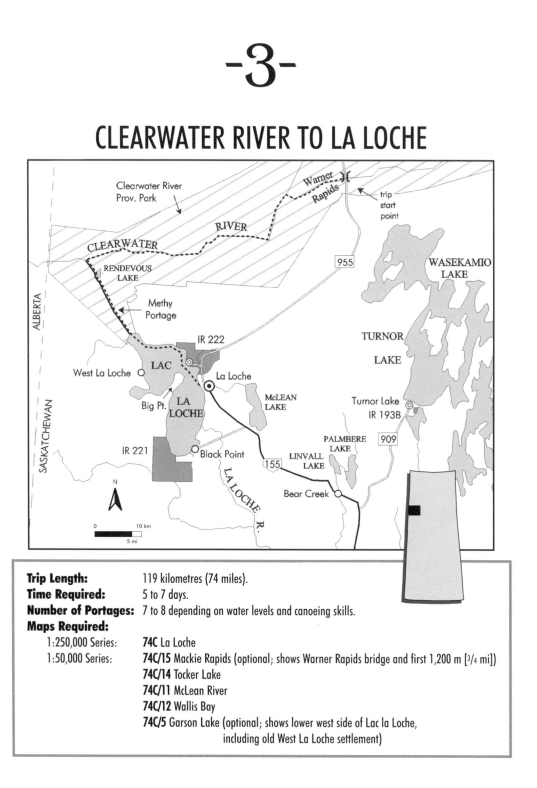

Trip Length:	119 kilometres (74 miles).
Time Required:	5 to 7 days.
Number of Portages:	7 to 8 depending on water levels and canoeing skills.
Maps Required:	

1:250,000 Series: **74C** La Loche

1:50,000 Series: **74C/15** Mackie Rapids (optional; shows Warner Rapids bridge and first 1,200 m [³/₄ mi])
   74C/14 Tocker Lake
   74C/11 McLean River
   74C/12 Wallis Bay
   74C/5 Garson Lake (optional; shows lower west side of Lac la Loche,
          including old West La Loche settlement)

About the Trip

The route for this trip runs 80 km (50 mi) westward down the Clearwater River from where Road 955 crosses the river at Warner Rapids to the north end of Methy Portage. It then goes 19 km (12 mi) southeast over Methy Portage. From the south end of the portage, it winds 1 km (2/3 mi) down a creek running into Lac la Loche. Finally, it goes 19 km (12 mi) southeast across Lac la Loche to end at the community of La Loche.

The Clearwater section of this trip was never part of the old voyageur highway across Saskatchewan. Only that section of the river downstream from Methy Portage—a short, 14-km (9-mi) paddle into present-day Alberta—was on the voyageurs' main travel route. Accordingly, Methy Portage might be seen as the correct starting point for this guide. However, the portage has no road access, and canoeing down from Warner Rapids is the best way to reach its north end. Getting to the north end lets you head southward under load and begin Saskatchewan's voyageur trail like a true *homme* (or *femme*) *du nord*.

This trip is not for everyone. The first 48 km (30 mi) of the Clearwater downstream from Warner Rapids has difficult whitewater requiring advanced skills. And, Methy Portage is long and difficult, calling for a great deal of physical stamina. Further, both the Clearwater and Methy Portage are remote and lightly travelled. If you run into trouble, you may not see help arrive for several days.

The whitewater below Warner Rapids would make this trip extremely difficult in an upstream direction. Experts, especially those with strong poling skills, might be able to go upstream, but our description of the route will assume that you are travelling downstream.

Water levels can be low on the Clearwater. In 1986, we were on the river at its seasonal peak, yet we still found the water was often only 50 cm (20 in) deep through rock gardens. The river ordinarily peaks in late May or early June, so you may want to plan your trip to start during this time.

The whitewater between Warner Rapids and Contact Rapids (where the Clearwater leaves the Precambrian Shield) will give you a chance to improve your paddling skills. The main rapids and falls all have portages, but there are several lesser rapids without portages that offer good challenges.

The scenery on the Clearwater is spectacular and, in our opinion, the best of the entire guide route. From Warner Rapids to Contact Rapids, the river has numerous rapids, a fine set of falls, and a gorge between vertical rock cliffs up to 25 m (80 ft) high. At Contact Rapids, the whitewater is left behind, and the river slows down to meander across the floor of a broad valley sided by well-treed slopes over 150 m (500 ft) high. The patchwork patterns of green along the high valley walls provide a view not seen elsewhere in Saskatchewan.

Camping is excellent between Warner Rapids and Contact Rapids, especially on the portages. Between Contact Rapids and Methy Portage, there are only limited camping possibilities. Methy Portage itself offers good camping at each end and partway across at Rendevous Lake.

Notwithstanding the Clearwater's attractions, the real highlight of this trip is historic Methy Portage, the most famous portage in Canada. After Indians first showed it to Peter Pond in 1778, the portage was quickly recognized as the vital link needed to create a truly transcontinental fur trade. Thereafter, for a full century, it played a key role in the operation of the voyageur highway. Since the portage trail has changed very little over the years, hiking or carrying its length will allow you a very special glimpse into the world of the voyageur.

You may want to see Methy Portage, a main segment of this trip, yet avoid the rigours of coming down the Clearwater and then crossing the portage with your whole outfit. Although you cannot get to Methy Portage by road, you can reach its south end by launching your canoe at La Loche and paddling 19 km (12 mi) northwest on Lac la Loche and 1 km (2/3 mi) more up a small access creek. You can then leave your canoe and explore the length of the portage with either a day hike or an overnight excursion.

The natural grandeur of the Clearwater and the historic importance of Methy Portage have received official recognition. In 1936, the Historic Sites and Monuments Board of Canada placed a commemorative plaque at the mouth of the Clearwater. Years later, in 1974, Methy Portage was declared a National Historic Site by the Canadian government, and a stone cairn and plaque marking the occasion were placed near the south end of the portage. In June 1986, the Clearwater was designated a Canadian Heritage River. On August 1, 1986, the river and adjacent lands between Lloyd Lake and the Alberta border were designated a Saskatchewan Wilderness Park.

STARTING POINT

The starting point for this trip is where a one-lane steel bridge crosses the Clearwater River at Warner Rapids 65 km (40 mi) north of La Loche. From Prince Albert, you can reach La Loche by driving just over 500 km (300 mi) northwest on paved Highways 3, 55, and 155. From La Loche, the final 65 km (40 mi) north to Warner Rapids are on Road 955, a good gravel road built to service the Cluff Lake uranium mine further north.

If you arrive at the Warner Rapids bridge late in the day and need a place to camp, you will find a provincial campground on the north shore of the Clearwater River, 500 m (550 yd) upstream from the bridge. The access road to the campground is just north of the bridge on the east side of Road 955.

At the immediate north end of the bridge, on the west side of Road 955, there is a fish filleting shack where you can unload your canoe and gear. From the shack, a trail leads 50 m (55 yd) west to the Clearwater. Here, downstream from the main part of Warner Rapids, you can launch your canoe from a small, sandy notch crowded by shore willows.

Note that if you have only Map 74C/14 for your start, you will not see the Warner Rapids bridge since it is 1,200 m (¾ mi) upstream from the map's eastern edge (and hence on Map 74C/15). The map on page 71 shows the area where you will begin your journey.

Clearwater River

The Clearwater River begins at Patterson and Forrest lakes in northwestern Saskatchewan and then runs south and west for roughly 370 km (230 mi) to empty into the Athabasca River at Fort McMurray, Alberta. As it is a tributary of the Athabasca, its waters eventually make their way to the Arctic Ocean.

Little is known about the Clearwater's first inhabitants, but the earliest fur trade accounts suggest that in pre-European contact times, they were Athapascans. Writing in 1781, presumably from information received from explorer Peter Pond, Alexander Henry the Elder referred to the Clearwater River as the "River Kiutchinini."[1]

If "Kiutchinini" (possibly *kâ-ayahcininiw*) is from a Cree reference to "strangers," as we guess to be the case,[2] it seems a non-Cree people (presumably Athapascan) once lived or at least travelled on the river.

In accounting his travels, fur trade explorer Alexander Mackenzie wrote:

> When this country was formerly invaded by the Knisteneaux [Cree], they found the Beaver Indians inhabiting the land about Portage la Loche [Methy Portage]; and the adjoining tribe were those whom they called slaves. They drove both these tribes before them...[3]

Henry's name for the river and Mackenzie's brief statement are not much to go on, especially since Henry and Mackenzie were not reporting first-hand knowledge. But the two fragments suggest that the ancestors of Athapascan-speaking Beaver now living in Alberta and British Columbia and possibly another Athapascan group once lived in the Clearwater region of northwestern Saskatchewan.

While the Cree may not have been the Clearwater's first inhabitants, they no doubt arrived on the river a long time ago. At least as early as 1715, Cree people were known to be in the region. These Cree, perhaps best referred to as Athabasca Cree, had ties to other Cree groups, but early writings suggest that they may have spoken a distinct "r" dialect of the Cree language. Eventually, the Athabasca Cree abandoned the Clearwater, leaving little behind. Quite possibly, though, the Cree-style pictographs found on the river south of Lloyd Lake were painted by them.[4]

By the late 1700s, Dene people had migrated southward to occupy all of the Clearwater upstream of Methy Portage, as well as parts of the upper Churchill—perhaps territory they had frequented in former times. They were drawn south by the opportunities presented by the advancing fur trade. Their movement was facilitated too by the terrible smallpox epidemic of 1781 that left much of the southern fur country thinly populated.[5] In the initial stages of this migration, they may have simply used the Clearwater to move back and forth between their northern homeland and the south. In time, however, they became permanent settlers in the region, and the river became much more to them. Today, the Clearwater Dene, who now live mainly on Lac la Loche, refer to the Clearwater as *Des Nethay*, meaning the "great river."

The first white man to see the Clearwater was Peter Pond, who came north across Methy Portage in 1778. Other traders soon followed when they learned that the Clearwater downstream from Methy Portage led to the rich Athabasca fur country. These white men knew the Clearwater River by a variety of names including Little, Pelican, Kiutchinini, Swan, Clearwater, "Wash-a-cum-mow" (*wâsêkamâw*, Cree for "clear water") and Little Athabasca.[6]

Curiously, the name Clearwater, which is now centuries old, is something of a misnomer. When the Clearwater begins as a small stream in the north, it meanders through a vast, peaty marsh where it takes on a weak tea tinge which persists all the way to Methy Portage. But tea-tinged or not, the Clearwater is famous for its sparkle and pristine freshness, so its name suits well enough.

WARNER RAPIDS TO METHY PORTAGE

Warner Rapids

The narrow steel bridge at Warner Rapids has an odd history. It was put in place in 1973 when the road to the Cluff Lake uranium mine was being built. However, its origins go back to 1909 when it first served as a truss in a bridge over the Battle River at Paynton, Saskatchewan.

The term Warner Rapids can be loosely applied to a 4-km (2½-mi) section of the Clearwater in the vicinity of the bridge, but the main rapids are those right at the bridge—a

Map 3.1   Warner Rapids Bridge

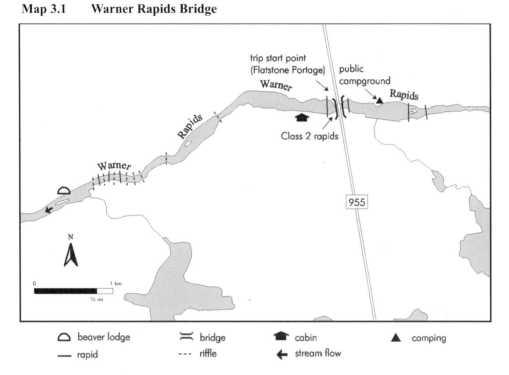

place long known to the Dene as *Tthaykalas Hoteth*, meaning "flatstone portage." These strong, Class 2 rapids begin about 30 m (33 yd) upstream of the bridge, pass beneath it, and then continue on for another 80 m (88 yd) or so with some big standing waves.

To begin your trip with a little whitewater practice, you can take your canoe upstream along a portage on the north side of the river and put in at a low shelf of bedrock extending out into the water. You can then shoot the rapids by going down a wide tongue left of centre. For a more measured start to your trip, you can carry your canoe and gear west from the bridge's fish filleting shack in order to embark below the rapids.

Down from Warner Rapids Bridge

Downstream from the bridge, quiet water will let you take stock of your surroundings. The shoreline here is thick with willows, sweet gale, and the occasional tamarack. Back from the shore, where the terrain is mainly sand studded by small outcrops of Shield rock, there are jack pines as well as some birch, spruce, and aspen.

You will pass a trapper's cabin on the south shore 500 m (¹/₃ mi) below the bridge, and 500 m (¹/₃ mi) further on, you will come to where the river narrows and swings its course from west to southwest. At this point, you will leave Map 74C/15 to go onto Map 74 C/14.

Right after the swing to southwest, you will encounter a shallow, riffly rapid about 200 m (220 yd) long calling for some alertness (74C 215075). Quiet water follows for about 750 m (½ mi), and then minor rapids and riffles extend for about 1 km (²/₃ mi). Not far past the minor rapids, there is a beaver house on the north shore, beyond which you can expect 3 km (2 mi) of calmer water.

When you have come 6.5 km (4 mi) from the bridge, you will encounter what the Dene call *Ts'oo Chogh Tthaybah*, or Big Spruce Rapids (74C 168060). These are major rapids divided by an island. Be ready to land on the island to reconnoitre or to put in at the portage on the river's north shore.

Big Spruce Rapids

The Class 3 rapids in the north channel are not suitable for open canoes. They are quite short, but they start with a difficult drop. Experts with spray covers might consider going down this drop on a course close to the island, but we advise ordinary canoeists not to do so.

The longer, Class 2 rapids in the south channel are difficult, but when water levels are high enough, advanced canoeists may choose to run them after scouting a course from the island. If you so decide, you may start down the centre and then move quickly left to avoid a small ledge. About halfway down, you can eddy out into a quiet pool on the left side of the channel to check your course. You can then continue down through the shallow lower section of the rapids by moving back to the centre of the current and seeking out the narrow gaps between large, submerged rocks.

On May 29, 1986, the first day of our long trip down the guide route, we ran down the south channel successfully. But finding a clear passage was tricky, and we therefore recommend that canoeists take advantage of the portage on the north shore of the north channel.

Portage #1 - Big Spruce Portage (± 125 m / 135 yd)

This portage begins about 25 m (27 yd) upstream from the start of the rapids in the north channel. Its upstream landing is a low, mud bank at a 2-m (6-ft) break in the alder growth on the river's north shore. The current here is fast, but the river near shore has a firm, sandy bottom only about 30 cm (1 ft) deep. It is therefore easy to stand in the water to unload gear onto shore.

The portage trail is in very good condition. It rises gently from the upstream landing to a good jack pine campsite. It then continues through sandy, jack pine terrain until it descends somewhat steeply to its downstream end.

The downstream landing is poor and requires canoeists to reload in the water to avoid big rocks in the water near shore. Reloading is also made difficult by the great many alders and willows that get in the way.

Down from Big Spruce Rapids

After Big Spruce Rapids, the Clearwater makes a slight jog and then continues southwest with a good current but no rapids for 4.5 km (2¾ mi). It then divides around a large island over 1 km (²/₃ mi) long—known locally as *Noo Chogh*, or "big island" (74C 128035 to 118027). The channels down both sides of Big Island are shallow but easily navigable. The river right channel, though it is almost a continuous riffle, seems to have fewer rocks than the left channel, so we would recommend it as the better of the two options.

As soon as the two island channels reunite, there is a short, minor rapid where you will have only to watch for a few half-submerged rocks. Below this minor rapid, there is quiet water for 1 km (²/₃ mi) and then a short riffle. Approximately 500 m (¹/₃ mi) further on, the river makes a 90-degree right turn to run northwest.

Map 3.2   Confluence of Descharme River

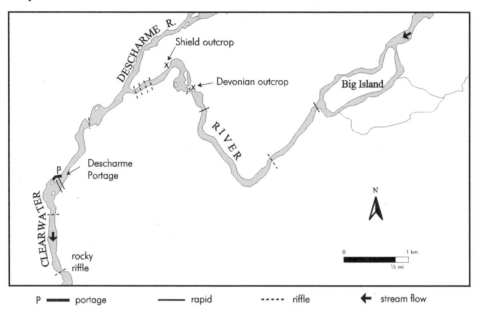

About 1.25 km (¾ mi) downstream from the 90-degree turn, there is a moderate, Class 1 rapid about 50 m (55 yd) long (74C 099026). Though it is not difficult, this rapid has some bad rocks down its left side. To avoid these, it is convenient to work over to the river right shore with a back ferry and then later move back to the centre of the current.

Perhaps 300 m (330 yd) below the moderate rapid, there is a riffle. Here, along the river right shore, you may notice an outcrop of either limestone or dolomite, something quite different than the Precambrian Shield outcrops in the area. This new rock dates to the Devonian Period of geological time, extending from 408 to 360 million years ago, when a vast body of water known as the Elk Point Sea covered the region and laid down great beds of precipitates. The Clearwater River has the only significant outcrops of Devonian rock in Saskatchewan.[7]

At the Devonian outcrop, the Clearwater makes a sharp left turn to run southwest. In this direction, you will find about 600 m (⅓ mi) of modest current followed by 400 m (¼ mi) of faster current and riffles. The riffles end at a junction where the Descharme River, coming down from the north, flows peacefully into the Clearwater. The Descharme, which flows from Descharme Lake some 25 km (15 mi) to the north, is known in Dene as *Thlooh Deszay*, or "whitefish river."

About 750 m (½ mi) downstream from the mouth of the Descharme River, there is a minor rapid about 50 m (55 yd) long (74C 082024). It is really not much more than a riffle and will not pose any problems for alert canoeists.

Descharme Rapid

About 1.75 km (1 mi) down from the Descharme River, there is a more substantial, Class 2 rapid which we will refer to as "Descharme Rapid" (74C 077015). This is a broad rapid about 75 m (82 yd) long with many boulders down the river left side and some down the right. However, down the centre of this rapid, there is a line through moderate standing waves that is quite straight and rock-free. If you examine this line in advance, you might choose to run it. Otherwise, land on river right for a portage.

Portage #2 - Descharme Portage (± 90 m / 99 yd) (optional)

This portage's upstream landing is about 10 m (11 yd) up from the start of the rapids. It is a poor landing that will require you to stand in the current while you unload your gear onto the river bank.

The portage begins by rising up a fairly steep bank. It is then in good condition as it runs through sandy, jack pine terrain. At its downstream end, it is again fairly steep.

The downstream landing is a canoe notch cut into the shore. This notch is just in front of a small island in a quiet cove west from the foot of the rapid.

Down from Descharme Rapid

About 300 m (330 yd) downstream from Descharme Rapid, there is a short, choppy riffle. This riffle is followed by approximately 1 km (2/3 mi) of swift current that ends with a rather rocky riffle. You can then expect quiet water the rest of the way to Gould Rapids, another 5 km (3 mi) distant.

About 2 km (1¼ mi) south from the rocky riffle, you will see a trapper's cabin on a sandy ridge along the river's east shore (74C 074981). This cabin formerly belonged to Pierre Lemaigre (now deceased) who had his main cabin on the lower end of the Descharme River. As with all trapline property, the cabin and any equipment here should remain untouched.

Before you get to Gould Rapids, you will begin to see, off on river left, the high, southeast wall of the Clearwater Valley. This escarpment and its counterpart 3 km (2 mi) to the northwest rise about 100 m (325 ft) above the valley floor. Further on, their heights increase to over 200 m (650 ft). Water erosion would not ordinarily carve a valley so spectacular. However, when the last glaciers retreated from the region about 10,000 years ago, the Clearwater served as an escape channel for meltwater ponding in front of the glaciers. As this great volume of meltwater washed west, it carried soil and sand with it and left a giant trough in its wake.[8]

But so much for past geological events. As you draw near to Gould Rapids, you will have to pay close attention to your present situation. Gould Rapids are dangerous and must be approached with caution.

Both Maps 74C and 74C/14 show a large island that splits the Clearwater into two channels immediately above Gould Rapids. The proper course past this island is down the west (river right) channel, since the east channel ends in a bad drop over a ledge. However, the west channel itself has a moderate rapid about halfway down, where a small point on the west shore pinches into the channel. This rapid does not have a portage, and it can be run provided it is first scouted from shore. One option for running is to hug the west shore staying west of a tiny islet not shown on either Map 74C or 74C/14. A second option is to take a straighter, though rockier, course to the east of the tiny islet.

No matter how you come down or get by the preliminary rapid, you should continue on by staying close to the west shore. About 250 m (275 yd) down this shore, you will come to the portage around Gould Rapids.

Gould Rapids

The major whitewater making up Gould Rapids, which are strong Class 3 rapids, begins about 350 m (380 yd) downstream from the start of the portage around the rapids or about 175 m (190 yd) downstream from the south tip of the large island mentioned above. This white-water, which has a full complement of big waves, boulders, chutes, ledges, and holes, extends with very little interruption for about 700 m (770 yd).

The Dene refer to Gould Rapids and the major falls 2 km (1¼ mi) further downstream col-lectively by the appropriate name of *Tthabah Nethay*, meaning "the grand rapids."

It may be that some experts properly equipped might be able to run parts of Gould Rapids. After we examined these rapids, however, we decided that they were well beyond our abilities and accordingly chose to portage them. We advise others to portage as well.

Portage #3 - Gould Portage (± 1,250 m / 1,370 yd)

The main start for this portage is a 2-m-wide (6-ft) canoe notch directly southwest from the downstream tip of a small, well-wooded island (shown on Map 74C/14 at 066953) located between the large island and the west shore. You will find the canoe notch concealed by shore willows until you draw near to it. Though inconspicuous, the notch makes a good landing. It has a gentle mud slope that allows canoes to be pulled up easily. From it, the portage trail climbs southwest for 20 m (22 yd) and then levels out.

Map 3.3   Gould Rapids and Smoothrock Falls

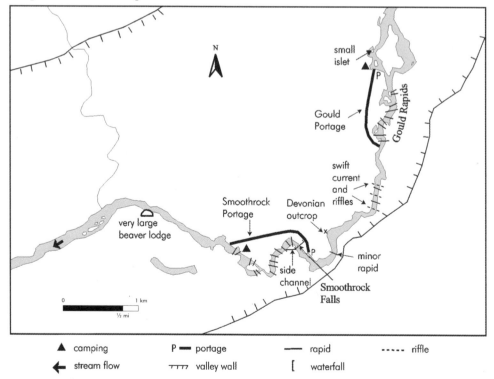

If you wish to camp at the upstream end of the portage, you can watch for three small canoe notches located a short distance before, or north of, the main landing. About 35 m (38 yd) inland from these notches, there is an excellent, open camping area amid widely spaced jack pines. From this campsite, a trail leads 70 m (77 yd) in a southerly direction to join the main portage.

Some canoeists may want to continue downstream past the main portage landing to reduce the portage distance by about 300 m (330 yd). If you choose this option, you can first move down the river right shore through some swift water and minor rapids until you are just past the south tip of the large island. Then, with the river now reunited in a single channel, you can continue south about 175 m (190 yd) to where the river again divides around two small islands. Taking the river right channel, you can pass down about 25 m (27 yd) of very swift, moderate rapids to enter a quiet pool about 150 m (165 yd) long that ends in a constricted chute. You may then land on a shelf of bedrock jutting into this quiet pool in order to begin the portage. By walking inland about 120 m (130 yd), you will meet up with the main portage trail.

Our view is that the option just described may be a little dangerous. A canoeist approaching the two channels created by the two small dividing islands might accidentally go down the dangerous river left, or east, channel. Better to play it safe and carry the extra 300 m (330 yd).

Gould Portage is in very good condition overall. Most of it runs through sandy jack pine forest interspersed with outcrops of granitic Shield rock. There are a few wet spots, but these are not serious. Near the downstream landing, the portage forks, with the main trail going left down a steep descent to the water. (The right fork is a blazed but indistinct trail 1,000 paces long, perhaps made by upstream travellers.) The downstream landing is a poor, rocky one in a small eddy below the rapids.

Down from Gould Rapids

Below Gould Rapids, the Clearwater runs fast between walls of Shield rock for about 1 km (2/3 mi). You will have little time to enjoy the scenery here, but you cannot miss seeing colourful splashes of orange lichen, especially on the east wall. When we descended this little canyon on May 30, 1986, we also saw remnants of the past winter's snow and ice along the east wall.

As the current slows down, you may notice an outcrop of Devonian rock in a quiet eddy on river right (74C 060932). From this outcrop, it is about 200 m (220 yd) further to where the river briefly narrows to a width of about 75 m (82 yd). Here, there is a short, ripply rapid that can be run without difficulty.

From the short rapid, the river runs quietly but with a current, as it bends from south to northwest towards major falls occurring less than 500 m (550 yd) onward. If you went over these falls, you would never again have a use for this guide. You should therefore be ready to put in at the portage on river right.

Smoothrock Falls

As mentioned, the Dene consider these falls to be part of Gould Rapids and apply the name *Tthabah Nethay*, or "grand rapids," to both the rapids and the falls. Neither Map 74C nor Map 74C/14 names the falls, but for some years, they have been unofficially known to canoeists as Smoothrock Falls.[9] Whatever name you give them, the falls are spectacular. With an incredible thunder, the Clearwater's flow plunges 10 to 15 m (30 to 50 ft) downward over steps of pink granite. On its way, it crashes and boils violently wherever a rock cauldron or other obstruction impedes its free passage. When it completes its main descent, it runs out into a bed of brawling, boulder-strewn rapids.

Smoothrock Falls Side Channel

If you have 1:50,000 Map 74C/14, you will note that a small side channel branches off from the river left shore just above the falls and runs west for perhaps 200 m (220 yd) before rejoining the main channel. We have never explored this side channel, but canoeist Bill Jeffery says it is a fascinating place. Though the side channel handles only a small and variable volume of water, there is sometimes enough flow to produce a picturesque waterfall. The channel also features several natural kettles—some large enough to stand in—formed by the action of the current swirling stones and gravel in a circular motion. According to Bill, who has seen a lot of the North, "It's just a beautiful place."

Greg Marchildon at the head of Smoothrock Falls.

Notwithstanding our warning about the falls, you may want to explore the side channel. But remember that it is close to the brink of the falls. Also keep in mind that you will later have to come back upstream and across to river right to take the mandatory portage.

Portage #4 - Smoothrock Portage (± 1,400 m / 1,530 yd)

This portage, which bypasses the falls and 1 km (²/₃ mi) of rapids below, begins at a 2-m (6-ft) break in shore alders on river right 5 m (5½ yd) downstream from a low beaver lodge that is about 150 m (165 yd) upstream from the head of the falls. The landing is a slope of dirt and grass. Though this slope is somewhat steep, you will be able to drag your canoe up it with little trouble.

The portage runs through a mixed forest comprising a great deal of jack pine and some spruce, poplar, and birch. The trail is generally good, though it is steep in places, fairly rocky, and occasionally wet. Along it, you will see many outcrops of pink granite blackened by lichens and some interesting boulders of considerable size. Near its downstream end, you will also find an excellent, spacious campsite on a sandy jack pine ridge overlooking the rapids below.

The portage ends at a grassy slope (which roses and tiger lilies decorate in July) in a small cove at the foot of the rapids. The river bank here has a notch of sorts for loading canoes, but it is not the best since the sandy shore edge here is embedded with small rocks.

Down from Smoothrock Portage

Below Smoothrock Portage, the Clearwater runs quietly west for some distance. You can therefore relax and enjoy the scenery. About 1 km (²/₃ mi) from the portage, you will see a huge beaver lodge sloping against the south (river left) shore—probably the work of many beaver generations. About 2 km (1¼ mi) further downstream, on the north shore, there is another good-sized beaver lodge. Also along the north shore, but well back from the water, there is a fine vista created by a chain of green hills rising up from the valley floor.

About 500 m (550 yd) downstream from the second large beaver lodge, there is a short, minor rapid (74C 010932). It is of little consequence and can be run easily.

About 1 km (²/₃ mi) downstream from the minor rapid, on the north or river right shore, there is a bedrock shelf that rises back from the water to a height of 4 m (13 ft) (74C 999936). Though this spot has little in the way of tent space, it would make a very good lunch or rest stop.

About 500 m (550 yd) past the bedrock shelf, the Clearwater sends a small side channel south along a large island. The main, navigable channel to the north begins with a narrows about 30 m (33 yd) in width (74C 994937). Here, there is a short but serious Class 2 rapid with a ledge on river right. Provided water levels are high enough, this rapid can be run left of centre down a good smooth tongue ending in moderate waves. However, before adopting this option, you should first land at a bedrock outcrop south of the rapid to scout.

Just less than 1 km (²/₃ mi) downstream from the short rapid, the river funnels into a spectacular gorge (74C 985932). The gorge is choked with major rapids, so a portage is mandatory. Be ready to land on river right some distance upstream of the gorge.

Bald Eagle Gorge

The gorge, which is not named in English but which is known in Dene as *Det'awnichogh Tthabah*, meaning "bald eagle rapids," is indeed a fine sight. Here, the Clearwater rushes between sheer cliffs of weathered granite, or perhaps granitic gneiss, that rise 20 to 25 m (65

Map 3.4   Bald Eagle Gorge

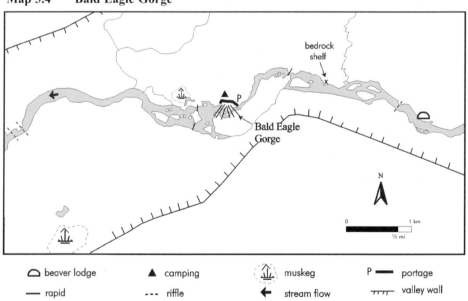

If you hike along the north (river right) rim of Bald Eagle Gorge, you can watch for a large nest of sticks about three-quarters of the way up the cliff opposite (on the north side of an island in the gorge). This nest has been abandoned when we have seen it, but according to Pierre Lemaigre of La Loche, it was built by bald eagles. How fledgling birds could ever leave this nest and survive the rapids below is a mystery!

to 80 ft) above the water. The cliff walls are colourfully painted with orange, black, and green lichens that thrive on the spray from the rapids below.

Like Smoothrock Falls upstream, the gorge provides excellent photo opportunities. The portage does not follow right along the gorge, but you can walk in from the portage and find good vantage points for pictures.

Portage #5 - Bald Eagle Portage (± 380 m / 415 yd)

This portage starts from a slight eddy on the river right shore about 130 m (140 yd) upstream from preliminary rapids leading into the gorge. Right next to the eddy, there is fast water moving towards the gorge, so we recommend a cautious approach. The upstream landing, which shows as an 8-m (25-ft) break in the shore vegetation, is a gently sloped bank of sandy soil. The bank is cut vertically at the water's edge, so you will find it hard to drag your loaded canoe up it. You will likely have to stand in the water near shore and unload your gear to the bank before taking your canoe out.

The portage climbs from the upstream landing and then runs through a forest of jack pine and birch. It is steep in spots but in very good condition overall.

About 230 m (250 yd) along the portage, there is a very good campsite set amid jack pines. This is a sandy site, but it has interesting outcrops of bedrock scattered about. Travellers have also found enough loose rock to build a good fire pit. The site's only drawback is that water must be brought about 150 m (165 yd) from the portage's downstream end.

At its downstream end, the portage drops steeply to a small eddy just north of a massive outcrop of bedrock marking the foot of the gorge. In the shadow of the outcrop, you will find a tiny gravel beach with room for canoes to re-embark one at a time.

Bald Eagle Gorge.

Down from Bald Eagle Gorge

About 300 to 400 m (330 to 440 yd) downstream from Bald Eagle Gorge, you will come to an island with rapids on both sides. On the island's north side, a short rapid occurs in a rock-walled channel about 25 to 30 m (27 to 33 yd) in width. This rapid has a bad boil in mid-channel, but we found a good passage down it next to the north or river right shore. On the island's south side, there is a broad, shallow rapid. We have not canoed down this, but it looks runnable along the south or river left shore. You may run either side of the island, but we recommend you first scout whichever option you select.

Below the island rapids, the Clearwater runs quietly west and then southwest for 3 km (2 mi). Some swift current and whirlpools then occur at a narrows. And, about 200 m (220 yd) further on, a minor, ripply rapid occurs. After the ripply rapid, the river again runs quietly for a further 1,250 m (¾ mi). It then bends southward, and almost immediately, is interrupted by a long series of rapids known collectively as Simonson Rapids.

Simonson Rapids

The 5-km (3-mi) section of the Clearwater comprising Simonson Rapids is roughly N-shaped with the river first running south, then northwest, and then south again. For most of this distance, shallow, rocky rapids of minor to moderate difficulty alternate with stretches of quieter water. In low water conditions, canoes may have to be waded or lined past some of the rapids. However, in average to high water, advanced canoeists who keep a good lookout and occasionally stop to scout ahead will be able to manoeuvre a course down all the rapids except two which will call for portages.

The first required portage, which (not knowing its local name) we refer to as Simonson

Map 3.5   Simonson Rapids

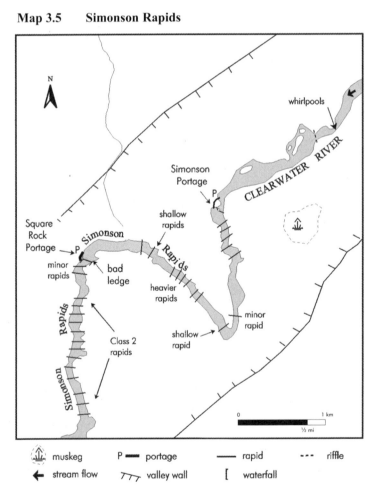

muskeg   P ▬ portage   —— rapid   - - - riffle
← stream flow   ⊤⊤⊤ valley wall   [waterfall

Portage, is at the very start of Simonson Rapids (74C 939920). The river here narrows to about 80 m (88 yd) and divides around a rocky island in mid-stream. Ledges span most of the river in a line even with the upstream end of the island and create major rapids which, in our opinion, should not be run.

Portage #6 - Simonson Portage (± 80 m / 88 yd))

This portage begins at an inconspicuous break in the vegetation on the river right shore about 75 m (82 yd) upstream from the rapids. The portage trail is in good condition. It ends at a muddy but reasonable landing in the willows bordering a quiet cove west from the foot of the rapids.

Down from Simonson Portage

Not far below the portage, broad, shallow rapids begin and continue for about 500 m (1/3 mi). Though long, they are not difficult. They are followed by about 500 m (1/3 mi) of quiet water that ends at a short, minor rapid. When you are past this short rapid, you will approach an elbow where the river makes a sharp turn to the northwest.

An early edition of the provincial canoeing guide booklet for the Clearwater suggested that canoeists might avoid the remainder of Simonson Rapids by portaging south from the elbow to the McLean River and then following that river downstream to where it joins the Clearwater below Simonson Rapids.[10] On May 31, 1986, we found that a canoeist had in fact scrabbled through the shore willows on the south side of the elbow and then blazed a trail to the McLean. The blazed trail was through sandy, jack pine terrain that was quite park-like. However, as the trail went 1,500 m (1 mi) before striking the McLean, we decided it was not a practical option.

More rapids occur in the river reach northwest of the elbow turn. First is a rock-strewn, shallow rapid that is not too difficult. It is followed by perhaps 300 m (330 yd) of quieter water and then by about 150 m (165 yd) of moderate rapids which, at least at reasonable water levels, can be run down the centre. After a brief interval of quieter water, moderate rapids extend for about 300 m (330 yd). These are heavier rapids that will require you to manoeuvre adroitly to avoid rocks and small ledges. They are followed by about 200 m (220 yd) of quieter water and a further 150 m (165 yd) of shallow, minor rapids. The river then settles down as it begins to bend from northwest to west in advance of a more abrupt turn southward.

When the Clearwater turns southward, it is spanned by a major ledge having the Dene name of *Tthay Naht'ahthee*, or "square rock" (74C 924913). The ledge has a drop of perhaps 2 m (6 ft) and extends from the river left shore to a small island on river right. Since neither the ledge nor the narrow channel behind the island offers any feasible passage for canoes, a portage across the island is necessary.

Portage #7 - Square Rock Portage (± 50 m / 55 yd)

The main starting point for this portage is a bedrock shelf on the northeast tip of the small island on river right. You may, however, sneak your canoe down the southeast shore of the island and disembark in a little cove just above the lip of the ledge. This option, though somewhat risky, will put you on the main portage at its midway point and thereby cut your carrying in half. The portage, which runs along the southeast side of the island, is a poor, overgrown trail barely distinct enough to follow. It ends at the foot of the island where fast water and minor rapids begin immediately.

Down from Square Rock Portage

The minor rapids below Square Rock Portage last for perhaps 200 m (220 yd) and then give way to a similar distance of quiet water. When the interval of quiet water ends, the final section of Simonson Rapids begins.

This last section is a stretch of almost continuous, moderate Class 2 rapids well over 1 km (²/₃ mi) long. (On the 1:50,000 scale maps, the rapids begin in the lower left corner of 74C/14 and cross to the upper left corner of 74C/11.) The rapids are runnable, but they demand constant alertness and much manoeuvring to avoid rocks. By the time you get through them, you will be ready for a breather.

About 350 m (380 yd) downstream from the end of Simonson Rapids, you will see some lively rapids on river left (74C 925893). These are not on the Clearwater. Rather, they are at the mouth of the McLean River which tumbles into the Clearwater from the east. They signal that you are roughly opposite the start of a portage on the west shore that bypasses Contact Rapids, the last rapids before Methy Portage.

Contact Rapids

We have not found written evidence of why Contact Rapids are so named. Perhaps it is because they mark the southwestern perimeter, or contact edge, of the Precambrian Shield. Downstream from Contact Rapids, any rock outcrops occurring along the Clearwater are much younger formations than the ancient Shield rock.[11]

Contact Rapids are major rapids that curve south, then west, then northwest in a rough arc about 1,500 m (1 mi) long. (On the 1:50,000 scale maps, they begin in the upper left corner of 74C/11 and then cross west to the upper right corner of 74C/12.) The current provincial canoe trip booklet for the Clearwater gives a detailed account of how canoeists might shoot Contact Rapids.[12] However, we have not gone down them, and our own view is that they are too big for the ordinary canoeist.

Map 3.6   Contact Rapids and Portage

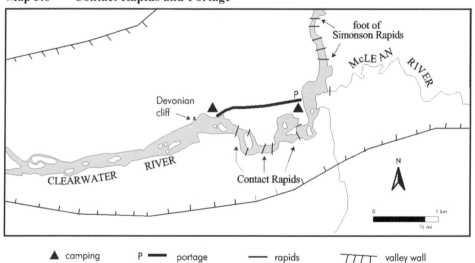

Jack Hillson, a canoeist from North Battleford, Saskatchewan, has told us that he and his son John tried to run Contact Rapids during high water in the summer of 1991. He said that they capsized in big waves soon after starting down and lost hold of their canoe in the upset. Swimming their best, they were unable to make it to shore until the current had carried them to the foot of the rapids. They did later recover their canoe downstream, but by then it was badly damaged.

With our own view reinforced by Jack's experience, we encourage canoeists to portage past Contact Rapids.

Portage #8 - Contact Portage (± 1,350 m / 1,475 yd)

The start of this portage shows as a sandy path rising up from the west (river right) shore of the Clearwater across and somewhat south from the mouth of the McLean River (74C 922891). The path is south of a bare sand bank about 6 m (20 ft) high that runs for some distance along the west shore. It is also 200 to 300 m (220 to 330 yd) north from the head of the rapids.

At the portage's upstream end, there is ample camping space amid the jack pines on the sandy terrace above the path from the river. The portage itself is in excellent condition. For the most part, it is a dry, level, and sandy trail through a park-like jack pine forest. About 250 m (270 yd) from the downstream end, it crosses a small creek bridged by poles. In this vicinity, there are aspen poplars.

The portage's downstream end is a big, grassy slope with a view of the foot of the rapids. In early July, you find tiger lilies here. The slope does not have many level tent spaces, but it makes a good camping area.

Contact Rapids to Methy Portage

Embarking from Contact Portage, you will leave the Shield bedrock behind. Shortly, though, you will have a chance to see a good example of younger, Devonian bedrock. About 200 m (220 yd) or so from the portage, along the north (river right) shore, an impressive dolomite cliff about 20 m (65 ft) high rises up from the forest floor.

Below Contact Rapids, the Clearwater takes on an entirely new character. For the next 32 km (20 mi) down to Methy Portage, it wanders across the floor of a broad, high-sided valley having a "valley-in-valley" form.[13] As earlier mentioned, the major carving of this valley occurred when it served as an escape channel for glacial meltwater during the last glacial retreat. Since then, however, there has been continued erosion as the river current—whose speed now varies from 2 to 5 km (1 to 3 mi) per hour—has cut deeper into what was the bed of the early, post-glacial river. This further erosion has created a second, much smaller valley within the first. It is characterized by frequent meanders and steep cut banks which rise as much as 6 m (20 ft) or more above the water.

The high walls of the Clearwater Valley, which rise up to 200 m (220 yd) or more above the valley floor, have a substantial effect on local vegetation. They create a humid microclimate in the valley by trapping the evening mists off the river and drawing in above-average rainfall. The extra moisture keeps the valley lush throughout the summer. This is especially evident along the valley walls where bands of light-coloured poplar and birch alternate with bands of darker conifers to produce rich patterns of green. Bare spots occur only where the steepness of some slopes has caused the soil and vegetation to slide or slump downwards.

At river level, the vegetation differs from that of the valley walls. Willows often crowd the shoreline. The low islands in the river are also thick with willows.

You will now encounter many more birds than before. You may also see some of the animal life abundant in the valley. Besides the smaller water animals such as beaver, muskrats, mink, and otter, you may see moose, bear, or white-tailed deer. The many bends in the river can give you the advantage of surprise as you watch for wildlife.

The willowy shores reduce the number of good campsites between Contact Rapids and Methy Portage. About 6 km (3¾ mi) down from the rapids, however, you will find good camping on a flat, grassy terrace above a 2-m-high (6-ft) sand bank on the north side of the river (river right) (74C 857884). And, about 10 or 11 km (6 or 7 mi) further on, another good campsite occurs in a grassy clearing above a 1.5-m-high (5-ft) sand bank also on river right, just before the river makes a sharp elbow turn from south to west (74C 778880). Still further on, more terraces above sand banks provide other camping possibilities.

As you draw near to Methy Portage, you will see a trapper's cabin on river left (74C 706867) where the river makes a horseshoe bend to the southeast. From this cabin, it is about 1.5 km (1 mi) further to the portage's northern terminus.

Trapper's cabin on south shore of Clearwater River, near Methy Portage.

At one time, canoeists could locate Methy Portage by looking for a fire tower standing on the north rim of the Clearwater Valley, more or less opposite the portage. Now, that landmark is gone. The tower was moved in the fall of 1989 to a location south of Tocker Lake, about 45 km (28 mi) to the east.

Long before the fire tower, the north shore across from the portage was the location of a very early establishment of the Montreal traders. When Peter Fidler arrived at the north end of Methy Portage on May 20, 1792, he noted:

> … a lopped pine on north side, and old French small house—but none remaining in it—it was built for the purpose of keeping provisions in to meet the canoes at the Methy Carrying Place on their return from the Grand Portage—The provisions were brought down Peace river in July or the beginning of August and then sent directly to this place, for the above purpose, where they remained until the arrival of the canoes.[14]

The landing at Methy Portage is a 4-m-wide (13-ft) boat notch cut into a 2-m-high (6-ft) sand bank on the south (river left) shore (74C 697864). As this notch is actually just inside the mouth of a small creek running into the Clearwater, it is somewhat screened from the river by a band of willows, sedges, and horsetails growing on a low spit forming the north bank of the creek. If you keep a good lookout, however, you should find the notch without any great trouble.

Methy Portage

Methy Portage crosses the height of land dividing two of North America's major drainage basins. At its north end, the Clearwater River ultimately drains to the Arctic Ocean, while at its south end, the waters of Lac la Loche make their way to Hudson Bay. Except for the steep valley wall at its north end, Methy Portage has no section that is particularly difficult. Indeed, the trail is actually much better than most. But good footing cannot compensate for distance. A load that is light at the outset and still bearable an hour later can become painful further down the trail. Add heat, insects, and yet more distance, and simple pain can become mind-numbing misery.

The early Indians who originally blazed the portage trail known to the Dene as *Hoteth Choghe*, meaning "big portage," likely saw it as a useful connector for regional travel. However, when Indian guides brought Peter Pond here in 1778, white traders almost immediately recognized the portage as a gateway to the farthest reaches of the North-West. And from the time Pond first saw Methy Portage, the voyageurs had a new test for determining who was a true *homme du nord*. About 19 km (12 mi) in length, Methy Portage was the longest portage faced on the road into the North-West. Any voyageur able to carry his full share of canoe and cargo across it earned bragging rights that would last into his old age.[15]

When we crossed Methy Portage on June 2 and 3, 1986, we carried our canoe and gear over in two trips. With too many good books and too much extra food on our backs, we were near to collapse when we reached the south end. But subtracting the 1-km (²/₃-mi) respite of Rendevous Lake from our distance, we had tramped only 54 km (34 mi). In contrast, the early voyageurs would have made three to four trips carrying either two 40-kg (90-lb) *pièces* or a share of a North canoe each trip—up to 126 km (78 mi) with 72 km (45 mi) under load![16]

Quite clearly, Methy Portage was the worst obstacle on the old water highway to Fort Chipewyan, whether one started in Montreal or York Factory. The voyageurs might travel better than 50 km (30 mi) a day on much of the highway, but when they came to the portage, speed was reduced to a crawl. According to James Keith of the Hudson's Bay Company, writing in 1823, "loaded Canoes of 25 Packages cargo and 5 men usually take 5 days."[17]

So why did the traders use Methy Portage at all? The simple truth was that, although it was a bottleneck, it was the only practical avenue to the fur riches of the North-West. Soon after Peter Pond first crossed the portage, traders began a search for an easier way to reach Lake Athabasca and the lands beyond it. By 1800, they had already explored the Mudjatik, Garson, and Fond du Lac rivers as possible access routes, but these proved unsatisfactory.[18] Alternative routes were eventually found, but Methy Portage continued to play a key role in fur trade transport right until the advent of steamboats and railroads.

The North End

Landing at the boat notch on the Clearwater's south shore (74C 696865), you will find that the north end of Methy Portage is a grassy meadow reaching back about 50 m (55 yd) to the woods and running about 300 m (330 yd) along the river. As yet, only a few aspen and balsam poplars encroach into the meadow. This was no doubt once a major staging area, but there is now no sign of that former activity except a few shallow depressions where buildings may

have once stood. We recommend the north end of the portage for camping. The grassy meadow gives room for any number of tents. Most importantly, the river provides water which is in short supply on the portage.

The grassy clearing has not always been the start of the portage. The very first fur traders, and likely early native travellers before them, commonly paddled through a swamp south of the Clearwater to shorten the portage by 500 m (550 yd) or so. On Maps 74C and 74C/12, this swamp shows as a small oxbow lake lying just east of the head of the portage.

We did not get far into the swamp before willows stopped us. However, 800 to 900 m (880 to 990 yd) south on the portage we found an old trail that branched to the northeast and led to a small clearing. We did not explore further, but it may be that this trail once connected to the swamp.

On May 20, 1792, Philip Turnor and his party came up the Clearwater on their way back east from Lake Athabasca. They had not been across Methy Portage before, since they had earlier approached Lake Athabasca via a difficult route up the Garson River. Describing their approach to Methy Portage, Turnor wrote:

> ... then put Robt Garroch on shore on the South side to look for the Methy carrying place as we had been informed by the Canadians that its upon this spot but very difficult to find ... then stoped [upstream] with intent to stay all night fired several guns and was after some time answerd by Robert Garrock at a little distance down the river he then came within call and informed us that we had passed the carrying place we returned and took him in and proceeded down to the swamp which leads to the carrying place enterd the swamp which is about thirty yards wide at the entrance ... went to within a 100 yards of the end of the bay [in the oxbow] and landed on the left hand side at the carrying place upon a peice of fine meadow and put up at 9 1/2 PM...[19]

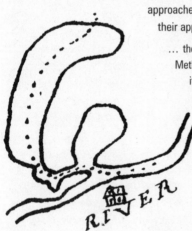

HBCA / E.3/1 fo. 50 (N14867)

Sketch of the approach to Methy Portage from the Clearwater River, in Peter Fidler's journal, May 20, 1792.

In his own journal, Peter Fidler, one of Turnor's companions, confirmed the Canadians' advice that the portage was hard to find: "it is by accounts very intricate to find, by any person who has never seen it by reason of having 2 crooked small swamps to paddle across—after they leave the river..." In a marginal sketch he drew the swamp and plotted the course through it, leaving no doubt that the main swamp was the oxbow lake on today's maps.[20]

The Valley Wall

Today, the portage heading south from the grassy meadow is easy to find. It shows as a clear path through the tall white spruce bordering the south side of the meadow. At first, it goes over level ground, but within a kilometre, it begins its infamous climb of the Clearwater Valley's south wall which, based on the contour lines on Map 74C/12, is close to 200 m (650 ft) high. The climb is accomplished by a long series of switchbacks cut into the valley wall. Though the switchbacks seem never-ending, they are well designed and produce a much gentler grade than any direct approach up the side of the valley.

Before the construction of the switchbacks on Methy Portage, the portage trail was much steeper than it is today. In 1844, Lieutenant John Henry Lefroy of Toronto crossed Methy Portage in the course of doing a magnetic survey of the North-West. In a letter home to his sister, he first commented on the excellent view of the Clearwater Valley from where the portage came over the valley rim and then continued: "The descent from the point of view to the river is so precipitous and difficult, particularly when rendered slippery by rain, that you wonder how it were possible to get a clumsy and heavy canoe down it, on mens shoulders."[21]

Eventually, the use of ox carts on the portage provoked improvements to the valley slope. Ox carts could move goods back and forth between the portage's south end and the valley rim, but they could not risk the steep trail into the valley. It was thus necessary to shuttle loads from the valley rim to the Clearwater either by more controllable sleds or by ordinary manpower. Switchbacks would have to be carved into the valley wall before carts could roll safely from one end of the portage to the other.[22]

Henry Moberly, perhaps best known for establishing Fort McMurray for the Hudson's Bay Company in 1870, is credited with building Methy Portage's switchbacks. In 1874, while still in charge of Fort McMurray, he was given the responsibility of overseeing the portage[23] which was then, according to an HBC chief factor, in a "wretched state."[24] He immediately took control and, by 1875, had the steep valley slope re-contoured.[25] This much needed improvement came late in the day for the portage, but over the following decade, it allowed ox carts to move a tremendous amount of freight over the portage without transshipping at the valley rim.

With or without an oxcart, you will in time reach the top of the valley wall where you will be treated to a splendid view of the valley below. Many early travellers wrote of the view from a lookout called the "Cockscomb," a knife-edged ridge on the portage trail. It seems the ridge was either levelled off or bypassed during the switchback construction since the present track does not have a ridge fitting early descriptions such as that of Philip Turnor:

NA / C002477

"Portage La Loche between Lac La Loche and the Clearwater River, July 16, 1825," watercolour over pencil by Sir George Back.

came to ridge about two yards wide at the top the sides of which are very steep and not less than a Hundred yards to the bottom on either side and if a person was to make a slip to either side he would be shure of being at the bottom before he stoped…[26]

Perhaps because the valley was so different from the surrounding country, travellers frequently extolled the prospect seen from above. In a letter to Sir George Simpson dated July 5, 1848, explorer John Rae gave a description typical of many:

Not having crossed to the west end of the portage until this morning, I was much struck with the splendid view down the valley of the Clear water River. The beautiful effect of light and shade on the variously colored foliage, the undulations of the sides of the valley and the pure water showing itself here and there over and between the branches of the trees, looking like sheets of polished silver produced a scene which I have seldom or never seen surpassed.[27]

Rendevous Lake

Not quite 6 km (3¾ mi) from the Clearwater, and 2 km (1¼ mi) southeast from your climb out of the valley, you will come to the northwest corner of Rendevous Lake (we use the official spelling), known in Dene as *Sheth Tthee Too*, meaning "head of the hills lake." Here, at a beach of small stones, you can put your canoe back in the water for a brief but welcome break from carrying. Another 1 km (²/₃ mi) of paddling will take you to the south end of the lake where you can pick up the portage trail again.

If you are travelling northwest across Rendevous Lake towards the Clearwater, you will see the northwest landing as a clear break in the shoreline with the portage visible behind it. You will reach the landing before the shoreline turns to run northeast.

Rendevous Lake would be a happy sight to tired packers even if it were a black swamp. It is made extra pleasant by being a pretty little lake. The whole south shore is sandy with an old dune rising as high as 4 to 5 m (13 to 16 ft) in the lake's extreme southeast corner. The lake water is clear, cold, and great for swimming. We are not so sure of the fishing potential. In 1792, Peter Fidler said the lake had small pike,[28] but we have not caught any.

While the northwest landing has a small campsite with room for a tent, Rendevous' best campsite is immediately west of the dune in the lake's southeast corner, where a sandy clearing lies back from a good sand beach (74C 731812). The clearing has no definite boundaries, but it is roughly 50 m by 50 m (55 yd by 55 yd) and has ample room for camping. Here, for centuries, native travellers camped on their way across the portage. Similarly, countless voyageurs also stopped to rest from their work. Now, though, there is little visible sign of that early activity. The only obvious artifact from previous days is an iron band—

Our 1986 camp at Rendevous Lake on the historic south shore clearing.

Rendevous Lake as seen from the south shore campsite.

from a cart or wagon wheel—that presently serves to circle a fire pit.

From Map 74C/12, you may note that while Rendevous Lake drains north to the Clearwater, the small lake southwest of it drains to Lac la Loche. Without leaving the camp clearing, you can stand directly on the divide separating the Arctic and Hudson Bay watersheds.

To Simpson's Camp

From Rendevous Lake, it is just over 11 km (7 mi) south to a small stream (74C 784717) which we will refer to as Simpson's Camp. This distance is over level, sandy ground with the trail good to excellent in most places. The woods along the trail are mainly jack pine and aspen poplar though there are some black spruce in lower areas.

We recommend that when you leave Rendevous Lake, you take drinking water with you since Simpson's Camp is the next reliable water source. There is sometimes standing water along the way, but this cannot be counted on. When we portaged the southern section on June 3, 1986, we took no water and suffered for it. Luckily, we found a small puddle of water in the track about 5 km (3 mi) south from the lake. A bear had walked through the puddle earlier in the day, but we lay down on our stomachs and drank as much as we could hold.

Sometimes, the voyageurs could not find even a puddle. Richard King, surgeon to George Back's expedition to the Arctic, arrived at the south end of Methy Portage on August 9, 1833. He first went to the north end of the portage and then returned to this section the next day to check on his voyageur packers:

> we paid a visit to the men, in order to encourage them in their laborious duty. Owing to the dry weather we had of late experienced, the pools, which are generally to be found in low situations about the woods, were entirely drained. Even the *sphagnum*, or bog-moss, which acts as a sponge in retaining rain-water, was dug up and squeezed to no purpose; in addition to which, the thermometer in the sun indicated a temperature of 110° Fahrenheit. We found the men in a high state of fever, and rather dead than alive, from excessive thirst; yet not a murmur escaped them. … Several of the men were much weakened, and William Rowland entirely disabled. …

After King and a companion had brought kettles of water to the men, he learned that some had thought to go for water but decided not to for fear others might finish the portage ahead of them. Such an event would have been cause for embarrassment for the rest of the voyage.[29]

When we portaged south from Rendevous Lake in 1986, we saw recent signs of the fur trade. Here and there, we found small stick shelters, or cubbies, left over from the previous season's trapping. Though simple structures, these shelters are effective in both protecting bait from winter snowfall and drawing fur animals into traps. Since they can sometimes be used for more than one season, they should be respected as trapline property and left intact.

South along the portage, you will also pass a large muskeg area east of the trail. Interestingly, this natural feature is noted in the 1786 journal of Montreal trader Cuthbert Grant. Grant and his party were on Methy Portage from May 22 to 29, 1786. South from Rendevous Lake, Grant wrote:

> Wensday 24 in the morning I went to the other end of the Portage to See if the lack [Lac la Loche] was Clear but I found it Still Covered with Ice our people Slept at the little lack—

> Thursday 25 St Germain Derry Jolleybois & I Came to the end of the Portage to fish our people Slept at the Bon Dieu de Jos Gray—

> Fraiday 26 we Sent some fish to the people in the Portage they Sleept a little Beyond the Grand Maskege—

> Saturday 27 our people Slept a little this Side of the Grand Maskege—the Ice Disappeared[30]

As you move south on the portage, you can watch for faint ruts left behind by the big wooden wheels of Red River carts from the late fur trade era. These ruts are visible only in a few places, such as this section (right) photographed during our 1986 trip.

Simpson's Camp

After the 11-km (7-mi) march from Rendevous Lake, you will come to a pole bridge (74C 784717) over a little stream flowing east across the portage. The stream, bordered by large aspen and white spruce, is a small tributary of Portage Creek which runs into Wallis Bay on Lac la Loche. Though barely 2 m (6 ft) wide, it is perfectly clear and very cold. Whether you dip a drinking cup or put your face right in, you will not be disappointed.

The stream crossing must have been an important stopping place for weary voyageurs. We know for sure that on the evening of September 13, 1820, George Simpson stopped here on his first trip into the North-West. Heading north from Lac la Loche, he wrote:

> proceeded about one mile on the Portage and encamped near the little Rivulet: it is usual for the *Bourgeois* on his first visit to this Portage to treat the men with an extra dram, otherways he is subject to the unpleasant process of shaving (as practised on board Ship in crossing the line), and as ancient voyaging customs must be respected, I indulged the people with a bottle of rum, and they have honoured me by naming the spot 'Le campement de Monsr. Simpson'; the early part of the evening was extremely calm and mild, but about nine O'Clock a sudden gust of wind came on (which blew the Tent down and the ridge pole nearly fractured my skull) and was followed during the Night by a violent Tempest with Rain.[31]

Given the major role that George Simpson later played in the history of the Hudson's Bay Company, one might rightly wonder how the company would have fared through the 1800s if Simpson's tent pole had in fact stove his skull in.

The South End

From Simpson's Camp, it is only 1,300 m (¾ mi) to Methy Portage's south end. As you draw near it, you will first come to a sandy clearing, on the west side of the portage, where a few large jack pines grow.

About 125 m (140 yd) further southeast, there is a clearing on high ground to the east of the portage. Though it is now small and overgrown by slim poplars, it was the site of a Hudson's Bay Company transport depot from about 1874 to 1888. While the HBC simultaneously operated a nearby post on Lac la Loche, the transport depot was needed to store goods and supplies and to maintain livestock used in the portage's freighting operations.

Excavations at the depot site by archaeologist Donald Steer in the early 1970s uncovered remains of living quarters, two storehouses, and an animal stockade. From his study of the area, Steer concluded that this was likely the area where wagons and carts were loaded and unloaded during freighting operations. It was apparently not general practice to take the wagons and carts much farther southeast along the portage.[32]

Yet another 100 m (110 yd) southeast along the portage, you will come to where Methy Portage ends on the west bank of a small creek that runs into Wallis Bay on Lac la Loche. The Dene have sensibly named this creek *Hoteth Des*, or "portage creek." A still visible notch cut into the bank for canoes and boats indicates where the voyageurs must have transferred packs to and from the water.

Nowadays, at a point about 20 m (22 yd) downstream from the notch, a small pole bridge crosses the creek and blocks passage of canoes. It is therefore necessary to veer from the portage about 25 m (27 yd) before the creek and follow a path along the creek's west bank until you are just below the bridge. The path is in fair shape, but you must watch out for holes caused by beavers undermining the creek bank.

About 30 m (33 yd) or so below the small bridge, there is a low beaver dam across the creek. If the water is high, you may pull your loaded canoe over this dam. If it is not, you will want to extend your carry along the west side of the creek until you are below both the bridge and the dam. The same advice applies in reverse should you arrive from Lac la Loche.

Methy Portage in the Canoe Era

For forty-five years, from 1778 to 1823, fur trade voyageurs (at least in summer) reached Methy Portage strictly by canoe. This was the golden age of the birchbark canoe in North America. Canadian voyageurs working for Montreal-based companies made summer voyages that were truly incredible. Canoes would leave Lake Athabasca in spring with the winter fur harvest and paddle out to Grand Portage or, as later organized, to a forwarding depot at Rainy Lake. Turning around on about August 1, they would then return to the Athabasca in a race against freeze-up. In some years, over two dozen North canoes would make the long round trip.[33]

The name "Rendevous Lake" may conjure up images of voyageurs from the north and the south meeting on Methy Portage to exchange packs of furs and trade goods. However, during the canoe era, there was actually no established rendezvous on the portage. Meeting plans were sometimes made, but these *ad hoc* arrangements did not always work out.

In 1786, the North West Company's Cuthbert Grant made the earliest recorded effort to make a rendezvous at Methy Portage. That spring, Grant left Peter Pond's post on the lower Athabasca River to take eight canoes loaded with 162 packs of furs down to Rainy Lake. When he got to the north end of Methy Portage, he left two canoes there, believing that he would meet two canoes from Île-à-la-Crosse at the south end. However, when the Île-à-la-Crosse canoes did not show up, Grant had to rush eight men back to the Clearwater for the canoes left behind. The men made the return trip in under twenty-four hours, but Grant had to pay them a bonus of 100 livres each for their efforts.[34]

The failure to rendezvous at Methy Portage meant that canoes had to be carried from one end of the portage to the other, minus the short paddle across Rendevous Lake. This carrying was no small matter. On a regular portage, two men could carry a North canoe, but on a long portage such as Methy, four were ordinarily required for the task. When Philip Turnor and his men went south across Methy Portage in late May 1792, Peter Fidler wrote:

> ... & then brought up the Canoes, which is by far the worst & hardest job of all—we tried at first to carry them with the mouth down ward upon the shoulders of the men but we found it particularly inconvenient on account of the narrowness & unevenness of the Track—we then carried them the old usual way with the mouth upward, resting upon the shoulders of 2 men, one at each end—which at short distances were relieved by 2 others.[35]

The early voyageurs could expect to carry three to four loads across Methy Portage—both when they passed south with fur and when they passed back north with trade goods. In the case of smaller, four-man crews, the need to send all hands across with the canoe likely guaranteed four trips per man. By the end of a fourth trip, a birchbark North canoe might well have seemed more like the straw that breaks the camel's back than the centrepiece of a golden age.

Introduction of York Boats

In 1820, George Simpson, newly hired as the Hudson's Bay Company's Acting Governor in Rupert's Land, voyaged into the North-West as far as Lake Athabasca. Simpson quickly established himself as a shrewd manager and a man obsessed with economy. Though he admired the voyageur canoe, he soon decided it should be discarded wherever possible in favour of the more profitable wooden York boat. Wooden boats had been tried out on the Churchill River as early as 1799 when the Hudson's Bay Company sent boats inland from Churchill Factory to Île-à-la-Crosse.[36] By 1820, they had not yet reached into the far North-West, but George Simpson felt they would be practical there. On November 30, 1820, after having established himself at Lake Athabasca, he wrote to his superior, William Williams: "Boats would be of essential benefit here, they can with ease be sent to Portage La Loche, McKenzie's River, and the foot of the Mountain, if you could therefore provide a Boat Carpenter he would be a valuable servant."[37]

It took only a short time for Simpson to see that his suggestion was acted upon. On May 21, 1823, four newly made boats departed Fort Chipewyan with fur cargoes destined for York Factory.[38] Under the system being inaugurated, these boats were left at the north end of Methy Portage with their crews re-embarking in other craft at the south end. The crews then continued to York Factory and later made a return to Fort Chipewyan, arriving at the latter on September 29.[39]

The Hudson's Bay Company's 1823 experiment proved a success. The four boats returning to Fort Chipewyan that fall brought in 209 *pièces* of trade goods. Ten canoes sharing the transport work brought in a total of 220 *pièces*.[40] The stark reality was that the boats had outshone the canoes. Henceforward, the HBC would have only limited use for North canoes on its main line into the North-West.

The new boat system was good for the economizing Simpson, but it was hard on the voyageurs crossing Methy Portage. True, the voyageurs did not have to wrestle the heavy York boats over the portage—a different set of boats was kept on each end of the portage to avoid such labour. But this advantage was more than offset by the extra *pièces* the York boats carried. Instead of three or four trips across Methy, voyageurs were now looking at four, five, or even more.

The voyageurs also lost the respite of paddling across Rendevous Lake. Unless a free boat or canoe should happen to be at the little lake, they now had to carry their loads along the low sand ridge that skirts the lake's south and west shores—a rim of dry ground 5 to 10 m (15 to 30 ft) wide between the lake on one side and boggy muskeg on the other. As they trudged along the sandy rim, the voyageurs must have cursed Simpson's love of economy and the added suffering it brought them.

The Rendezvous

Initially, even though there was one set of York boats for the north side of Methy Portage and one for the south, the men manning them made the entire round trip from Fort Chipewyan to York Factory and then back. This involved the men leaving boats in storage at either end of the portage when they were not in use. By May 14, 1824, a boat storage house large enough for eight boats had been built at the north end of the portage.[41] A similar storage house may also have been built at the south end of the portage.[42]

The round trip from Fort Chipewyan to York Factory and back was a challenge since the distance involved was at the outer limit of how far boats could travel in a single season. Any attempt to extend the round trip could easily result in boats being stopped short of their destinations by fall freeze-up, jeopardizing a whole year's returns. So how was the Hudson's Bay Company to extend its operations into the farthest North-West?

The Council of the Hudson's Bay Company's Northern Department soon struck upon a solution for supplying its most distant posts. It directed that, starting in 1826, a special brigade of York boats, later known as the "Portage la Loche brigade,"[43] would take trade goods to Methy Portage where they would meet with boats from the Mackenzie River and exchange their trade goods for furs. This was the beginning of the famous Methy Portage rendezvous.

As the rendezvous system was refined, the pattern was for the men of the Portage la Loche brigade, comprised mainly of Métis tripmen from Red River, to leave their Red River homes in the spring and row their lightly laden boats to Norway House—the HBC's advance depot at the north end of Lake Winnipeg. There, they would pick up trade goods and work their way upstream via the Saskatchewan, Sturgeon-weir, and Churchill rivers. At Methy Portage, they would rendezvous with the Mackenzie River brigade in late July or early August. They would then return with their payloads of fur to York Factory after about a month of travel. At York Factory, they would pick up trade goods for the following season and transport these to Norway House where they would be cached for the following spring. They would then return south on Lake Winnipeg to winter at Red River.[44]

The sandy south shore of Rendevous Lake soon became the established meeting place for the Portage la Loche and Mackenzie River brigades. The site allowed for a roughly equal division of labour. While the Portage la Loche men had more distance to carry, the Mackenzie River men had to deal with the Clearwater's steep valley wall. If the former did perhaps have a greater share of the work, they could at least then boast that fact when they met with their northern counterparts to argue who was or was not an *homme du nord*.

In addition to the Portage la Loche and Mackenzie River brigades, brigades serving the Athabasca District—a region comprising Lake Athabasca, Great Slave Lake, and the Peace River—used Methy Portage during the rendezvous period. The Athabasca brigades continued to make a round trip each summer from Fort Chipewyan to Norway House (to where goods had been advanced from York Factory) then back again.[45] These through brigades would not necessarily see anyone on the portage, but there were likely times when chance allowed them to join the rendezvous and share a drink or two.

The rendezvous' importance faded in the late 1840s and early 1850s when horses and oxen were introduced to Methy Portage to haul freight. The horses and oxen were not entirely reliable at first, so voyageurs no doubt continued to carry some packs to and from the rendezvous through a transition period. Eventually, however, by about the mid-1850s, ox cart freighting was sufficiently established to allow an end to most portaging.

Like the birchbark canoe, the rendezvous has endured as a colourful symbol of the hard times and good times of the voyageur life. At Rendevous Lake, those times past are not so very distant. Here on a summer evening, you can almost catch the "*Salut!*" of men ready to drop their *pièces* and tap a rum keg with old friends.

The *Poses*

During both the canoe era and the York boat period, the voyageurs relied on a system of *poses* to obtain some relief from Methy Portage's crushing labour. From the French word *poser,* meaning "to put down or to lay down," these were resting places where heavy loads would be put down. The stages between these *poses* varied in length, but one source puts them at "500 to 600 yards each."[46] Principal *poses* no doubt developed where a natural feature made it attractive to stop. The constant caching of loads on these same spots would have kept them clear of underbrush and convenient to use. The voyageurs knew these principal *poses* by name.

The earliest mention of specific *poses* on Methy Portage comes from the North West trader Cuthbert Grant (see excerpts from Grant's 1786 journal on page 90) but the most detailed list of Methy's *poses* comes years later from Sir John Richardson. On June 28, 1848, Richardson arrived at the portage on his way to the Arctic to search for the missing Franklin expedition. Regarding the *poses*, or at least the principal ones in use at the time, he wrote:

> I subjoin the voyagers' names for the several resting-places on the portage, premising, however, that the halting-places vary both in number and position with the loads and strength of the carriers, and that the names are often transposed.
>
> Methy Lake (Lac la Loche).

Thence to	*Petit Vieux*	2557	paces
"	*Fontaine du Sable*	3171	"
"	*La Vieille*	4591	"
"	*Bon Homme ou De Cyprès*	3167	"
"	*Petit Lac*	3238	"
"	*De Cyprès ou La Vieux*	4302	"
"	*La Crête*	1283	"

| " | Descente de la Crête | 1984 | " |
| " | La Prairie | 300 | "[47] |

The *poses* listed by Richardson no doubt had intervening *poses* to break the carrying into smaller stages. While these may have had names as well, such names are now lost.

Methy's *poses* have now been largely reclaimed by nature, but you may still reliably locate some of them. Rendevous Lake and what we have referred to as Simpson's Camp are easy to identify. On certain hot days, you might also find La Vieille (the voyageurs called the wind "Old Woman") where a welcome breeze sometimes reached the portage trail and cooled the voyageurs' brows.

Indians on the Portage

Though the voyageurs were ordinarily proud of their ability to withstand all hardship, Methy Portage's agonies were great enough to cause them to search out whatever relief might be available. One of the first options was to hire Indians on an *ad hoc* basis to assist with the carrying.[48] This sub-contracting was not a trading company budget item, but some voyageurs were willing to pay the cost from their own wages.

With little regard for its own men, the Hudson's Bay Company's Northern Council, headed by George Simpson, eventually banned the practice of Indian packers on Methy Portage. Indians had long been known as tough packers, so it was not a question of their qualifications. Rather, the company worried that Indians would earn so much on the portage that they would quit trapping fur. As well, it feared that the voyageurs, or tripmen, would engage in private trading if they mixed with the Indians during portaging operations.[49]

It is clear that some HBC officers saw the ban on hiring Indians on the portage as short-sighted. On January 1, 1837, Chief Factor Edward Smith at Fort Chipewyan wrote to George Simpson and other officers of the HBC's Northern Department and reported on his summer trip inland from Norway House:

> The usual severe and unavoidable duties in Portage La Loche were got through—not without difficulty. Several of the men at that stage of our voyage, particularly after getting up and carrying along the [La Loche] River were ailing, criple or incapacitated. We were under the necessity of overlooking their employment of some Indians who happened to be here to assist them. In so doing I am well aware that it was contrary to a resolve in Council but the detention that the incapacity of the men as mentioned would have caused the whole Brigade, the risk of Outfits being stoped, the certainty at the time that the Indians would not be of any service to their Post— was the reason of allowing it in that instance…[50]

Ironically, when the Northern Council banned Indian labour from Methy Portage, George Simpson must have taken a "do as I say and not as I do" approach to the issue. In crossing Methy on his way to the Pacific in 1828, he had enlisted the help of ten Dene men to help his party make the portage in one trip![51]

Horses, Oxen, and Carts

The Hudson's Bay Company was not, however, opposed to the notion of using draft animals for hauling freight across Methy Portage. As early as 1820, even before the company merged with the North West Company, horses were being considered. Prior to George Simpson making his first trip to Lake Athabasca, his superior, Governor William Williams, gave him the following direction:

> To leave four men and a Superintendent to improve the Portage at Lac Laloche in such a way that Horses and Carts may be employed to convey Goods across, Spades, Pick Axes, and other utensils should be sent with the men; could a Fisherman be spared it would be advisable to send one to support the Party; some pemican may be sent [from] Isle ala Crosse.[52]

Simpson was usually quick to get things done, and he arranged to have John Clarke of the HBC post at Île-à-la-Crosse supply the portage with horses and carts for the 1821 season. However, other events must have interfered, since it was some years before draft animals and carts became a reality.

The first cart on Methy Portage was actually a man-powered "truck" built by the men of John Franklin's second overland expedition to the Arctic in 1825. Before leaving England, Franklin had had three boats of mahogany and ash—one twenty-six feet long and two twenty-four feet long—built to withstand the icy seas the expedition would encounter on the Arctic Ocean. These boats were similar to North canoes but their heavier weight was a drawback. Referring to the expedition's crossing of Methy in early July 1825, Franklin wrote:

> The boats were the heaviest and most difficult articles to transport. One of the small boats was carried on the shoulders of eight men, of whom Mr. Fraser undertook to be one, as an example to the rest. Another of the same size was dragged by other eight men; and the largest was conveyed on a truck made for the purpose on the spot, to which service the lame were attached. ...

> With reference to the Methye Portage I may remark, that, except the steep hill at its western extremity, the road is good and tolerably level, and it appeared to us that much fatigue and suffering might have been spared by using trucks. Accordingly two were made by our carpenters at Fort Chipewyan in 1827, for the return of the Expedition, and they answered extremely well. I mention this circumstance, in the hope that some such expedient will be adopted by the Traders for the relief of their voyagers, who have twice in every year to pass over this ridge of hills.[53]

The fur trade was slow to pick up on Franklin's lead. When the voyageurs finally did get some extra help, it was from pack horses rather than carts. In 1842, possibly the first year horses were used on Methy Portage, a Métis named "Old Cardinal" had thirty-four pack horses on the portage to assist with freighting.[54] And in 1845, the Council of the HBC's Northern Department resolved that:

> two Servants of the Company be stationed with a band of about 40 horses on the shores of Lac La Loche so as to be in attendance at the proper season, for the purpose of transporting the Goods and Returns on that Portage free of all charge to the crews and that C.T. [Chief Trader] Campbell be instructed to take necessary steps to carry this object into effect.[55]

Pack horses were an improvement to Methy Portage's transport, but they were not entirely trouble free. At times, they were "running wild as Deer through the Woods."[56] And in the fall of 1847, all of the Hudson's Bay Company's horses at Lac La Loche died of disease, as did another fifteen or twenty horses owned by an "Indian" who leased them out for portage work.[57]

In the 1850s, locally built ox-drawn carts of the Red River design replaced pack horses on Methy Portage. In 1852, the Hudson's Bay Company directed Chief Trader George Deschambeault of Île-à-la-Crosse to procure eight oxen from Fort Pitt for use on the portage.[58] In the years to follow, carting proved practical, and more oxen were assigned to the portage. While a pack horse was limited to loads of about two *pièces,* a cart pulled by an ox (or a horse) could handle eight to ten *pièces.*

As freight volumes on Methy Portage grew, so did the dependence on oxen. In 1875, this dependence threatened to shut down the bulk of transport into the North-West. That year, the thirty-seven oxen to be used on the portage were being wintered at Fort McMurray at the junction of the Clearwater and Athabasca Rivers. In early April, an ice jam on the Athabasca caused the river to rise 57 feet in less than an hour. The result was that all but one of the oxen drowned. Henry Moberly, who was in charge of the local Hudson's Bay Company post, barely managed to find enough replacement oxen and horses at Lac la Biche to save the season.[59]

After the 1875 flood, carts hauled freight over Methy Portage for another decade. By this time, the trail had seen considerable improvement, especially where it dropped steeply to the Clearwater, and it handled larger volumes than ever before. It is estimated that just prior to 1886, when Methy finally lost most of its business to other routes, ox carts were hauling approximately 100,000 kg (220,000 lb) of freight across the portage each season.[60]

METHY PORTAGE TO LA LOCHE

The 20-km (12-mi) route between the south end of Methy Portage and La Loche, being 1 km (²/₃ mi) down Portage Creek and 19 km (almost 12 mi) across Lac la Loche, is the last leg of the trip from the Warner Rapids bridge to La Loche. It can, however, also be a trip in itself for canoeists who paddle out from and back to La Loche in order to explore Methy Portage. The round trip from La Loche is an excellent option for those lacking the advanced skills needed to come down the Clearwater or for those wanting to hike the portage free of a heavy load.

At the south end of Methy Portage, Portage Creek is only 5 m (16 ft) wide and closed in by willows on both sides. It then follows a zig-zag course on its way to Lac la Loche. Yet, it has good depth and is big enough to allow canoes free passage.

Since Portage Creek shortens Methy Portage by 1 km (²/₃ mi), the early fur traders must have had considerable appreciation for it. At the same time, they sometimes commented on its limited suitability for freighting. On May 25, 1792, Peter Fidler wrote:

> came to the Creek again & the end of the portage, here we push the Canoes into the Creek & proceed down to the Methy Lake — creek very narrow scarce sufficiently wide to permit a Canoe turning in it — very crooked & all willows...[61]

The shrewd George Simpson, heading north from Lac la Loche on September 13, 1820, noted the creek's modest size yet also recognized that it could float a York boat:

> proceeded to Portage la Loche. The entrance from the Lake is by a little shoal zig-zag muddy stream for about half a mile to the landing place, but sufficiently large to admit a fifty piece boat...[62]

As these accounts of Fidler and Simpson indicate, once you start down Portage Creek, you will have many short turns to make. After a paddle of about fifteen minutes, you will come to a fork in the channel. The proper route is then down the wider branch on stream right. At the fork, the channel widens to about 25 m (80 ft), so from here on, steering is easier.

About 100 m (110 yd) or so from the mouth of Portage Creek, you will come to a grassy clearing on stream left that is about 45 m (50 yd) wide and about 70 m (77 yd) deep. Here, a stone cairn built by the Historic Sites and Monuments Board of Canada in 1974 supports a plaque explaining the historical significance of Methy Portage. The plaque also serves as a graffiti board and rifle target. In the past, the cairn clearing was not likely a favourable spot for permanent establishments since its elevation is low relative to the water. No doubt, though, it has seen a great deal of use as a temporary camp. While low and surrounded by a black spruce swamp, it is a reasonable campsite with room for many tents. Should strong winds prevent you from setting out on Lac la Loche, you might find it valuable.

If you paddle to Methy Portage from La Loche, you will be able to use the stone cairn as a landmark. Keep in mind, however, that although the cairn suggests it marks the south end of the portage, this is not the case. Three snowmobile trails lead away from the clearing, but they are not part of the portage. Though the most westerly trail joins Methy Portage, it is too swampy and overgrown to have any practical summer use. Methy Portage properly begins 1 km (²/₃ mi) up Portage Creek!

Lac la Loche

From Methy Portage to its outflow into the La Loche River, Lac la Loche accounts for 26 km (16 mi) of the voyageur highway. As maps show, it is divided into two halves by a major peninsula jutting out from its southwest shore. The peninsula and an island off the tip of it break the sweep of the prevailing northwest winds. Notwithstanding this, the lake remains dangerously prone to the buildup of big waves. Before you commence a traverse either to or from La Loche, make sure you have fair weather.

For as long as anyone knows, Lac la Loche has been named after the burbot (*Lota lota locustris*), an odd-looking fish also known as the maria (pronounced "ma-ruy-a"), ling, or freshwater cod.[63] *La loche* is the French name for the fish, and the word "methy" (or *mithay*) is the Cree equivalent. The Dene name for the lake, *Ttheentaylas Too*, means "little burbot lake."

On March 11, 1820, John Franklin arrived at Lac la Loche for the first time. In the narrative of his journey, he says of Lac la Loche:

> This is a picturesque lake, about ten miles long and six broad, and receives its name from a species of fish caught in it. This fish, the methye, is not much esteemed; the residents never eat any part but the liver except through necessity, the dogs dislike even that. The tittameg [*atihkamîk* or "whitefish"] and trout are also caught in the fall of the year.[64]

The burbot or "methye" that Franklin mentions are still found in the lake. Whitefish, northern pike, suckers, and some walleye also occur, but the trout are now gone.

Oddly, Lac la Loche's geography has apparently changed since the early days of the fur trade. Sketch maps drawn by Peter Fidler in late May 1792 (reproduced below and on the following page) indicate that the northeast end of the lake's dividing peninsula was once a large island. Though Fidler's island has been questioned,[65] his uncanny powers of observation were not likely wrong. Moreover, John Franklin's map from his expedition of 1819-1822 also shows the end of the peninsula as an island. Significantly, Franklin's map would have been based in part on his dog sled journey on March 13, 1820, up the west side of the lake and across the base of the present peninsula.[66]

The early fur trade may have had some high water years, or perhaps,

HBCA / E.3/1 fo. 52 (N14794)

the La Loche River outflow channel was then not cut so deep as now. Whatever the case, it seems that any water lying over the base of the present peninsula would have been shoal, as suggested by the "grass" legend on Fidler's one sketch. When Philip Turnor passed this way with Peter Fidler, he identified the peninsula as an island but made it clear that the canoe route through Lac la Loche ran to the north of it.[67]

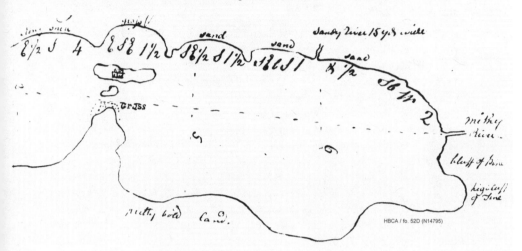

HBCA / fo. 52D (N14795)

Facing page and above: Sketch maps of Lac la Loche drawn by Peter Fidler, May 26-29, 1792.

Wallis Bay

From Portage Creek, you will enter Lac la Loche by first passing over a sandy shoal at the mouth of the creek and then paddling southeast into Wallis Bay. In Dene, Wallis Bay is appropriately named *Hoteth Tl'awzee*, meaning "portage bay."

The northeast shore of Wallis Bay was the site of a very early North West Company house on Lac la Loche. After leaving Methy Portage on May 26, 1792, Philip Turnor mentioned the post in his journal:

> the creek opens to about 30 yards wide at the Lake which we enterd at 11 1/4 AM the Lake is very shoal off the mouth of the creek went into the Methy Lake EbS 1 1/2 mile to a point leaving a bay 1/2 mile deep to North and the Lake 1 1/2 mile wide to South *at this point the Canadians formerly had a temporary house as while they were upon the Methy carrying place the rivers was frozen over so they returned to this place to fish untill the river was fit to walk upon they then hauled their goods to the Athapescow Lake* went nearly along the side of the Lake EbS 3/4 mile EbS 1/2 mile across a little bay then EbN 1/2 mile along the shore and put up at 1 1/2 PM not being able to proceed farther for Ice fore part of the day Wind Variable Southerly at 1 1/2 PM the Wind came to NW fresh Gale with heavy rain and continued showery all the afternoon before we went on shore we set two nets and in the afternoon got 70 Suckers or Carp and 5 Jack fish the South part of the Lake seems very full of Ice Mr Ross shot one swan and myself another.[68]

It is possible that the Hudson's Bay Company built its first post on Lac la Loche in the Wallis Bay area over the winter season of 1809-1810. It is known that the HBC traders Richard Sutherland and David Garson were stationed somewhere on Lac la Loche that season.[69] While we have found no reference as to where their post might have been, it might well have been in the general vicinity of Methy Portage.

It is also possible that both the Hudson's Bay Company and the North West Company built posts in the Wallis Bay area in 1820. Both competitors had posts in the south part of Lac la Loche in the 1819-1820 winter season, but it seems that they moved their respective establishments further north during the summer of 1820. George Simpson may have found the re-located posts in or near Wallis Bay when he made his scathing journal entry of September 13, 1820:

> Left our encampment [at head of La Loche River] at five A.M., strong wind and shipping much water; got to Mr. Clarkes establishment in the Lake at 10 A.M.; one Perring in charge, where I found a very fine band of Indians, to whom I made a speech and gave some Rum & Tobacco; ... The greater part of this band has migrated from Athabasca, numbers are expected to follow, and I suspect there will be very few left: this establishment interferes very much with Fort Wedderburne [HBC post on Lake Athabasca], and is not likely to do good to the Trade generally, and therefore in my opinion should be with-drawn. Perring the man in charge is totally unworthy the trust reposed in him, and should be dismissed the service; he is on terms of intimacy with Frazer the N.W. Clerk in charge of the opposite post, who he has supplied with fish the greater part of the season; he is also an habitual drunkard, and enjoys himself with his friend Mr. Frazer at the Company's expense on the liquor intrusted to his charge; Mr. Frazer finds him a very convenient social neighbour, and as he has not the means of reciprocating, he spends his Evenings very pleasantly over a flagon in Mr. Perrings Tent. I have given this fellow a very serious lecture… Took leave of this Gentleman who is certainly one of the Company's worst bargains, and proceeded to Portage Laloche.[70]

We do not believe Perring's 1820 post could have been in the south part of Lac la Loche if it took Simpson five hours to reach it from the head of the La Loche River. On the other hand, paddling as far as Wallis Bay, a distance exceeding 20 km (12 mi), could account for five hours in hard going. It may also be noted that when Simpson returned south on May 29, 1821, he made it from Methy Portage to the HBC's La Loche post in two hours, even though there were problems with ice.[71]

A week after Simpson had passed through on September 13, 1820, one John McLeod arrived at the HBC's La Loche post to help out. In a letter back to the HBC establishment at Île-à-la-Crosse dated September 25, 1820, he indicates that new construction was planned:

> I have now all the men off in different Quarters [hunting] but it is very little they can bring, and I am inclined to think that it will do us more harm than good as it will put us entirely on the Back ground with the building—not a single stick cut as yet for the building—to every Indian as they arrive I must give a little Rum, which keeps them & us in constant uproar.[72]

Earlier, Simpson had left orders at Île-à-la-Crosse that four men would be left at La Loche to work on improving Methy Portage the following summer.[73] Though John McLeod's new building might have been meant for the general trade, it was possibly meant to headquarter an influx of new workers. If the latter is true, McLeod was likely building somewhere in the north part of the lake.

When we came down Wallis Bay on June 4, 1986, we saw no sign of the ancient North West Company house or any other fur trade post. We did, however, see a more recent ruin on the southwest side of the bay. Here, at the point where the shoreline turns south and the bay opens to the main part of Lac la Loche, there is a clearing of more than a hectare in back from the stony shore. In the clearing, there stands a one-and-a-half-storey house made of squared timbers and fronted with a verandah. The house was obviously built by skilled hands, though the passage of time has now caused the roof to collapse.

Hudson's Bay Company post at West La Loche, September 1908.

West La Loche

On the west shore of Lac la Loche, not quite 4 km (2½ mi) south from Wallis Bay, a few small shacks in a clearing of two or three hectares mark where the community of West La Loche once stood. On Map 74C, you will see the site marked as "La Loche West." Map 74C/12 does not show it since it is about 2 cm (¾ in) or 1 km (²/₃ mi) below the bottom of the map. If you have Map C/5, you will see it marked as "La Loche West" near the map's upper margin.

Though West La Loche seems somewhat off the beaten path, the Dene of Lac la Loche have long favoured it as a place to live. Significantly, even while the community is essentially now abandoned, they still refer to it as *Kwoeⁿ*, meaning "the village." In days past, the Dene no doubt found that the local landscape suited residency, but they might also have found it a good meeting place. Map 74C shows what looks to be a snowmobile trail running from West La Loche to La Loche's sister community of Garson Lake 25 km (16 mi) to the southwest. We suspect that that trail follows on or near a much older track. If this is so, West La Loche is at what would once have been a three-way junction where the Garson Lake and Methy Portage tracks met.

West La Loche was also favoured as a post site by fur traders, although it is impossible to say when the site may have first been used by traders. Possibly, the Sutherland and Garson post of 1809-1810 was situated here. Likewise, it may be that the posts Simpson saw in 1820 were also here.

After the Hudson's Bay Company and the North West Company merged in 1821, the new Hudson's Bay Company soon shut down all trading operations on Lac la Loche, likely after the 1822-1823 season.[74] Over the next thirty years, it may sometimes have had men stationed at or near Methy Portage to help with portage operations, but there are no records of an established post in the area.

Eventually (at least by 1853), the HBC recommenced trading on the lake with a new post at West La Loche under the charge of an interpreter named Antoine Morin.[75] By this time, horses and oxen were being routinely used on the portage, and this called for both animal care and the maintenance of carts and harnesses. As well, the HBC felt a post in the area would cut down on illicit trading by their own tripmen.[76]

For whatever reason, the HBC's management was not entirely pleased with West La Loche's performance. As early as 1873, there was a recommendation that the post be abandoned and any necessary operations moved to the south end of Methy Portage.[77] Another recommendation was that it be moved to Bulls House on Peter Pond Lake.[78] Yet another was that it go to Big Point, situated further east on Lac la Loche.[79]

Some efforts were made to shift West La Loche's operations to Methy Portage, but the recommendations to quit the post were never really carried out. It may be that the men who actually worked at the post resisted a move. But why would they not gladly move to Methy Portage when they so often had to travel 10 km (6 mi) to attend to matters there? The following are typical of the entries in the Portage La Loche [West La Loche] post journals:

> [June 24, 1879] … Seeing 11 boats pass the Point au Mongrain [Big Point] I started for the Portage today.
> [June 25, 1879] … I was employed at the Portage today receiving & giving out Cargoes to 11 Boats all of which got off before sun-set. I came back to the Post to-night.[80]

Arguably, the men at West La Loche wanted to have a refuge from the confusion of the portage's summer traffic. Or perhaps they preferred their view of the open lake over the crowded banks of Portage Creek. They may also have been reluctant to leave behind improvements won through years of hard work. Frank J.P. Crean, an explorer sent out by Canada's Department of the Interior, visited West La Loche on September 17, 1908:

> The map shows this post as being at one end of the Portage. It really is six miles from there, south. The Hudson's Bay Company's buildings stand in a large clearing and the situation is most picturesque. A large growth of merchantable spruce forms a back ground which adds considerably to the appearance of the whole. A garden of about one acre is fenced with a rail fence. This garden looked splendidly on the 17th of September. The potatoe tops were not touched by frost.[81]

Story has it that the Hudson's Bay Company post at West La Loche finally came to an end in 1936 when a local man stole some furs from the post and then burned the post down to hide the theft. At that time, the HBC had just bought out the rival Revillon Frères whose operations were at the village of La Loche on the east side of Lac la Loche. So, rather than rebuild at West La Loche, the HBC moved to the Revillon Frères facilities on the other side of the lake.[82]

West La Loche survived as a considerable community even after the Hudson's Bay Company left. Father Bertrand Mathieu, O.M.I., a long-time resident of La Loche, told us that when he arrived at La Loche in 1950, there were still about 100 people living at West La Loche. However, since then, with the road and other services all going to La Loche, West La Loche has dwindled away.

When we stopped at West La Loche on June 4, 1986, we met a dozen Dene youth at an outdoor fire boiling a large pail of tea and another full of duck eggs. From talking to them, we learned that they had just come over from La Loche by skiff for a bit of an outing. The only permanent residents left at West La Loche were Alex Janvier, Joe Lemaigre, Joe's wife Monique—all in their old age—and a solitary brown horse that had the meadow grass all to itself.

Big Point

When you cross to the east side of Lac la Loche, you will pass near the northeast shore of the large peninsula that divides the lake in two. This peninsula, though it was once known locally as Old Sylvestre's Point,[83] is today referred to in Dene as *Hoocheenla Chogh*, meaning "big point."

On June 4, 1986, we found a large flock of white pelicans fishing the shallows between Big Point and the island lying to the northeast. During the three days we camped in the vicinity, the pelicans continued to favour the same spot. They would sometimes lift ponderously from the water to visit elsewhere, but they would always return to their place near the island.

Big Point has its own fur trade history since it was the site of a North West Company post that operated from about 1789 to about 1791. Philip Turnor and Peter Fidler, after being hemmed in by ice at Methy Portage for two-and-a-half days, passed this way on May 29, 1792. Turnor's journal reads:

> Tuesday at 4 AM we got underway in the Lake after having tried for our other net [swept away by ice] without success went to a point on the Et side E3/4S about 4 1/2 miles leaving a kind of double bay about 3/4 mile deep to North went nearly along the shore EbS 1/2 mile and EbN 1 mile a Pine Island about 1/2 mile from the shore the Lake seems about 5 miles wide at this place with a large Island well coverd with pine near the North shore upon which the Canadians formerly had a house but did not find it good for provision…the course over the Methy Lake is nearly SE and runs on the North side of the large Island that the Canadians had their House upon…[84]

In 1971, archaeologist Donald Steer of the University of Saskatchewan located the site of the North West Company post. During the 1971 and 1972 summer seasons, he and a crew excavated the site and discovered that the post had been a large, three-room log building measuring 43 feet long and 28 feet wide and having two stone fireplaces and two cellars. Artifacts found on the site helped confirm its identity and show that it probably operated for two to three years. Some of the artifacts, such as three stone arrowheads, were of native manufacture and suggest that European trade goods had not supplanted native technologies to any great extent at the time the post operated.[85]

Donald Steer also found evidence of more recent activity at Big Point. Besides cellar depressions left from late-nineteenth-century cabins, he identified the site of a Roman Catholic chapel built in 1877 by Oblate missionaries working out of Île-à-la-Crosse. Although this chapel lasted until being torn down in 1891, it never actually had a resident priest and was in fact only used to give two "missions."[86]

Clearwater River Dene Nation

Directly opposite Big Point, on a headland coming out from Lac la Loche's north shore, you will find a sizable Dene community known as Clearwater River (its Dene name, *Ne-hoo-ed-zay-k'ay-yuy*, in our rough phonetics, simply means "the Reserve") which serves as the home base and headquarters of the Clearwater River Dene Nation (CRDN). CRDN has reserve lands here (Reserve 222), at the southwest corner of Lac la Loche (Reserve 221), and on the northeastern shore of Peter Pond Lake (Reserve 223).

Although CRDN lands lie within the territorial boundaries of Treaty No. 10 signed in 1906, its treaty origins go back to 1899 when Adam Boucher, a Dene leader, signed an adhesion to Treaty No. 8 at Fort McMurray.

Boucher's people became known as the Portage la Loche Band, but they were not at first allocated any of their treaty land entitlement and remained occupying traditional lands in both Alberta and Saskatchewan. It was not until 1970 that three parcels of reserve land were finally transferred to the Portage la Loche Band.

In the initial transfers, Reserve 222 was to the north of Linvall and Palmbere Lakes some distance southeast of Lac la Loche. In 1981, however, a trade was made whereby 222 became re-established at its present location opposite Big Point. In 1984, by which time people were beginning to settle there, 222 became known as Big C Reserve after then-Chief Frank Piché, who was nicknamed "Big Chief" or "Big C" due to his robust size. This name continued until June 23, 1994, when the Clearwater River Dene Nation name was adopted to describe the First Nation and its land.

Since 1993, Chief Roy Cheecham has been head of CRDN, succeeding Chief Frank Piché. CRDN now has over 1,100 members, and about 600 of these live at the Clearwater River community. The community has the First Nation's administration offices, a school with about 175 students from kindergarten to grade nine, a centre opened in May 1999 for treating alcohol and drug abuse, and a store selling groceries, dry goods, and gas.[87]

PHOTO BY DOUG CHISHOLM

Aerial photo of Clearwater River Dene Nation community taken September 4, 1999. Big Point shows in upper left of photo.

Dog Island

The only real island on Lac la Loche lies roughly halfway between Big Point and the Big C community. Anyone familiar with the layout of northern communities might guess this is Dog Island, or, as the Dene say it, *Thlee^n Noo*. This is where, in the days before the snowmobile, the sled dogs of La Loche were kept for the summer. On the island, they would still require periodic feeding, but they would be much less a nuisance here than in the village.

To La Loche

From Dog Island, it is about 4 km (2½ mi) further to where the village of La Loche lies along the lake's east shore. If you paddle in the general direction of the Roman Catholic church standing near the shore, you will be able to land near the centre of the village where you may end your trip or else buy new supplies for a continuation of your voyage.

LA LOCHE TO BUFFALO NARROWS

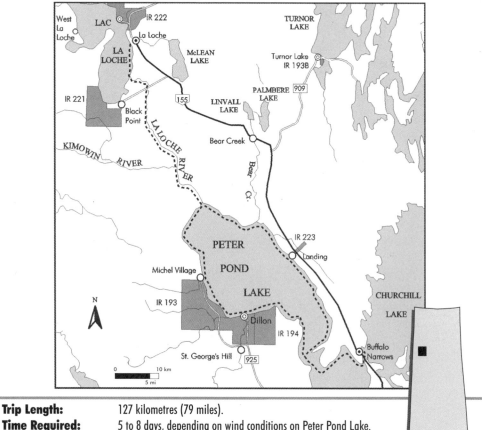

Trip Length:	127 kilometres (79 miles).
Time Required:	5 to 8 days, depending on wind conditions on Peter Pond Lake.
Number of Portages:	None. Considerable wading may be required on the La Loche River.
Maps Required:	
1:250,000 Series:	74C La Loche and
	73N Buffalo Narrows
1:50,000 Series:	74C/6 McLean Lake
	74C/3 Hay Point
	73N/14 Michel (optional; needed for route down west side of Peter Pond Lake)
	74C/2 McCoy Lake (optional; needed for route down east side of Peter Pond Lake)
	73N/15 Dillon
	73N/16 Buffalo Narrows

ABOUT THE TRIP

The route for this trip begins at the community of La Loche and follows the east shore of Lac La Loche to the outflowing La Loche (or Methy) River, which it traces for 56 km (35 mi) to Peter Pond Lake. Canoeists can then choose to follow either the east or west shore of Big Peter Pond Lake (the lake's large, northern lobe) to reach Little Peter Pond. From Little Peter Pond, the route passes through the Kisis Channel to arrive at the community of Buffalo Narrows.

This trip was once as much a part of the old voyageur highway as any other section of the guide route. In modern times, however, it has not seen much canoe traffic. The often shallow La Loche River in the first half of the trip and huge Peter Pond Lake in the second half of the trip deter many canoeists. Nonetheless, the trip is an interesting one and well worth paddling.

Travel on the La Loche River is dependent on water levels. In extreme low water conditions, the river could become difficult or even impassable. We therefore recommend that you plan to paddle the river early in the season and also check on water conditions in advance.

Peter Pond Lake, which accounts for nearly 60 km (38 mi) of the trip, is the most dangerous lake on the entire guide route. Its great size and its exposure to the northwest make it extremely hazardous when the wind comes up. Anyone travelling this lake should have good weather sense and mature judgment.

Because of the shallow rapids on the La Loche River and the big water of Peter Pond Lake, we suggest that you have advanced tripping skills before tackling this trip. We would add, though, that on this trip, good common sense can help make up for some lack of previous canoeing experience. At reasonable water levels, a careful attitude should allow you to paddle or wade down the shallow rapids on the La Loche River without mishap. And, *provided you wait for good weather*, you may safely come down Peter Pond Lake by coasting either the east or west shore.

Upstream travellers will need to do considerable tracking and wading in order to ascend the La Loche River. Since tracking and wading upstream is never easy, we strongly recommend that you have well advanced canoeing skills before doing this trip in an upstream direction.

An important historic site on this trip is the former location of Bulls House where the La Loche River empties into Peter Pond Lake. This is where, in the latter part of the 1800s, the Hudson's Bay Company wintered oxen for use in hauling carts on Methy Portage during the summer.

A scenic highlight is the east shore of Peter Pond Lake. Here, a fine sand beach runs unbroken for many kilometres. Elsewhere in the world, such a beach would be lined with high-rise hotels, but Peter Pond's climate and relative remoteness have thus far saved it from such a fate.

If you choose to travel down the west shore of Peter Pond Lake instead of the east, you will pass by the small Dene communities of Michel Village, St. George's Hill, and Dillon. They typify northern Saskatchewan's smaller communities.

Camping possibilities along the trip route are variable. Since the trip lies outside of the Shield, bedrock sites are not available. Moreover, certain marshy sections of the La Loche River have no camping at all. However, except through these marshy sections, good campsites can usually be found.

The starting point for this trip is the community of La Loche located 510 km (317 mi) northwest of Prince Albert. From Prince Albert, you can reach La Loche by going 44 km (27 mi) west on Highway 3, then northwest 168 km (104 mi) on Highway 55 to Green Lake and then, finally, about 300 km (186 mi) northwest on Highway 155. The entire route is paved. At La Loche, you can turn left off La Loche Avenue onto Descharme Street and follow Descharme west past the Northern dry goods store to launch your canoe where a boat notch makes a break in Lac la Loche's willowy shoreline.

Community of La Loche

Early Times

The La Loche community's recorded history is not so old as that of West La Loche, but we suspect that the townsite has been favoured as a place to stay or visit for generations. For one thing, we have seen the incredible pike spawning run that happens in Saleski Creek in early spring each year. During the run, breakfast, dinner, and supper would be easily had with a net, snare, or spear. We also note that current topographical maps show the townsite as a jumping off point for land trails heading to places such as Wasekamio Lake and Turnor Lake. If these present trails follow old trails (as is likely the case, given the Dene's historical affinity for cross-country trips), the townsite would have been a logical place for early travellers to rendezvous.

Our Lady of the Visitation Mission

In more modern times, the Roman Catholic church can be credited with drawing people to live at present-day La Loche. The first Catholic priests visited Lac la Loche in 1845, and thereafter, Oblates from Île-à-la-Crosse did mission work on the lake from time to time. Eventually, in April 1895, Father Jean Marie Penard arrived to live full-time at La Loche, adopting the name "Our Lady of the Visitation" for his mission. The mission has continued to this day.

Over the years, the mission has relied upon the work of many Oblate priests and brothers. It has also depended on the Grey Nuns who came in 1943 to teach, nurse, and perform other tasks. Two priests stand out for the length of their tenure. One is Father Jean-Baptiste Ducharme, who was in charge of the mission from 1916 until his retirement in 1950. The other is Father Bertrand Mathieu who arrived in 1950 and stayed until being transferred in 1987.[1]

On our 1986 trip, we were able to spend time with Father Mathieu—a most interesting man. He told us that after coming to La Loche in 1950, he spent thirteen winters visiting his parish with a team of four to six fish-fed sled dogs. In summer, he used a single pack dog for help and company as he went on overland treks on Dene trails to places as far as Turnor Lake and Garson Lake. He would reach Turnor Lake in a single day even though the trail was over 50 km (32 mi) long and had a great deal of wet muskeg! Father Mathieu could recall when La Loche's mission community had included three priests, two brothers, and the Grey Nuns. However, the other priests and brothers had transferred away (the last brother due to Parkinson's disease) and the Grey Nuns had left in 1981, so Father Mathieu now worked alone.

Fur Trading

When the Oblate mission was first established at La Loche, the Hudson's Bay Company was some distance away at West La Loche. This opened up an opportunity for competitors. By 1901, the trading firm "Marcelin and Co." from Île-à-la-Crosse had a trader stationed at La Loche and was causing enough trouble to force the HBC to think about moving its West La Loche post to Big Point.[2] An even greater threat came some time later when the French company, Revillon Frères, went into business at La Loche. Competition from Revillon Frères continued until the HBC took over Revillon in 1935. When the HBC's own post at West La Loche burned down in 1936, it moved across to La Loche and into the Revillon buildings.[3] For the 1937–38 trading season, the HBC called upon trader Syd Keighley, who could speak Dene, to manage its new La Loche post. In his memoir *Trader Tripper Trapper*, Keighley reflected on his year at La Loche:

> La Loche post was small. The dwelling house and store were both two-storey log buildings. I had one clerk. The only other white resident was the Catholic priest, Father Ducharme [whom Keighley did not like]....

> Because of my love of hunting, an attractive feature of the La Loche area was that it had some of the best duck country in Canada. At that time one could shoot a meal from the front door of the house almost any day and lakes back of the post were always loaded with ducks. Fishing was always good, whitefish and pickerel being especially abundant.

> Several times during the winter, I chartered Cecil McNeil to fly me to the native camps to pick up furs and leave plentiful supplies. This kept the natives trapping. We flew as far as Lake Athabaska in the north, west into Alberta and south to Whitefish Lake [Garson Lake]. I had my first experience at buying squirrels, which the trappers killed in the thousands. I never knew there could be so many. We paid ten cents each for the skins, whether damaged or undamaged and shipped them in bales of three thousand. Squirrels were something new on the market then. Other principal furs were mink, fox, lynx, coyote, beaver and muskrat.[4]

The HBC continued operating at La Loche until 1987 when it sold off its Northern Stores to the new North West Company.

PHOTO BY DOUG CHISHOLM

Aerial view of La Loche taken September 4, 1999.

Map 4.1   Community of La Loche

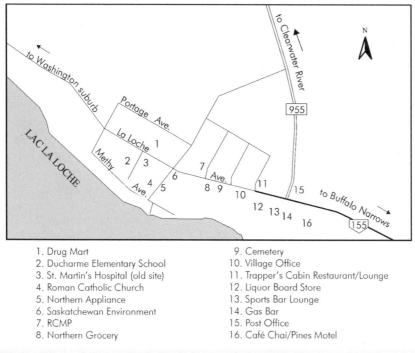

1. Drug Mart
2. Ducharme Elementary School
3. St. Martin's Hospital (old site)
4. Roman Catholic Church
5. Northern Appliance
6. Saskatchewan Environment
7. RCMP
8. Northern Grocery

9. Cemetery
10. Village Office
11. Trapper's Cabin Restaurant/Lounge
12. Liquor Board Store
13. Sports Bar Lounge
14. Gas Bar
15. Post Office
16. Café Chai/Pines Motel

La Loche Today

Father Mathieu told us that when he first arrived in 1950, La Loche was an isolated community of about 700 people. Since then, there have been many changes. A road was built to the village in 1963, telephone service began in 1974, and television was introduced in 1976. The community, designated a "Northern Village" in 1983, now has a population of about 2,000 people,[5] mainly Métis and non-treaty Dene. People live in the central part of the village, as well as in suburbs with names like "Washington" (so-called because its first house was white), "Seattle," "Spokane," "Poplar Point," and "Other Village."

La Loche is often mentioned as a place of high unemployment, large social problems, and poor prospects. It is true that some of the community's socio-economic problems are now too big to be solved by an upturn in squirrel prices. However, La Loche also has much going for it. The village's schools—Ducharme Elementary and Dene High—are renowned for their first-rate education of local youth, and community-based companies such as Methy Construction are creating at least some jobs. As well, the Dene language remains strong; young people still speak it fluently. We can also say that people in La Loche are as friendly as you will meet anywhere.

For canoeists, La Loche offers several services. There is an airstrip just south of the village, and Air Mikisew has a float plane base at Saleski Lake. The Northern Store operates both a grocery and a non-grocery outlet. There are also confectioneries, a drug store, two restaurants, a fried chicken outlet, gas stations, two motels, a Liquor Board store, an RCMP detachment, a Saskatchewan Environment office (where topographical maps can be found), post office, St. Martin's Hospital (a new hospital, replacing an older facility, was officially opened on November 15, 2001),[6] and Our Lady of the Visitation Roman Catholic church. Currently, the village does not have a bank or a laundromat.

LA LOCHE TO PETER POND LAKE

Saleski Creek

Once you embark from La Loche, but before you actually leave the community's environs, you will pass the mouth of Saleski Creek, which flows out of Saleski Lake situated 1 km (²/₃ mi) northwest of La Loche. If you are a bird watcher, you will find it worthwhile to make a side trip up this little creek, since it shelters a rich variety of bird life. When we paddled the creek on June 7, 1986, we saw terns, magpies, kingfishers, blackbirds, crows, a bittern, and a variety of ducks. We also heard many songbirds, though they were invisible in the thick shore willows. At the head of the creek, Air Mikisew of Fort McMurray, Alberta, now operates a water base where it keeps a de Havilland Beaver on floats.[7]

Lac la Loche

South from La Loche, the canoe route follows the east shore of Lac la Loche. This shore is very low and appears marshy in places. About 5 km (3 mi) south of La Loche, however, it becomes sandy with some dune activity back from the beach. Though the whole shore is exposed to westerly winds, the sandy section is suitable for camping and lunch breaks.

On June 7, 1986, we were astonished by the number of pike we saw as we paddled south. It was as if someone had marked the shallow lake bottom with a grid of squares measuring 5 m (15 ft) or so to a side and had then stationed a pike wherever the corners of the square met. These fish, intent on basking in the warm sun, barely moved as our canoe passed over them. But they responded quickly enough to a lure. Around lunchtime, we made a single cast from the canoe and immediately had a 1.5-kg (3-lb) pike on the line. In short order, we were on the beach with our catch set up on a fire of dried willow twigs.

In 1986, we found that C & M Airways, the air company then maintaining the float plane base at Saleski Lake, besides having a Beaver in the water, also had a Norseman tied up at the dock. We talked to Marvin Bather, who ran C & M, and learned that the wood-and-fabric plane had been built in 1946 and that it was then the only Norseman still working in Saskatchewan. Sadly, though, C & M's Norseman has now met its end. In the fall of 1989, it experienced an engine fire at Cree Lake and was destroyed by flames.

The exposed east shore of Lac la Loche would have made a poor location for a fur trade post. Records indicate, however, that the Hudson's Bay Company and the North West Company each had a post on the lake's west shore. John Franklin noted these posts on March 11, 1820, when he arrived at Lac la Loche by dog sled:

> Quitting the river [La Loche] we crossed a portage and came upon the Methye Lake, and soon afterwards arrived at the trading posts situated on the western side of it. These were perfect huts, which had been hastily built after the commencement of the last winter.[8]

Franklin's expedition map clearly marks these posts as being on the west shore of the southern part of Lac la Loche. However, as noted in the previous chapter, it seems that the posts were moved to the northern part of the lake just a few months after Franklin's visit.

La Loche (Methy) River

Just over 3 km (2 mi) south from where the sand beach begins on the east shore, Lac la Loche drains to the east via the La Loche River. This river is also commonly known as the Methy, from the Cree name for the burbot. To the Dene, it is *Ttheentayl Des*, which yet again means "burbot" or "maria" river.

Your passage down the La Loche River will depend greatly on current water levels. In high water, it is possible to travel the entire 56 km (35 mi) to Peter Pond Lake without getting out of your canoe. At lower levels, considerable wading may be required down sections of rocky shallows. In extremely low water, long sections of portaging might be necessary.

During the fur trade, the La Loche River was regarded as one of the more difficult sections of the voyageur highway. Its difficulties were noted by George Simpson travelling upstream on September 11, 1820:

> 11th, Portage de Pinnet.—Monday: Did not embark [from Peter Pond Lake] on account of the Rapids until five A.M., the water very low and much time occupied in polling up, and repairing the damage which our Canoe had sustained.—The Water was so low in this River some years ago that the N.W. Brigade could not proceed, they were therefore under the necessity of bringing their Athabasca Indians to this place in order to be equiped, and part of their goods was hauled by Dogs in the course of the Winter, a very expensive and laborious business: here I fear our boats [York boats which were being considered for the route] will meet with difficulty in dry seasons, but as they are intended to come in early while the Waters are high, there will be less danger. Made Decharge la Barrier, Decharge Sepulcre [Tomb Rapids], the latter is the worst piece of road I ever travelled, it is three miles in length, and the last mile a perfect swamp, filled with stumps of Trees three feet deep: the poor fellows carry two pieces each the whole length of this Discharge. Encamped at seven O'Clock.[9]

Down from Lac la Loche

From Lac la Loche, the La Loche River's outflow can be difficult to spot. In 1986, we overshot it and ended up at the little settlement of Black Point, 4 km (2½ mi) south down the lake. Nonetheless, by keeping a careful watch, you can find it in a corner to the south of a swampy point. Here, about 200 m (220 yd) of bulrushes stand in front of the outflow, but a clear channel with a noticeable current provides a good passage to it.

In its first 6 km (3¾ mi) east from Lac la Loche, the La Loche River meanders considerably. Its shores are low and lined with cattails, horsetails, and willows. The river here runs with

Aerial photo of Black Point taken September 4, 1999. Signs of a recent forest fire surround the community.

PHOTO BY DOUG CHISHOLM

a current of 1 to 2 km per hour (about 1 mi per hour). Even at ordinary water levels, it has spots as shallow as 30 cm (1 ft) and is rarely deeper than 1 m (3 ft). However, since the bottom is sandy, it provides reasonable passage for canoes.

In a later trip, while paddling in early October, we had the good fortune of seeing five tundra swans floating serenely with the current about 5 km (3 mi) downstream from the lake (74C 995519). They apparently saw the marshy river as a good place to feed and rest as they migrated south from the Barrens.

First Rapids

Not quite 6 km (3¾ mi) from Lac la Loche, the river bends right to run south-southeast, and the land becomes higher (74C 007516). At the bend, head-sized rocks extend into the river from the right shore, and these mark the beginning of shallow, rocky rapids that continue for about 750 m (½ mi). To get down these rapids, you can expect to alternate between wading and paddling.

 Those travelling the route upstream (from Buffalo Narrows to La Loche) can expect to wade most of the way through First Rapids.

As you start down the rapids, you will see two cabins on the river left shore. Passing the cabins, you will encounter the remains of two broken-down bridges, about 100 m (110 yd) apart, that were apparently once part of a bush road across the river. You may have to lift over the upstream bridge, but you will find the downstream bridge essentially washed out.

An old portage starts on river right, where the head-sized rocks extend into the river. It follows high ground and is in generally good condition except that it is now obstructed by considerable windfall. Though this portage has seen little or no recent use, it has clearly seen heavy traffic in the past and may be Simpson's "Portage de Pinnet."[10] In 1986, we followed it for over 500 m (⅓ mi) downstream without reaching the end of it.

Black Point Road

Approximately 1 to 2 km (about 1 mi) downstream from the shallow rapids, you will come to a road bridge crossing the river (74C 012497). The road was built between 1988 and 1990 to link the small Dene settlement of Black Point,[11] situated in the southeast corner of Lac la Loche, with Highway 155. Canoes can pass under the bridge without difficulty.

The Long Marsh

From the Black Point bridge, the La Loche River flows for over 20 km (12 mi) through a swampy marsh, where its banks are mainly bordered by wet sedge meadows. As Map 74C/6 clearly indicates, the river's zigzag meanders make the route a great deal longer than its crow-fly length. Typically, the river is 10 to 15 m (30 to 50 ft) wide with a shallow, sandy bottom. You will get some help from a current of 1 to 2 km (about 1 mi) per hour.

If you are travelling upstream, this current should not present serious problems. At most, you may have to move from one shore to another on occasion to avoid the channel's strongest flow.

Because the river rarely moves close to high ground, it has very few dry campsites. There is, however, a particularly good site at a clearing on river right 9 km (5½ mi) downstream from the Black Point bridge, marked from a distance by tall spruce, aspen, and jack pine (74C 013444). When you get to the south side of the clearing, you will see a well-worn path leading up to it from a narrow break in the shore willows. The level clearing is 40 m (44 yd) across and thus has lots of room. In late summer, it also has blueberries in abundance.

On June 9, 1986, after travelling about 2 km (1¼ mi) downstream from the blueberry campsite, we came across a Cessna 152 airplane upside down in the sedge meadow on river right (74C 015434). Earlier, Marvin Bather at C & M Airways in La Loche had told us that a student pilot out of Fort McMurray had disappeared June 6 on his first cross-country solo. We expected the worst as we approached the plane, but the pilot was not to be found anywhere. When we were finally able to report our find, we learned that the pilot had been rescued unharmed by helicopter the day before we came on the scene.

Soon after we left the Cessna crash site, by which time the La Loche's tight meanders had opened up into longer reaches, a small thunderstorm passed overhead. We did not think it worthwhile to take cover (there was none anyway), but we did jump when thunder cracked just above and behind us. Within minutes, we saw smoke rising from where lightning had hit the bush 400 m (¼ mi) away. We then watched as a helicopter and water bombers from Buffalo Narrows arrived on the scene. By the time they had the flames out, the La Loche River had given us enough excitement for one day!

About 15 km (9 mi) downstream from the Black Point bridge, there is another good campsite on river right (74C 023410). It is a large, grassy area over 2 m (6 ft) above the water. Beavers have helped keep it clear of aspen growth. From the grassy campsite, it is another 7 km (4⅓ mi) to where the river's character begins to change. The sedge meadows along the shores now give way to willow and alder thickets that close in the banks. The river also twists and turns more frequently again, and there is some increase in current and depth.

About 4 km (2½ mi) downstream from where the willows and alders begin to close in the banks, you can watch for a good campsite under tall black spruce on the river right shore (74C 062371).

Tomb Rapids

The black spruce campsite marks where the river's character changes yet again. Starting from here and continuing for just over 6 km (3¾ mi), the current runs faster and is often interrupted by minor rapids and rocky shallows.

As noted above, Simpson referred to these rapids as "Decharge Sepulcre." Sir John Richardson's later reference to them as "Rapid of the Tomb (La Cimetiere)" is of particular interest to botanists. After seeing the rapids on June 27, 1848, he wrote:

> At the Rapid of the Tomb (La Cimetiere) several pitch or red pines (Pinus resinosa) grow intermixed with black spruces, one of them being a good-sized tree. This is the most northerly situation in which I saw this pine, and the voyagers believe that it does not grow higher than the River Winnipeg.[12]

Today, red pine is not thought to grow further west than southeastern Manitoba, but since Richardson was such a careful observer, it is difficult to discount his report.

Descending Tomb Rapids in an average year, you will likely find it necessary to get out of your canoe several times to wade. This will not be entirely pleasant. One note from our 1986 trip reads: "Wading down those rapids was bad. Falling into holes 4 feet deep. Rocks slippery. Current strong. Mosquitoes everywhere."

At higher water levels, you may be able to avoid wading by running down the several strong minor rapids that occur. In running the rapids, you will have to keep a good lookout for rocks, sweepers, and broken beaver dams.

If you are travelling upstream, Tomb Rapids will present a serious challenge. You may find yourself tracking or wading up the whole section. However, while this will be difficult and will demand advanced skills, a half-day's work should see you up past the last rapid.

Tomb Rapids have significant beaver activity, especially in their lower half—from the top of Map 74C/3 to 3 km (2 mi) downstream—where aspen and balsam poplar are common along the river banks. Beavers have done extensive clearcutting along the banks and have used some of the wood to build several dams across the river. Interestingly, as you will see from remnants of a half-dozen old dams, the river's current has washed out successive generations of these dams. We wonder if the La Loche River beavers build dams each autumn simply to insure they have good ponds for their winter survival. If this is so, they may not care if the dams are later washed away by spring runoff.

Since Tomb Rapids make up the most difficult section of the La Loche River, early native travellers and the voyageurs often would have portaged them or made a *décharge* in low water. We have not searched for the old portage, but we have looked at sections of an abandoned bush road that runs back from the river right shore. It may be that this road follows the same general path as the old portage.

Down from Tomb Rapids

Tomb Rapids end as quickly as they begin. At a point where a small stream joins the La Loche from river left (74C 104330), the rocks end, the channel deepens, and the river becomes placid. The final 1.3 km (¾ mi) to the Kimowin River confluence is easy paddling.

The La Loche River flows into the Kimowin at a right angle. In the corner formed by the La Loche's right shore and the Kimowin's river left, you will find a large, level clearing a metre (3 ft) or so above the water that is good for camping. Beavers have mowed down most of the aspen that once grew here. Fortunately, they have ignored a magnificent old spruce that soars skyward from the centre of the clearing.

Kimowin River

The Kimowin River and its main tributary, the Garson River, have been used by natives for centuries to travel between the La Loche River and what is now Alberta. From Philip Turnor, we know that both the Cree and Dene were familiar with the Kimowin-Garson route as a region where moose and buffalo were plentiful. Both nations knew the route as the Swan River—the Cree calling it "Wa-pe-sue a See-pe" (or *wâpisiwi-sîpiy* in today's orthography) and the Dene, *Caw-coos a Dez-za*.[13]

Despite its importance to the Cree and Dene, the Kimowin was never developed as a regular fur trade route. In 1791, it was first seen by white men when Philip Turnor and his party went up it en route to Lake Athabasca. Turnor had originally planned to travel via Methy Portage, but he was told that the poor hunting in that direction would not allow his party to live off the land. At the Kimowin confluence on June 2, 1791, he wrote:

> Mr Mackensie Mr Lerue [explorer Alexander Mackenzie and one Laurent Leroux of the NWC] and the Southern Indians [Cree] all assured us that we should not be able to get any kind of provision beyond the Methy carrying place and that on this side we should only be able to get a few fish and we have not Seven days provision left Mr Lerue informed us that the Indians had told him that there was a better way to the west of the Methy carrying place and which parts off at this place the Southern Indians confirmed it and said both Buffalo and Moose are plenty in that track in which our Chepawyans concur and say they know most of the way being only part of one river which they have not seen but know both ends of it and as we are to go before the current we cannot miss the way though if it should prove full of falls and no person knowing them it may prove tedious as well as dangerous but want of Provision will oblige us to try it.

Turnor and his party then proceeded up the Kimowin in the company of several Dene guiding them. They later carried on up the Garson River and then down the Christina River to the Clearwater. As predicted, they had excellent hunting along the way. However, they also found the route to be so difficult, it was thereafter dismissed as a practical trade route.[14]

Down from the Kimowin

After the La Loche and the Kimowin merge, the augmented La Loche River is deep and 30 m (33 yd) or more in width. The current is imperceptible at first, but further down, especially in high water, it may approach 5 km (3 mi) per hour. Poplars and willows grow right down to the water on both banks. There are also some good stands of spruce. About 500 m (1/3 mi) down from the confluence is a trapper's cabin on the river left shore (74C 100321). In the 4 km (2½ mi) down from the cabin, you will encounter—at least at average water levels—seven or eight minor rapids (possibly producing the "Decharge de la Barrier" referred to by George Simpson) where the river runs over stony shallows. In 1986, we waded through four of these. Low water conditions would likely require more wading, while high water would drown out all the rapids.

Upstream paddlers can expect to do considerable wading on approaching the confluence. However, since the river gradient is not great, the wading is not as difficult as at Tomb Rapids.

From the end of the minor rapids (74C 106289), it is just over 10 km (6 mi) to Peter Pond Lake. In this distance, the La Loche River gradually widens to 50 m (55 yd) and then 75 m (82 yd) and grows more placid. The bottom is generally sand or mud, low grassy islands occur, and rocks are few. In short, this is easy paddling.

Bulls House

Towards the La Loche River's mouth, the land becomes lower. However, 1 to 2 km (about 1 mi) before the mouth, good, cleared tablelands stand on both shores. A first clearing of about 2 hectares (5 acres) on the river right shore (74C 162253) has two abandoned cabins. One-half km (⅓ mi) further down on the same shore, a second clearing has two modern cabins (74C

166251). Across the river, on river left, there is a more extensive grass clearing of about 4 to 5 hectares (10 or 12 acres) (74C 167253). This clearing has no cabins, but it has several cellar depressions and a Roman Catholic cemetery (shown above) at its extreme east end.

The earliest mention of fur trade activity at the mouth of the La Loche River comes from Peter Fidler who noted that, "in 1795 the Canadians built a House about 2 miles from the Lake [Peter Pond] up the Methy river on SWt side—but only remained at it one winter." It was apparently a very temporary establishment.[15]

Years later, the area of the clearings became a community known to its Dene inhabitants as *Des Chagh,* simply meaning "the mouth of the river." It was also commonly known as Bulls House—so called because the Hudson's Bay Company here wintered the oxen it used on Methy Portage. The site was favoured for keeping livestock since feed was more plentiful here than at Methy Portage. In particular, the slough grass growing at Hay Point on the north shore of Peter Pond Lake would have been a source of winter forage. Oxen were likely kept at Bulls House from the early 1850s until 1873 when they were shifted to Fort McMurray.[16]

Bulls House was never a major fur trade post, but the Hudson's Bay Company considered it a convenient location for business. Even after it was no longer required for wintering oxen, Bulls House was maintained as a small-scale trade operation. An HBC report for 1897, perhaps a typical year, mentions that as an outpost of West La Loche, Bulls House collected furs valued at 924 Made Beaver in the preceding season.[17]

As late as the mid-1930s, as many as five homes were still occupied at Bulls House. At this time, Bulls House had a small store—possibly an independent operation—run by Bob Woods, a former chef who had once cooked on the Athabasca River steamboats. In about 1935, Bob Woods left his wife Flora and four young children at Bulls House in the care of a friend named Sam Seright and headed for parts unknown. He was never to be heard from again. Not long after his departure, most people at Bulls House moved over to the growing community of Buffalo Narrows.

From 1928 onward, and especially through the 1950s and 1960s, the Buffalo Narrows area was a major centre for mink ranching in northern Saskatchewan. At least one mink ranch was operated at Bulls House by Robert Geutre.[18] If you explore the grassy clearings, you can still find mink cages which were abandoned after low prices caused the industry to collapse. Cages can be found on both sides of the river, so it is likely that Bulls House had more than one ranch during the ranching period.

La Loche River Outflow

Down from Bulls House, the La Loche River's left shore is low and willowy and would make poor camping. However, while the river right shore is also low, it is sandy and provides good camping opportunities.

On June 1, 1791, Philip Turnor and his upstream party arrived at the outflow and had a chance meeting with Alexander Mackenzie coming downstream. The two parties camped together—likely on the sandy river right shore. In his journal, Turnor wrote:

> at 7 PM *Mr Alex Mackensie the Master* of the Athapiscow Lake settlement and its dependances arrived with one Canoe in which he had 20 Packs of furs besides his own things which is not common for a Canadian Master to have as they mostly keep their own Canoe for their own things he informed me that he had Fourteen Canoes more following him deeply loaded...

Significantly, though Mackenzie was delivering furs to Grand Portage, he was en route to London to study surveying and astronomy in preparation for his famous expedition to the Pacific in 1793.[19]

PETER POND LAKE

The present Dene name for Peter Pond Lake is *Ttheentaylcho Too*, meaning "big burbot (maria) lake."[20] However, the oldest known name for the lake is actually Buffalo Lake. Peter Pond, for whom the lake is now named, made the very first record of the lake's name when he used the legend "Beef Lake" on his 1785 map of North America.[21] Similarly, Philip Turnor said that the lake was "called by the Southern Indians Mis-toose-Sask-a-ha-gan and by the Chepawyans A-gid-da Too-ah or Buffalo Lake."[22] The ancient name has persisted to the present day with residents of Buffalo Narrows routinely calling the northern part of Peter Pond Lake "Big Buffalo" and the southern part "Little Buffalo."

Peter Pond is by far the most dangerous lake found between Methy Portage and Cumberland House. It is a huge lake divided into two parts by a narrows—larger "Big Buffalo" or "Big Peter Pond" in the north and smaller "Little Buffalo" or "Little Peter Pond" in the south. The most direct water route between the La Loche River inflow and the lake's outflow into the Kisis Channel measures 58 km (36 mi). There are no islands for protection on Big Peter Pond and only a couple well off the main track on Little Peter Pond. It is therefore absolutely critical to avoid long traverses. If you were to capsize in the middle of Peter Pond, you would perish very quickly in the cold water.

Professor J. Mitchell of the University of Saskatchewan at Saskatoon visited Peter Pond Lake in 1943. He wrote that, "There is a tradition that one must propitiate the spirit of Big Buffalo by throwing in a spruce bough when entering its waters. The magic words are, 'Shake hands, Big Buffalo.' We failed to do this and were storm bound two full days at Buffalo River."[23]

Because you cannot simply set out in a straight line traverse down Big Peter Pond, you must choose to coast either the east or west shore until you get to the narrows leading to Little Peter Pond. Both shores are options, but the somewhat longer west shore provides better wind protection from the prevailing northwest winds. We will describe both shores beginning with the east.

EAST SHORE OF BIG PETER POND

The trip southward along Big Peter Pond's east shore is actually first east-southeast along the north shore, then southeast for a long distance and finally southwest along Thompson Peninsula. Keeping reasonably close to shore along this route, you will paddle at least 50 km (31 mi) to reach the tip of Sandy Point where the narrows to Little Peter Pond begins. The time needed to paddle this distance will greatly depend on the weather. Be ready to drink tea for hours on shore if the wind gets up.

In 1986, we paddled down the west shore, so we saw the east shore only from a distance. When we paddled the east shore a decade later, Peter Pond Lake was higher than normal and the shoreline was considerably flooded. We therefore did not see nearly as much sand as we had seen while flying over the area on previous occasions. We suspect you will find more sand beaches than we mention here.

The shore eastward from the La Loche River is generally low and willowy with some sections lined with ice-shoved stones. At Hay Point, 5 km (3 mi) east-southeast from the river mouth, the willows are interrupted by extensive meadows of wild slough grass. As mentioned, hay from here, though not a high quality fodder, would have been a staple in the diet of any Methy Portage oxen overwintered at Bulls House.

The northeast corner of Big Peter Pond is particularly marshy with bulrushes offshore. However, after turning and heading more directly southeast for about 5 km (3 mi), you can expect to find the occasional sand beach. These beach areas might make reasonable campsites.

Big Peter Pond is large enough to have a fair amount of flotsam make its way to the east shore. Of all the things trapped in the shore willows, the wrecks of old plywood skiffs—as many as a dozen—are the most obvious. The wrecks are a good indicator of how popular skiffs are on the "West Side" of northern Saskatchewan. Because they are both seaworthy and cheap to build, these locally made boats are favoured for commercial fishing and general transportation. They are heavy, but weight is not critical since they can run all the way from Bulls House to Dipper Rapids without a portage. With their high prows and bright paint, they have become a colourful symbol of West Side navigation.

As you paddle southward, you may also catch the odd glint of wire strung in the poplars and spruce back from the shore. This wire is left over from a telephone line strung north from Buffalo Narrows. Likely built in the 1940s, it served as an extension of a provincial government telegraph line running from Meadow Lake to Buffalo Narrows. The telephone line ran north around Peter Pond Lake to Bulls House from where branch lines extended to both La Loche and Dillon.[24]

Landing

About 13 or 14 km (8 or 9 mi) down from the northeast corner of Big Peter Pond, you will come to a place marked on some maps as "Landing." The land here was transferred to the Portage la Loche Indian Band (now the Clearwater River Dene Nation) as a reserve in 1970 towards satisfaction of treaty land entitlement.[25] A number of people lived on the reserve in the 1970s, but most have now relocated to Lac la Loche. Arriving by canoe, you will see a boat launch and a gravel road leading up from it. The road runs about 3 km (2 mi) northward to connect with Highway 155.

Birch Point

Southeast from the Landing boat launch, the shore remains mainly low and willowy. Then, about 10 km (6 mi) from the boat launch, the shoreline turns southwest to run out to the end of what the maps name as Birch Point. From the turn onward, there is a good sand beach with the shore rising to 4 m (13 ft) high back from the beach. About 400 m (¼ mi) before the end of the point, where a small cove indents the shore, there is a very good campsite with shelter for tents amid aspen and birch (73N 481024).

Big Buffalo Beach

When you round Birch Point to go southeast again, the shore is once more low and willowy. However, after 3 km (2 mi), the shoreline makes a right turn and begins a long, 10-km run southwest along Thompson Peninsula to the end of what the maps call Sandy Point. The entire 10 km (6 mi) to Sandy Point is a sand beach known locally as "Big Buffalo Beach." Though it has some scrub growth in places, the beach is really quite excellent.

About 4 km (2½ mi) down the beach, you will come to where a lookout platform for sightseers has been built on the dunes above the beach. Back from the platform, a boardwalk leads to a vehicle cul-de-sac reached by an access road coming off Highway 155 just north of Buffalo Narrows. At the cul-de-sac, there is a good public picnic area that has pedestal campfire grates and outdoor toilets.

In the vicinity of the lookout platform, dunes rise to a height of 6 m (20 ft). Dune formations can also be found further down the shore, and hiking the dunes offers a welcome break from paddling. The dune ecology is fragile, and care must be taken not to disturb any vegetation.

The tip of Sandy Point, which is mainly bulrushes and willows, marks the southern extremity of Big Peter Pond.

WEST SHORE OF BIG PETER POND

From the La Loche River, it is just over 10 km (6 mi) due south to a shoulder-like point known as "Headquarters" (74C 166130) on Big Peter Pond's west shore. A straight-line traverse to the point may be tempting, but it will take you as much as 4 km (2½ mi) offshore. Coasting the shore is much safer and will add less than an hour of paddling.

For 2 to 3 km (about 1½ mi) down from the river, the shore is sandy with aspen and jack pine back from the shore. Camping possibilities are therefore good. Further down, the shore remains sandy but willows occur in places. We have not scouted the shore carefully here, but we expect good sandy campsites do exist.

As you move towards Headquarters, you can see the Grizzly Bear Hills, sometimes called the Buffalo Hills, off to the southwest. Since the region of the Grizzly Bear Hills is remote and wild country, grizzlies and buffalo might very well be successfully reintroduced there. For now, though, you can camp Big Peter Pond's west shore without fear of either a grizzly attack or a buffalo stampede.

In a country that is exceedingly flat, the Grizzly Bear Hills are a prominent landmark, and early travellers often commented on them. When Philip Turnor passed the mouth of the Dillon River heading north on June 1, 1791, he wrote:

a hill appears WbS called by the Southern Indians Mis-ta-hay Mus-qua Wau-chu and by the Chepawyans Hot-hail-zaz-za Sheth or the Grizil Bear Hill."[26]

On Turnor's return this way on June 6, 1792, his companion Peter Fidler marked the hills on a sketch map. Fidler's sketch is reproduced at right.

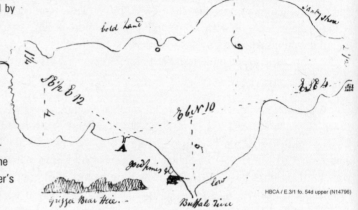

HBCA / E.3/1 fo. 54d upper (N14796)

Headquarters

After gradually turning from south to east, Big Buffalo's west shore makes a sharp right turn around a shoulder to head south-southeast. As mentioned, the area of the turn is known as Headquarters. In 1916, the McInnes Fish Company of Edmonton came to the Buffalo Narrows area to run a commercial fish operation. It was here at the shoulder point that the company set up its "headquarters" with bunkhouses for its men and barns for horses employed in freighting fish.[27]

When we arrived at Headquarters on June 9, 1986, we did not see any sign of the old fishing establishment. However, in a shallow bay just west from the turn, we found an excellent sand beach and a picnic shelter at the end of a rough vehicle track coming from the south. We made a good camp here and caught two pike for supper. Later that evening, we had company when a half-dozen young men from Michel Village arrived in an old car to party. We knew a couple of them, so we stayed up to talk a while. But we were fast asleep in our tent long before our visitors shut things down.

To Michel Village

From Headquarters, it is 7 km (4⅓ mi) south to Michel Village. The shore south is stony and backed by a mixed wood of poplar, spruce, and willow. There are also some sections of sand beach, so camping opportunities do exist.

Wooden bridge over creek near Michel Village.

Marked as "Michel" on Maps 73N and 73N/14, Michel Village is a small settlement comprised mainly of non-treaty Dene. It sits back from a good sand beach on a sandy terrace perhaps 8 m (25 ft) above lake level with spruce and jack pine surrounding it. People have apparently lived here for several decades, but the population grew substantially in the late 1970s. This growth brought an all-weather road and a power line from Dillon in 1983. In 1986, about 125 people lived in the community. More recently, while the community has maintained its status as a "Northern Hamlet," its population has dropped to about seventy-five residents.[28]

Michel Village has a Roman Catholic church, a community hall, a hamlet office, and the Buffalo Hills School for kindergarten to grade nine students. It does not have a store, gas station, or other commercial establishment. For groceries and the like, you will have to paddle southeast to Dillon.

To Dillon

As you move towards Dillon, you will find that the shoreline continues with no irregular bays or peninsulas—"hanging in a easey sweep" as Philip Turnor described it in 1791.[29] It is similar to that north of Michel Village—often stony, but with sandy sections that might allow camping.

The most direct route between Michel Village and Dillon is 12 km (7½ mi), while the safer route along the shore is perhaps 14 km (9 mi). In 1986, we made a modest traverse from a point south of Michel across to Dillon. At first, a light northwest wind allowed us to put a tarp up as a sail. Soon, though, the light wind grew stronger, and we were in as much trouble as we could handle. Dropping our sail and taking to our paddles, we barely succeeded in keeping our canoe from swamping as big rollers took us up, down, and up again. When we were finally thrown ashore with the surf at Dillon, we were all too aware that our traverse had been a huge mistake.

Frank Crean's September 1908 photo of Dillon shows cabins, drying racks, a horse and dogs.

Dillon and the Buffalo River Dene Nation

Dillon, a community of over 600, is situated on land belonging to the Buffalo River Dene Nation and serves as that First Nation's home base. In Dene, it is known as *Ayjere Des Chay*, or "buffalo river mouth," from its location at the mouth of *Ayjere Deszay*, the "buffalo river"—now the Dillon River. The origin of the current English name "Dillon" is unknown to us. We do know that it was already used to name the community on top- ographical maps in the 1930s and that in 1942, the Hudson's Bay Company changed the local post's name from "Buffalo River" to "Dillon."[30]

The earliest recorded information regarding Buffalo River comes from Peter Fidler's journal entry made June 6, 1792. Though this entry makes no written comment on the area, an accompanying map of his party's route through Big Peter Pond shows a house just west of the mouth of the "Buffalo River."[31] This house, perhaps abandoned when Fidler passed, would have been built by Montreal traders since the Hudson's Bay Company had not yet built posts so far inland.

In the early 1800s, the Hudson's Bay Company made some efforts to trade at Buffalo River. By 1820, just before the merger of the HBC and the North West Company, it seems that both companies had posts in operation here. John Franklin, arriving here by dog team on March 6, 1820, wrote:

> we arrived at the establishments which are situated on the western side of the lake, near to a small stream, called the Beaver [*sic*] River. They were small log buildings, hastily erected last October, for the convenience of the Indians who hunt in the vicinity. Mr. Mac Murray, a partner in the N.W. Company, having sent to Isle à la Crosse an invitation to Mr. Back and me, our carioles were driven to his post, and we experienced the kindest reception. These posts are frequented by only a few Indians, Crees and Chipewyans. The country round is not sufficiently stocked with animals to support to [*sic*] many families, and the traders almost entirely subsist on fish caught in the autumn, prior to the lake being frozen. The water being shallow, the fish remove to a deeper part, as soon as the lake is covered with ice. ...

> Mr. Mac Murray gave a dance to his voyagers and the half-breed women; this is a treat which they expect on the arrival of any stranger at the post.[32]

It is likely that after the HBC and NWC merged, the new HBC, now lacking any competition, would have seen no need to continue a full-fledged post at Buffalo River. However, by 1903, the HBC's Île-à-la-Crosse post began operating an outpost at Buffalo River with Charles Eugene Bélanger as manager, and in 1916, this out- post became a post in its own right. The HBC was then fast losing its trade monopoly. As early as 1907, Revillon Frères was set up in Buffalo River, and in 1919, the fur trading Lamson and Hubbard Company was also present.[33] Though this competition was short-lived, it indicates that Buffalo River was eventually fre- quented by more than just "a few Indians" as was apparently the case in Franklin's time.

According to teacher Monique Sylvestre of Dillon, oral history has it that the current community got its start in the latter part of the 1800s when two Dene brothers and their families settled here after finding buffa- lo to hunt and fish to catch. They were in time joined by other Dene, but Monique Sylvestre notes that one of her own great-grandfathers, father to her grandfather George Grosventre (Benjamin), was in fact a Gros Ventre (Atsina) Indian who had come from the south to the Buffalo River area in order to trap and had then stayed.

A century ago, the Buffalo River Dene were part of about 200 Dene known as the Clear Lake Band. This Band entered into treaty on August 28, 1906, when their leader, Chief Raphael Bedshidekkge (Campbell) signed Treaty No. 10 with federal Treaty Commissioner James McKenna at Île-à-la-Crosse. In 1933, the Clear Lake Band became known as the Peter Pond Lake Band. In 1972, the Band separated into the Buffalo River Band and the Turnor Lake Band to reflect the geographic locations of its members. These bands are now known as the Buffalo River Dene Nation and the Birch Narrows First Nation respectively. The Buffalo River Dene Nation occupies Reserve land in and around Dillon and is headed by Chief Elmer Campbell.

Today, Dillon is a modern, growing community. A road was built, and power and telephone services were installed in the early 1980s. The community has a store (though the former HBC store was closed in 1987), a gas station, a nursery-to-grade-twelve school, a medical clinic, and St. Andrew Roman Catholic Church.

St. George's Hill

On our 1986 trip, we took a side trip up the Dillon River to visit the small community of St. George's Hill. Soon after starting out, we were surprised to pass a herd of eleven horses grazing in a riverside meadow. We were later to learn that the Dillon area then had about seventy horses and a like number of cattle. Ranching in the bush!

Advancing about 5 km (3 mi) upstream, we next came to a cluster of houses on the river bank. This was not St. George's Hill but an area known as "44." Its odd name comes from the fact that when Monique Sylvestre's grandfather George Grosventre and his brother Michel built the first two small cabins here, the cabins perched on the bank—when viewed from the river—together looked like the number 44.

About one or two km (roughly 1 mi) upstream from 44 and just up from a bridge and power line crossing the river, we came to where St. George's Hill occupies a sandy clearing some 5 to 6 m (16 to 20 ft) above the river on the river's westerly shore. Upon landing, we found that the community's main focal point, at least for young people, seemed to be the local pool hall which boasted two snooker tables. We spoke to some of the youth there and then went on a short walking tour before going back to our canoe and returning downstream.

St. George's Hill is a relatively new community built on land just outside the Buffalo River Dene Nation's Reserve boundary. Its Dene residents are closely related to their neighbours at Dillon, but they are mainly without treaty status. According to Monique Sylvestre of Dillon, her aunt and uncle Marie and Michel Bekkattla became St. George's Hill's first settlers in about 1950 and one "Stone" Lemaigre and his family, as well as others, arrived some time later. Monique says she has heard of two possible origins for the hamlet's name. One is that it recognizes a Catholic priest from Dillon named Father George who blessed some of the hamlet's first homes. The other is that it recognizes a carpenter named St. George who built some of those first homes.

Nowadays, St. George's Hill has the municipal status of "Northern Hamlet." It currently has about eighty-five residents. It has a school that offers kindergarten to grade nine as well as upgrading classes. Given its small population base, it has little else in the way of services.

Horses at Dillon, 1986.

Pierre-Marie Noltcho and his handmade birch-bark canoe in 1986.

Dillon's Birchbark Canoe

The day after we arrived in Dillon in 1986, we attempted to move on towards Buffalo Narrows though the northwest wind was still strong. We first forced our way north beyond the breakers and then tried to progress by quartering northeast. We soon found, however, that things were as bad as the day before. We therefore turned to run south and come ashore just past the eastern edge of Dillon.

As we were setting up camp on the beach where we landed, an elderly man came to us from further up the bank and, with the same friendliness we had already seen in Dillon, offered us a tarp to use as a windbreak for our camp. He also invited us to come up to his place the next morning for a visit.

The following morning, we took up the old man's invitation and visited him at his home not far from our camp. We learned that he was 78-year-old Pierre-Marie Noltcho (the father of Monique Sylvestre). Most interesting to us, we learned that he was descended from a long line of birchbark canoe builders and that two years before, he had actually built a small birchbark canoe (pictured left) using skills he had learned from his father as a young man. We were fascinated, since despite our interest in the birchbark canoe, we had never before seen one.

The canoe was not quite 4 m (13 ft) long and built entirely of natural materials. The ribs and planking were of hand-hewn spruce, while the birchbark cover was laced together with spruce roots and sealed with spruce gum. Pierre-Marie told us that he had taken the stitch pattern for his lacing from two pieces of an old birchbark canoe that had been found on the beach by a relative in 1979. He showed us these pieces of ancient rind and how the stitch holes on their edges matched those on his canoe. Pierre-Marie said his little canoe had been water-tested and found to be tippy but usable. Though small, it did look like a practical craft for a single hunter travelling on protected waters. Our own view was, though, that it really belonged on display where people could admire it. Happily, things have worked out in that regard. Since we visited Pierre-Marie, Alex Robertson of Robertsons' Trading in La Ronge has purchased the canoe and has it hanging amid his store's excellent collection of northern crafts and memorabilia.

West from Dillon

From Dillon, it is 7 km (4⅓ mi) west-northwest to Willow Point. The shoreline here has both sandy and stony sections. The sandy sections provide good opportunities for camping.

As we were moving towards Willow Point on June 12, 1986, we met with a half-dozen western grebes scattered on the waves. A bit smaller than loons, these pretty birds with curved white necks reminded us of miniature swans out for a day in the sun. Though we hoped to see them again, this meeting on Big Peter Pond was the only time we saw them that summer.

At Willow Point, the shore turns right to run southeast. This will put the prevailing wind at your back which is preferable to a side wind. Nonetheless, the lake remains dangerous in this area. We were reminded of this in 1986 when we saw two wooden crosses along the shore inscribed with the names "Roland Toulejour" and "Edward Montgrand" and the date "May 23, 1970." After our experience coming into Dillon, it was not hard for us to imagine how the lake might have claimed these men.

Old Fort Point

About 6.5 km (4 mi) from Willow Point, you will come to a pointed headland where the shoreline, after a short sweep northeast, again turns right to run south-southeast (73N 417999). Two km (1¼ mi) to the south, both Maps 73N and 73N/15 mark another headland as "Old Fort Point."

Old Fort Point is where a North West Company trader named Graham wintered in 1790-91. Philip Turnor noted the location of Graham's winter quarters while passing north on May 31, 1791:

> then went NW 3 1/2 miles to a point [Old Fort] on [SW] shore the land on this side rather bold and well coverd with Pine Asp &c went round the point and put up in a small sandy bay at the place Mr Graham wintered at, at 9 PM Wind Variable Westerly strong Gale with cloudy weather.[34]

Graham had collected twenty packs of beaver pelts from Cree trappers during the 1790-91 winter season. In April, 1791, he and his men hauled these pelts over the ice to the narrows between Peter Pond and Churchill Lakes so that they could be taken out by canoe in advance of Peter Pond Lake's late breakup. On May 20, he brought the fur to Île-à-la-Crosse by canoe for forwarding on to Montreal. Unfortunately, he was to drown a short time later while canoeing at Île-à-la-Crosse.[35]

Old Fort Point has seen other activity since Graham was here. About 500 m (⅓ mi) south from the tip of the point, there is a clearing (73N 429978) where a hectare of brome grass grows on a terrace 3 m (10 ft) above the stony shore. There are old cellar depressions in the clearing, but no clear clues as to their origins.

South from Old Fort Point

From Old Fort Point, the western shore of Big Peter Pond runs due south towards the narrows leading to Little Peter Pond. In most weather situations, it is best to hug the west shore all the way into the narrows and then follow it as it curves eastward. This will bring you to the end of the unnamed headland that faces Thompson Peninsula on the opposite shore. If you have fair weather, you can then make a traverse of 1.5 km (1 mi) across the narrows to Thompson.

Coming down from Old Fort Point, the west shore is very stony. However, there are sandy spots that could be used for camping. A particularly good campsite (73N 454895) where we stayed June 12, 1986, is about 200 m (220 yd) west from the northernmost tip of the unnamed headland. Here, a sandy beach fronts a grassy clearing edged by poplars.

Map 4.2   Big and Little Peter Pond Lakes

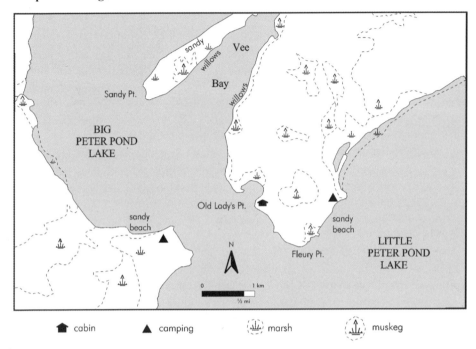

cabin ▲ **camping** 🔱 **marsh** 🔱 **muskeg**

Old Lady's Point

On the east side of the narrows between Big and Little Peter Pond, about 1 km (²/₃ mi) northwest of what Maps 73N and 73N/15 call "Fleury Pt.," there is a large clearing with cabins and a sizable garden (73N 473900). Known locally as "Old Lady's Point," it is named after Suzanne Montgrand, who died many years ago but whose small cabin still stands.

The most senior resident at Old Lady's Point's has more recently been Mary Laliberte, born about 1908. In the fall of 1936, Mary and her husband were travelling north by canoe to return to their home at Bulls House. They had come from Île-à-la-Crosse where Mary had given birth to a son George. Sadly, they had also stopped at Buffalo Narrows on their way back to bury an older son who had died the same day George was born. After the burial, they had continued towards home with the infant George, but at Old Lady's Point, they were stopped by new ice. They then took steps to camp here until freeze-up might insure safe winter travel. Somehow, though, what was to be a short sojourn turned into a permanent stay. Until the year 2000, when she finally moved into Buffalo Narrows, Mary (aided by grown-up sons, including George) kept house right where the ice first stopped her, her husband, and baby George.

LITTLE PETER POND

From the south tip of Fleury Point, it is a straight-line traverse of over 10 km (6 mi) across the north end of Little Peter Pond to the entrance of Kisis Channel, the narrows leading to Churchill Lake. This traverse, which crosses a broad expanse of open lake, is not safe for canoes. It is much better to follow the shore northeast from Fleury Point towards Gran Bay at the far north end of Little Peter Pond. When appropriate, you can then cut across to the eastern shore with a shorter, safer traverse.

About 1 km (2/3 mi) northeast from the south tip of Fleury Point, there is a sandy beach. Excepting the beach area, neither the northwest nor the northeast shore of Gran Bay appears suitable for camping. For the most part, the shores are either stony or low and brushy.

There is a small sand beach fronting a grassy picnic area (73N 579907) 1 km (2/3 mi) northwest from the entrance to Kisis Channel and another sand beach (73N 592902) on the south side of the channel entrance. These beaches would make good lunch stops. However, since they also likely see some good after-the-bar parties arriving from Buffalo Narrows, they might be very poor overnight camps.

Kisis Channel

Kisis Channel, not quite 3 km (2 mi) long, is deep and wide with no current that will present difficulty to either downstream or upstream travellers. Known locally as the "Kiezie Channel," its name comes from Buffalo Narrows' first permanent residents, Martial and Charlotte Kiezie. Martial was a Cree from Cold Lake, Alberta, while his wife Charlotte was a

Map 4.3   Kisis Channel area

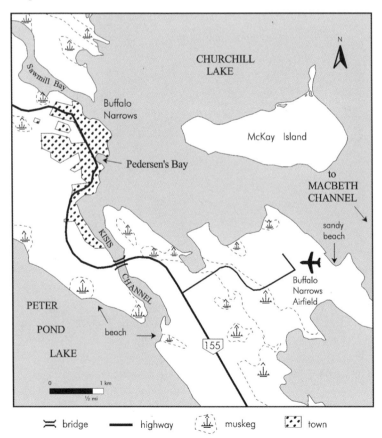

Dene from Fort Resolution. In 1895, soon after meeting and marrying in Île-à-la-Crosse, they moved to Buffalo Narrows and settled near where Highway 155 now enters the village's main business section.[36]

Halfway down the channel, you will pass under the bridge that allows Highway 155 to continue north to the Buffalo Narrows community. When an all-weather road first reached here in 1957, a ferry was used to take vehicles across the channel. The ferry operated until the current bridge opened in the fall of 1980.[37]

At the mouth of the channel, you may turn north to paddle 600 m ($1/3$ mi) or so up Churchill Lake's west shore to Pedersen's Bay, a small bay adjacent to Buffalo Narrows' downtown. Here, you can land at the government dock to either end your trip or resupply for the next leg of your voyage.

-5-

BUFFALO NARROWS TO ÎLE-À-LA-CROSSE

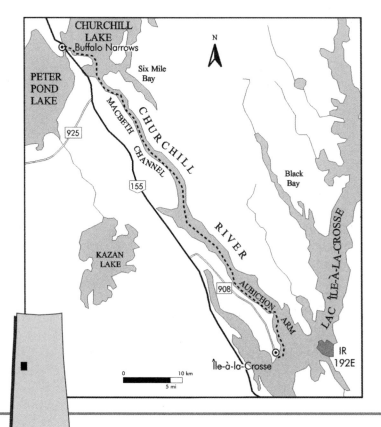

Trip Length:	64 kilometres (40 miles).
Time Required:	2 to 3 days.
Number of Portages:	None.
Maps Required:	
1:250,000 Series:	73N Buffalo Narrows
	73-O Île-à-la-Crosse
1:50,000 Series:	73N/16 Buffalo Narrows
	73N/9 Kazan Lake
	73-O/12 Black Bay
	73-O/5 Lac Île-à-la-Crosse

ABOUT THE TRIP

From Buffalo Narrows, this trip begins with an 8-km (5-mi) paddle along the south shore of Churchill Lake. It then continues in a southeasterly direction down the canal-like MacBeth Channel and Aubichon Arm all the way to Île-à-la-Crosse. Since this route has good wind protection and no rapids or significant current, it will suit canoeists who have only modest paddling skills or who prefer flatwater over whitewater.

As the route is all flatwater, the trip can be done in either direction. Headwinds may be more common in an upstream direction, but given the route's sheltered nature, they are not likely to cause anyone significant problems.

The route is rarely more than 5 km (3 mi) away from Highway 155, which runs on a parallel track off to the southwest. It is thus not what most people would consider remote wilderness. On the other hand, the highway absorbs practically all of the traffic between Buffalo and Île-à-la-Crosse. You can therefore expect to paddle the route in relative solitude.

Camping possibilities are limited. The route is all south of the Shield, so there are no bedrock campsites. The shores are often lined with ice-shoved stones and backed by steep, aspen-clad banks. There are, however, occasional sand beaches and other spots where you may overnight.

STARTING POINT

The starting point for this trip is the village of Buffalo Narrows which is 407 km (253 mi) northwest of Prince Albert via paved Highways 3, 55, and 155. At Buffalo, you can launch your canoe at or near the government dock on Pedersen's Bay, a small bay next to the main downtown area.

Community of Buffalo Narrows

Pre-Contact History

Since the Buffalo Narrows area has seen more archaeological work than much of northern Saskatchewan, it is known that people have been here a long time. Projectile points in the "Angostura" style (8,000-7,500 BP) and some in the "Early Side-notched" style (7,000-5,500 BP) have been found at Buffalo. A single "Oxbow" (5,500-4,500 BP) projectile point has also been found here. And, several "McKean" phase (4,200-3,700 BP) and some "Pelican Lake" phase (3,000-2000 BP) projectile points have been found in the region.[1]

About 2,000 years ago, a culture known as the "Taltheilei" reached into the Buffalo Narrows region from further north. This culture is thought to represent the ancestors of today's Dene. Later, about 1,000 years ago, a pottery-making culture originating on the southern prairies arrived at Buffalo Narrows. This "Narrows" culture featured distinctive pots having a cord-roughened exterior and a single row of puncture marks around the rim. Finally, starting as early as 700 years ago, another pottery-making culture known as the "Selkirk"—belonging to the ancestors of today's Cree—invaded the Churchill basin and continued until European contact. Large Selkirk sites containing thousands of potsherds have been found along the Kisis Channel.[2]

The various projectile points from the different ages—whether they be from spears, atlatl darts, or arrows—make it clear that the first peoples in the Buffalo region were hunters. They would have hunted the wood bison that once roamed the area and would have known that bison came to the Kisis Channel in order to cross from one side of Peter Pond and Churchill lakes to the other. These hunters no doubt frequently stayed here. Perhaps they knew the strait as *mostos wapâsihk*, the present Cree name for Buffalo Narrows, or its equivalent in whatever tongue they spoke.

Fur Trade Posts

Oddly, although Buffalo Narrows must have been a very recognizable waypoint on the old voyageur highway, it did not have trading posts (at least none that we know of) during the early fur trade era. It was not until 1888 that the Hudson's Bay Company finally established an outpost here. That year, its Île-à-la-Crosse post sent Charles Lafleur and another man to Buffalo to counter competition from independent traders. Thereafter, the HBC maintained an outpost at Buffalo which operated—perhaps with some breaks—under the supervision of Île-à-la-Crosse until 1916 and then Buffalo River (Dillon) until 1942. A full post was finally set up in 1942 to capture more of the business generated by the growing commercial fishing industry. This post continued in operation until 1987 when the HBC transferred it to the new North West Company.[3]

Early Residents

The earliest written reference we have seen of any building at Buffalo Narrows comes from the Irish adventurer and military man, William Francis Butler, who passed this way in February 1873, on his way from Red River to the Pacific coast. Arriving here from Île-à-la-Crosse by dog sled, he wrote:

> Rivière Cruise was passed, Lac Clair lay at sundown far stretching to our right into the blue cold north, and when dusk had come, we were halted for the night in a lonely Indian hut which stood on the shores of the Detroit, fully forty miles from our starting-place of the morning.[4]

It is known that a cemetery was established at Buffalo in the 1880s and that Dene families, who later moved to Dillon, lived here around this time.[5] However, as mentioned in the last chapter, Martial and Delia Kiezie, who arrived in 1895, are considered to be the community's first permanent settlers. The Kiezies, along with Martial's brother Pat, were the only residents for a time. However, as commercial fishing and then mink ranching began in the area, more and more people arrived. When a school was established at Buffalo in the early 1930s, people naturally migrated in from outlying areas such as Bulls House so that their children could get an education.[6]

Buffalo's early residents and its later immigrants created a Métis population not to be found elsewhere in northern Saskatchewan. Many of the first immigrants were Île-à-la-Crosse Métis born of the old fur trade. But trapping and commercial fishing prospects also brought in a small army of Scandinavian bachelors. These two groups intermarried with each other, with Dene families already in the area, and with other immigrants from diverse places, such as Quebec, the United States, Scotland, and Armenia.

Commercial Fishing

Much of Buffalo Narrows' early growth stemmed from commercial fishing. As North American fish markets developed in the early 1900s, northern fish became much sought after. In 1916, the McInnes Fish Company of Edmonton established itself at "Headquarters" on the west side of Big Peter Pond Lake. Soon after, in 1918, Tom Pedersen, a former merchant seaman from Odda-Hardanger, Norway, started commercial fishing at Buffalo Narrows. As time would prove, Buffalo's location between Peter Pond and Churchill Lakes made it an ideal centre for fishing operations. For years, the two big lakes combined produced well over a million pounds of fish annually. Nowadays, commercial fishers are permitted to take fewer fish than in the old days, but they still net large quantities of pike, walleye, and whitefish from the two lakes.[7]

In 1943, Waite Fisheries Ltd. of Big River, founded by John Waite, built a fish filleting plant at Buffalo. In

Tom Pedersen, first commercial fisherman at Buffalo Narrows.

the same era, Rizer Fisheries also had a plant, but only the Waite operation has survived. After Waite's first plant burnt down in 1951, second-generation Len Waite built a new plant which employed as many as forty to fifty workers. It continued filleting operations until the 1975-76, when it converted its Buffalo operation to a packing plant. Headed now by fourth-generation John Waite, who took over from his father Richard Waite, the plant currently takes deliveries from forty to fifty fishers and ships their catch to the Freshwater Fish Marketing Corporation in Winnipeg for processing.[8]

Norwegian Ole Jacobsen, born circa 1880, a trapper and mink rancher at Buffalo Narrows.

Mink Ranching

In the mid-1900s, when dress fur was more in fashion than at present, an abundant fishery allowed Buffalo Narrows to become the mink ranching capital of northern Saskatchewan. Mink ranching—where mink, selectively bred to produce particular colours, are raised in pens for the value of their pelt—was an effective way to add value to the local fish catch. In colder weather, a single mink could eat up to 1/3 kg (3/4 lb) of a mix of ground fish and imported cereal each day. This used up a huge amount of fish, including fish plant offal and fish such as suckers (which were cooked to remove toxins) which might have had no other ready market.

The mink ranching era started in 1928 when Norwegian Halvor Ausland began raising mink on the Deep River (MacBeth Channel) from wild mink and stock imported from Quebec and the United States. Others followed his lead, including Tom Pedersen who, in the early 1940s, started the first ranch right in Buffalo. When mink ranching reached its peak in the late 1950s and early 1960s, the Buffalo region had as many as thirty-three ranches having a combined total of 21,000 mink.

Ranch-raised mink prices were highly dependent on the fashion of the day. By the late 1960s, prices fell as fashion designers turned their attention to artificially dyed furs, synthetic furs, and other materials. The result was that by 1970, there were only eight mink ranches left in the Buffalo area. Within another five years, the last ranch had shut down, and a major chapter in Buffalo's history was over.[9]

Aerial photo of Buffalo Narrows as it was in 1950.

Buffalo Narrows Today

With the economic activity generated by fishing and mink ranching, Buffalo Narrows took on a town-like character much sooner than most communities in northern Saskatchewan. By the 1940s, stores, hotels, and cafes were serving the public. In the same decade, Buffalo residents had a local school board (formed in the 1930s), a Ratepayers Association, Red Cross and Hospital Ladies Aid groups (instrumental in the opening of an outpost hospital in 1947), and even a Boy Scouts program.

Religion was important to Buffalo's first residents. Catholic Oblate Father Louis Moraud (later recognized for his work among the English River Dene) is credited with being the community's first clergyman. He is said to have first arrived in 1930 to establish a mission—to be called St. Leon Le Grand—and built the community's first church in 1932. Not long after, in 1939, the Northern Canada Evangelical Mission arrived in Buffalo whereupon two men, Stan Collie and Isaac Reini, built its first church. In 1956, the Presbyterian Church came to Buffalo; its first church, St. Mark's, was built here in 1958. Today, all three of these early churches remain active in the community.[10]

Since early on, Buffalo residents have put an emphasis on communication. The first post office was started in the 1930s and run out of a store kept by Tom Pedersen. Service was at first sporadic, but in the late 1930s, M & C Airways began flying mail in on a monthly basis. Also in the 1930s, a telegraph line was built to connect Buffalo to the south, and in 1939, a single telephone line was strung to link Buffalo with Île-à-la-Crosse. The first local newspaper, a small four-pager, was started by the Northern Canada Evangelical Mission some time after the Mission arrived in 1939. Later, in 1947, the Buffalo Narrows School started a paper called the "The Narrows Narrator," which published at least until 1950. Television arrived in 1974-75, and today there is also a local radio station.

A big event in Buffalo's development was the construction of an all-weather road in 1957. At first, the road required a ferry to take vehicles across the Kisis Channel, but in 1980, a modern bridge was opened to replace the ferry. Also in 1980, a major airport was completed on the large peninsula east of the Kisis Channel.[11]

By 1971, Buffalo had a population of over 1,100.[12] Some people then moved away as mink ranching went into decline. However, the population again grew as Buffalo benefitted from government initiatives started by the Department of Northern Saskatchewan (formed in 1972). Government jobs were to become important to the local economy and continue so to this day. Many jobs now come from Buffalo's role as a forest fire suppression centre. The local Correctional Centre, built in the 1980s, also provides jobs. At the same time, traditional industries like commercial fishing and forestry remain important to the community.

Nowadays, with the municipal status of "Northern Village," Buffalo Narrows has a population of about 1,250.

Services

Buffalo Narrows offers canoeists a wide range of services. These include an airstrip, two air charter companies (Courtesy Air and Voyage Air), Northwestern Helicopters, Northern store, Petit's Lumber & Hardware, a post office, North West Credit Union (opened in 1991, this is the only credit union or bank on the guide route), churches, public health clinic (staffed by four nurses; an Île-à-la-Crosse doctor is in four times a week), pharmacy, gas stations, laundromat, Rosie's Dining & Lounge, fast food outlets, taxis, Kingfisher Bay Motel, Liquor Board Store, Buffalo Narrows Hotel (with bar), a six-member RCMP detachment, and a Saskatchewan Environment office that sells local topographical maps.

Map 5.1   Community of Buffalo Narrows

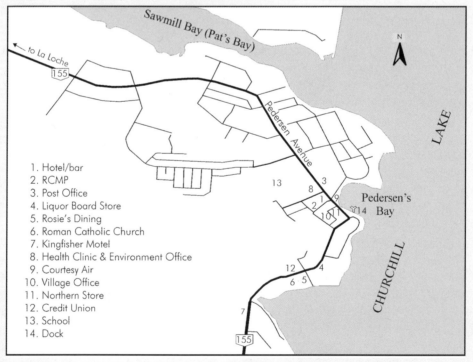

1. Hotel/bar
2. RCMP
3. Post Office
4. Liquor Board Store
5. Rosie's Dining
6. Roman Catholic Church
7. Kingfisher Motel
8. Health Clinic & Environment Office
9. Courtesy Air
10. Village Office
11. Northern Store
12. Credit Union
13. School
14. Dock

Buffalo Narrows to Île-à-la-Crosse

Churchill Lake

Measuring 40 km (25 mi) from north to south and occupying 559 sq km (216 sq mi), Churchill Lake is (after Peter Pond Lake at 777 sq km) the second biggest lake on the entire route.[13] As maps show, much of the lake is wide open with little wind protection. Fortunately, however, the old voyageur highway only cuts across the southwest corner of the lake. This short, 8-km (5-mi) passage does not require a major traverse.

When Philip Turnor and his party first saw Churchill Lake on May 30, 1791, Turnor referred to it as "a lake called by the Southern Indians Wash-a-cum-mow Sack-a-ha-gan or Clear water Lake and by the Chepawyans Eg-ga-zah Too-ah or Egg Lake."[14] The early fur traders chose to adopt the Cree name: Alexander Mackenzie referred to it as "Lake Clear," while George Simpson called it "Lac Clear."[15] Since the 1930s (or earlier), the lake has been officially known as Churchill Lake, but this new name has not gained general acceptance. Today, people of Buffalo Narrows still commonly call the lake Clear Lake, while Dene in the area keep to their original Egg Lake.

The early voyageurs, with their keen sense of geography, suspected that Churchill Lake's long sweep northward might lead them to a detour around the back-breaking Methy Portage. They were correct in their suspicions, but the detour they found proved impractical. As George Simpson wrote in 1820:

> Along the N.E. of Lac Clear I understand there is a communication to Athabasca, which avoids Portage Laloche, it was explored by the X.Y. Compy. but found very circuitous.[16]

We have not seen any record of a fur trade post on Churchill Lake during the early fur trade.[17] However, in the early 1900s, Churchill Lake saw a flurry of trading activity at its north end where a narrows leads to present-day Frobisher Lake (formerly "Island Lake"). Here, on the east side of the narrows at Indian Reserve 193A, there was a small community known as "Clear Lake," complete with its own Roman Catholic mission. In 1921, according to an HBC Archives map plan, the Clear Lake community had no less than three trading establishments operating—the Lamson and Hubbard Company, Revillon Frères, and the Hudson's Bay Company!

The Lamson and Hubbard Company must not have survived long after 1921 since the HBC bought up that company in 1923-24. Similarly, HBC records indicate that in 1932, the HBC abandoned its own buildings and moved into those of Revillon Frères, suggesting Revillon had by then closed. In the early 1930s, the HBC operation at Clear Lake had the status of a full post with outposts of its own at Buffalo River and Island Lake. But it was later downgraded to an outpost of the Buffalo Narrows post and then finally shut down altogether in the 1960s. At some date, possibly when the HBC outpost closed, the Clear Lake community was also abandoned.[18]

Birch Narrows Dene Nation

Churchill Lake is part of the traditional territory of the Birch Narrows Dene Nation which presently has its home base and administrative centre at Turnor Lake, about 45 km (28 mi) by air due east of La Loche. As mentioned earlier, this Dene group first entered treaty as part of the Clear Lake Band at Île-à-la-Crosse on August 28, 1906, when their leader, Chief Raphael Bedshidekkge (Campbell) signed Treaty No. 10. In 1933, the Clear Lake Band became known as the Peter Pond Lake Band. In 1972, the Peter Pond Lake Band separated into the Buffalo River Dene Nation and the Birch Narrows First Nation. The latter First Nation now has just over 500 members, most of whom reside at Turnor Lake, and is headed by Chief Robert Sylvestre.

Southwest to MacBeth Channel

Paddling out from Buffalo Narrows, you will first go eastward for about 3 km (2 mi), passing between McKay Island to the north and the Buffalo Narrows Airport peninsula to the south. You will then turn southeast along the shore of the airport peninsula to move towards the head of the MacBeth Channel. The navigation here is straightforward, but you must take care not to accidentally enter Six Mile Bay which runs just east of and parallel to the MacBeth Channel. Since Six Mile Bay looks a lot like the proper channel, you could go a long way down it before noticing any mistake.

The shores east and southeast from Buffalo are generally stony, so camping possibilities are limited. However, about 1.5 km (1 mi) southeast from the north tip of the airport peninsula, you will find a small sand beach on an inside corner where the shore jogs 90 degrees to the northeast (73N 625913). You can camp here if you do not mind its proximity to the airport.

From the corner campsite, it is just over 3 km (2 mi) to the head of the MacBeth Channel. Immediately west from the entrance to the channel, there is another sand beach that offers very good camping (73N 637886).

Starting at the extreme south end of Churchill Lake, the MacBeth Channel runs 25 km (16 mi) southeast to connect Churchill Lake with Lac Île-à-la-Crosse. The channel is a quiet, canal-like waterway with a width that varies between 350 m (380 yd) and 1 km (2/3 mi). It has no current to speak of, which suggests that it has considerable depth. Indeed, to the early fur traders, the channel, in conjunction with the Aubichon Arm downstream, was known as the "Rivière Creuse" or "Deep River." The Deep River name remains in common usage to this day, though it now applies only to the MacBeth Channel and not the Aubichon Arm.[19]

Topo maps show the MacBeth Channel as the start of the Churchill River which, from Churchill Lake at its head, flows 1,500 km (900 mi) to Hudson Bay. The river is named after Lord John Churchill (1650–1722), a brilliant British military commander (and ancestor to Sir Winston Churchill), who served as the HBC's third governor from 1685 to 1692.

The MacBeth Channel does not figure largely in the journals of the early traders. For the voyageurs, the distance northwest from Île-à-la-Crosse was a leg of easy paddling hardly amounting to a full day's work. One record of a voyageur passage through the channel can be found in the journal of Archibald McDonald who accompanied HBC Governor George Simpson on a canoe trip to the Pacific in 1828. After leaving Île-à-la-Crosse on August 5, 1828, McDonald wrote:

> Got under weigh at half-past three a.m. with unusual glee in the three canoes. Just as we were putting ashore for breakfast, Cadotte cast up with his three boats from the Portage [Methy] with 157 packs and 3 kegs Castorum, the returns of the McKenzie's River District for outfit 1827. ... Dined at the narrows of Lac du Boeuf at three. Head wind all day.[20]

In a single day, Simpson's voyageurs had paddled the length of our chapter route despite being slowed by a head wind and Simpson's discussions of company business with the Cadotte brigade. And they still had much of their work-day ahead of them!

As you go down the MacBeth Channel, you will note that the shores have stony edges and banks that rise quite steeply back from the water. The banks, treed mainly with aspen, are generally 2 to 5 m (6 to 16 ft) high, but they occasionally rise to 10 m (over 30 ft). Camping possibilities are therefore limited. However, about 4 km (2½ mi) down the channel, you can watch for a campsite on channel right where the channel makes a slight jog north. Here, there is a small sand beach about 20 m (22 yd) wide which offers a good place to stay (73N 669860). Just under 2 km (1¼ mi) further on, still on channel right, there is a grassy clearing (with old cellar depressions) which would provide good camping for larger groups (73N 684854).

Downstream from the cellar depression clearing, the stony shores and steep banks—still mainly wooded with aspen—continue to discourage camping. But within 12 km (7½ mi), you can watch for a sandy beach on channel left that would make a good campsite (73N 756772). And 750 m (½ mi) further on, another small beach on the same shore offers a second camping option (73N 762767).

Halvor Ausland Mink Ranch

About 600 m (¹/₃ mi) down from the second sandy beach, you will come to a large clearing on the channel left shore. This was once the mink ranch of Halvor Ausland, born in Evge, Norway, in 1902. In 1928, he became the first mink rancher in the Buffalo Narrows area. When we stopped here in 1986, the ranch was long-abandoned, but there was still much to see. We found a wharf made out of giant logs lashed together with steel cable, a main residence made of squared logs covered with siding (which burned down in about 1989), a second residence, a feed house, a pumphouse, a concrete base for a power plant, and hundreds and hundreds of mink cages in open-sided sheds.

When we visited with Vital Morin of Île-à-la-Crosse in 1986, he told us that before World War II, Ausland's was also a stopping place for the teamsters who hauled freight north to Buffalo Narrows each winter and then brought fish back south. Horses would be fed and kept overnight in stables here on the two-day trip between Île-à-la-Crosse and Buffalo. This continued until about 1940 when cat swings, and later trucks, put an end to horse freighting.

Halvor Ausland is credited with kick-starting Buffalo's mink ranching industry. Not only did he start the first ranch, but with an interest in genetics, he developed a breeding program to improve the value of ranch-raised pelts. His program originated a "palomino" strain of mink having a light brown or orange colour. He assisted new ranchers by selling them breeding "trios" consisting of a male and two females and also gave out advice when asked. He sold his

ranch to George Williams in 1961 before mink prices dropped and then eventually moved to White Rock, B.C. After he died, his ashes were returned to the Deep River and spread here at his old ranch.[21]

Old house (as seen in 1986) on the Deep River where Halvor Ausland started the area's first mink ranch in 1928.

*Abandoned
mink cages at
the old
Ausland site
on the Deep
River.*

Aubichon Arm

Eight km (5 mi) downstream from the Ausland ranch, the MacBeth Channel widens considerably as it continues southeast. The wider channel, officially named the Aubichon Arm, has much the same character as MacBeth Channel but is considered to be part of Lac Île-à-la-Crosse.

Just as the channel begins to widen, there is a small sandy point on the channel left shore. This point would make a suitable lunch spot or even campsite.

About 500 m (1/3 mi) down from the sandy point, both Maps 73N and 73N/9 show a building legend in a small bay on the left shore. This was once the home of Joe and Mary Walzer, originally from Melfort, Saskatchewan, who came here in the 1930s to fish and trap. Like Halvor Ausland, they also ran a stopping place for teamsters. Later, they went into mink ranching, but in the early 1950s, they sold their operation to Carl Sernes and his son Ray. The Sernes family, who were of Norwegian descent, raised mink through the 1950s and then, after losing many mink to a distemper-like disease, sold their operation to Kelly Shatilla of Buffalo Narrows. Later, in 1962, the Department of Natural Resources had a sawmill here, and old slabs left from this operation are still visible. Nowadays, with the site abandoned and a grassy clearing left behind, you may choose to camp here.[22]

Three km (2 mi) southwest from the Sernes's mink ranch, both Maps 73N and 73N/9 show an inlet named Watchusk Bay (*wacask* is "muskrat" in Cree) with a building legend on the south side of the entrance. The maps' building legend marks where John Thompson of Big River, a man of Icelandic descent, came in 1956 to set up a mink ranch. In 1958, John was joined by his son Fred and later by his son Jack, and at one time, the family had as many as 8,000 mink. Fred left the mink ranch in 1973 to work for the Northern Municipal Council and then to sit as an NDP Member of the Legislature from 1975 to 1995. Jack continued mink ranching until 1978, but then he too quit when the collapsed market for ranch-raised mink showed no signs of recovery.

Jack Thompson remained at Watchusk Bay, and in 1980, he started an outfitting camp here called Silver Pine Resort. When we stopped in 1986, we met with Ron Thompson, one of Jack's younger brothers who was working at the camp for the summer, and learned that Silver Pine had a total of ten cabins. Jack has since sold the camp to outfitters from Alberta, but he continues to reside at Watchusk Bay.

Down from the Thompsons' old place, the Aubichon Arm has little to offer in the way of camping for several kilometres. On June 17, 1986, having paddled into the black of night, we made a poor camp in the rocks and brush of the channel right shore, near to the right edge of Map 73N/9. Had we gone just over a kilometre further, we may have made out a sandy beach (just past a small, claw-shaped point) on the same shore where camping would have been much better (73-O 114575). When we stopped at this beach the next day, a brown mink with a white blaze on its chest swam up and came ashore long enough to look us over. We wondered if the mink might be descended from the ranch mink who sometimes escaped from their cages to join their wild cousins.

Seven km (4½ mi) downstream from the beach where we saw the mink, there is another beach—a narrow band of sand and gravel—on the north side of a square-cornered point jutting from the channel right shore (73-O 164525). And 750 m (½ mi) further east and south, there is a better sand beach that would make a good campsite (73-O 165521). Finally, just over 1 km (²/₃ mi) further south, there is yet a third sandy beach, albeit a rather low and willowy one (73-O 170580).

McKay Point (Hoffman's Point)

If you stay on the channel right shore as you approach Île-à-la-Crosse, you will finally come to the peninsula that marks the southwest side of the Aubichon Arm's entrance into greater Lac Île-à-la-Crosse. In early times, this peninsula was known as "La Pointe des Gens de Terre."[23] The name "Gens de Terre" perhaps refers to Indians, i.e., "people of the land." If so, the name may originate from early Cree and Dene staying here when they came to Île-à-la-Crosse to trade.

Clearly, the peninsula was itself the home of at least one of Île-à-la-Crosse's early fur trade posts. The late Dr. P.E. Lavoie, Medical Superintendent for Île-à-la-Crosse, who was keenly interested in local archaeology and history, wrote in a report dated December 2, 1935, to historian Arthur S. Morton: "Last summer on the pointe 'Gens de Terre' ... I have dug in an old cellar that every one knows to be on the site of an old post of the Hudson's Bay Post." Examining the cellar of what had been a "20 ft. x 30 ft.," two-chimneyed building, Dr. Lavoie had found five unused copper kettles, ten tin plates, old axes, and other articles suggestive of a post. His report to Morton also mentioned that he understood there to be the remains of a different HBC post just north of the one he excavated. Dr. Lavoie theorized as to the precise identities of these posts, but as we will suggest in the next chapter, more work needs to be done before definite names can be put to post sites in the Île-à-la-Crosse area.[24]

The peninsula has a small Protestant cemetery. A few of the tombstones from the 1930s bear Scandinavian names—likely those of white trappers who came north in the early 1900s. There are more recent graves as well.

Nowadays, the Gens de Terre peninsula is locally known as "McKay Point" after Annie McKay—said to have been a most attractive woman—who made her home here for many years in the early to mid-1900s. In her old age, Annie McKay sold her land on the point to Dr. Meinrad Hoffman who, with his wife, was to live here for many years. The peninsula is thus now often called "Hoffman's Point."

Dr. Hoffman was born in the German town of Frankenstein (now part of Poland) before World War I. He eventually emigrated to Canada and, as a doctor, made his way to Île-à-la-Crosse in 1954 where he took up the medical practice left vacant by the retirement of Dr. Lavoie in 1953. (A Dr. Honig managed the practice in 1953-54.) For the next 20 years, Dr. Hoffman was to be the only doctor serving Île-à-la-Crosse and the surrounding communities.

The challenges that solo practitioners such as Dr. Lavoie and Dr. Hoffman must have faced can hardly be overstated. Dr. Hoffman, now in his 80s but still working out of Calgary, is modest about his work but admits that the long hours and isolation at Île-à-la-Crosse were challenging. With no other doctor available for a second opinion, he handled everything from head colds to surgeries. For surgeries, his anaesthetist was a very capable Grey Nun nurse who would administer ether to the patient. Dr. Hoffman says that ether is the safest anaesthetic in primitive operating conditions, but its smell tends to panic some patients. To overcome this difficulty, his anaesthetist would first feed *eau de cologne* into the ether mask to get a patient relaxed and breathing properly.

Dr. Hoffman's practice was rather broad by today's standards. Ron Clancy, a fur trader at Pinehouse in the late 1950s, can recall Dr. Hoffman flying into Pinehouse to run an emergency dental clinic. A chair was set up in Clancy's office, and people who had been too long in pain quickly formed a line that extended right out of the trading store. Dr. Hoffman first went down the queue to administer Novocaine and then, after borrowing a galvanized pail from the trade store for use as a spittoon, went to work "yarding" teeth out. By the end of the day, the teeth and blood in the pail were enough to make a tooth fairy cringe, but Dr. Hoffman's patients could finally claim relief from the agonies of toothache.

Despite a busy practice, Dr. Hoffman found time for other things at Île-à-la-Crosse including the collection and study of traditional native medicines. He was also interested in agriculture and, after the Catholic mission sold its cattle, he kept a bull at McKay Point that local Métis with cattle could use for breeding. He was also involved in civic affairs and spent ten years as mayor or overseer of the village. Somehow, he also found time, in 1967-68, to have a large house, placed with a fine view of the village, built for himself and his wife on McKay Point.

In 1974, by which time his wife had died, Dr. Hoffman left Île-à-la-Crosse to live in Germany for a time and later, from 1979 onward, to practise medicine at St. Martin's Hospital in La Loche (1979-1983) and then at Calgary. His house was therefore vacant and boarded up when we arrived here in 1986. We camped on the shore near his house, hoping he would not mind our stopping.

Dr. Hoffman's house and land has since been purchased by Ken Cornett and Carol Miller of Île-à-la-Crosse. They now operate the property as a "bed and breakfast" under the name Rainbow Ridge Outfitters. Besides bed and breakfast, they offer unserviced campsites and a canoe outfitting service which has become popular with canoeists from Europe.

To Île-à-la-Crosse

From the tip of McKay Point, it is just over 1 km (²/₃ mi) southwest to the older part of the Île-à-la-Crosse community, where the village's main services will be found. To reach this area, you can steer towards either a public boat ramp which leads up to the local Northern store or to a public dock situated about 300 m (330 yd) southward.

-6-

ÎLE-À-LA-CROSSE TO PATUANAK

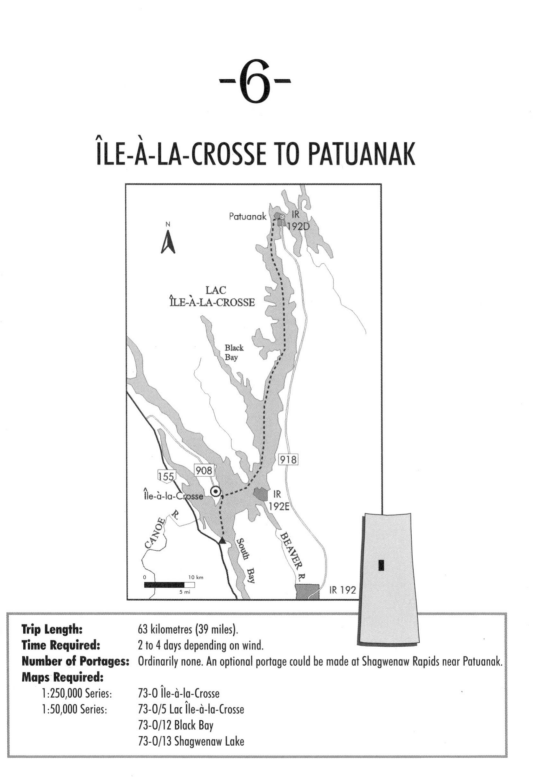

Trip Length: 63 kilometres (39 miles).

Time Required: 2 to 4 days depending on wind.

Number of Portages: Ordinarily none. An optional portage could be made at Shagwenaw Rapids near Patuanak.

Maps Required:

    1:250,000 Series: 73-O Île-à-la-Crosse

    1:50,000 Series: 73-O/5 Lac Île-à-la-Crosse

                               73-O/12 Black Bay

                               73-O/13 Shagwenaw Lake

About the Trip

This is a big lake trip which follows a track almost due north on Lac Île-à-la-Crosse from the Île-à-la-Crosse starting point to the extreme north end of the lake. In most places, the lake is only 3 to 4 km (2 to 2½ mi) wide with shorelines near at hand. Accordingly, in fair weather, you can proceed with only modest canoeing skills. But the wind quite often funnels down the length of the lake to create dangerous conditions. At such times, you will need enough good sense to put ashore and wait for better weather. In 1986, we were windbound near Île-à-la-Crosse for three days.

Since this is a lake trip, "upstream travel" is not a problem. Indeed, upstream travellers can expect some advantage from having the prevailing winds at their backs.

Île-à-la-Crosse village, with its fur trade history, is a highlight of this trip. First established as a post by Montreal fur traders in 1776, it went on to become the command centre of the Hudson's Bay Company's English River District and a major pemmican supply depot on the old voyageur highway. Today, its Métis population represents the fusion of fur trade cultures. The village is also Saskatchewan's second oldest community (only Cumberland House is older).

Lac Île-à-la-Crosse lies south of the Shield in a low relief country treed mainly with aspen interspersed with a few spruce. Most often, the shorelines have narrow, stony beaches backed by wooded banks. Camping opportunities are therefore limited, but sandy beaches offer some possibilities.

The lake has a rich fishery which favours several species of fish-eating birds. Birdwatchers can expect to see many pelicans, gulls, terns, and cormorants.

Starting Point

There are two possible starting points for this trip. The first option is to set out from the village of Île-à-la-Crosse, which is 384 km (239 mi) northwest of Prince Albert via paved Highways 3, 55, and 155, and paved Road 908. When you reach the village of Île-à-la-Crosse, you will first pass through a northern section of the community which, despite its level geography, is known locally as "Snob Hill." If you continue southward, the main road will take you about 500 m (⅓ mi) across a marsh to an older part of the community. Once over the marsh, you can take the first turn left (just before the provincial government building) to follow a road along the lakeshore. This road will bring you first to a pier where there is a boat ramp and then, about 300 m (330 yd) further on, to a public dock. Either the boat ramp or the dock could serve for launching canoes.

The second option is to start this trip from a provincial campground situated on Lac Île-à-la-Crosse's South Bay (73-O 195376). The campground can be reached by turning east off Highway 155 about 32 km (20 mi) north of the "Beauval Forks" onto a marked gravel access road and proceeding 1.5 km (1 mi) to the lake. Here, possibly after an overnight stay, canoes can be launched from a broad sandy beach. Leaving from South Bay will require you to paddle north an extra 9 or 10 km (5½ or 6 mi) to reach Île-à-la-Crosse, but it will cut down on the length of your vehicle shuttle.

Community of Île-à-la-Crosse

The Name

The community of Île-à-la-Crosse, like the lake surrounding it, takes its French name from nearby Big Island where, at the time the first traders arrived, natives played the game of lacrosse. The Canadian voyageurs called the game la crosse because the stick used by the players reminded them of a Catholic bishop's staff or *crosse*. John Richardson, on Franklin's expedition of 1819-22, described the Cree manner of playing lacrosse:

> An extensive meadow is chosen for this sport, and the articles staked are tied to a post, or deposited in the custody of two old men. The combatants being stript and painted, and each provided with a kind of battledore or racket, in shape resembling the letter P, with a handle about two feet long, and a head loosely wrought with net-work, so as to form a shallow bag, range themselves on different sides. A ball being now tossed up in the middle, each party endeavours to drive it to their respective goals, and much dexterity and agility is displayed in the contest. When a nimble runner gets the ball in his cross, he sets off towards the goal with the utmost speed, and is followed by the rest, who endeavour to jostle him and shake it out; but, if hard pressed, he discharges it with a jerk, to be forwarded by his own party, or bandied back by their opponents, until the victory is decided by its passing the goal.[1]

Though the Île-à-la-Crosse name has long had common usage, the community is still also known as "Sakitawak." In Cree, *sâkitawâhk* means "the river mouth." In the case of Île-à-la-Crosse, it is taken to mean the place where rivers meet—the Canoe River, the Deep River, and the Beaver River join here to flow north into the Churchill. To the Dene, who visit Île-à-la-Crosse on a regular basis, Île-à-la-Crosse is known as *Kwoe^n*, simply meaning "a village" or "a place where people stay."

Map 6.1   Île-à-la-Crosse area

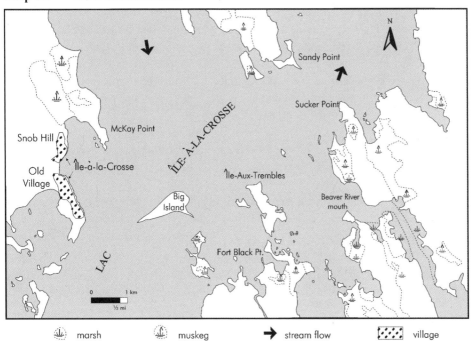

Fur Trade History

At first glance, Île-à-la-Crosse does not look like an ideal location for a fur trading post. It is on a low-lying spit of land which, excepting some high ground at the south tip, seems hardly high enough to withstand flooding. Moreover, most of the land lying north from the spit is a muskeg devoid of trees large enough for firewood. Nonetheless, from a fur trade perspective, Île-à-la-Crosse was well located. Referring to its environs, Alexander Mackenzie wrote:

> The situation of this lake, the abundance of the finest fish in the world to be found in its waters, the richness of its surrounding banks and forests, in moose and fallow deer, with the vast numbers of the smaller tribes of animals, whose skins are precious, and the numerous flocks of wild fowl that frequent it in the spring and fall, make it a most desirable spot for the constant residence of some, and the occasional rendezvous of others of the inhabitants of the country, particularly of the Knisteneaux [Cree].[2]

Île-à-la-Crosse had the advantage of being at the hub of major summer and winter travel routes. The Deep River, which led to the rich North-West, was particularly important. However, the Beaver River was also important since it allowed a way to bring pemmican—the fuel of the fur trade—from the buffalo plains to the voyageur highway. Brigades that had last resupplied at Cumberland House could take on enough pemmican at Île-à-la-Crosse to reach Fort Chipewyan or, in the case of the Portage la Loche brigade, to go to Methy Portage and back.

The first post at Île-à-la-Crosse was established in 1776 by Thomas Frobisher and the veteran woodsman Louis Primeau. Earlier that summer, Thomas Frobisher, his older brother Joseph, and fellow Montrealer Alexander Henry had been lower down on the Churchill where they had intercepted Dene trappers from the Athabasca country as those trappers brought their 1775–76 catch out to trade. The Frobishers and Henry had succeeded in trading for all the Dene fur they wanted. However, not wanting to lose this bonanza to competitors, the Frobisher concern decided a house near the Dene would be a good way to keep their future trade.

While Joseph Frobisher and Alexander Henry left to transport their fur to Montreal, Thomas Frobisher and Louis Primeau stayed behind to get ready for the coming season. Originally, the plan was for Frobisher and Primeau to go all the way to Lake Athabasca to build a new post. However, as we know from a map of Peter Pond, the post was actually built on the peninsula where Île-à-la-Crosse stands today. Though situated short of the original goal, the Île-à-la-Crosse post was still deeper into the North-West than any previous trading establishment. Once completed, it was operated through the winter of 1776–77 by Primeau, while his employer Thomas Frobisher was otherwise busy on the Saskatchewan River.[3]

The precise location of the 1776 post is not known. However, the late Dr. P.E. Lavoie, historian and medical superintendent for Île-à-la-Crosse, felt that the post was most probably located at the south end of the Île-à-la-Crosse peninsula in the vicinity of the present-day Catholic church or south of it in the small bay adjacent to the Catholic cemetery.[4]

Written records are scarce, but it is thought that after the 1776–77 season, the Frobisher-Primeau post site saw more or less continuous occupation by Montreal traders.[5] Though Louis Primeau had spent time at Montreal in 1777–78 (a rare trip to the city), the fall of 1778 found him heading back into the North-West to winter with Venant St. Germain at Île-à-la-Crosse on behalf of the Frobishers.[6] Four years later, in 1782–83, Peter Pond was at Île-à-la-Crosse where he could escape some of the controversy of the previous season (in March, 1782, he had been involved in the death of trader Etienne Wadin on Lac la Ronge).[7] And, from 1784 to 1791, Patrick Small (father to Charlotte Small, wife of explorer David Thompson) traded here on behalf of what was now the North West Company with approximately thirty men under his command.[8]

While Patrick Small was at Île-à-la-Crosse, he faced two years of competition from no less a figure than Alexander Mackenzie, then a partner in the small Montreal firm of Gregory, McLeod & Company. Arriving in 1785, Mackenzie had set himself up in Île-à-la-Crosse, while a partner, John Ross, went into the Athabasca to compete with Peter Pond trading for the North West Company. Mackenzie competed with Small at Île-à-la-Crosse through the winters of 1785–86 and 1786–87. However, early in 1787, there was an incident in the Athabasca where one of Peter Pond's men, one Péché, shot and killed John Ross in a dispute over who should have the right to trade with some Dene hunters. When this news got to Grand Portage, the NWC and Gregory, McLeod & Company quickly agreed to merge under the NWC name to avoid any further calamity. Alexander Mackenzie, now with the NWC, was transferred to serve as Peter Pond's assistant in Athabasca, while Île-à-la-Crosse remained under Patrick Small.[9]

The Hudson's Bay Company did not have a presence at Île-à-la-Crosse until the arrival of Philip Turnor and his party on October 7, 1790. Turnor recorded the event in his journal:

> came to Mr Smalls House about 1 PM. where we were very kindly received by Mr Small who offered us two Houses in his yard as we intend staying here this Winter and having no intention to trade any thing but Provisions and three of our men unfit for any kind of duty Viz Hugh Lisk not able to walk from a violent swelling in the knee which seems full of matter Peter Brown very bad with a terrible cut in his foot and Robt Garroch with a violent bruised heel and as we can never be in a worse condition to build a place we thought it best to accept the offer...[10]

It is quite possible that the "two Houses" offered to Turnor were older cabins dating back to the early Montrealers, perhaps even to the initial Frobisher-Primeau occupation. Whatever the case, the houses were only temporary accommodation since Turnor and his companions renewed their journey to the Athabasca on May 23, 1791.[11]

It is interesting that the sketch map Peter Fidler made of Île-à-la-Crosse (below) while he was with Philip Turnor shows two separate post locations—a house with a flag in what is now the southern part of Île-à-la-Crosse and another house in present-day Snob Hill (73-O 168482). It is likely that the house with the flag represents Patrick Small's NWC post. But what of the more northerly house Fidler marked? Assuming Small's post was on the same ground occupied by Frobisher and Primeau and then Pond, it is quite possible that the northerly house was where Alexander Mackenzie traded for Gregory, McLeod & Company in the 1785–86 and 1786–87 seasons. Mackenzie might therefore have been the first European to reside at Snob Hill.

HBCA E.3/1 fo. 55 lower (N14797)

Peter Fidler's sketch showing Aubichon Arm
and two trading posts at Île-à-la-Crosse.

The Hudson's Bay Company did not make a concerted effort to establish itself at Île-à-la-Crosse until 1799, and when it did, North West Company pressure tactics made it very difficult for the HBC to gain a toehold. In 1799, the HBC sent William Linklater with six men to Île-à-la-Crosse where they built a post a short distance from the NWC post. However, by Christmas, the NWC's strong grip on the local trade had caused Linklater and his men to abandon their new post and join fellow HBC traders stationed at Green Lake. While Linklater later returned to Île-à-la-Crosse, the NWC continued to hamper the HBC's efforts to trade. The HBC finally gave up and withdrew completely from Île-à-la-Crosse in the spring of 1806.[12]

Records are scant, but it seems that in 1809, the Hudson's Bay Company may have sent Peter Fidler to Île-à-la-Crosse to re-establish a post there. Fidler and his men were certainly at Île-à-la-Crosse for the winter of 1810–11. By this time, competition between the HBC and the North West Company was growing fierce. John Duncan Campbell, in charge of the NWC's Île-à-la-Crosse post (located less than 150 m or 165 yd to the south of Fidler's) and his men, most notably the rough young Scotsman, Samuel Black, did everything they could to make life miserable for the HBC men. The HBC had its property destroyed and stolen, and Black would often settle discussions with his fists.[13] Although Fidler and Campbell were quite civil to each other on a personal level, even dining together on occasion, this had no effect on the NWC's campaign of intimidation.[14] Finally, on June 4, 1811, after a last night of non-stop NWC harassment, Fidler and his men quit their Île-à-la-Crosse post. Fidler wrote:

> At 8 AM we all Embarked for Churchill Factory in 3 Boats & 16 men—before we went away swept out all our Houses very clean, extinguished the fires, shut the Doors & Windows all in & closed both Gates into the Yard & barred them ... As we took up our nets after we left the House & about 3/4 mile from it & in sight—numbers of Canadians Climbed over our Stockades—then the French officers followed with many Indians thro' the Gate that the Canadians had unbarred who went over the Stockade first—when we had travelled about 4 Hours we saw a large smoke ascending exactly in the Direction of our House—& we suppose that it is the Canadians who have set it on Fire...[15]

So much for sweeping the floors.

Île-à-la-Crosse's role as a fur trade hub prevented the Hudson's Bay Company from ignoring it for long. In the fall of 1814, it sent Joseph Howse to again establish a post at Île-à-la-Crosse. Howse still found NWC competition strong, and tension was high—so high that in February 1815, both Howse's accountant, James Johnston, and an NWC labourer were killed in a shooting incident in which Samuel Black had some involvement.[16] But Howse was able to gain a foothold at Île-à-la-Crosse, and his work was carried forward by three men: Robert Logan, who built a replacement post in the fall of 1815 and managed it in 1815–1816; John McLeod, who stayed in 1816–1817; and then the colourful John Clarke (a former NWC man), who arrived in 1819. Clarke was ambitious and built another replacement post in 1820, which became known as Fort Superior.[17] He was also inclined to meet the NWC on its own terms as is evidenced by George Simpson's remarks recorded on April 20, 1821:

> I regret to learn that disturbances of a serious nature are breaking out at Isle ala Crosse, and I cannot help thinking that they in a great measure arise from Mr. Clarkes own folly; instead of opposing the enemy by judicious, cool, and determined measures, he encourages broils & squabbles between the Officers & men, and for his amusement sends a parcel of Bullies which have no other effect than giving our Opponents a pretext for renewing their former aggressions in other parts of the Country where we are less able to contend with them:— The N.W. Co. are not to be put down by Prize fighting, but by persevering industry, Economy in the business arrangements, and a firm maintenance of our rights...[18]

But whether Simpson approved of Clarke's approach or not, Clarke was able to see the HBC's Île-à-la-Crosse post successfully through the final days of the competition between the HBC and the NWC which at last ended with the merger of the two companies in 1821.

Unfortunately, from the information we have seen, we are unable to give precise locations for the various pre-1821 posts in the Île-à-la-Crosse area. At best, we can provide a list (which may not be complete) of posts that appear to have existed (see Table 6.1).

Table 6.1   Pre-1821 Fur Trade Posts in the Île-à-la-Crosse Area

DATE	TRADER	FIRM
1776	Louis Primeau	Frobishers
1784	Patrick Small	NWC
1785	Alexander Mackenzie	Gregory, McLeod
1790	Philip Turnor	HBC
1798	Alexander McKay	NWC[19]
1799	William Linklater	HBC
1802 (?)	Samuel Black (Fort Black)	XY Company
1809 (?)	Peter Fidler	HBC
1814	Joseph Howse	HBC
1815	Robert Logan	HBC
1820	John Clarke (Fort Superior)	HBC

From 1821 onward, indeed from 1814, the HBC operated continuously at Île-à-la-Crosse until it sold off its Northern Stores to the new North West Company in 1987. For much of this period, the Île-à-la-Crosse post was pivotal to the HBC's trade—particularly as a pemmican depot delivering pemmican brought from the south via the Beaver River to the passing fur brigades and as an administrative centre. From 1822 to 1824, it was headquarters for the HBC's "Île-à-la-Crosse District" and from 1824 to 1895, for its "English River District."[20]

The HBC sometimes had to deal with competitors at Île-à-la-Crosse, especially during the early 1900s when the French company Revillon Frères and smaller enterprises enthusiastically entered the fur trade. Revillon operated a post at Île-à-la-Crosse as part of its

NA / PA 18067

Hudson's Bay Company dwelling house at Île-à-la-Crosse in 1919.

Prince Albert district. The Lamson and Hubbard trading company was also here for a time, albeit with limited success. Harold Kemp (who would later be a Revillon man at Stanley Mission) took his wife and two young sons to Île-à-la-Crosse in 1920 to trade for Lamson and Hubbard. But as the candid Kemp put it, "The Ile à la Crosse interlude was an authentic flop. I shall always associate it with a half-empty store, a fight to retain the few customers we had, and a sense of utter frustration." Eventually, the HBC would, in 1923–24, absorb all Lamson and Hubbard operations and, in 1936, take over Revillon Frères' fur trade operations in Canada. In keeping with the company's "Here Before Christ" image, the HBC at Île-à-la-Crosse managed to survive all comers.[21]

In the post-1821 era, seemingly in 1843, the HBC moved its operations to what is now the Snob Hill area of Île-à-la-Crosse (73-O 481168) and remained there until 1950, when it moved its store near where the present "Northern" store is situated.[22] In 1972, a new store was built on the current Northern store location. This new store burned down in 1985 and was rebuilt on the same site in 1986. The rebuilt store was transferred to the new North West Company in 1987 and now continues under that company's "Northern" trade name.

The Métis

The fur trade has had a tremendous impact on the people of Île-à-la-Crosse. Indeed, it has shaped their very identity. Because it was a fur trade hub, Île-à-la-Crosse saw many European and Euro-Canadian traders and voyageurs stay long enough to marry local women and raise families. The traders were mainly English or Scottish, while their voyageurs were most often either Orkneymen or French Canadians. The women were mainly Cree but some were Dene. The marriages—whether solemnized by fur factor, priest, or *à la façon du pays*—ordinarily produced children, and these children in time became a vibrant community of Métis.

Marriages of French Canadian voyageurs to Cree women were the most numerous and, as a result, the local Métis culture has strong French and Cree roots. This is most apparent in the language spoken. It is a distinct form of *y* dialect Cree sometimes known as "Cree Michif." In Michif, the basic language structure is Cree, but a great many words, especially nouns, are French in origin.

Many notable Métis have had connections to Île-à-la-Crosse. Charlotte Small, born at Île-à-la-Crosse to Scotsman Patrick Small of the North West Company and his Cree wife, was married to the great explorer David Thompson at Île-à-la-Crosse on September 1, 1785, and thereafter, during a marriage that lasted nearly sixty years, accompanied Thompson on many of his travels.[23] And, the paternal grandparents of Métis leader Louis Riel were married in Île-à-la-Crosse in 1815.[24]

Roman Catholic Mission

On September 10, 1846, two Oblates, Father Taché (later a bishop) and Father Lafleche, arrived in Île-à-la-Crosse from St. Boniface to establish the first Roman Catholic mission in Saskatchewan—"Chateau St. Jean," named after St. John the Baptist. That first winter, they were assisted by the elderly HBC post manager, Roderick Mackenzie (a different Roderick than the cousin of Sir Alexander Mackenzie), who gave them a roof over their heads and helped them learn Cree and Dene. With this early support, they were soon able to develop a mission (at the present mission site) that would deliver religion, education, and health care.

The Oblates were greatly helped in their work by the Grey Nuns, the Sisters of Charity. The first nuns—Sisters Agnes, Pepin, and Boucher—came to Île-à-la-Crosse on October 6, 1860, and within two days had established a convent to be called "Saint Bruno." Almost immediately, they began offering medical services, and by November 26, 1860, they had opened a boarding school for twenty-five students. Since then, excepting an absence from 1905 to 1917, the Grey Nuns have been working in Île-à-la-Crosse.

Sara Riel, Louis Riel's sister, joined the Grey Nuns at Red River in 1866, becoming the first Métis Grey

Nun. In 1871, she travelled to Île-à-la-Crosse to join its convent. Here, adopting the name Sister Marguerite Marie, she worked until dying of poor health in 1883 at the young age of 34. Her grave (photo right) is marked with a simple headstone in the Catholic cemetery.[25]

Though the HBC post at Île-à-la-Crosse would have drawn people to settle in the village, the Catholic mission must also have acted as a magnet. Some hint of this can be found in the reminiscence of Tom Natomagan who was born at McKay Point at Île-à-la-Crosse in about 1890:

> As far back as I can remember, I was about twelve years old, when we used to come to Sakitawak by dog sled. We used to come from far to go to midnight Mass. We didn't use tents. We slept out in the open. There were only about three houses. We never used to have houses, just teepees. They just didn't want to make houses. The people who lived in houses were called "house people." They couldn't believe we lived in teepees. Later, some old men started building houses until, finally, everybody had a house.[26]

Île-à-la-Crosse Today

Some of the old ways at Île-à-la-Crosse—freighting by water in summer and by horse team and sleigh in winter—lasted well into the twentieth century. The late Stan Durocher told us that, in the mid-1930s, one of his first wage jobs was removing rocks from the Beaver River to allow barges easier passage. Similarly, elders like Vital Morin, a well-known community leader in Île-à-la-Crosse, can remember that, up until the 1940s, horse swings originating in Big River hauled winter freight up northern Saskatchewan's "West Side." By about 1940, a rough road was cut along the east side of Lac Île-à-la-Crosse to bring goods by vehicle as far as Fort Black. Then later, in 1958, the present all-weather road was built to Île-à-la-Crosse.

Nowadays, Île-à-la-Crosse is a "Northern Village" with a population of about 1,500 people,[27] almost all of whom are of fur trade Métis descent. Originally, most Île-à-la-Crosse Métis lived in scattered locations around the lake, where they might find favourable fishing, hunting, and trapping. As these people moved into the village, they first built homes on the southern peninsula where the earliest trading posts had been. The peninsula area—which some see as having a northern "Town" section, a middle "Mission" section, and a southern residential section called "Bouvierville"—remains the heart of the village. However, in recent decades, people have settled north of the peninsula in an area where there was formerly only the pre-1950 HBC post and little else. As modern houses were built here, the area took on the name "Snob Hill." The area is now the village's main residential area, but it keeps the Snob Hill name.

Though some men still trap each winter, Île-à-la-Crosse's old economy based on fur and freighting has given way to a mix of enterprises. Commercial fishing, wild rice harvesting, fire suppression work, some cattle ranching, an alcohol and drug abuse treatment centre, and a garment factory now offer employment opportunities. As well, as in most northern Saskatchewan communities, many men and women fly in to the northern uranium mines where they typically work on a "week in/week out" rotation.

Because of its size, Île-à-la-Crosse offers visiting canoeists a wide range of services. These services include an airstrip, Île-à-la-Crosse Airways (McKay Point), grocery and dry good stores, gas stations, the Northern Sunset Motel (Snob Hill), Rainbow Ridge bed & breakfast (McKay Point), Lisa's Cafe (Snob Hill), a fried chicken outlet, an RCMP detachment, a Saskatchewan Environment office (where you can purchase topographical maps), a post office, St. Joseph's Hospital (which includes a pharmacy), and St. John the Baptist church.

Map 6.2   Île-à-la-Crosse (Old Village)   **Map 6.3   Île-à-la-Crosse (Snob Hill)**

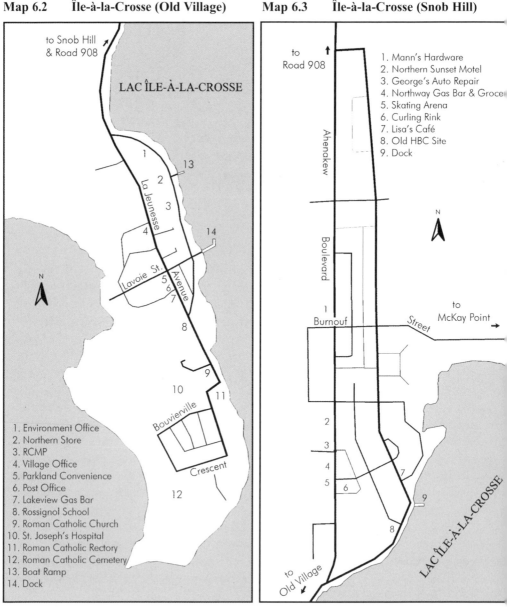

to Snob Hill & Road 908

LAC ÎLE-À-LA-CROSSE

La Jeunesse

Lavoie St.

Avenue

Bouvierville

Crescent

1. Environment Office
2. Northern Store
3. RCMP
4. Village Office
5. Parkland Convenience
6. Post Office
7. Lakeview Gas Bar
8. Rossignol School
9. Roman Catholic Church
10. St. Joseph's Hospital
11. Roman Catholic Rectory
12. Roman Catholic Cemetery
13. Boat Ramp
14. Dock

to Road 908

Ahenakew

Boulevard

Burnouf

Street

to McKay Point

to Old Village

LAC ÎLE-À-LA-CROSSE

1. Mann's Hardware
2. Northern Sunset Motel
3. George's Auto Repair
4. Northway Gas Bar & Grocery
5. Skating Arena
6. Curling Rink
7. Lisa's Café
8. Old HBC Site
9. Dock

ÎLE-À-LA-CROSSE TO PATUANAK

Lac Île-à-la-Crosse

As is most clearly shown on 1:250,000 Map 73-O, Lac Île-à-la-Crosse, or *sâkitawâhk sâkahikan* ("where rivers meet lake") and *Kwoe^n Too-ay* ("where people stay lake") by its respective Cree and Dene names, is a very long lake, stretching over 85 km (53 mi) from south to north. Starting from the village of Île-à-la-Crosse, the lake makes up about 60 km (38 mi) of the old voyageur highway.

Because the lake is narrow, you need not stray far from shore as you paddle it. However, the north wind can funnel down the lake and create dangerous whitecaps. When this happens, you will have little choice but to wait for calmer conditions.

Big Island

A nearly full moon rises over Lac Île-à-la-Crosse.

When you embark from Île-à-la-Crosse to head north, you will pass by Big Island, known locally as "La Grosse Île." This was the island where local Indians had a lacrosse field when the first European traders arrived. The island rises up to a height of perhaps 15 m (50 ft) at its centre. However, on its southeast corner, there is a large sandy meadow tapering off into a spit, which would have made a good playing ground.

The sandy meadow on Big Island, where early residents probably played lacrosse.

Fort Black

Both Maps 73-O and 73-O/5 mark "Fort Black" on Lac Île-à-la-Crosse's east shore, 2 to 3 km (about 1½ mi) southeast from Big Island. We have not found accounts of any such post in fur trade journals. However, oral histories make it clear that this was the post of Samuel Black—the same man who acted as the North West Company's tough guy at Île-à-la-Crosse.

Black did not begin his career with either the NWC or the HBC. Rather, he immigrated to Canada from Scotland in 1802 to work as a clerk for the XY Company (also known as the "New North West Company")—the company formed in 1800 when Montreal traders known as the "Potties" joined with explorer Alexander Mackenzie who had broken with the NWC.[28] The late Dr. P.E. Lavoie of Île-à-la-Crosse, who excavated the Fort Black site in the 1930s, believed that Black initially built his post for the XY Company but may also have kept it operational on behalf of the NWC—running it parallel to the NWC's main Île-à-la-Crosse post—for some time after the XY Company merged into the NWC on November 5, 1804.[29]

Much more recently, in the 1950s, Fort Black was the site of a Mid-Canada Line radar station—a Cold War initiative meant to detect incoming Russian missiles. Though the station had a brief lifespan, its construction created a temporary Fort Black community having its own "Fort Black Co-op" store. After the station closed in 1957, this store was moved over the lake ice to Île-à-la-Crosse.

Île-aux-Trembles

Immediately north from the Fort Black site is a large island having the map name of Île-aux-Trembles. It is known locally as "La Pointe du Tremble," "Poplar Point Island" and also "Poplar Island." Métis family names associated with the island include Desjarlais and Kyplain.

When we stopped at Île-aux-Trembles on June 22, 1986, we first met George Kyplain Jr. and two companions unloading pike, walleye, and suckers from a skiff. We then went inland towards the centre of the island where we visited with George's parents who were busy outside their cabin salvaging floats and leads from an old fishing net.

After introductions, George Sr. took us on a tour of his island mink ranch. George had over 100 female mink with litters, as well as seven males kept for breeding purposes. The mink ranged in colour from brown to blue to black. George told us that he had had mink for twenty-five years and was now one of only two mink ranchers left in Saskatchewan (the other being at Dore Lake). George said that low prices had very nearly shut down the industry, but he added that a good black pelt would still fetch $75—double the $35 paid for an average pelt.

George Kyplain, Sr., holding a mink

Nora and Fred Darbyshire.

Beaver River

Two km (1¼ mi) east from Île-aux-Trembles, you will find the mouth of the Beaver River or, as it is known in Cree, *amisko-sîpiy*. When we stopped at the mouth of the Beaver River on June 22, 1986, we had the good fortune of meeting Fred and Nora Darbyshire at their home. Fred, a northern legend who started trapping in 1924, had spent most of his life, first with his cousin Ed Theriau and later with his wife Nora, in the vast country between Cree Lake and Wollaston Lake. Ed Theriau, who had also kept a home at the Beaver River mouth, was now deceased, but Fred at 86 and Nora at 70 were both in excellent health. They invited us in to lunch, and we spent the next two hours spell-bound by stories of the old North.[30]

Of all the junctions on the Saskatchewan portion of the old voyageur highway, the Beaver River's inflow to Lac Île-à-la Crosse is one of the most important. The Beaver River, with its connections to the southern plains, provided a way to bring pemmican—the fuel of the voyageurs—to Île-à-la-Crosse where it could be used to resupply passing brigades.

In the later stages of the fur trade, the Beaver River also played a role in bringing trade goods into the North-West. In 1874, the steamer Northcote was built to transport goods up the Saskatchewan River. And, in 1875, a cart road was built, seemingly along an old Indian track, from Fort Carlton on the North Saskatchewan to Green Lake. It then became possible to bring goods to Fort Carlton by steamer, move them to Green Lake by ox cart, and finally take them north down the Green and Beaver rivers by boat to Île-à-la-Crosse. Some goods still came to Île-à-la-Crosse from Cumberland House via the old voyageur highway, but from 1876 on, the Beaver handled a share of the incoming freight.[31]

Sucker Point and Sandy Point

Two km (1¼ mi) north of the Beaver River mouth, still on the lake's east shore, you will come to a thumb-like peninsula known as "Sucker Point." The tip of Sucker Point is Indian Reserve 192E which belongs to the English River Dene Nation based in Patuanak to the north.

About 1.5 km (1 mi) northeast of and directly opposite Sucker Point, on the west side of the lake, both Maps 73-O and 73-O/5 mark "Sandy Point." This area may have been the site of one or two of Île-à-la-Crosse's early fur trade posts. Though little is known in this regard, Dr. P.E. Lavoie of Île-à-la-Crosse understood that the earliest HBC post (the William Linklater post) and also a competing NWC post were somewhere west of the point. Similarly, Fred Darbyshire had been told there was once an HBC post here.[32]

Whether or not Sandy Point was ever a post site, it has long been a stopping place for travellers. Indeed, it is likely that voyageurs coming inland would stop here to spruce up before making their entrance to Île-à-la-Crosse. This was the case on August 4, 1828, when George Simpson arrived here on his way to the Pacific with two lightly loaded canoes, each with a crew of nine men. His companion Archibald McDonald wrote, "Breakfasted and changed at Point au Sable. Arrived at Fort of Isle à la Crosse by eleven a.m."[33]

Sandy Point was once also one of Lac Île-à-la-Crosse's many small Métis communities. In days past, families with the surnames of Morin, Lariviere, and Gardiner all lived here. They were occasionally joined by others, and at times, the community had as many as six or seven families. Though Sandy Point is no longer a year-round community, some families still have houses here and stay through the summer.

You will find good camping possibilities along the sand beach on the south side of Sandy Point, east from some houses. We note, though, that a slough behind the beach might be a real mosquito factory.

North from Sandy Point

Two km (1¼ mi) north from Sandy Point, across the mouth of what the maps call Mogloair Bay,[34] you will come to a peninsula known as "Bélanger Point" or *Bélanger minawâ-tim* (73-O 238519). Once home to a Bélanger family, Vital Morin of Île-à-la-Crosse would later operate a mink ranch here.

Two km (1¼ mi) north-northeast from Bélanger Point, you will come to yet another point along the lake's west shore (73-O 254535). Here, a sand beach extends back west for about 100 m (110 yd) along the south side of the point. Despite a lack of firewood, this beach offers even better camping than Sandy Point.

Continuing further north, both the east and west shores of the lake are generally stony. Typically, the shores consist of a narrow band of ice-shoved stones backed by a margin of sand too narrow to camp on and, further back still, a fairly steep bank that may rise anywhere from 1 to 5 m (3 to 16 ft). The adjacent forest is predominately aspen with a few spruce scattered here and there.

The ice-shoved shores limit camping possibilities. However, about 9 km (5½ mi) north from Sandy Point, you will find a beautiful sand beach in a shallow cove along the west shore (73-O 240583). The beach, which is about 150 m (165 yd) long, has room for many tents.

Two-and-a-half km (1½ mi) north from the little sand beach, there is a large island close to the west shore. Just north of the island, and south of the opening to Black Bay, there is a foot-like peninsula coming from the west shore (73-O 237627). The toe of this peninsula was once home to an Austrian named Frank Fisher who, in the 1930s, trapped at Cree Lake and was responsible for guiding northern author A.L. Karras and his brother Abe on their first trip to Cree Lake in 1935. Fisher, who was a bachelor all of his life, raised mink for many years here at the mouth of Black Bay.[35]

In 1986, two km (1¼ mi) north from Black Bay, we found an active bald eagle nest along the west shore. This was directly across from "Little Gravel Point" on the east shore, known as *Tsi-gra-weh* in local Michif (73-O 288665).

Halfway Lake

Eight km (5 mi) north from Little Gravel Point, you will come to where both Map 73-O and 73-O/12 mark "Halfway Point." One km (⅔ mi) further north from the point, there is a good-sized island which is locally known as "Halfway Lake." The island was another one of Lac Île-à-la-Crosse's favoured living places. Irene Desjarlais of Île-à-la-Crosse grew up at Halfway Lake. The daughter of Nap Johnson (born in 1915 at Sucker Point) and his wife Margaret (née Kyplain), Irene says that the island had horse stables and served as one of the stopping places for teamsters who, up until about 1940, hauled freight north from Big River with horse-drawn sleighs in winter.

Halfway Lake offers good camping on its west shore in an old clearing where cabins once stood (73-O 298756). Here, you will find a boat notch cleared from the shoreline rocks where canoes can be pulled up. In the clearing, you will find grassy spaces for many tents. You will also find many raspberries and gooseberries to pick in midsummer.

Gully Reef

Six km (3¾ mi) north from Halfway Lake, a rocky reef will indicate to those with 1:50,000 maps that they have moved north from Map 73-O/12 to Map 73-O/13. Marked as "Gully Reef" on Map 73-O/12, there is no confusion as to where the name comes from since it glistens white with droppings from gulls and pelicans. Lac Île-à-la-Crosse has white pelicans up and down its length. Interestingly, however, Fred Darbyshire told us that though the pelicans favour the lake for fishing, they do not nest here.

A commercial fisherman pulling a net at the north end of Lac Île-à-la-Crosse, near Patuanak.

Gravel Point

Yet another 6 km (3¾ mi) north, you will come to the pointed heel of a foot-like peninsula coming out from the west shore (73-O 288878). Though not identified on topographical maps, the pointed heel is well known as "Gravel Point," similarly known in Cree as *asinîskâs minawâtim* and in Michif as *Graweh.* The gravelly point, about 100 m (110 yd) long, has no doubt been a stopping place for centuries. It would make a good lunch spot or campsite.

Mike Durocher, who grew up at Sandy Point and later commercial fished on much of Lac Île-à-la-Crosse, has told us that for commercial fishing purposes, Gravel Point marks an unofficial resource boundary between the Île-à-la-Crosse Métis and the Patuanak Dene.

From Gravel Point north to Patuanak, camping opportunities in this section are limited, since both the east and west shores are most often edged by ice-shoved, head-sized rocks. However, not quite 6 km (3¾ mi) north of Gravel Point, you can watch for a modest beach of gravel and small stones on the east shore (73-O 284935). Though nothing special, it would be adequate for a lunch stop or even a camp. Behind a ridge about 15 m (50 ft) back from the shore, there is a low area where tents could be set up. We have not camped here, but on June 23, 1986, we caught a good pike off the shore and picked saskatoons on the ridge.

Shagwenaw Rapids

When you reach within 1 km (²/₃ mi) of the extreme north end of Lac Île-à-la-Crosse, the lake bends right to run eastward into a funnel-shaped outflow channel. Over the course of 2 km (1¼ mi), this channel narrows until Shagwenaw Rapids—marked on both Maps 73-O and 73-O/13—begin.

The name "Shagwenaw"—which apparently dates to pre-contact times—is a Cree name (*sâkwânâw*) denoting narrowness.[36] Describing the voyageur highway in an upstream direction, Alexander Mackenzie wrote, "Then Shagoina strait and rapid lead into the Lake of Isle à la Crosse…"[37] Mackenzie would have learned the name "Shagoina" only a decade after white traders first reached this far inland.

The Dene who now occupy the Patuanak region know Shagwenaw Rapids as *Buhneech'eree Tthaybah* which translates roughly as "tearing rapids." The name also conveys a sense of "water breaking through" or "where the water broke through." According to Joe Black, formerly of Patuanak, Dene legend has it that a giant beaver once lived on Lac Île-à-la-Crosse. He had a large house in the southern part of the lake, the remains of which now form Big Island. He also had a large dam at Shagwenaw Rapids to hold in the lake water and enlarge his domain. One day, however, the pressure of the built-up water burst the dam, and the giant beaver's work went for nought. The discouraged beaver then apparently left the country, leaving behind his Big Island lodge and rocks strewn down Shagwenaw Rapids where his dam had been.

Shagwenaw Rapids extend for about 350 m (380 yd). They are Class 1 rapids which should not present any problems for canoeists who stay alert. Patuanak people run skiffs up and down the rapids routinely on a course down river centre, and this is the best route to follow. The biggest waves occur at the foot of the rapids, but they are not difficult to handle at normal water levels.

If you are travelling upstream, you may want to investigate a possible portage trail on the south (river right) shore. It begins at a 3-m (10-ft) break in shore willows about 50 m (55 yd) down from a rocky spit at the foot of the rapids and runs along the rapids. However, as the trail is not in good shape, we suggest you avoid any carrying by taking your canoe up along the south shore with a combination of wading, tracking, and paddling.

To Patuanak

From the foot of Shagwenaw Rapids, you will paddle less than 1 km (²/₃ mi) southward down a run-out channel to reach the community of Patuanak on Shagwenaw Lake. Here, after proceeding a short distance south past the Roman Catholic church and the remains of a large dock, you can put in at a sand beach east of the local Northern store.

-7-

PATUANAK TO PINEHOUSE LAKE

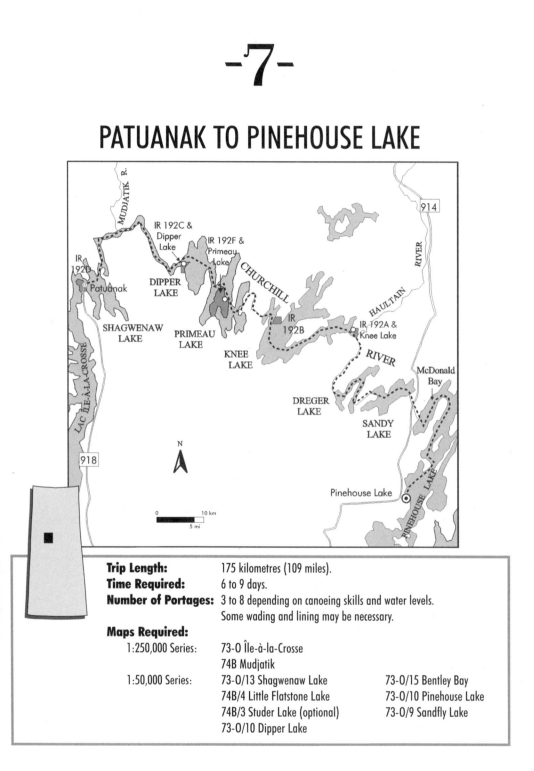

Trip Length: 175 kilometres (109 miles).
Time Required: 6 to 9 days.
Number of Portages: 3 to 8 depending on canoeing skills and water levels.
Some wading and lining may be necessary.

Maps Required:

1:250,000 Series:	73-O Île-à-la-Crosse
	74B Mudjatik

1:50,000 Series:

73-O/13 Shagwenaw Lake	73-O/15 Bentley Bay
74B/4 Little Flatstone Lake	73-O/10 Pinehouse Lake
74B/3 Studer Lake (optional)	73-O/9 Sandfly Lake
73-O/10 Dipper Lake	

ABOUT THE TRIP

This trip requires advanced canoeing skills and good judgment. There are several challenging rapids, and a couple of these lack good portaging options. Further, some of the lakes on the trip, most notably Dipper Lake and Knee Lake, call for traverses that are prone to dangerous wind conditions.

Upstream travel on the trip route is difficult and should be left to experts equipped with the skills of the old voyageurs. In an upstream direction, there are strong currents to deal with in several places. A particularly bad section is the channel between Sandy Lake and McDonald Bay which is almost continuous fast water. In low water conditions, the current can be even worse in places as the river recedes from its usual, broad channel into a narrower, more restricted one.

The scenery on this trip changes from west to east. Downstream from Patuanak, the Churchill runs through level terrain wooded mainly with aspen poplar. Further east, after the river enters the Shield, the shore relief becomes somewhat bolder, and more spruce mixes in with the aspen. Finally, on Pinehouse Lake, rugged outcrops of bedrock predominate to create the classic Shield scenery for which the Churchill is famous.

Camping opportunities on this route are limited since many shorelines are jumbled with head-sized stones and backed by dense thickets, but a few good campsites will be mentioned.

The trip route is off the beaten track compared to those sections of the Churchill further downstream. You may encounter some Dene from Patuanak fishing or hunting along the way, but you will not likely see many people at all. Between Patuanak and Pinehouse Lake, there are indeed three small, neat and tidy Dene settlements—Dipper Lake, Primeau Lake, and Knee Lake. These are, however, now occupied only on a seasonal basis by former residents who have taken up permanent homes in Patuanak. They persist largely as nostalgic reminders that this section of the Churchill was once busier than it is today.

The trip route was once home to a most amazing individual—Oblate missionary Father Louis Moraud. For half a century, from 1916 to 1965, he ministered to the Dene of the Churchill, building churches wherever they were needed. His church at Knee Lake, still well-preserved, is a particularly poignant monument to his work.

One aboriginal rock painting site occurs near the end of this trip. Located on the east shore of McDonald Bay, the large bay at the northeast corner of Pinehouse Lake, this site is the most westerly of the Churchill's many rock painting sites.

STARTING POINT

This trip begins at the Dene community of Patuanak located 407 km (253 mi) northwest of Prince Albert. From Prince Albert, you can reach Patuanak via Highways 3, 55, 155, 165, and Road 918. The route is paved except for 90 km (56 mi) of gravel on Road 918.

At Patuanak, you will first come to the off-Reserve, hamlet side of the community and the local hamlet office. If you continue north past the office for 2.5 km (1½ mi), you will pass onto the Reserve side of the community and arrive at Patuanak's Northern store. Here, from a beach a short distance east of the store and about 50 m (55 yd) south of the remains of a large public dock, you can launch your canoe onto Shagwenaw Lake.

Community of Patuanak

Patuanak is a Dene community that serves as home base to the English River Dene Nation (ERDN). It occupies a large peninsula bounded by Lac Île-à-la-Crosse to the west, Shagwenaw Rapids to the north, and Shagwenaw Lake to the east. The main, northerly part of the community is on Indian Reserve 192D, land belonging to the ERDN. A smaller section, sometimes called "La Ronge" or "Little La Ronge,"[1] lies south of the reserve and has the status of a "Northern Hamlet." The reserve side of the community has a population of about 800, while the hamlet side has just under 100 people. Currently, Chief Alfred Dawatsare (who succeeded Chief Archie Campbell in November 2001) heads the ERDN, while Margaret Aubichon is mayor of the hamlet. Almost all of the residents, whether they live within the reserve or the hamlet, are treaty status members of the ERDN.

Local Dene people refer to Patuanak as *Buhneech'eree*, a name adopted from the rapids immediately upstream. The name "Patuanak"—which is a shortened version of the Cree word *wapâciwanâhk* describing a long narrows with current or rapids—may be a kind of back translation of "Shagwenaw," the original Cree name (denoting narrowness) for the upstream rapids. On a map based on 1892 explorations, surveyor J.B. Tyrrell translated Shagwenaw Rapids as "Narrow Rapids."[2] The *wapâciwanâhk* name could be an alternate original Cree name for the Patuanak area, but it is also quite possible that it originated from someone translating the English name "Narrow" back into Cree. The Patuanak name—or at least "Wahpachewanack"—was in use as early as 1907,[3] though the local Hudson's Bay Company post, first known as "Pine River," did not adopt the "Patuanak" name until 1950.[4]

English River Dene Nation

The English River Dene Nation takes its name from that given to the Churchill River by Montreal trader Joseph Frobisher in 1774 who, when first seeing the river at Frog Portage, recognized the fact that the English Hudson's Bay Company already had a post downstream where the river entered Hudson Bay.[5]

Like the other Dene First Nations already discussed in this guide, the English River Dene are descended from Dene who, in pre-contact times, occupied the tundra–forest transition zone of northern Saskatchewan and exploited migratory herds of barren ground caribou. The southern limit of these early Dene has not been clearly defined, but it is generally thought that it did not come as far south as the Churchill or, if it did, then just barely so.

In the late 1700s, the Dene were attracted south by the fur trade. Ordinarily, they may have expected some opposition from resident Cree groups, but those groups had been devastated by the great smallpox epidemic of 1781. The Dene were therefore often able to move into country that had few, if any, people left. It was not long before the Dene were trading at Île-à-la-Crosse and travelling well south of it.[6] They also moved downstream on the Churchill, seemingly even as far as Stanley Mission.[7]

At some stage, likely in the late 1800s, the various Dene groups became less nomadic, and their identities became connected to specific territories. A group that became known as the English River Dene occupied a large region extending east along the Churchill from Patuanak to beyond Knee Lake, south to the Beaver River, and north to Cree Lake. On August 28, 1906, Chief William Apesis and Headmen Joseph Gun and Jean Baptiste Estralshenen of the English River Dene met with federal Treaty Commissioner J.A.J. McKenna at Île-à-la-Crosse and signed Treaty No. 10 on behalf of their people.[8] Later, Reserve lands owing pursuant to the treaty, including six parcels along the Churchill, were transferred to the First Nation.

In the first years after Treaty 10 was signed, the English River Dene remained highly mobile—living in tents and going where they wished to fish, hunt, and trap. In the 1940s, however, new changes—including the advent of commercial fishing, a Northern Fur Conservation Program which introduced defined trapping areas, and a provincial welfare system—tended to restrict people's nomadism and attract them into communities.

Along the guide route, people settled at Patuanak, Dipper Lake, Primeau Lake, and Knee Lake. Further changes took place in the 1960s. In 1968, a school set up at Patuanak drew people there. At the same time, the introduction of snowmobiles allowed people to live mainly in Patuanak and still work their distant traplines. By the early 1970s, most English River Dene had moved from the outlying areas into Patuanak.[9]

Fur Trading

In the early fur trade era, Patuanak was not a trading post centre. At most, it would have had the occasional outpost operating under the supervision of a parent post at Île-à-la-Crosse. This changed, it seems, some time after 1900 when the French company Revillon Frères arrived here and spurred the Hudson's Bay Company to meet its competition with at least an outpost. According to elder Martin Smith of Pinehouse, oral tradition has it that in the early 1900s, prior to the great flu epidemic of 1918, two brothers named Kenny and Jimmy McDonald traded in opposition to each other at Patuanak for the HBC and Revillon Frères respectively.[10]

Eventually, the HBC set up a permanent post at Patuanak. On October 1, 1921, Charles Eugene ("Blooch") Bélanger and six other HBC men arrived from Île-à-la-Crosse by scow and moved into an old house purchased for use as temporary quarters. Revillon Frères was also then operating at Patuanak, and the HBC's new post—called "Pine River"—was likely a response to continuing competition from Revillon. This competition is hinted at in HBC post journal entries, such as the one for October 21, 1921: "Old Matchee won over to the good cause today, and does quite a bit of buying."[11]

From 1921 to 1936, the HBC's Pine River post was managed by its founder, "Blooch" Bélanger, who had previously managed other HBC operations (Buffalo River, Souris River, and Île-à-la-Crosse) on the guide route. He was succeeded as manager by Alex Ahenakew who ran Pine River from 1936 to 1947. It was a rare thing for a Cree Indian such as Ahenakew to be an HBC post manager, but Ahenakew had the advantage of education, having studied divinity at Wycliff College in Toronto. Ahenakew was succeeded by other managers who operated the post (named "Patuanak" after 1950) for the HBC until it and other HBC Northern stores were transferred to the new North West Company in 1987.[12]

Father Louis Moraud, O.M.I.

No discussion of Patuanak would be complete without mention of an extraordinary Oblate priest named Father Louis Moraud. Born in Quebec in 1888, Father Moraud first began visiting the English River Dene in 1916 from his base at the Catholic mission at Île-à-la-Crosse. In 1930, he became resident priest at Patuanak and, in 1937, built his first church here. Until his death in 1965, he devoted all of his time to travelling and working among the English River people. According to Patuanak's Frank McIntyre:

> He was a real wilderness man, that Father Moraud. Other priests take holidays or

SAB / STAR-PHOENIX COLLECTION / S-SP-B 182-9

Father Louis Moraud, circa 1950.

The Roman Catholic Church at Patuanak, built by Father Louis Moraud.

retreats, but he never took a holiday, and used to say "travelling around is my holiday."

He was a tough old man, that little priest. Even in cold weather he would wash in the lake, and at forty below he would wash in the snow. He never complained, even if sick, but just carried on with his work. He always carried a box along for his equipment for saying mass. Even at fifty below he'd be up at six in the morning saying mass under the stars![13]

Father Moraud is buried in the Catholic church yard at Patuanak. His life has been commemorated in the name given to the Catholic mission and the community's "St. Louis School."[14]

Aerial photo of Patuanak looking westward, taken September 4, 1999. Lac Ile-a-la-Crosse is in background; channel into Shagwenaw Lake is in front.

Patuanak Today

Over the past century, change has come rapidly to Patuanak. Since the signing of Treaty No. 10, it has evolved from a seasonal stopping place to a community of over 800 people. The opening of the community's first school in 1968 (expanded to offer classes to grade twelve in 1999) was a major impetus to growth. Construction of an all-weather road to Patuanak in 1977[15] had a similar effect. While the community is still remote, it now has many of the same amenities available in larger centres to the south. At Patuanak, canoeists will find an airstrip, a Northern store (which sells fuel), a medical clinic with two nurses (doctors visit from Île-à-la-Crosse twice a week), a post office, a two-member RCMP detachment (established in 1996), ERDN's administration centre, St. Louis School, and the Roman Catholic church. Provincial Environment officers from Beauval visit Patuanak as required and work out of the ERDN administration centre, but they do not maintain a regular office. While Patuanak has had restaurants in the past, it does not have one at present.

Map 7.1   Patuanak (main village)

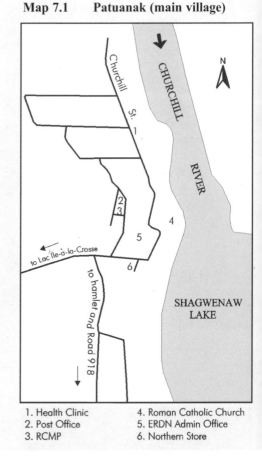

1. Health Clinic
2. Post Office
3. RCMP
4. Roman Catholic Church
5. ERDN Admin Office
6. Northern Store

PATUANAK TO PINEHOUSE LAKE

Shagwenaw Lake

Shagwenaw Lake's name is one of some antiquity. Over 200 years ago, Alexander Mackenzie found the lake already known as "Shagoina Lake."[16] The name comes from the rapids joining Lac Île-à-la-Crosse and Shagwenaw Lake which, as mentioned above, take their name from a Cree word denoting narrowness.[17] The Dene name for Shagwenaw Lake is *Buhneech'eree Too-ay*. This name, which can be loosely translated as "tearing lake," has a different translation than the Cree, but it also comes from a description of the rapids between Lac Île-à-la-Crosse and Shagwenaw Lake.

Shagwenaw Lake is a good-sized lake, but the old voyageur highway makes only a short, 3-km (2-mi) traverse across the north end of it. When you begin this traverse from Patuanak, you may find it hard to see where the Churchill leaves Shagwenaw Lake since the outflow is around a finger-like point that appears to be part of the parallel shoreline lying east of it. If you head generally northeast by east, however, you will soon find the exit.

Paddling northeast from Patuanak, you will pass near two of Shagwenaw Lake's several islands. The first (73-O 312007), located north along the west shore of the lake, is known in Dene as *Ayjere Noo-awzsay*, meaning "cow island." The second (73-O 322999), a tiny island slightly south of the midpoint of your traverse, is known in Dene as *K'ee Noo-awzsay*, meaning "little birch island."

The large island lying just over 1 km (⅔ mi) southeast from Little Birch Island is called *Noo Aylay* in Dene and Shaggy Island (73-O 327985) in English. Both names describe the island's irregular shoreline.

At the outflow of Shagwenaw Lake, you will enter a wide channel lined by aspen poplar and a few spruce. The Dene call the outflow area *Nee-ho-aw*, a reference to the lake entrance being reached by someone coming from downstream. The outflow channel has no current to speak of.

Two km (1¼ mi) north from Shagwenaw Lake, the river channel makes a sharp elbow bend to the right. The point on the inside, or south side, of the bend is known in Dene as *Toteenay The Tlee[n]*, meaning "where the white man lies" (73-O 334036). Story has it that a white man was buried here after dying from eating a celery-like poisonous plant—likely water hemlock.

Cross Island

Six km (3¾ mi) further north, the Churchill divides around an island (73-O 331088) known in Dene as *Dechent'uy Noo-ay*, meaning "cross island." If you paddle down the east side of this island, you will see a path that leads up from the shore to a raised clearing hidden behind a screen of shrubs and small trees. You will also see a tall steel cross, perhaps 8 m (25 ft) high, rising up from the clearing.

Map 7.2   Churchill River from Cross Island to Leaf Rapids

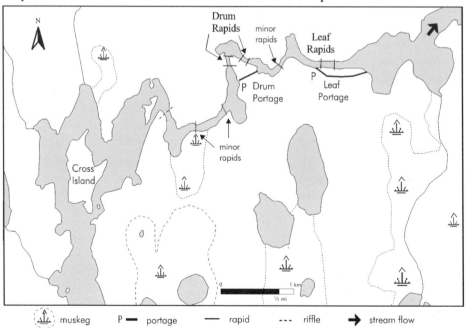

The cross site is very good for camping. Surrounding the cross is a level, grassy clearing bordered by aspens and a few fine old jack pines. This clearing has room for many tents. And, as an added bonus for fall travellers, it can be one of the best blueberry patches in northern Saskatchewan.

Cross Island took on its present religious significance during the North-West Rebellion of 1885. During the Rebellion, the Oblate missionaries at Île-à-la-Crosse, receiving word of the recent killings of two priests and others at Frog Lake, worried that fighting might spread from the south to Île-à-la-Crosse. As a precautionary measure, they moved north from Île-à-la-Crosse and sheltered on Cross Island until the Rebellion had run its course.

Father Moraud was responsible for erecting a wooden cross (later replaced by the present steel one) on Cross Island to commemorate the Oblates' stay there.[18] The people of Patuanak have since used Cross Island as a place for worship. When we camped on the island in 1986, we found a wooden altar and lectern set up near the cross. That altar has now given way to the elements, but the cross site still has religious significance to the people of Patuanak.

At the downstream end of Cross Island, you will leave Map 73-O (or Map 73-O/13) and go onto Map 74B (or Map 74B/4). Just after this map change, the Churchill divides around a small island (74B 340096) and then makes a sharp elbow turn to the right. In low water, the channel southeast of the small island can be choked with rocks, so you may want to stay west and north of the island as you move downstream. Some current occurs off the island's north tip, but it will not cause you any difficulty.

After the elbow turn at the small island, the Churchill runs southeast for 500 m (1/3 mi). Halfway down this short reach, there is some fast water which, in low water, takes the form of a minor rapid about 40 m (44 yd) long (74B 342096). If you stay alert and keep to the centre, you will have no trouble with this rapid.

The Churchill next makes a 90-degree left turn to run northeast. Shortly after this turn, there is a minor rapid (74B 346094) followed by about 300 m (330 yd) of swift current and then a second minor rapid (74B 350096). In low water, the two minor rapids and the swift current between them tend to merge into one continuous minor rapid about 600 m (1/3 mi) long. The people of Patuanak refer to the two rapids together as *Dee-yay-thee-yay Tthaybawzsay* which, loosely translated, simply means "the first little rapids." The main channel down these rapids begins by zigzagging right and then left, but it then keeps a line left of centre. The waves of the second rapid are somewhat bigger than those of the first, but both rapids and the swift current between them can be run by average canoeists who stay alert.

Two large boulders on river right, belonging to a large but ordinarily submerged boulder field, mark the end of the second of the two minor rapids. From here, you will have about 300 m (330 yd) of quiet water before reaching Drum Portage on river right (74B 352099).

If going upstream, you will be able to wade or line up the swift current and minor rapids between Drum Portage and Cross Island. However, in high water conditions, when normal shorelines are flooded out, wading and lining these sections may be extremely difficult. Likewise, in the opposite situation of very low water, when much of the Churchill's bed becomes a jumble of exposed rock and the river retreats into a narrower and swifter channel, wading and lining may be equally difficult.

Drum Rapids

Drum Rapids likely take their name from the drumming roar they produce. This notion has some support in that the early fur traders called the portage past the rapids "Portage Sonnant"[19] (*sonnant* is a French word meaning "sonorous.") The name may have derived from a similar Indian name. However, the Dene today simply call the rapids *Hochela Khlay Hoteth Tthaybah*, meaning "rapids where the portage goes over the point."

These major rapids begin 500 m (⅓ mi) or so downstream from the previous minor rapids. They occur where the Churchill changes direction from north to southeast in a sharp elbow turn to the right around a point. Being a double set, they have one section upstream of the sharp turn and a second one downstream from it.

The first section, which is about 200 m (220 yd) long and ends just as the river turns right, earns a Class 3 rating. In this section, the river's main channel, a 30-m-wide (100-ft-wide) trough flowing down the right, is quite straight with relatively few obstructions. However, as the channel here has a steep gradient, the rapids in it are very swift and dangerous.

The second section, around the corner from the first, is also about 200 m (220 yd) long. The rapids here have some big waves, and they have a particularly bad hole about halfway down on river left. However, at Class 2, they are not so difficult as those in the first section and advanced canoeists would find them navigable in a line running generally right of centre.

Interestingly, men from Patuanak run their skiffs both up and down Drum Rapids. (Indeed, they run all the rapids between Patuanak and Dipper Rapids.) But they only do so with considerable skill and an awareness of the risk involved. In 1986, we found a tall wooden cross erected on the right shore of the rapids' first section where it could watch over boatmen and remind them of the hazards at hand.[20]

In 1986, we scouted both sections of Drum Rapids from shore and then ran down them with an unloaded canoe. Although we made our way down the rapids all right, the ride was a good deal faster than expected. We decided that Drum Rapids would best be portaged by everyone.

The cross erected at Drum Rapids (shown here as it was on September 24, 1992) is a reminder to paddlers of the danger there.

Historically, it seems, Drum Rapids were sometimes run by the voyageurs. When Peter Fidler arrived at Drum Rapids with Philip Turnor on his way downstream on June 11, 1792, he recorded in his journal, "This fall is commonly shot in going down, with light Canoes." However, it should be noted that Fidler, Turnor, and their party themselves chose to portage here rather than shoot the rapids.[21]

A more recent mention of Drum Rapids can be found in A.L. Karras's book *North to Cree Lake,* in which Karras describes his experiences trapping with his brother in northern Saskatchewan in the 1930s. The Karras brothers made their first trip down the Churchill in the summer of 1935 guided by an Austrian named Frank Fisher, a veteran trapper familiar with northern Saskatchewan. In describing this trip, Karras writes:

> We were on the Churchill again and travelling with a strong current. Soon we heard the boom of Drum Rapid somewhere ahead. Frank piloted us in to shore at the head of the rapid where we unloaded some of the heavy goods to lighten the boats. Then we ran the rapid. Somehow I misjudged the channel. My boat passed through great white-maned waves which clubbed the boat from all sides. Luckily I made it to the bottom after taking a good deal of water aboard.[22]

Portage #1 - Drum Portage (±325 m / 355 yd)

This portage begins on river right about 300 m (330 yd) downstream from the previous minor rapid and 275 m (300 yd) upstream from the head of Drum Rapids. It is not easily visible, but if you watch, you will see its upstream end as a 4-m (12-ft) break in the shore willows. In front of this break, shore rocks have been moved aside to give canoes a better approach to the portage. The small channel created leads to a gentle, grassy landing.

At the upstream landing, there is a small, grassy camping area in the willows that would have room for four to five tents. Though this might be a bad place for mosquitoes, it is a reasonable spot. The portage itself has been worn deep by centuries of use, and it remains in very good condition. It passes through an open wood of small aspen and is generally level. When it reaches the far side of the point it crosses, it makes a gradual drop down to the water.

There is a good campsite for small parties at the downstream end of the portage. It does not have much level ground for a tent, but compensating for this deficiency is a fine view of the river as it runs out from Drum

In 1986, we found a woodchuck, pictured at right, sunning itself near its burrow in a bank alongside Drum Portage.

Rapids and then turns around a bend downstream. The downstream landing is a broad beach of small stones located in a quiet eddy down from the rapids. It is very convenient for loading and unloading canoes.

Rapid Downstream from Drum Rapids

About 300 m (330 yd) downstream from Drum Rapids, after the river bends to the northeast, there is a small, ripply rapid (74B 357102) known in Dene as *Des Eneehaw-zay*, meaning "where the river lifts up." There are Dene stories of a lurking danger here, but the rapid can be easily run by alert canoeists.

If you are travelling upstream, you will want to wade up the river right shore (on your left) of the small rapid. This will better allow you to reach the eddy at the foot of Drum Rapids Portage.

Continuing downstream from the small rapid, it is another 500 m (⅓ mi) or so to Leaf Rapids. As there is fast current over this distance, canoeists must now stay alert in order to land safely above Leaf Rapids, preferably on the river right shore. A landing is necessary because Leaf Rapids require careful scouting or else a portage.

Leaf Rapids

Leaf Rapids are known in Dene as *Etthen Des Tthaybah*, meaning "caribou river rapids," because they are just upstream of the Mudjatik River which the Dene refer to as *Etthen Deszay*, (the "caribou river").

Joe Black, who was raised at Dipper Lake and who spent many years on the Churchill as one of its best commercial fishers, says that lake trout are occasionally caught at Leaf Rapids and at Drum Rapids upstream. Since trout are not normally caught on the upper Churchill, he believes the Leaf and Drum trout must be migrants from the Mudjatik River.

These are long rapids extending about 800 m (½ mi). They warrant a Class 2 rating, but their difficulty depends a great deal on water levels. In high water, it is possible to ride down them well clear of submerged rocks and boulders. However, in low water, when whole fields of rocks and boulders break the surface, the rapids can be a treacherous obstacle course. At such times, canoeists have three options: 1) those with good advanced skills may shoot the rapids; 2) less advanced canoeists may wade or line their canoes along the south shore; 3) cautious and less skilled canoeists can portage past the rapids on the south shore.

> Upstream travellers have two options at Leaf Rapids. One option is to wade or track canoes along the south shore (deftness and caution are required). The alternative is to use Leaf Portage.

A journal entry by Philip Turnor going upstream on October 5, 1790 (the water at this time of year must have been near the freezing mark) indicates that his party chose to wade and line canoes at Leaf Rapids:

> then went S 1/2 mile and SW 1 mile in a part with grassey marshey sides and came to the mouth of a small river on NE side called Teak a Seepe or Deer River [Mudjatik River] this river leads towards the Athapiscow Country but is full of falls and shoals the Canadians have examined it and find it not fit for large Canoes, then went SSW 1/2 mile, asps on both sides and came to a fall or strong rapid [Leaf Rapids] and led the Canoes 3/8 mile on South side then paddled 1/4 mile and handed 40 yards on south side then paddled 200 yards to the foot of the carrying place [Drum Rapids Portage], and carried 350 yards through burnt woods on south side good carrying.[23]

Portage #2 - Leaf Portage (± 875 m / 955 yd) (optional)

This portage begins at a 4-m (13-ft) break in the willows of the river right shore some 40 to 50 m (44 to 55 yd) upstream from the head of the rapids. In 1986, a large aspen poplar standing about 10 m (11 yd) up the river bank showed where the portage trail led off into the woods.

When we hiked this portage in 1986, we found that it had some windfall but was otherwise in good condition. Indeed, we could not have wanted a nicer walk. The narrow, well-worn portage path rustled with leaves that had fallen the previous autumn from the aspen and birch overhead. Alongside the path, there were many understorey plants including sarsaparilla, Labrador tea, bunchberries, blueberries, ground cranberries, and twinflower. Also, because the path followed a bank perhaps 15 m (50 ft) above the water, we had a good view of Leaf Rapids below us. As we finally came to the path's downstream end, we passed through a large wild raspberry patch. Right at the downstream end, we found a clearing about 20 m (22 yd) across with plenty of room for camping.

> If you arrive from downstream, the end of the portage shows as a grassy clearing behind some shore willows. You can gain access to this clearing at a good landing about 40 m (44 yd) southeast from some rocks marking the foot of the rapids. You will have no trouble reaching the landing as the current up to it is not strong.

Mudjatik River

Not quite 2 km (1¼ mi) downstream from Leaf Rapids, you will come to where the willow-lined Mudjatik River runs into the Churchill from the north, which confluence is known in Dene as *Etthen Des Dee^n Ee^n Lee^n*, meaning "where the Caribou River flows in." The Mudjatik drains a sandy region lying south of Cree Lake, so its current is laden with a great deal of sand and silt. When the Mudjatik joins the Churchill, much of this sediment load settles out into shallow sand bars that extend some distance downstream on the Churchill. In low water conditions, you may occasionally ground on these bars.

The Mudjatik River

The first official survey of the Mudjatik was made by J.B. Tyrrell on behalf of the Geological Survey of Canada. In his official survey report, Tyrrell describes how difficult it was to go up the river:

> On the 1st of July, 1892, we entered the mouth of the river, which was then at extreme high water, and began the toilsome ascent of its rapid current. The water was up in the willows, which almost everywhere overhung the channel, so that it was impossible to track the canoes with a line from the banks. Poling was also out of the question since the bed of the channel is composed of shifting quicksand. It was, therefore, necessary to ascend entirely with paddles, keeping close to the banks, and occasionally clutching the low bushes...[24]

In editing the journals of Philip Turnor, a project of his later years, Tyrrell makes further reference to the Mudjatik and explains how the river got its present name:

> It is interesting to know that at this early date [1790] the energetic fur collectors of the North West Company, here called "Canadians," had examined this river [the Mudjatik] in an attempt to find an easier and shorter route to Lake Athabaska than that over the Methy portage and down the Athabaska river. In 1892, a hundred and two years after Turnor's visit, I ascended the river to its source, crossed the watershed, paddled over Cree lake, and descended Cree and Stone rivers to Lake Athabaska. In order to distinguish it from the many other A-tick [atihk is Cree for "caribou"] or Cariboo rivers in western Canada, I called it Mudjatick [macatihk], or Bad Cariboo river. ... Both it and the Cree river which flows northward from the watershed at its source, are too swift and shallow for economic navigation by large canoes.[25]

Despite the Mudjatik's difficult navigation, several white trappers used it during the 1930s to move into northern Saskatchewan where they could find a better living than the Great Depression would allow them in the south. A.L. Karras's *North to Cree Lake* provides an excellent firsthand account of the experiences of these men, including what it was like to travel up the Mudjatik.[26]

Of course, long before any white man saw the Mudjatik, it would have been well-explored by natives. Who these first people were is not known. However, given clues such as the early existence of the Cree name "Teak a Seepe" [atihko-sîpiy], it seems probable that the Cree were the people inhabiting the Mudjatik watershed in the period before European contact. If they were not, they at least occupied the area immediately to the west.[27]

The Mudjatik River is now Dene territory and has likely been so since the early 1800s. For the Dene, the river, which they know as *Etthen Deszay*, has an interesting early history as a transportation route. Oral tradition has it that throughout the 1800s and up until about 1875, Dene who wintered in the area southeast of Cree Lake used the Mudjatik as part of a fascinating summer migration cycle. Every spring, these Dene would make canoes and then paddle down the Mudjatik and up the Churchill until they came to Île-à-la-Crosse. When they reached that settlement, they would camp on nearby Big Island and spend the month of July trading, fishing, and socializing. They would then continue south via the Beaver River until they reached Lac la Plonge and then Dore and Smoothstone Lakes. There, they would end their southward journey and begin to move back towards home.

To make their return trip, the Dene would first travel north via the Smoothstone River and Pinehouse Lake, then turn east to go downstream on the Churchill. Finally, they would paddle north again, sometimes up the Bélanger River but more commonly up the Foster River, to reach their wintering grounds just before freeze-up ended canoe travel for the year.[28]

In 1986, we met two Dene families living in two canvas wall tents at their fishing camp near the mouth of the Mudjatik. Jean-Marie and Rose Gunn (Rose in photo right) and the family of Philip Wolverine (photo below) showed us how to smoke whitefish and how the fish can be made into pemmican. When we continued on our way, they gave us several

smoked whitefish to add to our food box. We soon discovered that these whitefish gave us considerably more paddling energy than the pike and walleye we ordinarily ate. Philip Wolverine was later to provide us with many of the Dene place names for the Churchill.

Upper Deer Rapids

About 3.5 km (2 mi) downstream from the mouth of the Mudjatik, you will come to the first rapids of the two-part Deer Rapids, which the Dene refer to collectively as *Nuhkay Tthaybawzsay* or "two little rapids." Early fur trade references to modern-day Deer Rapids are vague. One exception is that of Sir John Richardson who, while passing upstream on June 24, 1848, in search of the lost Sir John Franklin, referred to Deer Rapids as "the Angle Rapid (*Rapide de l'Equerre*)."[29] Perhaps the current name for the rapids derives from the nearby Mudjatik River, formerly the Caribou River, since, at one time, northerners commonly referred to caribou as deer.

The first rapids, or Upper Deer Rapids, begin where the Churchill bends left around a point (74B 415122). Here, on river right, you will see outcrops of rusty pink granite as the Churchill now enters the Precambrian Shield. Upper Deer Rapids are serious Class 2 rapids, but they can be shot by advanced canoeists after careful scouting from the right shore. To position yourself for scouting, you may advance southeast towards the rapids through 100 m (110 yd) or so of rapid current. This will bring you to a small, V-shaped eddy on river right where a tiny streamlet trickles into the Churchill from the south. You can pull into this eddy, which is roughly adjacent to the head of the rapids proper, and then disembark to scout from shore.

To run Upper Deer Rapids, you can start out down a main tongue at river centre or down a passage near the river right shore. You can then proceed by staying generally right of the rocky shallows off the point on river left. However, after 100 m (110 yd) or more, you will

Map 7.3   Upper Deer Rapids and Lower Deer Rapids

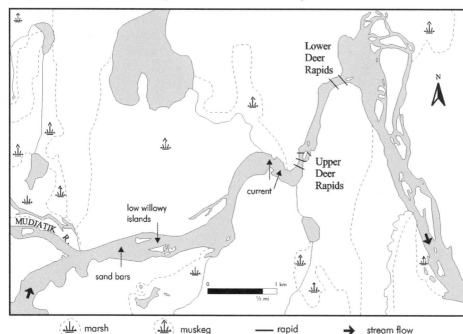

marsh   muskeg   —— rapid   → stream flow

come to where a massive granite knob, about 3 m (10 ft) high, pushes out from the right shore. Here, you will have to veer left to avoid bad whitewater near the knob and eddy lines below it. Past the knob, you will have some further swift current, some minor rapids alongside a small island, and then a return to quiet water.

Ordinarily, one would expect to find a portage past rapids as difficult as Upper Deer Rapids, but we have seen no record of one and have not found one on our own. Cautious canoeists will therefore have to wade and line to get their canoes past the rapids. We suggest that canoes could be waded, lined, and sometimes carried along the bouldery river right shore. We should note, however, that when Philip Turnor, Peter Fidler, and their party went up these rapids on October 5, 1790, they "led the Canoes S to W 1/4 mile strong current shoal and full of great stones"[30] with the canoes being led on the river left side.[31]

Of course, upstream travellers will also be required to wade and track to get their canoes past the rapids. We have never done this, so we have no clear advice on which shore to take. You might perhaps follow Turnor's example and go up the northwest shore.

One km (²/₃ mi) of quiet water, known in Dene as *Nuhkay Tthaybawzsay Rutahrray* ("between the two little rapids"), intervenes between Upper Deer Rapids and the next rapids, which we will refer to as Lower Deer Rapids. Between the two sets of rapids, you can watch for bedrock lunch spots on the banks of the river left shore. These do not have very good landings or much in the way of tent space. (Since our 1986 trip, players or fans from Patuanak's hockey team, the Pats, have painted the rocks at one spot with a great deal of graffiti.) Still, if you want a break between the rapids, the river left shore does provide reasonable stopping.

Lower Deer Rapids

Lower Deer Rapids (74B 422135) extend for about 200 m (220 yd) and end just as the Churchill bends sharply right to run southeast. Like their upstream counterparts, these are serious Class 2 rapids with some hazardous rocks and many large waves. When we ran these rapids on June 25, 1986, we were surprised by the size of the waves once we saw them up close and even more surprised after a couple came over our gunwales. Nonetheless, we suggest that advanced canoeists may run these rapids, possibly on a course near the river right shore, provided they first land and scout them carefully.

Cautious paddlers have the option of portaging Lower Deer Rapids. An overgrown trail on river right, which is either an old portage or a game trail, runs along the main length of the rapids, though it dwindles out as it goes downstream. This trail has no obvious landing point at either end, but you could strike inland at any convenient point to find it. If you should miss it, you may easily pick a path of your own choosing since the aspen and balsam poplar woods here are mainly free of underbrush. Canoeists could also wade or line their canoes down the rapids. The north shore might be preferable for wading and lining. It was the choice of Philip Turnor and his companions when they ascended the rapids on October 5, 1790.[32]

> Upstream travellers can follow Turnor's example and wade and track their canoes along the north shore. The other option is, of course, to seek out the trail described above and portage.

Down from Lower Deer Rapids

Downstream from Lower Deer Rapids, the Churchill settles down as it flows lazily south-southeast through low, level country for several kilometres. In this distance, aspens and some spruce grow back from the river, but the river's stony shorelines are generally thick with willows. While the slow current here allows for good paddling in either direction, the shore terrain offers no camping to speak of.

If you are using the 1:50,000 map series, you will notice that the Churchill leaves Map 74B/4 to cut across the lower left corner of Map 74B/3. Since this corner crossing accounts for less than 2 km (1¼ mi) of easy paddling, you may choose to proceed without Map 74B/3 and resume your map reading in the upper left corner of Map 73-O/14. Two km (1¼ mi) downstream from the top of 73-O/14, there is a narrows the Dene refer to as *Horeeⁿ dareeⁿ*, meaning, appropriately enough, "the narrows" (73-O 452068).

Ten km (6 mi) or so downstream from Lower Deer Rapids, the Churchill makes a 90-degree turn eastward and immediately divides around a small island (73-O 471040). The river's main flow goes around the south side of the island, but there is normally sufficient water on the north side to allow canoes to pass.

From the 90-degree turn, it is only 600 m (⅓ mi) to Dipper Rapids. Since these are very dangerous rapids, canoeists of all skill levels should prepare to put ashore on river left.

> Both sides of the small island above Dipper Rapids have fast current, so upstream travellers may have to wade a short distance here to advance. Stronger canoeists could perhaps get up the current with some hard paddling.

Dipper Rapids

Dipper Rapids have been known by various names over the years. If we can judge by the names they gave the portage past the rapids, the early voyageurs knew the rapids as "la Puisse" ("mighty")[33] and also "des Pins" ("spruce").[34] Much later on, writing in 1934 as editor of the journals of Philip Turnor, J.B. Tyrrell referred to the rapids as having both the name Pelican and the name Dipper.[35] The Dene today refer to Dipper Rapids by the name *Horuhchaghe Tthaybah*, meaning "pelican rapids." This name might have been borrowed from the Cree who lived in the region before the fur trade; if so, it could be of considerable antiquity. On the other hand, if the name is of strictly Dene origin, it may not be so old as the early voyageur names.

The rapids, which have an elevation drop of roughly 3 m (10 ft) over a distance of about 400 m (¼ mi), are the most serious rapids found between Patuanak and Pinehouse. They start as swift water where the Churchill has to flow through and around two jumbles of rock that form a broken line across the river channel. Below the rock jumbles, which may have only two or three boulders exposed in high water, swift current and lesser rapids extend for some distance. But then, at a point where a square thumb of granite juts out from the north shore, the river thunders down over a major ledge and churns itself into white foam. Only 30 m (33 yd) downstream, it drops again over a second ledge that recharges the turbulence. Quieter water then follows for 100 m (110 yd) or so. Finally, towards the foot of the rapids, rocks and big waves interrupt the quieter reach and produce a last section of bad whitewater.

Dipper Rapids Lore

The Patuanak Dene do *not* run their skiffs up or down Dipper Rapids. To our knowledge, Joe Black, formerly of Dipper Lake, is the only man ever to have run a skiff through the rapids. In the early 1970s, as many as twenty to thirty skiffs were on their way to Patuanak from fishing down river. As they arrived at Dipper Rapids together, there was considerable congestion as men waited to take their skiffs over the portage on the railway built for that purpose. Joe was in line for the railway when, with the confidence of youth, he decided he could jump the queue by running his skiff up the rapids. With men watching from the rock above the rapids, he somehow succeeded in driving his boat all the way to the top. Amazed by what they had seen, two more men had Joe pilot their skiffs up the rapids before Joe decided he could not press his luck further. Though he also drove his skiff down the rapids later that same summer, neither he nor anyone else has since tried to take a skiff through the rapids in either direction.

Father Moraud is the one man known to have survived a trip down the rapids in a canoe. As the story goes, Father Moraud and four other men were travelling downstream to Dipper Lake with a load of lumber in a freighter canoe. When they reached Dipper Rapids, the four men accompanying the priest were able to disembark at the portage. However, before Father Moraud could do so, the heavily laden canoe was swept out into the current and down the rapids. Miraculously, Father Moraud, standing in the front of the canoe like a doomed sentinel, survived what must have been a most incredible ride. When his anxious companions rushed to the foot of the rapids, they found that, while the canoe's motor had been lost, the priest, the canoe, and its lumber cargo were all intact.[36] No one should risk repeating Father Moraud's adventure! All canoeists should portage along the north shore of Dipper Rapids.

The portage railway at Dipper Portage, autumn, 1992.

Portage #3 - Dipper Portage
(± 375 m / 410 yd)

As you approach this portage from upstream, you will see its start area as a small, grassy clearing on river left (73-O 477040). You will also notice the portage railway that runs up from the water, across the clearing, and off into the woods in an easterly direction. A boat ramp at the head of the railway serves as the upstream landing.

You will have to exercise caution and stay as close to the shore as possible as you paddle to the upstream landing. There is some current right up to the landing, and the landing itself has only the slightest eddy protection. There is swift current only 5 or 10 m (5 or 10 yds) out from the landing.

The grassy clearing at the start of the portage makes a reasonable campsite. It has a gradual slope and a few rocks here and there, but tent spaces can be found.

In 1986, we found the portage railway, which had been last rebuilt in 1975,[37] in some disrepair. However, in 1988, men from Patuanak gave it a major upgrade. The railway now has its angle iron rails running on timbers underlain with actual railway ties. This improved construction easily supports the heavy-duty rail car used to haul skiffs and freight over the portage.

When the railway was first built in 1960,[38] it began further downstream than it does now. Indeed, its starting point was just above the most dangerous part of the rapids. You can still see where the path of this older railway joins with the current railway and portage.

You may be tempted to use the rail car for transporting your canoe and gear over the portage, but we would advise you to carry your things instead. The rail car is heavy and hard to control for those who are not used to it. In 1986, we loaded our outfit onto the car and started pulling it east along the railway. Unfortunately, when we came to the slight downhill slope at the end of the portage, our best efforts could not keep the car under control. In the resulting crash, our only spare paddle was broken and the barrel of our camera's zoom lens was dented.

The railway's terminus, located just below the foot of the rapids, serves as the portage's downstream landing. Here, it is possible to camp on a flat terrace north from and some 6 to 8 m (20 to 25 ft) above the level of the railway. This terrace, which is thinly wooded with small aspens, has a great deal of room for tents. Its disadvantage is that it is only accessible by a very steep track up the bank alongside the railway.

Upstream travellers will have to paddle against some current to reach the landing. However, if you stay close to the north shore, you should not find this current too troublesome.

Down from Dipper Rapids

About 700 m (770 yd) downstream from Dipper Rapids, where the Churchill bends south, there is a section of fast water some 75 m (82 yd) long. In low water, this stretch develops good-sized waves. Even then, though, the channel down river right remains deep and rock-free.

Whether in high or low water, upstream travellers will likely have to wade or track up part of the fast water below Dipper Rapids. Those with the proper skills might try poling as mentioned by Peter Fidler in a journal entry made as he travelled downstream with Philip Turnor on June 11, 1792: "then arrive at a Carrying place [Dipper Rapids Portage] upon the north side 440 yards over. Pretty good carrying, but stony towards the upper end. a very steep fall here—Then in the river as before, ESE 1/2 a rapid 250 yards set it up with poles in 1790...."[39]

Just below the fast water, the Churchill bellies out as it makes a broad turn east and then north. According to Philip Wolverine of Patuanak, the Dene refer to this expansion in the river as *Guh-taray Too-ay*, meaning "rabbitskin lake," with the name being derived from the nickname of an old man who once lived here.[40] At one time, the Hudson's Bay Company had a post, perhaps only a small outpost cabin, somewhere on the east shore of the lake. In about 1910, the post and other buildings in the vicinity burned to the ground.[41]

You may note that Map 73-O marks a settlement called "Pine River" on the west end of Rabbitskin Lake. This is a cartographic error. There has never been a settlement on the spot indicated. To confuse things further, the name Pine River actually has applied to both the upstream community of Patuanak and the Knee Lake settlement further downstream.[42]

Downstream from Rabbitskin Lake, for the last 4 km (2½ mi) to Dipper Lake, the banks of the Churchill are low and marshy. Since the river slows here, much of its sediment load has settled out to form numerous islands. If you are a bird-watcher, this is a good place to take it easy and look around. Picking your way through the maze formed by the islands, you will find the willowy shorelines teeming with blackbirds and other songbirds. In front of your canoe, you will see any number of ducks with their growing broods.

Dipper Lake

In 1934, J.B. Tyrrell referred to this lake both as Pelican Lake and Dipper Lake.[43] The Dene today maintain the use of the name Pelican Lake, which they say as *Horuhchaghe Too-ay,* but Dipper has become the standard English name for the lake.

The canoe route across Dipper Lake is a 4-km (2½-mi) traverse with almost no wind protection. Paddlers attempting this traverse in blowing conditions could easily swamp amid rows of marching whitecaps. Swamping might well be fatal, so the traverse should be saved for fair weather. Though they offer only slight wind protection, there are two islands just south of the traverse line that can serve as waypoints for paddlers. The first, 1 km (2/3 mi) southeast from the mouth of the river, is a mass of steep, bare Shield rock that contrasts sharply with the generally low shorelines around the lake. It is known in Dene as *Tthay Kulay Noo-ay,* or "flat rock island." The second, about halfway across the traverse, is also a Shield rock island, but it is not so rugged. It has emergency camping possibilities at its southwest corner and on its east side. It is known in Dene as *Ghe-aw[n]-zee[n] Tthay Kulay Noo-ay,* or "farther flat rock island."

Peter Fidler's sketch of Dipper Lake and Primeau Lake.

Dipper Lake History

The early fur traders considered Dipper Lake and present-day Primeau Lake to be all one lake, which they referred to as Primeau Lake. Likely the oldest written record of a name for this double lake is in Philip Turnor's journal entry for October 4, 1790, wherein he refers to entering "Nick-ey-thut-tins-Sack-a-ha-gan or Lewis Primoes Lake."[44]

Louis Primeau, a quite remarkable French fur trader, had his name attached to the double lake after he built a post, actually somewhere on the west side of Dipper Lake, in 1775 and used it as his wintering quarters during the winter of 1775–76.[45] Primeau, as we shall explain later, had, in 1774, built a post at Frog Portage for the Frobisher brothers, fur traders from Montreal. The post at Frog Portage had the distinction of being further into the North-West than any previously constructed. When Primeau went up the Churchill in 1775 and built at Dipper Lake, once more under instructions from the Frobishers, he could again claim that his post was further advanced than any that had come before.[46]

Not much is known about Primeau's post on Dipper Lake. It was likely a hastily built log structure not meant to last more than a season or so. Nonetheless, since Hudson's Bay Company records suggest two Montrealer or "Pedler" canoes went to Primeau Lake in 1775 and since those canoes would ordinarily be manned by at least four men apiece, Primeau may have had as many as eight men to help with construction. Such a crew—even allowing for time taken to procure food—may have built a house of considerable size.

In January 1776, Joseph Frobisher and Alexander Henry, both "Pedlers" from Montreal, paid a visit to Matthew Cocking, who was in charge of the Hudson's Bay Company post at Cumberland House, and mentioned Primeau's post to him. Cocking's journal entry for January 21, 1776, reads:

> They tell me that they did hear in the Fall from the two Canoes left by Frobisher in the Thopiskow Indians Country last summer, They were intended to have gone a considerable distance up a River that way to Trade but the account recieved from them informs that they had gone but a little way & were scarce of Provisions.[47]

Clearly, though, Primeau's post was active through the 1775–1776 season. On April 20, 1776, Cocking spoke to an Indian family that had arrived at Cumberland House from Amisk Lake. In his journal, Cocking writes, "They inform me that one of the Master Pedlers with Eight Men went off last month hauling Rum for the two Canoes who are residing in the Thopiskow Indians Country."[48] And, on June 27, 1776, while recounting in his journal a report he had received from his man Robert Longmoor regarding Longmoor's trip to the "Pedlers Settlement" at Frog Portage, Cocking further writes:

He [Longmoor] found two of the Master Pedlers [Alexander Henry and a Frobisher, likely Joseph] were gone up with a Supply to the upper settlement [Primeau's post] sometime, the Master left at the House (the Elder Frobisher)[sic., likely Thomas Frobisher] did invite him in and offer him any assistance he might want which he refused except partaking of a little Food. On the 16th the two Masters returned from above, accompanied by Lewis Primo who had resided at the Upper Settlement...[49]

But what of the other name Turnor gave for the lake—"Nick-ey-thu-tins-Sack-a-ha-gan"? Seemingly, it is the same as the Cree *nikî-thôtinisin sâkahikan*, meaning "I was caught in the wind lake" or "windbound lake" and apparently derives from Primeau's Cree nickname. It fortuituously serves as a useful reminder that Dipper Lake is potentially dangerous.

Dipper Lake Settlement

On the west shore of Dipper Lake, 2 km (1¼ mi) south from where the Churchill runs into the lake, stands what was once the community of Dipper Lake (73-O 521031), referred to in Dene simply as *Tthaybah Chahrray*, meaning "the foot of the rapids." There are about a half dozen cabins here, and the settlement area remains neatly cared for. For the most part, however, the cabins are now occupied only on a seasonal basis by people with permanent homes in Patuanak.

The fact that Louis Primeau chose to build his 1775 post in the vicinity of the Dipper Lake settlement site suggests that the area has long been a favourite gathering place for native people. But in those early days, the hunting life would not have allowed for a permanent settlement here. According to information collected by ethnographer Robert Jarvenpa, who worked among the English River Dene in 1971 and 1972, it was not until about 1900 that Dene from the Churchill region began to build log homes at Dipper Lake and at Primeau Lake and Knee Lake further downstream.[50]

Once people started to settle at Dipper Lake, fur traders no doubt established themselves nearby. As already mentioned, there was a post just upstream from Dipper Lake at Rabbitskin Lake for an unknown period up to about 1910. In subsequent years, the Hudson's Bay Company apparently continued to trade at Dipper Lake. Some proof of this comes from a brief entry in the company's Pine River (now Patuanak) Post Journal for October 10, 1921: "Dispatched Dipper and Elbow [Knee] Lake Outfits per Gilbert Deertooth and James Paul, early this morning."[51]

A major event occurred at Dipper Lake in 1949 when the energetic Father Moraud built the first of three churches he was to construct in three consecutive years at points on the Churchill downstream from Patuanak.[52] When we stopped at Dipper Lake on June 26, 1986, we were able to examine Father Moraud's church here even though it was then in the process of being dismantled and converted into a storage shed. The main section of the church, which had been re-roofed as the shed, measured roughly 6 m by 8 m (20 by 25 ft). What had once been a storey-and-a-half back section—now detached from the main section and standing off to one side—measured roughly 6 m by 2.5 m (20 by 8 ft). The belfry, which had been lowered to the ground and was now also standing to one side, was nearly 4 m (13 ft) high and fitted with galvanized metal shingles and a wooden cross on top. We had come too late to see the church as it once was, but it was still evident that Father Moraud had been both a good architect and a good carpenter.

Father Moraud had wanted his Dene parishioners to stay in their traditional hunting grounds and outlying communities. His church-building projects went some distance to meet that end. However, as underscored by the dismantling of the Dipper Lake church, modern-day pressures eventually led to the gradual abandonment of several small English River communities. A main pressure was the need to give children proper access to schooling. When St. Louis School opened in Patuanak in 1968, people from outlying communities naturally migrated to that centre.[53]

Old cemeteries commonly survive as memorials to abandoned communities. Dipper Lake's cemetery lies 1 km (²/₃ mi) south of the settlement site near a winter trail that leads into McEachern Lake to the west (not named on Map 73-O). Because of its proximity to the cemetery, the Dene know McEachern Lake as Dene *Thee-ay Too-awzsay*, or "dead people's lake."

Primeau Lake

Once you have completed your traverse of Dipper Lake, you will come to a narrows (73-O 570040) leading into a bay or channel which, for convenience, we will refer to as part of adjoining Primeau Lake. In low water, the narrows actually becomes a broad, ripply rapid, but it remains easily navigable by canoe.

The point on the south side of the narrows is known in Dene as *Say-Tsee-yay William Awzsay Hochela*, or "old William point," after an old man who lived there many years ago. The point has an exposure of red granite which, at least at ordinary water levels, would make a good lunch spot. It might also serve as a campsite though it does not have much room for tents.

The Dene know Primeau Lake by different names, including *G'es Gkuzay Too-ay*, which means "poplar channel lake," and *Tthaybahtee Too-ay*, which means "the lake before the rapids." The rapids referred to in this latter name are Crooked Rapids, just downstream from the lake's outflow.

As maps will show, Primeau Lake is more a zigzag of long bays and peninsulas than it is a lake. It therefore has a very long shoreline. However, since the canoe route through the lake simply crosses the mouths of the main bays, it is really not that circuitous. It is only 17 km (11 mi) from the narrows out of Dipper Lake to Otter Island where Primeau Lake has its outflow. From the narrows out of Dipper Lake, the old voyageur highway runs south for 5 km (3 mi) down a channel having low shores wooded mainly with aspens. A long bay continues much further south, but the highway itself makes a sharp left turn around a point to head northeast. After going 1.5 km (1 mi) northeast, it then bends to the right around another point to once again run south. As the highway leads on, the land becomes higher than before, and the aspen woods become mixed with more spruce.

Primeau Lake Settlement

What was once the community of Primeau Lake (73-O 614965) now consists of a few cabins spread along the west shore of the lake directly below the "u" in "Primeau" on Maps 73-O and 73-O/14. In Dene, the settlement site is called *G'es Gkuzay*, or "poplar channel," because the adjacent channel is lined by poplars. As in the case of the Dipper Lake settlement, the buildings and yards here are neatly kept. Again, however, the cabins are occupied only on a seasonal basis. In 1986, we visited the cabin of an elderly couple named Joe and Eleanor Solomon, who advised us that they spent only their summers at Primeau Lake.

In 1950, a year after building at Dipper Lake, Father Moraud built a church at Primeau Lake.[54] Located up a slope overlooking the lake, the church was about 6 by 8 m (20 by 25 ft), with a side wing, perhaps the rectory, of about 4.5 by 3.5 m (15 by 12 ft). It was of good frame construction over a stone foundation and finished with shiplap siding painted white. When we saw it in 1986, it was being remodelled into a cabin.[55]

Otter Island

Primeau Lake's outflow channel begins in the southeastern part of the lake and runs north-northeast. As you move into the outflow channel, you will pass a tiny island, and then, 1 km (2/3 mi) further north, you will come to a larger island. This larger island is known in Dene as *Nahnbee-ay Noo-awzsay*, meaning "otter island" (73-O 650949). We did not see otters here, but we found their beaver cousins well established with a lodge built against the east side of the island. You might find Otter Island suitable for camping. The beavers have cut down the aspen on a high knoll at the north end of the island. The clearing they have created has room for tents.

Crooked Rapids

Crooked Rapids, commencing 3 km (2 mi) north from Otter Island, are known in Dene as *Tthaybah Thaywahrray*, meaning "crooked rapids," and also *Denechawzay Tthaybah*, meaning "elbow rapids." The rapids, which are in three distinct sets, occur where the Churchill makes a square turn back on itself as it corners from north to east and then to south. The rapids are runnable, but those of the second set require advanced to expert skills. Many canoeists will thus want to bypass the rapids in their entirety by taking the portage, which we will describe shortly, across the thumb of land that forms the river right shore of the rapids.

The initial rapids are immediately before the river's first right turn. These are minor, Class 1 rapids having rocks down the left but good water down the right. In low water, they should

Map 7.4   Crooked Rapids and Crooked Portage

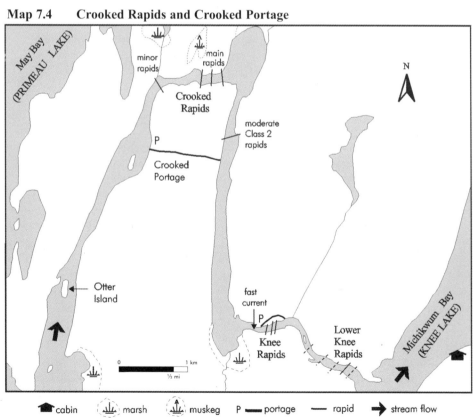

be looked at before being run. Ordinarily, though, they can be run right of centre without difficulty. After the initial rapids, a section of fast water about 600 m (1/3 mi) long will bring you to the second rapids. You will have to stay alert in the fast water and steer to shore in time to do a mandatory scouting of these major, Class 2 rapids.

The second rapids are long. They extend, at least in low water, some 400 m (¼ mi) to where the river turns sharply to the south. Throughout their length, they flow down an even gradient, but they nonetheless have some big waves and bad rocks that demand careful manoeuvring. The best course to shoot is to the left, or north, of a small, rocky island. There is boiling whitewater north of the island, but a navigable path 15 to 20 m (50 to 65 ft) wide lies between it and the island. From the foot of the second rapids, the river runs for about 700 m (770 yd) to reach the third and final rapids. It should be noted, however, that this intervening water is not placid. Rather, it contains tricky fast sections and sometimes even minor rapids.

The third rapids, which we rate as Class 2, are about 100 m (110 yd) long. They are not as difficult as the second rapids though they do have medium to big waves and do warrant scouting from shore. A navigable path of good depth begins down the centre and runs to the right of a rubbly island. It then veers left and thus avoids some boulders to the right near the foot of the rapids.

Peter Fidler has left us with an early account of Crooked Rapids. As he travelled downstream from Primeau Lake on June 11, 1792, he wrote:

> went down a river with strong current & several very bad shoal rapids 100 yds wide—NbE 1 1/2—ENE 3/4 two very bad rapids, led up in 1790 on South side but now necesseated to carry the rapids are so very shole 250 yards at the upper end we carried—a small Island in the middle of the river when the water up you shoot on the N side of it, commonly the Canadians make a portage on S Side of 1370 yards long to avoid these 2 rapids & 2 more, a little way below, when the water is shole.[56]

The Canadian portage that Fidler referred to is most likely the portage in use today. We recommend it to those wanting to avoid the hazards of the rapids described above and, of course, to upstream travellers.

Portage #4 - Crooked Portage (± 1,200 m / 1,310 yd)

The upstream start of this portage (73-O 663968) is on river right about 200 m (220 yd) northeast of a willowy island located 1 km (2/3 mi) upstream from the first section of Crooked Rapids. It can be hard to find since it shows only as a vague break in the shore willows. Moreover, the healthy growth of bulrushes, horsetails, and sedges in front of the shore may have no break at all. You may have to search a bit to find the mud landing that slopes gently up to the portage.

There is a small clearing behind the shore willows hiding the start of the portage. This clearing is nothing special and may attract mosquitoes at times, but it does have space for a couple of tents. The portage trail itself goes through a pleasant mixed wood of aspen, birch, spruce, and jack pine. It has not seen much use in recent years and has considerable windfall. It would not, however, be confused for a game trail, and it is in good condition overall.

Another small camping area exists at the downstream end of the portage. This is a level, grassy clearing behind the shore alders and willows. In early summer, tiger lilies bloom here.

Coming from downstream, you may also have trouble finding the portage (73-O 673967). Its east end is perhaps 200 m (220 yd) downstream of the third rapids and just within sight of them. You can work up the river's west shore until the shore makes a slight, 10-m (11-yd) jog to the west. From this jog, it is another 20 m (22 yd) north to where an inconspicuous break in the shore alders and willows identifies the portage.

Down from Crooked Rapids

From Crooked Portage, the Churchill flows south for 2 km (1¼ mi) down a narrow channel. It then makes a 90-degree turn to the east and the current becomes significantly stronger for about the next 100 m (110 yd). A ridge of pink granite running out from the river left shore then marks the start of a portage bypassing some major whitewater known as Knee Rapids. All canoeists should land on the upstream side of the ridge of pink granite to reconnoitre.

Because of the strong current, upstream travellers will be required to do some wading to advance up the first 100 m (110 yd) above Knee Rapids.

Knee Rapids

The journals of Philip Turnor and Peter Fidler provide two early accounts of Knee Rapids. If nothing else, these accounts underscore the extreme pains the early voyagers would go to in order to avoid a portage and the high degree of skill they must have had in handling a canoe. On October 3, 1790, while he and his party were travelling upstream out of Knee Lake, Philip Turnor wrote:

> and came to a part about 200 yards wide went W 1/4 mile very strong current set up it with poles then paddled 200 yards, then led the Canoes on north side 1/4 mile near West up the lower part of a fall [Knee Rapids] to a rock at the head of it, then carried 20 yards over the rock this fall is very bad at the lower part being very full of large stones, frequently most of the cargoe is carried the whole length of the fall, the Canadians run this fall down, enter on south side and cross directly to the north not good...[57]

When Turnor returned this way going downstream on June 11, 1792, his companion Peter Fidler, who had also been with him on the upstream journey, wrote:

> then East 1/2 and came to another Carrying place on N side 10 yards over a rock—we shot it down and carried nothing—sometimes the Canoes are led up all the way on the South side & so avoids the Portage—we carried here in 1790—NE 1/2 a strong rapid & very large stones very bad handing—steep rocks on the South side—ESE 1/2 Three short rapids led them all up in 1790 on the N side—all the 3 is not more than 200 yards long, but bad owing to the very large stones, sometimes the Canoes is upon a Stone & the next step you take are up to the middle in the water—high steep banks on both sides of the river below the Carrying place.[58]

Knee Rapids, which are known in Dene as *Tthaychelay Tthaybah*, meaning "rocky rapids," are major, Class 3 rapids extending 350 to 400 m (380 to 440 yd). Throughout their length, they have rocks, boulders, low ledges, and medium to large waves. The waves are especially large at the lower end of the rapids.

Some experts might shoot these rapids after carefully scouting them from shore. There appears to be a course that starts on river right, swings left, and then returns to the right again. But when we looked at Knee Rapids in 1986, we decided that they were too difficult for us. We opted for a portage.

Although the whole north shore of the rapids has been burned off in a forest fire, the area of the rapids remains picturesque. The rapids themselves glisten brightly on a sunny day. And, the "steep rocks on the South side" referred to by Fidler rise into a promontory 8 to 10 m (25 to 30 ft) high near the foot of the rapids. In 1986, on the north shore, across from the high promontory, there was an active bald eagle nest in the top branches of a tall, fire-damaged jack pine.[59]

Portage #5 - Knee Portage (± 375 m / 410 yd)

At its upstream end, this portage begins in a corner created by the ridge of pink granite running out from the river's north shore, right above the main rapids. The bare and spacious granite ridge provides plenty of room for unloading. Unfortunately, the portage itself is as bad as any between La Loche and Cumberland House. Due to the rocky nature of the north shore, it has likely never been good. Alexander Mackenzie said of it, "The portage of the same name [as Knee Lake] is several hundred yards long, and over large stones."[60] A classic understatement! The portage has been made worse by the forest fire that burned the north shore in the early 1980s and all but obliterated the original trail. In 1986, we could find no more than a short remnant of it and thus had to pick our way through a jumble of broken boulders and crisscrossed windfall as best we could.[61]

The downstream end of the portage is not much easier to find than the portage itself. What might be considered the downstream landing is a rocky shore roughly opposite the high promontory on the south side of the river. Since this landing area has no good place to beach or moor a canoe, it may be necessary to stand in the water to load or unload gear.

Lower Knee Rapids

Below the main part of Knee Rapids, the Churchill bends right to flow southeast. About 200 m (220 yd) from the bend, there is a small island, and from this island, it is just over 1 km (2/3 mi) further to where the river enters Michikwum Bay (*mihcikwan* is Cree for "knee") on Knee Lake.

At ordinary water levels, the entire distance from the small island to Michikwum Bay, which we refer to as Lower Knee Rapids, has fast water and minor rapids. At lower water levels, this section of river increases in intensity and becomes one continuous series of rapids. The rapid marked on both Map 73-O and Map 73-O/14 near Michikwum Bay is the most difficult whitewater (73-O 690936). In low water, with submerged rocks and medium-sized standing waves, it earns a Class 2 rating and warrants scouting from shore.

If you do not have good, advanced canoeing skills, you may decide to stay close to shore and wade or line parts of Lower Knee Rapids. The river left shore appears to offer the best wading.

Going upstream, you will have to wade or track up all of Lower Knee Rapids. Again, the river left shore appears to be the best option. Once the small island is reached, you may paddle the rest of the distance up to the downstream end of Knee Portage.

Knee Lake

Knee Lake's name likely predates the coming of the white man. When Philip Turnor first saw the lake on October 2, 1790, he referred to it as "U-che-Quan Sask-a-ha-gan [*ohcikwan sâkahikan*] or Knee Lake,"[62] no doubt an already existing name. The name is suitable, since a major peninsula coming down from the northeast gives the lake the shape of a sharply bent leg complete with thigh, knee, and shin bone. In Dene, Knee Lake is known as *Tsho Deszay Too-ay* with the words *Tscho Deszay* being the name of the Haultain River. While *Deszay* means "river" and *Too-ay* means "lake," the origin of the word *tscho* is apparently not known.[63]

Knee Lake is a big lake accounting for a full 24 km (15 mi) of the old voyageur highway. The area is well-treed with a mixed forest dominated by aspen and spruce. Much of its shoreline is made up of large, head-sized stones, but the shore also has notable Shield rock outcrops.

As you leave Michikwum Bay on the west side of the lake and enter what Map 73-O/14 calls Knox Bay, you will see two small islands in your path. The south end of the more westerly island has room for a tent and would serve as a campsite for a single canoe in a pinch. There are not many trees here, so it could be windy. On the other hand, this might be a real plus when the mosquitoes are bad.

Two km (1¼ mi) due south from the westerly island, a peninsula, which is part of Knee Lake Indian Reserve 192B (a reserve of the English River Dene),[64] forms the east side of the entrance between Knox Bay and the main part of Knee Lake. A small, gravelly beach on the westernmost corner of this peninsula would make a good lunch spot (73-O 710915). The aspens back from the beach would also have room for one or two tents.

From the gravelly beach, it is a long, 5-km (3-mi) traverse to the southwest end of the large peninsula—known in Dene as *Hochela Chogh* or "big point"—that shapes the inside bend of Knee Lake's knee. A few islands in the first half of this traverse provide some wind protection. Even so, the traverse is a dangerous one that should be attempted only in good weather.

Optional Route on Knee Lake

In rare circumstances, you may gain some wind protection on Knee Lake by paddling northeast up the main part of the lake and then portaging across the base of the lake's dividing peninsula to enter Bentley Bay, the shin bone part of the lake. If you opt for this route, you can watch for an old airplane crash site on a stony point about 3 km (2 mi) up the west shore of the lake's dividing peninsula. In 1977, pilot Rod Brock, flying a de Havilland Beaver, was hauling fish on a foggy morning when he flew into the point and was killed. The Beaver's engine and the rear halves of its pontoons still sit on the stony shore. More wreckage is strewn in the aspens further inland.

Portage #6 - Knee Lake Portage (± 650 m / 710 yd) (optional)

The portage starts from the bay lying immediately north of the narrow base of Knee Lake's dividing peninsula. More precisely, it begins from the southeast corner of a little bay 50 m (55 yd) wide and 100 m (110 yd) deep, which bay in turn is in the southeast corner of the bay first mentioned. (The portage begins about 300 m further east than where indicated on Map 73-O. It is not marked on Map 73-O/15.) The landing has a band of sedges in front of it, but it is visible as a 3-m (10-ft) break in the shore willows.

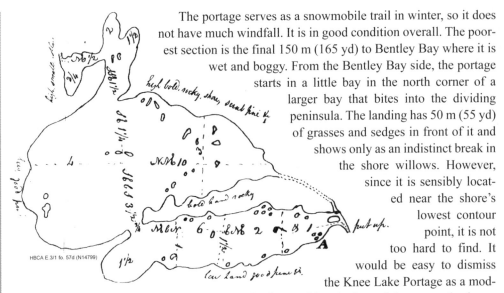

The portage serves as a snowmobile trail in winter, so it does not have much windfall. It is in good condition overall. The poorest section is the final 150 m (165 yd) to Bentley Bay where it is wet and boggy. From the Bentley Bay side, the portage starts in a little bay in the north corner of a larger bay that bites into the dividing peninsula. The landing has 50 m (55 yd) of grasses and sedges in front of it and shows only as an indistinct break in the shore willows. However, since it is sensibly located near the shore's lowest contour point, it is not too hard to find. It would be easy to dismiss the Knee Lake Portage as a modern-day snowmobile trail, but it actually dates back to prehistoric times. It is accurately shown on a map (reproduced above) sketched by Peter Fidler on June 12, 1792.

Main Route on Knee Lake

If you follow the old voyageur highway through Knee Lake, you will find that the southwest tip of Knee Lake's dividing peninsula is a massive bastion of Shield rock. Well before you reach here, you will see that a tall steel cross stands high on the bald crown of the promontory and guards the lake below. This cross was erected by Father Moraud who, we can guess, wanted to assure his far-flung parishioners that they were never really alone.

The cross promontory is separated from the main part of the peninsula by a small bay that cuts into the northwest shore of the peninsula. If you enter this protected bay, you will find good camping on a sand beach about 100 m (110 yd) long (73-O 742871).

There is another good camping area on a sand beach on the southeast side of the peninsula (73-O 742869), directly across from the beach on the other side. This beach, which we highly recommend, is much like the first one, but it has the advantage of facing the morning sun.

Going up Bentley Bay, you will find other spots with camping possibilities. About 8 km (5 mi) up the bay, there is a slope of smooth bedrock on the southeast shore that would make a good campsite (73-O 810894). Just over 3 km (2 mi) farther, on an anvil-shaped peninsula on the opposite, northwest shore, a broad shelf of pink granite sloping down into the water makes another good campsite (73-O 835916).

If you keep to the southeast shore of Bentley Bay, you can watch for a bald eagle nest on the south end of an island (73-O 837899) lying southeast from the anvil-shaped peninsula on the northwest shore.

As you draw to within 1 km (2/3 mi) of the east end of Knee Lake, you will come to a large island known in Dene as *Noo Chogh*, or "big island." The main travel route along the south side of the island is *Noo Chogh Gkuzay*, or "big island channel." According to Joe Black who has fished extensively in this area, the channel is an excellent place to catch whitefish in the summer.

Knee Lake Settlement

On the extreme eastern shore of Knee Lake, you will find a settlement site identified by Maps 73-O and 73-O/15 as Elak Dase Indian Reserve 192A. The name "Elak Dase" is a misnomer. The region's only *Elehk Des* ("floating muskeg river") is a tributary of the upper Mudjatik; such a river is not known to exist near Reserve 192A. The correct Dene name for the settlement is *Tsho Deszay Che*, which refers to its being at the mouth of the Haultain River. In English, the settlement was at one time commonly referred to as Pine River.[65] In recent times, it has been known as either Elbow Lake or Knee Lake with the latter name now the more common.

The settlement comprises a small church and a dozen cabins scattered along a grassy slope about 4 to 5 m (13 to 16 ft) above the lake level. Like the cabins at Dipper Lake and Primeau Lake, the ones here are now mainly occupied on only a seasonal basis by people with permanent homes in Patuanak. Again, though, while the settlement is for the most part deserted, it is kept neat and tidy by those who stay here from time to time.

Since the settlement site is on the best high ground available near the mouth of the important Haultain River, it has likely been a well-used camping spot for centuries. However, like its sister communities upstream, it did not become established as an actual community until late in the fur trade. Louis George of Patuanak, who was raised at Knee Lake, told us (consistent with Robert Jarvenpa's information) that he understood people first settled at Knee Lake around 1900 or so.[66]

As already noted, there is a record of the Hudson's Bay Company sending a trading outfit to Knee Lake in 1921. At some point, possibly after 1921, the company operated a store at Knee Lake on a seasonal basis for roughly twenty-five years.[67] For at least part of its life, the store was run by JB (Jean Baptiste) George.

Knee Lake's small outpost store would not have provided full-time employment for its operator. When JB George ran it, he also trapped, fished, and raised livestock. JB's son Norbert George has reflected on his father's livestock operation:

> Knee Lake was a good area for trapping and fishing ... and there were big grass meadows there. My dad brought in two cows from Beauval mission by scow, to get started. When I was a kid we had thirty-five or forty head of cattle, and four teams of horses—boy that was a lot of work! I remember cutting hay by hand all day long—that was good exercise![68]

For the tireless Father Moraud, the Knee Lake settlement marked the southeastern corner of his vast parish. For years, stopping with his necessary accoutrements in a portable wooden box, he said mass at Knee Lake under the open sky. In 1951, however, he was able to build a proper church at Knee Lake—his third church in three years—for use during his visits to the community.[69]

Norbert George, circa 1950.

As already mentioned, Father Moraud's wish that his Dene parishioners stay in their small communities has not been fulfilled. When we arrived on Knee Lake on June 28, 1986, we found only three families staying there. They were then working at various locations around the lake, so when we stopped at the actual settlement, we found only a very old woman present. She was kneeling on the grass scraping a moose hide with hand-crafted tools she had unwrapped from a brightly coloured cloth. She spoke no English, and we spoke no Dene. But we needed no language to understand that, for this woman, Knee Lake was home.

Father Moraud's church at Knee Lake, shown at right, has fared better than his ones at Dipper Lake and Primeau Lake. While the small rectory next to the church has been converted into a cabin, the people of Knee Lake have preserved the white-painted, clapboard church exactly as Moraud left it when he died in 1965. High in the steepled belfry, the church bell waits ready to ring. In the church's interior, below, a statue of Christ still beckons worshippers to the altar, and the Stations of the Cross still line the walls. Near a window,

a "Pictorial Catechism" poster, the work of Alberta priest Father Lacombe, shows the ladders one might take in life to reach either heaven or hell. If one takes a seat on one of the wooden pews, with only the wind to touch the quiet, it is easy to imagine Father Moraud in his robes speaking to the Dene people he loved so much.[70] The small church at Knee Lake still serves as a place of worship for the Dene. While you may want to visit the church and linger for a while, be sure to leave it as you found it.

South from Knee Lake

From the Knee Lake settlement site, the Churchill drains southward. The river here is broad with a lazy current. The shores, especially on river left, are generally low and willowy. The occasional sandy cutbank rises as high as 2 m (6 ft), but even in these instances, the land behind is wet and marshy. The low terrain limits camping opportunities between Knee Lake and Dreger Lake. But there are some campsites, and they will be noted below.

Haultain River

Just 2 km (1¼ mi) south from Knee Lake, the Churchill is joined from the north by a major tributary, the Haultain River, which rises in the country southeast of Cree Lake. Like the Mudjatik River, the Haultain carries a load of sand and silt into the Churchill. At its mouth, the Haultain has major sand bars that are exposed to view in low water.

As mentioned previously, the Dene name for the Haultain is *Tsho Deszay*. To English speakers, the river was, at least for a time, known as the Pine River. However, in 1892, the river was given its current official name by explorer J.B. Tyrrell. In editing the journal of Philip Turnor, Tyrrell noted:

> About a mile below Knee lake, or Lac Genou, they [Turnor and his party in 1790] passed the mouth of Pine river, a stream three hundred feet wide, which discharges into Churchill river over a bar of sand. In order to distinguish it from the many other Pine rivers in this country, I bestowed on it the name of Haultain river, after Sir Frederick Haultain, Chief Justice of the province of Saskatchewan.[71]

The Haultain is navigable by canoe. Philip Wolverine of Patuanak has said that it was once a favoured canoe route by white trappers. The Dene themselves must also have canoed the river. Traditionally, however, they may not have paddled it as much as one might expect. The topography east of the Haultain allowed for the use of land trails as an alternative to canoe travel. In reference to this region, Alexander Mackenzie wrote:

> It may also be considered as a most extraordinary circumstance, that the Chepewyans, go North-West from hence to the barren grounds, which are their own country, without the assistance of canoes; as it is well known that in every other part which has been described, from Cumberland House, the country is broken on either side of the direction to a great extent: so that a traveller could not go at right angles with any of the waters already mentioned, without meeting with others in every eight or ten miles...[72]

Down from the Haultain

Two km (1¼ mi) south from the Haultain's mouth, the Churchill bends 180 degrees to run back north for a short distance. This bend is known in Dene as *Hon Wahrray,* meaning "the sharp bend." Typical of Dene naming, this name does not seem particularly unique. However, Joe Black says that the Knee Lake people have named every twist and turn in their part of the Churchill in such a way that no two bends would be confused in conversation.

One km (²⁄₃ mi) past the Sharp Bend, you will come to a point where a small side channel branches away from the west shore (73-O 901877 to 898855). Your map will show this channel running south for about 2 km (1¼ mi) before it rejoins the Churchill's main flow. In 1986, we did not canoe this route since Map 73-O/15 suggests that it is unnavigable. But the early explorers did not have modern maps to dissuade them from searching out shortcuts. On October 2, 1790, Philip Turnor actually explored this side channel in an upstream direction. Though he found it canoeable, he concluded it offered no real saving of travel time.[73]

Camping

On the main river channel, about 1.5 km (1 mi) downstream from the start of the side channel just referred to, you will find a good campsite alongside a small eddy on the river left shore (73-O 905862). At the eddy, Shield rock slopes up from the water to a height of about 4 m (13 ft). There is room for tents among the small aspens on top of the Shield outcrop.

About 1.75 km (1 mi) further downstream, there is a very good campsite located on river left (73-O 898845), about 30 m (33 yd) upstream of a high promontory of grey rock. This campsite is on a low ledge near the water. Up from the ledge, on a level-topped rock knoll, there are spaces for many tents. Another 100 m (110 yd) downstream from the ledge campsite, you may find a bald eagle nest in the aspens on the river left shore.

Below the ledge campsite, camping possibilities continue to be generally poor. However, 6 km (3¾ mi) downstream from it, there is a further site on river left (73-O 866817). Here, an outcrop of pink granite hidden by shore bulrushes is crested by a bluff of aspens. Amid the thinly spaced aspens, there is level ground for camping.

Short Cut to Dreger Lake

One km (²/₃ mi) downstream from the aspen bluff campsite, the Churchill divides around a large island. Halfway down the left (east) side of this island, a side channel (73-O 857802) branches off to the south, while the main channel flow swings northwest to stay close to the island. The side channel takes a short cut of about 3.75 km (2¹/₃ mi) to Dreger Lake, while down and back on the Churchill's sweeping bend to the south is about 9 km (5½ mi). Though the short cut is only about 20 m (22 yd) wide, the voyageurs used it regularly to save over 5 km (3 mi) of paddling.

Early fur trade explorers knew the shortcut channel as the Grass or Grassy River, a name apparently learned from the Cree.[74] The name no doubt referred to the sedges and water grasses thick along the channel's low banks. The Dene today simply refer to the channel as *G'etzalghay Neeⁿ-leeⁿ Deszay,* meaning "the short cut."

The Short Cut is a fascinating place, hidden and remote from the main river. It doubles back and forth in so many tight meanders, you may wonder if it really has an exit. But while its maze-like turnings may seem endless, this little byway is a good paddle. Rich shore vegetation crowds in on both sides, and wildlife signs are frequent. Each bend up ahead offers a chance to surprise a duck, beaver, or muskrat.

As you travel down the Short Cut towards Dreger Lake, the channel branches into a north and a south fork. Ordinarily, both forks have good depth for canoes. In 1992, however, likely because of unusually low water levels, beavers had a dam across the north fork making the slightly longer south fork the better route option.

The Short Cut has a current similar to that in the main channel coming down from Knee Lake. While it may be 2 to 3 km (about 1½ mi) per hour, it should not present a problem for upstream travel.

Robert Hood of the Franklin expedition saw the Short Cut in late June 1820, as he and his companions travelled upstream. He wrote:

We were detained in Sandy Lake, till one P.M., by a strong gale, when the wind becoming moderate we crossed five miles to the mouth of the river, and at four P.M. left the main branch of it, and entered a little rivulet called the Grassy River, running through an extensive reedy swamp. It is the nest of innumerable ducks, which rear their young, among the long rushes, in security from beasts of prey. At sunset we encamped on the banks of the main branch.[75]

Map 7.5   The Short Cut and *wâkâhonânisihk*

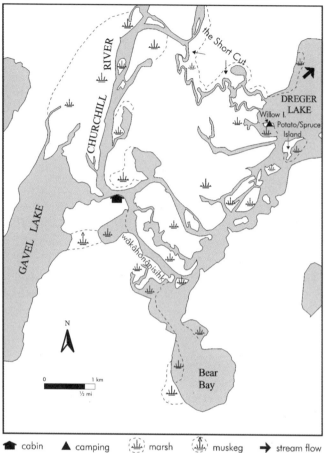

cabin 🏠   camping ▲   marsh 🌿   muskeg 🌿   stream flow ➡

Wâkâhonânisihk

If you do not take the Short Cut to Dreger Lake but continue south in the main channel, you will find that the shores remain low. There is higher ground and some Shield rock back from the river, but the shores are lined with willows, cattails, horsetails, and sedges. Blackbirds and ducks are everywhere.

About 3.5 km (2 mi) downstream from the Short Cut, the main channel makes a sweeping, 180-degree bend to turn northeast. This broad bend has the Dene name of *G'estaree^n-lee^n*, meaning "where the river flows to the poplar bank." It has also long been known by the Cree name of *wâkâhonânisihk*, meaning "the curving river place."[76]

Although *wâkâhonânisihk* was ordinarily bypassed by the voyageurs, it did play a role in the latter days of the fur trade. From the 1890s to around 1915 or 1916, the Hudson's Bay Company operated a winter post here to serve a mainly Dene clientele. This post was known variously as "Wakenanci," "Wadaouanis," "New Souris River" (to distinguish it from the older Souris River post at the north end of Pinehouse Lake) and also, confusingly, as "Souris River." During part of the same period, Revillon Frères operated a competing post in the vicinity.[77]

Besides being accessible via the Churchill, *wâkâhonânisihk* could also be reached by a winter trail coming from two separate points on the south end of Pinehouse Lake. After the two branches of this trail joined west of Yost Lake, it ran northwest through a chain of small lakes and entered into "Bear Bay" (*maskwa wâsâw* in Cree) which lies directly south from *wâkâhonânisihk* (73-O 860740).

When we came to *wâkâhonânisihk* on June 28, 1986, we found a good rock shelf in front of a small trapping cabin on the south side of the river bend. This was just east of the inflow channel from Gavel Lake. It was late, so we stopped to camp in the absent trapper's front yard. We fished from the rock shelf for supper. Supper and then some! The first fish to take a hook was a 7-kg (15-lb) pike, which was large enough to provide that night's supper as well as breakfast and lunch the next day.

Two days after we camped at *wâkâhonânisihk*, we chanced to meet Louis George of Patuanak who had been raised at Knee Lake. He said he understood that there had once been two trading stores near where we had caught the large pike. He also said there had once been a store where the Short Cut rejoins the Churchill's main flow. We have since learned from Joe Black that one of the stores at *wâkâhonânisihk* was a Hudson's Bay Company post. We can speculate that the neighbouring store there was a competing Revillon Frères establishment. It is harder to guess who may have operated the store at the Short Cut's mouth.

Dick Hansen of Pinehouse can recall when three Dene families lived at *wâkâhonânisihk*. It is his recollection that these families moved away in the 1940s.

Dreger Lake

Dreger Lake begins where the two forks of the Short Cut run into the Churchill's main channel coming from the south. The canoe route through the lake first runs 3 km (2 mi) northeast and then makes a sharp elbow turn to the right to run almost another 6 km (3¾ mi) southsouthwest.

In the old fur trade journals, Dreger Lake is sometimes not mentioned by name. However, it seems that the voyageurs knew the lake as Lac Croche,[78] obviously a reference to its elbow turn. The present Dene name for the lake is *G'estaree^{n}lee^n Too-ay*, meaning "poplar bank lake." The present Cree name for the lake, similar to the voyageur name, is *wâkâhonân sâkahikan*, or "curved lake."

According to Martin Smith of Pinehouse, the tip of the long peninsula creating Dreger Lake's elbow turn is known locally by the English name "Jigger Point," because a jigger used to run fish nets under the ice was once left there for a period of time. When Martin was a small boy in the late 1920s, the name was already in use.

The lake's shores are not marshy, but they are low without much relief. For the most part, the shoreline is made up of ice-shoved stones lying against a band of willows. Aspens and a few spruce and jack pine grow on slightly higher ground behind the willows.

Camping

Dreger Lake's shoreline offers poor camping. However, the small island (73-O 873787), known in Cree as *nîpisiy ministikos* or "willow island," lying immediately southeast of the twin outflows of the Short Cut, offers some possibilities. The east tip of the island has a low bedrock slope with enough room for a single tent. Room for an extra tent or two might be found in the willows behind the bedrock slope.

There is a somewhat larger island (73-O 876783) lying 300 m (330 yd) southeast of the small island. The Dene know this island as *Labada Noo-ay* or "potato island," while its Cree name is *minahiko-ministik* or "spruce island." We have not explored this larger island, but it may have some camping prospects.

Other camping possibilities occur where Dreger Lake makes its sharp elbow turn to the right at Jigger Point. On the northernmost point of the peninsula causing the turn, there is a low shelf of sloping bedrock in front of some level ground that might be used for tenting (73-O 899806). Then, around the peninsula and 500 m (⅓ mi) to the south, there is room for a tent in a clump of aspen and balsam poplar on a bedrock ridge that rises about 3 m (10 ft) above the water (73-O 899800). This ridge is open to the breeze and would be relatively free of bugs. Finally, another 250 m (270 yd) further south, there is a third possible campsite where a sheet of bedrock slopes gently up from the water (73-O 899798). This is a good site, but it is difficult to reach since it is behind a screen of bulrushes and horsetails.

Dreger Rapids

Dreger Lake's outflow is down the lake's eastern shore nearly 6 km (3¾ mi) south from its elbow turn. Although Map 73-O does not show it, an island about 500 m (⅓ mi) wide divides the outflow into two channels. Both channels have minor rapids commonly referred to as Dreger Rapids. The Dene refer to Dreger Rapids as *Buhneech'eree Tthaybawzsay*, meaning "lesser tearing rapids." Here, "lesser" distinguishes the rapids from Shagwenaw Rapids upstream which have a similar Dene name that differs only in its "greater" connotation.

The channel northeast of the island has a depth of only about 50 cm (20 in) at normal water levels. This depth is enough to float a canoe. However, just over halfway down the channel, there is a shallow rapid that requires about 40 m (44 yd) of wading. Moreover, in low water years, the whole channel can dry up completely.[79]

The channel southwest of the island carries the Churchill's main flow and is the better route for canoes. It has only a few riffles and very minor rapids extending a distance of about 100 m (110 yd). These should not present any problems for alert canoeists. However, in low water conditions, canoeists may have to descend next to the river right shore where the greatest depth and best navigation will be found.

Where the riffles and minor rapids of the southwest channel begin, there is a prominent rock about 1 m wide and 2 m long (3 by 6 ft) situated to the right of the current's centre line. It is all white from bird droppings and has the apt local name of Pelican Rock.

Today, Dreger Rapids marks the approximate territorial boundary between the Dene of Patuanak and the Cree Métis of Pinehouse. Before the fur trade began, the upper Churchill was inhabited by Cree. Later, though, fur trade influences brought the Dene down from the north and onto the Churchill. The Dene eventually established themselves on the upper Churchill at least as far downstream as Pinehouse Lake and possibly even to Stanley Mission. In the early 1900s, however, they retreated back upstream to the region above Dreger Rapids.[80]

Dreger Rapids to Sandy Lake

From Dreger Rapids, the voyageur highway runs northeast for 5 km (3 mi) down a wide channel leading to Sandy Lake. The shores of this channel are similar to those of Dreger Lake. They do not offer much in the way of camping possibilities.

Since the channel is wooded mainly with aspen, it is an attractive place for beavers. There is a good-sized beaver lodge along the channel's north shore.

The channel opens up into Sandy Lake where a sandy point juts out from the south shore (73-O 935777). This point makes a good lunch spot or campsite. Canoes can be landed on a beach on the east side of the point. If you wish to camp here, you will find room for several tents in an open meadow behind a thin screen of willows backing the beach. The meadow does not offer much shelter from the wind, but on a bad night for mosquitoes, this could be a bonus.

Sandy Lake

From the sandy point, the voyageur highway continues eastward for 8 km (5 mi) through Sandy Lake. Despite its name, Sandy Lake's shores are not particularly sandy. Rather, they consist mainly of head-sized, ice-shoved stones. The lake's main feature is a ridge of high, rocky land running along its southeastern shore. This ridge is well-treed with spruce and aspen, and it gives the whole lake a pleasing aspect.

Churchill River Wilderness Camps is an outfitting camp at the southwest end of Sandy Lake (73-O 907742). On June 30, 1986, we stopped here and had a pleasant visit with the owner, Glen Skocdopole, and the camp manager, Eddie Tihonen. While we had coffee, Gord Wallace, a well-known northern bush pilot, landed with his family in a de Haviland Beaver on floats. Gord easily gave us the history of the camp since he had built it in 1976 and owned it until selling it to Glen in 1982.

When we continued eastward in 1986, the fire tower shown southeast of Sandy Lake on Map 73-O/10 was clearly visible. It was later dismantled, but a replacement tower was built in approximately the same location in 1996. Known as the Granite Tower, it is presently the only fire tower in active service on the guide route.

As you near the east end of the lake, you will see two sand beaches on the south shore about 1 km (2/3 mi) southwest of the lake's outflow (73-O 005769 & 008773). Both of these beaches make good lunch spots or campsites. In low water, the more westerly beach may be the preferable of the two since it is less likely to be stranded by wet foreshore flats.

When you reach Sandy Lake's outflow, you will find a small island in the mouth. The south side of this island is shallow and rocky. The north side of the island is therefore the better route option. There is some current here, but it is not strong. You may paddle either down or up along the island's northeast shore without difficulty.

HBCA E.3/1 fo. 58 lower (N14800)

When Peter Fidler descended the Churchill with Philip Turnor in June of 1792, he referred to Sandy Lake as "the Cross Lake."[81] However, the lake's current name may have been in use even then. When George Simpson made his first trip into the North-West in 1820, he recorded the lake's name as "Lac de Sable," meaning "sandy lake."[82] And, though the Dene name for the lake is *Nunadoothee Too-awzsay*, or "little snake lake," its present Cree name, which might well go back to antiquity, is *yîkawiskâw sâkahikan*, also meaning "sandy lake."

Map 7.6   Sandy Lake's outflow, Road 914, and Upper and Lower Snake Rapids

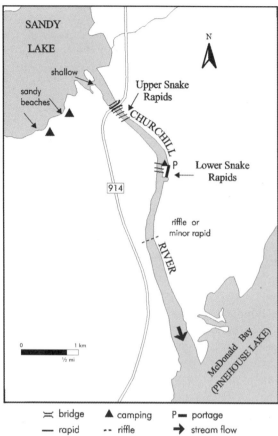

SANDY LAKE

shallow

sandy beaches

N

Upper Snake Rapids

CHURCHILL

914

P   Lower Snake Rapids

riffle or minor rapid

RIVER

0   1 km
½ mi

McDonald Bay (PINEHOUSE LAKE)

≍ bridge   ▲ camping   P▬ portage
— rapid   -- riffle   ➜ stream flow

Snake Rapids

The general name Snake Rapids, translated from the Cree name, *kinîpik pâwistik,* applies to the length of the 5.5-km (3½-mi) channel between Sandy Lake and McDonald Bay on Pinehouse Lake. The rapids include two main rapids—which we will presently describe as Upper Snake Rapids and Lower Snake Rapids—and also considerable fast water.

Both Maps 73-O and 73-O/10 show a portage trail along the northeast shore of Snake Rapids which provincial *Canoe Trip #1* says was an old winter road ending at McDonald Bay.[83] In 1986, we were not able to locate this road. We did find that a rough vehicle track started where the maps show the head of the portage on Sandy Lake (73-O 016780) and then went east to Highway 914, but it did not appear to be what we were looking for.[84] Anyway, since the old winter road would be long and likely far back from the river, it would hardly serve as a practical portage.

The high ridge running along the northeast side of the rapids might be a better portage option. It is thinly wooded and tracked with game trails that allow for reasonable hiking. But again, a portage along the ridge would be lengthy, and climbing up to and down from the ridge would be difficult.

For downstream travellers, therefore, we suggest three options for dealing with Snake Rapids: 1) experts may run the entire length of Snake Rapids provided careful scouting is done; 2) those with advanced but less than expert skills may run Upper Snake Rapids and then portage Lower Snake Rapids; or 3) cautious canoeists may line down Upper Snake Rapids and then portage Lower Snake Rapids.

If you are travelling upstream, we recommend you track or wade your canoe up the southwest (river right) shore. A less attractive option would be to track or wade up the more difficult northeast (river left) shore, climbing up to the high ground inland to portage when necessary.

Snake Rapids in Voyageur Accounts

The oldest existing written reference to Snake Rapids comes from Alexander Henry the Elder who, in 1776, arrived here with his partner Thomas Frobisher as they searched for Indians to trade with. With the exception of Louis Primeau and perhaps a few others, no white men had yet been this far into the North-West. In his account of his trip up the Churchill, Henry, using the voyageurs' French name for the rapids, wrote:

> On the fifth day [from Frog Portage], we reached the Rapide du Serpent, which is supposed to be three hundred miles from our point of departure. We found white-fish so numerous, in all the rapids, that shoals of many thousands were visible, with their backs above the water. The men supplied themselves by killing them with their paddles. The water is clear and transparent.
>
> The Rapide du Serpent, is about three miles long, and very swift...[85]

Henry's reference to Snake Rapids is noteworthy since it is his only mention of a geographical feature upstream of Frog Portage by name. In fact, the clear reference to Snake Rapids has helped historians trace Henry and Frobisher's route.

For the fur traders and their voyageurs, especially those going upstream, Snake Rapids made for hard going. Ascending the Churchill on September 30, 1790, Philip Turnor made reference to Snake Rapids in his journal:

> enterd the Ca-na-pick See-pee [kinîpiko-sîpiy] or Snake River which is about 150 yards wide land very low and coverd with willows, sides grassey went NW 1 mile easey current NNW 1/2 mile strong current and came to the snake fall handed the Canoes on SW side 1/4 mile NW very strong current and bad bottom being all large stones and very slippey, then went WNW 1/4 mile moderate current then handed the canoes at a fall WNW 1/4 mile current and bottom much the same as at the other fall land low all this river, enterd a lake [Sandy Lake] about 2 mile wide...[86]

Two years later, on June 13, 1792, while travelling downstream, Turnor's companion Peter Fidler mentioned the rapids in a similar vein:

> Then entered Snake River, about 70 yards wide ... ESE 3/4 led 1/2 mile of it on S Side in 1790 SSE 3/4 another very bad rapid as the last, led 1/3 mile on S Side in 1790—River here 100 yards wide—at this last rapid high rocks on the East side the stones are very slippey here with a green slime which makes these 2 rapids very bad to hand the Canoes up—besides the Stones are large & the poles are very difficult to keep from fastening amongst them...[87]

Robert Hood and other members of the Franklin expedition went up Snake Rapids on June 26, 1820. Making light of their difficulties, Hood wrote:

> From the Serpent to the Sandy Lake, it [the Churchill] is again confined in a narrow space by the approach of its winding banks, and on the 26th we were some hours employed in traversing a series of shallow rapids, where it was necessary to lighten the canoes. Having missed the path through the woods, we walked two miles in the water upon sharp stones, from which some person was incessantly slipping into deep holes, and floundering in vain for footing at the bottom; a scene highly diverting, notwithstanding our fatigue...[88]

Upper Snake Rapids

These rapids are 500 m (1/3 mi) downstream from Sandy Lake at a point where a highway bridge now spans the Churchill. The bridge is part of Road 914, commonly called the Key Lake Road, which connects the community of Pinehouse 25 km (16 mi) to the south with the Key Lake Uranium Mine another 200 km (124 mi) to the north. The road reached the Churchill in 1979, and the bridge was built in 1980.

The rapids, which we rate as Class 2, begin about 300 m (330 yd) upstream of the bridge and continue a similar distance below the bridge. They begin in a minor way but build into medium-sized standing waves closer to the bridge with the biggest waves occurring just past the bridge. About 50 m (55 yd) down from the bridge, there is a small ledge and related boil on river right which are best avoided. The rapids are a fast ride, but they have good depth and can be run by most canoeists on a course more or less down river centre.

It is difficult to scout Upper Snake Rapids on foot because large stones line the shores. These stones also make it difficult to line or track canoes though it is possible to do so along the right shore and even under the bridge. (It would be very hard to scramble up and over the highway embankment at the bridge.) Given the poor footing, lining or tracking calls for great caution.

Some motorists camp near the bridge, but the camping possibilities are limited. Moreover, for paddlers, the swift current of the rapids makes it hard to put a canoe into shore. If you do wish to stop at the bridge to camp or just look around, the best place to put in is at a slight eddy on river right about 100 m (110 yd) downstream from the bridge. From the eddy, a trail leads about 50 m (55 yd) up to a small clearing and then a short distance further to the highway.

Down from Upper Snake Rapids

From Upper Snake Rapids, you can ride a strong but flat current 1 km (2/3 mi) southeast to reach Lower Snake Rapids. As the river begins to bend right, you should be sure to move to river left in order to make a mandatory stop in the quiet water above a small island that juts out from the river left shore adjacent to the rapids.

Lower Snake Rapids

These major rapids, which vary from Class 2 to 3 depending on water levels, begin even with the north end of the small island on the river left shore and then run their strongest for about 150 m (165 yd) along the west side of the island. Down their west (river right) shore, the rapids are shallow over a bottom of large stones. Nearer to the island, they are wilder as they go around and over large rocks and ledges. A most notable feature is a strong boil about 65 m (70 yd) down from the top of the island. It warrants real respect.

In 1986, we ran Lower Snake Rapids down the shallow west shore. In low water, however, this would not be possible, and shooting the rapids would hence require a more difficult run down the main flow. If you opt for such a run, you might choose to start down a tongue on river right and then move left to pass east of the strong boil. But before you run Lower Snake by any route, we urge you to scout them carefully to insure a safe passage.

To scout the rapids or to portage them, you should steer into the quiet pool northeast of the top of the small island. You can then land at a bedrock slope on the island shore.

Portage #6 - Snake Portage (± 100 m / 110 yd)

To start this portage, paddle south down the quiet pool as far as possible before landing on the Shield rock of the island. There is no danger of being swept downstream here since the island is almost a peninsula with very little water flowing down its east side.[89] From the Shield rock, you can head generally southwest to find the portage. You will find good camping around the head of the portage. There is not much room for tents, but the Shield rock provides good living space. The area is also good for fishing and exploring.

The portage is indistinct at first until two or more trails join into a single, narrow track. This track has very bad footing since it is embedded with rocks and boulders. In places, there is hardly room for a foot to fit.

The downstream end of the portage is on the west side of the island just below the main part of the rapids. It also has very bad footing because of rocks. You will have to wade a few metres around large shore rocks to reach a place suitable for relaunching.

Depending on water levels, anywhere from 100 m (110 yd) to 300 m (330 yd) of lesser rapids and swift water continue downstream from the portage. You can negotiate this water by first keeping close to the island shore and then moving over to centre as the channel there clears of rocks.

Above, the upper portion of Lower Snake Rapids, taken in low water conditions in the fall of 1992.

Left, at Lower Snake Rapids, you will see an interesting jumble of square-cut boulders on the west side of the portage island. Some stand up to 3 m (10 ft) high.

Down from Lower Snake Rapids

One km (²/₃ mi) downstream from Lower Snake Rapids, you will encounter a riffle (73-O 024749) that can be a 200-m-long (220-yd) minor rapid at lower water levels. This riffle is best run down the deeper river right side.

From the riffle, the river channel broadens slightly, and there are no more rapids. After 2 km (1¼ mi), the channel opens into McDonald Bay.

McDonald Bay

McDonald Bay is known in Cree as *sîkwâyâw wâsâw*, or "below the rapids bay." Though considered part of Pinehouse Lake, the bay is itself larger than many lakes, being 2 km (1¼ mi) wide and nearly 14 km (9 mi) long. From the Snake Rapids channel, you will traverse northeast for about 6 km (3¾ mi) across the middle section of the bay to reach its easterly shore and the narrows leading into Pinehouse Lake.

Although McDonald Bay lies perpendicular to the prevailing northwest winds, it is very open and can be dangerous on windy days. The traverse of the bay should only be made after carefully assessing weather conditions.

Kamkota Lodge, a fishing camp operated by outfitter Kerry Ukrainetz, stands on the west shore of McDonald Bay just south from the bottom of the Snake Rapids channel. The camp was started by Philip Tinker of Pinehouse and operated by him until Kerry took it over in 1996. It is accessible by vehicle from Road 914 and could offer valuable emergency help if you run into trouble in the vicinity.

McDonald Bay Rock Paintings

On McDonald Bay's easterly shore, just over 2 km (1¼ mi) southwest from the narrows to Pinehouse Lake (73-O 067751 estimated), there are rock paintings on a rock outcrop rising up from the water's edge. In this vicinity, there are two rock outcrops separated by about 40 m (44 yd) of bush. The paintings are on the more northerly outcrop on a rock face with a slightly negative incline and a west-northwest orientation. In 1986, the lowest paintings were roughly 150 cm (5 ft) above the water.

The seven figures visible on the rock face are all very faint and difficult to make out. They comprise a wavy line that could be either a snake or a lightning bolt, what looks to be a boat with a mast, a moose-like animal, and four different thunderbirds.

The paintings here are significant in that they are the furthest upstream of any of the ancient rock paintings known to exist along the Churchill. They are the first paintings dealt with in Tim Jones's book, *The Aboriginal Rock Paintings of the Churchill River*.[90]

As with all of the Churchill's rock paintings, these on McDonald Bay are of obscure age and origin. Arguably, though, the boat figure here offers a clue about age. If the figure represents a York boat rigged with a sailing mast, it would not predate the early 1800s when York boats were first introduced on the Churchill. Of course, the figure may not be a boat of any kind, and, even if it is a York boat, the other paintings may not date to the same era. The boat's mast has the brightest coloration found in any of the paintings, so the boat may be the most recent work in the McDonald Bay group.

On to Pinehouse Lake

If you leave McDonald Bay and paddle about 300 m (330 yd) into the narrows leading to the main part of Pinehouse Lake, you will find a good campsite in a small indent on the southwest shore of the narrows (73-O 084766). Here, screened by a few bulrushes, there is a low shelf of bedrock about 20 m (65 ft) wide and 15 m (50 ft) deep that will provide reasonable space for smaller canoe parties.

Another 1.5 km (1 mi) due east, there is a second possible campsite on the opposite, or northeast, shore of the narrows (73-O 099767). This site is at a sand beach about 50 m (55 yd) wide. It has room for several tents.

A large, three-sided island lies at the southeast end of the narrows to Pinehouse Lake. The Cree name for the island is *kâ-wapâhk ministik*, meaning "narrows island." The west side of Narrows Island can be a dry channel in low water, so you may wish to avoid this side even if you are turning south to the community of Pinehouse.

If you do not plan to stop at Pinehouse but want to follow the old voyageur highway down the Churchill, your course lies east-northeast for 15 km (9 mi) across the top end of Pinehouse Lake.

If you are going to Pinehouse, either to end your trip or to resupply, you will head 25 km (16 mi) south into the main body of the lake. As you move southward, you will have to make use of your map to navigate around the lake's many islands. However, once you are within 10 km (6 mi) of Pinehouse, you will be able to see a telecommunications tower on the west shore of the lake. The tower is in fact within the bounds of the community and thus serves as a good landmark.

As far south as the community, Pinehouse Lake is within the Precambrian Shield, but the local Shield rock is not particularly rugged. Paddling south, you will find many places where the bedrock slopes gently up from the water and allows for good camping.

When you near Pinehouse, you will have a fair view of the community since it is built on a sandy slope rising up from the lakeshore. You will see St. Dominic's Roman Catholic Church with its aquamarine metal roof and, about a block south from the church, a sand beach where you can conveniently land. From the beach area, a road leads directly to the centre of the community and then on to Road 914.

-9-

OTTER RAPIDS TO STANLEY MISSION

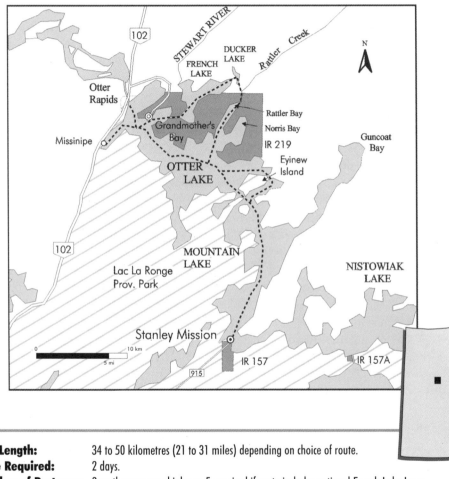

Trip Length: 34 to 50 kilometres (21 to 31 miles) depending on choice of route.
Time Required: 2 days.
Number of Portages: 2 on the voyageur highway. 5 required if route includes optional French Lake Loop.
Maps Required:
    1:250,000 Series: 73P Lac la Ronge
    1:50,000 Series: 73P/10 Otter Lake
                           73P/9 Guncoat Bay
                           73P/8 Nistowiak Lake

ABOUT THE TRIP

This trip takes a track through Otter Lake and Mountain Lake—two of the Churchill's medium-sized lakes. Since it has good wind protection and no whitewater paddling, the trip is especially well suited for canoeists with only modest skills. It can normally be completed in either an upstream or downstream direction in a single weekend.

A great advantage of this trip is that it allows for variations. For example, you can leave the ordinary route across Otter Lake and make a one-day detour north of the lake on what we will describe as the French Lake Loop. Or, in crossing Otter Lake, you can make a half-day side trip to visit the Rattler Creek rock painting site. Or, you can avoid the commonly used Stony Mountain and Mountain portages between Otter Lake and Mountain Lake by taking what we will describe as the Northeast Route. Using these variations or others you might think of, you can tailor a trip that will fit your time schedule and, if you fashion a loop trip, save the trouble of a vehicle shuttle.

But one warning. Though this trip allows for modest canoeing skills, it does require good map and compass reading. Irregular shorelines and dozens of islands make it easy to get lost. Once you start out, you will want to know where you are on your map at all times.

Boat and canoe traffic can be frequent along the route. Local people travel by boat between Missinipe, Grandmother's Bay, Stanley Mission, and their summer camps on a regular basis. Recreational fishing boats are also common, and many canoe parties paddle here in July and August. Despite all this, if you extend common courtesy to others you chance to meet, you will not likely find that the traffic detracts from your own voyage.

The scenery is excellent. Since both Otter Lake and Mountain Lake are entirely within the Shield, they have deeply indented shorelines and numerous islands which display a fine pattern of mixed woods and rugged rock outcrops. Between the lakes, spectacular falls occur as the water from Otter Lake drops 9 m (30 ft) to reach Mountain Lake.

Camping possibilities are very good. Some campsites will be mentioned, but you will no doubt find others on your own. Most sites are on bedrock.

Aboriginal rock paintings are a special attraction on this trip. Paintings occur at the Rattler Creek site just north of Otter Lake and at four different sites on Mountain Lake. These sites, in combination with yet another site on Mountain Lake that is downstream from Stanley Mission, form a concentration of paintings rivalling that found in the Kinosaskaw Lake and Black Bear Island Lake area.

STARTING POINTS

The main starting point for this trip is at Otter Rapids, 325 km (202 mi) north of Prince Albert. From Prince Albert, you can reach Otter Rapids by driving 240 km (149 mi) north on paved Highway 2 to La Ronge and then continuing another 85 km (53 mi) north on Highway 102. The route north of La Ronge is paved for 30 km (19 mi) but then becomes a winding gravel road. Once on the gravel portion, you will need to watch for trucks hauling loads to and from Saskatchewan's northern uranium mines.

At Otter Rapids, you can reach the launch area by first crossing east over the bridge spanning the rapids and then turning right into the provincial campground at the end of the bridge.

The highway and the campground have obliterated part of the old canoe portage along the east shore of the rapids. However, in the southwest corner of the campground, you will find where the interrupted portage continues southward to its downstream end. If you follow this path for about 225 m (245 yd), you will come to a wide, gravelly landing in a quiet inlet lying east of the foot of the rapids. Here, you can put your canoe onto Otter Lake.

To reach a different launch site, you can follow a trail that branches left from the main portage about 125 m (135 yd) south from the campground. The side trail leads to a grass and mud landing about 70 m (77 yd) east of the main landing. This secondary landing is useful when low water conditions make the main landing very stony.

Leaving Otter Portage, you will first proceed south along the shore on your left. Initially, you will have to stay alert as you pass through turbulence running out from the foot of Otter Rapids. Within a few minutes, however, you will be on flat water and safely underway.

An alternate starting point for this trip is the hamlet of Missinipe—which will be mentioned shortly in more detail—situated in Walker Bay, the westernmost arm of Otter Lake. About 5.5 km (3½ mi) south of Otter Rapids, a sign on Highway 102 marks where a short access road runs southeast into Missinipe. If you follow this main road through the hamlet and stay on it as it curves southward, you will come to a government dock where canoes can be launched in a quiet back bay on the Walker Bay arm.

Missinipe

The community of Missinipe *(misi-nipiy)*, which means "big water," takes its name from the centuries-old Cree name for the Churchill River. Tucked away in the westernmost corner of Otter Lake, it is about 4 km (2½ mi) off the main canoe route. While it is not used as a canoe trip start point as often as Otter Rapids, you may decide to begin your voyage here or perhaps stop to buy last-minute items on your way to Otter Rapids. If you are in the middle of a trip, you can make a short detour into Missinipe to resupply.

Missinipe is a summer resort community with the municipal status of "Northern Hamlet." In the winter, it is a quiet place of about forty souls. In summer, its population swells into the hundreds as fishers, canoeists, and other tourists come to see the Churchill and points north.

Bill's Camp and Thompson's Camps

Missinipe is a young community. The present townsite was all bush until 1961 when an all-weather road reached Otter Rapids and made the townsite accessible by vehicle. That summer, Bill Chanin, a former RCMP officer, and his helper Ralph Anderson began clearing land for a tourist camp in an area just southeast of the present-day public beach. Before long, Bill was able to start operating at Missinipe under the name Bill's Camp.

Bill was to have competition right away. While he was setting up in 1961, outfitter Gary Thompson began building another camp at Missinipe. As well, George Sewell, working for Red's Camps of La Ronge, moved into a tent nearby to develop yet a third operation. Though the Red's Camps endeavour was short-lived, Bill Chanin and Gary Thompson both became well established. Before long, they had Otter Lake on the map as a sport-fishing destination.

In 1972, Gary Thompson brought an air charter service to the community, and he now has a twin Otter, a single Otter, three Beavers (including a turbo), and a Cessna 185 operating under the name Osprey Air. In 1974, he bought out Bill's Camp and combined it with his own Thompson's Camps. Today, Thompson's Camps is the largest outfitter in Saskatchewan with room for over 150 guests at Missinipe. Every spring, this capacity helps Missinipe metamorphose from a quiet hamlet into a bustling summer resort.

Churchill River Trading Post

In 1968, Paul and Delia Jacobsen opened a store, cafe, and gas station in Missinipe. In 1984, the Jacobsens passed the business on to their son Leo and his wife Sherry who continue to operate it under the name "Churchill River Trading Post." The Trading Post is a grocery, general store, and gas station. It also serves as the community post office with mail coming from La Ronge on Mondays and Thursdays. Next door to the Trading Post, the Jacobsens have a snack & ice cream bar that is open during the summer months. After a week or so of fish and Kraft dinner, you might find the ice cream tastes pretty good!

Horizons Unlimited

Although Missinipe has developed primarily as an outfitting centre for sport fishers, it is also the capital of canoe outfitting in Saskatchewan. At Missinipe, Ric and Theresa Driediger, friends of the late Bill Mason, operate "Horizons Unlimited" to offer a full range of services to canoe trippers.

Ric guided his first canoe trip on the Churchill River in 1973 and has been at it ever since. In 1976, he and others started a non-profit corporation called Wilderness Trails Inc. to take church groups canoeing on the Churchill. In 1979, Horizons Unlimited Wilderness Services was started as a profit wing of Wilderness Trails. Horizons began by doing canoe trips on the Churchill River, the Foster River, and the Nahanni River.

By 1981, Horizons was based at Missinipe. In 1986, it purchased a rival Missinipe company, Churchill River Canoe Outfitters. CRCO had been in business since 1959 and, after being taken over by Peter Whitehead of Regina in the mid-1960s, had become Saskatchewan's foremost canoe outfitting service. CRCO had continued to grow under Paul Wilkinson who owned it from 1976 to 1986. Hence, when Horizons bought CRCO, its own operations expanded considerably.

Since 1986, Horizons has added a substantial canoe instruction program focusing on whitewater paddling and canoe tripping. Guided canoe trips continue to be offered on most northern Saskatchewan rivers, some rivers in northern Manitoba, and some trips in the Northwest Territories. A large fleet of Royalex canoes and everything else one would need to go on a canoe trip are available for rent, as are cabins and fishing boats. Horizons also makes and sells the Campfire Tent (made popular by Bill Mason in his books and films) and beautiful cedar strip epoxy canoes crafted by Theresa Driediger in the Chestnut Prospector design.

To a large extent, the success of Horizons Unlimited over the years has been because of the competency and skill of its staff and guides. Instructor and canoe trip guide Kevin Schultz has worked for Horizons since 1981. His skill as an instructor and canoe trip guide continues to bring clients back. Sheila Archer, who has worked for Horizons since 1986, brings to the company unquenchable enthusiasm, laughter, and a great deal of skill. Many other staff have contributed to Horizons over the years.

Horizons' Ric Driediger stands out as one of the Churchill's staunchest friends:

> The Churchill River is a very special place. It is a unique wilderness area. It has incredible recreational potential. It is the home of many native people who still live a traditional lifestyle. The Churchill has a rich history. I want to see it preserved!

Services Available

Missinipe's services include Thompson's Camps which provide accommodation, Horizons Unlimited which provide canoe outfitting and rental cabins, Osprey Air which has float planes and wheeled aircraft, and Churchill River Trading Post with groceries, snack bar, postal service, and gas pumps. Other facilities include a public beach, a public campground, and a government dock. Although the La Ronge provincial Environment office has a storage yard and summer maintenance staff at Missinipe, it does not operate a regular office here.

Map 9.1   Missinipe

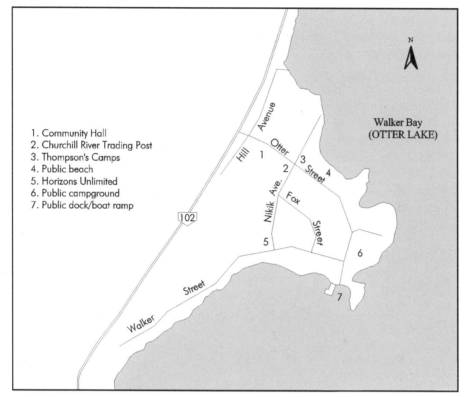

1. Community Hall
2. Churchill River Trading Post
3. Thompson's Camps
4. Public beach
5. Horizons Unlimited
6. Public campground
7. Public dock/boat ramp

MAIN ROUTE FROM OTTER RAPIDS TO MOUNTAIN LAKE

Otter Lake

Otter Lake, which takes its name from the Cree equivalent *nikiko-sâkahikan*, is a classic Shield lake. Its main shoreline twists in and out of numerous bays and skirts around just as many odd-shaped peninsulas. To add to this confusion, over 150 islands take up space inside the bays and between the headlands. Soil cover is poor on both the mainland and the islands, and outcrops of bare bedrock are common. Somehow, though, the entire lake supports strong stands of spruce, jack pine, aspen poplar, and birch. The result is a shore panorama of grey rock and green forest.

The bedrock shores provide many good campsites. Local Cree residents, using old-time white canvas wall tents, occupy some of these sites as summer camps, but you should ordinarily have no trouble finding a good one for yourself.

The main canoe route across Otter Lake runs for 16 km (10 mi) from Otter Rapids to Stony Mountain Portage at the southeast end of the lake. If you have good weather, you can use your map to select the shortest way between the lake's many islands. If you have wind to contend with, you will no doubt want to alter your course to take advantage of whatever wind protection you can find.

Grandmother's Bay

About 4 km (2½ mi) southeast of Otter Rapids, you will find the Cree community of Grandmother's Bay,[1] *kohkominânihk* in Cree, spread along the north shore of Otter Lake. It is the first of two Lac la Ronge Indian Band centres you will encounter on the Churchill, the other being Stanley Mission another 30 km (19 mi) downstream.

For as long as anyone knows, La Ronge Band members have lived in and around Grandmother's Bay. In 1970, the area was formally transferred to the La Ronge Band for reserve land as part settlement of the Band's outstanding treaty land entitlement.[2] Since then, many families from the general area and Stanley Mission further downstream have settled here. The community is now home to almost 300 Band members.

In 1982, a power line was built to bring electricity to Grandmother's Bay from Highway 102.[3] In 1996, a 12-km (7½-mi) access road was completed to link it to the highway,[4] and a year later, regular water and sewer facilities were developed. The community has a local Band office, Nihithow Awasis School (kindergarten to grade nine), an Anglican church, and a Health Clinic able to provide emergency first aid. While the community currently has no store, residents expect to have a Co-op store and gas bar up and running in 2002.

Beyond Grandmother's Bay

At Grandmother's Bay, you will have the option of proceeding northeast into Grandmother's Narrows to begin a loop that runs through French Lake and Ducker Lake and then back into Otter Lake. This option, which requires an extra day to paddle, will be described later as the French Lake Loop.

If you stay on the main canoe route across Otter Lake, you can paddle generally southeast from Grandmother's Bay for 12 km (7½ mi) to reach Stony Mountain Portage. However, if you have a half day to spare, you may wish to take a side trip requiring an extra 13 km (8 mi) of paddling (round trip total) to visit the Rattler Creek rock painting site northeast of Otter Lake's Rattler Bay (73P 274640). Choosing this option, you will find that a forest fire has burned from the north end of Rattler Bay to a point about 1 km (²/₃ mi) up the Stewart River (73P 282648). This fire—named the "Regina" fire—occurred in 1998, a bad year for fires, and burned off a large part of the country to the east.

Rattler Creek Rock Paintings

The Rattler Creek rock paintings (73P 287656), 2 km (1¼ mi) northeast of Rattler Bay, are at the junction of the Stewart River and Rattler Creek. Once you arrive here, you will see a very steep rock outcrop about 11 m (36 ft) high on the west bank of the Stewart River just opposite the mouth of Rattler Creek. The paintings are along the foot of this outcrop.

The most southerly group of paintings occurs about 1 m (3 ft) above the water on a rock face protected from the rain by its negative incline. The four figures here include a weasel-like animal, a caribou, a very faint insect-like creature with seven legs on each side, and an unidentifiable creature with splayed limbs.

To the right 1 or 2 m (about 5 feet) but still on the same inclined rock face, there is another group of paintings. This group's most vivid figure is a beaver situated on viewer's left. Below and to the right of the beaver, there are two complex objects, each adorned with fringes, which rock art expert Tim Jones suggests are carrying bags or medicine bags.[5] Just to the right of the two ringed objects, there is the faint front half of an open-mouthed animal of unknown species.

Map 9.2   Rattler Creek area

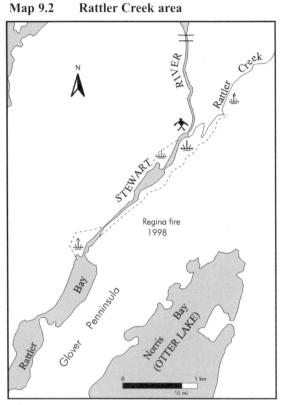

marsh   muskeg   — rapids   rock paintings

About 30 cm (1 ft) to viewer's right of the open-mouthed animal and about 2 m (6 ft) above the water, you will find a single figure painted on a rock face projecting 40 to 50 cm (16 to 20 in) forward from the face already described. The single figure here is very faint but appears to be a small, tailed animal of some kind.

Again, about 25 cm (10 in) to viewer's right of the small, tailed animal, there are more paintings on yet another rock face projecting about 10 to 15 cm (4 to 6 in) forward from the last face. These paintings consist of two groups of interconnected designs and other areas of faded pigment. It appears that the interconnected designs have been painted over earlier, faded paintings. Neither the interconnected designs nor the areas of faded pigment are decipherable.

The last group of paintings occurs on a vertical face about 40 m (44 yd) north of the indecipherable paintings. The main figure in this group is a very

Aerial view (looking north) of the Rattler Creek rock painting site, autumn 1998. The rock paintings are on the cliff just down from the confluence of Rattler Creek (flowing from right) and the Stewart River. Signs of 1998's "Regina" fire can be seen in the bottom half of the photo.

PHOTO BY DOUG CHISHOLM

faded, bison-like animal located level with an old high water mark (about 80 cm [30 in] above the actual water level when we were here on July 30, 1986). Above and to viewer's left of the bison, there is a vivid but unidentifiable patch of pigment. And finally, below the patch, there is a little more pigment having no recognizable form.

Beyond Rattler Creek

Whether or not you visit the Rattler Creek rock paintings, you will soon reach the southeast end of Otter Lake where a big island blocks the way to Mountain Lake. Map 73P does not name this island, but Map 73P/10 gives it the name Eyinew Island. Local Cree people simply call this island *misi-ministik*, meaning "big island." Operating like a giant stopper, it manages to keep the water level on Otter Lake some 9 m (30 ft) higher than that on Mountain Lake. Some water does, of course, escape down either side of Eyinew Island. These escape routes provide two possibilities for reaching Mountain Lake. One option is to paddle to the southwest end of Eyinew Island and then portage past Robertson Falls and Twin Falls via Stony Mountain Portage and Mountain Portage respectively. The other option is to paddle to the northeast end of Eyinew Island and portage past two major falls marked but not named on official maps.

The shorter, southwest route crossing Stony Mountain and Mountain portages was the route used by the voyageurs. It has since become the main route used by modern-day canoeists. Nonetheless, the less popular northeast route is an excellent option and will be described later.

Assuming you stay on the main route, you will quickly draw near Robertson Falls and Stony Mountain Portage. Should you approach this area with the aid of Map 73P/10, you may be tempted to avoid the portage by running either of two sets of rapids (not accurately shown on Map 73P) occurring south of Reid Island, about 1 km (²/₃ mi) east of Robertson Falls. The channel southwest of Reid Island (73P 262563) may in fact be runnable by experts, but we would not recommend it for the average canoeist. After scouting it and seeing that it had submerged rocks, bad ledges, and several sweepers, we decided it was not for us. As for the channel southeast of Reid Island (73P 268563), it has bad falls at its foot making it impassable for canoes. We think canoeists should avoid both these channels.

Map 73P/10 also shows a portage 1 km (²/₃ mi) east of Robertson Falls that bypasses both Robertson Falls and Twin Falls. This portage does in fact exist as a boat pullover. In Cree, it has the sensible name of *piyak onikâhp*, meaning "one portage." It starts from Otter Lake in a small, rocky bay and runs about 325 m (355 yd) to where it ends in the bay lying northeast of Twin Falls. The portage is wet at the northwest end and steep at the southeast end but otherwise in very good condition.

Unfortunately, strong currents at the foot of Twin Falls make *piyak onikâhp* impractical for canoeists. Downstream paddlers leaving the portage have capsized in these currents. And, at least in high water, upstream paddlers simply cannot paddle fast enough to work their way up to the portage. We recommend that you land at *piyak onikâhp* only from the Otter Lake side and then only for the purpose of hiking to view Twin Falls.

Robertson Falls

Robertson Falls are named on Map 73P/10 and marked as Stony Mountain Portage on Map 73P. From the maps, you will see that they connect Otter Lake with a small, unnamed lake lying between Otter Lake and Mountain Lake. They are wide, beautiful falls broken into

Robertson Falls, viewed from downstream, July 1986.

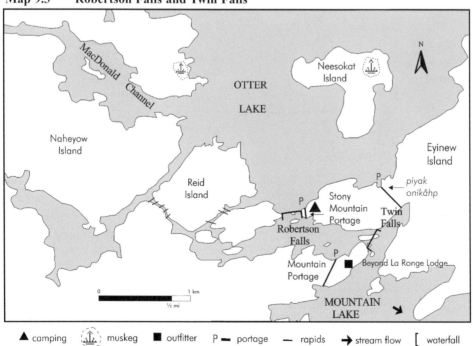

channels by a number of rocky islets. Since they produce an elevation drop of perhaps 4 m (13 ft), you will have to portage past them.

Portage #1 - Stony Mountain Portage (± 85 m / 95 yd)

This portage, which bypasses Robertson Falls on channel left, begins east of the falls at a point about 40 m (44 yd) up the shore from some preliminary rapids. As you approach, you will see the portage climbing up over bedrock and passing through a stand of tall spruce. Once at the portage, you will have to unload your canoe before hauling it ashore, but a convenient rock ledge allows you to do this without getting your feet wet.

The portage is a little steep at both ends. And, at the Otter Lake end, it has some white clay fill that becomes very slippery when wet. Otherwise, though, it is in excellent condition.

Along the portage, there are several very good campsites. If it is late, you may wish to stop here since these sites are better than any camping possibilities at Mountain Portage.

Map 9.3   Robertson Falls and Twin Falls

MacDonald Channel

OTTER LAKE

Neesokat Island

N

Naheyow Island

Eyinew Island

Reid Island

P

Stony Mountain Portage

piyak onikâhp

Twin Falls

Robertson Falls

P

Mountain Portage

Beyond La Ronge Lodge

MOUNTAIN LAKE

0   1 km
½ mi

▲ camping   muskeg   ■ outfitter   P ▬ portage   — rapids   → stream flow   [waterfall

Travelling upstream, you will find Stony Mountain Portage about 50 m (55 yd) east from the falls. You may also land just 10 m (30 ft) east from the falls and follow a somewhat narrower alternate path towards Otter Lake.

Below Robertson Falls

From Stony Mountain Portage, it is only 500 m (¹/₃ mi) southeast across a small, unnamed lake to where Mountain Portage crosses over a peninsula to Mountain Lake. The portage allows canoes to bypass dangerous Twin Falls situated 500 m (¹/₃ mi) to the northeast between the portage peninsula and Eyinew Island.

Portage #2 - Mountain Portage (± 285 m / 310 yd)

This portage begins in a tiny cove about 100 m (110 yd) southeast of some red cabins belonging to an outfitting camp called Beyond La Ronge Lodge. The start shows clearly as a wide break in the trees along the shore. Its landing is a dirt bank that becomes quite slippery when wet. The actual portage trail, however, is level and in excellent condition.

If you arrive from Mountain Lake, Mountain Portage can be hard to see. You will find it in a cove 300 to 400 m (under ¼ mi) southwest of the outfitting camp. The downstream landing is just northeast of some bulrushes in the corner of the cove. Although inconspicuous, this landing has a gentle, grassy slope that is very good for pulling canoes up.

Beyond La Ronge Lodge

This outfitting camp is situated between the canoe portage and Twin Falls. When we stopped here on July 31, 1986, it impressed us as a neat and tidy operation. The hospitable owners, Ron and Karen Cojocar, told us that the camp was started in about 1960 by a bush pilot named Dennis Kelly who was later killed in a plane crash.[6] The camp then passed through different hands until the Cojocars took it over in 1980. The Cojocars ran the camp until 1994 when they turned it over to Andy and Beatrice Fecke of Melfort, Saskatchewan. The Feckes then ran the camp for several years. But recently, in 2001, the Cojocars returned to Beyond La Ronge Lodge to operate it as they had before.

Beyond La Ronge Lodge is on another portage connecting the small, unnamed lake with Mountain Lake. This is a good portage that is shorter than the canoe portage. However, its southeast end is so steep that the camp actually has a stairway built down to its dock on Mountain Lake.

Twin Falls

Twin Falls, known in Cree by the equivalent *nîsôstîw pâwistik,* are 350 m (380 yd) northeast of Beyond La Ronge Lodge. They send the combined flow from the Reid Island rapids and Robertson Falls onward and downward into Mountain Lake. Notwithstanding their name, the falls, at least in high water, actually drop down three channels created by two small dividing islands. Since the southernmost channel is only 5 m (16 ft) wide, the falls' name apparently derives from the main, north channel and the secondary, middle channel.

If you wish to make a side trip to view Twin Falls, we suggest the following options:

1) you can hike to the falls via *piyak onikâhp*. If you follow that portage from Otter Lake to its Mountain Lake end, you will find a foot path leading southwest from the portage to the falls;

2) you may be able to canoe from Stony Mountain Portage, land somewhere upstream of the falls and then walk to a good vantage point. However, since we have not done this, we warn that it may not be safe; or

3) you can paddle towards the foot of the falls from the Mountain Lake side and then land on the shore opposite and southeast from the falls. From here, you can hike around the edge of the bay lying northeast from the falls until you connect with the foot path leading from *piyak onikâhp*.

When Peter Fidler passed here returning down the Churchill with Philip Turnor on June 19, 1792, he wrote down his impression of the falls:

> then go down the river SE 1/3 & cross it & carry over a hill on the South side 180 yards [Mountain Portage]—the hill steep both ways—at this carrying place, the main fall [Twin Falls] is about 1/3 mile off & is the largest one I ever saw in any part of this Country. In falls in two places, both perpendicular … it is awfully grand terrifying to look nearly at it.[7]

Peter Fidler's account sheds some light on the voyageurs' portage past Twin Falls. Philip Turnor's journal adds similar information. When Turnor and his party passed here going upstream on September 24, 1790, (almost two years before Fidler's remarks on the return trip), he wrote:

> went NbE 7 miles in a lake called by the Canadians the Lake of the bald stone this part of the lake about 1 1/2 or 2 mile wide then turned between Islands leaving a large opening ahead full of Islands went NWbW 3/4 mile NW 3/4 mile, NWbN 2 1/2 miles and WNW 3/4 mile and came to carrying place about 1/4 mile south of a fall, called the hill carrying place [Mountain Portage], … carried 180 yards over a hill through the woods, rockey bad landing at the lower side of the carrying place, went W 1/4 mile in a small bay and came to a fall and carried 100 yards over a rock on north side [Stony Mountain Portage], not good, enterd a lake called the Ne-keek Sack-a-ha-gan [*nikik sâkahikan*] or Otter Lake….[8]

The accounts of both Fidler and Turnor seem to give a fair description of the outfitting camp portage and not the present-day canoe portage.

Curiously, members of John Franklin's first overland expedition to the Arctic seem to have used yet a third portage when they passed here going upstream on June 19, 1820. Robert Hood, one of Franklin's officers, left this account:

> we found ourselves in a confused mass of islands [on Mountain Lake], through the openings of which we could not discern the shore. The guide's knowledge of the river did not extend beyond the last portage [at Stanley Rapids], and our perplexity continued, till we observed some foam floating on the water, and took the direction from which it came. The noise of a heavy fall, at the Mountain Portage, reached our ears, at the distance of four miles, and we arrived there at eight A.M. The portage was a difficult ascent over a rocky island, between which and the main shore [Eyinew Island?] were two cataracts, and a third in sight above them, making another portage. We surprised a large brown bear, which immediately retreated into the woods…[9]

Although Hood's group may have mistaken the portage peninsula for an island, the above quote suggests that the group portaged over the little island northeast of the 5-m-wide (16-ft) channel. This island would make a very bad portage. The lack of a guide might explain how Hood's group could have missed the portage used by Turnor's party.

Map 9.4   French Lake loop

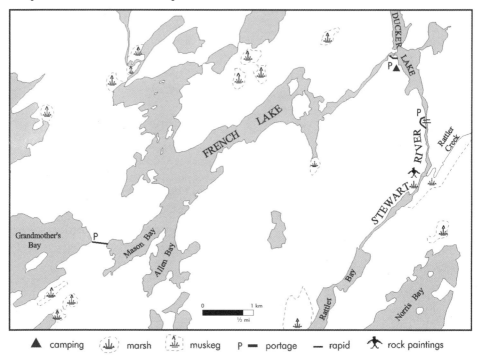

▲ camping   marsh   muskeg   P ▬ portage   — rapid   🕺 rock paintings

OPTIONAL FRENCH LAKE LOOP

As mentioned earlier, you need not paddle directly from Grandmother's Bay to the southeast end of Otter Lake. Rather, you can turn northeast into Grandmother Narrows to paddle a loop that takes you through Grandmother's Bay, French Lake, and Ducker Lake, and then down the Stewart River back into Otter Lake. This loop will add three portages and 12 km (7½ mi) of extra paddling to your trip. But on the plus side, it is off the main track, it has a first-class campsite, and it goes right by the Rattler Creek rock painting site. If you have an extra day to spare, we recommend the detour.

Once you have gone up Grandmother Narrows into Grandmother's Bay, you can paddle to the easternmost extremity of the bay where there is a portage into French Lake, or as the Cree say, *môniyâw sâkahikan*.[10]

Portage #0.1 - Grandmother's Bay Portage (± 360 m / 400 yd)

To locate this portage from the Grandmother's Bay side, you can first watch for a stand of aspen poplars growing near the start of the portage (73P 218642). Upon drawing nearer, you can head for a clear break in the shore bulrushes and cattails that will allow you passage to the portage's good mud landing.

The portage, which passes through a pleasant, mixed wood forest, is in excellent condition over its entire length.

From the French Lake side, you will find the portage in the northwest corner of Mason Bay (73P 222641). Though the landing is inconspicuous from a distance, it is visible close up as a narrow canoe notch cut into the shore mud. This notch makes it easy to unload canoes.

French Lake to Ducker Rapids

From Grandmother's Bay Portage, you can paddle northeast on French Lake for just over 5 km (3 mi) to where the lake enters a narrow outflow channel. You can then go a further 2 km (1¼ mi) to where the channel drains into Ducker Lake via a set of rapids. We will refer to these rapids as Upper Ducker Rapids to distinguish them from more rapids, to be called Lower Ducker Rapids, occurring south of Ducker Lake.

Upper Ducker Rapids

This rocky little cascade drops at least 3 m (10 ft) over a distance of about 80 m (88 yd). At its top end, it is about 10 m (30 ft) wide, but this narrows to as little as 2 m (6 ft) in places. Navigation by canoe is impossible, so a portage (on channel right) is required.

Portage #0.2 - Upper Ducker Portage (± 100 m / 110 yd)

From the channel out of French Lake, this portage shows clearly as a break in the shore alders about 20 m (22 yd) south from the head of the rapids. Here, the shoreline consists of quaggy mud embedded with a few rocks, so the landing is poor. Although the portage trail has a number of clay hummocks laced with tree roots, its general condition is good.

The Ducker Lake end of this portage is 150 to 200 m (165 to 220 yd) east and south around a corner from the foot of the rapids. Seen from Ducker Lake, it shows as a clear break in the shore willows and alders. The landing area is wet and muddy but free from rocks.

If you follow a footpath 90 m (100 yd) north from the Ducker Lake end of the portage, you will arrive at an excellent campsite looking out over the lake. It has two or three tent spaces amid black spruce and jack pines growing on a rise back from the shore. From this rise, the bedrock slopes down to a cooking area and then down some more to the water's edge. The whole campsite is roomy and well laid out, so we recommend it as an overnight stop.

If you fish, you can cast from the shore of the campsite to catch northern pike. Or, you can walk about 75 m (82 yd) east to the foot of the rapids to try for walleye.

PHOTO BY HILARY JOHNSTONE

Lower Ducker Rapids,
September 6, 1992

Lower Ducker Rapids

If you go past Upper Ducker Rapids and proceed south on Ducker Lake, the lake soon narrows to become what is the final section of the Stewart River. The river in turn quickly narrows to create what we will call Lower Ducker Rapids. Like the upper rapids, these rapids are too rocky and shallow to allow passage by canoe and thus call for another portage.

Portage #0.3 - Lower Ducker Portage (± 200 m / 220 yd)

This portage starts on river right at a bedrock landing about 30 m (100 ft) upstream from the head of the rapids. The trail is steep in places and also has some clay hummocks and bad tree roots to watch out for. Nonetheless, its overall condition is good.

> If you are travelling upstream, you will see the downstream end of the portage as a clear break in the shore vegetation about 25 m (80 ft) west of the foot of the rapids. The landing here is a firm, gentle slope made from a mixture of mud and gravel.

Rattler Creek Rock Paintings

From the foot of Lower Ducker Rapids, it is just over 1 km (²/₃ mi) to where a 5-m (16-ft) break in the horsetails on river left indicates the mouth of Rattler Creek. Just opposite the creek mouth, a very steep rock outcrop on the west bank of the Stewart River marks the Rattler Creek rock painting site, which has been described earlier.

Below Rattler Creek

Past the Rattler Creek rock paintings, the Stewart River will take you southeast for another 2 km (1¼ mi) to where it empties into Rattler Bay on Otter Lake. Once you are back on Otter Lake, you can paddle southeast to rejoin the main canoe route and proceed towards Stony Mountain Portage. If you prefer, however, you can travel in a more easterly direction to take the optional Northeast Route into Mountain Lake.

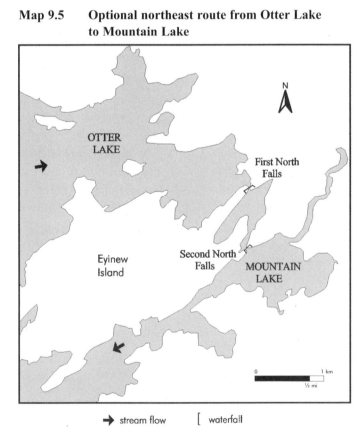

Map 9.5   Optional northeast route from Otter Lake to Mountain Lake

OTTER LAKE

First North Falls

Eyinew Island

Second North Falls

MOUNTAIN LAKE

N

0   1 km
½ mi

➡ stream flow   [waterfall

OPTIONAL NORTHEAST ROUTE FROM OTTER LAKE TO MOUNTAIN LAKE

If you have already travelled the main route from Otter Lake to Mountain Lake or if you just want to avoid traffic on the main route, we recommend you take the route around the northeast end of Eyinew Island. Besides having the advantage of being off the main track, it also has the scenic attraction provided by two major falls.

The channel and the falls northeast of Eyinew Island have no official names, though the first falls are commonly called North Falls. The local Cree refer to the route as *sîpânakiciwan,* meaning "a side channel." We will simply refer to the channel as the Northeast Route and the falls as First North Falls and Second North Falls.

First North Falls

These falls begin at a 75-m-wide (250-ft) gap in Otter Lake's easternmost shore. As soon as the lake's water escapes through this gap, it drops 1.5 m (5 ft). The channel controlling the flow then narrows to about 25 m (80 ft), and a second drop of 1.5 m (5 ft) occurs. Following the second drop, the channel narrows even more to end in a chute of boiling white water about 30 m (100 ft) in length.

First North Falls, August 1987.

If you go over First North Falls, things will go very badly. You should therefore take the portage (on channel left) northeast of the falls.

Portage #1A - First North Falls Portage (± 160 m / 175 yd)

As you approach this portage from Otter Lake, you will first see only a shoreline of black spruce. Closer in, however, you will see a low, rock island about 50 m (55 yd) long in a small cove lying just north of the head of the falls. This island is in front of the portage. South of the island, lake current is moving towards the falls, but you can avoid it by paddling around the north end of the island. Once you thus round the island, you will see the portage's rocky landing about 35 m (38 yd) north from the head of the falls.

The portage is steep in places but in good condition. It leads to quiet water about 30 m (100 ft) east from the foot of the falls. Here, a bedrock landing allows you to float your canoe parallel to the shore for either loading or unloading.

Below First North Falls

From First Falls, it is 500 m (1/3 mi) due south across a small, unnamed lake to where a narrow island about 75 m (82 yd) long partially blocks the channel draining the lake. Although riffles and swift current occur down both sides of this island, you can, with a little extra caution, proceed down either side without landing to scout. At the lower end of the island, you can continue on without stopping through about 50 m (55 yd) of minor rapids. You will then have about 200 m (220 yd) of quiet water before arriving at Second North Falls.

Second North Falls

These falls, which discharge into Mountain Lake, are actually twin falls occurring on either side of an island about 100 m (110 yd) wide. The northeasterly falls are about 30 m (100 ft) wide and drop more than 2 m (6 ft) over their 30-m (100-ft) length. They could be classed as rapids, but by any name, they are much too dangerous for canoes.

At the opposite end of the island, the southwesterly falls are about 20 m (22 yd) wide. They comprise a 1-m (3-ft) fall followed by about 50 m (55 yd) of rocky, lesser rapids. Like the northeasterly falls, these are too dangerous for canoes.

Second North Falls can be avoided by a portage across the dividing island.

Portage #2A - Second North Falls Portage (± 75 m / 82 yd)

This portage begins on a good bedrock landing about 20 m (22 yd) up the shore from the head of the southwesterly falls. The portage trail is in very good condition. It leads to a point on the lee side of the island about 20 m (22 yd) south of the foot of the northeasterly falls where a bedrock shelf provides another fine landing.

Below Second North Falls

Once you are past second North Falls, it is just over 3 km (2 mi) southwest on Mountain Lake to where the Northeast Route rejoins the main canoe route at Cow Narrows.

MOUNTAIN LAKE TO STANLEY MISSION

Mountain Lake

From Mountain Portage, Mountain Lake extends 17 km (11 mi) to Stanley Mission and another 5 or 6 km (about 3½ mi) down to Stanley Rapids. This entire distance is very good canoeing. The lake's rugged shores of Shield rock and its many islands are scenic and also create protected passages for canoes to follow. Appropriately, the lake's Cree name is *kâ-wapâwakâhk*, meaning "a place full of narrows."

As it does not have any mountains, we have to puzzle as to how Mountain Lake got its English name. Writing in 1790, Philip Turnor said the voyageurs called the lake "the Lake of the bald stone."[11] However, in the same era, Alexander Mackenzie already knew it as "Lake de la Montagne."[12] It may be that the voyageurs simply exaggerated the lake's "bald stone" geography to arrive at the mountain name.

The shores of Mountain Lake are steep enough to have attracted aboriginal rock artists. As on Black Bear Island Lake, there is a rich concentration of sites. Four sites have been found between Mountain Portage and Stanley Mission, and a fifth occurs between Stanley Mission and Stanley Rapids.

Map 9.6   Mountain Lake

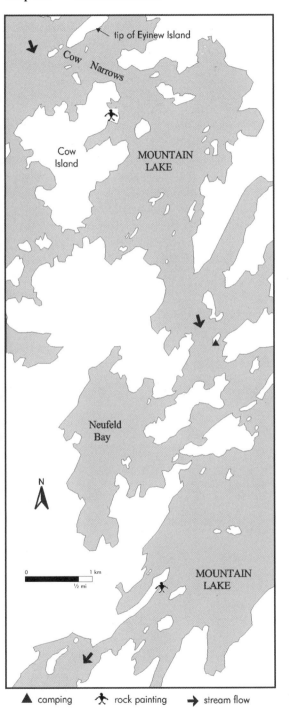

tip of Eyinew Island

Cow Narrows

Cow Island

MOUNTAIN LAKE

Neufeld Bay

N

0   1 km

½ mi

MOUNTAIN LAKE

▲ camping   🏃 rock painting   ➡ stream flow

Cow Narrows Rock Paintings

Two km (1¼ mi) southeast of Twin Falls, a strait known as Cow Narrows runs along the north shore of a large island having the same name. Rock paintings occur, at grid reference 73P 297545, on the east side of the northeast tip of the island. They are about 2 m (6 ft) above the water on an exposed outcrop that slopes back from the shore to a height of about 8 m (25 ft).

Though the paintings themselves are very faded, unthinking graffiti writers have made them only too easy to find. The symbols "EDM," "RC," and "83," written in green paint, stand out just to viewer's left of the paintings, and the name "PHIL" and a large heart, both in red paint, actually touch the bottom of the paintings.

While the paintings here are very faded, it is still possible to make out a human figure connected to a bison (hence the name "Cow"?) by two lines. The connecting lines make the paintings unusual since such lines do not occur in any of the other pictographs described in this guide. Tim Jones, Saskatchewan's authority on aboriginal rock art, says the lines resemble markings seen in Ojibwa birchbark pictography representing magical control possessed by shamans.[13]

Beyond Cow Narrows

If you are using Map 73P/10, which ends soon past Cow Narrows, you may wonder how best to proceed downstream from the narrows. The simplest course is a straight line south-southeast to the bottom right-hand corner of your map. Continuing in the same direction, you will almost immediately pass into the most expansive part of Mountain Lake. From here, your route will run southwest, encroaching onto the upper left hand corner of Map 73P/8 for about 1 km (⅔ mi) and then crossing onto Map 73P/7.

Coming down from Cow Narrows, you will see various camping possibilities. Some of these are occupied as summer camps by families from Stanley Mission, but others are usually available. There is an inconspicuous but good site (73P 312510) with room for up to four tents on a small island 750 m (½ mi) northwest from the lower right hand corner of Map 73P/10.

Mountain Lake Peninsula Rock Painting Site #1

On the west shore of Mountain Lake, a thin, finger-like peninsula points northeast towards Guncoat Bay. The first of two rock painting sites on this peninsula can be found on the peninsula's southeast shore roughly 350 m (380 yd) southwest from the peninsula's tip. At this point (73P 303475), a shore cliff rises about 10 to 12 m (30 to 40 ft) above the water. In the foreground of this cliff, a pie-shaped rock face rises about 3 m (10 ft) above the water.

There are three paintings in the centre of the pie-shaped rock face. Starting on viewer's left, the first is an indecipherable pattern of dots and lines being made even more obscure by an ongoing invasion of small green and blackish brown lichens. To the right of this figure, there is a deer-like animal having a long, sinuous antler coming from its head. Finally, still further to the right, there is a short, curved line with a dot above it.

Mountain Lake Peninsula Rock Painting Site #2

About 45 m (50 yd) south of Site #1, another shore cliff, spattered with blackish lichens, rises some 14 m (45 ft) above the water. Here, in the cliff face, there is a noticeable 1-m (3-ft) deep recess lined with rock tripe. To the viewer's left of this recess, there are two small rock paintings. The first shows a human form with a tail-like appendage between its legs. The second, about 20 cm (8 in) below the first, is so faint it can hardly be made out, but it appears to be a smaller version of the first.

Map 9.7   South end of Mountain Lake

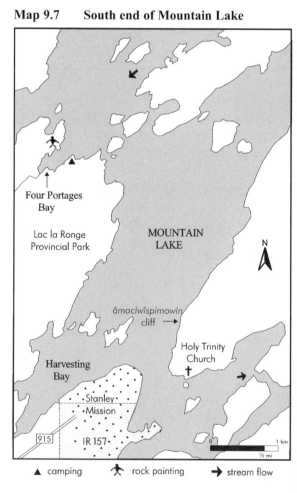

▲ camping   🏃 rock painting   ➔ stream flow

Four Portages Bay

Lac la Ronge Provincial Park

MOUNTAIN LAKE

N

âmaciwîspimowin cliff ➔

Holy Trinity Church ✝

Harvesting Bay

Stanley Mission

915   IR 157

0   1 km
½ mi

Coat of Arms of the North West Company 1783-1821

Frances Anne Hopkins, Canoes in a Fog, Lake Superior, 1869, *Collection of Glenbow Museum, Calgary Canada*

Frances Anne Hopkins, Canoe Manned by Voyageurs Passing a Waterfall, 1869.

Frances Anne Hopkins, Voyageurs at Dawn / Voyageurs à l'aube, 1871.

Frances Anne Hopkins, Shooting the Rapids / Descente des rapides, 1879.

Trapper's cabin on south shore of Clearwater River, downstream from Warner Rapids, 1986.

Smoothrock Falls, Clearwater River, 1986.

Downstream end of Bald Eagle Gorge, Clearwater River, 1986.

Clearwater Valley, viewed from Methy Portage, 1986.

Cessna 152 crashed on the La Loche River, 1986.

Sand beach on Aubichon Arm, 1986.

Commercial fisherman from Patuanak pulling net at north end of Lac Île-à-la-Crosse.

Patuanak youth, 1986.

Rose Gunn smoking whitefish at camp near the confluence of the Churchill and Mudjatik rivers, 1986.

Cabins at Dipper Lake, 1986.

Cabin and toboggan at Dipper Lake, 1986.

Plywood skiff at Pinehouse, 1992. Skiffs are common on northern Saskatchewan's "West Side."

Large boulder in the shape of a bear's head on Sandfly Lake, noted by explorer Alexander Mackenzie in the late 1700s. Photo taken July 27, 2001.

Silent Rapids rock painting site, Black Bear Island Lake, 1986.

High Rock Narrows rock painting site #2, face #7, Black Bear Island Lake, 1986.

Aerial photo of High Rock Narrows, taken September 23, 1998. Note the early smoke of a forest fire started by campers near the more westerly of two High Rock Narrows rock painting sitess.

PHOTO BY DOUG CHISHOLM

Helicopter with firefighting crew at Rock Trout Rapids, 1986.

Holy Trinity Church, Stanley Mission, 1986.

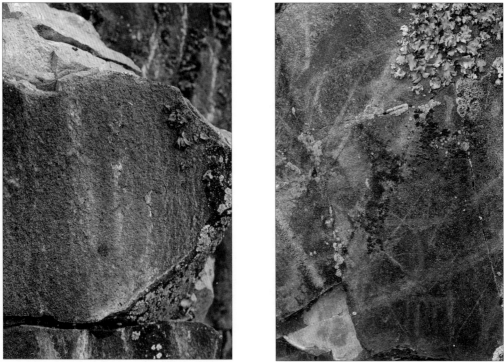

Four Portages rock painting, Mountain Lake, 1986 (left) and Rattler Creek rock paintings, 1986 (right).

Peter Ballantyne Cree Nation summer camp at the east end of Trade Lake, 1986.

Hand-painted sign on Lindstrom Lake, showing the way to Frog Portage, 1986.

Pullover rack at Second Pot Hole Rapid, 1986.

Rock painting at Medicine Rapids, 1986.

Limestone rubble on shore of Amisk Lake, 1986.

Last cabin at the old Beaver City site on Amisk Lake, 1986.

Saskatchewan Centennial Canoe Quest (SCCQ), June 20, 2005, Day 1: Team River Women, *the fastest women's team, moves down the La Loche River. From left to right: Viki Cirvencic, Renée Carriere (bow), Bernadette McKenzie, Veronica Favel (stern), Deanna McKay, and Debbie Chadwick. Photo credit: Gill Gracie, Aurora Communications, La Ronge*

SCCQ, June 23, 2005, Day 4: Cutting up moose meat for a community supper at Patuanak. Photo credit: Kevin Waddell, Cumberland House

SCCQ, June 28, 2005, Day 9: Solomon Carriere's Opimiskaw, *the fastest team overall, in Otter Rapids. From left to right: Jeff Kolka (bow), Solomon Carriere, Dennis Fosseneuve, Glen McKenzie, Bruce Barton, and Bill Torongo (stern). Photo credit: Thomas Porter Photographics, Prince Albert*

SCCQ, June 29, 2005, Day 10: Teams line up for the morning start at Grandmother's Bay, Otter Lake. Photo credit: Gill Gracie, Aurora Communications, La Ronge

SCCQ, June 29, 2005, Day 10: Captain Ralph Caribou (left) with Pukatawagan's Team Rock *cross the portage at Potter Rapids to leave Nistowiak Lake.*

SCCQ, July 2, 2005, Day 13: Opimiskaw *leads the race out of Pelican Narrows followed by Cumberland House's* Roger Carriere Classic *and Peter Ballantyne Cree Nation's* Otawacikiwak #1 *(far left). Photo credit: Gill Gracie, Aurora Communications, La Ronge*

SCCQ, July 3, 2005, Day 14: Canoes at Leaf Rapids, Sturgeon-weir River. Teams in foreground are, left to right, Peter Ballantyne Cree Nation's Otawacikiwak #2, *Pukatawagan's* Team Rock, *and* Opaskwayak Cree Nation Men. *Photo credit: Jeff Henderson, Flin Flon*

SCCQ, July 4, 2005, Day 15: La Ronge's O-Kehtay-o-Pimiskaw-wuk *in "Old Yellar" reach the finish line at Sturgeon Landing in 10th place. From front to back: Sid Robinson (bow), James Irvine, Kent Pointon, Warren Kelly, Gerry Morin, Glenn McKenzie (stern). Photo credit: Thomas Porter Photographics, Prince Albert*

Four Portages Rock Painting

This pictograph, the last on the way to Stanley Mission, is on the west side of a small bay at the mouth of the stream running into Mountain Lake from Hunt Lake. If you wish to visit it, you can paddle along the west side of the small bay until you come to a shore cliff about 12 m (40 ft) high (73P 266444). You can then search this cliff for a small, greyish-black rock face about 60 cm (2 ft) wide and about 30 cm (1 ft) high positioned about 2 m (6 ft) above the water.

In the centre of the greyish black rock face, there is a pictograph of a solitary stick man having an extremely long torso and two faint marks to viewer's left of his head. The stick man is very simply drawn. But perhaps because he is still a vivid rusty red or because he stands all alone, he makes a strong impression on those who see him.

Though he is now hidden from most of the Churchill's traffic, the stick man looks out on a canoe route that was once an important link between the Churchill and Lac la Ronge. Starting from the stick man's small bay, aptly known as Four Portages Bay, the route crosses four portages to reach Lac la Ronge. After centuries of use, the route lost much of its significance in 1978 when Stanley Mission became accessible by an all-weather road.

Camping

Before leaving Four Portages Bay, you may wish to examine an excellent campsite (73P 268442) directly across the bay from the stick man pictograph. This site is marked by a 25-m (27-yd) ridge of bedrock that slopes down from the woods to the water. Back in the woods, you will find room for two or three tents. The ridge of bedrock provides lots of space for all kinds of camping activities.

PHOTO BY HILARY JOHNSTONE

Âmaciwîspimowin Cliff

From Four Portages Bay, it is only 4 km (2½ mi) to Stanley Mission. As you paddle this distance, you will have a good view of *âmaciwîspimowin* cliff located on the east shore of Mountain Lake just 1 km (2/3 mi) northeast of Stanley Mission. This cliff is a massive rock face rising straight up out of Mountain Lake. It is too high for us to give an accurate eye estimate of its height, but contour lines on Map 73P/7 show that it and the hill crowning it reach 60 m (200 ft) above lake level.

Âmaciwîspimowin cliff, summer 2000.

In Cree, *âmaciwîspimowin* means "shooting arrows uphill." There are many stories, not always consistent with each other, as to the origin of the name. We will set out an account provided to us by Allan Charles, a school-teacher native to Stanley Mission.

According to Allan, Cree people lived near *âmaciwîspimowin* long before the coming of the white man. In summer, family groups would gather in the area to take advantage of the good fishing and to spend time visiting friends and relatives. At the end of the summer, everyone would again divide into family groups to go off to their winter hunting grounds.

Once the fall dispersal began, an age-old custom required each family paddling north to stop at the foot of *âmaciwîspimowin* and have its strongest hunter shoot an arrow to the top of the cliff. If the chosen hunter put his arrow to the top of the cliff, it meant hunting would be good up north. The family could then continue its journey to its usual wintering area. On the other hand, if the hunter was weak and his arrow fell back from the cliff face, it was a sign that the trip north would be a poor one. The family would then abandon its journey and stay at or near Mountain Lake where it could at least rely on the fishery for survival.

It is said the *âmaciwîspimowin* tradition ended when the first Anglican missionary came to the Stanley Mission area. While in the company of a family ready to head north, the missionary was allowed to shoot the ritual arrow to the top of the cliff. However, the missionary failed in his attempt, and his arrow fell back from the cliff. Weak-muscled or not, the missionary was a man of strong belief and quickly declared that his God would intervene and insure a good trip north. With his coaxing, the family did in fact continue north and actually had a good winter's hunt. When this news spread, *âmaciwîspimowin* had to make room for the Anglican faith.

Stanley Mission

At Stanley Mission, you can disembark at the public dock situated just south of the northeast corner of the community. The public dock leads up to a gravel parking lot where you will find plenty of room to stretch your legs and sort out your gear.

-10-

STANLEY MISSION TO PELICAN NARROWS

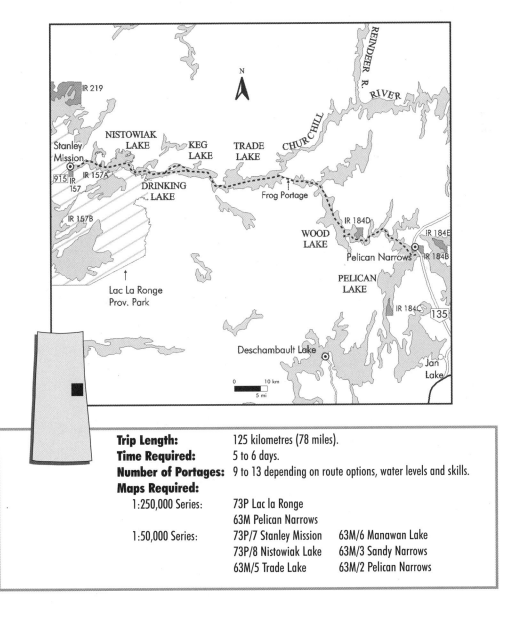

Trip Length: 125 kilometres (78 miles).
Time Required: 5 to 6 days.
Number of Portages: 9 to 13 depending on route options, water levels and skills.
Maps Required:
   1:250,000 Series: 73P Lac la Ronge
                     63M Pelican Narrows
   1:50,000 Series: 73P/7 Stanley Mission   63M/6 Manawan Lake
                     73P/8 Nistowiak Lake   63M/3 Sandy Narrows
                     63M/5 Trade Lake   63M/2 Pelican Narrows

ABOUT THE TRIP

The trip route first follows a chain of lakes forming part of the Churchill River. It then crosses south over a divide to continue through lakes that are part of the upper Sturgeon-weir River. Big lakes and major rapids make the route challenging, but the lakes have reasonable wind protection and portages bypass the bad whitewater. If you are travelling downstream, you can undertake this trip with a combination of modest canoeing skills and mature common sense.

Though the route is mainly lake travel, an upstream trip calls for advanced canoeing skills. Going upstream, it can be difficult to paddle up to and away from the portages that bypass the rapids between lakes. This is especially true in high water conditions.

The route is entirely within the Shield. Its lakes thus have irregular shorelines and numerous islands. Shield bedrock is commonplace and provides many good campsites.

East from Stanley Mission, there is considerable boat traffic from local residents and sport fishers. You are also likely to see other canoe parties. Further downstream, especially from Drinking Lake onward, the traffic becomes much lighter.

Even in the remoter areas of the trip route, you will see cabins and summer camps belonging to local residents. Significantly, these habitations belong to two different First Nation groups. From Stanley, you will first travel through lands long used by the Lac la Ronge Indian Band. Later, from Trade Lake and onward, you will pass through country traditionally occupied by the Peter Ballantyne Cree Nation.

At the start of the trip, Holy Trinity Church at Stanley Mission makes a memorable stop. Built in the 1850s by Anglican Reverend Robert Hunt, it has some very fine architecture. It is also the oldest building in Saskatchewan.

Even older than Holy Trinity Church are several rock paintings made by early aboriginal inhabitants of the route. The paintings at Stanley Rapids are likely the most visited pictographs in northern Saskatchewan. Other paintings occur on Keg Lake, Manawan Lake, Wood Lake, and Muskike Lake (at Medicine Rapids).

Another notable feature is historic Frog Portage where the trip route crosses the height of land between the Churchill River and the Sturgeon-weir drainage. During the fur trade, the portage was a crucial gateway on the voyageurs' road to the North-West.

STARTING POINT

The starting point for this trip is the community of Stanley Mission located about 320 km (199 mi) north of Prince Albert. From Prince Albert, you can reach Stanley Mission by driving 240 km (149 mi) north on Highway 2 to La Ronge, then continuing 44 km (27 mi) north on Highway 102 and then turning to go a final 36 km (22 mi) east on Road 915. The roads are paved to a point 30 km (19 mi) north of La Ronge and then gravelled for the last 50 km (31 mi) to Stanley Mission.

At Stanley Mission, you can drive to the northeast corner of the community where you will find a large gravel parking lot that looks out across the Churchill towards Holy Trinity Church on the far shore. At the edge of this parking lot, there is a provincial government dock where canoes can be launched without difficulty.

Community of Stanley Mission

Stanley Mission takes its Cree name, *âmaciwîspimowin,* from the nearby "shooting arrows uphill" cliff. The "shooting up" legend (told on page 274) suggests that Cree people have favoured Stanley Mission as a place to live since ancient times. While it seems they did share the region with Dene from the late 1700s to the late 1800s,[1] it is thought that Cree speaking a *th* dialect have been here for centuries.

As noted earlier (page 212), the Stanley Mission Cree originally entered into treaty as part of the James Roberts Band. There was then a period—from 1910 to 1949—when they had their own identity as the Amos Charles Band. In 1949, they again joined the James Robert Band to form the Lac la Ronge Indian Band.

The Stanley Mission Cree are closely connected to other members of the La Ronge Band. At the same time, however, people associated with Stanley have tended to occupy a different geographic area than those centred on La Ronge. In very general terms, Stanley people have traditionally lived west to Nipew Lake, north to the Wathaman country, east to Trade Lake, and south to parts of Lac la Ronge. Of course, Brabant Lake and Grandmother's Bay lie within this area, and they too have their own geographic footprints.

Nowadays, Stanley has a population of about 1,500 with most of those people living on Indian Reserve 157. Fewer than 200 people live on the northern, off-Reserve side of the community which is usually called the "Hamlet Side" (though it is actually a "Northern Settlement") or the "McLeod Side" (after the main families living there). At one time, many Stanley people, notably the McLeods, did not have treaty status. However, under amendments made to the federal Indian Act, almost all Stanley residents are now treaty members of the Lac la Ronge Indian Band.

Holy Trinity Church

Stanley Mission's history as an actual settlement dates to the arrival of the Anglican Church. The Church first sent native catechist James Beardy to the Churchill–Lac la Ronge area in 1845 and then catechist James Settee in 1846. When these men found that the region's Cree had an interest in the Christian message, the Church sent Englishman Robert Hunt, an ordained clergyman, into the area. Arriving in 1850, Hunt initially established himself on Lac la Ronge, where he looked for a mission site that had good fish, game, and agricultural potential and that was also accessible by the far-flung Cree. Within a year or so, however, he determined that the Stanley area was better able to meet those needs.[2]

Between 1854 and 1860, Hunt completed Holy Trinity Church—a splendid architectural work—on the north shore of the Churchill, directly across from present-

NA / PA 18348

View of Holy Trinity Church and the settlement of Stanley Mission, 1920.

day Stanley Mission.[3] The church's construction was described years later by Robert Hunt's son, Reverend Stather Hunt, himself an Anglican clergyman in England:

> With Indian labor and the help of a half-breed carpenter named Sanderson, my father built that church. In fact, he named the place after our ancestral home, Stanley Park. Every board, every nail that went into the building was made on the spot. The lumber was whipsawn from logs out of the forest and the nails were cut and headed by hand. The only materials that were shipped out from England were the big door hinges and the colored glass for the windows.[4]

Holy Trinity Church now stands as the oldest building in Saskatchewan. In recent times, it has seen significant restorative work. In 1977, it was transferred to the province of Saskatchewan to be administered as a historic site. Major repair work began in 1981 and continued for several years. On June 21, 1988, a new steeple over 8 m (25 ft) high, a replica of the original, was lifted onto the church by helicopter to replace a "temporary" steeple that had replaced the original in the 1920s. The following year, on September 15, 1989, a new bell made in Cologne, Germany, was installed in the bell tower to replace the original that had been removed to parts unknown in the 1920s.[5]

As you start from Stanley Mission, you may wish to stop and admire the church and walk through the adjacent cemetery, both of which are still used by the Stanley community.

Holy Trinity Church, Stanley Mission, August 1, 1986.

Fur Trade History

The earliest fur trade activity in the Stanley Mission area was concentrated 15 km (9½ mi) downstream, where the Rapid River empties into the Churchill from the south. It was not until 1853, when Reverend Robert Hunt was preparing for the construction of Holy Trinity Church, that the Hudson's Bay Company decided to move its Rapid River post to Stanley. This was done under the supervision of Postmaster Samuel McKenzie who was to remain in charge at Stanley until 1863.[6]

The Hudson's Bay Company operated at Stanley through most of the last half of the 1800s. During this period, at least in the late 1880s, the HBC faced competition from Winnipeg traders, Stobart and Company. However, after the HBC brought in veteran trader Henry Moberly (the same man who had improved Methy Portage) to run its Stanley post from 1887 to 1889, Stobart and Company sold out and left. The HBC continued to operate a post at Stanley (still under the name "Rapid River") until 1894. In that year, because it was then reopening a post on Lac la Ronge, it closed its Stanley post, and for the next few years, the company only traded here on an occasional basis.[7]

In about 1901, the Hudson's Bay Company returned to trade at Stanley—first with an outpost and then, in 1916, with a full post. By 1921, both the Lamson and Hubbard trading company and Revillon Frères were competing with the HBC at Stanley, though it seems that Lamson and Hubbard sold out to the HBC that same year.[8] Revillon was to continue operating until the HBC took it over in 1936.

The early 1900s brought some hard times to Stanley. Solomon Merasty (whom we met at Pelican Narrows in 1986) told us that when the great 1918 flu epidemic struck Stanley in the winter of 1919-1920, approximately thirty people died. He arrived by dog sled just as the epidemic hit and spent the next weeks helping fur trader George Moberly (son to HBC man Henry Moberly) care for the sick and bury the dead. Since the ground was frozen, bodies had to be stored in Holy Trinity Church until there was time to dig proper graves in the cemetery.[9]

Two excellent books describe trading at Stanley in the 1920s. One is Syd Keighley's *Trader Tripper Trapper*, which describes Keighley's experiences as an HBC post manager at Stanley. The other is Harold Kemp's *Northern Trader* regarding his experiences as a post manager for Revillon Frères among people he described as "the finest in the North."[10] Keighley operated on the south side of the Churchill, while Kemp was on the north side near Holy Trinity Church. As the books ably describe, Keighley and Kemp were not always at their established posts. Both were masters at "tripping"—going on winter dog sled expeditions to buy fur right from the trapping camps, a practice the early traders described as trading *en derouine*.

PHOTOS BY HILARY JOHNSTONE

Residents of Stanley Mission display their wares: left, Flora Charles with a birchbark basket, May 1988; right, Mary Roberts and Betsy McKenzie with bannock and birch syrup, 1988.

In 1938, shortly after the HBC took over Revillon, Syd Keighley and an Italian named Joe Visentin set up an independent store to compete with the HBC. They continued in business until 1945 when they sold out to the HBC. A few years later, possibly in 1951, the HBC faced new competition when Saskatchewan Government Trading (SGT) shut down a store it had started at Birch Rapids and moved the operation to Stanley. As in the case of Pinehouse, Stanley's SGT store later became a Northern Co-op Trading store. Nowadays, the new North West Company's Northern store (the HBC's successor) faces stiff competition from Northern Co-op Trading's successor, the Amachewespemawin Co-op started in 1979. This Co-op now operates a retail store, opened in 1992, which has 14,000 square feet of space.[11]

Stanley Mission Today

In the 1920s, when people had "pitched off" to their traplines in the fall, Stanley Mission would have only its fur traders left behind.[12] Dramatic changes have occurred since then. New developments came especially fast after 1978, when an all-weather road reached the community, bringing with it all manner of things from the modern age.

At Stanley, canoeists will find the Co-op store, the Northern store, gasoline pumps, a fast food outlet, post office, a medical clinic with nursing staff, and a two-member RCMP detachment. Saskatchewan Environment officers from La Ronge visit Stanley, but they do not keep a regular office here. You will not find liquor outlets since Reserve 157 is a "dry Reserve" pursuant to a Band bylaw.

Map 10.1   Community of Stanley Mission

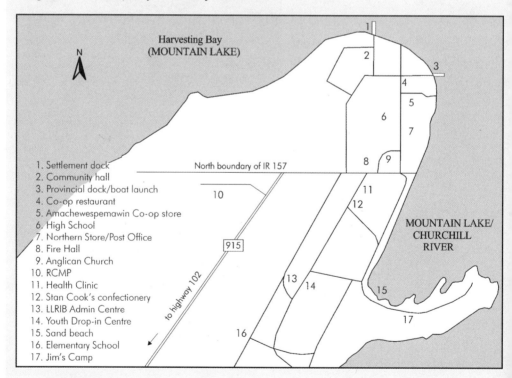

1. Settlement dock
2. Community hall
3. Provincial dock/boat launch
4. Co-op restaurant
5. Amachewespemawin Co-op store
6. High School
7. Northern Store/Post Office
8. Fire Hall
9. Anglican Church
10. RCMP
11. Health Clinic
12. Stan Cook's confectionery
13. LLRIB Admin Centre
14. Youth Drop-in Centre
15. Sand beach
16. Elementary School
17. Jim's Camp

STANLEY MISSION TO PELICAN NARROWS

Downstream from Stanley Mission

From Stanley Mission, the Churchill flows east-northeast for 5.5 km (3½ mi) to Stanley Rapids. In this distance, which might be considered an arm of Mountain Lake,[13] the river is as much as 1 km (²/₃ mi) wide. Its only significant current is 1.5 km (1 mi) east from Stanley in the narrows (73P 297411) north of Spencer Island (named on 73P/7). The Cree call the narrows *kâ-wapâcikociwasik*, meaning "where the narrows has current." Map 73P marks a portage here, but alert canoeists can paddle down the current without difficulty.

Likewise, it is also usually possible to paddle upstream past Spencer Island though in high water, this may call for a serious burst of power.

Stanley Rapids Rock Paintings

Less than 1 km (²/₃ mi) before Stanley Rapids, the Churchill narrows as it flows south of a finger-like peninsula pointing out of the northeast. On the southeast side of this peninsula (river left) and about 100 m (110 yd) downstream from its tip, you will see a jumble of rocks that have fallen into the water from a cliff about 10 m (30 ft) high. Just past here, two large square rock faces display several pictographs in a band 1 to 2 m (3 to 6 ft) above the water. In front of the paintings, some flat rock slabs offer good standing room to viewers (73P 324424).

Map 10.2   Stanley Rapids rock painting site, Stanley Rapids, and Drope Lake

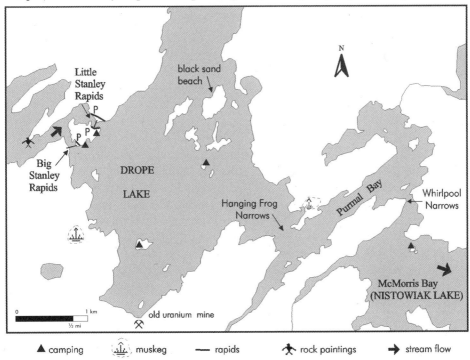

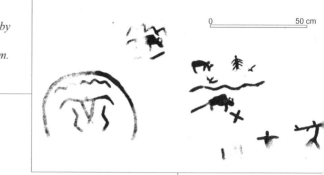

Sketches of Stanley Rapids rock paintings, reproduced from The Aboriginal Rock Paintings of the Churchill River *by Tim Jones, courtesy of Archeological Research, Royal Saskatchewan Museum.*

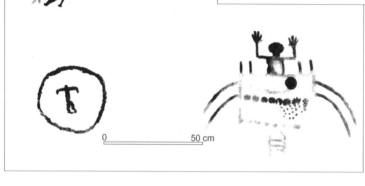

Starting on viewer's left, the first square rock face has a thunderbird with a horizontal wavy line above it and a vertical wavy line below each of its outstretched wings. The bird and the wavy lines are enclosed by a curved arc open to the bottom. To the right of the thunderbird painting, there are over a dozen other marks or figures. These include two bisons, what looks to be a grazing animal, an insect-like figure, and a small person with outstretched arms.

The second square rock face has a man shooting a rifle at a caribou-like animal that is being chased by either a wolf or a dog. In an area below the caribou-like animal, there is a circle enclosing what looks to be a dancing man. Finally, to the right, there is a complex figure that has a man with upraised arms standing in or behind a kind of raised box marked by various designs.

The rifle hunter on the second rock face is noteworthy since such figures are extremely rare in Shield rock art. With the exception of one other possible example in Ontario, the rifle hunter at Stanley Rapids is the only one known in the Canadian Shield. This may suggest that most Shield rock art predates the introduction of firearms. Of course, the rifle hunter here could not predate the late 1600s when Europeans first began trading from Hudson Bay.[14]

Stanley Rapids

About 500 m (1/3 mi) downstream from the rock paintings, the Churchill divides around an island to produce a north and a south channel. Rapids occur in both channels. While Maps 73P and 73P/8 use only the single legend "Stanley Rapids," the north rapids are commonly referred to as "Little Stanley" while those to the south are known as "Big Stanley."

The Cree refer to the main, south rapids as *napakihtako-pâwistik*, meaning "board rapids," and use a diminutive of the same name for the smaller north rapids. The story goes that, long ago, two white men accidentally went down the dangerous south channel instead of the north and drowned as a result. A thick wooden slab or board was used to mark their graves, and this gave rise to the rapids' Cree name.[15] It is not known when the drownings occurred, but they would have predated 1908 when Frank Crean, a federal government surveyor, referred to Stanley Rapids as the "Grave Rapid."[16]

The canoe route past Stanley Rapids is via the safer north channel, and we recommend this route. We will, however, mention both rapids in turn.

Little Stanley Rapids

Little Stanley Rapids in extreme low water conditions, July 1993.

These rapids handle a much smaller flow volume than Big Stanley, and in extreme low water conditions, they can be reduced to a trickle. Ordinarily, though, they consist of a 50-m (55-yd) section of strong Class 2 rapids followed by a second and final 50-m section of swift but easy rapids. At normal water levels, they can be run by advanced canoeists who have first scouted them from shore. The best course down is via a main tongue on river left which quickly drops about 50 cm (20 in) and then develops into good-sized rooster tails. A big knobby boulder in mid-channel marks where the rooster tails end and the final section of easy rapids begins. The course down river left avoids four separate rock ledges or spines that reach out from the river right shore.

During the fur trade, Little Stanley was seen as a *décharge* where canoes would be lightened of their loads.[17] It was perhaps sometimes a *décharge* in either direction, but good water levels may have allowed the rapids to be run without lightening of loads. After going down the rapids with Philip Turnor on June 19, 1792, Peter Fidler described how they were dealt with: "Carry on North side 90 yards part. The other part is taken up in the Canoe by handing along the shore. We now shot it down & put up here & set our net."[18]

Though Little Stanley Rapids can be run, many canoeists will want to bypass them using a short portage on river left or an even quicker boat pullover on river right.

Portage #1 - Little Stanley Portage (± 90 m / 99 yd)

This portage's upstream landing, which is gently sloped though with some rocks, can be found at a break in the river left shore willows about 60 m (65 yd) upstream from the head of the rapids. The portage itself was once in excellent condition but now suffers from underuse. At its downstream end, it drops quickly to a good landing of grass and mud adjacent to a sloping shelf of grey rock that is helpful in loading and unloading canoes.

Upstream travellers will find the portage's downstream landing, marked by the grey rock shelf, in a small indentation about 40 m (44 yd) upstream from Drope Lake. To reach the landing, it is necessary to advance past a riffle or minor rapid. Strong canoeists will be able to paddle up the riffle, but others may need to wade.

Portage #1A - Little Stanley Pullover (± 40 m / 45 yd)

The river right side of Little Stanley has traditionally been used as a boat pullover. In 1990, a pullover rack with wooden rollers was replaced by a deck of treated lumber fitted with sturdy blue synthetic rollers. From upstream, you can reach the pullover deck by advancing cautiously around a rocky point on river right and then paddling 50 m (55 yd) across a quiet cove lying south from the head of the rapids. You can then haul your loaded canoe over the rollers in mere moments. Downstream, the pullover ends in a narrow little bay which opens into the lower, easier half of the rapids.

There is also a portage trail about 130 m (140 yd) long running parallel to and some distance south of the boat pullover. Starting deep in the cove south of the head of the rapids and ending on Drope Lake, it is in excellent condition. It is not so efficient as the pullover, but it is often used by canoeists camping at Little Stanley.

Camping

Little Stanley's campsite, situated on the river right side of the foot of the rapids, is a very popular one. Overlooking Drope Lake to the east, it has room for many tents in open spaces cleared beneath some tall spruce. You may very well find canoeists or other campers here, but the area is large enough to accommodate more than one party at a time.

Boat pullover at Little Stanley Rapids.

Little Stanley is well known for its walleye fishing. Time spent casting below the rapids can often improve a supper menu.

Because the Little Stanley site is popular, special care should be taken to reduce the environmental impact of camping. Building a simple latrine in a suitable location is one practical measure that will help preserve the area for other users. Keeping firewood consumption to a minimum will also help.

Big Stanley Rapids

These are major, Class 3 rapids handling most of the Churchill's flow from Mountain Lake. Extending for about 40 m (44 yd), they occur where the south channel is reduced to perhaps 80 m (88 yd) in width and obstructed by a line of ledges and bedrock shelves. River left has the most obstructions, while right of centre the main flow dives into a hole that can grow to house-like proportions at some water levels. There is, however, a narrow slick of swift but navigable water right up against the river right shore—really a wall of rock about 10 m (30 ft) high. Stanley men who know the river run boats up and down the slick on a regular basis.

In recent years, some canoeists have been running Big Stanley. If you have expert skills and water levels are suitable, you may want to give it a try. The slick along the south wall provides a good route as long as you do not slip into the dangerous hole next to it. The river left shore also has a difficult S-pattern route that may be an option. Before choosing any route, however, you should first stop on the island and do a careful scout.

Portage #1B - Big Stanley Portage (± 65 m / 70 yd)

There is a portage past Big Stanley on river left. To reach it, it is necessary to skirt around a point extending from the island shore about 40 m (44 yd) upstream from the rapids. The current around the point creates some risk, but it is possible to paddle this current in either direction. Down from the point, the portage begins at a bedrock shelf about 5 m (or yd) north of the

PHOTO BY DOUG CHISHOLM

Aerial view looking west towards Stanley Mission, autumn 1998. Big Stanley Rapids in lower left; Stanley Rapids pictograph site at centre.

head of the rapids. There is again some current here, so caution is necessary when unloading or reloading canoes.

The portage trail is in very good condition though steep and rocky in one spot. It ends at a wide bedrock shelf about 30 m (33 yd) north from the foot of the rapids. The shelf has ample room for sorting out gear.

The downstream end of the portage has an excellent campsite with a well-used fire pit and a good view of the rapids. There is room for a couple of tents near the fire pit and room for several more in the woods to the north.

Drope Lake

Drope Lake is known in Cree as *sâkahikanisis*, which simply means the "little lake." It is actually a long lake from north to south, but the canoe route across its main part is a southeast traverse of only 3 km (2 mi). The crossing requires fair weather since most of the islands that could offer protection lie north of the traverse line.

You may wish to detour north to visit an unusual black sand beach on the north shore of the more easterly of Drope Lake's two largest islands (73P 349429). The beach was first mentioned to us in 1986 by Jeff Chiarenzelli, a geologist researching the age of local Shield rocks. The beach is about 75 m (250 ft) wide and 10 m (30 ft) deep. Though not large, it stands out as the only black sand beach (that we know of) on our route.

Camping

If you make a direct traverse southeast across Drope Lake, you will note two small islands lying just north of the midway point. The northwesterly island (73P 348420) is crowned by a grassy meadow large enough for several tents. About 4 to 5 m (roughly 15 ft) above the water and protected by only a thin ring of tall spruce, the meadow is fairly open to the breeze. This could make it a bit cool at times but might also help to keep mosquitoes down. The meadow can be reached from a landing of pink bedrock on the west side of the island.

Drope Lake Uranium Mine

Map 73P/8 shows buildings at the extreme south end of Drope Lake (73P 339400). This was the site of operations by a Toronto-based company, La Ronge Uranium Mines Limited. After prospecting revealed uranium in the area in 1949, work began with great enthusiasm to determine the extent of any ore bodies. Drilling was done, and pits and trenches were blasted into the local pegmatite rock. In 1954, a pilot mill was set up on the property, and there were plans to use Nistowiak Falls to generate hydroelectric power for the mine and mill.[19]

Mining operations were still in progress when Sigurd Olson passed this way in 1955. Olson observed:

> As we portaged Stanley Rapids and entered Drope Lake we could see a smudge of smoke, some buildings, and another uranium mine far to the southwest. The sun glittered on the shiny new roofs, and I could not help but think again of what Hemingway said about Africa, "A continent ages quickly once we come."[20]

Despite promoters' predictions that the Drope Lake find would be a world leader in uranium production, ore grades and volumes hoped for did not materialize. Operations did not continue much beyond when Olson passed by, and you will now see only the remains of some metal-clad buildings, some rusting equipment, and the blasted-out pits and trenches.

*Abandoned mine
at Drope Lake, 1986.*

Drope Lake to Nistowiak Lake

About 3 km (2 mi) southeast from Stanley Rapids, Drope Lake narrows briefly as it turns northeast around a finger-like point on river left and enters what Map 73P/8 calls Purmal Bay (73P 359411). The Cree know the point as *athîkis kâ-akocihk*, or "hanging frog point."

Two km (1¼ mi) northeast from Hanging Frog Point, there is a more constricted narrows where Purmal Bay leads into what Map 73P/8 calls McMorris Bay on Nistowiak Lake (73P 376415). This narrows is commonly known in English as "Frog Narrows," a name perhaps

Map 10.3   Hanging Frog Narrows to Nistowiak Lake

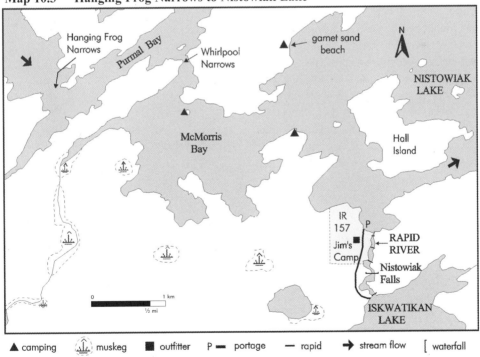

mistakenly borrowed from the "Hanging Frog" narrows 2 km (1¼ mi) upstream. The Cree call this narrows *kâ-mâthâciwasihk*, meaning a "place with fast current and whirlpools." Despite its Cree name, the current in the narrows should not present much difficulty for either downstream or upstream paddlers.

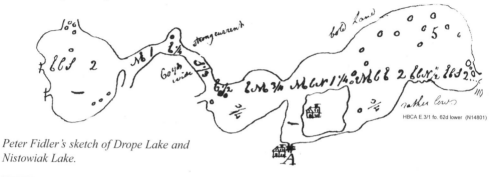

HBCA E.3/1 fo. 62d lower (N14801)

Peter Fidler's sketch of Drope Lake and Nistowiak Lake.

Nistowiak Lake

Nistowiak has a complicated shoreline and many islands, especially to the north. The canoe route avoids much of this confusion, however, by taking a more or less direct route of 9 km (5½ mi) east through the south part of the lake.

The lake's name represents the Cree word *nistowayâhk*, denoting the three-way junction formed by the Rapid River running into the Churchill from the south. In the days before roads, the Rapid River was an important waterway since its drainage was navigable by canoe as far south as present-day Prince Albert National Park. Indeed, it seems that early residents saw the Rapid River as a main branch of the Churchill and not just a simple tributary. After passing the mouth of the Rapid River on June 20, 1792, Peter Fidler wrote, "Then we go down the Missinnepee or Churchil River, here it only acquires that name & below, but it is the same waters that comes from the Isle a la Crosse."[21]

Maggie Ross of Stanley Mission at her family's summer camp at the east end of Nistowiak Lake, 1986.

Camping

Nistowiak has long been favoured as a place to live, and many Stanley people still spend a good part of their summers here. Several families have traditional campsites used year after year, but there are other good campsites available for the passing paddler.

One well-used site is on an island (73P 377408) about 500 m (¹/₃ mi) south and a bit east around a corner from the *kâ-mâthâciwasihk* narrows between Purmal Bay and McMorris Bay. This island has room for several tents amid some giant old spruce in a very level clearing about 2 m (6 ft) up from the water. Heavy usage has left no firewood on the island, but wood can be brought from the nearby mainland.

Another good site is on the south side of the narrows leading out of McMorris Bay where a broad shelf of pink granite comes down to the shore (73P 391406). Further back from the granite shelf, there is room for several tents in the shade of aspen and spruce. This site is particularly suitable for large groups.

Just over 1 km (²/₃ mi) due north from the pink granite site, another good site, suitable for larger groups, can be found at a 150-m-long (165-yd) sand beach in a shallow bay (73P 390417). At the beach's highwater mark, a skiff of sand having an unusual lavender hue—presumably of garnet origin—overlies sand of a more regular colour. Offshore from the beach, the lake has a gentle bottom which allows for good bathing.

Nistowiak Falls

Most canoeists passing through Nistowiak will want to make a slight detour southward to view Nistowiak Falls—where the Rapid River makes a final wild rush downward to join the Churchill. From Iskwatikan Lake[22] at their upper end to Nistowiak Lake, the falls and their related rapids produce a vertical drop of over 16 m (50 ft). The main falls, the best known in Saskatchewan, are spectacular. Thundering down a rock canyon, they turn the river white with foam and throw a rainbow mist high up the canyon walls.

To view the falls, you can land at Jim's Camp at the foot of the lowest rapids and hike up

Patsi Walton at Nistowiak Falls, 1986.

a 1.1-kilometre (1,200-yd) portage that runs along the west shore of the falls to Iskwatikan Lake. About halfway up the portage, side trails lead to vantage points overlooking the main falls. The vantage points are excellent, but keep in mind that they have no fancy guard rails. This is not a place to leave children unattended.

If you continue on to the top of the portage, you will see a small preliminary falls where the Rapid River leaves Iskwatikan Lake. These are sometimes called "Airplane Falls" in recognition of an incident which occurred in 1962. That summer, a Norseman, CF-SAM, had landed on Iskwatikan to pick up a crew of smoke jumpers working a fire in the area. The men boarded the plane near the head of Nistowiak's first falls, and the plane was cast off from shore. However, before the pilot could re-start the Norseman's engine, the current pulled the plane over the falls. The plane with its passengers then moved towards the main falls, but by good fortune, it grounded itself safely on shore just above the brink! A major salvage operation was needed to recover and repair the plane before it could be returned to service.[23]

Early Trading Posts

Because of its location, Nistowiak Falls was a natural place for early fur traders to station themselves. As Peter Fidler's sketch of June 20, 1792, shows, a post was located at the foot of the falls and another on the large island to the north (known in Cree as *nistowayâhk ministik* and as "Hall Island" on Map 73P/8). Fidler did not comment on the posts in his journal. However, if they were both operational when he saw them, they must have belonged to competing interests.

When David Thompson came to Nistowiak Lake in 1798, he noted two separate trading operations. On August 27, he reached "River aux Rapid where we found Roy by himself." Later, after a detour into Lac la Ronge, he proceeded upstream on the Churchill and a mile up from the mouth of the Rapid River "passed the Eng[lish] House of this summer on the right."[24] Roy would have been a Montreal trader, presumably with the North West Company, while the English House, possibly on Hall Island, would have been a Hudson's Bay Company establishment.

Much later, in 1828, Archibald McDonald of the Hudson's Bay Company, travelling upstream with George Simpson, noted that their party was able to pick up pemmican and dried meat at "the Rapid River House."[25] However, this house was likely a minor affair since during the period, the HBC's main operation in the area was a post at Lac la Ronge.[26] In 1830, the company decided to abandon its Lac la Ronge post in favour of one on Reindeer Lake without any mention of the Rapid River as a site option.[27] It was only when Reindeer proved unsuccessful that the company chose Nistowiak Falls as the best location for a new post. Minutes from the company's Northern Council meeting held at York Factory in 1831 read:

> The Post of Deer's Lake [Reindeer Lake] being found exceedingly inconvenient for the Crees of Lac la Ronge it is Resolved ... That it be abandoned and that a Post be established in its stead at the mouth of Rapid River which will accommodate the Crees of Lac la Ronge as also the Chipewyans of Deers Lake.

The Minutes also set out that the post would be in the charge of Clerk George Deschambeault.[28]

The new Hudson's Bay Company post, which could be seen from the Churchill's main canoe route when Sir John Richardson passed in 1848,[29] was maintained until about 1853 when, under the charge of Postmaster Samuel McKenzie, it was moved to an island near Stanley Mission.[30] The move to Stanley Mission was no doubt prompted by the construction of Holy Trinity Church at Stanley.

Jim's Camp

The land at the lower end of the portage past Nistowiak Falls is Reserve land belonging to the Lac la Ronge Indian Band. Since about 1980, Jim ("Big Jim") and Annie McKenzie of Stanley Mission, both well-known for their hospitality, have operated an outfitting camp here for both sport fishers and sightseers. The camp's cabins, built from spruce logs cut locally, are very popular and most often full throughout the summer.

If you stop at Jim's Camp, you may want to rent a cabin and enjoy the luxury of falling asleep in a real bed with the sound of rapids close at hand. You may also want to purchase basic grocery items at the camp store. If you simply pass through on the portage to see the falls, please keep the busy camp dock free of canoes and also respect the privacy of those staying at the camp.

Leaving Nistowiak Lake

From its southeast corner, an area marked as "Brown Bay" on Map 73P/8, Nistowiak Lake drains eastward into Drinking Lake through outflow channels passing on either side of a large dividing island. Canoeists may proceed: 1) down the main south channel which involves a portage past Potter Rapids; or 2) assuming reasonably high water levels, down the smaller north channel (not shown on Map 73P) which requires one or more short portages.

Map 10.4   Nistowiak Lake outflow channels

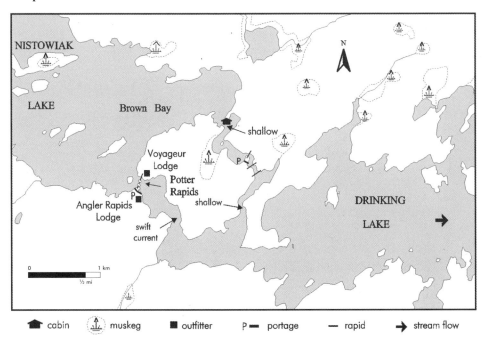

Potter Rapids

At the head of the south channel, which handles most of Nistowiak Lake's outflow volume, there are major rapids immediately downstream from a small island. The rapids are just over 100 m (110 yd) long and occur where two rocky islets subdivide the channel into three troughs. Each of the troughs has a fall-like drop of about 2 m (6 ft)—perhaps okay for a hot kayaker, but too dangerous for the ordinary canoeist.

During the fur trade, the portage adjoining the south channel rapids (on river right) was known as the "Rapid River Portage"[31] due to its proximity to the Rapid River's mouth upstream. Nowadays, the rapids are known in Cree as *kâ-pâscawakamosik* which, though the translation is difficult, apparently refers to a portage going over a rise and having sand at both ends. In English, the rapids are officially named on Map 73P/8 as "Potter Rapids," though they are just as often referred to as "Drinking Falls."

Since Potter Rapids are too dangerous for canoes, be sure to put in at the portage on river right.

Portage #2 - Potter Portage (± 100 m / 110 yd)

The portage past Potter Rapids is easy to find since it is situated right next to an outfitting camp called Angler Rapids Wilderness Lodge. When we saw the portage in 1986, it was equipped with a marine railway that allowed boats to be hauled back and forth on a small car. Later that same summer, however, the railway was removed and replaced by a roller system. But that roller system was not so sturdy, and it has now been replaced by a 2-m-wide (6 or 8 ft) boardwalk which has skid poles fitted into its deck at regular intervals.

> As an upstream traveller, you will encounter swift current before reaching Potter Portage. Coming up from Drinking Lake, you will find particularly swift current in the narrows about 750 m (½ mi) below the rapids (73P 461399). In places, this current is too strong to paddle up, so you will need to do at least some wading along the river right shore to get up through the narrows.

Fur trade journals suggest that the outfitting camp portage has been the preferred route out of Nistowiak Lake since pre-contact times. Peter Fidler passed this way with Philip Turnor going both upstream on September 23, 1790, and back downstream on June 20, 1792. Returning downstream, Fidler wrote:

> a Carrying place out of this Lake [Nistowiak] 110 Yards over on the South side—good carrying—but little firewood on the Carrying place that is dry—a heavy fall here river about 200 Yards wide—put up here for heavy rain[32]

Philip Turnor's journal entry for the same day echoes that of Fidler but also well shows how the early fur traders sometimes travelled on very short rations:

> 20th Wednesday took up our nets [at the foot of Little Stanley] but little success not having taken fish enough for breakfast at 4 1/4 AM we got under way went to the next carrying place [at Potter Rapids] carried over and put up at 7 1/4 AM it raining to hard to proceed remained all day we got a few jack fish at the foot of the fall which is a very heavy one, I mended our nets which stood much in need of it, in the morning Wind NE with a little rain at 9 AM the Wind shifted to NW and continued a heavy gale with rain all day[33]

Angler Rapids Wilderness Lodge

When we stopped at Potter Rapids in 1986, we met Jean and Joe Holowaty who owned the outfitting camp, then called Drinking Falls Lodge. The camp was originally built in the 1950s by the company operating the copper mine at Hunter Falls 10 km (6 mi) to the northeast. When the mine shut down, the camp was simply abandoned. It was then taken over by Jake Ernst in 1963. He operated the camp until 1971 when he sold it to Nick and Dorothy Fedun. The Feduns kept it until 1979 when they sold it to the Holowatys (except for cabins on the north side of the rapids which the Feduns retained).[34]

In 1987, Drinking Falls Lodge was sold by the Holowatys to Ginny and Mike Current of Denver, Colorado, who gave the camp its present name. For Mike, who had spent thirteen years in the NFL as an offensive lineman, the Churchill's tranquility was a welcome change from the limelight of professional football. In 1995, the Currents sold their interest in the camp to Joe Goodeyon from Chanute, Kansas. Joe is a good-natured businessman involved in the manufacture of oil field equipment. He somehow finds time to come north each summer to operate the camp every June and July.

Churchill River Voyageur Lodge

As noted, the cabins on the north side of Potter Rapids were formerly part of Drinking Falls Lodge. In 1979, when the camp was divided, Dorothy and Nick Fedun kept the north cabins and operated them under the name "Churchill River Leisure Lodge." In 1996, Leisure Lodge was sold to eight partners, some from La Ronge, who now operate it as "Churchill River Voyageur Lodge."

North Channel to Drinking Lake

The north channel is known in Cree as *sîpânakiciwanihk* which, roughly translated, simply means the "side channel." This channel handles only a small portion of Nistowiak Lake's outflow, and in low water conditions, it may have no flow at all. When it has little or no flow, it is best avoided since it then calls for four separate pullovers or portages. However, if it has at least a moderate flow, it is a reasonable alternative to the south channel.

If you are travelling upstream, you will appreciate not having to fight any significant current. But again, in low water, you may decide that the north channel adds more work than it saves.

Starting from Nistowiak Lake, the channel begins where a finger-like point, now occupied by a cabin, comes down from the northeast and creates a narrows about 20 m (65 ft) wide. From this point, the route is as follows:

1) At the initial narrows, adjacent to the cabin, a submerged berm of bedrock and broken rock spans the narrows. In low water, it may be necessary to pull or carry over this berm.

2) 600 m (1/3 mi) downstream from the initial narrows, at the toe of an L-shaped pond, a big shelf of pink granite marks where the channel pinches to as little as 3 m (10 ft) in width and produces about 50 m (55 yd) of twisting, unrunnable rapids (73P 471407). These rapids are bypassed by a 70-m (77-yd) portage situated about 70 m (77 yd) to the south. In 1986, this portage was newly fitted with a system of wooden rollers, but the rollers are now ready for replacement.

3) From the 70-m (77-yd) portage, it is about 75 m (82 yd) across a little pond to where a section of shallow, rocky rapids extends for about 125 m (140 yd) (73P 472406). Ideally,

canoes can be waded up or down these rapids. In low water, the rapids might call for a treacherous portage up the rocky streambed. In 1986, a wooden boardwalk was built on the river left side of the rapids, but this is now broken down.

4) 500 m (¹/₃ mi) further on, rocky shallows extend for about 40 m (44 yd) immediately before the channel opens onto Drinking Lake. At normal water levels, the shallows bear no mention, but in low water, they can be a dry rock garden.

Formerly, a portage of about 250 m (270 yd) long on river right bypassed the rapids in both #2 and #3 above. It started upstream about 15 m (50 ft) south of the head of the 70-m (77-yd) portage and ended downstream immediately below the #3 rapids. It led through mature black spruce and was in very good condition. However, a 1995 forest fire has obliterated the portage to the point where it is not presently a feasible option.

The best camping on the north channel is adjacent to the pink granite shelf mentioned in #2 above. The area has room for several tents amid a few tall spruce that survived the recent fire.

Drinking Lake

The Cree know Drinking Lake as *omîmîsiw sâkahikan*, meaning "fishfly lake." As for the current English name, its precise origin is not known. We have not seen the name "Drinking" mentioned in the earlier fur trade records. The first use we have come across is on the map in the 1909 report of surveyor Frank J.P. Crean.[35]

Though Drinking Lake has an irregular shoreline broken by many bays and peninsulas, the canoe track through it—12 km (7½ mi) of travel—takes an almost direct line along the lake's main west to east axis. The track has good wind protection, so you might reasonably expect to paddle it in two to three hours.

When we passed through Drinking Lake in 1986, two features caught our attention. The first was that a forest fire within the previous few years had burnt off the south shore and parts of the north shore further east. (Much of this area was reburnt in 1995.) The second was the number of bald eagles in the area. We saw at least a half-dozen adults who seemed attracted to the standing dead trees left by the fire.

Camping

Not quite 4 km (2½ mi) east from Potter Rapids, there is a small island near Drinking Lake's south shore (73P 490395). At the north end of this island, a bedrock spine rises up and back to a height of about 4 m (13 ft) above the water. The bedrock is suitable for cooking, drying clothes, etc. Further back, there is room for tents amid the island's black spruce which were spared from the fire that has burnt off the mainland shore.

Hunter Falls

Going through Drinking Lake, you may wish to detour 6 or 7 km (about 4 mi) to the northeast to visit Hunter Falls, sometimes known as Pitching Falls, on the Drinking River (named on Map 73P/8 at 73P 544437 but not on Map 73P). To see the falls, you can land on the east shore below some small rapids where a portage leads off to Pitching Lake. You can then follow the portage for about 150 m (165 yd) and then, using the sound of the falls as a cue, branch onto an indistinct trail and follow it for another 100 m (110 yd) to the falls.

The falls are only about 10 m (30 ft) wide and do not usually have a high flow rate. However, with an almost vertical drop of 6 m (20 ft) or more, they have enough white foam to look like a miniature Nistowiak Falls.

Hunter Falls was once the site of a fledgling copper mine. Copper was discovered here as early as 1924, though actual development work did not occur until the 1950s. An open pit and a shaft were then put in near the falls, while further work was done 2.5 km (1½ mi) to the northeast.[36] But ore grades or volumes must have been lacking, and the project was short-lived. Little sign is now left of the mine, but about 60 m (66 yd) south-west from the falls, you can still find concrete and timbers which appear to mark where the old shaft was sunk.

East on Drinking Lake

Exactly half way through Drinking Lake, you will come to a narrows about 150 m (165 yd) wide known locally as "Fishfly Narrows" (73P 514393). Though the whole of the Churchill's flow passes here, there is not enough current to cause problems for either down-stream or upstream paddlers.

More serious current develops 3.5 km (2 mi) further east where the lake divides around a large island marked as Healy Island on Map 73P/8 (73P 550388). The channel north of Healy Island is the common canoe path. It has a steady current which begins even with Healy Island's west end and continues to the island's east end, where a minor rapid extends across the channel (73P 555389). Alert canoeists can run this rapid by descending a broad, smooth slick flowing down river right. Though there is a narrow, navigable channel down extreme river left, it is perhaps best avoided since most of river left is obstructed by a submerged ridge of bedrock.

Map 10.5   Healy Island and east to Inman Channel and Jump Rapid

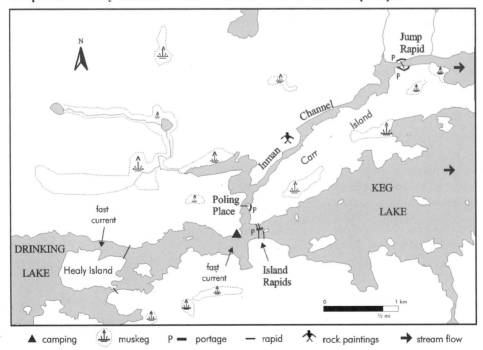

If you are travelling upstream, you may choose to work your way up either side of the north channel. If you take the Healy Island side of the channel, you will be able to paddle up most of the channel. However, at the minor rapid, you will have to do some difficult lining from the Healy Island shore, and 300 m (330 yd) further upstream, you will have to line or wade past another short section of current. If you take the north side of the channel, you may find better lining and wading since there is generally less current here. We have waded up the north side quite easily in low water, but we have not seen it up close in high water.

The channel south of Healy Island is broad except for one spot where it pinches in to a width of only 15 m (50 ft). Here, rapids extend for about 75 m (82 yd). Canoeists with modest whitewater skills may enjoy a fast run down these rapids, but they should first scout them from shore.

The south channel is not suitable for upstream travel—especially in high water. The rock bank on the south (channel right) shore is too steep for lining, and the water adjacent is too deep for wading. The channel's north shore is obstructed by a rock ledge that would force upstream travellers out into dangerous current in mid-stream.

Down from Healy Island

A further 1.5 km (1 mi) downstream from Healy Island, Drinking Lake narrows as it funnels towards Keg Lake. Just at its outflow, the current picks up considerably. This should not be a problem for alert and cautious downstream paddlers.

This faster current may present problems for those going upstream. It may be necessary to track canoes along the bedrock bank of the north shore.

At the extreme east end of Drinking Lake, there is a good campsite on the north shore right where the shoreline makes a rough 90-degree turn to run northward (73P 570391). Here, an extensive slope of bedrock rises 2 to 3 m (6 to 10 ft) to a level area where there is room for a couple of tents. We camped here in 1986 and found good walleye fishing in the offshore current.

To Keg Lake

Immediately northeast of the corner campsite, the exit channel out of Drinking Lake forks to present two separate ways into Keg Lake: 1) the northerly Inman Channel route; and 2) the southerly Island Portage route.

The Inman Channel is the recommended route for modern-day canoeists. On the other hand, the voyageurs ordinarily came and went via Island Portage, and in extreme low water conditions, this latter route is still to be preferred over the shallow Inman Channel. We will therefore mention both options in turn.

Inman Channel

The Inman Channel is a narrow strait separating Keg Lake's north shore from 4-km (2½-mi) Carr Island. In Cree, it is known as *sîpânakiciwanohk*, which, like the Cree name for the north channel between Nistowiak and Drinking Lakes, translates as the "side channel." As the Cree name suggests, the channel handles only a modest portion of the flow coming out of Drinking Lake.

About 500 m (⅓ mi) north from the corner campsite at its head, the Inman Channel has a minor rapid known in Cree as *natahâskosiwinisihk*, or the "poling place." At normal water levels, this rapid can be run down the centre by alert canoeists without any scouting. However, in low water, there may not be enough water to float a canoe loaded with gear and crew. In such case, some lining will be necessary.

Inman Channel, 1986.

Similarly, upstream travellers will have to line or wade up the rapid. The channel left shore is safer than the right for lining and wading upstream.

In more extreme low water conditions, there may not be even enough water to take a canoe through the Poling Place at all. If you have not then chosen to take the alternate Island Portage route, a short portage will be necessary.

Portage #3.1 - Poling Place Portage (± 80 m / 88 yd)

At its upstream end, this portage starts on channel right at an indistinct break in the shore willows about 30 m (100 ft) east from the head of the rapids. The trail has seen enough traffic over the centuries to provide a distinct path, though such usage has no doubt been sporadic. It ends on a good bedrock slope in a corner east from the foot of the rapids.

Down from the Poling Place

In 1999, there was an active bald eagle nest a short distance downstream from the Poling Place. It was situated on the Inman Channel's southeast shore directly across from where a bay leads off from the northwest shore.

Downstream from the Poling Place, the Inman Channel has no significant current until Jump Rapid situated 2.75 km (1¾ mi) further on. Indeed, excepting for the Poling Place and Jump Rapid, the length of the channel offers easy paddling for both downstream and upstream paddlers.

Inman Channel Rock Paintings

One km (⅔ mi) downstream from the Poling Place Rapid, there are aboriginal rock paintings on the Inman Channel's northwest (channel left) shore (73P 577403). As you approach, you can watch for a rounded, 2-m-wide (6-ft) rock to the right of mid-channel and then a jack pine–crowned cliff on channel left that rises about 5 to 8 m (20 to 25 ft) high and extends for 150 m (165 yd) or so to where the channel swings left and out of sight. The paintings are about 60 m (66 yd) down from the start of the cliff and just before the cliff becomes overgrown by trees and shrubs. They occupy an area about 1.5 m wide by 1.25 m high (about 5 ft by 4 ft) situated just over a metre (about 4 ft) above the water.

The painting area has up to a dozen different rusty red figures. Starting on viewer's left, they include a man with a large hunting bow, a snake-like diagonal line, a circle, an animal with what may be a large antler rack, two birdtrack-like designs, a large indistinct figure, and a small moose following a larger moose. Below these figures, there is a solid ball of pigment and also a bison. Finally, below the bison and touching it, there is an aquatic-like animal.

Jump Rapid

About 1.75 km (1 mi) northeast from the rock paintings, the Inman Channel narrows into a chute only 10 or 12 m (30 or 40 ft) wide (73P 592414). The channel's flow drops about 1 m (3 ft) as it sluices down the chute. In Cree, the resulting rapid is known as *kwâskohcipathihowinihk* or *kwâskohcipathiwin pâwistikos*, which, in short translation, means "jump rapid." The name derives from the fact that when local boats run down the rapid, they make a little jump as they go over the main drop.

Rating Jump Rapid is a difficult task. In extreme low water conditions, when almost no flow comes down the Inman Channel, you can actually paddle up the narrows where the rapid should be. On the other hand, in high water, the narrows can produce a boisterous Class 3 rapid suitable for experts only. At more normal water levels, you can expect to find a strong Class 2 rapid which may be run by advanced canoeists straight down a smooth, 3-m-wide (10-ft) tongue.

Given Jump Rapid's variable nature, anyone thinking to run it should first scout it from shore. For those choosing to portage, there are good options on both the north and south shores.

Portage #3.2 - Jump Portage (± 100 m / 110 yd)

The main canoe portage is on the north (channel left) shore. Its grassy upstream landing is about 50 m (55 yd) up the shore from the rapid in a small corner lying north of the channel's main flow. As you approach, you will readily see the portage climbing away from the landing and up a grassy bank. Once you have landed and are up the rather steep bank, you will find the portage in excellent condition.

> Paddling upstream, you may reach the portage by staying close to the channel's north shore. When you have passed two tiny islets and are just north of the foot of the rapid, you will come to a fine, flat slope of grey bedrock which serves as the portage's downstream landing.

Portage #3.2A - Jump Portage (± 35 m / 38 yd) (alternate)

On the south (channel right) shore of Jump Rapid, there is an alternate portage designed for boat traffic. Though not as safe as the canoe portage, some canoeists may want to take advantage of its shorter length.

This portage starts immediately to the right of the rapid, but it is possible to put in at a small sand beach 10 m (30 ft) further right so as to give the rapid a wider berth. The portage is a man-made affair created by shore rock being blasted out to a depth of about 1 m (3 ft) in order to make a suitable passageway for boats. The passage was formerly fitted with a pullover rack, but the rack is now gone.

At least in high water, many upstream paddlers will have a hard time going up the fast current below the foot of the boat portage. We therefore suggest that upstream paddlers use the regular canoe portage on the north shore.

Island Rapids

The main share of water coming out of Drinking Lake does not enter the Inman Channel. Rather, it passes down a short channel on the south side of Carr Island. This channel is divided into two smaller channels by two islands each about 120 m (130 yd) long—a westerly one of mainly bare rock and an easterly one with jack pine cover—that lie one ahead of the other and just left of mid-channel. The channels on either side of the islands are high-volume affairs and each has major rapids too dangerous to run.

If you choose to proceed via the Island Rapids channel, be ready to make a mandatory portage. Please note that the "Island Portage" legends on Maps 73P and 73P/8, which show a portage south of the rapids, do not correctly mark the historic canoe portage. The portage is in fact over the islands in mid-channel.

Portage #3A - Island Portage (± 120 m / 130 yd)

Going downstream, you can approach this portage by first paddling towards the head of the westerly mid-channel island. Here, since there is really no set portage trail, you can choose your own path. We recommend a route that starts in a little fjord on the west side of the westerly island. From the fjord, you can angle northeast along a spine of rock until you come to a safe put-in place at the foot of the rapids in the north channel.

Another option is to wade and paddle through a number of small sub-channels on the south side of the westerly island until you reach the easterly island. You can then portage across the easterly island to re-embark on the main body of Keg Lake.

For upstream paddlers, the route is the same in reverse. However, in extreme high water, Island Portage is best left to the strongest of upstream paddlers. As the current flow past the islands increases, it may become difficult to pull safely away from the head of the westerly island.

Channel south of Island Portage (looking west from islands) in low water, June 30, 1999.

PHOTO BY HILARY JOHNSTONE

Rock "kettle" at Island Portage, June 30, 1999.

PHOTO BY HILARY JOHNSTONE

Despite any risk associated with Island Portage, the Cree have likely used it for centuries. They now refer to the area as *ministik onikâhp pâwistikohk*, meaning "at the Island Portage rapids." Similarly, the early voyageurs had no hesitation in using the portage. The early maps and journals all indicate it was on the main canoe track with its name usually being given as "Portage de L'Isle"[37] or an equivalent.

If you use Island Portage, you can expect to see some peculiar natural features first recorded by Peter Fidler on June 21, 1792:

> Carry over an Island (Rocky) in the middle of the river, good carrying, called the Kettle carrying place—on account of several very round holes of a cylinderical form, from 1 to 5 feet in diameter perfectly smooth & round, some with a stone within loose—that has served to make the excavation by the falling waters and strong current moving the stone, and by its friction causing those kind of stone kettles above mentioned, these have been formed when these places have been the bottom of the river, now the rocks are above the surface 4 to 5 feet…[38]

Keg Lake

Measured from Island Portage to its outflow at Keg Falls, Keg Lake accounts for about 14 km (9 mi) of the old voyageur highway. It is an excellent canoeing lake since its many long islands produce a wide choice of protected passages for paddlers to follow. The islands do make it easy to get lost, so you will want to pay careful attention to your map as you proceed.

Greg Marchildon and Patsi Walton paddle calm water on Keg Lake, 1986.

On David Thompson's famous map of the West, Keg Lake is named as "Manito Lake"[39] which—with *manitow* denoting "God" or the "Great Spirit" in Cree—may have been the name in use when the first Europeans arrived. However, by the late 1700s, the portage at the falls immediately downstream was already known as "Portage de Bareel"[40] (Keg Portage). Perhaps in the same era, though exactly when is not clear, the lake itself also became known by the name "Keg" and the Cree equivalent, *mahkahk sâkahikan*.[41]

Keg Lake's name has a definite fur trade ring to it. The keg—typically an 8-gallon oak cask—was used extensively during the fur trade to move items such as liquor, grease, sugar, and gunpowder. Liquor kegs were especially prominent in early canoe cargoes.

Camping

Towards the east end of Keg Lake, camping options are limited. However, there is a very good campsite for two or three tents on a small island (63M 686396) 500 m (1/3 mi) west of Greig Island. A rather hidden trail on the north side of the island leads up to a good clearing surrounded by some old spruce dating back to the 1800s. Of late, the trees have suffered some from spruce budworm, but they have no doubt survived many such infestations.

To Keg Falls

The best route out of Keg Lake is via the channel along the southwest shore of Greig Island. Down this channel, swift current begins just upstream of a small islet in mid-channel. This current soon swings 90 degrees south towards Keg Falls. To avoid the falls, work your way down the Greig Island shore and then into the cove east of the falls where you can land at Keg Portage.

Map 10.6   Keg Lake outflow

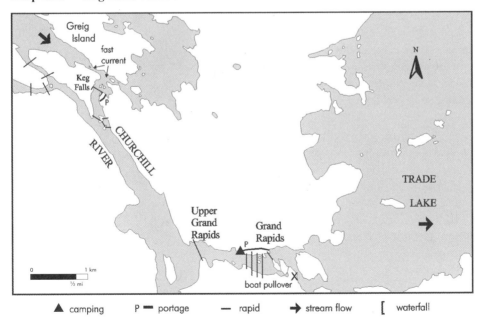

In low water conditions, you may find shallow rock gardens along the Greig Island shore downstream from the little islet. In this situation, you may decide to wade occasionally to stay close to shore. If you are a strong paddler, you may choose to stay in deeper, swifter water towards river centre.

If you are going upstream, you can leave Keg Portage and paddle north to Greig Island even though this involves cutting across fast current coming from the east side of the island. After turning northwest at Greig Island, you will have to ascend about 500 m ($^1/_3$ mi) of swift current to reach quieter water in Keg Lake. This can be done by doing some wading up Greig Island's southwest shore.

Keg Falls

Keg Falls, known in Cree by the equivalent *mahkahko-pâwistik*, occur where the flow channel narrows to about 100 m (110 yd) in width. Here, a ledge broken only by the odd jagged rock spans the channel and produces a nearly vertical drop of 1 to 2 m (3 to 6 ft). The drop is extremely dangerous, so all paddlers must portage.

Portage #4 - Keg Portage (± 80 m / 88 yd)

At its upstream side, Keg Portage begins in the cove on the river left or east side of the falls. Starting about 80 m (88 yd) to the left of the falls, it is easily visible as a clear break in the spruce and aspen growing on the shoreline. Near the landing, there is current moving towards the falls, so disembarking requires some caution.

In 1986, the portage had a pullover rack for boat traffic. It was in decay, but we were still able to drag our loaded canoes over it. Most of the rack has now disappeared, but even without it, the portage is easy to handle. Its only difficult section is a steep descent at its downstream end.

Patsi Walton at the downstream end of Keg Portage, 1986.

Travelling upstream, you will find Keg Portage simply by making your way up the east (river left) shore. Its downstream end is about 50 m (55 yd) below the falls. Though the run-out from the falls is close by, you should have no trouble reaching the portage.

Rapids Below Keg Falls

A few hundred metres below Keg Falls, rapids divided by an island extend for over 100 m (110 yd). Canoeists with modest whitewater skills can run these rapids. The best course is right next to the east shore of the channel east of the island (extreme river left).

Going upstream, you will not be able to paddle up these rapids. For Cree travellers going upstream, this was another *natahâskosiwinisihk*, or "poling place." If you are not a poler, you will find good wading along the east (extreme river left) shore.

Upper Grand Rapid

About 3 km (2 mi) downstream from the rapids below Keg Falls, the Churchill swings east. Right after this change in direction, a small rapid extends completely across the river. Though topo maps seemingly include it as part of Grand Rapids, it is quite separate from the main Grand Rapids farther downstream. We therefore refer to it as Upper Grand Rapid.

At this rapid, the river flows over a submerged ledge and drops about 50 cm (20 in). The ledge is remarkably uniform right across the river, but it does have some breaks where narrow chutes occur.

Advanced canoeists may scout this rapid from the south shore and then choose to run down one of the narrow chutes. One such chute is about 50 m (55 yd) from the south shore. However, narrow chutes can be hard to find at critical moments, so it may be safer to portage on the south shore.

Portage #5 - Upper Grand Portage (±2 m / yd) (optional)

Going downstream, you can reach this portage by hugging the south (river right) shore and paddling or wading down to just above the rapid. Here, a low finger of rock extends about 10 m (30 ft) from the south shore and joins with the submerged ledge in the river. Lining around the tip of the finger is hazardous, but a short portage of 1 to 2 m (about 5 ft) across the finger will take you safely past the rapid.

As an upstream traveller, you can also use the portage across the finger. It is possible to paddle up to the finger's lee side. However, after crossing the finger, you will likely have to wade up the south shore to quieter water before paddling again. Wading requires some caution because the stones here are very slippery.

An alternate portage, about 140 m (155 yd) long and in fair condition, runs further inland on the south (river right) shore. It starts at a low, grey rock about 60 m (66 yd) up the shore from the rapid. Its downstream end, overgrown with birch and dogwood, is in a cove below and to the south of the rapid. It has not seen much recent use, and at least at ordinary water levels, it is not a very practical option.

From Upper Grand Rapid, it is about 750 m (½ mi) to the main Grand Rapids. These main rapids require a portage, so be ready to land on river left.

Grand Rapids

The Cree name for these Class 3 rapids is *paskwatinaw pâwistik*, meaning "bald hill rapids." With no bald hill in the vicinity, the name seems odd. On the other hand, the name Grand Rapids, passed on to us by the voyageurs, is quite apt. Extending for a distance of about

Patsi Walton and Sid Robinson running Grand Rapids, 1986.

600 m (¹/₃ mi), the rapids are an obstacle course of rocks, ledges, and whitewater.

Besides being grand, the rapids can also be dangerous. Their potential danger is best underscored by a quote from Peter Fidler. Looking at the rapids on June 21, 1792, he wrote:

> a very strong fall, but not steep—several Canadians have been drounded here in running the Fall down—& one year in perticular a whole Canoes people were lost.[42]

In 1986, we ran a canoe without gear down Grand Rapids by following a course on river left. Although we made it down okay, our canoe banged over a submerged ledge a third of the way down, narrowly missed other hazards, and was finally hit by big waves near the bottom. At the end of our ride, we felt we had been more than a little lucky.

Confident canoeists may want to scout Grand Rapids and then make their own decision on shooting. We are of the view, however, that portaging is the only safe way to get past the rapids. We therefore advise all canoeists to use the portage found on river left.

Portage #6 - Grand Portage (± 630 m / 690 yd)

Going downstream, you can reach this portage by paddling towards some conspicuously tall spruce on the river's north shore. As you draw near them, you will find the portage's upstream landing some 100 m (110 yd) up the shore from the start of the rapids. It is in quiet water on the east side of a cove indenting the north shore. Not particularly convenient for canoes, the landing is a rough outcrop of dark bedrock rising up to higher ground about 3 m (10 ft) above the water.

Although the upstream landing does not provide very good access to the water, the high ground immediately above it makes a good campsite. Several giant spruce grow here. In the shade of their big branches, there are a number of tent spaces.

Campers who have read Kamil Pecher's *Lonely Voyage* may or may not look forward to spending a night on this portage. In his book, Pecher describes a solo kayak trip he took from Waterhen Lake to Cumberland House in about 1971. He claims that when he reached Grand Rapids, he found 40-cm-long (16-in) footprints on the portage trail and actually caught a glimpse of a sasquatch-like creature in the adjacent bush. Did Pecher see what he thought he saw? Maybe not, but his report makes for good talk when the campfire starts to throw shadows.

From the camping area, the portage runs through a mature forest of big spruce and aspen poplar. Though its length makes it demanding, it is a good hike. Minor hazards occur where slippery poles bridge a tiny water run and where the trail descends steeply to the downstream landing. Overall, though, the trail is in excellent condition.

If you are travelling upstream, you will find the downstream landing to the right of a 4-m-high (13-ft) rock wall that runs about 50 m (55 yd) north-northwest from the foot of the rapids. The landing is a small, stony area tucked in the corner created where the rock wall and the main shoreline meet at right angles. Here, a small eddy allows canoes to be unloaded in quiet water.

You may, however, find it hard to reach the downstream landing. You will not be able to paddle up along the north shore of the large island located downstream from the rapids because the current there is too strong. Instead, you will have to approach the landing by following the south shore of the island. Though you may have to do some wading along the island, you will eventually reach its upstream end. From here, you can cut over to the north side of the main channel and then go up the shore to the landing.

As you work your way upstream along the south shore of the big island, you may be tempted to make use of a pullover rack on the shore across from the island. This 150-m-long (165-yd) rack cuts across the peninsula (which is in fact divided into islands by four channels) jutting out from the south shore towards the foot of the rapids. It allows the local Cree people to navigate Grand Rapids by motor boat without having to go through the bottom section of big waves. However, as a canoeist, you will find the rack of no practical value because it does not connect with any feasible canoe route past the upper sections of Grand Rapids.

Trade Lake

Trade Lake's Cree name is *paskwatinaw sâkahikan*, meaning "bald hill lake," which corresponds to the Cree name for Grand Rapids. Nowadays, the name *paskwatinaw* is something of a mystery as the local landscape is presently well treed.

The current English name is easier to explain. As you may suspect, it stems from the fur trade. Its roots go back to 1774 when Joseph Frobisher, one of three fur trading brothers from Montreal, reached present-day Frog Portage at the east end of Trade Lake and traded with the Indians he encountered there. When news of his successful venture spread, the portage and the adjacent lake became known as Portage du Traite and Lac du Traite respectively.

Trade Lake is a big lake accounting for most of the 20-km (12-mi) distance between Grand Rapids and Frog Portage. Because of its overall size and because of its large expansion to the northwest, it can be a bad lake for wind. The first 6 or 8 km (4 or 5 mi) are especially dangerous. Accordingly, before you leave the shelter of the lake's west shore to start towards Frog Portage, you should be sure that you have good weather.

After you paddle east on Trade Lake for about 8 km (5 mi), you will come to a heart-shaped island about 500 m (¹/₃ mi) wide. On the south tip of this island, there is a triangle-shaped sand beach about 40 m (44 yd) wide. Back from this beach, commercial fishermen have built a plywood ice house. Near the ice house, the ground is level and only thinly wooded with black spruce. This level ground would make a very good campsite for larger canoe parties.

Four km (2½ mi) east from the heart-shaped island, you will come to Archibald Island, Trade Lake's largest island. Just off the northwest corner of Archibald Island, there is a smaller island with a bald eagle nest on its northwest shore.

At the extreme northeast corner of Archibald Island, there is a very good, albeit heavily used, campsite on a small point jutting north from the island. This campsite is accessible via a sheet of bedrock sloping into the water on the west side of the point. Just up from this sheet of bedrock, under the shelter of a few tall spruce trees, a large, level area provides room for a campfire and several tents.

Campsite on Archibald Island.

Peter Ballantyne Cree Nation

At Trade Lake, you will leave the traditional territory of the Lac la Ronge Indian Band and enter that of the *th*-dialect Peter Ballantyne Cree Nation (PBCN). PBCN's traditional territory is vast—running east to the Manitoba border, north to Reindeer Lake, and south to Sturgeon Landing. It has its main administration centre at Pelican Narrows, but it has land and members throughout northeastern Saskatchewan as well as in the city of Prince Albert. With about 6,700 members, it is Saskatchewan's second largest First Nation, just behind the Lac la Ronge Indian Band in size. From 1985 until 2001, Ron Michel of Pelican Narrows served as PCBN's chief. In April, 2001, Susan Custer, also of Pelican Narrows, was elected as its first female chief.

PBCN shares a common history with the Lac la Ronge Indian Band. As mentioned earlier, a large Cree band from the Churchill River region under headman James Roberts entered into treaty with the Canadian government on February 10, 1989, by signing an adhesion to Treaty 6. In the years to follow, families from the Pelican Narrows area added their names to the James Roberts treaty list. However, the Pelican Narrows families presented certain logistical problems since they were so far away from the James Roberts Band's base at Lac la Ronge. Accordingly, in 1900, Chief James Roberts and his council granted the Pelican Narrows people permission to split away to form a new band. A separation then took place with the new band at Pelican Narrows being named after its first chief, Peter Ballantyne. (A further division occurred in 1910 when a part of the Peter Ballantyne Band left to form the Mathias Colomb Band centred at Pukatawagan, Manitoba.) Like the Lac la Ronge Indian Band, PBCN has always been considered part of Treaty No. 6 even though most of its traditional territory lies within the geographic boundaries of Treaty No. 10.[43]

Northeast from Archibald Island, where Trade Lake begins to narrow, you may see white canvas wall tents pitched on islands you pass. These tents will belong to families of the PBCN who spend their summers hunting and fishing on the Churchill.

Down from Trade Lake

Just past the tent islands, Trade Lake has its outflow. This outflow is not a rapid or a fall but merely a narrows about 150 m (500 ft) wide. There is some current here, but it is not strong enough to cause problems for either downstream or upstream paddlers.

Downstream from Trade Lake's outflow, the Churchill moves slowly through a wide, lake-like channel. If you follow this channel east for 1.5 km (1 mi), you will come to a very important junction. Here, the Churchill swings north to continue on its way to Hudson Bay. But the canoe route to Pelican Narrows does not stay with the Churchill. Instead, it turns south to go across historic Frog Portage.

PHOTO BY DOUG CHISHOLM

Aerial view looking southward to Frog Portage, summer 1998.

Map 10.7   Frog Portage and area

STANLEY MISSION TO PELICAN NARROWS ■ 307

Farmer Charlie

At this juncture, some mention must be made of an unusual character named Charlie Planinshek who once lived on the north shore of the Churchill near Frog Portage. Born in about 1883, Planinshek was, it seems, from the eastern European town of Nis, Serbia. At a young age, he migrated to North America and shortly thereafter spent time in Mexico. Story has it that in Mexico, he joined the forces of the revolutionary fighter Pancho Villa. Eventually, for reasons unknown, he left Mexico and made his way to northern Saskatchewan.

We do not know when Planinshek arrived in the north, but it was not later than 1915. According to church records, he married Jane Mary Ballendine, aged 19, of Pelican Narrows, at Holy Trinity Church in Stanley Mission on July 26, 1915.[44] They settled near Frog Portage and, in the middle of the wilderness, started farming in a small but impressive way.

In 1924, C.S. MacDonald travelled by canoe up the Sturgeon-weir, across Frog Portage, and then down the Churchill to the Reindeer River as part of a Canadian government mapping operation. In an account of his travels, MacDonald says:

> we delayed for a minute or two at the home of Charles Planinshak, almost directly across the river from Frog Portage. This pioneer by dint of very hard work has carved a small farm out of the wilderness, raising good crops of vegetables and cereals and has even constructed the first and only grist mill on the Churchill River. For this he used two flat stones lying one upon the other, with a handle on the top stone for turning. Placing the grain between the stones he has ground out many bags of rough flour for which there is considerable demand amongst the Indians.[45]

In *The Lonely Land*, canoeing author Sigurd Olson recalls hearing a story of Planinshek using a moose to plough his clearing. Similarly, the ethnohistorian P.G. Downes, well-known for his travels in northern Saskatchewan during the 1930s and 1940s, heard stories of Planinshek using a bull moose and a dog in tandem to pull a sleigh.[46]

When we were in Pelican Narrows in 1986, the old people we met—including P.G. Downes's friend and travelling companion, Solomon Merasty—could not recall Planinshek having a moose trained to harness. They confirmed, however, that he was an extraordinary man known throughout the country as "Farmer Charlie."

Planinshek did not have the stay-at-home nature commonly found in farmers. In 1929, his wife having died in the winter just past, he left northern Saskatchewan to embark on an amazing canoe trip with his two children, Inez and Tony, then aged 8 and 6, and a man by the name of Frank O'Grady. In the two years to follow, Planinshek and his little crew canoed from northern Saskatchewan, down the Mississippi to the Gulf of Mexico, and then up the Atlantic coast to New York and Montreal. Quite a trip to take the kids on![47]

After his epic canoe journey, Planinshek returned to the north. He may have come back to Frog Portage briefly, but he did not settle here. Instead, he moved on, seemingly without his family, to Putahow Lake on Manitoba's northern border. In this isolated spot, he built a small, windowless hovel on an esker and then turned his energy to clearing several acres of land. When P.G. Downes visited him at Putahow Lake in 1940, by which time he was known as "Eskimo Charlie," he had at least two gardens, a corral built in an effort to domesticate caribou, and "stacks and stacks" of firewood he had hauled home in a four-wheeled wagon pulled by dogs.

All of Planinshek's ideas and enterprise came to an end when he died alone in his bunk at Putahow Lake in 1943 or 1944 of unknown causes. In 1945, some eighteen months later, RCMP Lance Corporal Marcel Chappuis discovered Planinshek's body and gave it a proper burial on the esker. As a parting gesture, Chappuis took flowers still growing in Planinshek's gardens and placed them on the grave.[48]

Frog Portage

Frog Portage is a short portage over even ground. Although it appears quite ordinary, it is no ordinary portage. Like Methy Portage, it crosses a height of land separating two watersheds. Lindstrom Lake, at the south end of Frog Portage, does not drain to the Churchill. Rather, it is one of the headwaters of the Sturgeon-weir River, which flows southeast to empty into the Saskatchewan River.

Historically, especially during the fur trade, the link that Frog Portage provided between the Churchill and the Sturgeon-weir was tremendously important. While the upper Churchill was for many years the best road into Canada's North-West, the lower Churchill was a poor complement since it had some sections that were very difficult to paddle. It was also too far north to provide critical connections to York Factory, Montreal, or the pemmican-rich prairies. On the other hand, the Sturgeon-weir, a tributary of the Saskatchewan, did lead to these major destinations. Frog Portage was thus a much needed gateway on the old voyageur highway. For a full century, from the 1770s to the 1870s, it handled a great part of the traffic entering or leaving the North-West.

As Methy Portage attests, it is often a hard task to cross the height of land between two watersheds. At Frog Portage, however, there is almost no height of land at all. The short hike from the Churchill to Lindstrom Lake is actually a gentle decline. Only a low ridge of granite along the Churchill's south shore prevents the river's waters from rushing south into Lindstrom Lake. Indeed, when the Churchill is high, water actually escapes over the lip of the granite ridge and runs down a stream bed on the west side of the portage.

When we crossed Frog Portage on August 6, 1986, the overflow was only a trickle. At times, however, the overflow has been an actual flood. Sir John Richardson crossed Frog Portage to the Churchill in 1848 on his way to search for the missing Franklin expedition. Though the portage was apparently dry enough in 1848, Richardson wrote of it:

> About forty years ago, in a season remembered especially for the land-floods, a gentleman was drowned on the Frog Portage by his canoe oversetting against a tree as he was passing from the Churchill River.[49]

More recently, in 1974, the portage experienced similar, albeit not so tragic, flood conditions.[50]

No one knows who first discovered Frog Portage. Perhaps an early traveller found it after stopping to puzzle over the mystery of the overflow channel. That was no doubt hundreds or even thousands of years ago.

The oldest story of the portage comes to us from Alexander Mackenzie. In describing the voyageur highway, with information he collected in the late 1700s, Mackenzie wrote:

> it is necessary to cross the Portage de Traite, or, as it is called by the Indians [Cree], Athiquisipichigan Ouinigam [now *athîki-sîpîhcikan onikâhp*], or the Portage of the Stretched Frog-Skin, to the Missinipe.... The Missinipi, is the name which it [Churchill River] received from the Knisteneaux [Cree], when they first came to this country, and either destroyed or drove back the natives, whom they held in great contempt, on many accounts, but particularly for their ignorance in hunting the beaver, as well as in preparing, stretching, and drying the skins of those animals. And as a sign of their derision, they stretched the skin of a frog, and hung it up at the Portage...[51]

In the past, some historians have taken this account of Frog Portage and some of Mackenzie's other writing as evidence that the Cree used European firearms to forcibly take the Churchill region away from an indigenous Dene population. The current view, however, is that the Cree have in fact lived along the Churchill since at least the early 1400s, long before Europeans entered the area.[52] Accordingly, Mackenzie's account—presumably derived from Cree oral history—raises many interesting questions about the Churchill's early inhabitants. The story's precise meaning remains a matter for campfire debate.

It is not known when the first white man came to Frog Portage, but it could have been a generation before Alexander Mackenzie. The veteran woodsman, Louis Primeau, for one, might very well have crossed the portage in 1766 when the Hudson's Bay Company, his employer at the time, sent him inland from York Factory in search of Indians with furs.[53] He, or perhaps another nomadic *coureur de bois* living with Indians familiar with the country, may even have been here earlier. Whatever the case, however, it was not until 1774 that Frog Portage really took its place in fur trade history.

In that year, a Hudson's Bay Company employee by the name of Joseph Hansom, was at Frog Portage, having been sent inland the year before by Moses Norton, the officer in charge of the company's Fort Prince of Wales at the mouth of the Churchill.[54] Accompanied by Indian guides, Hansom was to check on the competition from Montreal and to encourage Indians to come to Fort Prince of Wales to trade. Hansom got at least as far as Cumberland Lake. He then spent the winter of 1773-74 with Joseph Frobisher, Louis Primeau (who had by then deserted the HBC), and others in a house situated somewhere between Namew Lake and Cumberland Lake.[55]

Joseph Frobisher was a Montreal trader and therefore a Hudson's Bay Company opponent, but fur trade rivalry at this early date was still tempered by a spirit of cooperation. Moreover, since Hansom found that the native hunters he would need to survive were already in the employ of the Montreal concern, he had little choice but to seek lodging under Frobisher's roof.[56]

In the spring of 1774, Hansom headed north to Frog Portage where he would turn downstream towards Fort Prince of Wales. He no doubt intended to marshall together as many Indians as he could and have them accompany him on his return voyage. When he got to Frog Portage, however, Hansom discovered that the Montrealers had in fact started what was to be an invasion of the Churchill River country. His recent host, Joseph Frobisher, had got to the portage ahead of him and, with help from Louis Primeau and his other men, was siphoning furs from Indians who might otherwise have gone on to Fort Prince of Wales. Hansom could do little except to report this sorry state of affairs to his HBC superiors:

> On my Passage home saw a House in the Great River where Indians passes from all parts of the country; was greatly surprised to find it to be the Aforesaid Frobisher's He having come this Spring fourteen days Journey nigher hand then where he Wintered, which is about ten days Journey to York Fort, at my Arrival at the House found fifty Canoes of Indians all Drunk had Traded their goods and were going to return to their Relations; also heard that they Expected One Hundred more Canoes in a short time…[57]

Years later, Alexander Mackenzie explained how Frobisher's uncommon success gave the portage a new name, i.e., Portage de Traite or Trade Portage:

> The Portage de Traite … received its name from Mr. Joseph Frobisher, who penetrated into this part of the country from Canada, as early as the years 1774 and 1775, where he met with the Indians in the spring, on their way to Churchill, according to annual custom, with their canoes full of valuable furs. They traded with him for as many of them as his canoes could carry, and in consequence of this transaction, the Portage received and has since retained its present appellation.[58]

Not surprisingly, Joseph Frobisher was eager to repeat his initial success. Before he left Frog Portage in 1774 to take his payload of furs out to Grand Portage, he left Louis Primeau and three other men behind "to Build Part of a house in the Draft of Churchill River," apparently to expand or replace his original structure.[59]

Primeau followed his instructions and had a house up by fall, the first inland wintering post to be built this far into the North-West.

It is not known precisely where Primeau put Frobisher's house. In 1792, Peter Fidler, while crossing Frog Portage, reported that it was "at the east end of this Carrying Place." But since the portage runs more or less north to south, Fidler's directions are not clear. Harry Moody, an amateur archaeologist from Denare Beach (whom author Sigurd Olson meets at Frog Portage in his canoeing classic *The Lonely Land*), thought that he had found the site of Frobisher's house about 90 m (100 yd) west of the Churchill end of the portage. However, when an archaeological field crew with the Churchill River Study examined this site in 1973, it was not able to confirm Moody's conclusion.[60]

Wherever it was located, both Joseph and Thomas Frobisher spent the winter of 1774–75 in the house Primeau had just completed. By all accounts, they and their men had a hard and hungry time of it. As early as December, food was already in short supply. On December 16, 1774, Samuel Hearne at Cumberland House encountered some of the Frobishers' men and described their pitiful condition:

> in the afternoon 5 Frenchmen belonging to Mr Forbersher's crew calld at our house, as on their journey to Messrs Paterson Homes and Franceways houses [at Fort à la Corne on the Saskatchewan River] which are about 8 Days walk higher up the Theiscatchiwan, they inform me of Mr Forbersher and the Rest of his men being in great distress for want of Provisions which ware the reason of their leaveing the house. Those who came here ware in a Miserable condition having ben 20 Days from the house and killd nothing by the way.[61]

In the spring of 1775, the Frobishers did purchase furs from Indians coming down the Churchill. However, after they had taken these furs out to Grand Portage, they decided not to return immediately to Frog Portage. Instead, they came back, now in partnership with fellow Montrealer Alexander Henry (the Elder), only as far as Amisk Lake where they could winter near a fishery much better than that at Frog Portage.

In the spring of 1776, the Frobishers and Henry were quick to remember that Frog Portage was where the action was. In April, an advance team went to prepare a post at the portage, while another forty men followed on the first open water. At the portage, the traders found that very few Indians had arrived, so they decided to send a search party upstream on the Churchill to look for customers.

The searchers—Thomas Frobisher, Alexander Henry, six Canadian voyageurs, and an Indian woman as guide—were prepared to go as far as Lake Athabasca even though no white man had ever gone there before. As it turned out, however, they did not need to go that far. They met the Indians they sought at an unidentified lake located on the upper Churchill three days travel above Snake Rapids. After introductions and gift-giving all round, they escorted the Indians back to Frog Portage to trade.

Alexander Henry has described how the trade proceeded:

> The Indians [Dene] comprised two bands, or parties, each bearing the name of its chief, of whom one was called the Marten, and the other, the Rapid. They had joined for mutual defence, against the Cristinaux [Cree], of whom they were in continual dread. They were not at war with that nation, but subject to be pillaged by its bands.

> While the lodges of the Indians were setting up, the chiefs paid us a visit, at which they received a large present of merchandise, and agreed to our request, that we should be permitted to purchase the furs of their bands.

> They inquired, whether or not we had any rum; and, being answered in the affirmative, they observed, that several of their young men had never tasted that liquor, and that if it was too strong

it would affect their heads. Our rum was in consequence submitted to their judgment; and, after tasting it several times, they pronounced it to be too strong, and requested that we would *order a part of the spirit to evaporate*. We complied, by adding more water, to what had received a large proportion of that element before; and, this being done, the chiefs signified their approbation.

... it was in the course of this night, the next day, and the night following, that our traffic was pursued and finished. The Indians delivered their skins at a small window, made for that purpose, asking, at the same time, for the different things they wished to purchase, and of which the prices had been previously settled with the chiefs. Of these, some were higher than those quoted from Fort des Prairies.

On the third morning, this little fair was closed; and, on making up our packs, we found, that we had purchased twelve thousand beaver-skins, besides large numbers of otter and marten.

Our customers were from Lake Arabuthcow [Lake Athabasca], of which, and the surrounding country, they were the proprietors, and at which they had wintered.[62]

A Hudson's Bay Company man, Robert Longmoor, was actually camped at Frog Portage when the Frobishers and Henry traded here with the Indians. When he later reported to his superior, Matthew Cocking, at Cumberland House, Longmoor said that about 100 canoes laden with fur had come from upstream. Some of these apparently carried fur that Louis Primeau had already purchased while spending the winter of 1775–76 at a newly built "Upper House" located up the Churchill (presumably at what is now Dipper Lake). Nonetheless, Longmoor's report confirms that the canoes brought a great deal of fur still to be traded.

As Longmoor saw it, the rival Montrealers' trade at Frog Portage was far from being proper. By his account, during the first and second days the Indians were at the portage, they were only given liquor in trade. Then, on the second evening, when the Indians were drunk, the Frobishers and Henry had their men go into the Indian tents and remove all the bundles of fur they could find and haul them into their trading post. When the Indians awoke to the third and final day of trading, they had little choice but to accept whatever terms the Frobishers and Henry offered them.[63]

Henry and Longmoor leave us with different versions of what happened at Frog Portage in 1776, but both make it clear that the Montrealers conducted a very profitable trade at the portage that season.

After the 1770s, trade at Frog Portage dropped drastically as new trading posts belonging to both the Hudson's Bay Company and the Montrealers were built further inland. Yet, after the Frobisher post, the portage supported at least one other trading operation. Explorer J.B. Tyrrell, reporting on the portage as it was in 1894, wrote, "On the nearest island in the river was an old warehouse of the Hudson's Bay Company, while just to the west [the Moody site?] was the site of a very old trading establishment, of uncertain date."[64] When the Churchill River Study's archaeologists examined the site west of the portage in 1973, they found material indicating that the Hudson's Bay Company had operated a post on the site during the last half of the 1800s.[65]

Even when it no longer saw actual trade, Frog Portage remained a critical link in the voyageur highway. And today, it continues to handle local transportation needs. The Peter Ballantyne Cree routinely use it to go between Pelican Narrows and destinations on the Churchill and the Reindeer River. As they normally travel by sixteen-foot aluminum boat and outboard motor, they make the portage by loading their boat, motor, and gear onto a small but heavily built rail car stationed at the portage, and then pushing or pulling the car along its railway. Although the railway is a simple affair consisting of two lines of light angle-iron spiked to plank rails on a trestle of poles, it well serves its purpose.

Portage #7 - Frog Portage (± 330 m / 360 yd)

From the Churchill, the start of Frog Portage shows as a grassy clearing on the river's south shore. Two man-made features mark the clearing. One is a portage railway that runs up from the water's edge and then south across the clearing and into the woods. The other is a 4-m-high (12-ft) stone cairn in the southeast corner of the clearing built by the Historic Sites and Monuments Board of Canada to give travellers a brief history of the portage.

You may use the portage car to take your canoe and gear across Frog Portage. However, as the car is heavy, it can be dangerous if you lose control of it. It is safer simply to drag your canoe over the railway's evenly spaced pole ties. Or, you can make a regular portage using the footpath along the east side of the railway.

At the south end of the portage, you can make use of an unloading ramp and a wooden dock to re-embark on Lindstrom Lake. If you arrive at the portage from Lindstrom Lake, the ramp and the dock will serve to identify the portage.

On to the Sturgeon-weir River

As you dip your paddle into Lindstrom Lake, you will begin canoeing a chain of lakes and connecting

Portage railway at the north end of Frog Portage. The stone cairn is in the background.

channels whose waters flow southward to the Saskatchewan River. The chain is not officially known as a river until well downstream when maps finally name it as the Sturgeon-weir River. However, since the chain is all one waterway, it is reasonable to see its entire length as being the Sturgeon-weir. Thus considered, the Sturgeon-weir—from Frog Portage to Cumberland Lake—accounts for over 250 km (155 mi) of the old voyageur highway.[66]

The Sturgeon-weir is not a high-powered river. Nonetheless, since it joins the mighty Churchill with the broad Saskatchewan, it was a vital part of the old voyageur highway. Except when water levels were unusually low, it had enough water to float a North canoe, and that was all that was required of it.

The name Sturgeon-weir, of pre-contact origin, derives from the Cree once building a sturgeon weir in the southern part of the river.[67] The Cree now refer to the river by the abbreviation *namîw sîpiy*, meaning the "sturgeon river."

The largest lake along the Sturgeon-weir is Amisk Lake. Commonly, that part of the Sturgeon-weir upstream of Amisk Lake, or at least the first 70 km (44 mi) upstream, is referred to as the "West Weir." The part downstream from Amisk to Namew Lake is known as the "South Weir."

Lindstrom Lake

Lindstrom Lake begins as a channel only 20 to 30 m (65 to 100 ft) wide. With willows and cattails along its shores and yellow pond lilies on its surface, the channel looks more like a frog pond than a lake. Indeed, the Cree name for this section of Lindstrom Lake is *athîkis sâkahikanisis*, with *athîkis* meaning "frog" and *sâkahikanisis* meaning "a small lake or pond."

The gentle nature of this first part of Lindstrom Lake contrasts with the rugged shores of the Churchill just left behind. However, Lindstrom Lake and the other lakes making up the western Sturgeon-weir are in fact all within the Shield. As you proceed, you will again see bold shorelines of bedrock very similar to those found on the Churchill.

On June 21, 1792, Peter Fidler, while returning from Lake Athabasca to York Factory with Philip Turnor, made special note of the passage immediately southeast of Frog Portage:

> went thru this kind of swampy creek 3 miles between NNE & SSW making ESE 1 1/2 & came to another portage on S side 90 yards over the creek being choked up with large stones here—that in some years when the water is low the Canoe also must be carried—this swampy creek from 5 to 500 yards wide as below—went below the carrying place thru the same kind of creek 1 1/4 mile making ESE 3/4 & entered a small lake & put up.[68]

HBCA E.3/1 fo. 64 upper (N14802)

Peter Fidler's sketch of the area south of Frog Portage.

Alexander Mackenzie, who passed through Lindstrom Lake on many occasions in the late 1700s, has left a general description of the upstream route from Wood Lake to Frog Portage:

> The passage continues through an intricate, narrow, winding, and shallow channel for eight miles. The interruptions in this distance are frequent, but depend much on the state of the waters. Having passed them, it is necessary to cross the Portage de Traite, or, as it is called by the Indians, Athiquisipichigan Ouinigam [*athîki-sîpîhcikan onikâhp*], or the Portage of the Stretched Frog-Skin, to the Missinipi.[69]

Nowadays, the channel below Frog Portage is not so shallow or difficult as the above quotes suggest. This is because a small weir made of log cribs filled with rocks was built some years ago at the outflow of Wood Lake. This weir is a long 42 km (26 mi) downstream from Frog Portage, but it nonetheless serves to keep the water level as far back as Frog Portage slightly higher than natural. In 1986, taking some benefit from the weir, we had no trouble at all with shallow water as we paddled towards Wood Lake.

On August 6, 1986, we had a chance meeting with two paddlers in an old Chestnut canoe about 2 km (1¼ mi) southeast of Frog Portage. As we had not seen any other canoeists for a good while, we stopped for a visit. The paddlers turned out to be Allison Connell of Woodstock, New Brunswick, and his friend Mary-Ellen. They were camped for the summer on Manawan Lake to the east and were out on an excursion. They were familiar with the local area and some of its history. Allison was particularly well-acquainted with the writings of Prentice (P.G.) Downes who had had a special affinity for the country around Pelican Narrows. With no shortage of things to discuss, we let our canoes drift together in the light breeze and spent a pleasant hour in talk.

Not quite 3 km (2 mi) below Frog Portage, the "Frog Pond" comes to an end where a sizable expansion of it narrows into a channel, again only 30 m (100 ft) wide. At one time, the head of the channel was known as *athîkis pâwistikos*, meaning "little frog rapid," and Fidler's 90-yard portage ran adjacent to it along the southwest shore. Now, the little rapid is drowned out by the weir downstream, and no portage is necessary. In low water years, canoes may still scrape rocks here, but we do not expect that it gets any worse than that.

The channel out of the "Frog Pond" continues for 1 km (²/₃ mi) and then opens up into the main part of Lindstrom Lake. This main part, about 4 km (2½ mi) long, is known in Cree as *wîmistikôsiw sâkahikan*, meaning "white man's lake."[70] You will want to heed your map here since the lake has many islands which make navigation confusing.

Through Pixley Lake

At its easternmost point, Lindstrom Lake drains east into Pixley Lake via a small channel known in Cree as *âhâsiw wapâsihk*, or "crow narrows." In 1986, Martin Michel, a local trapper and fisherman, told us he understood the narrows had once had a portage. Peter Fidler, in his journal entry of June 21, 1792, does not mention a portage here but says, "a kind of smaller river 20 yards wide & grassy low swampy sides—& in the bend of it, it is stony & must be gone thru' with caution."[71] In all likelihood, before the weir was built at the outlet of Wood Lake, water levels at Crow Narrows sometimes called for a portage and sometimes only caution. Whatever the case, with the weir in place, there is now ample depth for canoes.

Pixley Lake itself is only 3 km (2 mi) long. You will find its outlet at the end of a bay that runs southeast. In Cree, the outlet is called *kistikân wapâsihk*, meaning "garden narrows."

There is a cabin on the south shore of Garden Narrows. In August 1987, a young man named Peter Ballantyne was staying here to harvest wild rice in the area. In his spare time, Peter was caring for an immature bald eagle which, he said, had fallen from its nest and into the water. While this eaglet could not yet fly, it was already an enormous size and strong enough to perch on a horizontal pole 1 m (3 ft) or so off the ground. Peter was feeding it a steady diet of walleye fillets and was planning to do so until it could fly and survive on its own. The eaglet appeared to be thriving, so perhaps it is now a white-headed adult with a nest site in the vicinity.

Manâwan nistowayâhk

Just 500 m (¹/₃ mi) northeast from Garden Narrows, you will come to an important junction known in Cree as *manâwan nistowayâhk*. The word *manâwan*, which also describes the large lake to the northeast, refers to a place for gathering eggs, while *nistowayâhk* means a three-way junction. At this junction, a canoe can travel northwest to Frog Portage, northeast to Manawan Lake, or southeast to Wood Lake.

Map 10.8 *Manâwan nistowayâhk* **area**

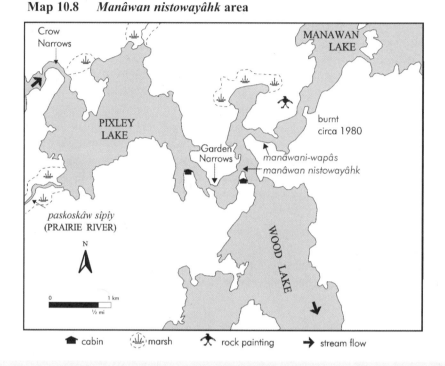

On August 6, 1986, we stopped at the peninsula forming the southern shores of *manâwan nistowayâhk*. Here, we had the good fortune of meeting Martin Michel and Frank Linklater who, with their families, were spending the summer at their cabins on the peninsula. They invited us to spread our maps out on a large wooden table outside Martin's cabin, and we then spent the afternoon learning local Cree place names. The kids who gathered around to listen could not help but laugh as we struggled with Cree pronunciation. But Martin and Frank were endlessly patient with us, and we came away with a wealth of knowledge.[72]

Martin and Frank told us that they had heard of trading posts once being located at *manâwan nistowayâhk*. One post site was said to have been on the peninsula where they lived. Another was said to have been due east from the north tip of the peninsula, on the other side of the narrows leading into Wood Lake. We have not seen any written reference to *manâwan nistowayâhk* having had a post. Nonetheless, as the junction is a natural meeting place, it probably supported at least a small outpost at one or more times in the past.

Manawan Lake Rock Paintings

From *manâwan nistowayâhk*, you can make a short detour into Manawan Lake to visit a rock painting site. To reach this site from *manâwan nistowayâhk*, first go 500 m (⅓ mi) north and then turn east to enter *manâwani-wapâs*, the narrow channel leading into Manawan Lake. Next, follow this channel east-southeast for 500 m and then turn northeast. The channel here expands into a small bay where you may note an old burn dating back to about 1980 on the eastern shore. If you paddle northeast up this bay for 500 m or so, you will come to another narrows that opens into Manawan Lake.

The rock paintings (63M 039366) are on the west shore of the narrows at the south end of a cliff that runs south to north along the shore for about 60 m (66 yd). They occur on two

Figure 10.1 Rough sketch of Manawan Lake rock painting—Face #1

separate rock faces which we will mention in turn.

Face #1 is a vertical face looking more or less to the east. It is about 3.5 m (12 ft) wide and rises vertically from the water for about 3 m (10 ft) before it begins to slope back. The paintings are in the bottom, viewer's left corner of the face and are all in a space measuring about 60 cm (2 ft) by 60 cm (2 ft). On August 6, 1986, the bottom of the lowest figure was about 40 cm (16 in) above the water.

The strangest painting here is a man about 15 cm (6 in) tall who appears to have no arms. From the man's shoulder, the one on viewer's left, a chain of eight drops are falling down to an indistinct horizontal object some 50 cm (20 in) below the man's shoulder. Next to the man's other shoulder there is a hunting bow about 10 cm (4 in) tall. There is also a small, solid ball of pigment 5 cm (2 in) to viewer's left of the man and a similar ball 2 cm (1 in) below him.

Unfortunately, the armless man paintings appear to have suffered from some deliberate chipping away of the rock face. Rock has been pecked away from the man's torso, his groin area, the lower right hand side of the bow and the ball of pigment below him.

Figure 10.2 Rough sketch of Manawan Lake rock painting—Face #2

The four other paintings on Face #1 are below and to viewer's right of the armless man. One figure is a horned or antlered animal about 15 cm (6 in) long, which might be a moose, though it lacks a bell beneath its jaw. Below and to the right of the moose, there is an animal 15 to 20 cm (6 to 8 in) long that could be either an ungulate lying down or a waterfowl swimming. Above this figure but not attached to it, there is a vertical line perhaps 12 cm (5 in) long. Finally, still further to the right, there is a figure about 15 cm (6 in) high that may be a frontal view of an animal face with pointy ears.

Face #2 is 3 to 4 m (10 to 12 ft) north of Face #1. It is a triangular face, just over 1 m (3 ft) wide at the base and about 2.5 m (8 ft) high, which, on August 6, 1986, was about 25 cm (10 in) above the surface of Manawan Lake. It

slopes back from the vertical and fronts southeast. The paintings here are towards the left side of the face and 1 m (3 ft) above its lower edge.

In the lower left corner of Face #2, an area cracking away slightly from the main face, there is a weasel-like creature about 16 or 17 cm (6 or 7 in) long. Three more figures lie just outside the area cracking away. About 20 cm (8 in) above the weasel, there is a faded, lichen-encrusted moose very similar in shape and size to the moose on Face #1. Just above this moose, there are some very faint lines arranged in the shape of an inverted triangle. Finally, about 16 or 17 cm (6 or 7 in) to the right of the weasel, there is a simple, rocket-like figure which might perhaps be a swimming beaver.

Wood Lake

Wood Lake is a large body of water accounting for 30 km (19 mi) of the old voyageur highway. From *manâwan nistowayâhk*, it first runs south-southeast in a long, open stretch for some 20 km (12 mi). Then, at a place called Grassy Narrows, it turns and runs east-northeast through a series of bay-like expansions for another 10 km (6 mi) to its outlet.

The lake's name is an old one. To Philip Turnor, the lake was "called by the Canadians the lake of the woods"; to Peter Fidler and also Sir John Richardson, it was "Woody Lake"; to Alexander Mackenzie, it was "Lake des Bois"; and to George Simpson, it was "Lac du Bois."[73] The present Cree name for the lake is *wîposkâw sâkahikan*, meaning "old burn lake." While the English and the Cree names may be unrelated, they might both derive from an ancient forest fire that left dead wood strewn in its wake.

Coming down Wood Lake from *manâwan nistowayâhk*, you will encounter several islands. For the most part, however, the lake is exposed to prevailing winds out of the north and west. You should therefore wait out any bad weather, especially before traversing to the east shore of the lake.

About 9 or 10 (5½ or 6 mi) south of *manâwan nistowayâhk*, you may notice cabins on a peninsula on the east shore of the lake (63M 077270). The Cree refer to this place as *âpihtawikamik*, meaning the "halfway place." On August 7, 1986, we stopped here and talked to a young woman named Judy McCallum who was busy washing clothes. She told us two families—that of her father John Charles and that of a Philip Charles—still lived at *âpihtawikamik* year round and trapped in the region each winter.

Wood Lake Rock Paintings

If you continue south from *âpihtawikamik* for about 6 km (3¾ mi), you will come to an island about 400 m (¼ mi) long lying about 150 m (165 yd) off the east shore of Wood Lake. The island occurs just before Wood Lake makes a major swing to the east. About two-thirds of the way down the east shore of this island, you will find three small rock paintings (63M 109223).

The rock paintings are where a rock outcrop on the island rises to a height of about 7 m (25 ft). Here, about 4 m (13 ft) above lake level, someone has scratched the initials "D.N.D." into the lichen growth. The rock paintings are on a vertical face directly below these initials. They are actually below an old waterline, and, on August 7, 1986, they were only about 25 cm (10 in) above lake level.

What might be seen as the main figure here is a rectangular figure in faint pinkish-orange measuring about 6 cm (2 in) by 6 cm (2 in). Since the top corners of the rectangle have fork-like extensions, the figure may represent a tent. About 3 cm (1 in) to viewer's

Figure 10.3 Rough sketch of Wood Lake rock painting

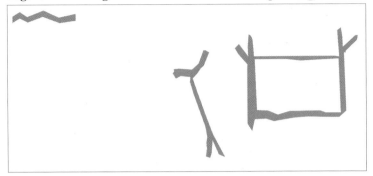

left of the tent, there is what looks to be a crude stick man in the same pigment as the tent. Finally, about 25 cm (10 in) above and 35 cm (14 in) to viewer's left of the stick man, there is an indistinct squiggly line about 6 cm (2 in) long.

We have been told that other rock painting sites occur farther down Wood Lake at Grassy Narrows, but we have not seen these sites.

Grassy Narrows

Both Maps 63M and 63M/3 show where Grassy Narrows will lead you out of the main part of Wood Lake and into the smaller, though more complex, eastern section of the lake. The name Grassy Narrows approximates the Cree name for the narrows which has the variants *opâwicikanaskos, opâwikocikanaskosîw,* and *opâwicikanaskosîhk.*

When we came to Grassy Narrows on August 7, 1986, we found a few cabins on the north shore of the narrows. The first person we met here was Eli Highway, an energetic man in his seventies, who hailed us from the roof of a new cabin he was building. He took time out from his construction to talk to us about the area and teach us some Cree. Later on, just down the shore, we got the same hospitality from Arthur McCallum who was hand-carving a new boat paddle from a piece of spruce.

Eli Highway, left, and Arthur McCallum, right, at Grassy Narrows in 1986.

From Eli Highway and Arthur McCallum, we learned that many members of the Peter Ballantyne Cree Nation have roots at Grassy Narrows. While most of these people now live at Pelican Narrows, some still come to Grassy Narrows to hunt, fish, and trap. Eli Highway told us that four or five families spent their summers at the narrows and that one family also stayed through the winter.

Interestingly, people at Grassy Narrows do not restrict themselves to hunting, fishing, and trapping. In 1987, Adam Highway, a commercial fisherman, was raising thirty-four chickens and fourteen domestic geese near his cabin at the narrows.

Beyond Grassy Narrows

Going east from Grassy Narrows, you will have to pay careful attention to your map. The eastern part of Wood Lake has many islands and irregular bays. If you lose your map location, you may find it hard to reorient yourself.

Less than 1 km (2/3 mi) east from Grassy Narrows, you will come to a large island. In low water years, there is not enough water to pass by the south end of this island, so a detour to the north is necessary. If you do detour to the north, you may still want to come back to the southeast corner of the island as there is a good campsite here (63M 159194).

About 1.75 km (1 mi) before the outlet of Wood Lake, there is a very good campsite for more than one tent on the north tip of a small island (63M 213220). This campsite has low, smooth bedrock reaching to the water's edge.

About 500 m (1/3 mi) past the island campsite just mentioned, there is a small island of rock about 40 m (44 yd) long (63M 216224). Almost bare of trees, it looks for all the world like the gently rounded back of a large, aquatic mammal. This little island is known in Cree as *sôniyâw ministikos*, meaning "money island."

According to Eli Highway, the name *sôniyâw ministikos* stems from an incident that occurred many years ago when a federal Indian Agent came to Pelican Narrows to make the annual treaty payment of $5 to each man, woman, and child covered by treaty. This Indian Agent made the required payments at Pelican Narrows and then left by canoe to proceed up the Sturgeon-weir. As luck would have it, a new baby was born in Pelican Narrows just after the Indian Agent had departed. The new father greeted the birth with both pride and alarm. Realizing that hard cash was slipping away from him, he got in his canoe and paddled as fast as he could to catch the Indian Agent. It took a good while, but at *sôniyâw ministikos*, he overtook the treaty party and claimed his bonus.

Beyond *sôniyâw ministikos*, a long arm of Wood Lake stretches far into the northeast. Be careful not to start down this arm by accident because, as your map will show, it leads to a dead end. To find the outlet of Wood Lake, you must turn southeast as soon as you pass *sôniyâw ministikos*.

There are campsites at the entrance of the bay leading to Wood Lake's outlet. You will find a small site with space for one tent on the southwest side of the entrance on the north end of a large island lying within the outlet bay (63M 223224). On the opposite side of the bay entrance, you will find a roomier site with space for several tents on a slim finger of land pointing out from the northeast shore (63M 225225).

Pot Hole ("Three Together") Rapids

Wood Lake drains to the southeast via a series of three short rapids occurring in quick succession. These rapids are the first of many you will encounter on the Sturgeon-weir. Although they are not very big, they are too boisterous to be navigable. Each of them requires a portage or pullover.

The Cree call the three rapids out of Wood Lake *kâ-niscoscîskik*, meaning "they are three together," but there is no well-established English name for the rapids. White travellers, from the past to the present, have usually only mentioned the rapids or their portages in general terms such as "the three galets [pullovers]" or "the three short portages."[74] However, from J.B. Tyrrell we know that, at least for a short time, the portages here were called "the Pot Hole Portages."[75] Since this name does not occur anywhere else along the Saskatchewan section of the old voyageur highway, we will revive it and apply it to both the rapids and their portages.

First Pot Hole Rapid

First Pot Hole Rapid, which acts as Wood Lake's outflow, is split by a small island about 225 m (250 yd) wide. On each side of the island, water flows into a channel about 10 m (30 ft) wide and then drops about 2 m (6 ft) to enter a quiet pond below.

Map 10.9   Pot Hole Rapids area

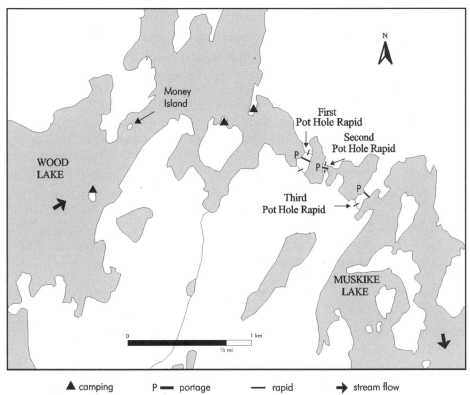

A main feature of the First Pot Hole Rapid is the man-made weir, already mentioned, that serves to keep Wood Lake, Manawan Lake, and the smaller lakes back as far as Frog Portage at a single, roughly constant level. The weir is a simple affair made of log cribs filled with rocks. These cribs extend across both the rapid's southwest channel and its northeast channel. In high water, water flows over the entire width of the weir in each channel. However, if the level of Wood Lake ever drops below the top of the weir, water can then only escape through a narrow notch built into the weir.

Adam Highway, an elder of the Peter Ballantyne Cree Nation, can recall the weir being built many years ago to reduce water fluctuations on the upstream lakes and thus increase their muskrat populations. With its simple but practical design, the weir ably accomplishes this original purpose. And, since it stabilizes the upstream lakes at a level slightly higher than normal, it also improves navigation through the shallow narrows leading to Frog Portage.

Portage #8 - First Pot Hole Portage (± 55 m / 60 yd)

From Wood Lake, this portage, which crosses the island dividing First Pot Hole Rapid, begins some 30 m (100 ft) to the right of the northeast channel of the rapid. It is equipped with a boat pullover rack made of spruce poles nailed crosswise over two parallel lines of support logs. If your canoe is reasonably sturdy, you can drag it loaded over this rack and save yourself the trouble of a regular portage.

It is possible to camp on the island which the portage crosses. We know from the journals of Philip Turnor and Peter Fidler that they and their party camped on this island on the evening of June 22, 1792, when returning from their two-year journey to Lake Athabasca. Philip Turnor's journal describes the day's journey:

22nd Friday at 3 3/4 AM got underway went about 1 mile and met 4 Canoes of Chepawyans went 2 mile more and found an other Canoe of Chepawyans from whom we got the flesh of a small Beaver went 3 miles and *met a Mr Mackie* [William McKay] *and three Canadians going to build a house at the Deers Lake that lays to the North of the Churchill river through which lake it is said there is a near way to the Athapescow Lake,* they had 7 or 8 Canoes of Che-pa-wy-ans with them from whom we got a little Moose flesh we then went about 9 miles and was obliged to put on shore the wind being to strong we lay by from 10 1/4 AM untill 2 1/2 PM at which time the Wind was not quite so violent we then went to the next carrg place [First Pot Hole Portage] carried over and put up at 8 1/2 PM Wind NW by W a heavy gale with flying clouds and a few showers of rain in the afternoon sailed the forepart of the day

23rd Saturday at 3 3/4 AM got underway and carried over the two next carrying places and handed down the one we carried part at in going up [Medicine Rapids] then put on shore to pitch our Canoes and was stoped by the rain about 2 hours...[76]

As mentioned, there is a quiet pond below First Pot Hole Rapid. It takes only a short paddle of about 150 m (165 yd) to cross this pond and reach Second Pot Hole Rapid.

Second Pot Hole Rapid

Similar to First Pot Hole Rapid, this rapid is divided by an island about 75 m (250 ft) wide. The island is mainly low bedrock, so it likely floods from time to time. Ordinarily, however, water flows around it down a northeast and a southwest channel. The northeast channel is about 5 m (16 ft) wide and has a short drop of perhaps 75 cm (30 in) over a natural ledge. The southwest channel is only 2 m (6 ft) wide and is essentially a fast chute.

Portage #9 - Second Pot Hole Portage (± 20 m / 22 yd)

This portage crosses the northeastern tip of the island between the two rapid channels. Again, it is equipped with a boat pullover rack. This rack starts in quiet water near the head of the northeast channel and ends in fairly fast water just down from the ledge in the channel. As before, you can drag your loaded canoe over the rack to avoid a regular portage.

From the foot of the northeast channel, it is not more than 400 m (¼ mi) across a second pond to the third rapid and portage.

Pullover rack at Second Pot Hole Portage, 1986.

Third Pot Hole Rapid

This last of the three Pot Hole Rapids occurs in the single channel that runs out the south end of the second pond and into Muskike Lake below. The rapid here has an overall drop of about 3 m (10 ft).

Portage #10 - Third Pot Hole Portage (± 50 m / 55 yd)

This portage also has a pullover rack. The rack's upstream end is about 140 m (150 yd) northeast of the outflow channel to Muskike Lake. An older, broken-down rack about 15 m (50 ft) closer to the outflow channel is now abandoned. You can use the newer pullover rack to avoid a regular portage.

If you are coming upstream, you will see a wooden dock about 10 m (30 ft) long where this portage begins. Of course, as with the other two portages above, the pullover rack itself makes it easy to spot the proper downstream landing.

There are a number of good campsites just below the portage. One of these will be only too easy to find as people have used brilliant red-orange paint to write their names and dates on the adjacent bedrock.

Muskike Lake

Muskike Lake—which takes its name from the Cree word *maskihkiy,* meaning "medicine" —is a pretty little lake running 2 km (1¼ mi) from north to south. It is best known for pictographs found at three sites in its outflow channel. These paintings are commonly referred to as the Medicine Rapids rock paintings, after the rapids located not far downstream.

Medicine Rapids Rock Paintings

Site #1 (63M 241202), which has the most elaborate of the Medicine Rapids rock paintings, is on the east side of the entrance to Muskike Lake's outflow channel. As you draw near, you will see a bald, round-topped rock hill over 25 m (80 ft) high on the east (channel left) shore. The paintings are at the foot of this hill on a 2-m-high (6-ft), negatively inclined rock face looking northwest. On August 8, 1986, this rock face, which rises up from a narrow ledge, was just less than 1 m (3 ft) above the water.

The six figures here make a fascinating group. The main figure is a bear-man (or wolf-man?), about 85 cm high (34 in), standing with his arms outstretched. This bear-man has two wavy, parallel lines running down his torso, which could signify his gullet or perhaps a swallowed snake. On viewer's left, below the bear-man's right arm, there is a vertical line about 60

Map 10.10   Medicine Rapids rock painting sites

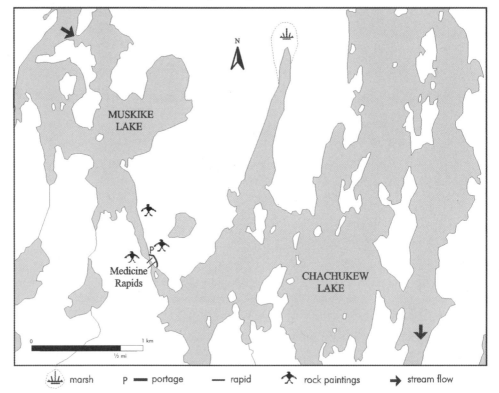

cm (2 ft) high that is forked at the top—perhaps a snake? Then below the bear-man's left arm, which is largely obscured by lichens, there is a small bear (or wolf) standing on its hind legs with its tongue or maybe part of a snake hanging from its mouth. Below the figures just mentioned, there is a wavy horizontal line about 90 cm (3 ft) long which may represent the ground. Above the figures, there is a similar horizontal line. Finally, above the upper horizontal line, there is a thunderbird having a height of about 20 cm (8 in) and a wing span of about 30 cm (12 in).

We cannot really know what the artist had in mind when he painted the bear-man scene, but the late Selwyn Dewdney, a rock painting authority, speculated that the painting might mean:

> I am Maskwa, the Bearman. In my dream I saw Missikinahpik, the great snake. His swiftness and power of life possess me. For in my dream I saw the Sacred Bear swallow the Great Snake. So I stretch my arms wide till the whole earth feels my power.[77]

Figure 10.4 Rough sketch of Medicine Rapids rock paintings—Site #1

Site #2 (63M 241199), on the west (river right) side of the channel leading to Medicine Rapids, is about 400 m (¼ mi) south from Site #1 and about 100 m (110 yd) upstream from the head of the rapids. As you approach this site, you can watch for the initials "G.C." and "G.B." written on the shore rock about 1 m (3 ft) above the water in what looks to be black tar. The rock paintings here are about 30 cm (1 ft) to viewer's left of these initials.

This site has only two simple figures. One figure, on viewer's left, is an unrecognizable patch of pigment about 30 cm (1 ft) high and 8 cm (3 in) wide. The other figure, just to the right of the first, is a wavy, vertical line about 50 cm (20 in) long.

Site #3 (63M 242199) is back on the east (river left) side of the channel leading to Medicine Rapids at a point about 30 m (100 ft) upstream of the rapids. Here, a 15-m-high (50-ft) gneiss outcrop with a few jack pine on its crown gives a slight bend to the shoreline. The outcrop has two separate painting displays.

The first display comprises five figures in a small area about 40 cm (16 in) wide and 30 cm (12 in) high on a nearly vertical rock face about 3 m (10 ft) upstream from the bend in the shoreline. On August 8, 1986, the lower edge of the display area was just less than 1 m (3 ft) above the water. Of the five figures, the most distinct, in a dark red pigment, are a diagonal line about 30 cm (12 in) long, an upturned arc about 12 cm (5 in) wide and an hourglass shape about 10 cm (4 in) high. To the lower left of these, there is a very faint paw print about 15 cm (6 in) long having a pad and four claws. Finally, to the lower right, there is a faint, unrecognizable shape about 15 cm (6 in) long suffering from the encroachment of green lichens.

The second display is about 6 m (20 ft) downstream from the first, just around the bend in the shoreline, and about 50 cm (20 in) higher above the water. The paintings or figures here, which are obscured by a good deal of lichen growth, form a kind of geometrical design.

Besides the rock paintings above Medicine Rapids, you will also see some graffiti. About 40 m (44 yd) above the rapids, on the rock of the west shore, someone has printed the words "MEDICINE RAPIDS" in bright orange-red paint. The words are accurate enough, but they seem out of place so near to the old pictographs.

Medicine Rapids

Figure 10.5 Rough sketch of Medicine Rapids rock paintings—Site #3, Display #1

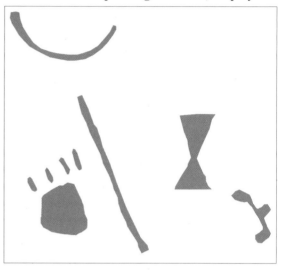

Figure 10.6 Rough sketch of Medicine Rapids rock paintings—Site #3, Display #2

Medicine Rapids, *maskihkiy pâwistik* in Cree, extend for about 85 m (93 yd) down a fast-flowing, narrow channel. The channel is sometimes not more than 5 m (16 ft) wide, and its navigable width is nearer to 2 m (6 ft). Fortunately, however, it is quite straight and has a line that is mainly free of rocks. On August 8, 1986, we watched local people lift the props on their

16-foot aluminum motor boats and then pole the boats down the channel. And Eli Highway, who stopped by while we were there, told us boats can also run up the channel.

As suggested by Philip Turnor, the voyageurs ordinarily treated Medicine Rapids as a *décharge*, at least when going upstream. In his journal, George Simpson refers to the rapids as the "Discharge des trois Petit Portagè," a name acknowledging the nearby Pot Hole Portages.[78] And, some years later, Sir John Richardson referred to it as "the Pelican lightening-place (*Demi-charge de chetauque*)."[79]

If you have advanced skills, you may wish to run, pole, or line Medicine Rapids after scouting them from shore. If you have more modest skills, you can portage on the east shore.

Portage #11 - Medicine Portage (± 85 m / 93 yd)

As a downstream traveller, you will find a good pullover rack begins on the east (river left) shore immediately above the rapids. If your canoe is sturdy, you can drag it fully loaded over the rack and thus make the portage in one trip. Or, you can make a regular portage over the walking trail that runs along the east side of the rack. This trail ends at a narrow pole walkway that extends about 25 m (27 yd) and improves the footing down to the water.

Going upstream, you will find the start of the pullover rack just at the foot of the rapids. There is some current here, so you may have to pole with your paddle to advance up to the rack.

Chachukew Lake and Pelican Lake

From Medicine Rapids, it is just over 9 km (5½ mi) to Pelican Narrows. The first 3 km (2 mi) or so of this distance are across the bottom end of Chachukew Lake, a lake lying off to the northeast. The final 6 km (3¾ mi), from the narrows leading south out of Chachukew, are along the top end of Pelican Lake, a big lake extending far to the south.

At one time, Chachukew Lake and Pelican Lake were considered to be a single lake. The Cree name for this lake was *cahcahkiw sâkahikan*, meaning "pelican lake." The early explorers and fur traders adopted this name and used either its English translation or "Chitique," a French rendition of the Cree (also spelled "Chatique," "Chetique," or "Chetauque").[80] In more recent times, the one lake became officially known as two separate lakes. The northern one then took the parent lake's Cree name, while the southern one took the English equivalent.

Today, the Pelican Narrows Cree refer to Chachukew Lake as *kâ-thôskâwakâk*, meaning "a place where there is soft sand." Pelican Lake and Mirond Lake, the next lakes downstream, are together known as *opâwikoscikan sâkahikana*, meaning the "fear narrows lakes." The story behind the Fear Narrows name will be told in the next chapter.

While the route through Chachukew Lake and Pelican Lake is not long, you can make it longer by getting lost. Below Medicine Rapids, the shorelines are deeply indented and the islands are numerous. It is very easy to stray north on Chachukew Lake and miss the proper channel south into Pelican Lake, so you will want to pay close attention to your map as you paddle.

Of course, modern maps make navigation much easier than it was during the early fur trade. Then, heavy reliance was necessarily placed on guides, either Indians or seasoned voyageurs who knew the route, and the lack of a guide could end an expedition. This reality was certainly on the mind of Philip Turnor of the Hudson's Bay Company when he and his survey party came to Pelican Lake for the very first time.

On September 20, 1790, Turnor and his companions were camped on the north shore of Pelican Lake, close to where the Anglican Church now stands in Pelican Narrows. The season was late, and they wanted to advance upstream to reach the faraway Athabasca country before freeze-up. However, they were unable to go any further because their Indian guide had just quit. They were only able to proceed when Patrick Small, the manager of the North West Company post at Île-à-la-Crosse, caught up to them with his brigade and kindly agreed to show them the way.

Malcolm Ross, one of Turnor's companions, recorded the event in his journal:

> I gave a treat of brandy to the Indian pilot last night, also a Coat & Blanket for his wife; he promised faithfully to stand by us, but this day when he was to embark his wife would not go, after all his promises we embarked at 1 P.M. after applying to Mr. Small for his assistance in showing us the Road, which we was obliged to do or else go back again, which I had very bad will to do.[81]

Peter Fidler, also with the party, later wrote about the same incident:

> The Pilot that was engaged to conduct us from Cumberland to the Isle a la Crosse deserted us 5 days journey from Cumberland House, in the Pelican lake, and the rest of the way we accompanied the Canadian canoes by the permission of Mr. Small on condition that we should not trade any skins from the Indians this winter that is past.[82]

If you do indeed follow your map carefully, you will soon approach the community of Pelican Narrows, built on the southern tip of a peninsula jutting into Pelican Lake. As you draw near, you will not see much of the community at first since a big island, by the Cree name of *cîpay ministik* or "ghost island," lies right in front of it. However, as you round the south tip of the island, where the local Roman Catholic cemetery is, you will begin to see buildings and roads.

If you plan to stop or end your trip at Pelican Narrows, you may choose to put in across and slightly north from the south tip of Ghost Island. Or, you can continue around the southwest corner of the community peninsula and put in at or near the public dock on the peninsula's south shore.

-11-

PELICAN NARROWS TO DENARE BEACH

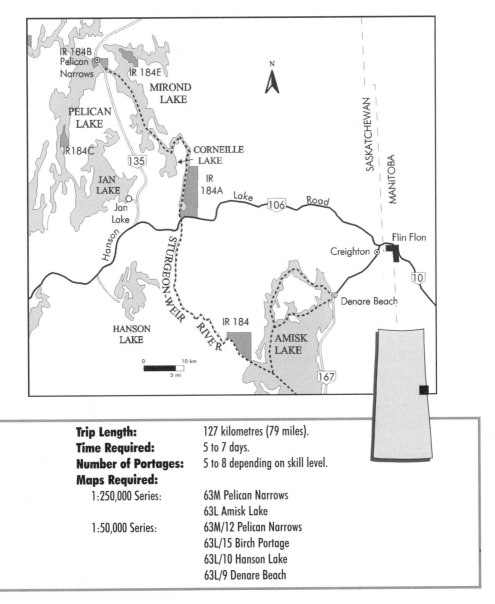

Trip Length:	127 kilometres (79 miles).
Time Required:	5 to 7 days.
Number of Portages:	5 to 8 depending on skill level.
Maps Required:	
1:250,000 Series:	63M Pelican Narrows
	63L Amisk Lake
1:50,000 Series:	63M/12 Pelican Narrows
	63L/15 Birch Portage
	63L/10 Hanson Lake
	63L/9 Denare Beach

ABOUT THE TRIP

This is both a big lake trip and a river trip. It begins with a voyage south on Mirond Lake, continues south on the Sturgeon-weir River and then ends with a long traverse northeast across Amisk Lake. The river requires only modest whitewater skills since it has an easy current over most of its length. It does have seven rapids, but they all have good portages. The big lakes present a greater challenge. The wind can make Mirond and Amisk extremely dangerous, so they require mature decision-making and may call for strong paddling skills.

If you are travelling upstream, you will not experience much extra difficulty. You may occasionally have to track or wade your canoe up the current, but this will not happen often.

The trip is not as remote as some. Coming down Mirond Lake, you are never far from Highway 135, and halfway through the trip, you will cross Highway 106. Later on, as you come onto Amisk Lake, you can expect to see fishing boats. Nonetheless, this is not crowded country, and you will still find some good peace and quiet.

There are some excellent campsites on this part of the route. The lakes offer several good bedrock campsites. The river also has good campsites at most of its portages.

STARTING POINTS

The starting point for this trip is the community of Pelican Narrows located 388 km (241 mi) northeast of Prince Albert. From Prince Albert, you can reach Pelican Narrows by travelling 79 km (49 mi) east on paved Highway 55 to Smeaton, then 258 km (160 mi) northeast on paved Highway 106 (the Hanson Lake Road), and finally 51 km (32 mi) north on gravel Highway 135.

At Pelican Narrows, you can launch your canoe onto Pelican Lake from the public dock at the south end of Bear Street—the main street running north to south through the community. You may also launch from a beach of coarse sand immediately east of the dock. You will then be ready to head east to the nearby narrows leading to Mirond Lake.

If you wish to avoid paddling the length of Mirond Lake, and shorten your trip by about 20 km (12 mi), you can start out from a boat launch located in the extreme southwest corner of Mirond Lake. This boat launch is on the east side of Highway 135 about 22 km (14 mi) north from Highway 106. It puts you on a small bay that is home to three sport fishing camps. Depending on your shuttle arrangements, you may wish to stop at one of the camps, which are all just up the road from the boat launch, to discuss starting out from the camp with your vehicle left in safe storage there.

Community of Pelican Narrows

When we reached Pelican Narrows late on August 8, 1986, it was pouring rain. We therefore rented a log cabin at Margaret and Eugene Klein's Seepeeseek Camp and guaranteed ourselves a dry sleep. The next morning, we met Louis Custer, then 70, who joined us at our cabin for coffee and a long talk. He told us that when he was a boy in the 1920s, Pelican Narrows had only about twenty houses. Back then, according to Custer, a free trader named Arthur Jan operated a post that was still in active use as part of Seepeeseek Camp's grocery store.

Louis Custer was himself a wealth of knowledge, but he also let us meet other community elders. Taking us down to the Old Folks Home, he introduced us to James and Elizabeth Sewap. When word got out that we were asking about the local history, other people stopped in at the Sewap's small suite to contribute to the general conversation. Much of the talk was in Cree, but through translation, we learned a great deal about life before the snowmobile and outboard motor.

Solomon Merasty, then 83, was one of the people who stopped by to visit while we were at the Sewaps'. Originally from La Ronge, he had lived at Pelican Narrows since 1929. Throughout the north, he had a reputation as a leading Cree linguist. He was also known as a traveller, and he had stories from many places on our paddling route. We were particularly fascinated by his recollections of his 1936 trip to Reindeer Lake with the American ethnographer P.G. Downes. Downes had greatly admired Solomon and had clearly seen him as a kindred spirit. On September 13, 1936, after paddling all day on Reindeer Lake in a driving rain, Downes wrote in his diary, "I wish I had enough money so that I might just wander on like this with the Indians, going nowhere, just wandering, seeing new country and new campfires. Solomon has very much the same desire, too."[1] Fifty years later, Solomon remembered Downes with high regard.

In discussing the Cree language, Solomon Merasty recommended we also talk to Father Beaudet, the local Oblate priest, whom he had been helping with translation work. So, after we left the Sewaps, we stopped in at the Catholic mission. Father Beaudet, originally from Victoriaville, Quebec, told us that he had first come to Pelican Narrows in 1946 for six months, had returned in 1959 for a three-year sojourn and had then come to stay in 1968. He modestly showed us his published translation of the New Testament into Cree which he had completed with help from Solomon Merasty. He also told us that he had just completed an 870-page French-Cree dictionary. When we noted that his work was published in fine italic calligraphy, he explained that what we saw was actually his own script. He had learned calligraphy and hand-scribed over 2,000 pages of Cree because he did not know how to type!

PHOTO COURTESY LYNDA HOLLAND AND LOIS DALBY

Solomon Merasty and P.G. Downes having lunch in 1936.

Early History

The oldest story about present-day Pelican Narrows relates to how it got its Cree name of *opâwikoscikanihk,* which translates into English as "fear narrows." The story dates back to the early fur trade and has been handed down through the generations in the oral tradition. There are different versions of the story, but they are all very similar. P.G. Downes recorded one account in 1939:

> a large band of Crees camped here for a permanent summer residence. All the men of the band packed up their furs and left for the east, possibly York Factory which was the nearest trading post at that time. This trip, an arduous and long one all the way to Hudson Bay, meant that the women and children must be left behind. Thirty tents were pitched upon the knoll where I was now seated. Thirty tents occupied the shore front.
>
> While the men were off on their trip to the trading post, strange Indians came up from the south, probably Blackfeet, and massacred the entire band except for two children whom they left on the small reef a few rods out in the lake from the present Roman Catholic Mission.
>
> When the men of the band returned shortly after the massacre, they found bodies floating along the shore. They pursued the killers down through Sandy Narrows to the south near Deschambault Lake. Catching up with them near a little creek there, they killed them all but the leader, whom they held for a special council. After some deliberation they cut off this man's hands and then, seizing him by the hair, they severed his head.[2]

Ron Merasty, a member of the Peter Ballantyne Cree Nation living in Prince Albert has recorded other variations of the story and has done a good analysis of it. After looking at extracts from the Hudson's Bay Company's York Factory Journals that refer to reports of inland massacres, Merasty is of the view that the Fear Narrows massacre quite likely occurred in 1730. He also concludes that the marauders were Sioux and not Blackfoot as Downes had thought.[3]

As the early Cree were highly mobile, it is difficult to know if the Cree involved in the Fear Narrows massacre were the direct ancestors of the Cree living at Pelican Narrows today. Whatever the case, research done by Ron Merasty shows that most Pelican Narrows families—such as the Ballantynes, Custers, Michels, Morins, and Sewaps—can trace their roots back to family members living here well over a century ago.[4]

Trading Post History

A half-century after the Fear Narrows massacre, the North West Company built the first trading post in the area right where the community is now situated. When Philip Turnor and his party moved north along the west side of the community peninsula on September 20, 1790, he noted they "passed a place where the Canadians formerly had a settlement."[5]

HBCA E.3/1 fo. 65 upper (N14803)

Peter Fidler's sketch of Pelican Lake and the NWC post on the site of present-day Pelican Narrows.

Similarly, when Turnor's party returned this way on June 23, 1792, his companion Peter Fidler referred to "an old Canadian house—it is now entirely down—built in a fine small sandy bay about the year 1779."[6]

In 1793, just a year after Fidler noted the broken-down Canadian house, the Hudson's Bay Company built its own house somewhere on Pelican Lake, possibly where Pelican Narrows is now. It survived until the

1798–99 season when it was operated by Thomas Linklater. However, Linklater faced stiff competition from a nearby North West Company post that winter, so the HBC abandoned its post in the spring.[7]

The Hudson's Bay Company then returned briefly to Pelican Lake in 1810–11 when George Charles, stationed at Manawan Lake, opened an outpost somewhere on Pelican to oppose North West Company traders there. This outpost probably operated for only a single season. The HBC was then absent for a time, but for the

SAB R-B9838(1)

The community of Pelican Narrows in 1922. The sign on the building to the left in the foreground reads "Hudson's Bay Company."

1818–19 season, at least, it had a post on Pelican Lake under the charge of John Pocock Holmes. Like his predecessors, Holmes had to deal with NWC competition which had by now escalated to a fierce level.[8]

When the Hudson's Bay Company absorbed the North West Company in 1821, George Simpson sharply reduced the number of fur trade posts in the country. As a result, Pelican Lake did not have an established trading post for the next several decades. In 1868, Louis Deschambault set up a short-lived post for the HBC on the lake, then in 1874, Antoine Morin finally established a permanent company post at present-day Pelican Narrows.[9] This post was still operating under the Bay flag when we stopped in 1986, but within a year, the HBC had sold it off with the rest of its Northern Stores Division. The store now survives on the 1874 site under the "Northern" name of the new North West Company which has salvaged the HBC's northern operations.

Going into the twentieth century, the Hudson's Bay Company could not maintain a trade monopoly at Pelican Narrows. In 1907, the Paris-based Revillon Frères opened a post at Pelican.[10] Wallace Laird was a Scotsman working as a Revillon trader at Pelican in the late 1920s. Later, referring back to the summer of 1928, he wrote, "In addition to us and the HBC, there was the free trader Arthur Jan, an RCMP detachment, a Saskatchewan Game Department officer, the Oblate missionary, and, for the summer, an Anglican Church school teacher."[11] Revillon Frères maintained a post at Pelican until the HBC took over its fur-buying operations in 1936.

Laird saw Pelican Narrows as a very friendly community with "a fair amount of socializing"—especially when members of the Peter Ballantyne nation came in from the surrounding country. Laird played the bagpipes and said of his Pelican audience, "The Crees preferred quicksteps and jigs, to which they kept time as they did to their Red River dances."[12]

Besides the Hudson's Bay Company and Revillon Frères, Pelican Narrows had other traders. In 1915, free trader Arthur Jan began operating at Pelican[13] and, as Louis Custer told us, operated at least into the 1920s. Another free trader at Pelican was Shorty Russick who, possibly starting as early as the 1920s, traded at Pelican until about 1953.[14] Russick (who died in 1983 at the age of 90) was well-known as both a trader and a world-class sled dog racer. In dog mushing circles, Russick is best remembered for having won the 200-mile World Championship Dog Derby at The Pas in 1924 in the record time of 23 hours, 42 minutes.[15] He and his team also placed third at the 1932 Lake Placid Winter Olympics, where sled dog racing was being showcased as a demonstration sport.[16]

In 1961, the Northern Co-op Trading Branch of Federated Co-operatives started trading in Pelican Narrows. Interestingly, it set up shop in the old log building that had served as Arthur Jan's store decades before. Renovations were done by the Co-op's Ron Clancy and a carpenter from Deschambault Lake named Matthew Eninew. The Pelican Co-op did not last, but the old Jan building went on to see other uses. When we were in Pelican in 1986, it was serving as Seepeeseek Camp's general store. Later still, it became a restaurant and was Pelican's only restaurant when it burned down in October 1998.

Church History

Like most northern communities, Pelican Narrows has seen the Roman Catholic church play a role in its development. The first Catholic clergy to pass this way were the Oblate Fathers Taché and Lafleche on their way to Île-à-la-Crosse in 1846. Later, other Oblate missionaries spent time in Pelican on an infrequent basis, with Father Legoff here during the spring of 1869, Father Gasté in 1874, and Father Blanchet in 1875. Father Bonald then spent the spring and summer of 1876 in Pelican. He returned in 1877 with Brother Labelle to build a small church. By 1878, the Oblates, with Father Bonald in charge, had permanently established what would be known as St. Gertrude's Mission in the southwest corner of the community. The Mission continues to this day but without a resident priest.[17]

The Anglican church has also had a role at Pelican Narrows. Anglican missionaries from Cumberland House and Stanley Mission first began working in the community in 1898. Reverend James Brown then directed construction of the first Anglican church in 1911. Since the Anglican church in Pelican never gained as many converts as the Catholics, it seems not to have had a resident clergyman for any length of time. It was active in the community, though, and established Pelican's first school in 1925.[18] Today, it still has a church on the peninsula at the southeast corner of the community.

Pelican was for many years a poor model for religious tolerance. The Catholics and Anglicans were sometimes bitterly divided, with the Catholics concentrated west of the present-day Northern store and the Anglicans to the east. In the early 1920s, some Anglicans even wanted to form their own Band separate from the Catholics.[19] The division was probably worsened later in the 1920s by the fact that Catholic children were sent to the residential school at Sturgeon Landing, while Anglican children often went to one in La Ronge. As late as the 1960s, some people still fostered the division, but happily, in recent times, religious differences are being put aside.

Pelican Narrows Indian Reserve 184B

As Maps 63M and 63M/2 show, part of the Pelican Narrows community is on "Pelican Narrows Indian Reserve 184B," while part is off-Reserve. Reserve 184B, belonging to the Peter Ballantyne Cree Nation, was set aside in 1930 towards partial satisfaction of PBCN's treaty land entitlement. Initially, Reserve 184B included 1,298 acres in a block running east from the east side of the community as well as two lots near to the Catholic church in the southwest corner of the community. In 1976, more lots near the church were made part of the reserve. More recently, there have been other transfers of community land to PBCN towards a final settlement of its treaty land entitlement. While Pelican Narrows continues to include some off-Reserve land considered a provincial "Northern Village," almost all of the community is now on PBCN land.[20]

Pelican Narrows Today

Pelican Narrows has changed a great deal since Louis Custer was a boy. An all-weather road came north to Pelican from the Hanson Lake Road in 1967. Other services followed. Today, the community has a population of about 2,500. Most residents are members of the Peter Ballantyne Cree Nation and have their homes on PBCN land.

At Pelican, canoeists will find a Northern store, Pearson Enterprises (with laundromat, confectionery and gas), Rising Phoenix Confectionery (with gas), Charles Confectionery (with gas), Custers' Confectionery, PBCN administration centre (housing the post office), medical clinic (staffed by nurses and visited by doctors from Flin Flon), churches, an eight-member RCMP detachment, Resources office, a public dock, Medicine Rapids Resort (with rental cabins and restaurant), Mista Noseyew outfitting (with cabins and restaurant, situated 3 km [2 mi] east) and Thunderbird Camps outfitting (offering remote fly-in sport fishing). The nearest airstrip for wheeled aircraft is several kilometres north of Pelican, but of interest to canoeists, Pelican Narrows Air Service keeps a de Havilland Beaver and a Cessna 185 on floats on Pelican Lake.

Map 11.1   Community of Pelican Narrows

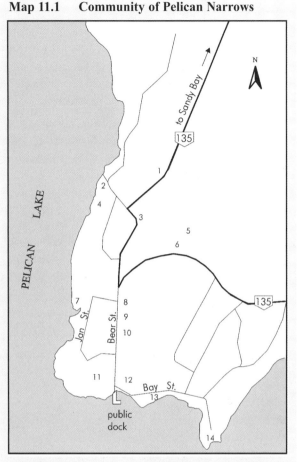

1. Pearson Enterprises
2. Fish Plant
3. Village Office
4. Pelican Narrows Air Service
5. Schools
6. Water Treatment Plant
7. Medicine Rapids Resort
8. RCMP
9. PBCN Admin Office/Post Office
10. Medical Clinic
11. Roman Catholic Church
12. Northern Store
13. Saskatchewan Environment
14. Anglican Church

PELICAN NARROWS TO DENARE BEACH

East on Pelican Lake

From the Pelican Narrows community, it is a short 2-km (1¼-mi) paddle east-southeast to the entrance to the narrows leading into Mirond Lake. Further on, a long island splits the narrows into a north and south channel. You may take either channel though the south channel provides the better passage. Since Highway 135 crosses the long island on its way to Pelican Narrows, you will go under a bridge no matter which channel you take.

The north channel is considerably smaller than the south channel. On the downstream side of the bridge, it has what looks to be the remains of an old stone fishing weir. In low water conditions, there may not be enough water over this weir to float a canoe. However, at normal water levels, you will pass down the channel without difficulty.

The south channel, both wider and deeper than the north channel, handles most of the flow out of Pelican Lake. Under the bridge here, you will find swift current calling for a sharp look-out, but it should not present any real difficulty.

> For upstream paddlers, we suggest the south channel as the better option. Energetic paddlers will be able to paddle up the swift current under the bridge at normal water levels. The north channel is not likely to present any great obstacle, but we have not tried it.

Mista Nosayew Camp

If you go down the north channel of the narrows, you will pass by Mista Nosayew Outfitters, a sport fishing camp, located on the shore north and west of the channel bridge (63M 339147). The camp, whose name means "big fish" in Cree (*mistanosîw*), was built in the 1960s as a community project inspired by a local trapper named Peter Linklater.[21] It is now owned and operated by the Peter Ballantyne Cree Nation with nearly a dozen cabins and a restaurant open through the summer months. You will also be able to find a pay phone here.

Mirond Lake

Two km (1¼ mi) west from the Highway 135 bridges, you will come to where the narrows opens up into Mirond Lake. The Cree refer to Pelican and Mirond lakes as twin lakes under the name *opâwikoscikan sâkahikana*, or the "fear narrows lakes." In 1792, Peter Fidler called it the "Stone Lake" or "Stony Lake," perhaps because of what he saw as "bare high rocks" along its shores.[22] Other early fur traders, however, knew the lake as "Heron Lake,"[23] or by its current name of Mirond Lake, which is from the French *mi-rond* meaning "half-round" or, according to Sir John Richardson, "half-moon."[24]

Mirond Lake is a large lake which, from the narrows out of Pelican Lake to Corneille Rapids in the south, comprises 19 km (nearly 12 mi) of the voyageur highway. Much of this distance is wide open to the north wind, so the lake can be extremely dangerous at times. In whitecap conditions, we strongly urge you to stay on shore where you can sleep, read, or find some other activity that will not drown you.

Mirond Lake has bold Shield rock shorelines and good depth—as much as 60 m (200 ft) in spots. Because of its depth, it is the last lake in the area to freeze in the fall but also the last to break up in spring. If you are travelling in early summer, you can count on it being colder than neighbouring lakes.

If you reach Mirond late in the day, you may wish to camp at a narrow island about 300 m (330 yd) long (63M 366143) that lies immediately east of the exit from the narrows. If it is unoccupied, you will find it has grassy spaces for a number of tents.

Heading southeast on Mirond, you can watch for a lobstick marker on an island (63M 400096) 6 km (3¾ mi) southeast from the narrows.[25] This is a big old spruce close to 1 m (3 ft) in diameter at its base that has had its trunk bared of branches for about 2 m (6 ft) below its high crown. Of course, since we last saw it, it may have succumbed to the elements.

If you are heading north from the lobstick island towards Pelican Narrows, you will see a telecommunications tower on the north horizon. The tower is east of the narrows to Pelican Lake, but it serves as a general landmark for travellers. So long as its guy wires stay secure, it should outlast its spruce and pine neighbours.

About 750 m (½ mi) southwest from the lobstick island, there is a small protected bay on the lake's west shore. This bay has a good campsite (63M 396089) featuring lots of bare bedrock for spreading out gear and general relaxation.

About 6 to 7 km (or 4 mi) south from the lobstick island, you will come to the entrance of a large, irregular bay back from the west shore. The rock peninsula on the north side of the entrance (63M 418034), which stands opposite an island sometimes called "Sewap Island," has an excellent campsite. The site, about 2 m (6 ft) above the water, is as level as a table top and has room for a small army. At the same time, it is well-protected by surrounding big spruce.

Continuing still further south, you will have to watch your map for the route out of Mirond Lake. To follow the voyageur track to Corneille Rapids, you must turn southeast into the bay above Corneille Rapids to avoid going to the south end of the lake. The turn southeast is not an obvious one. When Philip Turnor and his party came down Mirond Lake to Corneille Rapids on June 23, 1792, Turnor recorded that they "got to far South in Lake Merion and was forced to return against a very heavy gale of wind by which we lost 3 hours."[26]

There is in fact now a portage out of the south part of Mirond Lake and into Corneille Lake. We will describe it shortly as an alternative to the main Corneille Portage.

Map 11.2   South end of Mirond Lake and north end of Corneille Lake

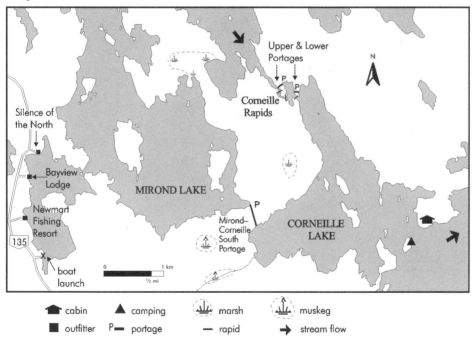

Fishing Camp Bay

If you do enter the south part of Mirond Lake, either by choice or by chance, you may wish to detour into a small bay in the extreme southwest corner of the lake. Here, you will find a cluster of three separate sport fishing camps—Silence of the North, Bayview Lodge, and Newmart Fishing Resort. The camps have been here a long time. Bayview was built in 1965 by Charles Lauterer, Newmart was built in 1967, and Silence of the North some time later.

At the camps, you can expect to find access to a telephone and Highway 135 (perhaps invaluable in an emergency). As well, you can expect that one or more of the camps will have a cafe, camp store, and canoe rentals. Current information on what you might find can be found in the *Saskatchewan Fishing & Hunting Guide,* published annually by Tourism Saskatchewan.

To continue downstream from Fishing Camp Bay, it is not necessary to go back north on Mirond Lake and regain the track to Corneille Rapids. Rather, once out of Fishing Camp Bay, you can turn south and then eastward to head to the extreme southeast corner of Mirond Lake where you will find a portage that leads to a bay on Corneille Lake. You can then paddle east to rejoin the old voyageur highway coming down from Corneille Rapids.

Portage #1A - Mirond–Corneille South Portage (± 340 m / 370 yd) (alternate)

From the southeast corner of Mirond Lake (63L 463957), this portage crosses to Corneille Lake along what appears to be an old winter freight road. The trail passes through park-like stands of mature aspen and jack pine, and is in excellent condition.

> If you are going upstream, you will find the portage (63L 63954) in the northwest corner of Corneille Lake's northwest bay. The portage is a good option for upstream travellers. Even though it is twice as long as Corneille Portage and adds 1.5 km (1 mi) of extra paddling to your route, it lets you bypass the current in the Corneille Rapids channel.

Corneille Rapids

The approach to Corneille Rapids is down a narrow channel that handles the whole of Mirond Lake's outflow. The river left side of this channel is shallow with big rocks on the bottom, so it is best to stay on river right until you reach the portage on river left.

About 240 m (260 yd) above the rapids, or 100 m (110 yd) above the portage, some fast current occurs, but this will not be problematic for downstream travellers.

> Upstream travellers, on the other hand, may have to wade here. The shallower, northeast shore (river left) might be preferable for wading.

Corneille Rapids, which occur in two separate parts, have had different names over the years. The Cree name for them is *âhâsiw pâwistik,* or "crow rapids." The matching current map name (*corneille* is French for "crow") suggests a Canadian voyageur origin. However, the early fur traders knew the adjacent portage as *Portage des Épinettes* or "pine portage."[27] We do not know when the name Corneille came into common English usage, but J.B. Tyrrell was using it by 1934.[28]

The first part of Corneille, a Class 2 rapid, begins where a large rock about 10 m (30 ft) long lies to the right of river centre. A smooth slick goes down the left side of this rock and ends in small to medium standing waves. It is possible to run down the slick. If you do so, you should stay as close to the large rock as possible since there is a rock garden to the left. When you reach the bottom, you can pull into a slight eddy on river right to consider how to deal with the second rapid.

The second part of Corneille, a Class 3 rapid, is over 100 m (110 yd) below and around a bend to the left from the first part. Here, the main flow swiftly drops 1 m (3 ft) as it goes down a channel 15 to 20 m (50 to 65 ft) wide on the left side of a 20-m-long (22-yd) islet. If you are an expert, you may decide to descend this main flow via a narrow route between bad rocks, but it is hard to get a good start down because of the way in which the current splits around the islet. Moreover, when you get to the bottom, you will have big standing waves to contend with.

Experts may scout Corneille Rapids and then opt to shoot them, but we recommend that everyone take the portage on the river left shore.

Portage #1 - Corneille Portage (± 160 m / 175 yd)

The upstream end of this portage is in a slight cove on river left about 140 m (155 yd) above from the first rapid. The portage is easy to identify since it is equipped with a pullover rack. You should have no difficulty crossing over from the river right side of the approach channel to the portage.

If you have a durable canoe, you can easily drag it over the pullover rack since the rack has no steep parts. For anyone wishing to make a regular portage, there is a very good walking trail alongside the rack.

The portage's camping possibilities are limited. There is a small, grassy camp space at its upstream end and another small, shaded one about 25 m (27 yd) further down the trail.

If you are travelling upstream, you will find the portage in the extreme northwest corner of the small bay lying north from the foot of the rapids. Again, the pullover rack is easy to spot.

Lower Corneille Rapid

From the lower end of Corneille Portage, you will travel only about 250 m (275 yd) southeast across the small bay or pond below Corneille Rapids before coming to a narrows which extends about 100 m (110 yd) and then opens into Corneille Lake. Just before the lake, the narrows has a short, Class 1 rapid with some medium-sized standing waves. With modest whitewater skills, you can run this rapid on a course right of centre which will get you past rocks which lie on either side.

When Philip Turnor and his party arrived at the narrows going upstream on September 20, 1790, Turnor recorded that they "enterd the river led the canoes 100 yards up a ripple in the mouth of it."[29] Cautious travellers might also choose to wade past the rapid or make a portage on the north, river left shore.

If you are going upstream, you might also choose to wade past the rapid or take the portage on the north, river left shore.

Portage #2 - Lower Corneille Portage (± 90 m / 99 yd) (optional)

The upstream end of this portage is about 10 m (30 ft) to the left of the start of the narrows. A line of willows extends out from the bank like a breakwater between the portage and the current flowing into the narrows. The portage is only in fair condition and is especially overgrown and indistinct towards its downstream end.

> If travelling upstream, you will find the portage's downstream end at a flat, sloping rock about 4 m (13 ft) wide located on river left about 20 m (22 yd) from the foot of the rapids. From the flat rock, you have to climb over some broken rock to gain the trail.

Corneille Lake

Corneille Lake accounts for just under 7 km (or 4 mi) of the old voyageur highway. From Lower Corneille Rapid, the canoe route runs south and then north around a peninsula forming the north shore of the lake. Map work is difficult here because the route crosses from the 63M maps to the 63L maps to go around the peninsula and then returns to the 63M maps. But you can keep on course by staying close to the peninsula and avoiding the main part of Corneille Lake off to the south.

The route through Corneille Lake offers good Shield camping. In 1986, we camped on the north tip of the first island (63M 478973) we came to below Lower Corneille Rapid. There is an even better site on the north tip of the island (63L 489962) lying 250 m (270 yd) southwest from the end of the north shore's main peninsula.

Dog Rapid

In its extreme northeast corner, Corneille Lake empties into what both Maps 63M and 63M/2 label as the Sturgeon-weir River. The lake's outlet is perhaps 60 m (200 ft) wide overall, but a small islet left of centre leaves the main, river right outflow channel with a width of about 25 m (27 yd). Here, on river right, a ledge produces a small, Class 3 fall or rapid having a vertical drop of a half metre (2 ft) or so.

The name Dog Rapid comes from the Cree name *acimos î-pa-pahkisihk*, which translates as "where the little dog went over the falls."[30] The name apparently describes an event from days long past since the name "Dog Rapid" was in use by at least the early 1930s.[31]

Running Dog Rapid solo, 1986.

It is possible to shoot over Dog Rapid's ledge and reach good water below it. However, the circulating wave below the drop could be dangerous. We strongly urge everyone to take the short portage on river right.

Portage #3 - Dog Portage (± 40 m / 44 yd)

The early fur traders called the portage past the rapid "Portage de L'Isle," "Petit Portage de L'Isle" or simply "Island Portage."[32] They gave the length of this portage as 15 or 20 yards[33]—less than half the length of the current portage. Philip Turnor, being more specific than most, recorded on September 19, 1790, that he and his party "came to a fall with a small Island in the middle carried part cargoe 20 yards being the length of the island and took the canoes up the fall with the remainder."[34] This leads us to suspect that the portage past Dog Rapid was formerly across the little islet in the channel. We have not, however, ever landed on the islet to look for a portage.

The upstream end of the current portage starts on river right about 70 m (77 yd) from the rapid. It is easy to spot since it is equipped with a pullover rack. If you have a sturdy canoe, you can use the rack to haul your canoe and gear across the portage in no time.

If you are travelling upstream, you will find the portage's downstream end in a little cove about 100 m (110 yd) southeast of the rapid. Your view of the portage may be blocked at first by a small island lying immediately in front of it.

Going across the portage, you will see that just to the south, there is a small side stream not more than 2 m (6 ft) wide running out of Corneille Lake. It is shallow, rocky, and sometimes even dry. However, at higher water levels, it is possible to sneak canoes through and thus avoid all carrying and hauling. Sigurd Olson and his friends did so on their classic 1955 canoe trip (described in Olson's *The Lonely Land*) down the Churchill and Sturgeon-weir.[35]

Although there are no campsites on Dog Portage, there is an excellent site on the second tiny island just below the portage (63M 515992). You will not likely find much in the way of firewood on the island, so wood should be brought from the main shore.

Sturgeon-weir River

Though we have earlier suggested that the Sturgeon-weir River might be seen as starting immediately below Frog Portage, topographic maps only apply the Sturgeon-weir name to that part of the river between Dog Rapid and its outflow into Namew Lake. Local people use the Sturgeon-weir name in a similar fashion, but they also frequently refer to the river upstream of Amisk Lake as the "West Weir" and that part of it downstream of Amisk as the "South Weir."

In describing the Sturgeon-weir from Dog Rapid down to Birch Portage, a distance of 18 km (11 mi), we can do no better than quote from Alexander Mackenzie. In describing the route upstream from Birch Portage to Dog Rapid, he wrote, "The Lake de Bouleau [Birch] then follows. This lake might with greater propriety, be denominated a canal, as it is not more than a mile in breadth."[36]

For the most part, the river down to Birch Portage has no current to speak of. The one exception is at a narrows (63L 537931) situated 7.5 km (4²/₃ mi) downstream from Dog Rapid. Here, where a rock islet divides the narrows into two channels, there is a section of strong current that will likely require upstreamers to wade their canoes. Both shores are suitable for wading up.

Down from Dog Rapid, the river's high shores are treed mainly with aspen, black spruce, and a greater than usual amount of jack pine. They offer little camping of particular note, but there are several places that would make passable campsites if you needed to stop.

Little Birch Lake

About 16 km (10 mi) down from Dog Rapid, the Sturgeon-weir expands into a small lake known in Cree as *waskway sâkahikanis,* meaning "little birch lake." This area has long been important to the Peter Ballantyne Cree Nation, and on January 23, 1930, the land on Little Birch's east shore was set aside as Birch Portage Indian Reserve 184A.[37] Grassy clearings on both sides of the lake entrance (63L 523844) show where there was once a settlement which, in the 1930s, was home to eight or ten families and also a trading store owned by the well-known Shorty Russick. A busy man, Russick ordinarily had "Oskachuk" ("Jack Pine") Thomas look after his enterprise at Little Birch Lake.[38]

The west, river right side of the old settlement site, where Russick's store was located, would make a good campsite. It has a grassy clearing near the shore and a second one further back. The clearings have lots of room for tents.

When Peter Fidler reached Birch Portage on June 24, 1792, he sketched the area and noted: "At the back of the Big Island [on Little Birch Lake] is a small river of about 4 Miles long that falls out of a pretty large Lake— several small rapids in the Creek."[39] Fidler is referring here to what is now the Wildnest River, which flows into the east side of Little Birch Lake. [40] This note—made on a day when his party covered over 50 km (31 mi)—is

Fidler's sketch of Little Birch Lake.

HBCA E.3/1 fo. 65d middle (N14804)

a good example of Fidler's uncommon ability to gather and record accurate information while travelling.

Birch Rapids

Less than 2 km (1¼ mi) from the old settlement site, you will come to Birch Rapids, known in Cree as *waskway pâwistik*. These major, Class 3+ rapids begin with a wild stretch of whitewater extending for about 100 m (110 yd). In this distance, the river makes a vertical drop of about 2 m (6 ft), and, in one place, narrows to a width of only 12 m (40 ft) or so. The rapids here do not appear rocky, but they have very large waves.

Below the first rapids, there is swift but quieter water for about 30 m (100 ft). More rapids then begin and extend for about 100 m (110 yd) through a channel about 20 m (22 yd) wide. These rapids, which look like a miniature version of Otter Rapids on the Churchill, produce a vertical drop of about 1 metre (3 ft). They are not as big as the first rapids, but they still have good-sized waves.

We have not tried to run Birch Rapids, and we have not talked to anyone who has. In 1986, Charlie Willetts, then operating Pawistik Lodge on Highway 106, told us that he was only aware of unsuccessful attempts to run the rapids. Experts may wish to use a fishing trail along the river right shore to scout the rapids with a view to going down them. We recommend, however, that most canoeists bypass the rapids via Birch Portage.

Portage #4 - Birch Portage (± 375 m / 410 yd)

Please make special note of the peculiar location of this portage's upstream landing. It is not along the river's flow channel! Rather, it is east of the rocky peninsula that juts north on the east side of the rapids channel (63L 523827). To reach the landing, paddle south about 600 m (⅓ mi) along the east shore of the peninsula until you are just west of a little point of rock and willows coming out from the shore. Here, you will see the portage trail leading up a grassy slope.

The portage is in excellent condition except for one muddy spot. It ends at a very good mud landing in a little cove on river left, not far below the rapids.

Map 11.3   Birch Portage area

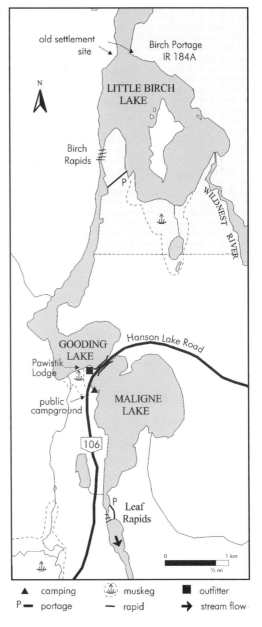

Sid Robinson at Birch Portage, 1986.

> Travelling upstream, you will encounter some current in the narrows downstream from the portage cove, but you should be able to paddle up it. As you reach the cove, the portage's lower landing and the portage itself are both easily visible.

Highway 106 (Hanson Lake Road)

About 2 km (1¼ mi) below Birch Portage, you will come to where the Sturgeon-weir widens somewhat to form what is now called Gooding Lake. This small expansion brings you immediately to a narrows spanned by two bridges (separated by a small island) on Highway 106. You may pass under either bridge since both have gaps in their cross-bracing that will allow boat traffic through.

> For upstream travellers, the current under the bridges is too strong to paddle up. It is therefore necessary to make a short carry of about 40 m (44 yd) to cross the highway. The area west of the west bridge is a suitable crossing point. Just watch for traffic!

Highway 106 is commonly known as the Hanson Lake Road after a large lake along it. The lake in turn is named after a Norwegian named Olaf Hanson who arrived in the area in 1919 to trap and later worked as a forest ranger. In the late 1950s, he was instrumental in scouting a route for Highway 106—a long awaited link between Prince Albert and Creighton—which was finally completed in 1962.[41]

Just west of the two bridges, on the north side of the highway, you will find Pawistik Lodge—an outfitting camp built in 1961 shortly prior to completion of the road. The camp operates through the summer months and has a small store where basic supplies can be purchased. It also offers canoe rentals.

Should you be starting a trip downstream from Highway 106, the provincial campground at the northwest corner of Maligne Lake, just west and south from Pawistik Lodge, will serve as a good departure point.

Maligne Lake

South of the Highway 106 bridges, the Sturgeon-weir again expands to form what maps refer to as Maligne Lake. This name is somewhat out of place here since, although the early voyageurs used the name "Maligne" for the Sturgeon-weir, it was really meant for the South Weir with its difficult rapids and swift current. To the voyageurs, who travelled upstream half of the time, the West Weir, with its slow current, was an almost ideal travel route.

From the bridges, Maligne Lake funnels southward for 2 km (1¼ mi) to where it drains down a narrow channel. As you enter the channel, be ready for rapids within 200 to 300 m (220 to 330 yd) (63L 519779).

Leaf Rapids

These Class 2 rapids, which take their name from the Cree *nîpîskâw pâwistik*,[42] extend for about 100 m (110 yd) down a reasonably straight course. They make a good run for advanced canoeists who first stop to scout a course. If you do decide to run them, you may wish to start down a broad tongue on river right and then move to river left to avoid medium-sized waves roughly halfway down. A final move back to river right will help you avoid large, submerged rocks on river left near the foot of the rapids. If you have only modest whitewater skills, we recommend a portage on river left.

The voyageurs likely ran Leaf Rapids as a matter of routine. Going upstream, they treated it as a *décharge* or a *demi-charge* where canoes would be lightened and then waded up the rapids. George Simpson referred to the rapids as the "Bouleau decharge" (distinct from "Bouleau Portage" just upstream), while Sir John Richardson referred to "the Birch lightening-place (*Demi-charge du bouleau*)."[43]

Portage #5 - Leaf Portage (± 200 m / 220 yd)

The portage starts on river left about 50 m (55 yd) upstream from the head of the rapids and 20 m (22 yd) up from a steel cable that suspends three orange-red cones over the river. The landing is a low shelf of bedrock that quickly gives way to a dirt bank that climbs gradually to a height of about 2 m (6 ft) and then rises at an even gentler slope.

Up from the landing, the trail leads through some fine black spruce. It is in excellent condition though a bit stony towards its lower end.

For upstream travellers, the downstream landing shows as a rocky break in the shoreline about 40 m (44 yd) east from the base of the rapids. The landing is a good gentle slope covered with a kind of gravel made from sharp, broken stones.

Down from Leaf Rapids

Downstream from Leaf Rapids, the Sturgeon-weir is narrower and has slightly more current than higher up. One km (²/₃ mi) below the rapids, there is a small riffle, and another kilometre further on, there is a 1-km (²/₃-mi) section with a modest current.

The riffle may require some upstream paddlers to wade along the east shore. The section of modest current will not present problems for upstream paddlers.

Halfway down the section of modest current, you will see a gravelly trail that leads up the east, river left bank to a large gravel pit, presumably used during the construction of Highway 106. Not far downstream from the trail up the bank, you will see a break in the shore willows and alders on river left. It connects to an old vehicle track that likely leads back to the gravel pit. About 15 m (50 ft) up from the shore break, you will find a grassy clearing amid jack pine and aspen that would make a pleasant camp for three to four tents.

Downstream from the gravel pit, the river banks are generally high and sandy with a good deal of jack pine cover. However, the actual shoreline is sometimes low and willowy, and sedge meadows occur in three places. When you reach the third sedge meadow, you can watch for a bald eagle nest in an aspen on the opposite, river left shore.

About 7 km (4¹/₃ mi) down from Leaf Rapids, you will come to Scoop Rapids. The sound of these rapids—which could be described as falls—will warn you in advance to watch for a mandatory portage on river left.

Scoop Rapids

These major rapids start where the flow channel narrows to roughly 15 m (50 ft) wide and then makes a quick 1-m (3-ft) drop over a rock ledge. The drop is followed by 20 or 30 m (25 or 30 yd) of churning whitewater cut by a bad diagonal trough. There is then another sharp 1-m (3-ft) drop over a second ledge, followed immediately by a very wicked hole. Wild, airshot turbulence then extends for another 30 m (or yd) before a more normal run-out begins.

It is common for some water to escape from the main rapids and flow over bedrock shelves that lie between the second ledge and the downstream end of the portage. These shelves are frequented by fish, especially suckers, that often find themselves semi-stranded in shallow depressions in the bedrock. Accordingly, in the early days of the fur trade, the portage was known as "Carp Portage." After passing the rapids on June 17, 1848, Sir John Richardson wrote, "At breakfast-time we crossed the Carp Portage, where there is a shelving cascade over granite rocks. The grey sucking carp (*Catastomus hudsonius*) was busy spawning in the eddies, and our voyagers killed several with poles."[44]

The name Scoop Rapids comes from the Cree equivalent, *kwâpahikan pâwistik*. This name, too, relates to the easy fishing offered by the bedrock shelves at the lower end of the rapids. John Morin, a Peter Ballantyne Cree Nation elder born on the Sturgeon-weir in 1925, says that when he was a boy, a "scoop," which was a dip net on a long pole, was kept at the lower end of the portage so that travellers might easily find a meal.

The abundant fishery has long made the rapids popular with pelicans. On June 24, 1792, Peter Fidler wrote, "A great number of Pelicans in the summer remain at the foot of the fall to catch fish—which they find plentifully."[45] Not much has changed in over 200 years. Every summer, a large group of pelicans gather on some low, flat rocks about 100 m (110 yd) downstream from the rapids. From the flat rocks, they can either swim up to the foot of the rapids in flotillas or use their wings to reach a vantage point higher up.

Scoop Rapids, June 1996.

PHOTO BY HILARY JOHNSTONE

Portage #6 - Scoop Portage (± 50 m / 55 yd)

At its upstream end, the portage begins in a quiet cove on river left at a point even with and 20 m (22 yd) to the left of the head of the rapids. It is easy to spot since it shows as a 4-m-wide (13-ft) mud path climbing up through a clear break in the aspen and balsam poplar woods. It has a very good mud landing.

The portage is in excellent condition although it can be muddy and slippery when wet. From the high midpoint of the portage, you can take a side trail eastward for about 50 m (55 yd) to a very fine camping area under some giant spruce and jack pines.

If you arrive from downstream, you will find the portage in a small cove east from the foot of the rapids. As you approach the cove, you will encounter some fast current, but a good eddy right next to the river left shore should allow you to gain the cove without difficulty. Once you cross the cove, a short paddle of 45 m (50 yd) or so, you will find the downstream landing just east of the fishing shelves.

Map 11.4   Scoop Rapids and Attree Lake

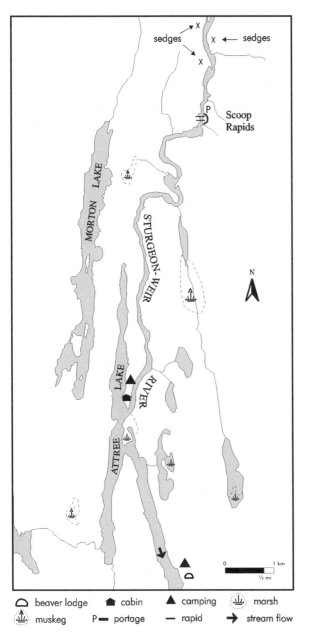

beaver lodge   cabin   camping   marsh
muskeg   P— portage   — rapid   → stream flow

Down from Scoop Rapids

Downstream from Scoop Rapids, the river channel has only a slight current and offers quiet paddling. A good mixed wood of spruce and aspen stands back from the river, but the shorelines are now lower than before. Willows, alders, and birch are common at the water's edge. You will see some bedrock outcrops, but these tend to be either small and brushy or too steep to allow landing. The nature of the shoreline limits camping possibilities.

About 450 m (500 yd) before the entrance to Attree Lake, a bare rock shore on river right marks the location of a good campsite (63L 505656). The shore here rises steeply for 1 m (3 ft), so it is not easy to land canoes. However, a grassed-over bedrock terrace about 2 m (6 ft) above the water provides good space for general camping activities. And behind the terrace, there is enough room for three or four tents.

South from the camp, you will soon pass a trapper's cabin on the same shore and then come to Attree Lake—a long thin lake running parallel to the Sturgeon-weir just beyond the river's west bank. The lake and the river share a common course for 1 km (²/₃ mi). You must then turn to river left to avoid going too far south in Attree Lake.

Peter Fidler's sketch of Attree Lake, June 24, 1792.

HBCA E.3/1 fo. 66 (N14805)

Peter Fidler noted the need to be careful in navigating at this point in the journey:

"two bays in the river ... which a person is very apt to go into if not taking particular notice & throws one a good while out of a persons way as the bays either way extend to a considerable distance."[46]

Robert Hood, here on June 15, 1820, did not consider Attree Lake a lake but called it the "Hay River"— which name likely derives from the wet sedge meadow on the Sturgeon-weir's east shore adjacent to the lake entrance. He also referred to the Sturgeon-weir upstream of Attree Lake as the "Great River" and that downstream of Attree as the "Ridge River."[47] Other early explorers did not leave a name for Attree Lake. Moreover, most used only a single name for the West Weir up and down from Attree Lake, though the name could vary from one explorer to another. Alexander Henry the Elder called it the "River aux Castors," while Peter Fidler and David Thompson called it the "Grass River."[48]

Below Attree Lake, the shores tend to be either steep bedrock or else low and marshy, so good campsites are to be cherished. One such campsite (63L 515620) is on river left 2.5 km (1½ mi) downstream from Attree Lake where the river has a slightly indented bay to the east. Here, canoes can be pulled up on a weathered bedrock slope. Up from the shore, there is room for several tents.

This part of the river has a current that does not normally exceed 1 km (⅔ mi) per hour. It is especially good beaver habitat. There is a beaver lodge on the river left shore 200 m (220 yd) downstream from the indented bay campsite. Other beaver lodges are further downstream.

Not quite 5 km (3 mi) down from the indented bay campsite, you will find another campsite (63L 544588) just past where the river jogs northeast and then bends to again run southeast. For some years, a nearly dead aspen of great size has identified the site, but it is now a doubtful landmark at best.[49] At the site, canoes can be landed on a 10-m (30-ft) strip of rough grey bedrock and then easily hauled up to a level grassy area near shore. About 30 to 40 m (33 to 44 yd) back from the water, there is a very good camping area with room for several tents amid mature aspen and spruce.

Next to the dying aspen campsite, Map 63L/10, marks the Sturgeon-weir as the "Snake River." This is likely a cartographic error since no early writings allude to this name. Nor is it presently known to Cree people familiar with the area.

Some 5 km (3 mi) down from the dying aspen campsite, you may begin watching the river right shore for a portage that bypasses Snake Rapids. All canoeists should stop at the portage to consider their options. Note that the portage starts about 500 m (550 yd) upstream of the rapids before a bend leading to them. If you can see the rapids, you have missed the portage!

Snake Rapids

The voyageurs knew Snake Rapids by different names. Alexander Mackenzie referred to it as "the Grand Rapid,"[50] while Sir John Richardson said it was known as the "Ridge Rapid."[51] The present-day name comes from the Cree equivalent, *kinîpik pâwistik*.

The voyageurs ordinarily treated Snake Rapids as a *décharge* where they lightened their canoes before taking them up or down the rapids. If water levels were high enough, lightening might not be necessary. Going downstream on June 24, 1792, a day when he and his companions had been on the water from 3:15 a.m. until 8:00 p.m., Peter Fidler wrote:

> This last [Snake Rapids] all a very shoal bad rapid led along the North side, & carried the things 450 yards over the worst of it so very shoal—when good water 3/4 of an hour good work to go up it with a Loaded Canoe. Fine high bank on N side, but little or no track thru the woods—put up here.[52]

Nowadays, Snake's Class 2 rapids may be run by advanced canoeists provided water levels are reasonable. In low water, manoeuvring becomes more difficult, and advance scouting is then advisable for anyone without expert skills.

The rapids begin with an upper section that starts about 500 m (550 yd) downstream from the portage and extends for about 200 m (220 yd). For the most part, this upper section consists of shallow rock gardens which are concentrated mainly on river right. To run this section, you can start down a broad tongue that runs left of centre but to the right of a 3-m-long (10-ft) rock situated close to mid-channel. Then be prepared to make a sharp turn to the left to keep

Map 11.5 Snake Rapids and Snake Portage

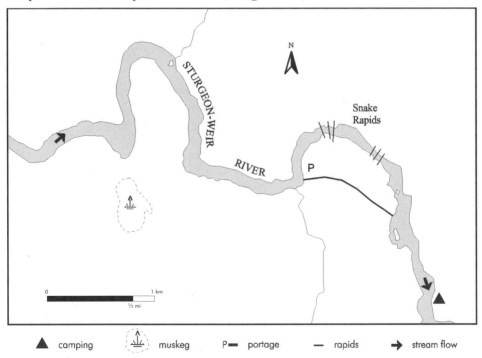

in the deeper water of the main flow. This will bring you close to the river left shore where you can stay until you are past the worst of the rock gardens.

After the upper section, you can expect only swift current and minor rapids for about 350 m (380 yd). Avoid some bad rocks on river right by following a broad tongue on river left. You will then go through about 100 m (110 yd) of minor rapids before reaching the final rapids which are short but more difficult than those upstream.

You can identify the final rapids by another large, 3-m-long (10-ft) rock in mid-channel. The river right side of the big rock is obstructed by rocks forming a kind of ledge. However, it is possible to thread your way through the rocks and medium-sized waves on river left or, with some luck, shoot through a narrow gap just to the right of the big rock.

Portage #7 - Snake Portage (± 1,050 m / 1,150 yd)

As mentioned, this portage (63L 581572) starts on river right about 500 m (550 yd) upstream from the head of the rapids. It is about 100 m (110 yd) down from where a small stream runs in at a low, willowy area on river right. The landing area is quite inconspicuous, but a watchful eye will see it as a small grassy clearing surrounded by poplars, alders, and a few willows. The landing is a gentle slope of mud and grass.

The portage has a very ancient aspect about it. It is a narrow footpath with shrubs crowding in on it, but it is well-worn and in excellent shape. The portage does not have any major campsites. However, the clearing at the upstream landing and another clearing about 35 m (38 yd) before the portage's downstream end both have room for a tent or two.

> Approached from downstream, the portage can be found about 450 m (500 yd) below the foot of the rapids. It is at the north end of a cove-like expansion on river right that has a sedge island at its centre. The portage is inconspicuous, but you will notice the landing as a grassy space about 5 m (16 ft) wide and 10 m (32 ft) deep. The landing has a good soft shore for pulling up canoes.

Down from Snake Rapids

One km (2/3 mi) downstream from Snake Rapids, there is a good campsite (63L 592561) on river left where a bedrock lookout stands about 3 m (6 ft) above the water. You can pull in behind a low shelf of bedrock running north from the lookout to find a mud and grass landing. At first, the site does not look like much, but a trail will lead you to an area suitable for several tents.

One km (2/3 mi) down from the campsite, Map 63L/10 shows where a small peninsula (which sometimes floods to become an islet) projects from the river right shore and narrows the river channel.

> There is swift current off the small peninsula, but strong paddlers will usually be able to paddle up it. If this is not practical, it should be easy to wade up to quieter water.

About 300 m (330 yd) further downstream, there is a tiny, 30-m-long (100-ft) island of rounded bedrock. It has only a few trees and is too small for camping, but it is an excellent place to stop for lunch. More fast current occurs at a good fishing narrows 1 km (2/3 mi) down from the 30-m-long island.

Some upstream paddlers may be able to muscle their way through the fishing narrows with just paddle power. But most will likely have to track or wade a short distance—perhaps best using the north, river left shore.

Continuing on through an area where the shores are lined mainly with willows and black spruce, you will come to two cabins on the river left shore situated in a good grassy clearing overlooking the river. You have now crossed the western boundary of Amisk Lake Indian Reserve 184 which was transferred to the Peter Ballantyne Cree Nation on January 23, 1930.[53] The Reserve reaches along the river left shore all the way to Amisk Lake.

Sport fishers often leave boats just above Spruce Rapids for easier access to the fishing upstream. The sight of these boats pulled up on the river banks will warn you that the dangerous rapids are near at hand. You can then be ready to put in at the portage on river left.

Spruce Rapids

Though the early voyageurs sometimes ran Spruce Rapids, they properly called for a full portage on river left. This was generally known as the "Pente Portage,"[54] with the French *pente* apparently meaning "slope," though Peter Fidler called it "the Eagle Carrying Place," while John Franklin and Sir John Richardson both called it the "Ridge Portage."[55] The current name for the portage matches its Cree name, *minahik onikâhp*.[56] Peter Fidler portaged here on his way downstream on June 25, 1792, and commented on the rapids, the voyageurs, and the local sturgeon:

> carried over the Eagle Carrying place on the North side 280 yards pretty good carrying—a bad fall, like going down a pair of stairs notwithstanding the Canadians shoot down it the light Canoes—this fall has something remarkable—as not a single Sturgeon was ever seen above it, in any part of this Track to the Athapiscow & Slave Lakes—altho they are plentiful close at the foot of it, & the Indians occasionally make a fishing weir here to catch them & other fish: the falls being so steep probably stops them from proceeding any further, or whether or not it may be owing to different water, food &c I cannot say but think that it is owing to the Fall being too steep.[57]

These major, strong Class 3 rapids produce a vertical drop of over 3 m (10 ft) in a distance of roughly 300 m (330 yd). They begin where a main vee passes by a rocky area on river right. After 100 m (110 yd), this vee passes between medium to large waves on river right and a ledge on river left. Then perhaps 30 m (100 ft) down from the ledge, there is a large square

In 1986, in the name of research, one of us took an unloaded canoe down the rapids on a course just to the right of the large square boulder. This turned out to be a mistake since the run was mainly uncontrolled. It was only thanks to the general seaworthiness of our humble Grumman Eagle and blind luck that canoe and paddler got to the foot of the rapids unscathed.

boulder about 10 m (30 ft) across in midstream with 40 m (44 yd) of big waves and canoe-eating rocks below it. More bad ledges and rocks follow on river right before the river bends to the left and finally settles down.

Experts may wish to scout the rapids and form their own opinion as to whether a run is feasible. An eddy below the ledge on upper river left and a section of smoother water next to the river right shore might offer two alternatives to the path just right of the square boulder. To scout the rapids from close-up, you may wish to take advantage of a narrow foot path on the river right shore, used mainly by sport fishers, that starts about 100 m (110 yd) above the rapids and then follows the shore for about 375 m (¼ mi) to a cove west from the foot of the rapids.

Our best advice is that all canoeists take advantage of the good portage on river left.

Portage #8 - Spruce Portage (± 275 m / 300 yd)

The upstream end of the portage begins on river left in a little cove separated from the head of the rapids by a rocky breakwater. The wide portage trail is clearly visible from the water. It starts at a mud bank which is cut away next to the water, necessitating a short step up.

The portage is broad, smooth, and in excellent condition overall. It has a campsite about 40 m (44 yd) from the upstream landing, and a larger site at its midpoint. This latter site has an established fire pit, level spaces for about six tents, and majestic aspen and spruce towering overhead.

> The portage's downstream end is about 40 m (44 yd) southeast from the foot of the rapids. It cannot be seen from further downstream, but once you are close, it is clearly evident. It has a good, gently sloped, mud landing.

Down from Spruce Rapids

About 500 m (⅓ mi) down from the rapids, there is a cemetery used by the Peter Ballantyne Cree Nation on river left. It has a good view of the river and is within earshot of Spruce Rapids. Most of the graves are marked with white-painted wooden crosses.

Cemetery near Spruce Rapids.

> Another 500 m (⅓ mi) past the cemetery, there is a short section of fast current, but upstream travellers will be able to paddle up it. The current from Spruce Rapids to Amisk Lake is generally somewhat stronger than further upstream though it ordinarily remains less than 2 km (1¼ mi) per hour.

Map 11.6   Spruce Rapids and area

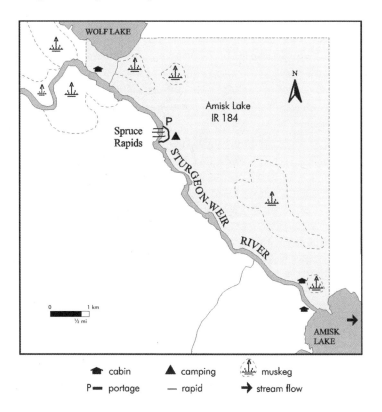

▲ cabin   ▲ camping   muskeg

P▬ portage   — rapid   ➔ stream flow

West Weir Mouth

Within 1 km (²/₃ mi) of Amisk Lake, you will see cabins on the river left shore. The present cabins are occupied on a seasonal basis, but this was once an established community of the Peter Ballantyne Cree Nation. John Morin, now of Prince Albert, an oral historian who has given us much of the history for the country between Pelican Narrows and Cumberland House, was born here in 1925. His parents were then based at Pelican Narrows, but they had stopped at the river mouth to visit when he was born. His own mother, Nancy (née Custer), had also been born here years before.

On the river right shore, about 300 m (330 yd) from the lake, there is a log patrol cabin belonging to Saskatchewan Environment and Resource Management. It is used from time to time by Conservation Officers based in Creighton.

If you approach the West Weir from Amisk Lake, you may have some difficulty seeing the river mouth. The river reaches northwest into a low area where the shores of willows and black spruce merge into one another. However, once you are close, you will recognize the river by its substantial width.

Frobisher-Henry Fort

The mouth of the West Weir is where the Montreal traders Joseph Frobisher, Thomas Frobisher, and Alexander Henry, along with forty men, spent the winter of 1775–76 while waiting to trade at Frog Portage in the spring. The Frobishers had previously left Louis Primeau and seven men at Amisk Lake to begin work on a wintering post, and it is quite likely that the Frobisher-Henry party wintered at Primeau's location.[58] Preparatory work by Primeau would have been most valuable since the Frobisher-Henry party did not reach the West Weir until November 1, 1775—a day before Amisk Lake froze over. There was then still plenty to do to prepare for winter. According to Henry:

> Our first object was to procure food. We had only three days' stock remaining, and we were forty-three persons in number. Our forty men were divided into three parties, of which two were detached to the River aux Castors, on which the ice was strong enough to allow of setting the nets....The third party was employed in building our house, or fort; and, in this, within ten days, we saw ourselves commodiously lodged. Indeed, we had almost built a village; or, in soberer terms, we had raised buildings around a quadrangle, such as really assumed, in the wilds which encompassed it, a formidable appearance. In front, was the house designed for Messrs. Frobisher and myself; and the men had four houses, of which one was placed on each side, and two in the rear.[59]

In 1953, amateur archaeologist Harry Moody actually discovered the old Frobisher-Henry fort in an area overgrown by forest. With the help of friends and a metal detector, he found numerous artifacts from the early fur trade—axe heads, knife blades, nails, broken glass, and the like. Most notably, Moody unearthed the remains of six fireplaces solidly built from flat pieces of limestone. The fireplaces fit the quad-rangle pattern described by Alexander Henry and leave no doubt as to the authenticity of Moody's find.[60] Moody also described pits dug for the winter storage of canoes at the Frobisher-Henry site, and these are still visible today. However, it does not seem that these were dug in 1775, since Henry wrote:

PHOTO BY HILARY JOHNSTONE

Remains of old fireplace at Frobisher-Henry post site.

> Our canoes were disposed of on scaffolds; for, the ground being frozen, we could not bury them, as is the usual practice, and which is done to protect them from that severity of cold which occasions the bark to contract and split.[61]

The canoe pits may have been dug a year or two later by a Captain James Tute and his men. Tute was at the Amisk Lake post for at least two winters beginning in 1776. On October 9, 1776, Matthew Cocking, in charge of the Hudson's Bay Company's Cumberland House post, wrote, "At noon arrived Two Canoes of Pedlers which are going to reside at Mr. Frobishers old Settlement in the Beaver Lake, the Masters name Captain Tute..."[62] Later, on February 17, 1778, William Tomison, Cocking's successor, wrote, "Late in the Evening (Captain Tuite) one of the Master Traders from the Beaver Lake came to the House begging the Favour to trade some Medicines; He being bad with the Veneral disorder..."[63]

Amisk Lake

Amisk Lake, which has since earliest record taken its name from the Cree word for beaver,[64] is one of the larger lakes between Methy Portage and Cumberland House. If you decide to go from the mouth of the West Weir to the head of the South Weir by the most direct route, you will paddle 19 km (nearly 12 mi) southeast. If you voyage from the West Weir to Denare Beach, you will paddle over 26 km (16 mi) to the northeast.

The lake is big enough to have lots of fish, and it has good populations of pike, walleye, and whitefish. But the fishery is not what it used to be. According to men who commercial fished the lake in the 1930s, Amisk then produced excellent lake trout. Gisli Norman of Denare Beach told us that in those early days, he and his fishing crew caught several trout weighing over 35 kg (75 lb). As well, Roland and Fred Robinson, who fished the lake in the late 1930s, have said that lake trout made up 40 percent of an average catch. Nowadays, whether because of simple overfishing or industrial pollution, the trout are gone. We can only hope that sufficient science and resources will eventually be available to bring them back and restore the lake to its earlier balance.

As you enter Amisk Lake from the West Weir, you will cross a line running from west to east that marks the southern boundary of the Precambrian Shield. Accordingly, the character of the lake you will see depends on your direction of travel. If you head southeast to the South Weir, the surface rock you see will be mainly Ordovician dolomite or limestone.[65] If you go to Denare Beach in the northeast corner of the lake, you will stay entirely within the Shield.

We will first mention the direct route to the South Weir and then describe the route to Denare Beach. We caution that both these routes can be hit by dangerous winds and thus need fair weather for safe travel.

Direct to the South Weir

South from the West Weir, the limestone you will see dates back to the Ordovician era of some 450 million years ago—making it roughly 100 million years older than the Devonian

Limestone cliffs on south shore of Amisk Lake, June 1996.

PHOTO BY HILARY JOHNSTONE

limestone seen on the Clearwater River. A good example of Ordovician rock is the "Tyndall stone" brought in from Manitoba to face the Legislative Building and other public buildings in Saskatchewan.[66] On Amisk Lake, Ordovician limestone shows occasionally in vertical cliffs and frequently at the water's edge in broken, platter-like pieces.

Eight km (5 mi) southeast from the West Weir, there are good limestone cliffs on the northwest side of a finger-like peninsula pointing northeast from the lake's south shore (63L 745414 to 753419). The cliffs are 4 to 6 m (13 to 20 ft) high and covered with orange lichens.

Three km (2 mi) further southeast, more limestone cliffs (63L 776407 to 779407) face north from the peninsula east of the entrance to Sturgeon Bay. These rise from 4 to 8 m (13 to 26 ft), and they too are covered with orange lichens. About 400 m (440 yd) south of the cliffs, towards Sturgeon Bay, there is a small beach of plate-sized limestones where a camp could be made. The beach has a limestone firepit, and back from the beach, there is room for one or two tents. On the next peninsula, 2 km (1¼ mi) yet further southeast, there is a second small beach of limestones (63L 794398). Perhaps too small for camping, it would make a reasonable lunch stop.

From the second small beach, a traverse of just over 2 km (1¼ mi) east-southeast across the mouth of Warehouse Bay, lying to the south, will bring you to the tip of a peninsula. From the tip, limestone cliffs rising as high as 8 m (25 ft) extend southwest towards Warehouse Bay for about 300 m (330 yd). Though considerably scratched with graffiti, these cliffs also have ancient rock paintings (63L 817389) which will be described in the next chapter.

Once you round the tip of the rock painting peninsula, you can follow the shore on your right for 3 km (2 mi) south-southeast to reach the head of the South Weir.

From the West Weir to Denare Beach

From the West Weir, the route across Amisk Lake to Denare Beach is all in the Shield. Here the rock outcrops, produced by ancient volcanic lava flows, often have a pale green hue not seen further west on the guide route. As well, they tend to be bolder and higher than Shield outcrops to the west. However, even though the shore rock sometimes rises steeply, good bedrock campsites are generally easy to find.

About 1.5 km (1 mi) east from the mouth of the West Weir, a portage (63L 704473) starts at an inconspicuous break in willows on the north shore and runs north for 600 m (660 yd) or so into the protection of Muskeg Bay. Saskatchewan's *Canoe Trip #14* booklet suggests that this portage could allow canoeists to avoid bad winds on the main body of Amisk Lake.[67] However, the portage—really a snowmobile trail—is not an option for canoeists. It goes through muskeg for about 460 m (500 yd) and then, at its north end, through a floating sedge marsh for another 150 m (165 yd) or so. We saw a red fox hunting the marsh by jumping from one tussock to another, but anyone taking a load there would quickly flounder in the mire.

If you avoid the portage into Muskeg Bay and continue around the heel of the foot-like peninsula lying east and north from the West Weir, you will find some camping possibilities. At the most southerly point on the heel (63L 712463), where we camped in 1986, you will find room for a couple of tents about 3 m (10 ft) above the water. One km (²/₃ mi) east, a small gravel beach (63L 722466) about 15 m (50 ft) long, though not ideal, also has room for a couple of tents. Another 400 m (440 yd) further east, at the extreme southeast of the heel, there is a good grassy camp (63L 726465) overlooking the water. Finally, 1.25 km (¾ mi) northeast from the grassy camp, on the northwest corner of a small island, there is a good Shield rock camp (63L 733476) 3 m (10 ft) above the water.

From the heel of the foot peninsula, you can first see the 250-m-high (825-ft) smokestack of Hudson Bay Mining and Smelting Company's smelter at Flin Flon, Manitoba, 17 km (10½ mi) northeast of Denare Beach. This tall sentinel, built in 1974, identifies your general direction of travel. However, a direct traverse towards the smokestack would be risky due to a lack of wind protection. It is much safer to go north along the west shore of Amisk Lake until you pull even with Missi Island.

As we headed north up the west shore in 1986, we were stopped by two officers from the Creighton Resources office, Jimmy Custer and Ed Gardiner, making a boat patrol of the lake. Jimmy Custer, nicknamed "Sugar," then had a reputation as a champion flour packer at northern winter festivals. In recent years, he has become known throughout the north as a winning sled dog racer (and shrewd dog trader).

Missi Island

Missi Island—which takes its name from the Cree prefix *misi-* meaning "big"—is a huge island occupying much of Amisk Lake's north end. It is large enough to have fourteen small lakes, several of which are a kilometre or more long.

The southwest tip of Missi Island is known as "Hudson Bay Point." As the name suggests, this corner of Missi Island was once the location of a Hudson's Bay Company post. We do not know the post's history except that it operated in the early 1900s to serve gold mining interests working at the Prince Albert Mine up Missi Island's "West Channel." The site apparently has some foundation rocks laid out "in two rows 70 feet long and 30 feet apart" marking where the HBC started but then abandoned a new building project, though we have not located them.[68]

From Hudson Bay Point, you have a choice of either: a) continuing north up the West Channel and then around the north side of the island; or b) heading east along the south side of the island. We have never paddled the more circuitous route north of the island, but we note that it is only 12 km (7½ mi) longer than the south route. We therefore suggest you might easily go either north or south of Missi to get to Denare Beach.

North around Missi Island

During the first half of the twentieth century, Missi Island was a magnet for those hoping to strike it rich prospecting for gold. Even Anahareo, wife of Grey Owl, staked some ground on the island during a 1934 sojourn away from her author husband.[69] If you are a prospector at heart, a detour around the north side of Missi—where the most gold prospects were found—would make a good trip. In advance of your excursion, it would be worthwhile to look at the stories collected by Berry Richards in *Gold and Other Stories,* as well as relevant government publications, to get the history of specific sites.[70] Saskatchewan's *Canoe Trip #41* booklet would also be useful.[71]

Up Missi Island's West Channel, there is a large island (63L 748632 to 749651) lying south of the old Prince Albert Mine peninsula. According to the late Harry Moody, the island is known as "Paddy's Island," after a prospector named Paddy Houlihan who lived there in the 1930s. The Cree apparently once knew it as *mîmîkwîsiwak ministik*, after their legendary water

Map 11.7   Early gold workings at north end of Amisk Lake

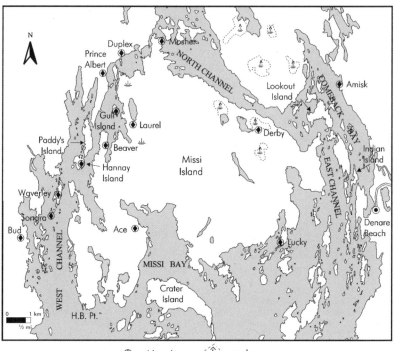

⬤ gold working   ⚓ muskeg

sprites. Story has it that both the *mîmîkwîsiwak* and the early natives procured rock painting pigment from the island. There is also said to be a pictograph site on the east side of the island, but we are not aware of it being seen in recent times.[72]

At the east end of Missi's North Channel, Lookout Island is said to be the highest vantage point on Amisk Lake and to have a good view in all directions. Back in 1933, a footpath was cut from a landing on the island's south shore up to the lookout. Harry Moody considered the lookout to be a mandatory stop for photographers.[73]

South Shore of Missi Island

If you choose to paddle east along the south side of Missi Island, you will have to sort your way through a large number of islands. It is likely most practical to go north of Crater Island, the largest island south of Missi, even though this could leave canoes exposed to winds coming out of Missi Bay to the north. East from Crater Island, there is good protection from the prevailing winds.

Crater Island was once known as "Pipestone Island" since Indians used a soapy chlorite schist from the island for making pipes. In 1932, Dr. J.P. Wright of the Dominion Geological Survey changed the name to "Crater"—presumably to reflect the island's volcanic past.

South from the extreme southeast tip of Crater Island, there are three long, thin islands. From north to south, the narrows they produce are "Pipestone Narrows," "Coyote Narrows," and "Basket Narrows." The first narrows takes its name from the old name for Crater Island. The second takes its name from the fact that coyotes frequent the narrows in winter. The third derives its name from when a Cree woman long ago stayed on the island south while her husband went off hunting. When the husband did not return on schedule, the woman began to fashion a canoe frame from willows with a view to making a craft she could use to leave the island. Before she was done, however, her husband returned to pick her up. Thereafter, passersby seeing the abandoned willow frame on the shore likened it to a large basket.[74]

Indian Island

As you draw near the Denare Beach bay, you will pass by an island (63L 871617 to 872629) lying just east of the entrance to the bay. Long favoured as a place to live by people of the Peter Ballantyne Cree Nation, the island is popularly known as "Indian Island."

Mary Morin, now of Prince Albert, recalls moving to Indian Island with her husband John in 1945, a year after their marriage, and living there for three years. During their stay, John had logging and mining jobs, while she cooked in a logging camp and also for Harry Moody who ran a small cafe, store, and post office in Denare Beach. The island then had seven houses occupied.

When we arrived here in 1986, the only home left on the island was that of Angelique and Bill Merasty (both since deceased).[75] We already knew of Angelique's reputation as one of the best of the old native birchbark biters—artists who fold thin layers of birch bark and then create intricate symmetrical patterns by biting through the layers—and we were anxious to meet her and discuss her work. However, when we stopped at the Merasty home, we found Angelique was getting ready to go to The Pas. After we had purchased two of her bitings, she excused herself to finish her travel preparations.

We understood Bill was also going to The Pas, but he was quite willing to sit down and talk about the local area, Angelique's work, and his own experiences. Originally born in La Ronge in 1914, Bill went to school at the Sturgeon Landing residential school for six years. He then moved to Pelican Narrows where he worked for the Hudson's Bay Company, Revillon Frères, and the free trader

PHOTO COURTESY GRAHAM GUEST

Angelique and Bill Merasty.

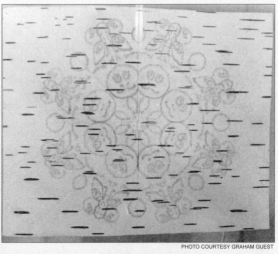

Left: Angelique Merasty creating a birchbark biting, shown above.

Shorty Russick. In 1938 or 1939, he moved to Indian Island and had kept a home here ever since. He also spent much of his time on his trapline at Balsam Lake to the west of Amisk and had as well worked and travelled elsewhere. At various times in the past, he had worked with Harry Moody doing archaeological work. Of particular interest to us, he had a clear memory of being with his wife and Harry at Frog Portage in the 1950s when the Sigurd Olson canoe party came through.

To Denare Beach

From Indian Island, it is a short paddle southeast into Denare Beach's protected bay, where you can stop to end your trip or resupply for the next leg.

-12-

DENARE BEACH TO STURGEON LANDING

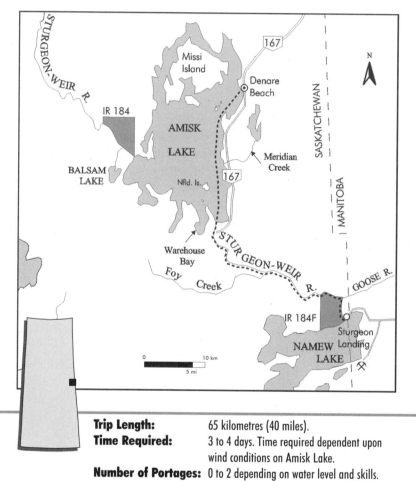

Trip Length:	65 kilometres (40 miles).
Time Required:	3 to 4 days. Time required dependent upon wind conditions on Amisk Lake.
Number of Portages:	0 to 2 depending on water level and skills.
Maps Required:	
1:250,000 Series:	63L Amisk Lake
	63K Cormorant Lake
1:50,000 Series:	63L/9 Denare Beach
	63L/8 Leonard Lake
	63K/5 Goose Lake

ABOUT THE TRIP

From Denare Beach, you will first paddle 27 km (17 mi) southward on Amisk Lake and then 38 km (24 mi) southeast on the Sturgeon-weir River, i.e., the "South Weir." The Amisk Lake leg has some island protection, but it is mainly open to the prevailing winds. It therefore requires good judgment to determine when paddling is safe. The South Weir has frequent rapids and sections of swift current. Most of the rapids can be handled with only modest whitewater skills, but their sheer number make them a challenge. Due to the wind risk on Amisk and the many rapids on the South Weir, we suggest this trip is most suitable for those with advanced canoeing skills.

Upstream travel on the South Weir would be extremely difficult, but it was a fact of life during the fur trade. An upstream trip would certainly provide insight into the voyageur experience. However, we do not recommend such an arduous task, and our route description will assume you are paddling downstream.

The South Weir becomes more difficult in low water and even impassable in extreme low water conditions. An early summer trip should insure good paddling. If you are planning a later trip, it would be useful to make advance inquiries as to the river level.

On Amisk Lake, you can expect to see some boats, but as the lake is large, they tend to be widely dispersed. On the South Weir, the shallow rapids discourage boat travel, so you are not apt to see any marine traffic at all.

Camping is variable. For the first 15 to 20 km (10 to 12 mi) from Denare Beach, the islands along the east shore of Amisk Lake offer some good Shield campsites. On the South Weir, good campsites are harder to find, but some do exist.

Limestone from the Ordovician era is an interesting aspect of the trip. In the southern part of Amisk Lake, the limestone sometimes outcrops in cliffs and often forms beaches of broken rubble. Down the South Weir, you can watch for places where limestone slab makes the river bed as flat as a table top.

There are aboriginal rock paintings at a site at the south end of Amisk Lake. While other such paintings mentioned in this guide occur in the Shield, these paintings are on a limestone cliff.

The head of the South Weir was once the site of a gold rush town called Beaver City. The town is now gone, but it is still possible to find where its buildings once stood above the river.

For most canoeists, the real highlight of this trip will be the many rapids on the South Weir. There are several that require alert manoeuvres, and a couple that call for advanced skills. They provide an excellent chance for canoeists to gain whitewater experience.

STARTING POINTS

The main starting point for this trip is the community of Denare Beach located 425 km (264 mi) northeast of Prince Albert. From Prince Albert, you can reach Denare Beach by travelling 79 km (49 mi) east on Highway 55 to Smeaton, 327 km (203 mi) northeast on Highway 106 (the Hanson Lake Road) to Creighton, and a final 19 km (12 mi) southward on Highway 167. The entire distance is paved.

At Denare Beach, you can start your trip from the protected, north-opening bay in front of the community—possibly launching from a public dock and boat ramp in the vicinity of Angell's Marina. Alternatively, you can drive down Spruce Street to the extreme south end of the community and launch your canoe at a public dock just past a fish packing plant (63L 878597). This latter option will put you south of and already outside of the community's front bay and will thus save you the 3 to 4 km (about 2 mi) of paddling otherwise needed to leave the bay and go around the peninsula forming it.

If you wish to avoid the big lake travel presented by Amisk Lake, you can drive 30 km (19 mi) south from Denare Beach via Highway 167 to the south end of Amisk Lake. Here, you can embark from one of three possible locations: 1) a government campground known locally as "Sandy Beach" (63L 847363), 2) a government picnic area at the southeast side of the entrance to the Sturgeon-weir (1 km west from Sandy Beach) (63L 835361), or 3) a government picnic area at a cul-de-sac where Highway 167 ends at the start of fast water on the Sturgeon-weir (63L 833357). These starting points will reduce the length of your trip by more than 25 km (16 mi).

Denare Beach

Denare Beach, often simply called "Beaver Lake," takes its unusual name from the former provincial Department of Natural Resources. An attractive community, it lies hidden in a secluded bay at the northeast corner of Amisk Lake. It is over 20 km (12 mi) northeast from the track of the old voyageur highway and was never a trading post in the early fur trade era. Nonetheless, a friendly village with many services, it is a good place to start or end a trip. It also makes a good waypoint if you are passing through Amisk Lake on a long trip.

In 1986, we canoed into Denare Beach just as an evening thunderstorm rolled in. Our plan had been to camp at the public campground north of the community. However, pulling into shore early to escape the building waves, we met up with one Roland (Roly) Chretien who invited us up to his place where we could stay the night out of the weather. Roly, as it turned out, was proprietor of "Roly's Store" in Denare Beach and, as suits a town merchant, was a most engaging raconteur. Over a bottle of Governor General's rum at his place and more drinks later at the local hotel bar (which has since burned down), he was able to tell us a good deal about Denare Beach and its residents.

Roly recommended that we speak to an Icelandic couple, Gisli and Lilje Norman, for a first-hand account of Denare Beach's early days. Accordingly, the next day, we visited 91-year-old Gisli and his wife Lilje at their home near the lake. Both were in excellent health and still busy with hobbies as diverse as taxidermy, fossil collecting, and Icelandic geneology.

Local History

Gisli told us that he first came north to commercial fish on Amisk Lake with a younger brother in 1927 after a time spent fishing on Lake Winnipegosis. When they arrived at Amisk, a trapper named Jack Geddes was the only person living at Denare Beach which, at the time, was known as "Sandy Beach." Fishing was good, and Gisli's four-man crew netted almost 40,000 kg (88,000 lb) of fish—mainly whitefish and large trout—in a single season. The profit allowed Gisli to go south and marry Lilje in 1928 and bring her back with him via the South Weir. At first, Gisli and Lilje lived on Vances Island in the centre of the lake. However, soon after, in 1931, present-day Denare Beach got its start when prospector Harry Moody and a partner started a store here. In 1933, Gisli and Lilje moved to what would become Denare Beach—building a home that would last them over a half century.

Around the time the Normans settled at Denare Beach, the community got a boost from a prospecting rush on Amisk Lake. In her book, *Devil in Deerskins*, the adventuresome Anahareo, wife of Grey Owl—who occasionally stayed with the Normans—describes arriving here by solo canoe in 1934 and finding a "claim-staking spree" going on. In

Above: Gisli and Lilje Norman, August 15, 1986.
Left: Grey Owl and Anahareo.

SAB / R-A 22531

the vicinity of the present village, she found "two stores, a fish camp, a mink farm, and a freighting company." At the same time, there was apparently a road or track to nearby Flin Flon since Amisk Lake prospectors were expected to go to the mineral recording office there for licences, etc.[1]

Denare Beach Today

Since the early 1930s, Denare Beach has evolved into a village of about 800 people.[2] In part a resort community, it is also home to people who make their living in the area—often with Hudson Bay Mining & Smelting at Flin Flon—and to more than a hundred members of the Peter Ballanyne Cree Nation having ties to Indian Reserve 184 at the mouth of the West Weir. These PBCN members live mainly in the southern part of the village, and on June 15, 2000, a ceremony at Denare Beach marked the transfer of some of this area to the PBCN as part of its treaty land entitlement. Currently, Mayor Carl Lentowicz—a former RCMP officer with many years of northern experience—oversees the village's affairs.

At Denare Beach, canoeists will find Bayside Store and post office (formerly Roly's), Angell's Marina Motel (marina, rooms, canoes), Rocky View Lodge (rooms, lounge, canoes), Raven's Roost Pub, Alpine convenience store (with gas), restaurants, excellent public swimming beach (centrally located), and a provincial campground (north of Rocky View Lodge). A special attraction is the Northern Gateway Museum on Moody Drive which displays a wide range of artifacts including many found by Harry Moody in his excavation of the Frobisher-Henry post at the mouth of the West Weir. The birchbark bitings of Angelique Merasty are also featured. In the fall of 1999, the museum began construction of a new addition to its existing facility.

Map 12.1   Community of Denare Beach

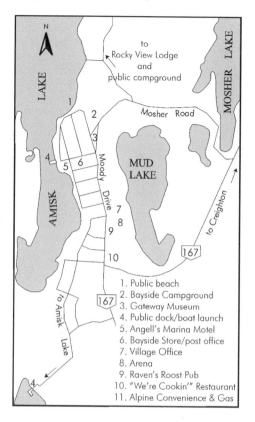

1. Public beach
2. Bayside Campground
3. Gateway Museum
4. Public dock/boat launch
5. Angell's Marina Motel
6. Bayside Store/post office
7. Village Office
8. Arena
9. Raven's Roost Pub
10. "We're Cookin'" Restaurant
11. Alpine Convenience & Gas

To Sturgeon Landing

South on Amisk Lake

Going south on Amisk Lake, you can stay generally close to the east shore and, for the first 18 km (11 mi) out of Denare Beach, take some wind protection from groupings of small islands. The rocky islands are part of what geologists call the "Amisk Group" which—consisting of ancient (nearly 2 billion years old) Precambrian rock of volcanic origin—represents the oldest rock in the region.[3] Besides wind protection, the islands also offer some good bedrock campsites.

You will cross the south boundary of the Precambrian Shield where Meridian Creek runs into Amisk Lake from the east. South from Meridian Creek, any visible bedrock is Ordovician limestone that dates from 505 to 438 million years ago. During the Ordovician Period, much of interior North America was covered by a shallow, equatorial sea that left behind layer upon layer of limestone. Some of the layers exhibit an array of marine fossils, and amateur palaeontologists can make some good finds.[4]

Newfoundland Island

If good weather prevails, you can traverse 4 km (2½ mi) southwest from the last of the Shield islands to Newfoundland Island—known as "Big Island" until 1949, when the provincial government renamed it to salute Newfoundland's entry into confederation.[5]

The northeast shore of Newfoundland Island has a beach of flat limestones backed by a 2 to 3-m-high (6 to 10 ft) limestone wall as multi-layered as a deck of cards (63L 823422).

From Newfoundland Island, you can travel almost due south for 2 km (1¼ mi) to reach an aboriginal rock painting site on the north tip of the peninsula separating Warehouse Bay from the head of the South Weir.

Amisk Lake Rock Paintings

On the northwest side of the peninsula between Warehouse Bay and the South Weir, limestone cliffs up to 8 m (25 ft) high extend back along the shore from the tip of the peninsula for roughly 300 m (330 yd). Some very faded rock paintings occur just to the left (north) of the centre of the cliffs at a point where the cliffs are fronted by a jumble of limestone blocks up to 2 m (6 ft) across. They occupy two small rock faces—each about 1.5 m (5 ft) wide and 50 cm

(20 in) high—stacked one above the other about 2 m (6 ft) above lake level. The faces show white under the protection of an over-hang in an area where the cliffs are mainly orange with lichens (63L 817389).

The upper face has a central figure consisting of a verti-cal rectangle about 25 cm (10 in) high and 10 cm (4 in) wide enclosing a short boomerang shape and showing other marks

Rock painting cliffs at south end of Amisk Lake, August 1986.

on its perimeter. To viewer's lower left of the rectangle, there is an extremely faded "ginger-bread man" shape with a straight line and another hint of pigment above it. Finally, to view-er's right of the rectangle, there is what could be either a thunderbird or a human.

The lower face has three human-like figures near its upper edge. Two of these figures, on either side of the face, are similar to the gingerbread character in the upper face though they might be interpreted as being thunderbirds. They seem to be standing on a connecting ground line of similar age. The third human-like figure stands between the other two at a level where the connecting ground line crosses his waist. His orange-pink coloration seems more recent than that of the other figures, yet the ground line seems to cross over his waist and suggests he may be of older vintage. Below the ground line, there are other small figures which, with the exception of a definite oval shape 10 to 12 cm (4 to 5 in) long, are difficult to make out.

The cliffs surrounding the rock paintings have been subjected to an incredible amount of modern-day graffiti, but the paintings themselves have escaped any overwriting. The main vandalism appears to be some deliberate scratching of the figures on the lower face, particu-larly the centre human-like figure. Natural weathering of these paintings seems to be much faster than with those in the Shield. In 1986, Dean Tait, a local outfitter, told us that twenty years earlier, the paintings had been considerably brighter. And, some of the figures we looked at in 1986 could scarcely be made out when we again saw them in 1996.

Warehouse Bay

The large bay south from the rock paintings takes its name from Hudson's Bay Company freighting operations. Just prior to 1900, the HBC cut a winter road between Cumberland Lake and Amisk Lake to avoid the necessity of having York boats bring freight up the difficult rapids on the South Weir. Horse teams pulling sleighs used the road to haul goods to the south

Map 12.2   The head of the South Weir

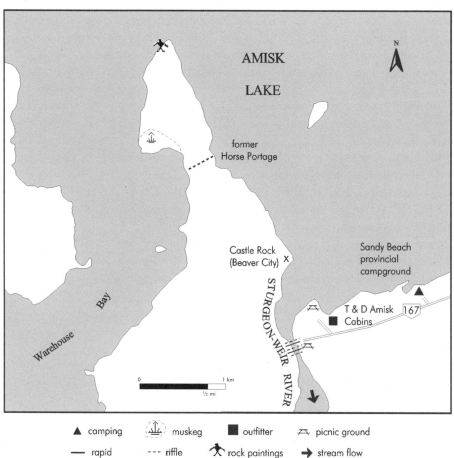

AMISK

LAKE

former
Horse Portage

Castle Rock
(Beaver City) X

Sandy Beach
provincial
campground

T & D Amisk 167
Cabins

Bay

Warehouse

STURGEON-WEIR RIVER

N

0   1 km
½ mi

▲ camping   muskeg   ■ outfitter   picnic ground

— rapid   --- riffle   rock paintings   → stream flow

end of Warehouse Bay, where it was stored in a large warehouse for later distribution by boat.[6]

Gisli Norman told us that the winter road had an extension from the warehouse location to Beaver City at the head of the South Weir. However, presumably before the extension was built, horse teams took freight to Beaver City via a trail which crossed the rock painting peninsula at a narrow spot 1.5 km (1 mi) south from its north tip (63L 822376). The trail was aptly known as "Horse Portage."[7]

Beaver City

Moving down the east side of the rock painting peninsula, you can identify the entrance to the South Weir by a limestone promontory on the west side of the entrance. Covered in orange lichens and rising to a plateau 5 or 6 m (16 or 20 ft) above the water, the promontory is known locally as "Castle Rock."

Between 1914 and 1918, the high ground above Castle Rock was the site of a small-scale boom town known as "Beaver City." After gold claims were first staked northwest of Missi Island in 1913, prospectors, developers, and dreamers flocked to Amisk Lake to strike it rich. Travelling by bush trail or canoe, they arrived at the head of the South Weir and used it as a jumping off point for their explorations.

Beaver City sprang up near Castle Rock to meet the gold rush's demand for services. Bunkhouses and stables were built to accommodate the many teamsters and horses hauling freight. The Hudson's Bay Company and Revillon Frères set up stores. Bill Hayes operated a boarding house, and a Saskatonian named Moore, the "Bannock King," went into business making and selling bannock. The town even had a detachment of the Saskatchewan Provincial Police![8]

Like so many boom towns, Beaver City collapsed almost as quickly as it arose. By 1918, the town was no longer where the action was, and it was all but deserted.[9] A British World War I veteran named Angus McDonald was its last resident. The bachelor McDonald was well-known for keeping as many as twenty dogs, relating both truth and fiction with a straight face, and always helping people out. He remained at Beaver City until World War II when he again served in the armed forces.

A humorous account of Angus McDonald's kindness and wry sense of humour can be found in Anahareo's *Devil in Deerskins*. In the late fall of 1934, after prospecting on Missi Island, Anahareo was travelling south again when she fell ill at Beaver City. While McDonald nursed her back to good health, she learned more about him:

> Angus' place was known as the "half-way" in the days before the railroad was built between The Pas and Flin Flon [1928]. All the machinery and supplies for the mining community had to pass through here on "swings" (horse and sleigh). Angus, in telling the story of how he got into the "hotel" business, said, "Them freighters were too damn lazy to make their own camp, so they used to come and stay here overnight. Sometimes this shack was so crowded you couldn't walk across the floor without stepping on somebody. So, I built a stable—my, I used to feel sorry for the horses, out there in the cold nights. I had plenty of hay for them too, but I told the freighters if they didn't want to get poisoned, they'd better bring their own grub."[10]

When we stopped at Beaver City in 1986, the only structures to be found were an old log cabin (without

a roof) and a kind of cellar built up against a limestone cliff. In the water just off Castle Rock, we also saw what looked to be an old winch crib fitted with a large cast iron gear about 1 m (3 ft) below the surface. It was perhaps used to winch freight up the shore.

The last cabin at Beaver City.

Camping

There is a government campground on the south shore of Amisk Lake, 1.5 km (1 mi) east of Castle Rock, known as Sandy Beach (63L 847363). There are also two government picnic sites nearer the head of the South Weir. The first is on a limestone slab (showing several interesting sea fossils) situated on the east side of the entrance to the river, immediately across from Castle Rock (63L 835361). The second is 500 m (1/3 mi) further south where Highway 167 ends on the east bank of the South Weir (63L 833357). Though the latter two sites are likely meant for picnickers arriving by road, you may want to use one of them for a lunch break. Both are equipped with fire grates and outdoor toilets.

T & D Amisk Cabins

This outfitting camp is on the south shore of Amisk Lake about 300 m (330 yd) southeast from the entrance to the South Weir. Built in 1957 by a man whose surname was Bouteiller, it was bought by Ted Tait in 1964 who passed it on to his son Dean and Dean's wife Bonnie in 1971. In 1992, the Taits sold the camp to Bruce Joa and his wife Janet (sister to Bonnie), and the Joas continue to operate it.

On August 18, 1986, we stopped at T & D and visited with Dean Tait. A big, friendly fellow, he was able to tell us a great deal about the local area. He had some excellent photographs including some of Verlen Kruger and Steve Landick who had passed through a few years before on an epic canoe voyage that took them over 40,000 km (25,000 mi) in three years.

Dean also impressed us with his fish filleting skills. Watching him work, we concluded he had to be one of the best filleters in the north. He told us that the best filleting knife is made by hand grinding an edge onto a hacksaw blade but that it takes hours and hours to work the hard steel.

Early Fur Trade House

The early fur trade journals do not describe any trading posts operating at the head of the South Weir. However, in 1792, Peter Fidler sketched a map showing a house in the general vicinity of T & D Amisk Cabins.[11] Perhaps this was a fishing cabin associated with the Frobisher-Henry post built at the West Weir in 1775. Or maybe it was an actual trading establishment built some years later—possibly built by Montrealers after they abandoned the post built at present-day Sturgeon Landing by Barthélemi Blondeau in 1778.[12] In his little house drawing, (shown on the next page) Fidler does not show a name over the door.

Dean Tait filleting a fish, 1986.

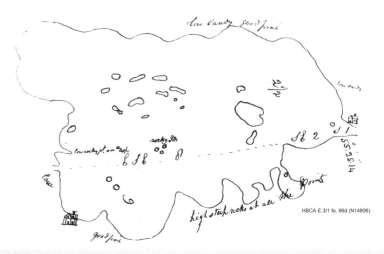

Fidler's sketch of Amisk Lake, made June 25, 1792. The head of the South Weir is shown at far right.

HBCA E.3/1 fo. 66d (N14806)

South Sturgeon-weir River

The Sturgeon-weir's name, which dates to antiquity, originated on the South Weir. When the HBC's Matthew Cocking reached the South Weir on October 3, 1775, en route to relieve Samuel Hearne at Cumberland House, he noted it as a "River where the Indians spear many Sturgeon every Summer."[13] Fifteen years later, while ascending the South Weir, Philip Turnor recorded that he and his party, "came to a rapid called the Nemew-kip-pa-ha-gan [*namîw kipahikan*] or Sturgeon Wear, the Indians frequently daming the river across at this place which is what the river takes its name from."[14]

After Turnor and his men spent a day-and-a-half paddling and wading up the South Weir, Turnor wrote:

> this river is in general very shoal but the water clear so that the stones can be seen though not easeely avoided, the bottom is of lime stone kind and like a honey comb which makes it very bad for the feet and our people led the Canoes about one sixth part of the whole river.[15]

The voyageurs knew the South Weir as *La Rivière Maligne*,[16] roughly meaning "the bad river," because of the tremendous effort it took to work canoes or York boats up the current. Although the Turnor party paddled and waded up the South Weir in 1790, voyageurs commonly used poles to go up the river. With some humility, Robert Hood left an account of ascending the river with poles on June 14, 1820:

> The Sturgeon River is justly called by the Canadians La Riviére Maligne, from its numerous and dangerous rapids. Against the strength of a rapid it is impossible to effect any progress by paddling, and the canoes are tracked, or if the bank will not admit of it, propelled with poles, in the management of which the Canadians shew great dexterity. Their simultaneous motions were strongly contrasted with the awkward confusion of the inexperienced Englishmen, deafened by the torrent, who sustained the blame of every accident which occurred.[17]

Two months after Hood, on August 27, 1820, George Simpson also went up the South Weir. His August 27 journal entry begins, "Started at day break and proceeded up Rivierre Mal-in, very appropriately named as it is a continual Rapid for about thirty miles, the poles in use nearly the whole way."[18]

Poling on the South Weir continued well into the twentieth century. Gisli Norman, who first went up the river in 1927, told us that he and a partner could take a canoe up all the South Weir rapids using ten-foot poles cut for the purpose. He said that poling was easy to catch on to though he was never able to match skills with the Indians who could even pole up the South Weir solo.

Down the South Weir

Fortunately, in a downstream direction, the South Weir is not a bad river at all. Its many rapids and sections of fast water produce a vertical drop of about 30 m (100 ft), but the drop is a gradual one spaced over the river's 38-km (23-mi) length—an almost ideal gradient for downstream paddling. Excepting Crooked Rapids and Rat Rapids, none of the rapids requires more than an alert lookout and basic whitewater skills.

The sheer number of rapids would make a narrative-style description of them confusing. We will therefore rely mainly on maps to illustrate where rapids or strong currents occur. As always, keep in mind that changing water levels may turn swift current into rapids and vice versa.

Old Bridge

About 500 m (¹/₃ mi) down from the South Weir's wide, upstream entrance, the river narrows and fast water begins.[19] About 80 m (88 yd) further downstream, Highway 167 comes to a dead end on river left. As you pass the highway, you may see vestiges of an old wooden bridge left over from a former winter road. The road's origins go back to 1947 when the citizens of Creighton and Flin Flon formed the Nipawin Winter Road Association in an effort to establish a road link to the south via Nipawin. After ten years of planning and work, a winter road was finally completed with the South Weir bridge being opened for traffic on November 24, 1957. Soon after, however, the new road's importance was eclipsed by the Saskatchewan government's decision to build the all-weather Hanson Lake Road which opened in the early 1960s. When ice later took out the South Weir bridge, there was no practical reason to replace it.

First Rapids

As noted, swift current begins about 80 m (88 yd) upstream from where Highway 167 reaches the South Weir. As you pass the highway, you will encounter minor rapids known in Cree as *nistam pâwistik*, or "first rapids," which continue for about 500 m (¹/₃ mi). The best course through them appears to be down river centre. Near the bottom of the rapids, you will have to avoid some bad rocks strewn across the width of the channel.

Crooked Rapids

Crooked Rapids, or *kâ-wâwâkâk pâwistik* in Cree, are incorrectly located on both Maps 63L and 63L/8. They are in fact less than 3 km (2 mi) south from First Rapids—about 3 km (2 mi) upstream from where the maps show them to be.

The rapids, which extend for just over 1 km (¹/₃ mi), begin with a stony riffle. Here, there is an almost continuous line of

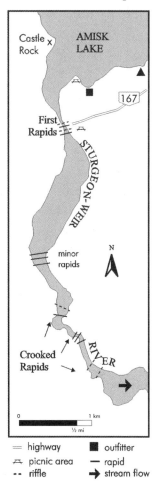

Map 12.3
From head of South Weir
to below Crooked Rapids

stones across the river channel. The water over the stones is very shallow, but there is a navigable passageway near the river left shore.

Less than 100 m (110 yd) below the stony riffle, a short rapid occurs where the river turns 90 degrees left. A broad limestone table covered by only a few centimetres (or inches) of water extends three-quarters of the way across the river from the river right shore. However, you will again find a reasonable passageway on river left.

Below the limestone table rapid, the river narrows and runs very swiftly southeast for 300 m (330 yd). Rapids then begin and continue for about 150 m (165 yd) in which distance the river bends right to run south-southeast. These rapids do not have particularly large waves, but they are very swift and have many bad rocks to avoid. While they can be run on a course more or less down river centre, they do call for advanced whitewater skills.

If you choose not to run the 150-m (165-yd) rapids, you may wish to wade your canoe down the shore. Another option would be to cut into the woods at a suitable spot on the west shore and make use a very old bush road—possibly dating back to the Beaver City era—that

Map 12.4   Below Crooked Rapids (63L 838323 to 63L 912278)

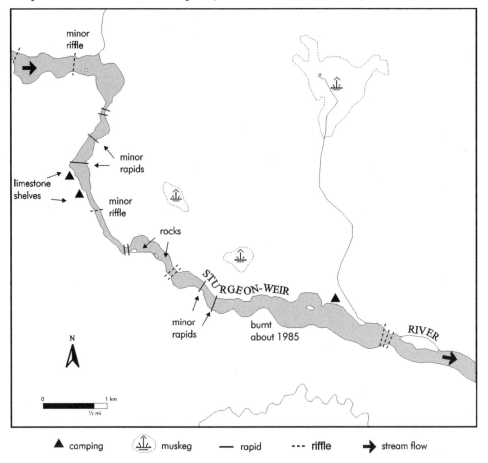

runs parallel to the river about 40 m (44 yd) inland. This road has some windfall, but it follows high ground here and is in reasonable condition.[20]

It may be that the old bush road overlies an older portage since Philip Turnor, ascending the rapids on September 16, 1790, wrote, "and came to a fall with a carring place 150 yards over on south side but the water being favourable led the Canoes on north side."[21]

Below the 150-m (165-yd) rapids, there is swift water for perhaps 300 m (330 yd) and then a final section of riffles or minor rapids that runs for about 150 m (165 yd). This final section has swift current and a great many rocks. The best course is down river centre or to the right of centre since there are rock fields on river left. In low water, some wading may be necessary to avoid hangups.

Camping

About 3 km (2 mi) downstream from Crooked Rapids, there is good camping on a flat limestone shelf on the river right shore. The shelf is about 20 m (65 ft) wide and elevated about 50 cm (20 in) above the water. There is room for three or four tents in the spruce woods back from the shelf (63L 848306).

There is a second good campsite on the river right shore about 250 m (270 yd) downstream from the first. Again, the campsite is fronted by a limestone shelf though the shelf here is cracked by wide fissures. This site has plenty of room for tents in a grassy clearing back from the shore, so it would suit larger parties (63L 849304).

It is likely that one of the limestone shelf campsites is where George Simpson camped on July 27, 1828, en route from York Factory to the Pacific with two light canoes manned by nine men apiece. Evidence of this comes from Simpson's companion, Archibald McDonald, who wrote that Simpson's party camped at "Sturgeon Rock" from where they travelled two hours the next morning to reach Amisk Lake.

A quote from McDonald gives some insight into what it was like to travel with the hard-driving Simpson. After the party had come from Cumberland House to Sturgeon Rock in a single day, McDonald wrote:

> Sunday, 27th.—Here [Cumberland House] took in, for the trip, each canoe a bag of common pemmican, and for the mess, a bag of dried meat (50 lbs.,) and 80 buffalo tongues, besides old and new potatoes, eggs, candles, and 4 gallons of spirits for the men. Got under weigh at half-past three, with fair weather, and a touch up of a favorite song chorused by both canoes. Breakfasted on one of the islands. Here the guide expressed a desire to have a better division of the men in favor of his own canoe, upon which, the Governor, in fairness to both, directed that they should be called out one by one by the two former, which was done, but ultimately placed both canoes nearly as they stood before the change made on the 17th. Entered *Riviere Maligne* about noon. On Rat Portage, passed two Indian lodges from Rat country; offered us a little dried meat which we declined, but gave them a dram and a little tobacco. Encamped on Sturgeon Rock below Beaver Lake. Water tolerably good in this river.[22]

Old Burn

Down from the limestone shelf campsites, the South Weir continues with more interruptions from minor rapids and riffles for another 3 km (2 mi). Then, after a final strong riffle, the river slows considerably. Here, and indeed for the next 8 km (5 mi) to the right margin of Map 63L/8, it is possible to paddle either up or downstream quite easily.

About 500 m (⅓ mi) down from where the river slows, you will come to a stand of small black spruce on the south shore which has been burnt off in a forest fire. The burn, which extends for about a kilometre along the shore, appeared fairly recent when we saw it in 1986.

At the downstream end of the burn, you will see a willowy island in the channel and, just downstream of it, a poplar-covered point on the north (river left) shore. In the lee of the point, there is a campsite left behind by firefighters (63L 889288). To reach the camp, it is necessary to climb a 2-m (6-ft) clay bank, but you will then find a good, spacious clearing beneath some towering spruce. The site is of particular value since there are few other developed campsites in the vicinity.

Down from Foy Creek

Just after Foy Creek joins the South Weir on river right, the river narrows with a resulting increase in current. However, over the next 2 km (1¼ mi), the current remains slow enough to permit upstream paddling.

One km (⅔ mi) down from Foy Creek, there is an old trapping cabin up from a grassy slope on river left. Made from small, unpeeled spruce logs, it is in a state of general disrepair.

The Weir Section

Crossing onto either Map 63K or 63K/5, you will find that the current again increases and that, within 1 km (⅔ mi), another section of minor rapids and riffles begins.

Map 12.5   Through the "Weir Section" (63L 905280 to 63K 100223)

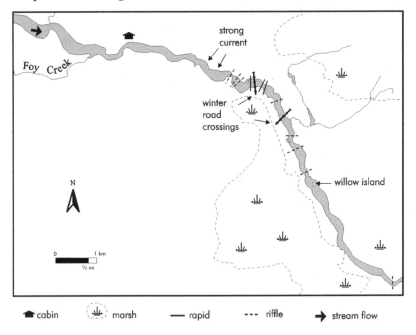

This section of rapids and riffles is significant because, according to Philip Turnor and Peter Fidler, it was at a particular place here that Indians built the sturgeon weir that gave the river its name. Going downstream on June 26, 1792, Peter Fidler wrote:

> now commences the middle & shoalest rapids of any in the whole river—near SE 1 1/2 in which are 5 rapids, & come to an open place in the river, about 300 yards wide, above this many being narrower—a fine barren ground bank on the North side, & steep, here is a dam of Stones built all across the river, to stop the Sturgeon, where a fishing weir was used annually some years back to be kept in repair to catch the Sturgeon before the Smallpox in 1781—from this spot the river derives its name. This is now a very bad shoal part to pass with the Canoes...[23]

We have not searched for or found any sign of the old weir, but you may perhaps spy some tell-tale rock debris still left from days past.

In 1986, the South Weir was not cut by any roads. Now, however, in the weir section, you will see where two wide winter roads—apparently logging roads—now cross the river about 1 km (²/₃ mi) apart from each other. More roads can be expected as a result of a 1999 decision of the provincial government to promote wide-scale logging in the northern boreal forest.

Near the end of the weir section, about 2.5 km (1½ mi) from its start, there is a 200-m-long (220-yd) island wooded with spruce, poplar, and birch. Down the river left side of this island, there is only a 5-m-wide (16-ft) channel. In the provincial canoeing booklet for the South Weir, *Canoe Trip #44*, Peter Gregg recommends the narrow channel as a navigable option in high water.[24] In 1986, we thought it was too narrow for a safe downstream run, but we found its flat limestone bottom was excellent for upstream wading.

Map 12.6   From below "Weir Section" to just above Rat Rapids (63K 100223 to 63K 160222)

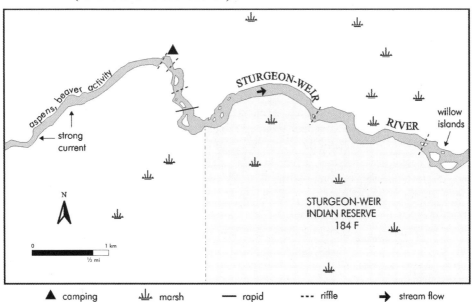

Down from the Weir Section

Below the wooded island, the river once more settles down and runs southeast for 4 km (2½ mi). It then comes to a tiny riffle where it bends to run northeast (63K 098222). Over the next 2.5 km (1½ mi), the channel narrows to about 60 m (66 yd) and the current strengthens, but there are still no rapids. You will have a good chance here to relax and enjoy the shore greenery. In the northeast run, the south bank is well-wooded with spruce, aspen, and the odd birch. The north bank is wooded mainly with aspen which have seen a great deal of beaver activity in recent years.

After its northeast run, the river bends sharply to the right to run south-southeast for 1 km (²/₃ mi), and riffles and minor rapids again occur. At the top of the bend, a limestone shelf about 30 m (100 ft) wide on river left would serve as a lunch spot or campsite for one or two tents (63K 121234). A quiet eddy on the downstream side of the shelf has good walleye fishing.

About 1 km (²/₃ mi) down from the limestone shelf, the river again bends sharply to run east-northeast. At this bend, you will pass the west boundary of Sturgeon Weir Indian Reserve 184F which was originally set aside for the Peter Ballantyne Cree Nation on May 24, 1925, and later augmented with small additions.[25] From here to Sturgeon Landing, all the land on the river right shore lies within the Reserve boundaries.

Rat Rapids

These rapids, known in Cree as *wacasko-pâwistik*, meaning "muskrat rapids,"[26] occur just 500 m (¹/₃ mi) before the South Weir makes a 90-degree right turn to begin its final run south to Sturgeon Landing. Though they are not named on either Map 63K or 63K/5, they are serious Class 2+ rapids which should be run only by those with strongly advanced whitewater skills.

The rapids begin immediately after the river jogs in an elbow turn to the right. Here, a willowy island about 100 m (110 yd) long runs parallel to the river left shore. The main current flows down a channel about 120 m (130 yd) wide on the river right side of the island. Much of it passes over a dangerous limestone ledge about 50 cm (20 in) high that extends from the top of the willowy island to within 20 m (22 yd) of the river right shore. Down from the ledge, there are minor rapids and rocks.

If water levels are suitable and you decide to run Rat Rapids, you can do so via a navigable passage about 10 m (30 ft) off the river right shore which will take you past the limestone ledge. Keep in mind, however, that once past the

Map 12.7
South Weir from Rat Portage to Sturgeon Landing

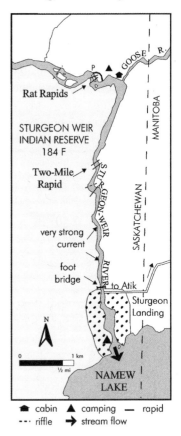

ledge, you will still have to deal with about 100 m (110 yd) of rapids that have some large submerged rocks to avoid—especially near their lower end.

On the river left side of the willowy island, there is a narrow channel which, at least at higher water levels, handles a considerable volume of water. However, its fast current and rocky rapids make it unnavigable for canoes.

We recommend that canoeists deal with Rat Rapids by portaging on river left.

Rat Portage (± 180 m / 195 yd)

To locate this portage's upstream landing, you can watch for a grassy slope on river left almost directly across from the elbow bend on river right. If you then continue down the shore from the slope for about 30 m (33 yd), to a point 75 m (82 yd) or so above the rapids, you will find the landing notch at an indistinct break in the shore willows and alders.

There is a trail leading up from the grassy slope to an old bush road that runs about 75 m (82 yd) inland from and roughly parallel to the portage. The bush road has likely been used as a portage by canoeists, but it is not the best since it swings away from the downstream landing.

The actual portage is overgrown and wet at its upstream end. It is then considerably better for the last 100 m (110 yd) where the vegetation is worn away to expose a flat limestone base. A lack of traffic in recent years has allowed brush to encroach on the pathway, but it remains in good general condition.

The downstream landing is at a 1-m-high (3-ft) shelf of limestone about 75 m (82 yd) down from shallow rapids on the river left side of the willowy island. It is easy to reach the water using natural steps in the limestone shelf.

A highlight of the portage is an expansive limestone table lying east from the downstream landing. The table makes an excellent campsite and is large enough to accommodate any number of paddlers. Should you decide to camp here, you can use any free time searching for fossils in the limestone or fishing for pike and walleye below the rapids.

The portage was extremely important during the fur trade as a rendezvous point. Travellers on the main voyageur highway could meet those from the Goose River, which enters the South Weir just 400 m (440 yd) below Rat Portage. When Philip Turnor was here in September 1790, he met Indians and also Robert Thompson and Patrick Small of the North West Company. His journal entries read:

> 14th Tuesday … came to a fall [Rat Rapids] carried 195 yards on north side good carrying place and put up at 9 1/2 AM found two Canadians at this place waiting for the Canoes coming up with goods one of them a Mr Tompson master of a settlement near the lower part of Grass river in the Port Nelson track, and five tents of Indians some belonging to Port Nelson river and others to the northward towards Churchill river all of them was very desireous to have us go to their country and make no doubt but either way would have answered in point of trade, traded some provisions

> … at 4 PM Mr Paterick Small [on his way to Île-à-la-Crosse] arrived with Ten Canoes of goods and put up by the side of us. Wind Westerly light breeze and clear

> 15th Wednesday 7 1/4 AM got underway our Indian pilot in company. left Mr Small settling goods for Mr Tompson to return to the Port Nelson track with…[27]

Goose River and the Rat Country

Just below Rat Portage, the Goose River empties into the South Weir from the northeast. About 40 m (44 yd) wide at its mouth, the Goose is not a large river. However, during the fur trade, when it was also known as the "Gray Goose River"[28] and the "Rat River,"[29] it was an important waterway.

In the century before any fur trade posts were built inland in northern Saskatchewan, the Goose River was the start of a canoe route commonly known as the "Upper Track" (Turnor's "Port Nelson track") that Indians used to reach York Factory on Hudson Bay. The route went up the Goose, across Cranberry Portage, and then down the Grass River.[30] Samuel Hearne made use of this track and came down the Goose River in 1774 on his way inland from York Factory to establish Cumberland House.[31] It was not until after 1774 that the track via Lake Winnipeg and the Hayes River became the main route to York Factory.

The Goose River was also used by traders to reach an area known as the "Muskrat Country," the "Rat Country," or simply "Les Rats" which lay east of the Sturgeon-weir River and between the Churchill and Nelson Rivers. In the late 1700s, the Rat Country was only sparsely populated—David Thompson calculated that in the years following the 1782 smallpox epidemic, there was only one soul for every 35 square miles—but its Cree inhabitants generated enough fur to attract stiff competition between the Hudson's Bay Company and the North West Company.[32]

Two-Mile Rapid

South from Goose River's inflow, the South Weir has only a modest current for 1.5 km (1 mi). There is then a minor rapid known locally as "Two-Mile Rapid" which is best run on river right. The rapid is not more than 100 m (110 yd) long and simply takes its name from being two miles distant from Sturgeon Landing. Traditionally, people would stop at Two-Mile for a lunch after having worked their way up all the fast current and minor rapids above Sturgeon Landing.

"Two-Mile Rapid," September 1992.

To Sturgeon Landing

About 500 m (⅓ mi) down from Two-Mile Rapid, and after an intervening section of riffles, there is another, last rapid that extends for about 100 m (110 yd) just before the river bends right. This rapid has small to medium-sized waves and many submerged rocks. The best course down is on river left to the left side of two low islets of limestone.

Below the last rapid, the river narrows and picks up speed. Indeed, riffles and whirlpools are almost continuous in the final 2.5 km (1½ mi) to Sturgeon Landing. With help from the swift current, you will soon arrive in the community.

-13-

STURGEON LANDING TO CUMBERLAND HOUSE

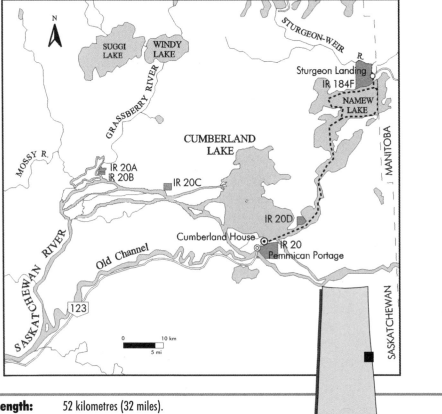

Trip Length:	52 kilometres (32 miles).
# of Portages:	None.
Time Required:	2 to 3 days. Time required will depend on wind conditions on Namew Lake.
Maps Required:	
1:250,000 Series:	63K Cormorant Lake
	63L Amisk Lake
	63E Pasquia Hills
1:50,000 Series:	63K/5 Goose Lake
	63K/4 Namew Lake
	63L/1 Archibald Lake
	63E/16 Cumberland House

ABOUT THE TRIP

Without any route variations, this trip would be rather impractical given the shuttle arrangements involved. It does, however, make a suitable conclusion to a longer trip on the voyageur highway. It might also be paddled in ways that reduce shuttle distances. For example, since the route has no current to speak of, an out and back trip could be made from either Sturgeon Landing or Cumberland House. It would also be practical to start at Sturgeon Landing and follow the voyageur highway through to The Pas.[1]

Since this trip is all flat water, with much of it having good wind protection, this is a suitable trip for canoeists with modest skills. The one caution is that Namew and Cumberland Lakes are big lakes that can be subject to bad winds. Especially in the case of Namew, mature judgment is called for in determining when it is safe to venture forward.

The route lies south of the Shield in a region noted for outcrops of Ordovician limestone—rock formed 500 to 450 million years ago beneath a shallow, tropical sea. The south shore of Namew Lake has especially interesting limestone cliffs. And in many places, flat limestone shelves along the shore provide good campsites.

A highlight of this trip is the starting point, Sturgeon Landing. A very pretty community, it has an interesting history as a fur trade post site, as a transfer point for ore hauling in the early 1900s, and as the location of a major residential school. Should you be windbound at Sturgeon Landing, there is much to explore.

An even greater highlight, especially from a fur trade perspective, is the end point, Cumberland House. Chosen by Samuel Hearne as the Hudson's Bay Company's first inland trading post, Cumberland House's strategic location made it a major hub of the North-West fur trade. It has survived to become the oldest community in Saskatchewan.

STARTING POINT

The starting point for this trip is the community of Sturgeon Landing situated northeast of Prince Albert. Somewhat off the beaten track, Sturgeon Landing is only accessible by road through Manitoba—via either Flin Flon or The Pas. From Flin Flon, you can reach Sturgeon Landing by travelling 98 km (61 mi) south on paved Highway 10 to the old railway siding of Atik and then 32 km (20 mi) west on a secondary gravel road. From The Pas, it is 58 km (36 mi) north on Highway 10 to Atik and then 32 km (20 mi) west.

At Sturgeon Landing, you can turn south on East Avenue, the main road through the community, and follow it past Sturgeon Landing Outfitters to where it ends at a public boat launch on the east side of the mouth of the Sturgeon-weir River. You can embark from the vicinity of the boat launch.

Community of Sturgeon Landing

Sturgeon Landing is a picturesque community. Divided by the swift-flowing Sturgeon-weir, it has been built on flat tablelands bordering both sides of the river mouth. The part of the community east of the river is accessible by road. It has an outfitting camp and store, as well as a school, an RCMP patrol trailer, and a few homes. The part west of the river—that marked as Indian Reserve 184F on Maps 63K and 63K/5—has only residential homes. The two parts of the community are joined by an unusual steel suspension bridge designed for pedestrian traffic only.

Fur Trade History

Sturgeon Landing was the site of a very early trading post. When Philip Turnor (making his first ever trip into the North-West) arrived at present-day Sturgeon Landing on October 10, 1778, he noted: "we found a Canoe belonging to Blondeaux a Canadian Trader, six men belongs to the Canoe which were building a House to Winter, there was one Tent of Indians with them."[2]

Though "Blondeaux"—Barthélemi Blondeau—actually spent the winter of 1778–79 on the North Saskatchewan just upstream from present-day Prince Albert,[3] his men at Sturgeon Landing had a successful season. In the spring of 1779, Turnor reported:

> . . . the Canoe which wintered in Pine Island Lake [Namew and Cumberland Lakes] has got Eleven Packs of Furs of 85lb or 90lb Wt ea consisting of Catts Beaver & Martins which the Honourable Companys Servants would have got all them Skins had there been men at Cumberland House to have sent to Tent by them as most of the Indians which they got the Furrs from was in debt to the Honourable Company and would not have had the impudence to have traded with the Canadians.[4]

On June 26, 1792, Peter Fidler noted "an old Canadian House here, but abandoned some years back—when they removed to the Beaver Lake." In an accompanying sketch, he marked the location of the old Blondeau post on the river right bank at the Sturgeon-weir's mouth.[5]

While we do not know of other early trading posts at Sturgeon Landing, its favourable location no doubt invited trading activity from time to time. However, since the trading centre of Cumberland House could be reached in a single day by either canoe or dog team, it is likely that any operations at Sturgeon Landing were small and temporary in nature.

HBCA E.3/1 fo. 68 (N14807)

Detail of Peter Fidler's sketch of the mouth of the South Weir and the Blondeau house.

Ore Haul Transfer Point

Sturgeon Landing saw a sudden burst of activity during World War I after a small but rich body of copper ore—some of it averaging over 20 percent copper—was discovered in 1915 just south of present-day Flin Flon, Manitoba. With war-time copper prices at twenty-six cents a pound, the discovery was developed and named the "Mandy Mine" (after the wife of one of the prospectors making the initial find).

Once ore was being mined, the challenge was to transport it to where it could be smelted. Quickly, a costly but workable system was put in place. Starting in the winter of 1916–17, mine ore was first loaded onto

Loading Mandy ore onto barges at Sturgeon Landing.

horse-drawn sleighs and taken over a winter road to Sturgeon Landing where it was stockpiled. When summer came, the ore was loaded onto barges which were then moved by steamboat through to Cumberland House and The Pas. At The Pas, the ore was transferred to trains which hauled it to smelters at Trail, British Columbia.

The Mandy Mine transport system was refined somewhat with the addition of steam tugs used to move ore from the mine to the south end of Athapapuskow Lake. This shortened the distance that ore had to be moved by winter road. Nonetheless, horse teams and sleighs were still needed to get ore all the way to Sturgeon Landing. In the winter of 1918–19, a total of 300 teams were hauling ore.[6]

The labour-intensive nature of the ore hauling kept Sturgeon Landing bustling. Horse barns, hotels, stores, and even a pool room sprang up. In 1918, Bill Hayes, who had been at Beaver City, moved to Sturgeon Landing and set up a store where a fine log home built by outfitter Roger Smith now stands. (The grave of Hayes's daughter Gwen, who died of poison at age six in 1924, can be seen in the community's older cemetery east of the river.) Another store was built by the American free trader Del Simons on the present-day elementary school site.

The World War I armistice brought lower copper prices and an end to the Mandy Mine. In 1920, the last mine ore was transported to The Pas, and Sturgeon Landing became a much quieter place. Even today, however, some signs of the Mandy Mine heyday still linger. The old haul road remains as a rough track running north along the east shore of the Sturgeon-weir and then along the south shore of the Goose River. In Sturgeon Landing, on the Sturgeon-weir's east bank, a rusty chain anchored in the earth marks where barges were tied up for loading from a stockpile. And, across on the west side of the river, a bare area of stained gravel marks where ore was also stockpiled.

Residential School Days

Sturgeon Landing did not stay quiet for long after the Mandy Mine shutdown. In 1926, Oblate priests and brothers, along with nuns from the Sisters of St. Joseph out of St-Hyacinthe, Quebec, opened a residential school in the community to teach girls and boys, both Cree and Dene, from northern Manitoba and Saskatchewan. Built on the west side of the Sturgeon-weir, it eventually accommodated well over 200 students and offered English instruction (and some French) up to grade eight.

The residential school was no ordinary school. It was a highly organized, self-sufficient operation complete with livestock, crops, gardens, sawmill and planer, blacksmith shop, shoe repair shop, and more. While nuns coordinated domestic tasks, Oblate brothers handled outdoor work with help from men hired from the community and the students themselves. Agricultural activities were particularly impressive. The school kept horses, pigs, chickens, and as many as one hundred cattle for meat and dairy products. Extensive gardens produced enough vegetables for all the school staff and students. Produce was overwintered in extensive root cellars. Interestingly, to help with communications, the school kept homing pigeons to ferry important messages to and from The Pas.

In early September 1952, mission staff began work on replacing the water tank that stood above the school in order to supply it with water pumped from the river. A local man started by using a hacksaw to cut away bolts securing the tank tower to its base. To speed up the work, one of the Oblate brothers arrived with a cutting torch and took over the task. Unfortunately, sparks from the torch fell into the school's generator room below and ignited a fuel source there. Within minutes, the whole school was ablaze. Everyone escaped safely,

PHOTO COURTESY JOHN AND MARY MORIN

The residential school when intact (left) and when ablaze in 1952 (below).

but the school was soon reduced to ashes. As the smoke cleared, students were relocated to The Pas. The Oblates then decided that rebuilding a school at Sturgeon Landing would not be practical since the community was still without road access and too cut off from the modern world.

For young students, especially those from far distant traplines, the residential school must have brought times of extreme

PHOTO COURTESY JOHN AND MARY MORIN

loneliness and hurt.[7] However, according to former students Louis Jobb and John Morin, there were also good times, and no child ever went hungry. While discipline was strict and students were kept busy, school staff were not abusive by the standards of the day.

John Morin spent eight years—from 1934 onward—at the residential school. He clearly remembers Brother Antoine from Germany, a rotund man with a Santa Claus beard, who ran the school shoe repair shop and was always quick to laugh as he patched the children's moccasins. Similarly, he fondly recalls an aged Oblate father who ran a small trapline with help from the older boys. The father's fur money all went to buy candy and Christmas presents for the children.

Nowadays, the residential school's green meadows can still be seen on both sides of the Sturgeon-weir. In a meadow on the west shore, the school's concrete basement is hidden by a screen of carraganas and maples gone wild. The basement once included a generator room, boiler room, student dining room and staff dining room (both to the south), kitchen, bakery, and separate washrooms for girls and boys. Exploring these rooms, one can well imagine the clatter, chatter, and reprimands of mealtimes so long ago.

Sturgeon Landing Today

After the residential school burned down, Sturgeon Landing continued as a mainly Cree community with as many as two hundred residents. However, in recent years, there has been out-migration—largely to Cumberland House and The Pas. When we stopped here in 1986, the population was down to about one hundred, and it has since dwindled to only a few homes divided between the east and west sides of the river. Those who remain speak either the *th*-dialect Cree of the Peter Ballantyne Cree Nation or the *n*-dialect Swampy Cree of Cumberland House.

Though the population of Sturgeon Landing may be at a low ebb, the Peter Ballantyne Cree Nation main-tains an extensive land base here. Indian Reserve 184F on the west side of the river was initially created in 1925 when

Map 13.1   Community of Sturgeon Landing

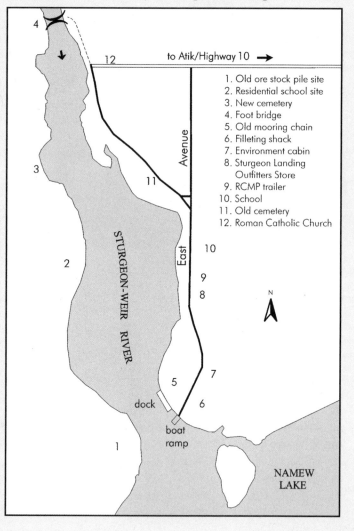

1. Old ore stock pile site
2. Residential school site
3. New cemetery
4. Foot bridge
5. Old mooring chain
6. Filleting shack
7. Environment cabin
8. Sturgeon Landing Outfitters Store
9. RCMP trailer
10. School
11. Old cemetery
12. Roman Catholic Church

5,538 acres were transferred to the First Nation. Smaller parcels were added to 184F in 1927 and 1969. More recently, in an effort to meet PBCN'S treaty land entitlement, much of the Sturgeon Landing community lying east of the Sturgeon-weir River has been made part of the reserve.[8]

With its low population, Sturgeon Landing lacks the services of larger communities. The community does have a grass airstrip (on a residential school meadow east of the river), a Roman Catholic church, a community hall (in poor condition), an elementary school, an outfitting camp, an RCMP patrol trailer (used on visits by the Creighton RCMP), a Saskatchewan Environment patrol cabin, and a government boat ramp and dock.

The outfitting camp, Sturgeon Landing Outfitters, situated between the RCMP patrol trailer and the Resources patrol cabin, is the community's main enterprise. Its origins can be traced back to the 1950s when Medric Poirier came to Sturgeon Landing and started a store north of the present camp store. Poirier then sold out to Bob Gale who in turn sold to Roger Smith in 1972. In Roger Smith's hands, the camp developed to have a store, cabins, campsites, and rental fishing boats.

Roger Smith eventually transferred the camp to current owner Jim Metz in 1997. Originally from Florida, Jim first came to the camp as an eleven-year-old in the early 1970s when his grandfather brought him north on a fishing trip. He came back in subsequent years, and in about 1973, still in his early teens, he started working for Roger Smith on a seasonal basis doing camp chores. When he finally purchased the camp, Jim was well acquainted with its operation.

The present camp store is an old building. In about 1975, it was moved during winter to its present site from the west side of the river where it had been part of the mission school complex. When it belonged to the mission school, it had a blacksmith shop on its main floor and Brother Antoine's shoe repair shop upstairs. Nowadays, as a store, it offers canoeists basic groceries and necessities. It is also the most practical place to find a telephone.

Namew Lake

Namew Lake is a big lake. By the most direct route between Sturgeon Landing and Whitey Narrows to the southwest, it accounts for 27 km (17 mi) of the old voyageur highway—fully half the distance between Sturgeon Landing and Cumberland House. In reality, the distance by canoe is even further since the direct route requires a long traverse open to the northwest wind. The traverse is much too dangerous for canoes, so a longer route coasting either the north shore or the east and south shores—adding perhaps 7 or 8 km (4 or 5 mi) of travel—is necessary.

When the first white fur traders arrived, they considered present-day Namew and Cumberland lakes and their connecting waters to be a single lake. Translating the Cree names for this lake, they knew it as either "Sturgeon Lake" or "Pine Island Lake" (also, more correctly, "Spruce Island Lake"). Soon, however, they began to recognize the lake as two separate lakes. They then restricted the Sturgeon name to the water east and north of Cumberland House and the Pine Island name to present-day Cumberland Lake.[9]

The lake sturgeon, or namîw, from which the lake takes its name, is a primitive bottom feeding fish having a long body covered with five rows of horny plates and a shark-like tail. It is slow-growing and requires fifteen or more years to reach sexual maturity. But it lives a long time, and with some specimens known to weigh over 68 kg (150 lb), it is Saskatchewan's largest fish. At one time, it was found throughout Namew Lake and up the Sturgeon-weir River

Limestone cliffs on south shore of Namew Lake, August 1986.

as far as Spruce Rapids. However, over the years, demand for its highly valued flesh and roe has caused a depletion of its stocks. While it may still occur accidentally in Namew, its Saskatchewan territory is now reduced to Cumberland Lake, the Saskatchewan River, and the Churchill River below Kettle Falls.[10]

Setting out on Namew Lake, you will find extensive cliffs of Ordovician limestone. About 4 km (2½ mi) south-southeast from Sturgeon Landing, the north side of Sturgeon Point has cliffs 10 to 12 m (30 to 40 ft) in height. Further south, more cliffs, averaging 4 to 6 m (13 to 20 ft) in height, range for 20 km (12 mi) along Namew's main south shore. Splotched with orange and black lichens, the vertical cliffs give a colourful and picturesque border to the lake.

The limestone cliffs offer good camping possibilities. The south shore cliffs are frequently fronted by flat limestone slabs where canoes can be pulled up and unloaded. Room for tents can be found on the thinly wooded tableland above the cliffs. Our one caution is that the south cliffs are exposed to the prevailing winds, and care must be taken to select a spot that offers adequate protection from a prolonged blow.

In 1986, we found a new nickel mine being built by Hudson Bay Mining and Smelting on the south shore of Namew Lake just 2 km (1¼ mi) east of the Manitoba border (63K 190108). When we talked to the workers on the site, we learned that the ore body to be mined was actually beneath Namew Lake. The mine's headframe was then half-built and a shaft had been sunk to about 200 m (650 ft), but work was being slowed by shaft flooding. Subsequent to our visit, we learned that the mine was finally commissioned on November 18, 1988, and remained in production until late October 1993.

Coffee and Tea Points to Cross Bay

Namew Lake's western shore is broken by a major peninsula which reaches eastward into the lake. The canoe track to Cumberland House passes south of this peninsula through a broad narrows about 2 km (1¼ mi) in breadth. The point on the northwest side of the entrance to the narrows is known locally as "Coffee Point" (63K 079117), while the point immediately opposite on the southeast shore is known as "Tea Point" (63K 095092).

Southwest from Tea Point, the cliffs of the southerly shore drop away, but limestone continues to outcrop in places. A noteworthy outcrop occurs about 4 km (2½ mi) southwest from Tea Point at the northern tip of a thumb-like peninsula jutting north from the main shore (63K 065068). Here, a broad limestone shelf about 1 m (3 ft) high runs along the west shore of the peninsula for over 100 m (110 yd). Then 5 to 10 m (20 to 30 ft) back from the shore, this shelf steps up 1 m (3 ft) to a second shelf that reaches back into scrubby woods. We highly recommend these shelves for camping since you are unlikely to find a better campsite in the remaining distance to Cumberland House.

Map 13.2   From Namew Lake to Cross Lake

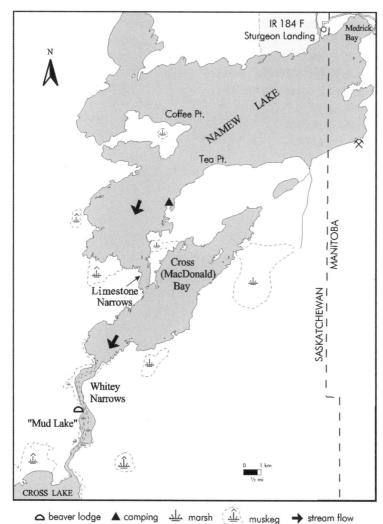

△ beaver lodge   ▲ camping   ⚓ marsh   ⚓ muskeg   ➡ stream flow

About 3 km (2 mi) southwest from the limestone shelves, the canoe track bends 45 degrees to run due south for 5 km (3 mi) through a narrows locally known as "Limestone Narrows." The narrows lead to a large bay identified on Maps 63K and 63K/4 as Cross Bay but more commonly referred to locally as "MacDonald Bay."

The canoe track goes southwest on Cross Bay between shores that are low but well treed with aspen, spruce, and willows. There are no limestone cliffs, but plates of broken limestone still line the water's edge. After 5 km (3 mi), the track reaches where Namew Lake drains southward into Whitey Narrows.

Whitey Narrows

Whitey Narrows is a sinuous passage that runs south for just over 8 km (5 mi) to flow into Cross Lake. Although the channel has some higher ground with small stands of fine spruce, its shores are generally low and often willowy. Camping prospects are poor.

The narrows takes its name from an early North West Company trader named White about whom very little is known. Peter Fidler's sketch made June 26–27, 1792, of the route from Sturgeon Landing to Cumberland House shows a house southwest of the south end of the narrows.[11] Referring to Fidler's sketch, J.B. Tyrrell observed that, "…beyond the Narrows on the right or west side, is a house probably built by White, the North West Company trader. From him these Narrows have ever since been called Whitey's Narrows."[12]

Halfway down its length, just past a beaver house on the west shore, Whitey Narrows expands somewhat and a swampy area opens to the east. This expansion has the Cree name of *asiskiy sâkahikanisis* or "mud lake." According to John Morin, a former Cumberland House resident, Mud Lake was once larger than it now is. When water levels were higher, it occupied much of what is now adjacent swamp.

As the name Mud Lake implies, the water in Whitey Narrows is not so clear as that in Namew Lake. As you draw nearer to Cumberland House, you can expect the water to grow ever murkier as the Sturgeon-weir's clean flow mingles with turbid water from the

HBCA E.3/1 fo. 68 (N14807)

Saskatchewan River. The Saskatchewan carries the effluent of many towns and cities, the run-off from chemical-dependent farmland and mercury from hydro dam reservoirs. This is the place to stop drinking the water alongside your canoe.

Cross Lake

Cross Lake is a small, roundish lake measuring 4 km (2½ mi) from north to south. In Cree, it is known as *kâ-pimicikamâsik* which, as we understand it, means "the lake is crosswise" or "the lake requires a crossing passage."

As already noted, Fidler's 1792 sketch and Tyrrell's interpretation suggest that the North West Company house built by White was on Cross Lake southwest from the foot of Whitey Narrows. Nowadays, there is a stand of spruce about 400 m (440 yd) southwest from the foot of the narrows. If we can assume that area vegetation has not changed much in the past two centuries, the spruce—which would make better building logs than the surrounding poplar—may mark the general location of White's house.

Cross Lake drains west-southwest via a broad channel. Both Maps 63E and 63E/16 identify the northwest side of the channel entrance as Spruce Point. Appropriately, there is a good stand of spruce in the area.[13]

Frobisher's House

Peter Fidler's 1792 sketch shows a second house on the south shore of Cross Lake. Though the sketch is somewhat skewed, the house appears to be at or near the start of Cross Lake's outflow channel to Cumberland Lake—more or less across from Spruce Point on the opposite shore. It is reasonably certain that this house was where the Montrealer Joseph Frobisher, along with Louis Primeau and sixteen other men, established himself during the winter of 1773–74.[14]

Frobisher's Cross Lake house is significant in that it was built in a year fur traders out of Montreal entered the North-West fur country in full force. They had not yet organized themselves into the North West Company. However, as historian Arthur S. Morton describes it, for the Montrealers, 1773 was a year "in which they crowded into Rupert's Land" and together produced "a great invasion of Pedlars."[15] Of special note, Frobisher's house was also the first house ever to be built north of the Saskatchewan River. It was to be the springboard for the Montrealers' quick advance up the Sturgeon-weir and Churchill rivers in the years to follow.

As luck would have it, the 1773–74 trading season was one in which the Hudson's Bay Company had only one trader inland. This was Joseph Hansom, who had been sent out from Fort Prince of Wales at the mouth of the Churchill. Reaching the vicinity of Joseph Frobisher's new house in late 1773, Hansom found himself hampered by the fact that local Indian hunters were under contract to Frobisher and his men. This meant that he could not hire the hunters he himself would need to survive the winter. What to do? Hansom pragmatically took room and board with his competitors at their Cross Lake house.

Budds Point

Cross Lake's outflow channel is about 1 km (2/3 mi) wide and leads about 7 km (4⅓ mi) to Cumberland Lake. The north side of this channel is a peninsula that looks remarkably like a human foot. At the arch of this foot, Maps 63E and 63E/16 show an Indian Reserve with Map 63 E/16 identifying it as "Budd's Point Indian Reserve 20D." At the toe, which extends into Cumberland Lake, the maps bear the legend "Budds Point."

Henry Budd

Budd's Point Indian Reserve and Budds Point commemorate Henry Budd and his descendants. Henry Budd, first known as *sâkâscîwîscam*, was born at or near Norway House in the early 1800s to an Indian father and Métis mother. When he was eight years old, the Anglican missionary John West brought him to Red River where he acquired his European name, formal schooling, and training as a catechist.

Early on, the Anglican Church recognized Budd as having superior talents. In June of 1840, the Church chose him to go to Cumberland House as a catechist to "collect some children for instruction and speak to the Indians on the subject of our missions." His initial venture at Cumberland House was poorly received, but it marked the beginning of the Anglican Church's work at Cumberland, as well as Budd's distinguished career with the Church.

Henry Budd.

In 1852, after further education, Budd was ordained to the priesthood and became the Anglican Church's first native minister in North America. Following his ordination, he continued with his earlier mission work in several northern communities including Cumberland House. In his later years, he endured much personal sorrow from several deaths in his immediate family. Despite this, he worked tirelessly for the Church until his own death from influenza in 1875.[16]

We do not know whether Henry Budd himself ever lived at Budds Point. However, Mary Morin of Prince Albert, who was raised at Cumberland House in the 1930s, says that she was told by her family that as many as eleven families once lived in the area just west of Budd's Point Indian Reserve. Most of these families were Henry Budd's descendants. They had horses, cattle, and large gardens, as well as a church and a school. Mary herself recalls people still living at Budds Point when she was a child. Though she is unable to recollect a school there, she can remember seeing a church.

Cumberland House Cree Nation

Budd's Point Indian Reserve 20D belongs to the Cumberland House Cree Nation (CHCN). The CHCN is descended from an indigenous group of *th*-dialect Cree, known as the "Basquia" (*opâskwêyâw*) Cree, and from *n*-dialect Swampy Cree who immigrated from present-day Manitoba. In the terrible 1781 smallpox epidemic, the Basquia Cree were nearly wiped out, and the Swampy Cree moved into the Cumberland region to fill the resulting void. Some surviving Basquia Cree no doubt intermarried with the incoming Swampy Cree. However, as these Basquia were few in number, the post-epidemic population eventually became Swampy Cree in character, and the Cumberland Cree today speak the *n*-dialect Swampy Cree language.[17]

The CHCN is a party to Treaty No. 5 (signed at Berens River, Manitoba, in 1875). Though not part of the original signing, the CHCN signed an adhesion to the treaty at The Pas, Manitoba, in 1876, after which the Cumberland House Cree were often referred to as the Albert Flett Band after Albert Flett, a Band councillor at treaty signing and later a chief. The Band formally adopted the "Cumberland House" name in 1930.[18]

Today, the CHCN has its main reserve and its administration centre at "Cumberland House Indian Reserve 20," situated just south of the village of Cumberland House. The First Nation has over eight hundred members with nearly half of these living on Reserve 20. Other members live in Cumberland House, Nipawin, The Pas, and elsewhere. Since 2001, Chief Pierre Settee has been head of the CHCN. A long-time chief, Chief Settee has returned to power after a break from 1999 to 2001, when Chief Walter Sewap held the CHCN's top office.

Tearing River

When you reach the entrance to Cumberland Lake, you will find to your immediate left the head of the Tearing River, known in Cree by the equivalent *tâtoskociwan sîpiy* or *tâtosko-ciwanisihk*. The Tearing River is the most easterly of three channels draining Cumberland Lake to the Saskatchewan River. During the fur trade, its 17-km (10½-mi) length was the main track used to link the lower Saskatchewan and the Sturgeon-weir flow coming down from Cross Lake. It was therefore an integral part of the voyageur highway.

On August 26, 1808, Alexander Henry the Younger of the NWC went up the Tearing River (what he calls the "Little English") in order to stop at Cumberland House:

> We soon came to Little English river, which falls into the Saskatchewan from the N.W. We here leave the latter river to proceed to our dépôt on the lake at the N. end of this little river. We began to ascend it; found the current very strong, with a winding passage among a number of channels, along which no kind of wood is to be seen. The land is low, covered with reeds, rushes, and long grass. On the banks grow some small willows, behind which appear many ponds and small lakes, full of wild fowl.... At the entrance to Sturgeon lake we put ashore on an island, whose black, rocky shore gave us reason to suppose we could put our feet once more on terra firma. Upon this island our north-bound brigades generally unload and proceed to Cumberland House for their supply of provisions; which, having brought, they load, and proceed N. along Sturgeon lake about 12 leagues to the entrance of Rivière Maligne; then up this river, and through a succession of lakes and rivers, to their respective destinations—some even to the Columbia, and others to McKenzie's river.[19]

The island where the voyageurs stopped at the head of the Tearing River was known to the voyageurs as "Athabasca Island."[20] We have not tried to locate it, but using the Henry reference, you may well be able to find it. Keep in mind, though, that with Cumberland Lake's modern-day lower water levels, the island may actually now be a peninsula.

Cumberland Lake

As noted earlier, the first fur trade explorers referred to both present-day Namew and Cumberland lakes as a single lake which they knew as either Sturgeon Lake or Pine Island Lake. Eventually, the Pine Island name became associated only with what is now Cumberland Lake. The Pine Island name continues to this day in an essentially equivalent Cree name for the lake, *kâ-ministiko-minahikoskâhk sâkahikan*, or "spruce island lake," though the lake is most often simply referred to as *wâskahikanihk sâkahikan*, meaning "house lake."[21]

The origin of the name Cumberland Lake goes back to 1774 when Samuel Hearne established Cumberland House as the Hudson's Bay Company's first inland trading post. The post was named for Prince Rupert, Duke of Cumberland, the first governor of the Hudson's Bay Company.[22] By 1790, Philip Turnor was using the name "Cumberland House Lake," and by 1793, David Thompson was using the shorter "Cumberland Lake."[23]

Cumberland Lake is a large lake measuring 20 km (12 mi) from north to south and roughly 15 km (9 mi) across at its base. It is fed mainly by the Sturgeon-weir River flowing in from the east and the Saskatchewan River flowing in from the west. It has three exit channels along its south shore—the Bigstone Cutoff, the Bigstone River, and the Tearing River—which all join back into the Saskatchewan as it continues eastward on a course lying just south of the lake.

The lake is shallow and has likely always been so. Philip Turnor, doing a circumnavigational survey in 1779, "found the Lake about 10 feet deep."[24] And, Alexander Henry the Younger, in going from the Tearing River to Cumberland House in 1808, "found the lake very shallow, and frequently got aground in the mud."[25]

Nowadays, the lake is even shallower than in former times. The main reason dates to about 1882 when the Saskatchewan River, at a place called Mosquito Point 50 km (31 mi) or so west from Cumberland House, became blocked by a spring ice dam and began cutting a new channel north of its "Old Channel." This "New Channel" drained north and east to empty into the west side of Cumberland Lake. As the New Channel accepted more and more water, the Old Channel—which had previously kept most of the Saskatchewan's flow south of Cumberland Lake—handled less and less volume.[26]

The routing of the New Channel into Cumberland Lake has produced shallowing in two ways. First, it has caused the natural cutting of a new outflow channel known as the Bigstone Cutoff to augment the Bigstone and Tearing rivers, the lake's two original outflows. The Cutoff's depth has allowed extra lowering of the lake. Secondly, the New Channel has delivered a huge sediment load which has settled onto the lake bottom. The combined effect of these two forces has been dramatic. Certain areas which were open water as recently as the 1930s have now become dry land, and beds of bulrushes continue to encroach further and further into the lake.

On the positive side, the diversion of the Saskatchewan into Cumberland Lake has created (or re-created if the diversion has occurred before) one of the best freshwater deltas in North America and some first-class wetland habitat. Nutrients arriving from upstream feed plants ranging from small phytoplankton to shrubs and trees. These plants in turn feed a wide array of life forms further up the food chain. While the lake may lack the scenic beauty of other lakes on the route, it has a much richer natural environment than most of those other lakes.

When it comes to fishing, anglers will likely find the lake's shallow, opaque water unattractive. Moreover, mercury levels in fish caught may restrict consumption. (Saskatchewan Environment offices can provide up-to-date advice on mercury contamination.) Nonetheless, fish stocks include pike, walleye, and whitefish, as well as goldeye. The lake also has sturgeon which are now absent from lakes further upstream on the route. However, with their numbers declining, sturgeon are currently protected from sport fishing.

For birdwatchers, Cumberland Lake presents a wide variety of both migrant and nesting wetland bird species. It is especially well known as a duck factory. Over a dozen kinds of duck nest on the lake and its environs with the most common being the lesser scaup, ring-necked duck, blue-winged teal, canvasback, mallard, and gadwall.[27]

Of the two dozen or so mammal species that stay or visit on Cumberland Lake, two deserve special mention. The first is the little muskrat which thrives in the lake's shallow water stands of bulrushes and cattails. It has long been the mainstay of local trappers and also an important local meat source. The other noteworthy species is the moose which, at times, has been more abundant in the Cumberland region than in any other part of Saskatchewan. It is locally valuable for both its hide and its meat.[28]

Unfortunately, over the past several decades, the Cumberland area's rich environment has been adversely affected by man-made changes. Hydroelectric dams built upstream on the Saskatchewan—especially the E.B. Campbell Dam built about 80 km (50 mi) to the west in the 1960s—have had a major impact on lake levels. Instead of having normal summer highs and winter lows, the lake now fluctuates according to how much water the electrical utility, SaskPower, chooses to hold back or release at its dams upstream. A major problem is that spring and summer hold-backs do not allow for the proper flushing and recharging of the delta and the lake. Other problems result from high volume releases; for example, in summer, nesting habitat may be destroyed, and in winter, muskrats may drown in their homes.

Another problem, already touched on, is that when the Saskatchewan River enters Cumberland Lake, it brings with it effluent from populated areas in both Alberta and Saskatchewan—including the urban centres of Calgary, Red Deer, Edmonton, Saskatoon, and Prince Albert. Too little is known about what comes down the river, but we expect some of it is quite nasty. We again suggest you not drink straight from the lake.

Map 13.3   South shore of Cumberland Lake

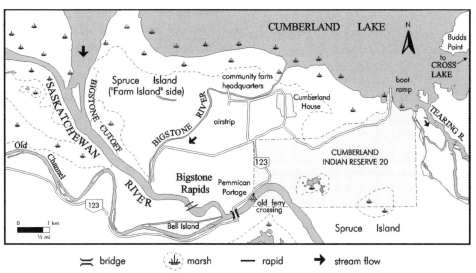

To Cumberland House

Going west from the head of the Tearing River, you will first pass where a road from Cumberland House leads to a boat launch at the end of a small point. From here, staying on the water, you can make your way west and then north by skirting along the northern edge of a great bulrush marsh. Even if you keep north of the bulrushes, you can expect to encounter some difficulty from water weeds. Odd as it seems, the bulrush marsh and the low land behind it was once a bay of open water. It was in this bay, approximately 2 km (1¼ mi) southwest from the boat launch just passed, that Samuel Hearne built the original Cumberland House in 1774.

When you have paddled 3 to 4 km (2 to 2½ mi) west and north from the boat launch, you can expect the northern edge of the bulrushes to bend to the west or southwest. After this bend, you can watch for a clear channel leading into the rushes on your left. This channel is kept free of rushes and weeds by motor boat traffic. If you turn south down it, you should eventually arrive at the head of the Bigstone River where you can land on the river left bank. This puts you right on the outskirts of Cumberland House and hence at the end of your canoe voyage.

Cumberland House

The community of Cumberland House is on the north shore of Spruce Island—a 25-km-long (16-mi) tract of low-lying land separating Cumberland Lake from the Saskatchewan River. Spruce Island is bounded on the west by the Bigstone Cutoff and on the east by the Tearing River, both of which flow from Cumberland Lake to the Saskatchewan. Immediately east of Cumberland House, the island is cut through by the 7-km-long (4¹/₃-mi) Bigstone River which, as another of Cumberland Lake's exit channels, runs from the lake and joins the Bigstone Cutoff on its way to the Saskatchewan.

In Cree, Cumberland House is variously known as *kâ-ministiko-minahikoskâhk* ("spruce island"), *mistiko-minahikoskâw* ("spruce bluff"), and *wâskahikanihk* ("the house"). The first two names derive from the tall white spruce which grow in the area. The last name commemorates the HBC's first trading post or "house" built here.

To first-time visitors, Cumberland House's location, surrounded by shallow waters and mosquito-infested marshes, may seem to be a poor one. However, with the waters and marshes producing abundant fish and game, local spruce providing excellent building logs, and the nearby rivers offering travel connections, the site has historically had real advantages over other places. Consequently, since being founded by Samuel Hearne in 1774, Cumberland House has survived to become the oldest continuous settlement in Saskatchewan.

History of Cumberland House

Cumberland House can trace its origin to a 1773 decision of the Hudson's Bay Company to establish an inland trading post to compete with Montreal traders who were intercepting North-West furs before they could reach the company on Hudson Bay. The HBC chose Samuel Hearne to travel inland from York Factory in 1773 to set up the post. A lack of canoes and Indian canoemen prevented Hearne from leaving in 1773 as planned, but the next summer, on June 23, 1774, he was able to set off in five small canoes with carpenter Andrew Garrat, trader Robert Longmoor, "upland leading Indian" Me-sin-e-kish-ac and five other Indians. After travelling from York Factory via the Grass and Goose rivers, he and his men reached Cumberland Lake on August 6, 1774. Hearne then spent three weeks exploring the southwest corner of Cumberland Lake and the Saskatchewan River as far downstream as The Pas looking for a place to build. Finally, on August 29, he decided on a spot (at approximately 63E 817809) about 2 km (1¼ mi) east-southeast from the present-day townsite. His journal entry for the day reads:

> Monday the 29th
> Bad Rainey Weather…after a long Consultation with the Indian Chiefs and others in Company, I determin'd to build the house, at least for the insewing winter, at a Part Call'd Pine Island Lake—it is the general opinion of those Indians that that Part will be more comodious both for Drawing the Indians to Trade as well as for Provisions then Basquiau [The Pas], it laying in the Middle between three Tribes [29]

Before starting to build, Hearne's party was joined by Bay men William Flett, Magnus Slater, and James Banks, who arrived with extra tools and supplies. Hearne was also to have had the help of Bay men Matthew Cocking, James Lisk, Isaac Batt, and Charles Isham, who had left from York Factory somewhat ahead of him. However, those men, dependent on natives going inland for their transportation, never reached Cumberland House at all that summer but instead ended up wintering far to the south at what is now Good Spirit Lake, Saskatchewan.

With his smaller than expected crew, Hearne started actual work on his new post on September 3, 1774. Hearne was no doubt very busy over the next weeks, but he still found time to make short entries in his journal. These give us a good sense of how the post work went:

Saturday the 3rd

Fine Pleasant Weather…[from the head of the Tearing River] we then went about 2 Miles to the Westward on the South side, when we came to a fine Bay, which seem'd very Comodious for building on, so we landed and I Pitch'd on the part I thought would be most convenient. The People Empd the Remaindor of the Day in Clearing a spot of Ground to Build a log Fort on for the Present. The Spot I Propose to build the Proper house on is fine and Levle, and tho not very high has seldom or Ever ben known to overflow by any of the Indians in Company. The Ground is stoney intermix'd with stiff Clay, the Woods on Each side for about one forth of a mile is fine Strait Pine intermix'd with Poplars and small Birch, but farther Backwards the woods are mostly Poplar, it has a Commanding view of Pine Island Lake for several miles Each way and is said to have some good fishing Places near…

Sunday the 4th

Ditto Wr…Carpenter and people Empd helveing of Hatchetts readey for going to work tomorrow

Monday the 5th

Ditto Weather. Carpenter and People Empd falling of wood for the Log Tent. This day 11 Cannoes of Grass River Indians came and pitch'd by us, of whome I Traded some Moose flesh and a few Parchment Beaver

Tuesday the 6th

Fine Pleasant Weather Wind at SW. The Carpenter and one man Empd arrecting the logg Tent, the rest of the People Carryin in loggs &c for that use

FRANKLIN ARBUCKLE / HBCA P-416 (N13495)

Painting by Franklin Arbuckle of Hearne building Cumberland House, 1774–75.

Wednesday the 7th
Ditto Wr. Carpenter and People Empd as before. The 11 Canoes of Indians who came the other Day Return'd to their Families. At Night almost finish'd the outside of the Logg Tent

Thursday the 8th
Ditto Wr. People Empd Caulking the seams of the Tent with Moss, and in the Evning we Remov'd all our goods &c into our new habitation[30]

In the days to follow, Hearne's carpenter fitted their "log tent" with doors and a floor. A storeroom was also added to the structure, as well as a 16-foot addition used to provide more living space. At the same time, besides taking time to find food for themselves and do some trading, the men started felling trees and squaring logs for a "Proper house" to be built early the next spring. They sometimes resented the twelve-hour workdays Hearne expected of them, but their efforts that first season created the beginnings of a Cumberland House settlement.[31]

Hearne and his men began work on a permanent post on April 6, 1775, using the logs they had collected throughout the winter. Hearne supervised the work until May 29 when he left (leaving carpenter Andrew Garrat in charge in his absence) to take furs out to York Factory. He arrived at York Factory on June 23—having been gone a year to the day—and then stayed two weeks before starting back for Cumberland. He got back to Cumberland on August 19 to find that the post construction had advanced well and was now at the roofing stage. Hearne resumed supervision of the work through the fall, but he was not to remain long. On October 4, 1775, Matthew Cocking (who had survived his previous winter at Good Spirit Lake to return to York Factory) arrived at Cumberland with a letter from Hudson's Bay Company officials advising that Hearne had been appointed chief of Fort Prince of Wales and that he, Cocking, was to take over at Cumberland. Within two days, in a race against freeze-up, Hearne was on his way to York Factory with the Indian canoemen who had brought Cocking inland. Cocking himself settled in for what was to be a two-year stay at Cumberland.[32]

Early Hardships

Right from the start, Cumberland House was noted for its incredible mosquito population. Fur trade journals do not often record complaints about insects, but the early Cumberland journals are an exception. In the fall of 1775, Hearne explains the problem his men were having in getting roof boards cut for the new post, saying, "The reason of our not geting a sufficient quantity of Plank cut emediatly on our arival ware oweing to the Meskittas being so thick that the People could not work in the woods."[33] Another entry, typical of others on the subject, is that of the HBC's George Hudson writing on June 18, 1781:

...Sent two Men to set two Sturgeon & two other small Nets, also to Overhaul one that was set before towards Evening they returned brought 20 Gold Eye'd fish and 4 small pike, the other two fell a little firewood for the Winter, but the Weather being very hot and Muschettos troublesome, came home and pitched part of the roof of the New house[34]

But the nuisance mosquitoes brought to Cumberland's early residents paled alongside the hardship and sorrow caused by disease, most particularly the smallpox that arrived in December 1781. Although the 1781 epidemic left the European traders largely untouched, it devastated the North-West's indigenous people who lacked immunity to it. News of the illness first reached Cumberland on December 11, 1781, and by Christmas Eve that year, William Tomison (George Hudson's successor at Cumberland) prophetically wrote, "...It is now spreading over the Whole Country, which will be a shocking affair as ever was known." For the two months to follow, Tomison's journal entries document the care of the sick and the burying of the dead at Cumberland. His entry for January 21, 1782, reads:

> 21st Monday. Wind N.W. a fresh Breeze, weather as Yesterday, sent James Wass to assist a sick Indian & bring him to the House, two men making a Sturgeon Net & the rest digging a Grave and buryed an Indian Woman that Died on the Plantation Yesterday Evening, late at Night 19 Starved Indians arrived, Indeed their Condition is too shocking to be described by pen, they have left severals on the Way, not able to walk & one died on the road, which they have brought here to be buried.[35]

To his credit, Tomison tried everything he could to save the Indians stricken with smallpox. He and his men provided food, lodging, and nursing care, but most often, this did not make up for a lack of any effective treatment for the disease. As Tomison put it, "…it cuts me to the Heart to see the Miserable condition they are in & not being able to Help them."[36] He and his men also had the task of burying those who died.

By mid-February, Tomison was reporting that all the "U,Basquiau Indians" [Basquia Cree] were now dead and that other Indian groups were hardly better off if their fates were known at all. Despite Tomison's assessment of the situation, it is likely that isolated pockets of Basquia Cree did in fact survive the smallpox to become part of the root stock of the present Cumberland community. Still, the death toll from the disease was incredibly high. It is something of a miracle that the survivors were able to pull themselves together into viable living units and once again engage in hunting, fishing, and trapping.[37]

As if the smallpox epidemic were not enough, the HBC's Cumberland post suffered further as a result of events at its York Factory supply base. On August 25, 1782, the French naval commander Lapérouse (France was at war with England) took over York Factory from HBC Governor Humphrey Marten and burned it to the ground. By this time, Tomison had already been in from Cumberland House to pick up supplies for the 1782–83 season. However, the French attack had a dire effect in the following year when the HBC's regular supply ship was late coming from London to York Factory. After coming for his 1783–84 trading supplies, Tomison waited anxiously at York Factory's deserted ruins until September 4, 1783, before returning to Cumberland empty handed. (The HBC supply ship did arrive a week after Tomison left.) Back at Cumberland, Tomison and his men, as well as their regular customers, faced a very difficult winter where ammunition and other necessities had to be bought from rival Montreal traders.[38]

A New Site

As it turned out, the original HBC post site chosen by Hearne was subject to periodic flooding. Accordingly, after fifteen years or so, by which time local firewood was growing scarce, the HBC decided to re-locate its post about 2 km (1¼ mi) eastward to where the present-day community now stands. The new post was started as early as 1789, but it took some years to complete. A day after Philip Turnor's exploration party arrived back at Cumberland House on June 27, 1792 (from its two-year excursion to the Athabasca), Turnor had a tour of the new post under construction. His companion Malcolm Ross reported:

> Messrs Turnor, Twatt [Orkneyman Magnus Twatt, in charge of the HBC's Cumberland post], Fidler & myself went to have a look at the new building which is a very fine house so far as it is come, but is very low as yet, and is not likely to go very fast up, on account of the fewness of the hands.

Despite delays, Magnus Twatt eventually did get the post finished, and by May 1794, it was in full operation.[39]

In 1793, just as the HBC was moving, the North West Company chose to build its first post at Cumberland

House on ground immediately northwest of the new HBC post. However, while the NWC no doubt wanted to cut into the HBC's share of the local fur market, it did not mount the fierce competition it did elsewhere. The two companies thus co-existed side by side in relative peace until they merged in 1821. Upon merger, the re-structured HBC continued using its own buildings since they were, according to James Leith, Chief Factor from 1822 to 1829, "large and tolerably well built, with a handsome dwelling-house, having glass windows, and what is still more uncommon in these parts, a gallery in front—the only instance of its kind I have yet seen in this country."[40]

The HBC remained at Magnus Twatt's building site for over 170 years. It finally abandoned the location and its traditional red-and-white buildings in 1966 when it moved into a new department store (now the Northern) situated about 500 m (1/3 mi) to the southwest.

Today, you can find the Twatt site by going to the Provincial Historic Park at the northeast corner of the Cumberland community. The precise layout of the earliest HBC buildings is now hidden under the turf, but an

old HBC powder house—built from local limestone in the 1890s—identifies the post's general location. If you visit the powder house, you need only walk about 50 m (55 yd) northeast to see a wave-cut bank marking what was once Cumberland Lake's south shore. Now, instead of lapping water, you will find a thick tangle of willows.[41]

The old Hudson's Bay Company powder house at Cumberland House.

Pemmican Supply Depot

When the North West Company built its Cumberland House post, it was interested in more than just the local furs. Early in the fur trade, it had been storing the pemmican supplies needed to fuel its passing brigades in a secret shore cache near present-day The Pas, Manitoba. One year, just prior to 1793, the brigades suffered when their guides were unable to find the cache. A decision was hence made to establish a reliable supply depot at Cumberland.[42] In his journal entry for August 26, 1808, the NWC's Alexander Henry (the Younger) wrote:

> This post is kept up by us less for the purpose of trade than for the convenience of a dépôt to supply our northern brigades. In the spring we bring down the Saskatchewan to this place from 300 to 500 bags of pemmican, and upward of 200 kegs of grease; part of the latter is taken to Fort William, while the whole of the former is required for our people going out in the spring and coming back in the fall.[43]

As the HBC opened up its own posts in the North-West, it too began to use Cumberland House to provide pemmican to its passing brigades and, indeed, continued to do so long after the 1821 merger. The company found that, much like Île-à-la-Crosse further west, Cumberland House was ideally situated for the collection and distribution of pemmican. Upstream from Cumberland, the North and South Saskatchewan rivers ran through prairies sustaining millions of buffalo. For as long as these buffalo roamed, they were harvested and converted into pemmican. This pemmican was floated downstream on the Saskatchewan's strong current and landed at the river bend directly south of Cumberland House. It was then taken overland (likely with help from horses or oxen) via "Pemmican Portage" to the HBC post where it could be given out to passing fur brigades.

Cumberland's role as a pemmican supply depot died with the buffalo. But today, a small settlement situated near where pemmican was originally landed on the Saskatchewan's north bank (downstream from the road bridge) is still known as Pemmican Portage.

The Steamboat Era

In 1874, the Hudson's Bay Company built the 150-foot steamboat *Northcote* above Grand Rapids where the Saskatchewan River entered Lake Winnipeg. That same summer, the big sternwheeler made her maiden voyage up the Saskatchewan as far as Fort Carlton and became the first steamboat ever to travel the river. In so doing, she introduced Cumberland House to an era of steam transport that would last for fifty years and bring new jobs to local residents. Some men found summer jobs on the boats, and many more had winter work cutting and stockpiling the cordwood the boats would burn on their summer voyages.

Steamboat travel on the Saskatchewan proved to be a challenge. The *Northcote* and later steamboats had to deal with shallow water, shifting sand bars, and rapids. The Cumberland area was a particular challenge. As luck would have it, within a few years of the *Northcote*'s maiden voyage, an ice dam at Mosquito Point upstream from Cumberland (discussed earlier on page 392) began to divert the Saskatchewan River away from its "Old Channel" and down a "New Channel" into the west side of Cumberland Lake. In 1882, the 190-foot steamboat *Manitoba* found the Old Channel too shallow for travel, and she thus had to pass down the recently cut New Channel. However, the New Channel itself branched into the Cumberland delta—a confusing maze of smaller channels that changed their location and depth from year to year. In the delta, a good river pilot was essential.[44]

Notwithstanding navigational hazards, steamboats came and went at Cumberland until 1925. Until then, one of the boats making regular stops was the Ross Navigation Company's 90-foot sternwheeler *Nipawin* launched at The Pas in 1917. The boat had cabin space for thirty-six passengers, but it also had a 35-ton cargo hold and could push additional payloads on barges, as it did in the Mandy Mine ore haul days. "Steamboat Bill" McKenzie, a Cumberland Métis born in 1901, went to work firing the

The Nipawin *was the flagship of the Ross Navigation fleet.*

A.J. DALRYMPLE / HBCA 1987/363-S-49/16 (N14881)

Old boiler for S.S. Northcote *in the park at Cumberland House, August 1986.*

Nipawin's boilers during her first summer and then worked aboard her every summer (the last several as ship's mate) until her retirement in 1924. He has described a typical run on the *Nipawin*:

> We had dinner at Cumberland House, supper at Sturgeon Landing, and then unloaded, even if it took until midnight Wednesday. The next morning we would wash the deck and wood up. We left Sturgeon Landing at Thursday noon, got to Cumberland Thursday night at supper-time and hit The Pas [connection between Cumberland Lake and the Saskatchewan was via the Bigstone River] at about 3 o'clock Friday morning. Then three, big, long whistles woke everybody up.[45]

You can see a reminder of Cumberland's steamboat era in the community's Provincial Historic Park. Here, two 5-m-long (16-ft) steam boilers and other pieces of metal work from the original *Northcote* are mounted on display. After her maiden voyage in 1874, the *Northcote* had kept busy working on the Saskatchewan River system. She then took part in the 1885 Riel Rebellion as a gunboat at the Battle of Batoche. However, only a year later, now recognized as being too big for the Saskatchewan's shallow waters, she was beached at Cumberland House and allowed to fall into ruin on a muddy shore. Her boilers and related hardware were later salvaged as mementos of Cumberland's steamboat days.

Other Influences

As mentioned earlier, the Anglican Church sent catechist Henry Budd to Cumberland House as early as 1840. Somewhat later, in the 1870s, the Roman Catholic Church sent Oblate Father M. Paquette to open St. Joseph's Mission at Cumberland and become its first resident priest. By this time, several Manitoba Métis—with names such as Carriere, Fosseneuve, and Goulet—had immigrated to Cumberland from Red River (where they had felt the pressure of increasing white encroachment) and established a significant Catholic presence. In 1888, Father Paquette was succeeded by Father Ovide Charlebois who directed construction of a small log school house in 1890 and a church in 1894. The little school house now stands as Cumberland's oldest building.[46]

Cumberland House's first school, built in 1890. Photo taken in August 1986.

Cumberland was another community where the French company Revillon Frères traded for furs in the early 1900s. From about 1906 to 1923, it had a store and warehouse south of the Catholic church. Harold Kemp, who would later spend most of his days with Revillon as a trader at Stanley Mission, got his start with the company at Cumberland in 1912 as a clerk under Paul Eugene Carré.[47]

In the late 1920s, Cumberland became a centre for law enforcement in northern Saskatchewan. In 1928, the RCMP sent Swiss-born Corporal Marcel "Chappy" Chappuis to operate a detachment at Cumberland. Previously, from 1918 to 1927, Chappuis had served with the Saskatchewan Provincial Police, and he had already earned a name for himself in police work. At Cumberland, he and special constables assisting him made legendary patrols by canoe and dog team to police the huge territory under their jurisdiction. One of Chappuis's special constables was Simeon Bloomfield, whom American P.G. Downes described as "a handsome halfbreed from Cumberland House who speaks beautiful Cree and English." On one patrol, between January and April 1938, Chappuis and Bloomfield travelled over 3,600 km (2,250 mi) on a dog sled trip that took them as far north as Lac Brochet, Manitoba. Undaunted, they made the same patrol the following winter. While Bloomfield left Cumberland to serve in World War II, Chappuis remained in charge of the local RCMP detachment until 1945.[48]

Since World War II, two other men—both from Cumberland—have had RCMP service records rivalling those of Chappuis and Bloomfield. Special Constable Charlie Fosseneuve (who, like Bloomfield, is a World War II veteran) served at Cumberland for twenty-six years between 1950 and 1976, and Constable Robert McAuley served here for twenty years from 1980 to 2000.

After World War II, Cumberland House, like other places in northern Saskatchewan, saw many changes. Fishing, hunting, and trapping remained important, but people began to spend less time on the land and water and more in town. Services like the outpost hospital built in 1940 made Cumberland an attractive place to live. The Family Allowance introduced in 1945 gave families added incentive to settle in one central location since payments were conditional on children attending school. While Cumberland grew, small outlying settlements such as the Barrier, Birch River, and Pine Bluff ceased to exist.

The provincial CCF government, elected in 1944, took an active interest in Cumberland House. It improved local education by having the province assume full responsibility for the local school. It also started a sawmill to produce building materials for the growing population. A government farm set up on the rich land west of the Bigstone River (this part of Spruce Island is now most often called "Farm Island") focussed on cattle production and brought in its first animals through the winter of 1946–47. Finally, steps were taken to improve the local muskrat habitat since muskrat pelts brought in cash and their carcasses were a major community food source. The federal government had begun building dikes and canals to control water levels in the vast muskrat marshes as early as 1939. The provincial government continued this work in cooperation with Ducks Unlimited which was working to improve Cumberland's role as a duck and goose factory. In the mid-1940s, Zeke Campbell of the province's Department of Natural Resources coordinated work in the marshes.

Construction of the Squaw Rapids (now E.B. Campbell) Dam upstream on the Saskatchewan River in the early 1960s caused problems for Cumberland House. The dam's reservoir increased mercury levels in fish. Water hold-backs and releases disrupted efforts to make marshes better for muskrat and waterfowl. The hold-backs and releases also made boating more complicated—a hold-back could reduce flow in an otherwise navigable channel to a trickle, while a release might wash away boats left on dry land. The years of frustration felt by local residents finally resulted in a court action for damages brought against provincial Crown corporations SaskPower and Sask Water. In 1988, the province reached a settlement with Cumberland House and the neighbouring Cumberland House Cree Nation whereby the communities would receive a compensation package worth an estimated $23 million. To administer the resulting funds, the communities have formed the Cumberland House Development Corporation (CHDC).[49]

In 1966, an all-weather road reached Cumberland House, giving it a new link with the outside. This road did not run right into the community. Rather, it stopped on the south shore of the Saskatchewan River opposite Pemmican Portage. A ferry (operated by Hilliard McKenzie when we used it in 1986) was therefore necessary to transport vehicles and goods across the river to the community. This meant that during each spring breakup and fall freeze-up, Cumberland was still without regular road access. Finally, after several years of lobbying by community leaders (in 1993, Lennard Morin, a former Cumberland mayor, trekked to Regina with a large wooden cross on his shoulder to underscore the need for a bridge), the provincial government built a bridge across the Saskatchewan River just upstream from the ferry crossing. The Cumberland House Bridge had its official opening on September 12, 1996.[50]

Cumberland House People

Cumberland House—much like Île-à-la-Crosse to the west—stands out as one of Saskatchewan's principal Métis communities. Its residents descend from a homegrown Métis population born of fur trade activity in the immediate area and from Métis immigrants who had their own fur trade origins. Métis from Red River came to the Cumberland area after the unrest of the 1869–70 "Red River Rebellion." More Métis came from St. Laurent, Manitoba, in the early 1900s to work at commercial fishing in and around Cumberland.[51] After years of mixing, residents now share a common ancestry that has Scottish/Orcadian, French Canadian, and Cree as its main components. The Cree component is especially strong, and most community members speak both n-dialect Swampy Cree and English.

Though it is close-knit and rather isolated, Cumberland House has had many of its citizens gain recognition on a broader stage. An early example is that of Alexander Isbister, born at Cumberland in 1822. Alexander's father Thomas was an HBC clerk from the Orkneys, while his mother Mary was the daughter of a Cree woman and HBC Chief Factor Alexander Kennedy. Thanks to the Kennedy family (Thomas was poor and, moreover, was killed by a bull at Norway House in 1836), Alexander was able to get a boyhood education in the Orkneys and at Red River. At sixteen, he interrupted his education for three years to work for the HBC at Fort Simpson and northward. However, he was then able to resume his education, eventually at the Scottish universities of Aberdeen and Edinburgh, to become a teacher, lawyer, and writer.[52]

In the twentieth century, Cumberland House contributed many men to Canada's armed forces in World War I and World War II—more than any other community on the route. Twenty-six men served in World War I, while thirty-three served in World War II. In both wars, there were Cumberland men who did not make it back from overseas. In 1946, Cumberland veterans organized the first aboriginal branch of the Royal Canadian Legion.[53]

In more recent times, Cumberland has produced several talented individuals. In politics, Cumberland native Keith Goulet has become the first aboriginal person to hold a post in Saskatchewan's provincial cabinet. Keith's cousin, Gerald Morin (son of our informant John Morin) was appointed a Saskatchewan Provincial Court judge in 2001. Yet another cousin, Solomon Carriere, is a world champion marathon canoe paddler.

Cumberland House Today

Cumberland House is now a modern northern community with a population of about 1,200. It has the municipal status of "Northern Village." Dale McAuley has been mayor of the village since late 1997 when he replaced Lennard Morin in the position. He and a council of six aldermen govern local affairs.

Map 13.4 Community of Cumberland House

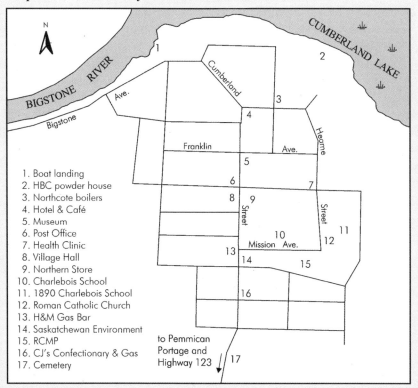

1. Boat landing
2. HBC powder house
3. Northcote boilers
4. Hotel & Café
5. Museum
6. Post Office
7. Health Clinic
8. Village Hall
9. Northern Store
10. Charlebois School
11. 1890 Charlebois School
12. Roman Catholic Church
13. H&M Gas Bar
14. Saskatchewan Environment
15. RCMP
16. CJ's Confectionary & Gas
17. Cemetery

Cumberland has its share of unemployment, and many families find it necessary to rely on government aid for their support. The community does, however, still obtain food and cash income from the traditional occupations of hunting, fishing, and trapping. In the fall, Cumberland is a mecca for moose and waterfowl hunters from all over North America, so local outfitters also earn money providing services to these visitors. Logging and wild rice harvesting provide other resource-based income. Cattle are raised on Farm Island west of the village. In the year 2000, the CHDC's community farm had about sixty cow-calf units, while three individual farmers—Donald Carriere, Norman Lambert, and Bert McAuley—had cattle herds of their own. Teaching, policing, and other community services provide a great many jobs. Other jobs come from the northern uranium mines; Cumberland workers are transported to and from the mines by air on what is usually a "week in–week out" rotation.

Cumberland House also has a resource-based business that is unique in northern Saskatchewan. Taking advantage of the Cumberland area's abundance of Manitoba maples, Joe Glaves, owner of CJ's Confectionery, runs a small maple sugar operation. Each spring, Joe taps a mature stand of maples growing naturally on CHCN lands in the vicinity of Samuel Hearne's original post site. After collecting a sufficient volume of sap, he evaporates it on site to make an excellent quality syrup. In the spring of 2001, he tapped approximately 2,500 maples. He now has plans to increase his maple syrup production and possibly expand into making birch syrup. Samples of Joe's syrup can be found at his confectionery.

Besides maple syrup, canoeists will find a good range of services at Cumberland. The community has an airstrip, Northern store, gas and convenience stores, Cumberland House Hotel with restaurant and bar, taxis, Saskatchewan Environment office, RCMP detachment, post office and a health centre with nursing staff (a Nipawin doctor comes in Mondays, Tuesdays, and Thursdays).

Cumberland has a small museum with some interesting artifacts and photos taken of archaeological work done at the original Hearne post site in the early 1990s. Outside the museum, there is a replica of a York boat which was built at the Saskatchewan Penitentiary in Prince Albert. Upon completion in 1993, it was rowed to Cumberland House where it was donated to the community. We happened to be in Cumberland for a short canoe trip in August 1993 and found the York boat moored on the Bigstone River. A close-up inspection of the boat and its massive oars confirmed for us that rowing a York boat would be no picnic.

If you wish to camp at Cumberland House, you will find camping options limited. The Historic Park at the northeast corner of the village offers one possibility, but you would need a vehicle to transport your gear to the park since it is now far back from the waters of Cumberland Lake.

From Cumberland House

Cumberland House marks the end of our route. If you have ended your trip here, you can (unless you live in Cumberland) head for home by driving south on Cumberland Street to connect with the road leading to Pemmican Portage and the Cumberland House Bridge. From the bridge, you can drive about 130 km (81 mi) southwest on Highway 123 (the first section is gravel) to join Highway 55 and the main provincial highway grid.

HILARY JOHNSTONE

APPENDIX A:
SUGGESTED PREPARATORY READING

CANOEING AND CAMPING

Anne Wortham Webre and Janet Zeller, *Canoeing and Kayaking for Persons with Physical Disabilities* (Springfield, VA: American Canoe Association, 1990).

Annie and Dave Getchell, *The Essential Outdoor Gear Manual* (New York: McGraw-Hill, 2000).

Gil Gilpatrick, *The Canoe Guide's Handbook* (Yarmouth, ME: DeLorme Mapping, 1983).

Will Harmon, *Wild Country Companion: The Ultimate Guide to No-Trace Outdoor Recreation and Safety* (Helena, MT: Falcon Press, 1999).

Cliff Jacobson, *Canoeing Wild Rivers: A Primer to North American Expedition Paddling* (Merrillville, IN: ICS Books, 1989).

Cliff Jacobson, *The Basic Essentials of Solo Canoeing* (Merrillville, IN: ICS Books, 1991).

Rolf and Debra Kraiker, *Cradle to Canoe: Camping and Canoeing with Children* (Erin, ON: Boston Mills Press, 1999).

Paul Landry and Matty McNair, *The Outward Bound Canoeing Handbook* (Vancouver: Douglas and McIntyre, 1993).

Bill Mason, *Path of the Paddle: An Illustrated Guide to the Art of Canoeing* (Toronto: Key Porter, rev. ed. 1995, orig. 1984).

Bill Mason, *Song of the Paddle: An Illustrated Guide to Wilderness Camping* (Toronto: Key Porter Books, 1994, orig. 1988).

Calvin Rutstrum, *North American Canoe Country: The Classic Guide to Canoe Technique* (Minneapolis: University of Minnesota Press, 2000, orig. 1964).

CHURCHILL RIVER

Tim E.H. Jones, *The Aboriginal Rock Paintings of the Churchill River* (Regina: Saskatchewan Museum of Natural History/Saskatchewan Department of Culture and Youth, 1981).

Peter Jonker, ed., *The Churchill: A Canadian Heritage River* (Saskatoon: University of Saskatchewan Extension Division, 1995).

FUR TRADE MEMOIRS

Sydney Augustus Keighley, *Trader Tripper Trapper: The Life of a Bay Man* (Winnipeg: Watson & Dwyer, 1989).

H.S.M. Kemp, *Northern Trader* (New York: Bouregy & Curl, 1956).

FUR TRADE CANOE ROUTES

Barbara Huck, *Exploring the Fur Trade Routes of North America* (Winnipeg: Heartland Press, 2000).

Eric W. Morse, *Fur Trade Canoe Routes of Canada/Then and Now* (Toronto: University of Toronto Press, rev. ed. 1979, orig. 1969).

NAVIGATING BY MAP, COMPASS, AND GPS

Cliff Jacobson, *The Basic Essentials of Map and Compass* (Old Saybrook, CT: Globe Pequot Press, 2nd ed., 1997).

Lawrence Letham, *GPS Made Easy: Using Global Positioning Systems in the Outdoors* (Seattle: Mountaineers Books, 1998).

David Seidman, *The Essential Wilderness Navigator* (New York: McGraw-Hill, 1995).

PADDLING NARRATIVES FROM THE ROUTE

Sigurd F. Olson, *The Lonely Land* (Minneapolis: University of Minnesota Press, 1997, orig. 1961).

Kamil Pecher, *Lonely Voyage: By Kayak to Adventure and Discovery* (Saskatoon: Prairie Books, 1978).

PLANT AND ANIMAL LIFE

Guide to the Forest Understory (Regina: Saskatchewan Department of Natural Resources/Forestry Canada, 1980).

Derek Johnson et al., *Plants of the Western Boreal Forest and Aspen Parkland* (Edmonton: Lone Pine/Canadian Forest Service, 1995).

Stephen Herrero, *Bear Attacks: Their Causes and Avoidance* (Toronto: McClelland & Stewart, 1999).

Jon M. Gerrard and Gary R. Bortolotti, *The Bald Eagle: Haunts and Habits of a Wilderness Monarch* (Washington, DC: Smithsonian Institution, 1988).

Jim Meuninck, *Basic Essentials of Edible Wild Plants and Useful Herbs* (Old Saybrook: CT: Globe Pequot Press, 2nd ed., 1999).

Dave Smith, *Backcountry Bear Basics: The Definitive Guide to Avoiding Unpleasant Encounters* (Vancouver: Douglas & McIntryre, 1997).

APPENDIX B:
CONTACTS

GENERAL

Canadian Recreational Canoeing Association
446 Main St. West
Box 398
Merrickville, ON, K0G 1N0
Phone: 1-888-252-6269 (toll free)
(613) 269-2910
E-mail: staff@crca.ca
Website: www.crca.ca

Canoe Saskatchewan
website: www.lights.com/waterways
(information on canoe routes in Saskatchewan, canoe camping and safety, history of routes, streamflow summaries, voyageur certificates and weather.)

AIR CHARTERS FOR CANOEISTS

Air Mikisew
Box 10
La Loche, SK, S0M 1G0
Phone: (306) 822-2022
Fax: (306) 822-2026
E-mail: mikisew@sk.sympatico.ca

Courtesy Air
Box 176
Buffalo Narrows, SK, S0M 0J0
Phone: (306) 235-4373
Fax: (306) 235-4622
E-mail: courtesy.air@sk.sympatico.ca
Website: www3.sk.sympatico.ca/courtesy/
Toll free 1-888-325-1313

Ile a la Crosse Airways Ltd.
Box 247
Ile a la Crosse, SK, S0M 1C0
Phone: (306) 833-2151
Fax: (306) 833-2251

Jackson Air Services
Box 1000
Flin Flon, MB R8A 1N7
Phone: (204) 687-8247
Fax: (204) 687-7694

Osprey Wings Ltd.
Box 419
La Ronge, SK, S0J 1L0 (base in Missinipe)
Phone: (306) 635-2112
Fax: (306) 635-2134

Pelican Narrows Air Services
Box 39
Pelican Narrows, SK, S0P 0E0
Phone: (306) 632-2020
Fax: (306) 632-2122

Ross Air
Box 10
Sandy Bay, SK S0P 0G0
Phone: (306) 754-2026
Fax: (306) 754-2202

Transwest Air
Box 320
La Ronge, SK, S0J 1L0
(bases in P.A., Saskatoon, Regina, and La Ronge)
Toll free for USA and Canada:
        1-800-667-9356 or 1-800-665-7275
La Ronge waterbase: (306) 425-5550
Website: www.transwestair.com

Voyage Air
Box 145
Buffalo Narrows, SK, S0M 0J0
Phone: (306) 235-4664   or
Box 5838
Fort McMurray, AB, T9H 4V9
Phone: (780) 743-0255
Website: www.voyageair.com
E-mail: bjobrien@sk.sympatico.ca

Canoe Clubs

Historic Trails Canoe Club
Box 3392
Regina, SK, S4P 3H1
Phone: (306) 543-7299

Saskatoon Canoe Club
Box 7764
Saskatoon, SK, S7K 4J1
Phone: (306) 343-0191
E-mail: saskatoon_canoe@canoemail.com
Website: www.sfn.saskatoon.sk.ca/sports/canoe

Pimiskatan Canoe Club
Box 1254
La Ronge, SK, S0J 1L0
Phone: (306) 425-2502 (Attn: Hilary Johnstone)

Canoe Outfitters

Horizons Unlimited Churchill River Canoe Outfitters
Box 1110
La Ronge, SK, S0J 1L0
(base camp actually in Missinnipe, SK)
Phone/Fax: (306) 635-4420 (Attn: Ric Driediger)
E-mail: ric.crco@sk.sympatico.ca
Website: www.churchillrivercanoe.com/

CanoeSki Discovery Company
1618 9th Ave. N.
Saskatoon, SK, S7K 3A1
Phone/Fax: (306) 653-5693 (Attn. Cliff Speer)
E-mail: info@canoeski.com
Website: www.canoeski.com

Rainbow Ridge Outfitters
Box 238
Ile a la Crosse, SK, S0M 1C0
Phone: (306) 833-2590 (Attn: Ken Cornett and Carol Miller)
Fax: (306) 833-2668
E-mail: ask@123math.ca

Water Levels

Sask Water Corporation
Victoria Place, 111 Fairford Street East
Moose Jaw, SK, S6H 7X9
Phone: (306) 694-3900
Website: www.saskwater.com/

Saskatchewan Environment Head Office

3211 Albert Street
Regina, SK, S4S 5W6 (head office)
Phone: (306) 787-2700 (year-round inquiry line)
Website: www.serm.gov.sk.ca
E-mail: inquiry@serm.gov.sk.ca

Saskatchewan Environment Northern Regional Offices:

Shield Eco-Region head office - La Ronge
1328 La Ronge Avenue
Box 5000
La Ronge, SK, S0J 1L0
Phone: (306) 425-4234
Fax: (306) 425-2580

West Boreal Eco-Region head office - Meadow Lake
Unit 1, 101 Railway Place
Meadow Lake, SK, S9X 1X6
Phone: (306) 236-7540
Fax: (306) 236-7677

East Boreal Eco-Region head office - Prince Albert
800 Central Avenue
Box 3003
Prince Albert, SK, S6V 6G1
Phone: (306) 953-2886
Fax: (306) 953-2502

Parkland Eco-Region head office
112 Research Drive
Saskatoon, SK, S7K 2H6
Phone: (306) 933-7950
Fax: (306) 933-8442

Topographical Maps

Information Services Corporation of Saskatchewan (SaskGeomatics Division)
300 - 10 Research Drive
Regina, SK S4P 3V7
Toll-free: 1-866-ASK-ISC1 (1-866-275-4721)
E-mail: ask@isc-online.ca
Website: www.isc-online.ca

Federal Publications Inc.
163 University Avenue
Toronto, ON, M5H 3B8
Phone: 1-888-433-3782 (toll free)
(416) 860-1611
E-mail: info@fedpubs.com
Website: www.fedpubs.com

APPENDIX C: SPELLING OF CREE AND DENE PLACE NAMES

In providing Cree names for geographical features, whether they be of the *y*, *th* or *n* dialect (the three Cree dialects found on the route), we make use of "Standard Roman Orthography" (SRO), a system designed specifically for the Cree sound system and now standard throughout most of Saskatchewan.

Cree words are reasonably easy to pronounce, since their sounds are not too different from those used in English. However, because some SRO symbols are not used in English, and because the pronunciation of some symbols or combinations of symbols do not necessarily correspond to the sound an English reader might normally expect, the following notes will be helpful:

a	sounds as the "u" in English "up";	*iw*	has a soft sound somewhat between the "ew" in "new" and the "o" in "go";
â	sounds somewhere between the "a" sounds of English "cat" and "father";	*îw*	approximates "ee-oo," with the "ee" sounding as in "meet" and the "oo" sounding as the Cree *iw*;
âw	sounds as the "ow" in "cow";		
ê	sounds long as the "ay" in "day" (this sound occurs only rarely in the *th* dialect);	*o*	sounds somewhere between the "o" of "boat" and the "u" of "put";
i	sounds short as the "i" in "it";	*ô*	sounds long as the "o" in "go";
î	sounds long as the "i" in "police" or the "ee" of "meet," and never the sound of long English "i" as in "kite" which is written "ay" in Cree;	*c*	usually sounds as the "ch" in "chat" or the "tch" in "catch," but may sound like "ts" in "cats";
		h	is always pronounced as an aspirate even when preceding another consonant.

****

Dene place names have presented us with a special challenge because the Dene language is very difficult for most English speakers to hear and pronounce. Moreover, our own knowledge of the language is extremely limited. What we do know is that Dene has sounds, such as the "greasy L," that simply do not exist in English and that it also makes use of glottal stops not used in English. As well, its vowels sometimes take on a distinct nasal quality similar to what one might hear in French. And, like Mandarin and Cantonese, Dene is a tonal language, i.e., the tone or pitch of a word can change its meaning. If you are Dene or a Dene linguist, you can no doubt point to other complexities in the language.

Given the Dene language's complex sound system, we wondered how best to transcribe the place names provided to us by Dene informants. We initially considered adopting a Dene orthography being developed for northern Saskatchewan. However, because this orthography uses symbols and marks that would be unfamiliar to most readers, we decided to use our own simplified phonetic renditions for the place names collected. Our renditions do not do justice to the Dene language, but they will give readers a readable approximation of the various names.

In our Dene names, we indicate glottal stops with an apostrophe where they occur. We also mark nasal vowels by adding a superscript *n* after the vowel. We have not marked high or low tones. Hence, although *sheth*, meaning "hill," is a high tone word, we do not indicate this in any way. Other explanation of our simplified system is as follows:

e	sounds short as in "let" (not long as in our Cree orthography);	*o*	sounds long as in "go;"
		oo	sounds as the "oo" in "soon"; and
ee	sounds long as in "meet;"	*tth*	sounds approximately like "t" and "th" together.

NOTES

CHAPTER ONE

1   Olson, *Lonely Land*, 26–27.

2   Henry (the Elder)'s *Travels and Adventures*, 327.

3   Saskatchewan, *Ecoregions of Saskatchewan*, 62, 79 and 98.

4   *Atlas of Saskatchewan*, 2d ed., 115.

5   Don Ryback (Environment Canada, Saskatoon), telephone interview, September 3, 1999.

6   Saskatchewan, *Boreal Shield Ecozone*, 54–55.

7   *Atlas of Saskatchewan*, 2d ed., 143–44.

8   Saskatchewan, *Boreal Shield Ecozone*, 51, 81.

9   Gerrard and Bortolotti, *Bald Eagle*, 57.

10   Our knowledge of the guide route's rock paintings, especially those on the Churchill, is based largely on the work done by archaeologist Tim Jones of Saskatoon. See Jones, *Aboriginal Rock Paintings*.

11   During the 1950s, the provincial government named geographic features, such as lakes, islands, and bays, after the 3,800 Saskatchewan men and women who lost their lives in World War II. Doug Chisholm of La Ronge has taken aerial photographs of many of these sites and has collected information on the persons they are named after. See *Their Names Live On: Remembering Saskatchewan's Fallen in World War II* (Regina: CPRC, 2001).

CHAPTER TWO

1   Innis, *Fur Trade in Canada*, 392.

2   *Canadian Encyclopedia*, 2d ed., vol. 2, 901–03.

3   *Atlas of Saskatchewan*, 2d ed., 23.

4   Meyer, "Churchill River Archaeology", 54–55; and *Atlas of Sasktchewan*, 2d ed., 23.

5   Epp, *Long Ago Today*, 44, 56, 60, 65–67.

6   Russell, *Eighteenth-Century Western Cree*. Russell details evidence that points to a lengthy Cree occupation of the route.

7   Smith, "Western Woods Cree," 267.

8   Honigmann, "West Main Cree," 227.

9   Smith, "Western Woods Cree," 259, 262.

10   Dale Russell has noted in conversation that the Cree vocabulary published by Alexander Mackenzie, likely learned during Mackenzie's early days at Île-à-la-Crosse, is in the *th* dialect.

11   Jones, "Writing on the Rocks," 11–13.

12   Jones, *Aboriginal Rock Paintings*; and *Atlas of Saskatchewan*, 2d ed., 29.

13   Thistle, *Indian-European Trade Relations*, 64–65, 68–69.

14   Ives, *Northern Athapaskan Prehistory*, chapter 2.

15   Smith, "Chipewyan," 283.

16   Dale Russell, conversations, 1997–1999.

17   Mackenzie's *Voyages from Montreal*, 151.

18   See Jarvenpa and Brumbach, "Southern Chipewyan Fur Trade History" (citing HBCA B.239/z/10, fos. 52a–57a) on 1838 census.

19   Mackenzie's *Voyages from Montreal*, 125.

20   Father Durand, conversation, July 2, 1986; and Martin Smith, conversation, July 28, 1998.

21   See Van Kirk, *Many Tender Ties*; and Brown, *Strangers in Blood*.

22   The HBC also hired some of its voyageurs (including both French Canadians and Iroquois) from Quebec, both prior to and after 1821, but only in small numbers. See Judd, "Mixt Bands of Many Nations," 129, 136–37.

23   See Nicks, "Orkneymen in the HBC." Also Judd, "Mixt Bands of Many Nations."

24   Crean, "Hats and the Fur Trade," 373–86.

25   NWC's *Documents*, 1–20; Morton, *History of the Canadian West*, 508–18; and Innis, *Fur Trade in Canada*, 194–203.

26   *Atlas of Saskatchewan*, 2d ed., 31.

27   See Galbraith, *Little Emperor* and Galbraith, "Sir George Simpson," 812. Also Rich's editorial introduction to Simpson's *Athabasca Journal, 1820 and 1821*, xl–xiv. Simpson was initially appointed Governor-in-Chief *locum tenens*, that is, as Deputy Governor to Governor William Williams. In 1821, he and Williams were appointed joint Governors. In 1826, when Williams returned to England, Simpson became sole Governor-in-Chief of the HBC's North American empire.

28   Simpson's *Athabasca Journal, 1820 and 1821*, 19.

29   Carlos, "Birth and Death of Predatory Competition," 156–83.

30   Simpson's *Athabasca Journal, 1820 and 1821*, 349–50.

31   Moberly, *When Fur was King*.

32   Gwyneth Hoyle, letter, October 24, 1988; and Newman, *Merchant Princes*, 208–14.

33   Newman, *Merchant Princes*, 394–99; and Town, *The North West Company*, 104–10.

34 William Auld quoted in Innis, *Fur Trade in Canada*, 159.

35 McKenney, *Sketches of a Tour*, 342–43

36 Ian and Sally Wilson, "Spirit of the Voyageur," 12.

37 Kent, *Birchbark Canoes*, I, 191–95.

38 Harmon's *Sixteen Years in the Indian Country*, 197–98.

39 Colin Robertson quoted in Rich's introduction to Simpson's *Athabasca Journal, 1820 and 1821*, xxxii.

40 Adapted from Nute, *The Voyageur*, 44–45.

41 Smith, *Alexander Mackenzie*, 38.

42 Quoted in Nicks, "Iroquois and the Fur Trade in Western Canada," 89.

43 HBC's *Journals of Hearne and Turnor*, 251.

44 Adney and Chapelle, *Bark Canoes and Skin Boats*, chapter 3; Van Kirk, *Many Tender Ties*, 61–62; and Kent, *Birchbark Canoes*, I, 14.

45 Mackenzie's *Voyages from Montreal*, 84–85.

46 Ibid., 99.

47 Morse, *Fur Trade Canoe Routes*, 22. In 1822, the HBC's Northern Council gave boat prices as, "Large new £30. Small £20. Second year large £15 & small £10 & third year taken off Inventories," suggesting boats lasted at least two full seasons (HBC's *Minutes of Council*, 27).

48 Rich in Simpson's *Athabasca Journal, 1820 and 1821*, 12n. Sources indicate that York boat loads and crews were highly variable. Rich's figures, which we use, appear to represent what was typical.

49 Morse, *Fur Trade Canoe Routes*, 32.

50 McDonald's *Peace River Journal [1828]*.

51 Downes, *Sleeping Island*, 48–49.

52 Harmon's *Sixteen Years in the Indian Country*, 197–98.

53 McDonald's *Peace River Journal [1828]*, 2.

54 See Van Kirk, "Louis Primeau" for Primeau's Cree name. The translation is our own based on information from Cree speakers.

55 Morton, *History of the Canadian West*, 267, 275.

56 HBC's *Journals of Hearne and Turnor*, 107.

57 NWC's *Documents*, 446–47; and HBC's *Journals of Hearne and Turnor*, 120n.

58 Henry (the Elder)'s *Travels and Adventures*, 260.

59 See Armour, "Alexander Henry [the Elder]."

60 In the *Canadian Encyclopedia*, 2d ed., vol. 2, 735–36, Richard C. Davis recognizes Alexander Henry (the Elder)'s narrative, *Travels and Adventures in Canada*, as being among the very best examples of "Canadian" exploration literature.

61 Quotation from L.G. Thomas's introduction to Henry (the Elder)'s *Travels and Adventures*, xii.

62 See C.S. Mackinnon, "Samuel Hearne." See also Hearne's *Journey from Prince of Wales's Fort*. The writing of this book was a major achievement for the semi-literate Hearne. In historian J.B. Brebner's words, Hearne was "blessed with an odd, judicious literary artistry which enabled him to write what is one of the classics of the literature of exploration, not only because it is an illuminating account of the country, its natural history and its inhabitants, but also because it conveys unconsciously a portrait 'in the round' of a very likeable and inquisitive, if somewhat timorous, man."

63 HBC's *Cumberland House Journals, First Series, 1775–79*.

64 Spry, "Matthew Cocking."

65 Gough, "Peter Pond"; and Innis, *Peter Pond*.

66 The full title of Alexander Mackenzie's book was *Voyages from Montreal on the River St. Laurence, through the Continent of North America, to the Frozen and Pacific Oceans; In the Years, 1789 and 1793. With a Preliminary Account of the Rise, Progress, and Present State of the Fur Trade of that Country*.

67 Lamb, "Sir Alexander Mackenzie"; Mackenzie's *Voyages from Montreal*; and Smith, *Alexander Mackenzie*.

68 Rich, "Philip Turnor"; and Tyrrell's introduction to HBC's *Journals of Hearne and Turnor*.

69 Allen, "Peter Fidler"; HBCA, E 3/1, Peter Fidler's journal; HBC's *Journals of Hearne and Turnor*; and MacGregor, *Peter Fidler*.

70 Nicks, "David Thompson"; Thompson's *Travels in Western North America*; and Tyrrell's introduction to Thompson's *Narrative* [Tyrrell, ed.].

71 Galbraith, "Sir George Simpson"; Galbraith, *Little Emperor*; and Rich's introduction to Simpson's *Athabasca Journal, 1820 and 1821*.

72 Simpson's *Athabasca Journal, 1820 and 1821*, 261.

73 Franklin's *Narrative, 1819–22*. See also *Franklin's Journals and Correspondence, 1819–1822*.

74 Hood's *Journal and Paintings*.

75 Richardson's *Arctic Searching Expedition*, I.

76 Back's *Journals and Paintings*.

77 Franklin's *Narrative of a Second Expedition, 1825–27*. See also *Franklin's Journals and Correspondence, 1825–1827*.

78 See also Neatby, *Search for Franklin*; Holland, "Sir John Franklin"; and Burant, "Robert Hood."

79 See Reid, "Tyrrell Museum of Palaeontology" in *Canadian Encyclopedia*, 2d ed., vol. 4, 2205.

80 Tyrrell and Dowling's *Athabasca Lake and Churchill River*.

81 See also Inglis, *Northern Vagabond*; Martyn, *J.B. Tyrrell*; Zaslow, *Reading the Rocks*; and McNicholl, "Joseph Burr Tyrrell" in *Canadian Encyclopedia*, 2d ed., vol. 4, 2205.

CHAPTER THREE

1 Henry (the Elder) in Burpee, *Search for the Western Sea*, 592.

2 See Dr. John Richardson in Franklin's *Narrative, 1819–22;* and Russell, *Eighteenth-Century Western Cree*, 189–90.

3 Mackenzie's *Voyages from Montreal*, 238.

4 For an analysis of the early Cree presence in the region, see Russell, *Eighteenth-Century Western Cree*, 153–71. Russell has doubts that a separate *r* Cree dialect existed given the lack of any detailed record of it (Russell, letter, July 13, 1998).

5 Russell, *Eighteenth-Century Western Cree*, 155, 171.

6 See NWC's *English River Book*, 19 ("little River"); Innis, *Peter Pond*, map ("Pelican River"); Henry (the Elder) in Burpee, *Search for the Western Sea*, 592 ("Kiutchinini"); Mackenzie's *Voyages from Montreal*, 128 ("by some called the Swan River, and by others, the Clear-Water and Pelican river"); HBC's *Journals of Hearne and Turnor*, 459 ("Wash-a-cum-mow Seepe or clear water river"); HBCA, E. 3/1, fo. 48d., Peter Fidler's journal, May 17, 1792 ("Little Athapescow"); and Simpson's *Athabasca Journal, 1820 and 1821*, 37 ("Little Athabasca River").

7 Saskatchewan, *Geological History*, 32–36, 91. Note that although this was the first Devonian outcrop we saw, geological mapping indicates outcrops as far as 5 km (3 mi) upstream, at the northeast end of Big Island. See Saskatchewan, *Sedimentary Geology of the La Loche Area*, figure 2.

8 Saskatchewan, *Geological History*, 79–81.

9 Saskatchewan, *Canoe Trip #40*, 6.

10 Ibid., 6.

11 Canada, *Devonian Stratigraphy of Northeastern Alberta and Northwestern Saskatchewan*, 6–8. The author, A.W. Norris, confirms Contact Rapids as the edge of the Shield, though he does not comment on the origin of the name.

12 Saskatchewan, *Canoe Trip #40*, 8–9.

13 Saskatchewan, *Sedimentary Geology of the La Loche Area*, 6.

14 HBCA, E. 3/1, fo. 50, Peter Fidler's journal, May 20, 1792.

15 Smith Portage on the Slave River, roughly 25 km (15 mi) long, might be named as a longer portage. However, in the early days of the fur trade, it was broken into shorter portages. Moreover, it is north from Fort Chipewyan and therefore somewhat beyond the main trunk of the voyageur highway.

16 The number of trips would depend mainly on crew sizes and cargo weights. Note, too, that a long portage such as the Methy would require four men to carry a North canoe rather than the two needed on shorter portages—hence an extra trip for two men.

17 HBCA, HBX B 39/a/22, fo. 24, "Athabasca Journal" of James Keith, quoted in Mackinnon, "Some Logistics of Portage La Loche," 57. We believe five days would be consistent with four trips over the portage.

18 See HBC's *Journals of Hearne and Turnor*, 355, regarding early NWC exploration of the Mudjatik River; and 370–88, regarding Philip Turnor's exploration of the Garson and Christina route (prompted by fear of starvation on Methy Portage rather than fear of labour). See also Thompson's *Travels in Western North America* on Thompson's exploration of the Fond du Lac.

19 HBC's *Journals of Hearne and Turnor*, 465–66.

20 HBCA, E. 3/1, fo. 50, Peter Fidler's journal, May 20, 1792.

21 Quoted in Kupsch, "A Valley View in Verdant Prose," 39.

22 Ells, "Portage La Loche," 142, note 5. And see Mackinnon, "Some Logistics of Portage La Loche," 59.

23 Moberly, *When Fur Was King*, 141–43, 151.

24 HBCA, B. 89/b/4a, fos. 8d.–19, Chief Factor William McMurray, "Remarks regarding the H.B. Co.'s Posts in Upper English River Dis.," Île-à-la-Crosse, January 10, 1873.

25 Ells, "Portage La Loche," 142, note 5.

26 HBC's *Journals of Hearne and Turnor*, 467.

27 *Rae's Arctic Correspondence, 1844–55*, 77. For an exhaustive review of descriptions of the Clearwater Valley see Kupsch, "A Valley View in Verdant Prose."

28 HBCA, E. 3/1, fo. 51, Peter Fidler's journal, May 22, 1792.

29 Quoted in Kupsch, "A Valley View in Verdant Prose," 38.

30 NWC's *English River Book*, 20–21.

31 Simpson's *Athabasca Journal, 1820 and 1821*, 36–37.

32 Steer, "A North West Company Trading Post," 130–32, 192–93.

33 The NWC had as many as thirty-one canoes from the Athabasca region travel out and back across Methy Portage in 1809 followed by two dozen or more in each of the subsequent five years (estimated from NWC's *Documents*, 260–77). In these years, the HBC did not have canoes in the far North-West.

34 NWC's *English River Book*, 18–21.

35 HBCA, E.3/1, fo. 51, Peter Fidler's journal, May 21, 1792.

36 Morton, *History of the Canadian West*, 453.

37 Simpson's *Athabasca Journal, 1820 and 1821*, 137.

38 Mackinnon, "Some Logistics of Portage La Loche," 56. Parker, *Emporium of the North*, 64.

39 HBCA, B.39/a/22, extracts from "'Athabasca Journal' by James Keith commencing from York Factory 1823," September 29, 1823. It is possible that in 1823, boats were not yet available for the outgoing Methy Portage to York Factory leg of the trip. If so, cargoes would have been transferred to canoes. In any case, four boats were ready at York Factory for the return trip inland (HBC's *Minutes of Council*, 43).

40 Parker, *Emporium of the North*, 64–65.

41 HBCA, B.39/a/22, extracts from "'Athabasca Journal' by James Keith commencing from York Factory 1823," April 5 and May 14, 1824.

42 Mackinnon, "Some Logistics of Portage La Loche," 56.

43 We use the term "brigade" loosely. The Portage La Loche brigade eventually became two or more smaller brigades to avoid congestion on the portages. For example, on July 25, 1861, guide Baptiste Bruce left Methy Portage for York factory with seven boats, while on July 29, 1861, chief guide Alexis Bonamis dit L'Esperance followed with seven more boats (HBCA, B.167/2/1).

44 Mackinnon, "Some Logistics of Portage La Loche," 56–57. See also Innis, *Fur Trade in Canada*, 291–92.

45 Innis, *Fur Trade in Canada*, 292.

46 McDonald's *Peace River Journal [1828]*, 9.

47 Richardson's *Arctic Searching Expedition*, I, 111–12. Richardson estimated 10 paces to equal 23

feet. It seems his paces were actually about 75 cm (30 in) in length, slightly longer than he estimated.

48 Indians were in fact hired as regular voyageurs and tripmen, especially later in the fur trade. Here, we refer to Indians who were not regular voyageurs or tripmen.

49 Mackinnon, "Some Logistics of Portage La Loche," 58.

50 HBCA, D5/4, fo. 222, letter, E. Smith (Fort Chipewyan) to Governor, Chief Factors and Chief Traders, January 1, 1837.

51 McDonald's *Peace River Journal [1828]*, 10.

52 Simpson's *Athabasca Journal, 1820 and 1821*, 3–4.

53 Franklin's *Narrative of a Second Expedition, 1825–27*, xxvi–xxvii (boat design), 3, 4.

54 Mackinnon, "Some Logistics of Portage La Loche," 58.

55 HBCA, B.239/k/2, fo. 34, quoted in Steer, "A North West Company Trading Post," 52–58.

56 HBCA, D5/18, fo. 520, C. Campbell to Governor, Chief Factors and Chief Traders, December 24, 1846, quoted in Mackinnon, "Some Logistics of Portage La Loche," 58.

57 Richardson's *Arctic Searching Expedition*, I, 108.

58 Steer, "A North West Company Trading Post," 52–58.

59 Moberly, *When Fur was King*, 152–53.

60 Mackinnon, "Some Logistics of Portage La Loche," 61.

61 HBCA, E.3/1, fo. 51d., Peter Fidler's journal, May 25, 1792.

62 Simpson's *Athabasca Journal, 1820 and 1821*, 36.

63 The name "maria", pronounced with a long "i" as "ma-ruy-a," is the name most commonly used in northern Saskatchewan.

64 Franklin's *Narrative, 1819–22*, 130.

65 Steer, "History and Archaeology of La Loche House," 19.

66 Franklin's *Narrative, 1819–22*, 130 and maps. Note, too, that after some of Franklin's men followed this way by canoe on July 4, 1820, Robert Hood wrote (p. 187 in Franklin's *Narrative, 1819–22*): "The lake is seventeen miles in length, with a large island in the middle."

67 HBC's *Journals of Hearne and Turnor*, 471.

68 Ibid., 469.

69 HBCA, B.89/a/2, Île-à-la-Crosse journal per Peter Fidler, June 9, 1810, and September 17, 1810.

70 Joseph Perring (or Perren) was a German, formerly a soldier in the De Meuron regiment. He joined the

HBC in 1817 and remained with the company until 1823. See Simpson's *Athabasca Journal, 1820 and 1821*, 35–36 (quote), 460 (Perring biography).

71 Ibid., 344.

72 HBCA, B.89/b/1, fo. 6–6d, letter, John McLeod to John Clarke, September 25, 1820.

73 Simpson's *Athabasca Journal, 1820 and 1821*, 32.

74 Steer, "A North West Company Trading Post," 47.

75 HBCA, Portage La Loche Search File.

76 Steer, "A North West Company Trading Post," 53–54. Though the 1853 date is not certain, Steer arrived at this date after a careful study of the HBC's *Minutes of Council*.

77 HBCA, B.89/b/4a, fos. a8d–19, Chief Factor William McMurray, report, Île-à-la-Crosse, January 10, 1873.

78 HBCA, B.167/e/4a, E.K. Beeston, "Inspection Report of Portage La Loche Post," August 28–30, 1897.

79 HBCA, B.167/E/5, Sedley B. Blake, "Report upon Trade of Portage La Loche Post, Outfit 1901."

80 HBCA, B.167/a/5, extracts from Portage La Loche Post journals, June 24, 1879, and June 25, 1879.

81 Crean, *Northland Exploration*, 32–33.

82 Lemaigre, "La Loche," 9. Lemaigre dates the fire in 1937, but HBC records suggest the move to the Revillon Frères buildings occurred in 1936, per letter from David Arthurs, HBC archivist, July 13, 1992. See also Keighley, *Trader Tripper Trapper*, 180.

83 Steer, "History and Archaeology of La Loche House," 19. Other names for the peninsula include "point Moryion" (HBCA, E.23/1, W.J. Christie's diary entry, September 28, 1872), and "Point au Mongrain" (HBCA, B.167/a/5, "Extracts from Portage La Loche Post Journals," June 24, 1879). The name "Old Sylvestre's Point" was in use as early as 1885 and likely referred to one Baptiste Sylvestre, a HBC employee (HBCA, B.167/A/4, extracts from "Journal of Daily Occurrences kept by Hudson's Bay Company for Portage La Loche Transport," August 14, 1885, and September 13, 1885).

84 HBC's *Journals of Hearne and Turnor*, 470–71.

85 In "History and Archaeology of La Loche House," Steer concludes (p. 31) that the house is the NWC establishment mentioned by Philip Turnor. This is quite likely correct. However, at least three other posts—an 1809 HBC post, an 1820 HBC post, and an 1820 NWC post—may have been situated in the vicinity. It is also possible that Big Point was the locale of a NWC post operating circa 1793–94 since, in a letter to his cousin Roderick McKenzie dated January 13, 1794, Alexander Mackenzie refers to the "Boy at Lac la Loche" (Mackenzie's *Voyages from Montreal*, 453). It is thus perhaps impossible for us to know the origin of Steer's "La Loche House" with absolute certainty.

86 Steer, "History and Archaeology of La Loche House," 19–21; and Ducharme, "Memoirs."

87 Lemaigre, "La Loche," 15–18; Barry, *People Places*, 34; and Walter Hainault (CRDN), telephone conversation, December 8, 1999.

CHAPTER FOUR

1 After leaving La Loche on June 30, 1987, Father Mathieu went to Wollaston Lake for seven years, replacing the legendary Father Jean Mégret, O.M.I. In 1995, Father Mathieu was transferred to Patuanak where he continues the work of the Church.

2 HBCA, B.167/e/5, "Report upon Trade of Portage La Loche Post, Outfit 1901, Sedley B. Blake in charge."

3 Lemaigre, "La Loche," 9; David Arthurs, HBC archivist, letter, July 13, 1992.

4 Keighley, *Trader Tripper Trapper*, 181–82.

5 Saskatchewan, *1999 Northern Local Government Directory*.

6 The earlier St. Martin's Hospital, started in 1981, was a modest facility occupying 15 ATCO trailers linked together. The new 24-bed facility has an estimated cost of about $10 million (per *The Northerner*, November 16, 1999, 1,2).

7 When we stopped at Saleski Lake in 1986, the water base there was being operated by C & M Airways. Pilots John Midgett and Grover Clark started C & M at La Loche in 1968. C & M pilot, Marvin Bather, along with two partners, then bought the company in 1989 and ran it under the name La Loche Airways (per Saskatchewan, *Wings Beyond Road's End*, 68–71). In the year 2000, La Loche Airways was taken over by Air Mikisew of Fort McMurray, Alberta. Air Mikisew's La Loche/Saleski Lake base is currently managed by pilot James (Jamie) Palmer.

8 Franklin's *Narrative, 1819–22*, 129.

9 Simpson's *Athabasca Journal, 1820 and 1821*, 35.

10 The name "Pinnet" may be from the French *épinette*, meaning "spruce."

11 Black Point is known in Dene as *Tat'luh*, meaning simply "at the bay." In 1998, Black Point's official population was 43 (per "Northern Settlement of Black Point" in Saskatchewan, *1998 Northern Local Government Directory*).

12 Richardson's *Arctic Searching Expedition*, I, 107.

13 HBC's *Journals of Hearne and Turnor*, 370–71. The word "kimowin" *(kimiwan)* is Cree for "rain" or "rainy." We have not been able to trace the origin of this current name.

14 Ibid., 370–88.

15 HBCA, E. 3/1, fo. 54, Peter Fidler journal, June 4, 1792. The fact that Fidler refers to a 1795 date (assuming no error) suggests he made a "fair copy" of his journal some time after his 1790–92 trip. Making a journal fair copy was a common practice of early travellers. It would have been especially important for Fidler since due to a lack of paper, parts of his field journals from 1790–92 were written on scraps of birch bark.

16 Mackinnon, "Some Logistics of Portage La Loche," 59–61.

17 HBCA, B.167/e/4, E.K. Beeston, "Inspection Report of Portage La Loche Post," August 28–30, 1897. HBC records from 1921 also refer to Bulls House as an outpost of West La Loche (HBCA, G7/6(4), "Plan of Bulls House Outpost," referred to by David Arthurs, HBC archivist, letter, July 13, 1992).

18 Wuorinen, *A History of Buffalo Narrows*, 50–52.

19 HBC's *Journals of Hearne and Turnor*, 369, 369n.

20 The name is similar to that for Lac la Loche, i.e., *Ttheentaylas Too*, meaning "little burbot lake."

21 Innis, *Peter Pond*, map. In Pond's day, the buffalo was commonly referred to as "beef."

22 HBC's *Journals of Hearne and Turnor*, 367.

23 SAB, Saskatoon, J. Mitchell to A.S. Morton, letter, September 21, 1943.

24 Ross, *The Manager's Tale*, 197.

25 Lemaigre, "La Loche," 18.

26 HBC's *Journals of Hearne and Turnor*, 368.

27 Wuorinen, *A History of Buffalo Narrows*, 17.

28 "Northern Hamlet of Michel Village" in Saskatchewan, *1998 Northern Local Government Directory*.

29 HBC's *Journals of Hearne and Turnor*, 368.

30 Cockburn, "To Great Slave and Great Bear," 139 (re topo maps); HBCA, Buffalo River/Dillon Post History.

31 HBCA, E. 3/1, fo. 54d., Peter Fidler journal, June 6, 1792.

32 Franklin's *Narrative, 1819–22*, 128 & map. Franklin's map of his 1819–20 travels shows only an NWC post at Buffalo River.

33 HBCA, Buffalo River Post History & Buffalo River Search File. Re Revillon Frères, the HBCA Search File contains an HBC journal entry from September 30, 1907, stating, "Frances and Family also arrived to take charge for Revillon Bros. Ltd."

34 HBC's *Journals of Hearne and Turnor*, 367.

35 Ibid., 363, 364–65, 367, 367n. And HBCA, E. 3/1, fo. 2d., Peter Fidler journal, May 31, 1791, re Graham's drowning. Fidler's journal, the fair copy of which was apparently prepared some time after 1791, does not make it clear whether Graham drowned in 1791 or 1792. However, it was likely 1792 since on June 8, 1792, Philip Turnor's party were treated kindly at Île-à-la-Crosse by one Graham acting as "Summer Master" of the post—probably the same Graham who had wintered at Old Fort Point in 1790–91 (per HBC's *Journals of Hearne and Turnor*, 474–75).

36 Wuorinen, *A History of Buffalo Narrows*, 3, 4. We presume "Kisis" is a cartographer's spelling of "Kiezie," but we have not confirmed this.

37 Wuorinen, *A History of Buffalo Narrows*, 26.

CHAPTER FIVE

1 Meyer, "Churchill River Archaeology," 54–56.

2 Ibid., 56–57; *Atlas of Saskatchewan*, 2d ed., 23–24.

3 HBCA, Buffalo Narrows Post History (re 1888–1942).

4 Butler, *The Wild North Land*, 108.

5 Wuorinen, *A History of Buffalo Narrows*, 2.

6 Ibid., 3.

7 Ibid., 4, 17–19. For 1990–1991, a year randomly chosen, Big Peter Pond had an annual quota of 136,000 kg (300,000 lb), Little Peter Pond 74,000 kg (163,000 lb), and Churchill 185,000 kg (408,000 lb) (per *The Saskatchewan Gazette*, May 18, 1990, 807, 830).

8 Wuorinen, *A History of Buffalo Narrows*, 18–20; *The Northerner*, La Ronge, Saskatchewan, May 9, 1992, 10; "John Waite Carries on Family Tradition," *Opportunities North*, Vol. 5, No. 1 (Jan/Feb 1998): 9.

9 Wuorinen, *A History of Buffalo Narrows*, 4, 21–28.

10 Ibid., 32–34.

11 Ibid., 25–42.

12 "Mink ranching important in Buffalo history," *The Northerner*, La Ronge, Saskatchewan, May 9, 1992, 9.

13 Lake areas from *The Canadian Encyclopedia*, 2d. ed., vol. 1, 426.

14 HBC's *Journals of Hearne and Turnor*, 366.

15 Mackenzie's *Voyages from Montreal*, 126; Simpson's *Athabasca Journal, 1820 and 1821*, 34.

16 Simpson's *Athabasca Journal, 1820 and 1821*, 34.

17 Innis, *Fur Trade in Canada*, 199, suggests Peter Pond spent the winter of 1782–83 (the season following his alleged shooting of Etienne Wadin) at Churchill Lake. But this seems unlikely since

Pond's own map puts him wintering at Île-à-la-Crosse that season (Innis, *Peter Pond*, map).

18 HBCA, Clear Lake Post History; HBCA, G.7/7, fo. 177, 1921 Plan; Innis, *Fur Trade in Canada*, 368, 372–73; Ross, *The Manager's Tale*, 109–10.

19 Mackenzie's *Voyages from Montreal*, 126 ("Riviere Creuse"); Simpson's *Athabasca Journal, 1820 and 1821*, 34 ("Rivierre Cruise"); Thompson's *Narrative*, [Tyrrell, ed.] map ("Deep River").

20 McDonald's *Peace River Journal [1828]*, 8–9.

21 Wuorinen, *A History of Buffalo Narrows*, 10, 21–23; Ross, *The Manager's Tale*, 107–09.

22 Wuorinen, *A History of Buffalo Narrows*, 12, 37.

23 SAB, Saskatoon, Dr. P.E. Lavoie to Arthur S. Morton, letter, notes & maps, December 2, 1935.

24 Ibid.

CHAPTER SIX

1 Richardson in Franklin's *Narrative, 1819–22*.

2 Mackenzie's *Voyages from Montreal*, 125.

3 See Henry (the Elder)'s, *Travels and Adventures*, 327; and HBC's *Cumberland House Journals, First Series, 1775–79*, 60, 93–94, 117–18, 149, 165–67, 257. And Innis, *Peter Pond*, map (re post location).

4 SAB, Saskatoon, Dr. P.E. Lavoie to Arthur S. Morton, letter & notes, December 2, 1935.

5 Morton, *History of the Canadian West*, 335. Morton suggests Île-à-la-Crosse was occupied continuously after 1776, but he does not cite authorities for this.

6 HBC's *Cumberland House Journals, First Series, 1775–79*, 257.

7 Innis, *Peter Pond*, map.

8 HBC's *Journals of Hearne and Turnor*, 330n; NWC's *English River Book*, xxxi (indicating Small had thirty men at Île-à-la-Crosse in 1786).

9 Mackenzie's *Voyages from Montreal*, 4, 10–12. HBC's *Journals of Hearne and Turnor*, 416–17, 417n.

10 HBC's *Journals of Hearne and Turnor*, 357.

11 Ibid., 365.

12 Longpré, *Île-à-la-Crosse, 1776–1976*, 9. Also HBCA, B.84/a/1, fo. 1–10, "Journal of Occurrences during an Expedition to Beaver River from Churchill Factory 1800 by William Auld" and HBCA, B. 179/a/3, fo. 5, "Reindeer Lake Journal by Joseph Spence," October 1, 1806.

13 After the merger of the NWC and HBC, Black had a significant career with the new HBC. He carried out major explorations in the Pacific region and rose to the rank of Chief Factor. However, perhaps in keeping with the phrase "what goes around comes around," he was killed while in his room at his

Kamloops post by an Indian on February 9, 1841. See Simpson's *Athabasca Journal, 1820 and 1821*, 429–30.

14 Longpré, *Île-à-la-Crosse, 1776–1976*, 9–12; MacGregor, *Peter Fidler*, 173–77. While Longpré and the HBCA Île-à-la-Crosse Post History put Fidler at Île-à-la-Crosse in 1809–10, Fidler's journal for that year does not survive. MacGregor hints that Fidler and his family were actually in the Reindeer Lake country that first year.

15 HBCA, B.89/a/2, fo. 36–36d., "Isle a la Crosse Journal" per Peter Fidler, June 3, 1811.

16 Arthur, "Duel at Île-à-la-Crosse," 46 (the "duel" describes a sword fight not related to the killings).

17 HBCA, Île-à-la-Crosse Post History; Anne Morton (HBCA) letter, September 1, 1999 (re Robert Logan); HBCA, B.89/a/4 and Simpson's *Athabasca Journal, 1820 and 1821*, 417 (re Fort Superior).

18 Simpson's *Athabasca Journal, 1820 and 1821*, 324.

19 Mackenzie's *Voyages from Montreal*, 476. McKay had earlier accompanied Alexander Mackenzie on his 1793 journey to the Pacific. He was later killed by Indians on the Pacific coast in 1811.

20 HBCA, Île-à-la-Crosse Post History.

21 Innis, *Fur Trade in Canada*, 368 (re Revillon at Île-à-la-Crosse) and 372 (re HBC purchase of Lamson & Hubbard); Kemp, *Northern Trader*, 85 (re work for Lamson & Hubbard).

22 Lavoie, December 2, 1935, gives 1843 as the supposed date of the HBC's move to the Snob Hill location. Consistent with Dr. Lavoie's date, the late Louis Bouvier of Île-à-la-Crosse, speaking to us on June 19, 1986, told us that the HBC had been at its Snob Hill site for about 100 years before moving south to a new location in 1949 or so. The HBCA's "Île-à-la-Crosse Post History" indicates the move south was in 1950.

23 HBC's *Journals of Hearne and Turnor*, 330n; Thompson's *Travels in Western North America*.

24 Longpré, *Île-à-la-Crosse, 1776–1976*, 33.

25 See ibid., 24–29, 33–35.

26 Ibid., 48. Tom Natomagan himself later settled at Pinehouse Lake where he raised a large Métis family.

27 Saskatchewan, *1999 Northern Local Government Directory*.

28 Simpson's *Athabasca Journal, 1820 and 1821*, 429–30 (re Black's hire with the XY Company). The XY Company got its name from the "XY" mark it put on its packs—a mark distinct from the "NW" the North West Company used to mark its packs. A good history of the XY Company can be found in Morton, *History of the Canadian West*, 508–18.

29 Lavoie, December 2, 1935.

30 The lives of Fred and Nora Darbyshire and Ed and Evangeline Theriau are set out in Karras, *Face the North Wind.*

31 Morton, *History of the Canadian West*, 698–99 (re old Indian track); Innis, *Fur Trade in Canada*, 343–44.

32 Dr. Lavoie mentions the two posts twice but does not give sources for his information (per Lavoie, December 2, 1935).

33 McDonald's *Peace River Journal [1828]*, 8.

34 "Mogloair" is possibly a misspelling of "Magloire." If so, it may refer to a Magloire Maurice who was born in the 1850s and lived to be a very old man. He spent many years employed by the HBC and was fluent in French, English, Cree, and Dene (per Cockburn, "To Great Slave and Great Bear," 135–36).

35 Karras, *North to Cree Lake* and Karras, *Face the North Wind*, ii–iii.

36 Cook et al, eds., *Nehithowewin*, 267; HBC's *Journals of Hearne and Turnor*, 356n.

37 Mackenzie's *Voyages from Montreal*, 124.

CHAPTER SEVEN

1 The Dene name for the town of La Ronge, on Lac la Ronge to the east, means a "bay," and the Patuanak hamlet has a small bay. From this rather weak connection, the hamlet has picked up the "La Ronge" nickname.

2 Tyrrell and Dowling's *Athabasca Lake and Churchill River*, map, opposite 120.

3 HBCA, Souris River Search File, letter from Île-à-la-Crosse to Thos. Bear, Dipper Post, November 6, 1907.

4 HBCA, Patuanak Post History.

5 Mackenzie's *Voyages from Montreal*, 120–21.

6 Jarvenpa and Brumbach, "Southern Chipewyan Fur Trade History," 152–54.

7 On June 17, 1792, Philip Turnor and his party met six canoes of Dene on Trout Lake. The Dene seemed familiar with the area and with happenings at Rapid River much further downstream. See HBC's *Journals of Hearne and Turnor*, 479–80. See also Moberly, *When Fur was King*, 175, re Dene trading at Stanley Mission. But note that Dene found downstream on the Churchill River may have arrived from the north via routes other than the upper Churchill, e.g. the Reindeer River. More research needs to be done in this regard.

8 Canada, *Treaty No. 10.*

9 See Jarvenpa, *Trappers of Patuanak*, 57–64.

10 Smith said that Kenny McDonald was later to trade at Île-à-la-Crosse, while Jimmy traded at La Loche.

They then both lost their families to the 1918 flu epidemic whereupon both moved north to Fond du Lac and started new families. Also see HBCA, Patuanak Post History re Patuanak as an outpost of Île-à-la-Crosse pre-1921.

11 HBCA, B.464/a/1, 3 & 6, Pine River Post Journal, October 1 and 20, 1921.

12 HBCA, Patuanak Post History; HBCA, unclassified, NSD Personnel Files, Box #1 (re Bélanger); Cockburn, "To Great Slave and Great Bear," 136 (re Ahenakew).

13 Guest, "Patuanak," 21 (re Moraud's life & McIntyre quote); Jarvenpa, *Trappers of Patuanak*, 51 (re church at Patuanak). But note Father Beaudet, O.M.I., in conversation on August 9, 1986, told us that Father Moraud was known to travel to eastern Canada wearing his cassock and moccasins to raise funds for his parish.

14 Father Moraud has not been officially canonized, but it is a common view in Patuanak that he will be one day.

15 Dennis A. Belliveau, letter, January 28, 1987.

16 Mackenzie's *Voyages from Montreal*, 124.

17 Cook et al, eds., *Nehithowewin*, 267; HBC's *Journals of Hearne and Turnor*, 356n.

18 Reynolds, "History of Patuanak," 69, 75.

19 Simpson's *Athabasca Journal, 1820 and 1821*, 31.

20 Philip Wolverine told us that the wooden cross at Drum Rapids had been moved there from Cross Island by John Lariviere. We assume that this was when the present steel cross on Cross Island was erected to take its place. In 1992, the wooden cross at Drum Rapids, about 3 m (10 ft) high, was grey and weathered but still standing.

21 HBCA, E. 3/1, fo. 56d., Peter Fidler journal, June 11, 1792.

22 Karras, *North to Cree Lake*, 90–91.

23 HBC's *Journals of Hearne and Turnor*, 355.

24 Tyrrell and Dowling's *Athabasca Lake and Churchill River*, 31.

25 HBC's *Journals of Hearne and Turnor*, 355n.

26 Karras, *North to Cree Lake*, 91–93.

27 See Russell, *Eighteenth-Century Western Cree*, 163–71.

28 Jarvenpa and Brumbach, "Southern Chipewyan Fur Trade History," 152–55.

29 Richardson's *Arctic Searching Expedition*, I, 101.

30 HBC's *Journals of Hearne and Turnor*, 354.

31 HBCA, E. 3/1, fo. 56d., Peter Fidler journal, June 11, 1792. Fidler made his journal entry respecting these rapids while travelling downstrem in 1792, but in so doing, he referred back to his party having

"led" canoes on the north side of the rapids while travelling upstream in 1790.

32 HBCA, E. 3/1, fo. 56d., Peter Fidler journal, June 11, 1792. Fidler again made his journal entry while travelling downstream. In doing so, he once more referred back to his earlier trip upstream in the fall of 1790, writing, "led 200 yards on the north side in 1790."

33 Mackenzie's *Voyages from Montreal*, 124. Also, Simpson's *Athabasca Journal, 1820 and 1821*, 31. The name "la Puisse" would seem to be related to the French word *puissant*, meaning mighty or powerful.

34 McDonald's *Peace River Journal [1828]*, 8. *Pins* is French for "pines," but note that the voyageurs often used *pin* to mean "spruce" and *cyprès* for "jack pine."

35 HBC's *Journals of Hearne and Turnor*, 354n.

36 Reynolds, "History of Patuanak," 56–57.

37 Saskatchewan, *Canoe Trip #1*, 5.

38 Reynolds, "History of Patuanak," 30.

39 HBCA, E. 3/1, fo. 56d., Peter Fidler journal, June 11, 1792.

40 Joe Black provided the name as *Guh-tha-theh*, which he translated as "rabbit feathers."

41 Jarvenpa, *Trappers of Patuanak*, 52. According to Jarvenpa's sources, the small lake was called "Rabbit's Hair Lake."

42 Ibid., 175.

43 HBC's *Journals of Hearne and Turnor*, 354n.

44 Ibid., 353. See also HBCA, E. 3/1, fo. 56d.–57, Peter Fidler journal, June 11, 1792.

45 HBC's *Cumberland House Journals, First Series, 1775–79*, 121.

46 HBC's *Journals of Hearne and Turnor*, 353–354.

47 HBC's *Cumberland House Journals, First Series, 1775–79*, 29.

48 Ibid., 43.

49 Ibid., 59–60.

50 Jarvenpa, *Trappers of Patuanak*, 48–49. Jarvenpa points out that what his Dene informants told him was corroborated to some degree by mapping done by surveyor J.B. Tyrrell in 1892 which shows houses marked on the west shore of Dipper Lake at or near the settlement site, the east shore of Dipper Lake, and at the Knee Lake settlement site.

51 HBCA, B.464/a/1, p. 4, Pine River Post Journal, October 10, 1921.

52 Jarvenpa, *Trappers of Patuanak*, 51.

53 Guest, "Patuanak," 23.

54 Jarvenpa, *Trappers of Patuanak*, 51.

55 By September 25, 1992, the church's conversion was complete, and it was being neatly kept as a cabin. The side wing had become an open air summer kitchen.

56 HBCA, E. 3/1, fo. 57, Peter Fidler journal, June 11, 1792. Fidler's description is somewhat hard to follow. His reference to "2 more, a little way below" seemingly refers to a minor rapid below the second rapids and also the third rapids.

57 HBC's *Journals of Hearne and Turnor*, 351.

58 HBCA, E. 3/1, fo. 57, Peter Fidler journal, June 11, 1792.

59 By 1992, the jack pine with the eagle nest had lost its hold on the rocky bank and had crashed to the ground.

60 Mackenzie's *Voyages from Montreal*, 124.

61 In 1992, the portage remained in essentially the same condition. If anything, it was in worse condition as more fire-killed trees had blown down.

62 HBC's *Journals of Hearne and Turnor*, 351.

63 We found the word *tscho* difficult to record phonetically. Philip Wolverine's pronunciation of it was closer to *schol*.

64 Philip Wolverine, one of our principal sources for local Dene place names, lived at Reserve 192B as a boy.

65 Jarvenpa, *Trappers of Patuanak*, 175n. The fact that the Knee Lake settlement was commonly known as Pine River can be confusing since the Hudson's Bay Company post at Patuanak was, up until 1950, officially known as Pine River.

66 See also Jarvenpa, *Trappers of Patuanak*, 49. Dene sources told Jarvenpa that Dipper Lake, Primeau Lake, and Knee Lake had their first log cabins built in about 1900.

67 Jarvenpa, *Trappers of Patuanak*, 52.

68 Guest, "Patuanak," 23.

69 Jarvenpa, *Trappers of Patuanak*, 51.

70 In the fall of 1992, the church remained essentially as we had seen it in 1986. The only change was that new steps had been built to replace a set that had become treacherous.

71 HBC's *Journals of Hearne and Turnor*, 351n.

72 Mackenzie's *Voyages from Montreal*, 123.

73 HBC's *Journals of Hearne and Turnor*, 350.

74 Mackenzie's *Voyages from Montreal*, 123; Simpson's *Athabasca Journal, 1820 and 1821*, 30; Hood in Franklin's *Narrative, 1819–22*, 184; and Richardson's *Arctic Searching Expedition*, I, 99.

Philip Turnor's journal indicates a Cree source for the name when he refers to the channel as being part of "the Mus-coo-see se-pee [*maskosiy sîpiy*] or Grass River." It seems Turnor and Peter Fidler applied the name to the entire distance between Knee Lake and Dreger Lake. See HBC's *Journals of Hearne and Turnor*, 350, and HBCA, E. 3/1, fo. 58, Peter Fidler journal, June 13, 1792.

75 Hood in Franklin's *Narrative, 1819–22*, 184.

76 See Jarvenpa and Brumbach, "Southern Chipewyan Fur Trade History," 161, for the spelling "wagaho-nanci."

77 Jarvenpa and Brumbach, "Southern Chipewyan Fur Trade History," 161.

78 Simpson's *Athabasca Journal, 1820 and 1821*, 31. A day later on the same voyage, Simpson also referred to part or all of present-day Primeau Lake as Lac Croche. This liberal use of the name must have been somewhat confusing in route discussions.

79 The channel was dry on September 28, 1992.

80 Jarvenpa and Brumbach, "Southern Chipewyan Fur Trade History," 161.

81 HBCA, E. 3/1, fo. 58, Peter Fidler journal, June 13, 1792.

82 Simpson's *Athabasca Journal, 1820 and 1821*, 30.

83 Saskatchewan, *Canoe Trip #1*, 7–8.

84 In 1986, there was an ice house for commercial fishing at the start of the vehicle track, but it has since been removed. We suspect the vehicle track was made by commercial fishers some time after the construction of Road 914.

85 Henry (the Elder)'s *Travels and Adventures*, 321.

86 HBC's *Journals of Hearne and Turnor*, 348–49.

87 HBCA, E. 3/1, fo. 58–58d., Peter Fidler journal, June 13, 1792.

88 Hood in Franklin's *Narrative, 1819–22*, 183–84.

89 On September 28, 1992, there appeared to be no water running on the east side of the island. However, as a black bear was met along the channel bed, investigation was cut short.

90 Jones, *Aboriginal Rock Paintings*, 12.

CHAPTER EIGHT

1 Father Durand died April 20, 1999, and was buried at the Oblate cemetery in Richelieu, Quebec (*The Northerner*, La Ronge, Saskatchewan, May 11, 1999, 34).

2 Father Durand, O.M.I. has suggested that the Pinehouse Lake Dene fell to an epidemic in 1900 or 1901 (per Durand, "History of Pinehouse", and also in conversation). However, Martin Smith believes the epidemic was the great influenza outbreak of 1918. See also Jarvenpa and Brumbach, "Southern Chipewyan Fur Trade History," 161, regarding the Dene presence in the area.

3 The use of the word "pine" to mean spruce was formerly common in the north.

4 HBCA, B.349/a/1, fo.7, Souris River Post Journal, September 22, 1933.

5 Durand, "History of Pinehouse."

6 The Government Trading store in Pinehouse was managed by Ron Clancy from 1955 to 1961. His experiences are set out in his book *True Lies of a Northern Fur Trader*.

7 Saskatchewan, *1999 Northern Local Government Directory*.

8 Richardson's *Arctic Searching Expedition*, I, 98, 98n.

9 The Cree *minahiko-wâskahikan sâkahikanihk*, literally "spruce house lake" but translated as "pine house lake," is now commonly used to refer to the lake.

10 Some Pinehouse residents consider the liver and eggs of maria (burbot) to be a delicacy. See Pinehouse, "Planning Project," 100–02, 177, 181.

11 Masson, ed., *Les Bourgeois*, I, 17.

12 Thompson's *Narrative* [Tyrrell, ed.], map.

13 HBCA, Souris River Search File & Souris River Post Journals; Jarvenpa and Brumbach, "Southern Chipewyan Fur Trade History," 160–61.

14 HBCA, Souris River Search File.

15 HBCA, unclassified, NSD Personnel Files, Box #1.

16 Wuorinen, *A History of Buffalo Narrows*, 9.

17 Mackenzie's *Voyages from Montreal*, 123, where Mackenzie refers to "the Lake des Souris." Also McDonald's *Peace River Journal [1828]*, 7, for use of *Lac de Souris*. And see HBC's *Journals of Hearne and Turnor*, 478, where Turnor refers to "Mouse Lake." Also HBCA, E. 3/1, fo. 59, Peter Fidler journal, June 14, 1792, for use of "Mouse Lake."

18 Simpson's *Athabasca Journal, 1820 and 1821*, 30. Simpson's journal refers to him passing through "Lac des Epingles" and then "Lac des Souris" on his voyage up the Churchill in 1820, his first trip into the North-West. It seems, perhaps because his voyageurs were using both these names for Sandfly Lake, he mistakenly applied the name Lac des Souris to a portion of Pinehouse Lake.

19 See Robert Hood in Franklin's *Narrative, 1819–22*, 183. And see Richardson's *Arctic Searching Expedition*, I, 97, for use of "Sand-fly Lake," June 22, 1848.

20 Mackenzie's *Voyages from Montreal*, 123.

21 Credit for identifying the glacial erratic as the stone bear head goes to Sid's wife Hilary Johnstone and daughter Haley Robinson who, while paddling by it, first noticed its resemblance to a bear's head.

22 Ibid., 122–23. And Simpson's *Athabasca Journal, 1820 and 1821*, 29 (Simpson uses a variant spelling "Canot Tournier" for the middle rapids).

23 Hood in Franklin's *Narrative, 1819–22*.

24 Robertson's *Correspondence Book*, 74–89.

25 Simpson's *Athabasca Journal, 1820 and 1821*, 348.

26 See Mackenzie's *Voyages from Montreal*, 123 where Mackenzie refers to "Portage des Epingles, so called from the sharpness of its stones." Also HBCA, E. 3/1, fo. 59, Peter Fidler journal, June 14, 1792, where Fidler says, "The stones upon this rocky carrying place very sharp resembling a honey comb, that the Canadians term it the Pin Portage." While these references might allude to the actual portage trail, we found the lake bottom at the upstream landing much more remarkable and the more likely source of the portage's name.

27 Barry, *People Places*, 31.

28 *The Northerner*, La Ronge, Saskatchewan, December 7, 1999, 1–2; October 30, 2001, 1–2.

29 Jones, *Aboriginal Rock Paintings*, 14.

30 HBC's *Journals of Hearne and Turnor*, 346n.

31 Mackenzie's *Voyages from Montreal*, 122.

32 HBC's *Journals of Hearne and Turnor*, 345.

33 Mackenzie's *Voyages from Montreal*, 122.

34 Jones, *Aboriginal Rock Paintings*, 17.

35 Jones, *Aboriginal Rock Paintings*, 22.

36 John McKay passed away in July 2000.

37 Richardson's *Arctic Searching Expedition*, I, 95. Sadly, on October 10, 1999, a 14-year-old boy died after mistakenly eating water hemlock while on a hunting trip with his brothers on Black Bear Island Lake.

38 Mackenzie's *Voyages from Montreal*, 122.

39 Simpson's *Athabasca Journal, 1820 and 1821*, 29.

40 HBC's *Journals of Hearne and Turnor*, 479.

41 Thompson's *Narrative* [Tyrrell, ed.], map.

42 Saskatchewan, *Canoe Trip #16*.

43 HBC's *Journals of Hearne and Turnor*, 344n. And NWC's *Documents*, 443.

44 HBC's *Journals of Hearne and Turnor*, 479–480.

45 Ibid., 344.

46 HBCA, E. 3/1, fo. 60d., Peter Fidler journal, June 18, 1792.

47 HBC's *Journals of Hearne and Turnor*, 344.

48 Ibid.

49 See Simpson's *Athabasca Journal, 1820 and 1821*, 29. See also Richardson's *Arctic Searching Expedition*, I, 96 for use of "Little Rock."

50 "Chief" is only an approximate translation for the Cree *okimâw*. The word *okimâw* can apply to any

person of influence, e.g., a fur trade factor or Indian Agent.

51 Keighley, *Trader Tripper Trapper*, 82. And Dale R. Russell, telefax, March 11, 1999. More research may clarify whether "Fine Cloth Lake" was either Mountney Lake or Nipew Lake.

52 Mackenzie's *Voyages from Montreal*. Also Simpson's *Athabasca Journal, 1820 and 1821*, 29. And Richardson's *Arctic Searching Expedition*, I, 96. David Thompson's famous map of the North-West does not show the portage, but it marks this section of the Churchill as the "Bank River" (Thompson's *Narrative* [Tyrrell, ed.], map).

53 HBCA, E. 3/1, fo. 61, Peter Fidler journal, June 18, 1792.

54 Thompson's *Narrative* [Tyrrell, ed.], 322–23.

55 Mackenzie's *Voyages from Montreal*, 122. To add to the confusion, it may be noted that Mackenzie was familiar with a Trout Lake on the Churchill. A letter to his cousin Roderick McKenzie is dated June 17, 1790, at "Lac la Truite" (Trout Lake), a location apparently 3 days travel downstream from Île-à-la-Crosse (ibid., 439).

56 Extreme highs and lows in water flows are rare. However, in 1993, summer water flows on the upper Churchill were less than half of the lowest summer flows recorded at any time in the preceding thirty years (Sask Water, "Environment Canada Hydrological Data"). On the other hand, in 1997, only four years later, summer flows on the upper Churchill were considerably higher than normal.

57 HBC's *Journals of Hearne and Turnor*, 343.

58 Ibid.

59 Ibid., 481. The term "handed" refers to voyageurs wading their canoe with hands on the gunwales.

60 Hood in Franklin's *Narrative, 1819–22*, 181–82.

CHAPTER NINE

1 Although the name "Grandmother" shows on Map 73P/10, "Grandmother's" is the common usage.

2 Howard DeLong, Saskatchewan Environment, telefax, June 13, 2000.

3 The line replaced an earlier generator-based system.

4 *The Northerner*, La Ronge, Saskatchewan, July 9, 1996, 3.

5 Jones, *Aboriginal Rock Paintings*, 60.

6 Kelly was a World War II paratrooper. In 1947, he became the first jumpmaster for Saskatchewan's firefighting "Smoke Jumpers." See Saskatchewan, *Wings Beyond Road's End*, 78; and *The Northerner*, La Ronge, Saskatchewan, August 19, 1997, 1–6. He was later killed when he crashed a bush plane into Great Bear Lake.

7 HBCA, E. 3/1, fo. 62, Peter Fidler journal, June 19, 1792.

8 HBC's *Journals of Hearne and Turnor*, 341–42.

9 Hood in Franklin's *Narrative, 1819–22*, 180–81.

10 According to Sam McKenzie, a Cree speaker from Grandmother's Bay, the Cree word *môniyâw* is commonly used to refer to a white person. However, in the present case, it refers to a French Canadian or Montrealer. *Môniyâw* is a Cree version of "Montréaler"—with the word reflecting the lack of an "r" in Cree.

11 HBC's *Journals of Hearne and Turnor*, 341.

12 Mackenzie's *Voyages from Montreal*, 121.

13 Jones, *Aboriginal Rock Paintings*, 59.

CHAPTER TEN

1 HBC's *Journals of Hearne and Turnor*, 479–80; Moberly, *When Fur was King*, 175.

2 La Ronge, *Our Roots*, 14–15. Also Holmes, "The Anglican Mission at Stanley and Lac la Ronge," 3.

3 La Ronge, *Our Roots*, 15. Also see commemorative plaques at Holy Trinity Church.

4 Kemp, *Northern Trader*, 131. From Kemp, it seems the name Holy Trinity comes from Hunt's home church in Kent, England.

5 *The Northerner*, La Ronge, Saskatchewan, June 19, 1988, 12–13. And "Keewatin Country," CBC radio broadcasts from La Ronge, June 21, 1988 and September 17, 1989. Many will recall that Holy Trinity Church's "temporary" steeple was topped by a weather-cock. This rooster, handmade from two pieces of tin sandwiched together, was not placed on the new steeple since it had not apparently not been on the original.

6 HBCA, Rapid River Post History, April 1989. Samuel McKenzie's father was the Scotsman Roderick McKenzie (not the cousin to Sir Alexander Mackenzie) who first joined the NWC but later became an HBC Chief Factor in charge of Île-à-la-Crosse. His mother Angelique was the daughter of an Ojibway chief. (See HBCA, Biog: McKenzie, Samuel; Simpson's *Athabasca Journal, 1820 and 1821*, 453–54.)

7 HBCA, Rapid River Post History, April 1989; Moberly, *When Fur was King*, 174–75; Ross, *The Manager's Tale*, 100.

8 Keighley, *Trader Tripper Trapper*, 71.

9 George Moberly was trading for a non-HBC concern—likely Lamson and Hubbard or Revillon Frères. Harold Kemp suggests bodies were buried in an old mine shaft on the little island right in front of Holy Trinity Church (Kemp, *Northern Trader*, 77), but Solomon Merasty said this is not correct.

Perhaps some were when Solomon was not in Stanley.

10 See Keighley, *Trader Tripper Trapper*. Also Kemp, *Northern Trader*.

11 Keighley, *Trader Tripper Trapper*, 191–98; Ross, *The Manager's Tale*, 119–20; *The Northerner*, La Ronge, Saskatchewan, June 10, 1992, 7.

12 Kemp, *Northern Trader*, 135.

13 Alexander Mackenzie referred to it as part of "Lake de la Montagne." See Mackenzie's *Voyages from Montreal*, 121.

14 Jones, *Aboriginal Rock Paintings*, 58, 65–66. Note that we use the term "rifle" to include any long firearm.

15 Kemp, *Northern Trader*, 244.

16 Crean, *Northland Exploration*, 23.

17 Mackenzie's *Voyages from Montreal*, 121 per "Décharge" and Simpson's *Athabasca Journal, 1820 and 1821*, 28 re "Rapid River discharge." See also Richardson's *Arctic Searching Expedition*, I, 94, who says, "At the lightening-place of the Rapid River, there is a fine precipice of granite fifty feet high, which is traversed by two magnificent veins of flesh-coloured porphyry-granite." Is he referring to the cliff on the south side of Big Stanley, and if so, did he see it in the course of travel or only on a side-trip?

18 HBCA, E. 3/1, fo. 63, Peter Fidler journal, June 19, 1792.

19 J. Gordon Copeland, president, La Ronge Uranium Mines Limited, letter to shareholders, and John C. Rogers, consulting geologist, report, March 30, 1954. Also J. Gordon Copeland, president, La Ronge Uranium Mines Limited, letter to shareholders, February 15, 1955.

20 Olson, *Lonely Land*, 180.

21 HBCA, E. 3/1, fo. 63, Peter Fidler journal, June 20, 1792.

22 The name "Iskwatikan" is apparently of Cree origin, possibly from *iskwâhtawâkan*, meaning a ladder or stairway, but its precise meaning is not known. Cree today call Iskwatikan Lake *wâposo-sâkahikan*, "rabbit lake." The Cree also formerly called the Rapid River the "Rabbit River" (SAB, Rev. H.E. Hives to Mr. Blewett, letter, Lac la Ronge, March 4, 1933). Given that in Cree, the letter "t" can approximate a "d" and the letter "p" can approximate a "b," we wonder if the name "Rapid" might derive from an early Cree pronunciation of the English "Rabbit."

23 Saskatchewan, *Wings Beyond Road's End*, 94–95.

24 HBC's *Journals of Hearne and Turnor*, 341n.

25 McDonald's *Peace River Journal [1828]*, 7.

26 HBC's *Minutes of Council*, 254.

27 Ibid., 254–56.

28 Ibid., 273–74.

29 Richardson's *Arctic Searching Expedition*, I, 92.

30 HBCA, Rapid River Post History, April 1989.

31 Mackenzie's *Voyages from Montreal*, 121. Simpson's *Athabasca Journal, 1820 and 1821*, 28.

32 HBCA, E. 3/1 fo. 63, Peter Fidler journal, June 20, 1792.

33 HBC's *Journals of Hearne and Turnor*, 340, 481.

34 When Sigurd Olson and his friends passed this way in 1955, they understood that the fishing camp at Potter Rapids had been built by the Drope Lake uranium mine (Olson, *Lonely Land*, 183, and Denis Coolican, diary, August 4, 1955, found at http://www.uwm.edu/Dept/MassComm/Olson/voyageur/1955_churchill_diary.htm). Since the Drope Lake and Hunter Falls mines both operated during the same period, the fishing camp might have served staff from both operations.

35 Crean marks the "Drinking R." in that river's present location (Crean, *Northland Exploration*, map).

36 Kupsch and Hanson, *Gold and Other Stories*, 261–62.

37 Mackenzie's *Voyages from Montreal*, 121. Simpson's *Athabasca Journal, 1820 and 1821*, 28.

38 HBCA, E. 3/1, fo. 63, Peter Fidler journal, June 21, 1792. Fidler's use of the name "Kettle" is an exception to the widespread use of "Portage de L'Isle" or an equivalent.

39 Thompson's *Narrative* [Tyrrell, ed.], map; *manitow* is the Cree word for God or the Great Spirit.

40 Mackenzie's *Voyages from Montreal*, 121.

41 The Cree *mahkahk* can mean a tub, keg, or barrel, and the lake's name is sometimes translated as "fish tub lake." However, it is safe to assume its earliest meaning was that of "keg."

42 Peter Fidler journal, June 21, 1792.

43 Merasty, "History of Pelican Narrows"; also La Ronge, *Our Roots*, 93; Barry, *People Places*, 33–34.

44 Anglican Church of Canada, Synod Office of the Diocese of Saskatchewan, Prince Albert, Saskatchewan. Planinshek's marriage certificate originally showed his birthplace as "Nisch, Servia," but this was then crossed out and replaced by the words "Filemon Somora [*sic*] Mexico." Though we give his birthplace as Serbia, Planinshek may indeed have been born in Mexico.

45 MacDonald, "Through Canada's Hinterland," 11.

46 Olson, *Lonely Land*, 198–99. Also Cockburn, "North of Reindeer," 43.

47 Cockburn, "North of Reindeer," 42–43. Also Keighley, *Trader Tripper Trapper*, 115.

48 Cockburn, "North of Reindeer," 42–43.

49 Richardson's *Arctic Searching Expedition*, I, 90n.

50 In August, 1974, the hydrological station upstream at Otter Rapids recorded a flow of 883 cubic metres (1150 cu. yd) per second. By comparison, the mean flow for August at the same station from 1964 to 1996 was 344 cubic metres (450 cu. yd) per second.

51 Mackenzie's *Voyages from Montreal*, 121.

52 Russell, *Eighteenth-Century Western Cree*, 153–71.

53 Louis Primeau had been a servant at the French posts in the North-West until the Seven Years War put an end to the French trade in 1759. Primeau, like some other French servants, then elected to adopt an Indian lifestyle and thus stay in the country. However, in 1765, he went to York Factory and took employment with the Hudson's Bay Company. That same year he went inland for the Company. Then, in 1766, he was sent to see the Beaver River which, it seems, would have required him to cross from Frog Portage in order to travel up the Churchill. See Morton, *History of the Canadian West*, 267, 275.

54 Hansom began employment with the Hudson's Bay Company in 1769. He remained with the Company until June 17, 1779, when he drowned in Grand Rapids (now the site of a hydro dam) where the Saskatchewan River runs into Lake Winnipeg. See HBC's *Journals of Hearne and Turnor*, 239–41.

55 It is possible that Joseph Frobisher's younger brother Thomas was also present during Hansom's stay in the winter of 1773–74. This is not entirely clear, but Matthew Cocking's journal entry for October 14, 1775 (Cocking was then in charge of the HBC post at Cumberland House) suggests that Hansom had stayed with both of the Frobishers in 1773–74 (HBC's *Cumberland House Journals, First Series, 1775–79*, 16).

56 Joseph Hansom, letter to HBC Governor and Committee, August 23, 1774, in HBC's *Journals of Hearne and Turnor*, 240n–241n.

57 Ibid.

58 Mackenzie's *Voyages from Montreal*, 120–21.

59 HBC's *Journals of Hearne and Turnor*, 121 (per Samuel Hearne).

60 Olson, *Lonely Land*, 203–05. Also Canada et al., *Churchill River Study: Archaeology Report*, 18–19.

61 HBC's *Journals of Hearne and Turnor*, 131 and 190. And HBC's *Cumberland House Journals, First Series, 1775–79*, 16 (per Matthew Cocking).

62 Henry (the Elder)'s *Travels and Adventures*, 322–24.

63 HBC's *Cumberland House Journals, First Series, 1775–79*, 59–65 (per Matthew Cocking, June 27, 1776).

64 HBC's *Journals of Hearne and Turnor*, 338n.

65 Canada et al., *Churchill River Study: Archaeology Report 19*, 18–19.

66 We measure the distance from Frog Portage to Cumberland House, without detour to Denare Beach, at 264 km (165 mi).

67 HBC's *Journals of Hearne and Turnor*, 330.

68 HBCA, E. 3/1, fo. 64, Peter Fidler journal, June 21, 1792.

69 Mackenzie's *Voyages from Montreal*, 120.

70 Note that the Cree *wîmistikôsiw* or *wêmistikôsiw* refers to a person who uses a wooden boat and sometimes translates as "Frenchman." See Cook et al, eds., *Nehithowewin*, 145; Charles, *Cree Language Dictionary*, 97; Faries, ed., *Dictionary of the Cree Language*, 83; and Wolvengrey, *Cree: Words*.

71 HBCA, E. 3/1, fo. 64, Peter Fidler journal, June 21, 1792.

72 Sadly, Frank was to drown about a year later when his snowmobile went through the ice on Pelican Lake.

73 HBC's *Journals of Hearne and Turnor*, 337; Richardson's *Arctic Searching Expedition*, I, 89; Mackenzie's *Voyages from Montreal*, 120; and Simpson's *Athabasca Journal, 1820 and 1821*, 25.

74 Mackenzie's *Voyages from Montreal*, 120 for use of "galets." And McDonald's *Peace River Journals [1828]*, 7 for use of "short portages."

75 HBC's *Journals of Hearne and Turnor*, 338n.

76 Ibid., 482–83.

77 Dewdney, *Indian Rock Art*, 4–5.

78 Simpson's *Athabasca Journal, 1820 and 1821*, 25.

79 Richardson's *Arctic Searching Expedition*, I, 89.

80 HBC's *Journals of Hearne and Turnor*, 335 ("pillicon Lake"); Mackenzie's *Voyages from Montreal*, 120 ("Chitique"); Henry (the Elder)'s *Travels and Adventures*, 256 ("Chatique, or The Pelican" re a Cree chief); Simpson's *Athabasca Journal, 1820 and 1821*, 25 ("Chetique"); and Richardson's *Arctic Searching Expedition*, I, 89 ("chetauque").

81 HBCA, B.9/A/1, Malcolm Ross journal, September 20, 1790.

82 HBCA, E. 3/1, fo. 2, Peter Fidler journal, May 30, 1791.

CHAPTER ELEVEN

1 Cockburn, "To Reindeer's Far Waters," 164.

2 Downes, *Sleeping Island*, 33.

3 Merasty, "History of Pelican Narrows," 15–27.

4 Ibid.

5 HBC's *Journals of Hearne and Turnor*, 336.

6 HBCA, E. 3/1, fo. 65, Peter Fidler journal, June 23, 1792.

7 Desnomie, "History of Pelican Narrows," 19.

8 Merasty, "History of Pelican Narrows," 171–73.

9 Desnomie, "History of Pelican Narrows," 20–22. And Ross, *The Manager's Tale*, 97.

10 Desnomie, "History of Pelican Narrows," 27.

11 Cockburn, "Revillon Man," 15.

12 Ibid.

13 Desnomie, "History of Pelican Narrows," 27.

14 Ross, *The Manager's Tale*, 183.

15 Cockburn, "Distant Summer," 97 (re Russick's age); Dennis Popaden, "Memories of Trappers' Festivals Past," *Ma-Mow-We-Tak: Sled Dog Racing Association Newsletter* 82 (February 1995): 1–2.

16 Peter Bowers, "Mushing's Olympic Efforts," *Mushing* 1, no. 2 (April/May 1988): 11–12.

17 Desnomie, "History of Pelican Narrows," 23–26. In 2000, the day-to-day care of St. Gertrude Mission was in the hands of pastoral ministers Roger & Elaine Poulin, also responsible for the RC church at Sandy Bay. An Oblate priest from Saskatoon visits Pelican Narrows and Sandy Bay monthly.

18 Desnomie, "History of Pelican Narrows," 36, 41.

19 Merasty, "History of Pelican Narrows," 78–81.

20 Ibid., 89–101; Roy Morin, PBCN, telefax, January 5, 2000.

21 Saskatchewan, *Churchill River Board of Inquiry Report*, 187–88.

22 HBCA, E. 3/2, fo. 65, Peter Fidler journal, June 23, 1792.

23 Hood in Franklin's *Narrative, 1819–22*, 179; McDonald's *Peace River Journal [1828]*, 6.

24 Mackenzie's *Voyages from Montreal*, 119 ("Lake Miron"). And Richardson's *Arctic Searching Expedition*, I, 84.

25 A lobstick, or "lopstick," is a spruce or pine that has had its lower branches removed to leave a distinctive tuft. A lobstick can be readily seen from a distance, and they were once commonly used as route markers. They are now seldom seen.

26 HBC's *Journals of Hearne and Turnor*, 483.

27 Mackenzie's *Voyages from Montreal*, 119 ("Épinettes"); HBCA, E. 3/1, fo. 65–65d., Peter Fidler journal, June 23, 1792 ("Pine"); McDonald's *Peace River Journal [1828]*, 7 ("Pine"); and Richardson's *Arctic Searching Expedition*, I, 84 ("Pine Portage (*Portage des Épinettes*)"). The use of *Épinettes* suggests "Pine" was meant to mean "Spruce."

28 HBC's *Journals of Hearne and Turnor*, 335n.

29 Ibid., 334.

30 Merasty, "History of Pelican Narrows," 166.

31 HBC's *Journals of Hearne and Turnor*, 335n.

32   Mackenzie's *Voyages from Montreal,* 119 ("Portage de L'Isle"); Simpson's *Athabasca Journal, 1820 and 1821,* 25 ("Petit Portage de L'Isle"); Richardson's *Arctic Searching Expedition,* I, 84 ("Island Portage").

33   HBC's *Journals of Hearne and Turnor,* 334 ("20 yards"); HBCA, E. 3/1, fo. 66, Peter Fidler journal, June 23, 1792 ("15 yds"); Tyrrell, ed., Thompson's *Narrative* [Tyrrell, ed.] map ("15 y.").

34   HBC's *Journals of Hearne and Turnor,* 334.

35   Olson, *Lonely Land,* 215.

36   Mackenzie's *Voyages from Montreal,* 119.

37   Merasty, "History of Pelican Narrows," 101.

38   The "Oskachuk" nickname is from the Cree *oskâh-tak,* meaning "jack pine." John Morin gives Thomas's first name as "John," though Gisli Norman of Denare Beach remembered it as "Henry."

39   HBCA, E. 3/1, fo. 66, Peter Fidler journal, June 24, 1792. Fidler's apparent error as to the length of Birch Portage is unusual.

40   A canoe trip on the Wildnest River is described in *Saskatchewan, Canoe Trip #22.*

41   Rosemary Nemeth, *Over the Narrow Hills: The Story of the Fishing Lakes* (Saskatchewan: Northern Saskatchewan Resources, undated), 5, 17. And Dennis A. Belliveau, letter, January 28, 1987. Some references give the Hanson Lake Road a later completion date, but the 1962 date seems most likely.

42   The Cree word *nîpîskâw* translates as "lots of leaves."

43   Simpson's *Athabasca Journal, 1820 and 1821,* 25; Richardson's *Arctic Searching Expedition,* I, 83.

44   Richardson's *Arctic Searching Expedition,* I, 83. We have not confirmed the sucker species referred to as "gray sucking carp."

45   HBCA, E. 3/1, fo. 66, Peter Fidler journal, June 24, 1792.

46   Ibid.

47   Hood in Franklin's *Narrative, 1819–22,* 178–79.

48   Henry (the Elder)'s, *Travels and Adventures,* 261 (*castor* is French for "beaver"); HBCA, E.3/1, fo. 66–66d., Peter Fidler journal, June 24 & 25, 1792; Thompson's *Narrative* [Tyrrell, ed.], map.

49   We last saw the aspen in 1996. It did not then look long for this world.

50   Mackenzie's *Voyages from Montreal,* 119.

51   Richardson's *Arctic Searching Expedition,* I, 80. Richardson referred to present-day Spruce Rapids and Snake Rapids as Ridge Portage and Ridge Rapid respectively. Richardson noted that Snake Rapids were said to be the highest point that sturgeon ascended in the river, but he was likely misinterpreting information applicable to Spruce Rapids.

52   HBCA, E. 3/1 fo. 66, Peter Fidler journal, June 24, 1792.

53   Merasty, "History of Pelican Narrows," 101.

54   Mackenzie's *Voyages from Montreal,* 119 ("Pente Portage"); Thompson's *Narrative* [Tyrrell, ed.], map; Simpson's *Athabasca Journal, 1820 and 1821,* ("Pente Portage").

55   HBCA, E. 3/1, fo. 66d., Peter Fidler journal, June 25, 1792. And Franklin's *Narrative, 1819–22,* map; Richardson's *Arctic Searching Expedition,* I, 80. Could the name "Ridge" be an English attempt to translate the French *pente*?

56   The Cree *minahik* is sometimes translated as "pine," but the portage's giant spruce suggest the word here has its common meaning of "spruce."

57   HBCA, E.3/1, fo. 66d., Peter Fidler journal, June 25, 1792.

58   In his journal entry of June 27, 1776, Samuel Hearne wrote that in the summer of 1775, Primeau and seven other men had been left to build a fort "within 2 Days walk of ours" (HBC's *Journals of Hearne and Turnor,* 190). A two-day walk would fit the distance from Cumberland House to the mouth of the West Weir. However, we cannot rule out the possibility that Primeau had built somewhere else on Amisk Lake—possibly at the head of the South Weir where, in 1792, Peter Fidler noted a pre-existing post (HBCA, E. 3/1, fo. 66d., Peter Fidler journal, June 25, 1792).

59   Henry (the Elder)'s *Travels and Adventures,* 261.

60   Moody, "Historic Sites in the Amisk Lake Area."

61   Henry (the Elder)'s *Travels and Adventures,* 261.

62   HBC's *Cumberland House Journals, First Series, 1775–79,* 94, 94n.

63   Tomison went on to say he offered up what medicine he had for free since Tute had previously treated HBC men with kindness. Ibid., 217. Tute's medical problems were not limited to veneral disease. He died of smallpox in 1781. See HBC's *Journals of Hearne and Turnor,* 159n.

64   Henry (the Elder's) *Travels and Adventures,* 260 ("Beaver Lake, or Lake aux Castors"); HBC's *Journals of Hearne and Turnor,* 331 ("Misk-a-Sask-a-ha-gan or Beaver Lake"). Today, the preferred northern Saskatchewan Cree spelling for beaver is *amisk.*

65   Dolomite is limestone that has been altered by the addition of magnesium ions to form a harder carbonate rock. Not being geologists, we will hereafter refer to dolomite, limestone and dolomitic limestone as simply "limestone."

66   See *Atlas of Saskatchewan,* 44–47. And *Saskatchewan, Geological History,* 28–32.

67   *Saskatchewan, Canoe Trip #14,* 4–5.

68   Moody, "Amisk Lake," 2.

69   Anahareo, *Devil in Deerskins*, 164–65.

70   Kupsch and Hanson, *Gold and Other Stories*. See also Saskatchewan, *Geology and Mineral Deposits of the Amisk-Wildnest Lakes Area*. And Saskatchewan, *Mineral Occurrences in the Precambrian of Northern Saskatchewan*.

71   Saskatchewan, *Canoe Trip #41*.

72   Moody, "Amisk Lake," 2. Note that some government maps erroneously name Paddy's Island as "Torrington Island."

73   Ibid., 4.

74   Ibid., 2–3.

75   Angelique Merasty died January 17, 1996. See Saskatoon *StarPhoenix*, 20 January 1996, A5. Bill Merasty passed away afterwards.

CHAPTER TWELVE

1   Anahareo, *Devil in Deerskins*, 164–65.

2   Official 1999 population was 776, per Saskatchewan, *1999 Northern Local Government Directory*.

3   Saskatchewan, *Geology and Mineral Deposits of the Amisk-Wildnest Lakes Area*, 22–36. And Saskatchewan, *Geological History*, 23–24.

4   Saskatchewan, *Geological History*, 28–32, 91.

5   Moody, "Amisk Lake," 3.

6   Ibid., 1. According to John Morin, in about 1970, the old winter road was re-opened so that Cumberland House hockey fans could travel by bombardier to watch Flin Flon Bomber hockey games.

7   Moody, "Amisk Lake," 2.

8   Ibid.," 1. Also Kupsch and Hanson, *Gold and Other Stories*, 231–34.

9   Inscription on government plaque at the end of Highway 167.

10   Anahareo, *Devil in Deerskins*, 165–171.

11   HBCA, E.3/1, fo. 66d., Peter Fidler journal, June 25, 1792.

12   HBCA, E. 3/1, fo. 67d., Peter Fidler journal, June 26, 1792.

13   HBC's *Cumberland House Journals, First Series, 1775–79*, 12.

14   HBC's *Journals of Hearne and Turnor*, 330.

15   Ibid.

16   Richardson's *Arctic Searching Expedition*, I, 76.

17   Hood in Franklin's *Narrative, 1819–22*, 178.

18   Simpson's *Athabasca Journal, 1820 and 1821*, 24–25.

19   Ending in 1996, a government hydrological station operated where the fast water begins at the head of the South Weir. It had a steel cable with orange marker cones suspended over the river. In 1999, final removal of station hardware was being scheduled. Per Dalvin Euteneier, Sask Water.

20   According to John Morin of Prince Albert, a bush road, which was complete with bridge crossings and corduroy, once ran along the west side of the South Weir from Sturgeon Landing to the old Beaver City site. When he first saw it in the 1930s, it was no longer in use and already growing up with vegetation in places. This road—distinct from the winter road to Warehouse Bay, Amisk Lake—was perhaps built during the Beaver City boom.

21   HBC's *Journals of Hearne and Turnor*, 331.

22   McDonald's *Peace River Journal [1828]*, 6.

23   HBCA, E. 3/1, fo. 68, Peter Fidler journal, June 26, 1792.

24   Saskatchewan, *Canoe Trip # 44*, 4.

25   Merasty, "History of Pelican Narrows," 101.

26   In the north and in trapping country generally, the term "rat" is the common term for the muskrat.

27   HBC's *Journals of Hearne and Turnor*, 329–30.

28   Ibid., 104.

29   Innis, *Fur Trade in Canada*, 440.

30   Morse, *Fur Trade Canoe Routes*, 39 (map), 45–47.

31   HBC's *Journals of Hearne and Turnor*, 104–105.

32   Thompson's *Travels in Western North America*, 106–07, 122. And Morton, *History of the Canadian West*, 440–41.

CHAPTER THIRTEEN

1   Described in Saskatchewan, *Canoe Trip # 15*.

2   HBC's *Journals of Hearne and Turnor*, 214. "Blondeau" was Barthélemi Blondeau. He was one of the earliest Montreal traders to come to the North-West after the British takeover of Canada in 176. See NWC's *Documents*, 427.

3   HBC's *Journals of Hearne and Turnor*, 217–218. Also see NWC's *Documents*, 427.

4   HBC's *Journals of Hearne and Turnor*, 234. "Catts" refer to lynx. A lynx pelt had the value of two beaver.

5   HBCA, E. 3/1, fo. 67d.–68, Peter Fidler journal, June 26, 1792.

6   Kupsch and Hanson, *Gold and Other Stories*, 59, 60, 65, 236–40. Also Barris, *Fire Canoe*, 195–96.

7   Miller, *Shingwauk's Vision*.

8   Merasty, "History of Pelican Narrows," 101.

9   Henry (the Elder)'s *Travels and Adventures*, 259 ("Sturgeon Lake"); HBC's *Cumberland House*

Journals, First Series, 1775–79, 12 ("Menistick Menihague-a-skow Spruce or Pine Island Lake" per Matthew Cocking); HBC's *Journals of Hearne and Turnor*, 214 ("Pine Island Lake" per Philip Turnor in 1778); Mackenzie's *Voyages from Montreal*, 118, and also Thompson's *Narrative* [Tyrrell, ed.], map (differentiating "Sturgeon Lake" and "Pine-Island Lake").

In 1790, Philip Turnor said the Indians knew present-day Namew Lake by a name translating to "lime stone Lake" (HBC's *Journals of Hearne and Turnor*, 328). But there is no other record of such a name, and its usage would seem to have been limited.

10   Saskatchewan, *Resource Reader*, 234; Saskatchewan, *Where to Fish*, 18.

11   HBCA, E. 3/1, fo. 68, Peter Fidler journal, June 26–27, 1792.

12   HBC's *Journals of Hearne and Turnor*, 485n.

13   Spruce Point's name may derive from the Cree equivalent *minahiko-miniwâtim*. Nowadays, however, local Cree speakers do not usually give Spruce Point any name at all.

14   HBC's *Journals of Hearne and Turnor*, 106 (Hearne), 115 (Hearne), 120n (Tyrrell), 240n–241n (Joseph Hansom); Morton, *History of the Canadian West*, 287–90. As noted earlier, it is possible that Joseph Frobisher's younger brother Thomas was one of the men wintering at Cross Lake in 1773–74. A journal entry by Matthew Cocking (in charge of the HBC post at Cumberland House) made October 14, 1775, suggests that the two Frobishers wintered together in 1773–74 (HBC's *Cumberland House Journals, First Series, 1775–79*, 16).

15   Morton, *History of the Canadian West*, 287.

16   Manitoba, *Reverend Henry Budd.*

17   But note that Dr. Richardson, in describing Cree life as he observed it at Cumberland House in the winter of 1819–20, used the *th* dialect in recording Cree words he had learned. Though Richardson's Cree informants may have been from elsewhere, his use of the *th* dialect could indicate that *th*-speaking Basquia Cree still had a recognizable presence at Cumberland as late as 1820. See Richardson in Franklin's *Narrative, 1819–22*, c. III.

18   Adopted from Barry, *People Places*, 22.

19   Henry (the Younger)'s *Manuscript Journals*, II, 471–74.

20   Simpson's *Athabasca Journal, 1820 and 1821*, 20.

21   Note that the English "Pine Island" is something of a misnomer originating from the early fur traders who often used the word "pine" to refer to spruce. The Cree *minahik* refers to spruce.

22   Barry, *People Places*, 22.

23   HBC's *Journals of Hearne and Turnor*, 328 (Turnor); Henry (the Younger)'s *Manuscript Journals*, II, 472n (Thompson).

24   HBC's *Journals of Hearne and Turnor*, 235.

25   Henry (the Younger)'s *Manuscript Journals*, II, 474.

26   Saskatchewan, *Cumberland House Historic Park*, 22; Peel, *Steamboats on the Saskatchewan*, 105–07; Barris, *Fire Canoe*, 64. We caution that it may be incorrect to assume that prior to the 1880s, the whole of the Saskatchewan flowed down the Old Channel. David Thompson referred to his 1786 trip up the Saskatchewan from Cumberland House saying his party "…continued for three days to proceed with the paddle up the alluvial channels to their end, where the River is one stream" (Thompson's *Travels in Western North America*, 85–86). This would suggest that the Saskatchewan had some kind of delta or braided stream formation upstream above Cumberland well before the 1880s diversion.

27   Townsend, "A Study of Waterfowl Nesting."

28   It has been estimated that the Cumberland region has a winter moose density of "1.6 to 2.0 moose per square mile," per Canada et al., *Churchill River Study: Synthesis*, 104. According to Tim Trottier, wildlife biologist at La Ronge, however, these figures from the Churchill River Study may predate the full impact of SaskPower's E.B. Campbell Dam on local moose habitat.

29   HBC's *Journals of Hearne and Turnor*, 97 (leaving York Factory), 113 (quote re choosing site). Hearne later wrote that Cumberland House was "comodiously situated between 4 Differant Tribes," 193.

30   Ibid., 114–15

31   HBC's *Journals of Hearne and Turnor*, 111–16, 142 (hours of work), 144 (start of proper house).

32   Ibid., 29, 144 (post building begins), 183 (Cocking arrives).

33   Ibid., 178.

34   HBC's *Cumberland House Journals, Second Series, 1779–82*, 198.

35   Ibid., 223–44.

36   Ibid., 231–32.

37   Ibid., 238, 298. But see Thistle, *Indian-European Trade Relations*, 64–65 re apparent survivors.

38   Saskatchewan, *Cumberland House Historic Park*, 14–15; Morton, *History of the Canadian West*, 333; Newman, *Company of Adventurers*, 274–80.

39   Simpson's *Athabasca Journal, 1820 and 1821*, 415; HBC's *Journals of Hearne and Turnor*, 237n, 487n; Richards, "Cumberland House," 109.

40   Saskatchewan, *Cumberland House Historic Park*, 20.

41   Richards, "Cumberland House," 113 (1966 move; age of powder house).

42 Morton, *History of the Canadian West*, 440.

43 Henry (the Younger)'s *Manuscript Journals*, II, 475.

44 Innis, *Fur Trade in Canada*, 343–44; Peel, *Steamboats on the Saskatchewan*, 106–09.

45 Christensen, "Steamboat Bill," 30; Barris, *Fire Canoe*, 196; *Opasquia Times* newspaper clipping, undated.

46 Saskatchewan, "Cumberland House Historic Park," 25–26; McKay et al., *A History of Cumberland House*, 8–10.

47 Richards, "Cumberland House," 112; Kemp, *Northern Trader*, 50.

48 RCMP Service Records, RCMP Museum, Regina; Downes, *Sleeping Island,* 48.

49 Regina *Leader-Post*, November 5, 1988, A1; Saskatoon *StarPhoenix*, July 23, 1996, A7.

50 Saskatoon *StarPhoenix*, August 8, 1993, 3 (re Morin's Regina trek); *The Northerner*, La Ronge, Saskatchewan, September 24, 1996, 6 (bridge opening).

51 Richards, "Cumberland House," 111–12.

52 Cooper, *Alexander Kennedy Isbister*.

53 Cumberland House cenotaph. And McKay et al., *A History of Cumberland House*, 18.

ABBREVIATIONS
used in Endnotes, Photography Credits, and Bibliography

CPRC   Canadian Plains Research Center, University of Regina
CRS   Churchill River Study
DCB   Dictionary of Canadian Biography, University of Toronto Press, Toronto
HBC   Hudson's Bay Company
HBCA   Hudson's Bay Company Archives, Public Archives of Manitoba, Winnipeg
NA   National Archives of Canada, Ottawa
NWC   North West Company
PAM   Public Archives of Manitoba, Winnipeg
SAB   Saskatchewan Archives Board

BIBLIOGRAPHY
of Primary, Government, and Secondary Sources

I. PRIMARY SOURCES

Archives

Hudson's Bay Company Archives, Public Archives of Manitoba, Winnipeg (HBCA)
Saskatchewan Archives Board (SAB), Saskatoon

Journals and Narratives of Traders and Explorers to 1900

Back, George. *Arctic Artist: The Journals and Paintings of George Back.* 1994. Reprint. Edited by C.S. Houston. Montreal: McGill-Queen's University Press, 1995.

Franklin, John. *Narrative of a Journey to the Shores of the Polar Sea, in the Years 1819-20-21-22.* London: John Murray, 1824.

Franklin, John. *Narrative of a Second Expedition to the Shores of the Polar Sea in the Years 1825, 1826, and 1827.* 1828. Reprint. Edmonton: Hurtig, 1971.

Franklin, John. *Sir John Franklin's Journals and Correspondence: The First Arctic Land Expedition, 1819–1822.* The Champlain Society, vol. 59. Edited by Richard C. Davis. Toronto, 1995.

Franklin, John. *Sir John Franklin's Journals and Correspondence: The Second Arctic Land Expedition, 1825–1827.* The Champlain Society, vol. 62. Edited by Richard C. Davis. Toronto, 1998.

Harmon, Daniel. *Sixteen Years in the Indian Country: The Journal of Daniel Williams Harmon, 1800–1816.* 1820. Reprint. Edited by W. Kaye Lamb. Toronto: Macmillan, 1957.

Hearne, Samuel. *Journey from Prince of Wales's Fort in Hudson's Bay to the Northern Ocean.* 1795. Reprint. Edited by Richard Glover. Toronto: Macmillan, 1958.

Henry, Alexander (the Elder). *Travels and Adventures in Canada and the Indian Territories between the Years 1760 and 1776.* 1809. Reprint. Edited by James Bain. Edmonton: Hurtig, 1969.

Henry, Alexander (the Younger). *New Light on the Early History of the Greater Northwest: The Manuscript Journals of Alexander Henry, Fur Trader of the Northwest Company, and of David Thompson, Official Geographer and Explorer of the same Company, 1799–1814, Exploration and Adventurer among the Indians of the Red, Saskatchewan, Missouri and Columbia Rivers.* 1897. Reprint. Edited by Elliot Coues. Minneapolis: Ross & Haines, 1965.

Hood, Robert. *To the Arctic by Canoe, 1819–1821: The Journal and Paintings of Robert Hood, Midshipman with Franklin.* Edited by C.S. Houston. Montreal: McGill-Queen's University Press, 1974.

HBC. *Cumberland House Journals and the Inland Journals, 1775–82: First Series, 1775–79; Second Series, 1779-82.* The Hudson's Bay Record Society, vols. 14-15. Edited by E.E. Rich. London, 1951.

HBC. *Journals of Samuel Hearne and Philip Turnor between the Years 1774 and 1792.* The Champlain Society, vol. 21. Edited by J.B. Tyrell. Toronto, 1934.

HBC. *Minutes of Council, Northern Department of Rupert Land, 1821–31.* The Hudson's Bay Record Society, vol. 3. Edited by R. Harvey Fleming. Toronto: The Champlain Society, 1940.

Mackenzie, Alexander. *The Journals and Letters of Sir Alexander Mackenzie,* including Mackenzie's narrative of *Voyages from Montreal on the River St. Lawrence through the Continent of North America to the Frozen and Pacific Oceans in the Years 1789 and 1793.* 1801. Reprint. Edited by W. Kaye Lamb. Toronto: Macmillan, 1970.

McDonald, Archibald. *Peace River: A Canoe Voyage from Hudson's Bay to Pacific by Sir George Simpson (Governor, Hon. Hudson's Bay Company) In 1828: Journal of the late Chief Factor, Archibald McDonald (Hon. Hudson's Bay Company) who accompanied him.* 1872. Reprint. Edited by Malcolm McLeod. Edmonton: Hurtig, 1971.

NWC. *The English River Book: A North West Company Journal and Account Book of 1786.* Edited by Harry Duckworth. Montreal: McGill-Queen's University Press, 1990.

NWC. *Documents Relating to the North West Company.* The Champlain Society, vol. 22. Edited by W. Stewart Wallace. Toronto, 1934.

Rae, John. *Rae's Arctic Correspondence, 1844–55: John Rae's Correspondence with the Hudson's Bay Company on Arctic Exploration, 1844–1855.* The Hudson's Bay Record Society, vol. 16. Edited by E.E. Rich. London, 1953.

Richardson, John. *Arctic Ordeal: The Journal of John Richardson, Surgeon-Naturalist with Franklin, 1820–1822.* 1984. Reprint. Edited by C.S. Houston. Montreal: McGill-Queen's University Press, 1985.

Richardson, John. *Arctic Searching Expedition: Journal of a Boat-Voyage Through Rupert's Land and the Arctic Sea in Search of the Discovery Ships under Command of Sir John Franklin.* 1851. 2 vols. Reprint. New York: Greenwood Press, 1961.

Robertson, Colin. *Colin Robertson's Correspondence Book, September 1817 to September 1822.* The Hudson's Bay Record Society, vol. 2. Edited by E.E. Rich. Toronto: The Champlain Society, 1939.

Simpson, George. *Journal and Occurrences in the Athabasca Department by George Simpson, 1820 and 1821, and Report.* The Hudson's Bay Record Society, vol. 1. Edited by E.E. Rich. Toronto: The Champlain Society, 1938.

Simpson, George. *Fur Trade and Empire: George Simpson's Journal [1824–25].* Edited by Frederick Merk. Cambridge, Mass.: Harvard University Press, 1931.

Thompson, David. *Travels in Western North America, 1784–1812.* Edited by Victor G. Hopwood. Toronto: Macmillan, 1971.

Thompson, David. *The Narrative of David Thompson.* The Champlain Society, vol. 12. Edited by J.B. Tyrrell. Toronto, 1916.

Thompson, David. *David Thompson's Narrative, 1784–1812.* The Champlain Society, vol. 40. Edited by Richard Glover. Toronto, 1962.

Tyrrell, J.B and D.B. Dowling. *Report on the Country between Athabasca Lake and Churchill River with Notes on Two Routes Travelled between the Churchill and Saskatchewan Rivers.* Ottawa: Geological Survey of Canada, 1896.

II. GOVERNMENT DOCUMENTS

Canada. *Treaty No. 10.* Reprint. Ottawa: Queen's Printer, 1966.

Canada. *Devonian Stratigraphy of Northeastern Alberta and Northwestern Saskatchewan. Memoir 313,* by A.W. Norris. Ottawa: Geological Survey of Canada, Department of Mines and Technical Surveys, 1963.

Canada. Saskatchewan and Manitoba. *Churchill River Study: Archaeology, Final Report 19.* CRS: Saskatoon, 1975.

Canada. Saskatchewan and Manitoba. *Churchill River Study: Synthesis.* CRS: Saskatoon, 1976.

Manitoba. *Reverend Henry Budd.* Winnipeg: Department of Cultural Affairs and Historical Resources, 1981.

Saskatchewan. *The Boreal Shield Ecozone: A Land of Lakes and Forests.* State of the Environment Report. Regina: Saskatchewan Environment, 1999.

Saskatchewan. *Canoe Safety and Ethics.* Regina: Saskatchewan Environment pamphlet, n.d.

Saskatchewan. Canoe Trip booklets issued by Saskatchewan Environment:

Canoe Trip #1: Île-à-la-Crosse to Otter Lake. Peter Gregg, revised 1977, reviewed in 1989 by Historic Trails Canoe Club, Regina, 13 pp.

Canoe Trip #5: Otter Lake to Pelican Narrows. Peter Gregg, reviewed in 1989 by Historic Trails Canoe Club, Regina, 10 pp.

Canoe Trip #14: Sturgeon-weir River (Mile 190, Highway 106) to Denare Beach. Peter Gregg, revised 1977, 6 pp.

Canoe Trip #15: Cumberland House to The Pas. Historic Trails Canoe Club, Regina, revised in 1971 by Peter Gregg, 3 pp.

Canoe Trip #16: Nemeiben Lake to Otter Lake. Peter Gregg, reviewed in 1989 by Historic Trails Canoe Club, Regina, 10 pp.

Canoe Trip #22: Pelican Narrows to Sturgeon-weir River (Mile 190, Highway 106). Historic Trails Canoe Club, Regina, revised in 1977 by Peter Gregg, reviewed in 1993 by Historic Trails Canoe Club, 12 pp.

Canoe Trip #40: Clearwater River (Warner Rapids) to Fort McMurray, Alberta. Johnson & Weichel consultants, reviewed in 1986 by Historic Trails Canoe Club, Regina, and updated in 1995, 12 pp.

Canoe Trip #41: Missi Island Loop on Amisk Lake. Peter Gregg, n.d., 6 pp.

Canoe Trip #44. Amisk Lake to Cumberland House. Peter Gregg, n.d., 5 pp.

Canoe Trip #52. Lac la Loche to Île-à-la-Crosse. Peter Gregg, 1976, 8 pp.

Saskatchewan's Voyageur Highway. Written with assistance of Historic Trails Canoe Club, Regina, 1991.

Saskatchewan. *Churchill River Board of Inquiry Report.* CRS: Saskatoon, 1978.

Saskatchewan. *Cumberland House Historic Park.* Historic Booklet No. 7. Regina: Department of Tourism and Renewable Resources, n.d..

Saskatchewan. *The Ecoregions of Saskatchewan.* Regina: Saskatchewan Environment and Canadian Plains Research Center, 1998.

Saskatchewan. *1999 Fishing & Hunting Guide.* Regina: Tourism Saskatchewan, 1999.

Saskatchewan. *Geology and Mineral Deposits of the Amisk-Wildnest Lakes Area, Saskatchewan.* Report No. 14. By A.R. Byers and C.D.A. Dahlstrom. 1954. Reprint. Regina: Department of Mineral Resources, 1970.

Saskatchewan. *Geological History of Saskatchewan.* Regina: Saskatchewan Museum of Natural History, 1989.

Saskatchewan. *Mineral Occurences in the Precambrian of Northern Saskatchewan (Excluding Radioactive Minerals).* Report No. 36. By L.S. Beck. Reprint. Regina: Department of Mineral Resources, Geological Sciences Branch, 1974.

Saskatchewan. *Northern Local Government Directory.* La Ronge: Saskatchewan Municipal Affairs, Culture and Housing, Northern Unit, 1998, 1999.

Saskatchewan. *Northern Municipal Directory.* La Ronge: Saskatchewan Municipal Affairs, Culture and Housing, Northern Municipal Services Unit, 2000.

Saskatchewan. *The Resource Reader.* Regina: Department of Natural Resources, Conservation and Information Branch, n.d.

Saskatchewan. *Sedimentary Geology of the La Loche Area, NTS Sheet 74 C.* Report No. 201. By D.F. Paterson, A.C. Kendall and J.E. Christopher. Regina: Saskatchewan Mineral Resources, 1978.

Saskatchewan. *Where to Fish: Central and Southern Saskatchewan.* Regina: Department of Parks and Renewable Resources, 1983.

Saskatchewan. *Wings Beyond Road's End: Airplanes over Saskatchewan's North.* La Ronge: Saskatchewan Education, Northern Division, 1992.

III. SECONDARY SOURCES

Adney, Edwin Tappan and Howard I. Chapelle. *The Bark Canoes and Skin Boats of North America.* Washington, DC: Smithsonian Institution, 1983.

Allen, Robert S. "Peter Fidler." *DCB.* Vol. 6: 249–52.

Anahareo. *Devil in Deerskins: My Life with Grey Owl.* Toronto: PaperJacks, 1988.

Armour, David. "Alexander Henry [the Elder]." *DCB.* Vol. 6: 316–19.

Arthur, Elizabeth. "Duel at Ile-à-la-Crosse." *Saskatchewan History* 27 (Spring 1974): 41-50.

Atlas of Saskatchewan. Edited by Ka-iu Fung. Saskatoon: University of Saskatchewan, 1969.

Atlas of Saskatchewan. 2d ed. Edited by Ka-iu Fung. Saskatoon: University of Saskatchewan, 1999.

Barris, Theodore. *Fire Canoe: Prairie Steamboat Days Revisited.* Toronto: McClelland and Stewart, 1977.

Barry, Bill. *People Places: Saskatchewan and its Names.* Regina: CPRC, 1997.

Brown, Jennifer H. *Strangers in Blood: Fur Trade Company Families in Indian Country.* 1980. Reprint. Vancouver: University of British Columbia Press, 1985.

Burant, Jim. "Robert Hood." *DCB*. Vol. 6: 327–29.

Burpee, Lawrence J. *The Search for the Western Sea: The Story of the Exploration of North-Western America*. 2 vols. Toronto: Macmillan, 1935.

Butler, William Francis. *The Wild North Land*. 1873. Reprint. Edmonton: Hurtig, 1968.

Campbell, Marjorie. *The North West Company*. Toronto: Macmillan, 1957.

Campbell, Marjorie. *Northwest to the Sea: A Biography of William McGillivray*. Toronto: Clarke, Irwin, 1975.

Canadian Encyclopedia. 2d ed., 4 vols. Edited by James H. Marsh. Edmonton: Hurtig, 1988.

Carlos, Ann. "The Birth and Death of Predatory Competition in the North American Fur Trade." *Explorations in Economic History* 19 (July 1982): 156–183.

Charles, Colin P. *Cree Language Dictionary: "Th" Dialect*. La Ronge: Lac la Ronge Indian Band, n.d.

Chisholm, Doug. *Their Names Live On: Remembering Saskatchewan's Fallen in World War II*. Regina: CPRC, 2001.

Christensen, Deanna. "'Steamboat Bill' of Cumberland House." *The Beaver* (Winter 1974): 28–31.

Clancy, Ron. *True Lies of a Northern Fur Trader*. Edited by Michael T. Clancy. Carrot River, SK: Simply Creative Designs by Donna, 1997.

Cockburn, R.H. "North of Reindeer: The 1940 Trip Journal of Prentice G. Downes." *The Beaver* (Spring 1983): 36–43.

Cockburn, R.H. "Revillon Man: The Northern Career of A. Wallace Laird, 1924–1931." *The Beaver* (February/March 1990): 12–26.

Cockburn, R.H. "To Reindeer's Far Waters: P.G. Downes' Journal of Travels in Northern Saskatchewan, 1936." *Fram: The Journal of Polar Studies* 1, no. 1 (1984): 131–76.

Cockburn, R.H. "To Great Slave and Great Bear: P.G. Downes Journal of Travels North from Île à la Crosse in 1938." Parts 1, 2. *Arctic* 38 (June, September 1985): 133–45, 231–43.

Cockburn, R.H. "Distant Summer: P.G. Downes' 1937 Inland Journal." *Fram: The Journal of Polar Studies* 2, no. 1 (1985): 31–119.

Cook, Cynthia et al., eds. *Nehithowewin [Cree Language Dictionary]*. La Ronge: Lac la Ronge Indian Band Education Branch, 1995.

Cooper, Barry. *Alexander Kennedy Isbister: A Respectable Critic of the Honourable Company*. Ottawa: Carleton University Press, 1988.

Cooper, J.I. "Jean-Étienne Waddens." *DCB*. Vol. 4: 757.

Crean, Frank, J.P. [Canada]. *Northland Exploration*. Ottawa: Department of the Interior, 1909.

Crean, J.F. "Hats and the Fur Trade." *Canadian Journal of Economics and Political Science* 28 (August 1962): 373–386.

Desnomie, May. "History of Pelican Narrows: Opawikoschikum." Typescript, 1973.

Dewdney, Selwyn. *Indian Rock Art*. Saskatchewan Museum of Natural History, Popular Series No. 4. Regina: Department of Tourism and Natural Resources, 1976.

Downes, P.G. *Sleeping Island: The Story of One Man's Travels in the Great Barren Lands of the Canadian North*. 1943. Reprint. Edited by R.H. Cockburn. Saskatoon: Prairie Books, 1988.

Ducharme, Father Jean-Baptiste. "Memoirs." Typescript, n.d.

Durand, Father. "History of Pinehouse." Typescript, n.d.

Ells, S.C. "Portage La Loche." *Canadian Geographical Journal* 12 (March 1936): 134–42.

Epp, Henry T. *Long Ago Today: The Story of Saskatchewan's Earliest Peoples.* Saskatoon: Saskatchewan Archaeological Society, 1991.

Faries, Ven. R. *A Dictionary of the Cree Language.* 1938. Reprint. Toronto: The Anglican Book Centre, 1986.

Galbraith, John S. *The Little Emperor: Governor Simpson of the Hudson's Bay Company, 1857–1885.* Toronto: Macmillan, 1976.

Galbraith, John S. "Sir George Simpson." *DCB.* Vol. 8: 812–19.

Gerrard, Jon M. and Gary R. Bortolotti. *The Bald Eagle: Haunts and Habits of a Wilderness Monarch.* Washington, DC: Smithsonian Institution, 1988.

Gough, Barry. "Peter Pond" *DCB.* Vol. 5: 681–86.

Guest, Graham. "Patuanak: Combining Old and New." *Denosa* (June 1982): 20–25.

Helm, June, ed. *Handbook of North American Indians: Subarctic.* Vol. 6. Washington, D.C.: Smithsonian Institution, 1981.

Holland, Clive. "Sir John Franklin." *DCB.* Vol. 7: 323–28.

Holmes, G. Hedley. "The Anglican Mission at Stanley and Lac la Ronge." Typescript, n.d.

Honigmann, John J. "West Main Cree." In Helm, ed., *Handbook of North American Indians: Subarctic*, 217–30.

Inglis, Alex. *Northern Vagabond: The Life and Career of J.B. Tyrrell.* Toronto: McClelland and Stewart, 1978.

Innis, Harold A. *The Fur Trade in Canada: An Introduction to Canadian Economic History.* 1930. Reprint. Toronto: University of Toronto Press, 1970.

Innis, Harold A. *Peter Pond: Fur Trader and Adventurer.* Toronto: Irwin & Gordon, 1930.

Ives, John W. *A Theory of Northern Athapaskan Prehistory.* Calgary: University of Calgary Press, 1990.

Jarvenpa, Robert. *The Trappers of Patuanak: Toward a Spatial Ecology of Modern Hunters.* National Museum of Man, Mercury Series. Canadian Ethnology Service Paper No. 67. Ottawa: National Museums of Canada, 1980.

Jarvenpa, Robert and Hetty Jo Brumbach. "The Microeconomics of Southern Chipewyan Fur Trade History." In *The Subarctic Fur Trade: Native Social and Economic Adaptations*, edited by Shepard Krech. Vancouver: University of British Columbia Press, 1984.

Jones, Tim E.H. *The Aboriginal Rock Paintings of the Churchill River.* Saskatchewan Museum of Natural History. Anthropological Series, No. 4. Regina: Saskatchewan Department of Culture and Youth, 1981.

Jones, Tim E. H. "Writing on the Rocks." *The Green and White: University of Saskatchewan Alumni Magazine* (Spring 1984): 11–13.

Jonker, Peter, ed. *The Churchill: A Canadian Heritage River.* Saskatoon: University of Saskatchewan Extension Division, 1995.

Judd, Carol M. and Arthur J. Ray, eds. *Old Trails and New Directions: Papers of the Third North American Fur Trade Conference.* Toronto: University of Toronto Press, 1980.

Judd, Carol M. "Mixt Bands of Many Nations." In *Old Trails and New Directions*, edited by Carol M. Judd and Arthur J. Ray.

Karras, A.L. *North to Cree Lake.* New York: Trident Press, 1970.

Karras, A.L. *Face the North Wind.* Don Mills: Burns and MacEachern, 1975.

Keighley, Sydney Augustus. *Trader Tripper Trapper: The Life of a Bay Man.* Winnipeg: Watson & Dwyer, 1989.

Kemp, H.S.M. *Northern Trader.* New York: Bouregy & Curl, 1956.

Kent, Timothy J. *Birchbark Canoes of the Fur Trade, Vol. I.* Ossineke: MI: Silver Fox Enterprises, 1997.

Kupsch, W.O. "A Valley View in Verdant Prose: The Clearwater Valley from Portage La Loche." *The Musk-Ox* 20 (1977): 28–49.

Kupsch, W.O. and S.D. Hanson, eds. *Gold and Other Stories as told to Berry Richards: Prospecting and Mining in Northern Saskatchewan.* Regina: Saskatchewan Mining Association, 1986.

Lamb, W. Kaye. "Sir Alexander Mackenzie." *DCB*. Vol. 5: 536–43.

La Ronge. *Our Roots: A History of La Ronge.* La Ronge: La Ronge Heritage Committee, 1981.

Leader-Post, The. Regina, daily newspaper.

Leighton, Anna L. *Wild Plant Use by the Woods Cree (Nihithawak) of East-Central Saskatchewan.* Ottawa: Canadian Ethnology Service, 1985.

Lemaigre, Evangeline. "La Loche: Its History and Development." Typescript, 1978.

Longpré, Robert. *Île-à-la-Crosse, 1776-1976.* Ile-à-la-Crosse: Sakitawak Bi-Centennial Committee, 1996.

MacDonald, C.S. "Through Canada's Hinterland." *Canadian Geographical Journal* 2 (January 1931): 3–20.

MacGregor, James G. *Peter Fidler: Canada's Forgotten Surveyor, 1769-1822.* Toronto: McClelland and Stewart, 1966.

Mackinnon, C.S. "Some Logistics of Portage La Loche (Methy)." *Prairie Forum* 5 (Spring 1980): 51–65.

Mackinnon, C.S., "Samuel Hearne." *DCB*. Vol. 4: 339–42.

Martyn, Katherine. *J.B. Tyrrell: Explorer and Adventurer: The Geological Survey Years, 1881-1898.* Toronto: University of Toronto Library, 1993.

Masson, L.R., ed. *Les Bourgeois de la Compagnie du Nord-Ouest.* Quebec: Imprimerie Générale, 1889.

McKay, Virginia et al. *A History of Cumberland as told by its own Citizens: 1774 to 1974.* Cumberland House: Cumberland House Bicentennial Committee, 1974.

McKenney, Thomas L. *Sketches of a Tour to the Lakes, of the character and customs of the Chippeway Indians, and of the incidents connected with the Treaty of Fond du Lac.* 1872. Reprint. Barre, MA: Imprint Society, 1972.

Merasty, Ron. "History of Pelican Narrows." Typescript, n.d.

Meyer, David. "Churchill River Archaeology in Saskatchewan: How Much Do We Know?" In *The Churchill: A Canadian Heritage River*, edited by Peter Jonker.

Miller, J.R. *Shingwauk's Vision: A History of Native Residential Schools.* Toronto: University of Toronto Press, 1996.

Moberly, Henry John. *When Fur was King.* London: J.M. Dent & Sons, 1929.

Moody, R.H. "Search for Historic Sites in the Amisk Lake Area." Typescript, n.d.

Moody, "R.H. Amisk Lake – Place Names." Typescript, n.d.

Morse, Eric W. *Fur Trade Canoe Routes: Then and Now.* 1969. Reprint. Toronto: University of Toronto Press, 1979.

Morton, Arthur S. *A History of the Canadian West to 1870-71.* 2d ed. Toronto: University of Toronto Press, 1973.

Neatby, Leslie H. *Search for Franklin.* Edmonton: Hurtig, 1970.

Newman, Peter. *Company of Adventurers*. Vol. 1. Vol. 2, *Caesars of the Wilderness*. Vol. 3, *Merchant Princes*. Markham, ON: Viking, 1985, 1987, and 1991.

Nicks, John. "Orkneymen in the HBC, 1780–1821." In *Old Trails and New Directions*, edited by Carol M. Judd and Arthur J. Ray.

Nicks, John, "David Thompson." *DCB*. Vol. 8: 878–84.

Nicks, Trudy. "The Iroquois and the Fur Trade in Western Canada." In *Old Trails and New Directions*, edited by Carol M. Judd and Arthur J. Ray.

Northerner, The. La Ronge, weekly newspaper.

Nute, Grace Lee. *The Voyageur*. 1931. Reprint. St. Paul: Minnesota Historical Society, 1955.

Nute, Grace Lee. *The Voyageur's Highway*. 1941. Reprint. St. Paul: Minnesota Historical Society, 1969.

Olson, Sigurd F. *The Lonely Land*. 1961. Reprint. Minneapolis: University of Minnesota Press, 1997.

Ouellet, Fernand, "Joseph Frobisher." *DCB*. Vol. 5: 331–34.

Parker, James. *Emporium of the North: Fort Chipewyan and the Fur Trade to 1835*. Regina: Canadian Plains Research Center, 1987.

Pecher, Kamil. *Lonely Voyage: By Kayak to Adventure and Discovery*. Saskatoon: Prairie Books, 1978.

Peel, Bruce. *Steamboats on the Saskatchewan*. Saskatoon: Prairie Books, 1972.

Pinehouse, Northern Village of. "Pinehouse Planning Project, Appendices 1 & 2." Typescript, 1987.

Ray, Arthur J. *Indians in the Fur Trade: Their Role as Hunters, Trappers and Middlemen in the Lands Southwest of Hudson Bay*. Toronto: University of Toronto Press, 1974.

Ray, Arthur J. and Donald Freeman. *"Give Us Good Measure": An Economic Analysis of Relations between the Indians and the Hudson's Bay Company before 1763*. Toronto: University of Toronto Press, 1978.

Reynolds, Margaret. "History of Patuanak." Typescript, n.d.

Rich, E.E. *Hudson's Bay Company*. The Hudson's Bay Record Society, vols. 21 and 22. London, 1958 and 1959.

Rich, E.E. *The Fur Trade and the Northwest to 1857*. Toronto: McClelland and Stewart, 1967.

Rich, E.E., "Philip Turnor." *DCB*. Vol. 4: 740–42.

Richards, Mary Helen. "Cumberland House: Two Hundred Years of History." *Saskatchewan History* 27 (Autumn 1974): 108–114.

Ross, Hugh Mackay. *The Manager's Tale*. Winnipeg: Watson & Dwyer, 1989.

Russell, Dale R. *Eighteenth-Century Western Cree and their Neighbours*. Archaeological Survey of Canada, Mercury Series Paper 143. Ottawa: Canadian Museum of Civilization, 1991.

Smith, James G.E. "Chipewyan." In Helm, ed., *Handbook of North American Indians: Subarctic*, 271–84.

Smith, James G.E. "Western Woods Cree." In Helm, ed., *Handbook of North American Indians: Subarctic*, 256–70.

Smith, James K. *Alexander Mackenzie, Explorer: The Hero Who Failed*. Toronto: McGraw-Hill, 1973.

Spry, Irene M. "Matthew Cocking." *DCB*. Vol.4: 156–58.

StarPhoenix, The. Saskatoon, daily newspaper.

Steer, Donald Norman. "History and Archaeology of the Historic Site of La Loche House." *The Musk-Ox* 12 (1973): 13–19.

Steer, Donald Norman. "The History and Archaeology of a North West Company Trading Post and a Hudson's Bay Company Transport Depot, Lac la Loche, Saskatchewan." Master's thesis, University of Saskatchewan, 1977.

Teed, L.M. and Rowe, J.S. *Saskatchewan Trees.* Saskatoon: Tri-Leaf Publications, n.d.

Thistle, Paul C. *Indian-European Trade Relations in the Lower Saskatchewan River Region to 1840.* Winnipeg: University of Manitoba Press, 1986.

Town, Florida. *The North West Company: Frontier Merchants.* Toronto: Umbrella Press, 1999.

Townsend, Gerald H. "A Study of Waterfowl Nesting on the Saskatchewan River Delta." *Canadian Field Naturalist* 80 (1966): 74–88.

Turnor, John Peter. "The La Loche Brigade." *The Beaver* (December 1943): 32–36.

Van Kirk, Sylvia. "Louis Primeau." *DCB.* Vol 4: 647.

Van Kirk, Sylvia. *"Many Tender Ties": Women in Fur Trade Society in Western Canada, 1670–1870.* Winnipeg: Watson and Dwyer, 1980.

Wagner, Henry R. *Peter Pond: Fur Trader and Explorer.* New Haven: Yale University Library, 1955.

Williams, Glyndwyr. "The Hudson's Bay Company and the Fur Trade: 1670–1870." *The Beaver* Special Issue (October 1983): 3–86.

Wilson, Ian and Sally. "In the Spirit of the Voyageur." *The Beaver* (June/July 1999): 8–16.

Wolvengrey, Arok. *nêhiýawêwin: itwêwina / Cree: Words.* Regina: Canadian Plains Research Center, 2001.

Wuorinen, Richard. *A History of Buffalo Narrows.* Buffalo Narrows: Buffalo Narrows Celebrate Saskatchewan Committee, 1981.

Zaslow, Morris. *Reading the Rocks: The Story of the Geological Survey of Canada, 1842–1972.* Toronto: Macmillan, 1975.

INDEX

Roly's Store, Denare B., 363, 364

Roman Catholic Church, Cumberland H., 400; Île-à-la-Crosse, 148–49; Lac la Loche, 103, 107; Pelican Narrows, 331, 332, 334; Sturgeon Lndg. residential school, 382–84; *and see* churches; Oblates of Mary Immaculate

Rosie's Dining & Lounge, Buffalo Nar., 134

Ross, John (Gregory-McLeod trader), 33, 53,145

Ross, Maggie, Nistowiak L., 288

Ross, Malcolm (HBC trader), accompanies Turnor / Fidler to / from Athabasca, 56, 99, 328, 397; contracts with guide, 328; Cumberland H., 397; praises Fidler, 57; shoots swan, 99

Ross Navigation Company, 399

Rossignol School, Île-à-la-Crosse, 150

Rowland, William (voyageur), 89

Roy (Montreal trader), 290

Royal Canadian Legion, 402

Royal Canadian Mounted Police (RCMP), 14, 18; Buffalo Nar., 134; Cumberland H., 401, 403; Île-à-la-Crosse, 150; La Loche, 109; Patuanak, 162; Pelican Nar., 333, 335; Pinehouse, 203; Stanley M., 280; Sturgeon Lndg. (patrol cabin only), 380, 384, 385

Royal Navy, Franklin, 61–64; Hearne, 50

Royalex canoes, 258

"rubbaboo," 48

runoff, spring, effect on water levels, 16

Rupert, Prince, Cumberland H. named for, 36, 391; forms HBC, 30

Rupert's Land, 30, 389; governor, 60, 92

Rupert R., 29, 30, 35

Russia, beaver from, 28

Russick, Shorty (trader / dog musher), 333–34, 342, 360

"Sable, Point au" (Sandy Pt., Lac Île-à-la-Crosse), 154

safety, bears, 17–18; checklist, 18; equipment required by law, 12; hypothermia, 19; life jackets, 18; lightning, 18; wind, 4, 18; scouting, 18; solo trips, 10

Saguenay R., 35

sails, fur trade canoes, 44, 48

Saint Jean, Louis (voyageur), 252–53

sâkâscîwîscam (Henry Budd), 390

Sakitawak (Île-à-la-Crosse), 143, 149

sâkitawâhk sâkahikan (Lac Île-à-la-Crosse), 151

sâkahikanisis (Drope L.), 286

Saleski Cr. / L., 107, 109, 110, 413 (n4–7)

sand dunes, Lac la Loche, 110; Peter Pond L., 119; Rendevous L., 88

Sanderson (carpenter), 278

Sandfly L., 199, 207–08, 210

sandhill cranes, 7

Sandy Bay (comm.), 335

"Sandy Beach" (now Denare B.), 363

"Sandy Beach" (prov. campground, Amisk L. S shore), 363, 367, 369

Sandy L., 157, 188, 191–93; camping, 191–93

Sandy Nar., Pelican L., 332

Sandy Pt., Lac Île-à-la-Crosse, 143, 153–54

Sandy Pt., Peter Pond L., 118, 119, 126

sâponikan pâwistik (Needle Rap. / Falls), 208

sâponikan sâkahikan (Sandfly L.), 207

Sarcee, 26

sarsaparilla, 5, 168

sash, voyageur, 39–40

Sask Water Corporation, 16, 401

Saskatchewan Environment, fishing licences, 8; Buffalo Nar., 134; Cumberland H. / L., 392, 403; Île-à-la-Crosse, 150; La Loche, 109; Missinipe, 258; Patuanak, 162; Pelican Nar., 335; Pinehouse, 203; Stanley M., 280; Sturgeon Lndg., 384, 385; topo maps, 15; voyageur certificates, 22; W Weir mouth, 353

Saskatchewan Fish Marketing Service, 203

Saskatchewan Fishing & Hunting Guide, 338

Saskatchewan Game Department, 333

Saskatchewan Government Trading / Northern Trading / Northern Co-op Trading, Birch Rap., 227, 280; Pelican Nar., 334; Pinehouse, 202, 280, 418 (n8–6); Stanley M., 280

Saskatchewan Legislature, 138

Saskatchewan-Manitoba border, maps, 1, 21, 329, 361, 376, 380, 387; nickel mine, 386

Saskatchewan Penitentiary, 403

Saskatchewan Provincial Police, 368, 401

Saskatchewan R., 93; bridge, 402; Cumberland L. drains to, 391, 394; Franklin, 63; HBC presence (pre-1774), 36; Hearne, 394; hydro dams, 392, 401; maps, 1, 30, 380, 393; Montrealer traders, 32; "New Chan." cut, 392; *Northcote*, 153, 399, 400; Old Chan., 392; pemmican supply route, 398; Simpson, 37; sturgeon, 386; Sturgeon-weir R. joins, 2, 309; water quality, 389, 393; *also see* N. Sask. R. *and* S. Sask. R.

Saskatchewan Voyageur Certificates, 22

Saskatoon, 1, 117, 393; shuttle distances from, 14

Saskatoon Berry L. / Saskatoon Bush L. (Trout L.), 227

saskatoons, 5, 156

SaskPower, 392, 401

(1778–79), 391, 392, 397; Deer Rap., 171–72; Devil Rap. / Port., 244, 247; Dog Rap., 341; Fort Chipewyan longitude, 55; Île-à-la-Crosse, 37, 145, 147; below Knee L., 187; Knee Rap., 181; Lac la Loche, 99, 103; Leaf Rap., Chur. R., 168; Lindstrom L., 314; Little Stanley Rap., 283; meets Mackenzie, 55; Methy Port., 86, 87–88, 92; Mirond L., 337; Mountain L., 265, 270; Otter Rap., 252; Patrick Small aids, 37, 56; Pelican L., 328, 332; Peter Pond L., 120, 121, 125; Pinehouse L., 204; Pot Hole Rap., 322; Potter Rap., 292; Primeau L., 176; Rat Port., 377; Rock Trout Rap., 232; Snake Rap., Chur. R., 194; S Weir, 370; Sturgeon Lndg., 381; sturgeon weir, 375; Trout L., 227, 229; Trout Port., 230; Tyrrell edits journal, 65; Twin Falls, 265; Wood L., 318

Tute, Captain James (Montreal trader), 354, 423 (n11–63)

Twatt, Magnus (HBC trader), 397, 398

Twin Falls, 262, 263, 271; discussed, 264–65

twinflowers, 5, 168

Two Lake I., NE of Nipew L., 241

Two-Mile Rap., S Weir, 376, 378

"Tyndall stone," 356

Tyrrell, J.B. (geologist / surveyor), bio, 65–66; Champlain Society president, 65; Corneille Rap., 338; Dipper L., 175; Dipper Rap., 173; edits Hearne / Turnor journals, 51, 58, 65; edits Thompson's narrative, 60, 65; Foster R., 213; Frog Port. posts, 312; Haultain R., 187; Mudjatik R., 65, 169; Patuanak, 159; photo of, 65; Pot Hole Port., 321; Whitey Nar., 388, 389

Tyrrell Museum of Palaeontology, 65

"U-che-Quan Sask-a-ha-gan" (Knee L.), 183

Ukrainetz, Kerry (outfitter), 197

United States, border, 62 (map); emigrants to Buffalo Nar., 131; ranch mink from, 132

United States Congress, receives Pond map, 54

Universal Transverse Mercator (UTM / grid) references, 15

University of Saskatchewan, 103, 117

University of Toronto, Tyrrell attends, 65

Upper Canada, Thompson moves to, 59

Upper Canada College, Tyrrell attends, 65

Upper Hudson House, Turnor, 56

"Upper Settlement" (Primeau's Dipper L. post), 177, 312

"Upper Track" (aboriginal canoe route), , 30, 49, 56, 378

upstream travel, difficulty of, 9, 16

uranium mines, Cluff Lake, 69, 70; Drope L., 281, 286–87; Key Lake, 195; northern employment, 149, 403; Hwy. 102, 256

Utik L., 30

Utrecht, Treaty of, 32

"valley-in-valley," 83

Vances I., Amisk L., 363

Vee Bay, Peter Pond L., 126

vegetation, guide route, 4–5

vehicle shuttles, 13–14, 142, 256; distances from Saskatoon / Regina / P.A. / La Ronge (grid), 14; environmental considerations, 19; P.A. to Denare B., 14, 362; P.A. to Île-à-la-Crosse, 14, 142; P.A. to La Loche, 14, 107; P.A. to Otter Rap., 14, 256; P.A. to Patuanak, 14, 158; P.A. to Pelican Nar., 14, 330; P.A. to Pinehouse, 14, 200; P.A. to Stanley M., 14, 276; P.A. to Sturgeon Lndg., 14, 380; P.A. to Warner Rap., 14, 69; Sturgeon Lndg. to Cumberland H. trip, 380

venereal disease, 354

vermillion, Mackenzie uses, 55

Victoria I., Arctic O., 62

Victoriaville, Quebec, 331

Villa, Pancho, 308

Visentin, Joe, 279

volcanism, Amisk L., 356, 358, 365

Voyage Air, Buffalo Nar., 134

Voyages from Montreal, Alexander Mackenzie, 56, 410 (n2–66)

voyageur certificates, 22

voyageur highway, 22; Churchill L., 135; Frog Port. link / gateway, 276, 309–12; Henry (Younger), 391; La Loche R.'s difficulty, 111; map of, 34–35; Methy Port. link / gateway, 68–69; Tearing R. link, 391; The Pas, 380

voyageurs, as guides, 39, 42; as interpreters, 39, 42; as symbol of fur trade, 29; "Canadian" / French Canadian, 39–42, 92, 148, 409 (n2–22); dancing, 122; drinking, 48; European, 27, 42; *hommes du nord*, 33; Iroquois, 42, 64, 409 (n2–22); *mangeurs de lard*, 33, 36, 37; Métis forebears, 27, 148; paddling, 85; portaging, 39, 46, 47–48, 85, 89, 92, 93, 111; private trading, 95, 101; Orkneymen, 148; red pine, 114; reminiscence of, 41; singing, 33, 39, 40–41, 48, 373; sketch of, 39; smoke breaks, 41, 48; stature, 39; work day, 45–48, 136

wacasko-pâwistik (Rat Rap.), 376

Wadin, Etienne (Monteal trader), killed, 53, 144

wild rice, 149, 315, 403

Wilderness Trails Inc., 258

Wilkinson, Paul (canoe outfitter), 258

Willetts, Charlie (outfitter), 342

Williams, George (mink rancher), 137

Williams, William (HBC governor), 92, 95, 409 (n2–27)

Willow I., Dreger L., 189, 190

Willow Pt., Peter Pond L., 125

willows, 5 *(numerous other entries throughout text)*

Wild Carrot I. (Craik I.), Black Bear Island L., 223

Wildnest R., 342, 343

wîmistikôsiw sâkahikan (main Lindstrom L.), 315

wind, Amisk L., 330, 355, 358, 362, 365; guide route, 4; Cumberland L., 380; *La Vieille*, 41, 48; Lac Île-à-la-Crosse, 142; Lac la Loche, 97, 98; Mirond L., 330, 336; Namew L., 380, 385, 386; Otter Rap. to Stanley M., 256; Peter Pond L., 106, 117, 118, 121, 124, 125; Pinehouse L., 203; respect for, 18; Trade L., 305; Wood L., 318

windbound, Primeau's nickname, 49; voyageurs, 48

Winnipeg, fish processing, 132

Winnipeg R., map, 34; red pines, 114

wintering partners, NWC, 36

wîposkâw sâkahikan (Wood L.), 318

Wisconsin glaciation, 24

Wisconsin R., 34–35

Wladyka Falls, Great Devil Rap., 242, 243

Wolf L., 353

Wollaston L., 34, 213; Thompson, 58

Wolverine, Philip, family, 170; Haultain R., 187; IR 192B, 417 (n7–64); Rabbitskin L., 175

wolverines, 6

wolves, 6

Wood L., 275; camping, 320, 321, 322; discussed, 318–21; Mackenzie (route upstream), 314; maps, 316, 321; rock paintings, 21, 276, 318–19; *manâwan nistowayâhk*, 315, 318; weir, 314, 315

woodchucks, 6, 166

woodpeckers, 7

Woods, Bob and Flora, 116

Woods / Woodland Cree, 26

"Woods, Lake of the" / "Woody Lake" (Wood L.), 318

World Wars I & II, Angus McDonald, 368; Cumberland H. servicemen, 401, 402; WW I copper demand, 381–82; WW II casualties honoured, 22, 409 (n1–11)

Wright, Dr. J.P. (Dominion Geological Survey), 358

XY Company (New North West Company), Black at Île-à-la-Crosse, 147, 152; explores Churchill L., 135; Fidler competes with, 58; formation, 33, 56, 152; Mackenzie's key role, 56, 152; merges with NWC, 33, 56, 152; name, 415–16 (n6–28)

y-dialect Cree, 25–26, 148, 201

yellow pond lilies, 5, 314

Yellowknife (Copper) Indians, 63

Yellowknife R., 62

yîkawiskâw sâkahikan (Sandy L.), 192

York boats, cargo capacity, 44, 93, 97, 136, 410 (n2–48); Cumberland H. replica, 45, 403; discussed, 44–45, 92–94; Fidler uses, 146; Lac la Loche, 102; life span, 44, 410 (n2–47); Métis, 42; portaging, 228; Orkneymen, 38, 42; rock painting depicts (?), 197; S Weir, 366–67, 370; Simpson promotes, 38, 44, 97, 111

York Factory, Cocking, 52, 396; Colen, 59; distance from Frog Port., 310; established, 30; Fear Nar. story, 332; Franklin, 63; Hearne, 394, 396; Henday, 36; d'Iberville captures, 30–31; Lapérouse captures, 397; lower Chur. R. remote from, 309; main route to, 378; maps, 30, 34, 62; Port. la Loche brigade, 93–94; Primeau, 49; Rock Depot inland, 60; supply ship late (1783), 397; transport to / from Methy Port. / Fort Chipewyan, 42, 85; Turnor draws plan of, 56; Turnor / Fidler returning to, 314; "Upper Track" to, 378

Yost L., 189

Yukon, Dene roots in, 26

Other books in the "Discover Saskatchewan Series"

Discover Saskatchewan: A Guide to Historic Sites (1998)
Discover Saskatchewan: A User's Guide to Regional Parks (1999)